HSING-I CHUAN

The Practice of Heart and Mind Boxing

Master James McNeil & Andrew Jackson

Published by Clink Street Publishing 2018

Copyright © 2018

First edition.

The author asserts the moral right under the Copyright, Designs and Patents Act 1988 to be identified as the author of this work.

All rights reserved. No part of this publication may be reproduced, stored in a retrieval system or transmitted, in any form or by any means without the prior consent of the author, nor be otherwise circulated in any form of binding or cover other than that with which it is published and without a similar condition being imposed on the subsequent purchaser.

ISBN:
978-1-912562-23-7

Dedication

It is with great honour that we write this book together. Without the help of Andrew and Julie Jackson this book would never be finished. We are hoping that after writing this book everyone who takes the time to read it will discover the wonderful world of internal arts attributed to Taoism.

After studying Hsing-I for at least forty years, I am again writing a book on this martial art with my student, Andrew Jackson, in honor of my teachers; Master Chiao Chang-Hung and Master Hsu Hong-Chi. I miss them both very much.

In my first book on Hsing-I, written in 1984, the final version that went to print was not complete as thirty six important pages were missing and also many pictures, including animals and teachers' names. The content of this book rectifies these omissions and includes many more very important facts about the art of Hsing-I that, to my knowledge have not been written in any another book to date.

I give thanks to my masters, for the wisdom they have bestowed on me and for the encouragement to practice and teach this treasured art. When I was in Taiwan or when they stayed in my home in California each year, they furthered my training and knowledge in the hidden secrets of Hsing-I, meditation and lovemaking.

Finally, I hope this book will help all kung-fu practitioners in their study of Hsing-I Chuan and keep this lineage alive for generations to come.

Master James W. McNeil, 2017

Acknowledgements

First and foremost, to my teacher, Master James McNeil for allowing, encouraging and supporting the writing of this book.

To Julie, my wife, for the countless hours spent at the computer, helping to organise my sometimes erratic writing style and thoughts. Also for taking many of the photographs contained in this book, setting them out and creating illustrations which help to demonstrate the content of this book and bring it to life.

To Beverley Richardson, PD Print, for her help in arranging and printing draft copies prior to publication.

To my senior brothers, Al Lam and Jim Doty for kindly writing the prefaces contained in this book.

To my senior brothers, brothers and sisters around the world who have given their time and support, providing innumerable photographs and opinions on the information contained in the book.

- Al Lam
- Jim Doty
- Gary Doty
- John Meiner
- Matt Schackno
- Tige Johnson
- Colin Kane
- Stephen Baker
- Ajay Kumra
- Mike Foster
- Brian Atkinson
- Simon Hill

I bow deeply to all involved with the utmost gratitude and respect.

Andrew Jackson

Contents

Part One: The History and Theory of Hsing-I Chuan

Chapter 1	Hsing-I Chuan – 'A True Internal Treasure'	3
Chapter 2	The History of Hsing-I Chuan	7
Chapter 3	The Connection between Hsing-I Chuan and the Tao	25
Chapter 4	The Internal Aspect of Hsing-I Chuan	39
Chapter 5	The Three Principle Stages of Hsing-I Chuan Training	59
Chapter 6	The Two Levels of Practice in Hsing-I Chuan	65
Chapter 7	Hsing-I Chuan and the Taoist Five Elements Theory	69
Chapter 8	The 'Six Styles of the Body' Theory of Hsing-I Chuan	115
Chapter 9	The Six Harmonies Theory of Hsing-I Chuan	121
Chapter 10	The Seven Stars of Hsing-I Chuan	127
Chapter 11	The Eight Fundamentals Theory of Hsing-I Chuan	131
Chapter 12	The Nine Essences Theory of Hsing-I Chuan	139
Chapter 13	The Twelve Animals Theory of Hsing-I Chuan	145
Chapter 14	Fighting Theory of Hsing-I Chuan	165

Part Two: The Practice of Hsing-I Chuan

Chapter 15	Hand Techniques of Hsing-I Chuan	179
Chapter 16	Foot Techniques of Hsing-I Chuan	201
Chapter 17	Stepping Methods of Hsing-I Chuan	213
Chapter 18	Stances of Hsing-I Chuan	225
Chapter 19	Opening and Closing Method of Hsing-I Forms	235
Chapter 20	Preparatory Forms – Ba Bu Da	243
Chapter 21	Five Element Fist Forms – Wu Chuan	269
	Metal Form – Pi Chuan	270
	Water Form – Tsuan Chuan	273

	Wood Form - Peng Chuan	279
	Fire Form - Pao Chuan	283
	Earth Form - Heng Chuan	286
	Five Element Chain Form - Wu Hsing	290
	Two Man Five Element Fighting Form/Wu Hsing I Er Ren	294
Chapter 22	Combined Forms of Hsing-I Chuan	299
	Linking Chain Form - Lien Wan	299
	Eight Form Fist Form - Ba Shih Chuan	309
	Basic Beginning Form - Chu Chi Chuan	321
	Three Gate Fist Form - San Guan Chuan	331
	Twelve Red Hammers Form - Sher Er Hong Chewi	340
Chapter 23	The Twelve Animals Forms	357
	Dragon Form - Lung Hsing	360
	Tiger Form - Hu Hsing	372
	Monkey Form - Hou Hsing	388
	Horse Form - Ma Hsing	400
	Tuo Form - Tuo Hsing	410
	Cock Form - Gi Hsing	416
	Phoenix Form - Tai Hsing	426
	Sparrow-Hawk Form - Yao Hsing	444
	Swallow Form - Yen Hsing	452
	Snake Form - Sher Hsing	464
	Eagle/Bear Form - Ying/Xiong Hsing	476
	Fighting Chicken Form - Dou Gi Hsing	484
Chapter 24	Lo-Shu Training	491
Chapter 25	Common Mistakes in Practice	497
Chapter 26	Five Element Staff	503
Chapter 27	Tien Gunn Exercises	529

About the Author - James W. McNeil

James W. McNeil has for over fifty years been learning, living and teaching the inner mysteries and secrets of the traditional, internal kung-fu arts. During history, such knowledge had normally been reserved for the elite few within the closed circles of the oriental Taoist societies. Until James McNeil came on the scene it was unheard of for any outsider, let alone a white American, to be accepted as a student by the great martial art masters of China and Taiwan. James McNeil has had the rare privilege to study with such greats as Master Hsu Hong-Chi, 'The Man With the Magic Hands' (Hsing-I & healing arts, Taoist sexual techniques), Master Chin Chen-Yen (Tzu Men-Chuan – the rare and deadly art of 'Poison Fingers'), Hsu Ting-Ming (Chinese psychic healing), Master Pan Wing-Chow (original Chen style Tai-Chi) and perhaps the greatest of them all, the legendary, Grand Master Chiao Chang-Hung (Little Nine Heaven Kung-fu, Shih Shui, Ba-Kua, advanced Taoist sexual techniques and mediation).

While his masters were alive James McNeil would go to Taiwan every year where they would teach him personally in the internal healing arts, but most of all Master Hsu and Mr Huang taught him personally for four long and intense years, training him in Taoist Lovemaking also known as the Taoist sexual techniques. Through continuous practicing and training hard he was handed down lineage of this method of practice. This honour is only handed down from Master to Student and one per generation. After Master Hsu's, unexpected death in 1983 James McNeil was excepted as the first and only American student of the Honorable Master Chiao Chang-Hung.

Honorable Grand Master Chiao was known as a living legend in martial arts for his remarkable skills and abilities and his foresight. Grand Master Chiao Chang-Hung taught James McNeil the oldest Taoist system known today, named Little Nine Heaven Wu Tao Kung-fu, along with Ba-Kua, and advanced Taoist sexual energy circulation for health, longevity and mediation, until his death in 2001.

An important aspect of the internal arts is the cultivation and manipulation of sexual energy for health, longevity and of course extraordinary pleasure. Since 1985 James McNeil has been sharing his wealth of knowledge on this subject with groups of people all over North America, Europe and China helping them to achieve superior sexual fulfillment and to treat sexual dysfunctions with simple, natural methods.

Master James McNeil and his work have been featured in articles and covers of magazines such as *Inside Kung-Fu*, *Inside Karate*, *Masters & Styles*, *Chi Master*, *Black Belt*, *Empty Vessel*, *Martial Arts Masters*, *Internal Arts* and *Orange Coast Magazine*, to mention a few, in addition to many local magazines, newspaper articles and foreign publications in England, Sweden, Poland, China and Italy. He has appeared as guest speaker for American Institute of Hypnotherapy conventions, World Research Foundation and Long Beach State University. McNeil has also taught at South Baylo College of Oriental Medicine, and John Bastyr Naturopathic College. He has appeared several times on television in the United States and Taiwan and has produced more than twenty DVD's and books about martial arts and sexual techniques. His informal and entertaining style is always well received and he has a knack for making almost anyone feel comfortable in an awkward situation. The multitude letters of gratitude and the great respect accorded him by his students attest to his skill and popularity as a teacher.

James McNeil is the director and founder of the Little Nine Heaven International Internal Kung-Fu Association. Students have travelled from all over, including every American state, England, Ireland, Scotland, Spain, Greece, Sweden, Poland, Canada, Russia, China, Japan, Burma, Vietnam, Malaysia, South Africa and many other countries, to come and learn from him. In more recent years he has travelled the world, aspiring to achieve his goal in keeping a promise made to his teachers to keep their arts alive. He has visited his students, helping them continue their training and to pass on his knowledge, unselfishly, to the next generation.

On New Year's Eve 1999, Grand Master Chiao Chang-Hung, in line with Little Nine Heaven tradition, officially passed on to his student James W. McNeil the title of 'Gate Keeper of the Little Nine Heaven Wu Tao System'. This honour established him as the next (34th Generation) lineage holder of the 'Xiao Jiu Tian Wu Tao', otherwise known as Little Nine Heaven Wu Tao.

It was the lifelong wish of Grand Master Chiao to spread the knowledge of the Little Nine Heaven Wu Tao system across the world and in fulfilment of this wish his student, James W. McNeil, has sought to make this wish a reality. Alongside teaching many students around the world this rare and ancient Taoist system, James W. McNeil achieved his own personal goal of returning the system back to its home in China where its knowledge was thought to have been lost for many decades.

In April 2016, the Chinese government was actively searching the world, looking to locate the next generation master of this system. It was then that James

W. McNeil was flown to China at the government's request where he was introduced to government officials and on providing legitimate documentation as proof of his lineage, was then officially recognised as Master James McNeil, sole descendant and next generation lineage holder of the Little Nine Heaven Wu Tao, the oldest Taoist system known today. He was taken to the original Little Nine Heaven Temple site, where his teacher and Grand teacher both lived and where his name will be officially recorded to the historical lineage of the system. He also visited the original family home of his teacher Grand Master Chiao, the first student to do this since Grandmaster Chiao's migration to Taiwan.

In October of the same year, Master McNeil retuned to QuingDao, China, where he was further recognised by the Chinese government as the next generation lineage holder of Little Nine Heaven Shih Shui and Taoist lovemaking system and was both a guest of honour and speaker at the first Chinese Sexual Health Conference held in over sixty-five years.

Following is a list of James W. McNeil's internal martial arts education:

1966-1973
Studied under Master Haumea (Tiny) Lefiti. Obtained the highest degree Black Belt given at that time for Splashing Hands fighting techniques.

1973-1977
Studied under Master Ralph Shun learning southern style Shaolin Five Animals, Wing Chun, Iron Hand and weapons. Obtained the rank of Master Instructor in June 1976.

1977-1984
Studied under Master Hsu Hong-Chi in Taipei, Taiwan. Received extensive training in the arts of Chi-Kung and Hsing-I. Was also taught Tui-Na, Acupressure massage, Taoist sexual techniques and meditation. Obtained a 4th degree Black belt in Hsing-I in 1983.

1983-1987
Studied under Master Chin Chen-Yen in Taipei, Taiwan. Trained in Tzu Men-Chuan system (Poison Fingers) and advanced training in Iron Hand.

1983-1996
Studied under Master Pan Wing-Chow, Taipei, Taiwan, since 1983. Trained in Chen style Tai-Chi.

1984-2001
Master Chiao Chang-Hung, Taipei, Taiwan. Receiving advanced training in Little Nine Heaven Kung-Fu consisting of fighting, sword and Shih Shui Kung. He was also taught Pa-Kua and advanced Hsing-I. Further training in Taoist Sexual techniques and high levels of Chi-Kung and Nei-Kung therapy, along with advanced Meditation.

James McNeil has obtained the following degrees in clinical hypnotherapy:

Bachelor of Clinical Hypnotherapy – American Institute of Hypnotherapy in 1988
Bachelor of Science Hypnotherapy – American Institute of Hypnotherapy in 1989
Doctorate of Clinical Hypnotherapy – American Institute of Hypnotherapy in 1990

Master James McNeil can be contacted through his website www.littlenineheaven.com

About the Co-author

Andrew Jackson MSc, BSc is based in Manchester, England. He is a qualified Chartered physiotherapist and a practitioner of Traditional Chinese Medicine. He has run a successful practice, with his wife, for over fifteen years. Treating the local community of all ages, for a wide range of health conditions and sports related injuries; using a unique combination of Chinese and Western Medicine.

He trained at the Northern College of Acupuncture in York, England and gained a Master of Science Degree in Acupuncture. He also attended the University of Salford, Manchester where he achieved a Bachelor of Science degree with Honours in Physiotherapy. He is a member of the British Acupuncture Council, Chartered Society of Physiotherapists and Acupuncture Association of Chartered Physiotherapists and the Danish Acupuncture Union.

He has written articles for magazines on acupuncture relating to the treatment of tinnitus and the use of moxibustion in Chinese Medicine. He has given talks and seminars across the country on Chinese Medicine and Internal Martial Arts and appeared on local and national radio talking about the use of Traditional Chinese Medicine within his practice. He regularly works with elite athletes from various sports, specialising in the use of acupuncture for treating muscular skeletal injuries.

Also based from his practice in Manchester, is the Little Nine Heaven UK Kung-Fu School, which Andrew heads up under the guidance of Master James McNeil, representing the Little Nine Heaven International Kung-Fu Association in the UK. At his school, he promotes and teaches the systems of kung-fu, Chi-Kung and health practices, taught to him by Master James McNeil. He continues to train as a private student with Master McNeil.

Preface

It is with great honour that I help co-write this book. Without the encouragement from my teacher, Master James McNeil, I would neither have found the courage nor discovered the wonderful world of internal arts attributed to Taoism.

This book has been a project, which has spanned over the last five years and aims to expand on previous written works by Master McNeil. It seeks to add layers of detail to existing knowledge and to show the true richness that the art of Hsing-I has to offer the serious practitioner. This book would not have been possible without the depth of information provided by my teacher.

It is my observation to date that most work pertaining to Hsing-I, translated or written directly in the English language, is very superficial and often simply repeats what has already been said before. This is not to say that the existing material is poor, just that it simply translates what has been written with very little explanation or expansion of its meaning. This maybe because traditionally the explanation was left to the teacher to orally pass to the student in the past. Many students now do not have regular access to a knowledgeable teacher to help correct and discuss their training on a daily basis, therefore it is my hope that this work will help whet the appetite of the Western speaking Hsing-I practitioner and provide a framework from which they can improve their understanding of Hsing-I in both theory and practice.

Further to this, it is the wish of my teacher, Master McNeil, that the lineage and content of Hsing-I, practiced by the Little Nine Heaven school and passed down through a rich heritage of highly ranked masters, is formally documented in Western language and made available to the general public – in particular students in Western speaking countries.

It is with quiet concern that I observe many of the classical internal arts in China being corrupted here in the West by teachers who seek to mix and match from different systems, creating hybrid systems that have very little in common with their original source, in my opinion losing the very soul and spirit originally attributed to them. It is the tradition and spirit of these ancient arts that makes them so special and without the discipline and respect this training creates in the student, these beautiful arts would simply be reduced to the mindless violence attributed to the more modern systems that are becoming popular today.

I have tried to the best of my humble abilities to take the already well written and documented theory of Hsing-I Chuan by my teacher and add to it from my knowledge of Chinese Medicine understanding, in the hope that the Western English-speaking student may understand more deeply the link to the Tao and Taoist theory that Hsing-I offers, how the body works from a Chinese energetic perspective and why Hsing-I has the ability to restore health within the human body and mind.

I am motivated in my desire to help preserve the classical teachings that are passed on to me by my teacher. In writing a book in this way, I have tried to tailor it to the Western mind set by demystifying the often confusing but beautiful language used within Taoism and Chinese Medicine and linking it to the practice of Hsing-I.

This book cannot promise to answer all questions associated with this deep and valuable art, in fact it may raise more questions than it answers, but I hope that by reading the information contained within its pages it motivates students to delve deeper into their own understanding and practice of Hsing-I. I also hope it will contribute to the slowly expanding range of literature available on this subject already published in English. Truthfully, no book or DVD can replace a genuine teacher of the internal arts of which there are few here in the West. I am lucky to have found one such teacher.

Thank you to my Sifu, for the wisdom he has bestowed on me and for the encouragement he has given me to write this book, also for providing personal notes and photographs from his teachers, some of which have never been seen publicly before and help to bring the content of this book alive.

Finally, I hope this book will help my fellow kung-fu brothers and sisters of our school in their study of Hsing-I Chuan and to keep this lineage alive for generations in the future.

Andrew Jackson
June 2017
Manchester, England
Andrew Jackson can be contacted through his website www.littleninheavenuk.com

2nd Preface

"I learned that from a book;" those of us who study with Master James McNeil know this phrase well. Yes, we all know that was said in jest and our teacher could not have learned what he just showed us from a book. That being said, I am delighted and grateful to see that he collaborated with my kung-fu brother, Andrew Jackson and others in our Little Nine Heaven family, to publish a comprehensive, illustrated book of Hsing-I Chuan as taught to him by Masters Hsu Hong Chi and Chiao Chang Hung.

Throughout the years, many martial styles have come and gone. Even among the styles that have survived, there are many that only focus on certain attributes and could not be considered as complete martial arts. For example, some styles excel in fighting but are not necessarily good for health cultivation; some styles have advanced techniques that suit experienced practitioners but lack good foundation-building methods to train beginners; some styles have a straightforward curriculum that simplify learning but lack the rich culture that make up an art, etc. Hsing-I Chuan is one of the few arts that has everything within itself; it does not need to look upon other styles to complement its training. It is simple to learn and does not take long to achieve results; yet it is so rich in contents and principles that one does not outgrow the art.

Hsing-I Chuan literally translates as Form-Mind Boxing. 'Form' is to train the external and 'Mind' is to train the internal. The two trainings complement each other. Without the correct form structure, physical condition, rhythm timing, etc., the mind cannot do much by itself. However, the style is also called Heart–Mind (心意) Boxing to emphasise the mental aspect of the art. Master McNeil always exhorts his students to "feel"! The focus is not in training 'visual' skill or even 'listening' skill; rather, the essence of the art is in training one's sensitivities. It actively trains our body to align and respond on contact but aims to hone our senses to react naturally without thinking. As one advances in this training, one's senses become more refined and precise. Feeling is no longer confined to the hands but any parts of the body. To exemplify this, let's look into the other nickname of this style: Walk–Mind (行意) Boxing. Practitioners of this style are known for their body methods and the mechanisms behind that come from training the legs. Hence, the name 行意 implies that one's kung-fu comes from mindful walking. For instance, to feel the "Strength comes from the ground" is not a matter of just sinking all the weight down in the legs. Rather, the feet need to constantly feel the ground and step in a delicate manner. It is so sensitive and precise that if one is to step on top of a leaf, one should be able to feel and line up with the stalk under the leaf and bounce off from that fine support. When one's form comes alive with feeling, the body and its movements truly become three-dimensional. From that point on, practice becomes interesting and one is considered entering the 'door'.

Hsing-I Chuan was blessed by a long heritage of masters that not only can 'walk the walk' but can also 'talk the talk'. Without their dedication to study and refine the philosophy, techniques, and theories behind the art, and then selflessly share their findings and experiences all in the spirit of preserving the art, we would not have such a rich repository of lore, tome, and referential resource available to Hsing-I practitioners for generations to follow. In fact, this benefit reaches far beyond one style.

For example, Tai Chi Chuan, renowned for its principles and theories, has an undeniable relationship with Hsing-I. Chen family's 14th generation descendant Chen Chang Xing adopted Hsing-I's nine theories into Chen Tai Chi theories that he passed down in Wen country. Chen family's 16th generation descendant Chen Xin, who wrote the universally acknowledged sourcebook of Tai Chi theory and techniques - "The Illustrated Canon of Chen Family Tai Chi Chuan", used the Hsing-I Boxing Manual as the base for his 3-3 Boxing Manual.

Although a small collection of these materials written in Chinese has been translated into other languages in recent years, a good English language book about Hsing-I Chuan is still few and far between. To this end, *Hsing-I Chuan, The Practice of Heart and Mind Boxing* is a work of intense scholarship that took years to complete. We hope it helps fill in the void in English Hsing-I literature and serve not only as a reference for the Little Nine Heaven family but also as a valuable resource that becomes widely accessible to the practitioners in the West.

Al Lam
April 2017
San Diego, California.

3rd Preface

It is with great pride and honour that I write this at the request of my teacher, Master McNeil, and my school brother, Andrew Jackson; I believe Andrew has done an excellent job in detailing the deceptively simple art of Hsing-I. I feel fortunate to be involved in this project in whatever simple way that I can. I have a nostalgic attachment to Hsing-I because it, along with Splashing Hands Kung-fu, was my first introduction to the Internal Arts over thirty-five years ago. Thus, began a lifelong journey of self-discovery and development that continues to this day. I have been fortunate over many years, to learn the full complement, of styles and practices that have been entrusted to Master McNeil by his teachers. The sheer volume of information imparted to me seems almost too much to comprehend at times and I truly believe that I would not be here today were it not for Master McNeil and kung-fu. Hsing-I was the beginning of it all.

My journey began in 1980 when my brother, Gary and I walked into the tiny school which was located in a nondescript industrial complex in Orange, California. My brother had discovered it the day before and thought there was promise here after observing a class. The head instructor was not present that day but my brother was impressed with the senior student standing in for him, called Al Lam. My brother and I went back together the following evening when the teacher was there. We had both been interested in martial arts since childhood and we had been on a mission for some time, trying to find a real martial arts teacher, whether it was kung-fu or any other style; we knew enough to know what we were looking for when we saw it.

The head instructor was there the next day and I think our inflated sense of our own abilities and lack of any real knowledge betrayed us. Although I cannot speak of my brother's thoughts, I was not really impressed with the teacher's appearance as he looked a very average guy, he was stocky with big forearms and appeared even a little out of shape. I remember thinking he wasn't very flexible as we watched him lead the class in warm-up exercises. At the time, my brother and I were both enamoured with images of Bruce Lee and really thought our own kicks were something special, however, we were in for a rude awakening.

I will never forget the first time Master McNeil slapped me; demonstrating different forms, he invited me to punch at his abdomen and I really had no concept of "helping the teacher in the demonstration" and I stepped in swinging for the fences. Using the opening move from the Five Elements forms, he slapped down on my forearm with both 'meaty' hands and a bright flash of white light exploded in my vision and when it cleared a second later, his huge index finger was drilled half way into my throat. He invited more punches and kicks and with great trepidation I complied a few more times. His hands were like butterflies made from bricks and I couldn't believe how much his soft touch hurt with so little effort on his part. Then it was my brother's turn.

Master McNeil told Gary to throw his best kick and Gary fired away but then limped off as he was struck in the ankle with perfect placement and timing by Master McNeil's oversized fist. As if that wasn't enough he invited me to freely hit him again. The stomach, ribs, kidneys, he didn't care and after about half a dozen increasingly frustrated punches and kicks later my hands and feet were sore and I was completely sold.

I was enthusiastic and dedicated, like a sponge, soaking up everything Master McNeil would teach me; Hsing-I, Splashing Hands, Chen Tai Chi, Little Nine Heaven Wu Tao, Ba Kua, Shih Shui, Iron Hand and all the meditations and chi kung exercises.

Eight years later, in 1988 I was fortunate enough to go to Taiwan with Master McNeil and compete in the Tang Shou Tao full contact tournament. While I was there, I visited my teacher's Masters in their homes and had the rare honour of learning the Tzu Men Chuan forms directly from Master Chin himself.

I was personally drawn to martial arts initially by the self-defence aspects and the skills I have developed under Master McNeil's tutelage have served me well over the years, however, the healing aspects of Hsing-I and the skill of Master Hsu Hong Chi have probably had the greatest impact on my life.

After the first few years of practise I began to have some issues with my lower back. I am not sure of the cause, possibly excessive supine leg lifts while lying on a concrete floor. Due to a problem with my lower spine involving the vertebrae and fascia sheath, the exercises had led to me having pain down my leg with weakness and numbness so this was affecting my ability to practice. This problem went on for some time and I started to get worried. At the time, Master Chi was over from Taiwan. He was visiting the Tang Shou Tao schools in California and he was sitting in on one of our training sessions one evening. He asked if anyone had injuries or other health issues that he could help with and several students came forward with some minor ailments and problems which he addressed with various Tui Na techniques. I then stepped up and described my problem and I could see his concern as he examined my back and the interpreter relayed my symptoms. It seemed that this wasn't just another run of the mill injury and I had his interest. The treatment required Master Chi and the help of two other people with the crux of the matter being that I was not allowed to bend over at the waist for three days while the fascia tissue grew back together, otherwise the vertebrae would just keep popping back out. This was challenging to say the least and he treated me again the next evening at class. The treatment was successful on the second session and my symptoms disappeared. Master Chi truly had the 'magic touch'.

This, of course, was just the beginning of my journey and development through practice of the internal arts. That is the development of energy that lies dormant within us all and can be cultivated through the art of Hsing-I. Throughout my life, there have been many 'ups and downs' but I am happy to still be a part of the Little Nine Heaven family that has been raised and perpetuated by our father, Master McNeil, and I will do the best I can to pass on this legacy and honour my teacher and grand teachers.

James Doty
November 2017
Arizona

Glossary

The study of Taoism, Chinese martial arts, Chinese culture and both Chinese and Western medicine involves the use of unique languages. Many of the terms used in this book are not used commonly in everyday English, therefore, the following glossary of keywords, terms, names of literature and subjects of history have also been elaborated on in this section. However, to understand these areas in more depth, further research would be required, as to fully explain them in this glossary would be beyond the scope of this book. It is, therefore, advisable for the reader to familiarise themselves with these terms and refer to if necessary before reading further on the subject of Hsing-I Chuan. For ease of reference, the keywords and terms have been categorised and placed in alphabetical order.

Historical Books and Texts

Art of War – Sun Tzu
The *Art of War* is an ancient Chinese military treatise attributed to Sun Tzu, a high-ranking military general, strategist and tactician. The text is composed of thirteen chapters, each of which is devoted to one aspect of warfare. It is commonly known to be the definitive work on military strategy and tactics of its time. It has been the most famous and influential of China's Seven Military Classics, and "for the last two thousand years it remained the most important military treatise in Asia, where even the common people knew it by name." It has had an influence on Eastern and Western military thinking, business tactics, legal strategy and beyond.

Classic of Categories (aka Leijing)
Zhang Jing-Yue (c.1563-1640; original name: Zhang Jie-Bin) had an immense influence on the development of TCM at a time when the Ming Dynasty was collapsing to give way to the Ching Dynasty. One of the major works coming from Zhang's years of learning and medical practice was the *Leijing* (a study of the *Neijing Suwen*). This massive piece of work contains thirty-two volumes and basically combined the contents of the *Neijing Suwen* with that of the *Lingshu*, rearranging them according to topical categories and adding lengthy explanations of difficult or controversial passages.

Neijing Suwen

The Yellow Emperor's Inner Classic of medicine (*Neijing Suwen*) is the most important ancient text in Chinese Medicine as well as a major book of Taoist theory and lifestyle. The text is structured as a dialogue between the Yellow Emperor and his ministers or physicians, most commonly Qíbó, but also Shàoyú. The *Neijing Suwen* departs from the old shamanistic beliefs that disease was caused by demonic influences. Instead the natural effects of diet, lifestyle, emotions, environment, and age are seen as the reasons for diseases to develop within the body.

San Ming Tong Hui (The Confluence of the Three Fates)

The Chinese Four Pillars of Destiny is a very old astrological technique. It has been in continuous use in China for nearly 1,400 years and has developed throughout the ages, specifically the Tang, Song and later Ming imperial dynasties. The most authoritative work on the technique is the book titled *San Ming Tong Hui* written by Wan Yu Wu of the Ming dynasty. This work contained instructions for many methods of divination.

Spiritual Axis (aka Lingshu Jing)

Lingshu Jing also known as *Spiritual Axis*, *Divine Pivot*, *Spiritual Pivot* or *Numinous Pivot*, is an ancient Chinese medical text whose earliest version was probably compiled in the 1st century BCE on the basis of earlier texts.

Spring and Autumn Annals

The *Spring and Autumn Annals* is the official chronicle of the State of Lu covering the period from 722 BCE to 481 BCE. It is the earliest surviving Chinese historical text to be arranged on annalistic principles. The text is extremely concise and, if all the commentaries are excluded, about 16,000 words long.

Su Nu Ching

The *Su Nu Ching* or *Classic of the White Madam*, by the Yellow Emperor is the ancient Taoist book explaining the hidden, higher purpose of reproduction and lovemaking. It contains secrets which help humanity enjoy life, improve life, love life and benefit from life. Specifically, it provides methods which heighten, intensify, and prolong lovemaking to strengthen the bond of love between couples.

Taoist Canon/Daozang

The 'Taoist Canon' consists of around 1400 texts that were collected circa CE 400. They were collected by Taoist monks of the period in an attempt to bring together all of the teachings of Taoism, including all the commentaries and expositions of the various masters from the original teachings found in the **Tao Te Ching** and

Zhuangzi. It was split into categories called 'The Three Grottoes'. These three divisions were based on the main focus of Taoism in Southern China during the time it was made, namely; meditation, ritual, and exorcism.

As well as the Three Grottoes, there were Four Supplements that were added to the Canon circa CE 500. These were mainly taken from older core Taoist texts apart from one which was taken from an already established and separate philosophy known as Tianshi Dao (Way of the Heavenly Masters). Although the above can give the appearance that the Canon is highly organised, this is far from the truth. Although the present-day Canon does preserve the core divisions, there are substantial forks in the arrangement due to the later addition of commentaries, revelations and texts elaborating upon the core divisions.

Tao Te Ching

The *Tao Te Ching* also simply referred to as the ***Laozi***, is a Chinese classic text. According to tradition, it was written around the 6th century BCE by the sage Laozi (or Lao Tzu, "Old Master"), a record-keeper at the Zhou Dynasty court, by whose name the text is known in China. The text's true authorship and date of composition or compilation are still debated, although the oldest excavated text dates back to the late 4th century BCE.

The text is fundamental to both philosophical and religious Taoism. Many Chinese artists, including poets, painters, calligraphers, and even gardeners have used the *Tao Te Ching* as a source of inspiration. Its influence has also spread widely outside East Asia, and is amongst the most translated works in world literature.

Historical Facts

Boxer Rebellion

The Boxer Rebellion was a pro-nationalist movement, which opposed foreign imperialism and the influence of Christianity within China between 1899 and 1901. The Righteous Harmony Society rebelled at a time when China was in a poor economic state with unrest ranging back to the Opium Wars and Christian missionary work, which undermined the weak Ching State, of the time. Boxer fighters converged on Beijing, forcing the foreigners to seek refuge in the Legation Quarter. In response to this aggression, the 'Eight Nation Alliance' brought in armed troops and defeated the Imperial Army, capturing Beijing, lifting the siege of the Legations.

Jin Dynasty 960-1234

The Jin Dynasty was founded by the Nuzhen tribes, who originated from the Changpai Mountain area. In 1115, a Nuzhen tribal leader, named Wanyan Aguda, unified the group and waged war constantly with the Liao Dynasty and Northern

Song Dynasty people. These battles resulted in the Liao army being completely defeated by the Jin army in 1125 and the Northern Song army were conquered in 1127. After that, the Jin Dynasty gradually unified the vast areas in the north along the Yellow River. During the late Jin Dynasty, rulers became corrupt and there was a dramatic surge in national uprisings. The Jin court in that period made enemies, including in these was the Mongolian Kingdom and in 1234, the Jin army was finally defeated and the Yuan Dynasty was founded by the Mongolians.

Jin Measurement
The Chinese Jin (also known as a 'catty') has a modern definition of exactly 500 grams. Traditionally about 605 grams, the Jin has been in use for more than 2000 years, serving the same purpose as 'pound' for the common-use measure of weight.

Kung-Fu
In Chinese, Kung means 'work' or 'achievement' and Fu can mean 'intensity'. It can be used in contexts completely unrelated to martial arts, and refers to any individual accomplishment or skill cultivated through long effort and hard work. It is only in the late 20th century, that this term was used in relation to martial arts by the Chinese community. Chinese martial arts, colloquially referred to as kung-fu have developed over the centuries and are often classified according to common traits, identified as 'families' (jiā), 'sects' (pài) or 'schools' (mén) of martial arts.

Pa Kua Zhang (aka Ba Gua Chang)
Translated into English as Eight-Trigram Palm, it is a form of internal martial arts, which is practiced by changing of the palms whilst walking in a continual circular motion. Its foundation is credited to Master Dong Haichuan (1796–1882).

Shaolin
Shaolin Temple is famous for its martial arts. Shaolin Kung-Fu refers to the traditional cultural system that has formed in the particular Buddhist cultural environment within the Shaolin Temple of Songshan Mountain in China over long history. It is based on a belief of Buddhism and fully reflects the wisdom of Buddhist religion. The martial arts practiced by monks in the Shaolin Temple are its major form of expression.

Taiji/Tai Chi Chuan
An internal form of martial art that is made up of a complex set of movements. The characteristics of the movements are flowing, relaxing and graceful in appearance, however the same moves can be lethal if applied in a fighting situation. Tai Chi Chuan is the most widely practiced form of the internal martial arts and can be practiced for health, meditation and self-defence.

Taoist Terms

Celestial Bodies
The Celestial Realm (Heaven) brings the energy of heat and light (Heavenly Chi) to the world. It defines our seasons, and brings celestial influences into the spheres of the Earth and humanity. The way of Heaven refers to the orbits and rules of the movements of the celestial bodies, such as the sun, the moon and stars. The Celestial Bodies have always played an important role in Taoism. Many of the earliest Taoist deities were star gods, and the highest gods of the Taoist pantheon are believed to dwell in different constellations in the sky.

Chi-Kung
Chi-Kung (pronounced 'chee-gung',) is translated from Chinese to mean 'energy cultivation' or 'working with the life energy'. Chi-Kung is an ancient Chinese system of postures, exercises, breathing techniques and meditations. Its techniques are designed to improve and enhance the body's chi level and chi flow.

Earth
The material realm of human existence and belongs to Yin. Earth is seen to include all the land, rivers and seas. It also includes the climate and all visible influences of the seasons. Within the human body, Earth pertains to all things below the level of the navel.

Five Elements-Wu Hsing
Taoists believe the five elements to be Wood, Fire, Earth, Metal and Water. Each element emulates an individual type of energy; each element has a Yin and Yang aspect. Human beings are products of Heaven and Earth and by the interaction of Yin and Yang, contain the combined chi of the five elements, not only in the body physically but emotionally within the mind and spirit.

Heaven
Within Chinese philosophy, Heaven is the immaterial realm, belonging to Yang. The realm of Heaven is seen to include the sun, moon, stars and sky. It also includes the atmosphere around us as well as invisible forces that influence the human body. Within the human body all which is above the navel corresponds to Heaven.

Hun
The spirit (Shen) of the liver is called the Hun or ethereal soul. It is the aspect of consciousness that continues to exist after the death of the body. The Hun is associated with the Wood element. As a person's internal practice deepens more

of the Po or physical aspects of consciousness are transmuted or used as support for the Huns subtler aspects and the person becomes closer to the chi of heaven and the Tao.

Little Nine Heaven Wu Tao (Hsiao Chiu Tien Wu Tao/Xiao Jiu Tian Wu Tao)
The Little Nine Heaven Wu Tao system is an internal method of Taoist cultivation and martial art. It consists of three skills; Ju Kung ('Nine Chamber Fist'), 'Chiankuan Jen' (swordsmanship), and 'Shih Shui' (bone-marrow washing). It is mainly based on the Confucian thoughts of the merging of heaven and man to transform one's disposition. In skill, it is based on the Tao's practice of the balancing between Yin and Yang to relax the tendons and bones, and to perform marrow washing. Even though its name translates to fist, it is an exclusive literature and a rich inheritance passed down through the centuries by word of mouth.

Macrocosm/Microcosm
Macrocosm is a Greek term used to describe a complex structure, such as the universe, regarded as an entirety, as opposed to Microcosms, which have a similar structure and are contained within the Macrocosm. It is a term commonly adopted in the West in relation to Taoism to describe the comparison between the universe and the human body.

Nei-Kung
Nei-Kung practice emphasises training the coordination of the individual's body and mind with the breath, known as the harmonisation of the inner and outer energy, creating a basis for developing and utilising internal power. Nei-Kung exercises involve cultivating physical stillness. The ultimate purpose of this practice is for the individual to become at one with Heaven or the Tao.

Ni-Wan Palace
Often termed 'Dust Pill'; it is a Taoist term for the upper Tan Tien, which is seen as an energy centre located within the brain.

Po
The spirit (Shen) of the lungs is called the Po or corporeal soul. It is the aspect of consciousness that dissolves with the elements of the body at the time of death. The Po belongs to the Metal element. Since the Po exists only within the context of a single lifetime, it tends to be associated with our immediate desires, as opposed to the Hun, which expresses more long-range commitments.

Shen (Mind/Spirit/Consciousness/Vitality)
Shen is an expression of life's activity. It encompasses the dimensions of mind, spirit, consciousness and vitality. Both chi and Jing nourish Shen, which is said to manifest in two ways. One is the mental state and thinking activities. The other is in the expression of physiological activities and pathological changes in the body. The element associated with Shen is fire as it resides in the heart and is seen to be 'the emperor' of the five organ related spirits. Shen of the heart is associated with the overall quality of our awareness, which can be perceived in the energy flowing through our eyes. When Shen is abundant the eyes will be clear, sparkling and responsive.

Shih-Shui Kung
Shih-Shui (pronounced she-sway), also known as 'bone-marrow washing' is a component of the ancient Taoist Little Nine Heaven Wu Tao system which originated in China almost 2000 years ago. Shih- Shui is an advanced form of Chi-kung/Nei-kung that focuses on strengthening the internal body and increasing sexual energy with a goal to optimise and preserve the health of the body, mind and spirit. It consists primarily of a series of special breathing and strengthening exercises along with specific energy circulation techniques.

Tan Tien
Traditionally, a 'Tan Tien' is considered to be a centre of chi or 'life force' energy within the body. The three Tan Tien's are important points of reference in Taoist based self-cultivation practices of exercise, breathing and meditation, as well as in martial arts and in Traditional Chinese medicine. Usually when discussing the Tan Tien texts are referring to the lower Tan Tien which is the focal point of breathing techniques as well as the centre of balance and gravity. The lower Tan Tien is seen to be located approximately two inches below the height of the navel in humans.

Tao/Taoism/Taoist
Tao is the term given to describe the way of nature. Tao is a cosmological and philosophical term that denotes the universe and all things within it as a whole. Taoism is the term given to the study of this philosophy. Taoists are those people who seek to study the Tao.

The Three Treasures (aka San Bao)
The Three Treasures is the name given to the combination of Jing, chi and Shen within the body.

Thrusting Meridian (AKA Ch'ung Mo)
The 'Thrusting Meridian' is the English term given to one of the most important channels of chi in Chi-Kung practice. It is located through the centre of the spine and starts at the perineum (Hui Yin point) and ends at the crown. (Baihui point). It penetrates many vital organs and glands including the spinal column and the brain.

Wuji
An important component of Taoist theory is the Chinese word used to describe the un-manifest aspect of Tao, or Tao-in-stillness. 'Wuji' is the undifferentiated timelessness which is represented by an empty circle. It refers to a state of non-distinction prior to the differentiation into Yin and Yang, out of which are born the ten-thousand-things, i.e. all the phenomena of the manifest world.

Yi
The spirit (Shen) of the Spleen is called the Yi, or intellect. Yi is associated with the earth element. The Yi includes our capacity to use our conceptual mind to exercise discernment and to form intentions. An unbalanced Yi can manifest as a kind of overthinking or 'pensiveness' that damages the spleen. A healthy Yi manifests as bright intelligence and understanding.

Yin and Yang
The terms Yin and Yang are used to indicate a duality or polarity in the universe that is reflected in human beings, on Earth, in nature and in the way everything relates to each other. The relationship between Yin and Yang is not static; it is flowing and dynamic with continual interaction between them.

Zhi
The spirit (Shen) of the Kidney is called the Zhi, or will and is associated with the element Water. Zhi is the minister in charge of the intention and effort required to accomplish things. This includes the effort and perseverance needed to succeed in a person's internal practice.

Traditional Chinese Medical Terms

Blood
Blood is the densest, fluid substance in the human body. It transmits nutrients and provides the material matrix for mental and emotional life. Within TCM, blood is seen to nourish the body and be Yin in nature. It is said to be stored in the liver, made by the spleen and propelled by the heart.

Chi
Chi is the essential ingredient that makes life possible. In humans, it represents vital energy, a unique energetic force that makes life sustainable on earth. In nature, chi is also present. Within humans, chi energy is seen to be a combination of both Yin and Yang circulating through pathways called meridians in the body.

Cold
In TCM terms, Cold may attack the external or internal parts of the body. Cold in the interior may be externally contracted or maybe internally generated, due damaged Yang. When Cold is externally contracted, it attacks the exterior and then it directly invades the interior, penetrating to deeper levels of the body. Once Cold is lodged deep inside the body, it tends to devastate Yang and can be life threatening.

Damp
In TCM terms, Dampness is localised fluid accumulation within the body associated with heat or disturbed organ function. It is a heavy, sluggish, Yin pathogenic influence that hinders and obstructs the flow of chi and blood. Internally generated dampness is caused when Spleen Chi is weakened. Damp can also be externally contracted when the body is too weak to protect itself when exposed to a damp environment such as getting wet from the rain or sweating.

Deficient
In TCM terms the state of deficiency within the body occurs when a basic substance is lacking or an organ has been weakened, thus becoming incapable of carrying out its normal function with chi and blood.

Dryness
In TCM terms, dryness may be of external or internal type. External dryness refers to externally contracted dryness when the body is too weak protect itself from weather changes. Internal dryness is due to the Zang/Fu's loss of Jing essence and depletion of fluids. External dryness may affect the interior parts of the body and interior dryness may also affect the exterior or superficial parts of the body such as the skin.

Du Meridian (aka Du Mai)
Translated in English as the 'Governor Vessel', it is one of the eight extra meridians of the body which runs up the back of the spine starting from the tip of the coccyx bone and the anus and ends at the inside of the upper lip of the face.

Excess
Within the human body and TCM principles, excess refers to too much Jing, Chi, Blood or Shen which leads to hyperfunction of any organ or physiological system.

Fire
In TCM the use of the terms Heat and Fire are based on the degree of manifestation. Fire is thought of as a more intense form of Heat. Fire is used to describe conditions with gross visible manifestations of heat such as red eyes, a flushed face, or bleeding. Fire usually relates to excess Yang or deficient Yin within the body.

Heat
Heat can accumulate in the interior of the body causing interior excess or dryness characterised by fever, constipation or abdominal pain that increases upon pressure.

Jing (Essence)
Jing is the indispensable substance from which the body is constructed and life activities maintained. Jing is composed of a prenatal Jing and postnatal Jing; both are closely related. Pre-natal Jing is reproductive Jing inherited from our parents. Post-natal Jing is the nourishment gained from food and water. Together they nourish the Zang Fu organs and are stored in the Zang organs. Many older texts translate Jing as 'Seminal Essence'.

Jing-Luo
Jing-Luo is a term used in TCM to describe the meridians or channels that form a network of energy pathways that link and balance the various organs. The meridians connect the internal organs with the exterior of the body and the person to the environment and the universe. They serve to distribute chi within the body, protecting the body against environmental imbalances.

Jin-Ye
Jin-Ye is a term used in TCM to describe all the liquids within the body. Jin-Ye protects, nourishes and lubricates the various tissues of the body. The Jin are the lighter-weight fluids that moisten and nourish the skin and muscles, while the Ye are the thicker, more viscous fluids of the bones, organs, brain and body orifices.

Ke cycle
The Ke cycle is the regulatory cycle pertaining to the five-element theory and applied when analysing how the body functions. It is where one phase or element regulates, inhibits and energetically oversees the functions of another element. For further details see the five-element chapter of this book.

Meridians
Meridians (Jing-Luo) are the western term for the pathways that carry chi, blood and fluids through the body. Most acupressure points are located on the meridians.

Rebellious Chi
TCM views Rebellious Chi as chi which flows in a disorderly way and against the normal direction. This causes the disease or illness in the body as the natural ordered flow of chi is hindered.

Ren Meridian (aka Ren Mai)
Translated in English as the Conception Vessel, it is the primary Yin meridian that extends along the front of the body. The Ren meridian originates in the uterus in females and in the lower abdomen in males, and emerges onto the surface of the body in the perineum. It ascends along the midline of the front of the body, ending in the groove just below the lower lip on the face. The Ren Meriden has a primary role in regulating menstruation and nourishing the foetus in females.

San Jiao (aka Triple Burner/Triple Warmer/Triple Heater)
There is no organ in western medicine which corresponds to San Jiao, but it is said to occupy the thoracic and abdominal cavities. It consists of three areas or 'Jiaos' as they are referred to in TCM terms.

Shang Jiao, the 'upper burner', is located in the thoracic cavity, above the diaphragm and it includes Fei (lungs) and Xin (Heart). It is associated with respiration.

Zhong Jiao, the 'middle burner', is located in the abdominal cavity, including Wei (stomach) and Pi (spleen). It is associated with digestion.

Xia Jiao, the 'lower burner', is located in the lower abdominal cavity and pelvic cavity, below the bellybutton, and includes Gan (liver), Xiao Chang (small intestine), Da Chang (large intestine), Shen (kidneys) and Pang Guang (bladder). It is associated with waste and elimination.

Seminal Essence (See Jing)
Seminal Essence is the English term for Jing and is the original substance of the body responsible for the construction of the body and generation of offspring.

Sheng Cycle
The Sheng Cycle is the sequence within the Five Elements theory that produces, supports and gives rise to another element or phase energetically. For further details see the Five Element chapter of this book.

Stagnation of Chi and Blood
In TCM terms, stagnation indicates chi or blood flowing weakly through an area, providing it with less than adequate nutrition.

TCM
TCM is an abbreviation for 'Traditional Chinese Medicine' and is commonly used to refer to the umbrella of arts that constitutes Chinese medicine practise. It covers a number of skills which are often practised in China as separate methods but can be united in that they all follow the same theoretical philosophy. These arts include acupuncture, Chinese herbal medicine, moxibustion, cupping and acupressure massage and many other effective adjuncts and methods attached to these major methods.

Triple Heater organ (aka Sanjiao organ)
This organ is not actually a physical organ like the other Zang/Fu but it serves to integrate the activities of all other organ networks within the body. The Triple Heater has its own meridian assigned to it and is one of the six Yang meridians whose function is to coordinate the functions of the three main body cavities, pelvis, abdomen and chest and the organs contained within them.

Turbid Chi
A Chinese medicine term used to describe 'waste' or 'dirty chi' created within the body. This type of chi can be a source of illness within and it should be sought to cleanse or expel Turbid Chi from the body to remain healthy.

Yang Deficiency
Yang deficiency occurs due to injury to the kidney and spleen. Yang deficiency manifests within the body as cold and systemic exhaustion with an aversion to cold. Yang deficiency indicates that something in the body is lacking, so simply wearing more clothing may not alleviate the symptoms.

Yin Deficiency
Yin deficiency occurs when Yin is deficient and fluids are depleted. Injury to kidney and liver causes Yin deficiency as these two organs serve as the reserve of Yin for the entire body. Severe or chronic Yang excess can also lead to Yin deficiency as the warming aspect of Yang will dry up the nourishing aspect of Yin.

Zang/Fu Organs
The Zang/Fu is the name given to the organ system of TCM. It is an extensive theory containing views on anatomy, physiology and pathology, as well as their own principles of diagnosis and treatment. The Zang organs are the heart,

pericardium, spleen, liver and kidney. They are classed as Yin, solid organs and store blood/essence.

The Fu organs are the large intestine, small intestine, bladder, gallbladder, triple heater and stomach. They are classed as Yang and are hollow organs. They move substances through the body.

Western Medical Terms

Abdominal cavity
The abdominal cavity is the cavity within the abdomen, the space between the abdominal wall and the spine. The abdominal cavity is not an empty space. It contains a number of crucial organs including the lower part of the oesophagus, the stomach, small intestine, colon, rectum, liver, gallbladder, pancreas, spleen, kidneys and bladder.

Cardiovascular System
The essential components of the human cardiovascular system are the heart, blood and blood vessels. It includes: the pulmonary circulation, a 'loop' through the lungs where blood is oxygenated; and the systemic circulation, a 'loop' through the rest of the body to provide oxygenated blood.

Diaphragm
The diaphragm is a muscle that separates the chest (thoracic) cavity from the abdomen. The diaphragm is the main muscle of respiration. Contraction of the diaphragm muscle expands the lungs during inspiration when one is breathing air in. We rely heavily on the diaphragm for our respiratory function so that when the diaphragm is impaired, it can compromise our breathing.

Foetus
An unborn offspring, developing from the embryo stage (the end of the eighth week after conception, when the major structures have formed) until birth.

Nervous system
The nervous system is the part of the body that coordinates the voluntary and involuntary actions of the person and transmits signals between different parts of their body. It consists of two main parts, the central nervous system (CNS) and the peripheral nervous system (PNS). The CNS contains the brain and spinal cord. The PNS consists mainly of nerves, which are long fibres that connect the CNS to every other part of the body. At its most basic level, the function of the nervous system is

to send signals from one cell to others or from one part of the body to others. The nervous system is susceptible to malfunction in a wide variety of ways, as a result of genetic defects, physical damage due to trauma or poison, infection, or simply aging.

Pathogen
A pathogen is a term used to describe any infectious agent that can produce disease.

Prolapse
Prolapse literally means 'to fall out of place'. In medical terms, prolapse is a condition where organs, such as the uterus, fall down or slip out of place. It is used for organs protruding through the vagina or the rectum or for the misalignment of the valves of the heart. A spinal disc herniation is also sometimes called 'disc prolapse' as it protrudes out from its natural housing between the individual vertebrae.

Thoracic Cavity
The thoracic cavity (or chest cavity) is the chamber of the human body that is protected by the thoracic wall (rib cage). The thoracic cavity includes the lungs as well as the cardiovascular system

Master James McNeil & Andrew Jackson

XXXIII

Part 1

The History and Theory of Hsing-I Chuan

Chapter 1

Hsing-I Chuan – 'A True Internal Treasure'

*'There are many paths to the top of the mountain,
but once there the view is the same.'*

Introduction

Hsing-I Chuan (Xing Yi Quan) is a Chinese boxing style of Taoist origin. Its name literally translates as 'mind form boxing' although it should be 'heart and mind boxing' as it is truly the heart that controls the emotions and fires the body's initial responses. Alongside Tai Chi Chuan (Taiji Quan), Pa Kua Zhang (Ba Gua Chang) and the rare system Little Nine Heaven Wu Tao (Xiao Jiu Tian Wu Tao), it is one of the four classical internal martial arts of China.

When discussing the internal styles, there is a common misconception that one internal art is superior to another. This is not true; the four internal arts are simply four different methods in which to obtain the same end result. Each of the aforementioned styles of boxing are very different in appearance but are connected by their link to classical Taoist philosophy, with the aim of uniting the body and mind through cultivation of chi to attain a higher level of being. Thus, Hsing-I, when practiced correctly, forms a complete art.

The aspect of martial boxing or self-defence in Hsing-I is somewhat a consequence of the training and when practiced correctly, the goal is to develop oneself spiritually rather than to attain an ability to fight an opponent in combat. Hsing-I is an internal art that is concerned with life, health and creativity rather than death, destruction and swelling of the self-ego, which is so often the focus of most martial training today. However, with guidance from a knowledgeable teacher and diligent practice of the systems movements, the creation of a strong and powerful body, alongside the ability to apply its movements in self-defence, are naturally developed. It is from this training that develops a martial art which is devastating in its application.

In the willingness to learn Hsing-I the practitioner should be motivated to practice for the purpose of health and self-development, as to spend many hours and years required to attain a high skill level purely to learn how to hurt someone, they will surely miscomprehend Hsing-I's true teaching. Over time the practice of Hsing-I will become a form of moving meditation, developing an internal awareness of one's self and also has a calming effect on the internal body helping the physical body to reconnect with the mind, which in today's stressful lifestyles most people have lost. This disconnection between the mind and body can lead to illness and premature death.

Any system that trains only the body remains working only at the physical level, no different than any other activity, such as aerobics or football. A system such as Hsing-I, which trains the body and the mind equally, allows the practitioner to surpass the physical or 'Jing' level of training, through to the energetic level or 'chi' level. By learning how to be aware of chi's existence within the body and how to develop it can significantly benefit the serious practitioner's overall health. When a student reaches a high level of practice it is said they will progress to the spiritual level or 'Shen' level, in search of what the ancient Taoists termed 'Immortality'.

Classical Taoist literature refers to Jing, chi and Shen as the 'Three Treasures' (San Bao), which are in essence all forms of the same energy substance just working at different levels of vibration within the body. As humans, we all possess these three forms of energy in varying amounts, but most of us have lost the ability to sense and use them efficiently. Taoist philosophy believes we are born with a given amount of each which comes from our parents and depending on their health at the time of our conception, reflects our overall constitution at birth. From the moment we are born, we start to use up this energy and depending on how hard we lead our lives, both mentally and physically, reflects on how much illness we may suffer and how long we can expect to live.

In the practice of Hsing-I and the Taoist internal arts, the practitioner's aim is to slow this depletion of chi and learn to cultivate it in order to restore it to its original levels, pre-birth. With correct practice of both physical and mental technique, correct breathing during practice of Hsing-I and following a regulated lifestyle, the advanced practitioner can achieve the health benefits developed by the Taoists of legend.

What are the Characteristics of Hsing-I Chuan?

The movements of Hsing-I are simple to look at. Classical literature states Hsing-I is easy to learn but hard to master. They mostly come and go in a straight line with one limb extending as the other reciprocally flexes with very few extra unnecessary movements. It is straightforward and direct in its actions, combining both soft and hard movements. Therefore, it conforms to the principle of Yin/Yang and when practiced correctly it is both balanced and beautiful to observe.

Hsing-I demonstrates speed and power, moving smoothly and directly in the most natural way. Its power is short and close to the body with twisting and drilling energy, in both attack and retreat. The systems footwork, body and hands are closely coordinated throughout its movements. The feet are solid and grounded, making a stable platform to strike, yet they are equally light and agile, depending on the situation. When coordinated, the body becomes strong and powerful and is forged by an equally strong will from the mind.

For self-defence, when applied correctly the techniques of Hsing-I are effective and dangerous; they can cause both external and internal injuries to the opponent and it is for this reason the method of training involves little free sparring and more single person or controlled multi-person exercises and forms to develop its technique. The practitioner cannot pull punches in this style because if they do it becomes ineffective and no longer demonstrates the true essence of the art.

Why Practice Hsing-I Chuan?

Hsing-I is excellent for conditioning the body internally and externally. The practice of the systems forms develops balance, coordination, timing and strong muscles. The drilling, twisting, rising and falling actions of the techniques can open the joints and stretch the muscles to their full range, encouraging increased chi and blood flow which in turn nourishes the tissues and benefits the health. The nervous system is developed through the coordination of heart, eyes, hands and feet during the forms movements and in time the mind and body combine to move as one.

Hsing-I also benefits the organs and the cardiovascular system with the combination of fast and slow movements inherent within the system serving to naturally increase the heart rate which improves circulation and chi flow throughout the body, in a controlled and beneficial way. Using correct abdominal breathing, it allows the lung capacity to be maximised and maximum oxygen intake nourishes the blood and subsequently, the body, reciprocally allowing maximum expulsion of carbon dioxide waste product out of the body. Abdominal breathing also maximises the use of the diaphragm and this more efficient action in turn moves and massages the organs from within. The physical movements of the various Hsing-I forms also enhance this massaging effect on the organs. In Traditional Chinese Medical (TCM) terms, this process increases the quality of chi and helps clear turbid chi from the body more effectively.

Hsing-I helps connect the mind to the physical body during practice. Intention and sensitivity within the body are developed as it is mental thought that drives the initiation prior to each movement. With skill, the practitioner can use their mind to guide their chi directly via the meridians to any part of the body as required and this method can be used for both healing and martial purposes.

Taoist philosophy states ***'The mind controls the chi and the chi commands the blood.'***

Importantly, Hsing-I can be practiced in both an energetic or gentle manner, therefore, it is never too late to begin study of this art. Therefore, people of all ages can practice and the system can be adapted to all abilities. Certain techniques have special characteristics in developing a practitioner's health and can aid specific ailments if practiced correctly. The health benefits of different techniques contained within the Hsing-I system will be discussed as appropriate throughout this book.

Chapter 2

The History of Hsing-I Chuan

Before reviewing the direct lineage history of Master McNeil, a brief overview of the different major lineages of Hsing-I found within the different geographic regions of China and their unique characteristics is discussed to help the reader understand the general development and spread of Hsing-I from ancient to modern times.

Introduction

Little is known about the original creation of Hsing-I. Before Li Lao-Nan (1802/1809? –1890) the factual history and lineage of Hsing-I is not clear. The following history comes from the commonly agreed version passed down through the Hsing-I community and from the past masters of this lineage. The masters' biographies discussed later in this chapter are only the ones directly connected to this line of succession and it is recognised that each of the masters mentioned below had many more students which are well documented and are not included in this book and it is with no disrespect to them that they have omitted them from the discussion below.

Historical information prior to Li Lao-Nan is mainly that of legend passed down through limited history books and word of mouth. It is for this reason there are considerable time gaps in the early history as written works are few and much forgotten. Literacy in the past was reserved for the elite, techniques were passed down in the forms taught and memorised through practice and this is how the styles of Hsing-I and their theories were preserved in ancient times.

Provinces of China and their Hsing-I Lineages

Hsing-I has three commonly agreed developmental branches which are Honan, Hebei and Shansi and derive their names from the provinces of China in which their founders originated. Each style has its own individual characteristics making it different from its counterparts, although all follow the same general theories and philosophical background.

Honan (aka He'nan/Henan)

Honan is a province of the People's Republic of China, located in the central part of the country. Although the name of the province means 'south of the river', approximately a quarter of the province lies north of the Yellow River. Honan is the birthplace of Chinese civilisation with over 5000 years of history, and remained China's cultural, economic, and political centre until approximately 1000 years ago. Numerous heritages have been left behind including the ruins of Shang Dynasty capital city Yin and the Shaolin Temple. Four of the 'Eight Great Ancient Capitals' of China, Luoyang, Anyang, Kaifeng, and Zhengzhou are located in Honan province.

Ma Xueli (DOB uncertain) is acknowledged as the founder of the Honan lineage of Hsing-I as we know it today. The Honan branch is known as the Muslim branch because it was handed down within the Chinese Muslim community to which its founder, Ma Xueli, belonged. Honan branch is sometimes referred to by practitioners as 'Six Harmonies Fist' (Xinyi Liuhe Quan) instead of simply Hsing-I Chuan. This may be attributed to the fact that the Muslim community of China was historically a closed culture and in order to protect them as a minority, opted to retain the older addition to the name of Hsing-I, Liuhe which refers to the six harmonies of the body.

Honan style is a very simplified style of Hsing-I as it has only Ten Animal forms which are extremely simplistic. The Five Elements are present only as concepts in this method, having no movement representations at all. Honan style is typically very aggressive in its application.

Hebei (aka Hubei/Hobei)

Hebei is a province of the People's Republic of China in the North China region. The name Hebei means 'north of the river', referring to its location completely above the Yellow River. Beijing and Tianjin Municipalities, which border each other, were carved out of Hebei. The province borders Liaoning to the northeast, Inner Mongolia to the north, Shansi to the west, Honan to the south, and Shandong to the southeast. A common alternate name for Hebei is Yanzhao, after the state of Yan and state of Zhao that existed here during the Warring States period of early Chinese history.

Li Lao-Nan (1802/1809?–1890) is acknowledged as the founder of the Hebei lineage of Hsing-I and it is probably the most widely practiced of the styles today. Schools of the Hebei branch emphasise powerful fist and palm strikes. Hebei style tends to be simple, slightly slower in appearance, utilising evasive footwork and is typically aggressive in its application.

Shansi (aka Shanxi)

Shansi is a province of the People's Republic of China, located in the North China region. Its name comes from the state of Jin that existed during the 'Spring and Autumn Period'. The name Shansi means 'mountain's west', which refers to the province's location west of the Taihang Mountains. Shansi borders Hebei to the east, Honan to the south, Shaanxi to the west, and Inner Mongolia to the north and is made up mainly of a plateau bounded partly by mountain ranges. The capital of the province is Taiyuan.

Ts'ao Chi-Wu (1665–?) is acknowledged as the founder of the Shansi lineage of Hsing-I as we know it today. This style was considered to be the original style. Further to this also from the Shansi province was Tai Lung-Pang (1713–1802) who became acknowledged as the founder of 'The Northern School' lineage of Hsing-I Chuan. Schools of the Shansi branch are typically fast and powerful. Shansi style tends to adopt a narrower stance, lighter footwork and be more evasive in application.

Map of China showing highlighted provinces in relation to the development of Hsing-I Chuan

The History of Master McNeil's Hsing-I Lineage

The following masters' biographies presented in this book have been referenced with *the Encyclopedia of Chinese Martial Arts*, published in 1998, and are commonly seen to be as accurate as possible although some dates are questionable and often there are conflicting facts within the available literature. There may be some discrepancies and debate with other lineages and biographies but until further factual evidence can be found we will present them as in this book.

Historical Timeline of Chinese Dynasties in relation to the Shansi Lineage of Hsing-I Chuan

ca. 2698–2597 BCE	Ancient China	Huang-Di (Yellow Emperor) Founder of the Internal Martial Arts
ca. 2100–1600 BCE	Xia (Hsia) Dynasty	
ca. 1600–1050 BCE	Shang Dynasty	
ca. 1046–256 BCE	Zhou (Chou) Dynasty	
	Western Zhou (ca. 1046–771 BCE)	
	Eastern Zhou (ca. 771–256 BCE)	Spring and Autumn Period (770–ca. 475 BCE)
		Confucius (ca. 551-479 BCE)
		Warring States Period (ca. 475–221 BCE)
221–206 BCE	Chin (Ch'in) Dynasty	
206 BCE–220 CE	Han Dynasty	
	Western/Former Han (206 BCE–9 CE)	
		Confucianism officially established as basis for Chinese state. (r. 141–86 BCE)
	Eastern/Later Han (25–220 CE)	
220–589 CE	Six Dynasties Period	Buddhism introduced to China
	Three Kingdoms (220–265 CE)	
	Jin Dynasty (265–420 CE)	
	Period of the Northern and Southern Dynasties (386–589 CE)	
581–618 CE	Sui Dynasty	
618–906 CE	Tang (T'ang) Dynasty	
907–960 CE	Five Dynasties Period	
960–1279	Song (Sung) Dynasty	Yueh-Fei (1103–1142)
	Northern Song (960–1127)	
	Southern Song (1127–1279)	
1279–1368	Yuan Dynasty	The reign of the Mongol empire

1368–1644	Ming Dynasty	Capitals: Nanjing and Beijing Chi Lung-Feng (1602–1680)
1644–1912	Ching (Ch'ing) Dynasty	Capital: Beijing T'sao Chi-Wu (1665–?) Tai Lung-Pang (1713–1802) Li Lao-Nan (1802/1809–1890) Liu Chi-Lan (1819–1889) Li Tsun-I (1847–1921) Shang Yun-Chang (1864–1938)
1912–1949	Republic Period	Capitals: Beijing, Wuhan, and Nanjing Liu Tsu-Yen Chang Chung-Feng (1902–1974) Hung I-Hsuang (1925–1993) Hsu-Hong-Chi (1934–1984) Chiao Chang-Hung (1912–2001)
1949–present	People's Republic of China	Capital: Beijing

Huang Ti 2698–2597 BCE

Huang Ti, the Yellow Emperor, reigned in China during the period 2698–2597 BCE and is revered today as one of China's most legendary rulers.

China's first art of war was initiated by Huang Ti. After many wars, he brought order to the land and it was from these wars that hand-to-hand and weapons fighting were developed to create the basis of the martial arts we practice today.

He also wrote two important books, one on Chinese medicine (*Neijing Suwen*) and a lesser-known text (*Su Nu Ching*) which deals with development of energy to maintain health and prolong life. It is said that upon his death Huang Ti ascended to Heaven on the back of a dragon and achieved immortality.

To this day Huang Ti is regarded as an important founder of Chinese Medicine and martial arts, particularly in relation to the Taoist philosophy that underpins them. He is said to have played an important role in collating and documenting a vast amount of factual evidence that still survives and is used to this day. It is for this reason the Little Nine Heaven School acknowledges him in its historical lineage as he had a major influence on all internal martial arts that derive from a Taoist background which includes Hsing-I Chuan.

Yueh Fei 1103–1142

The most commonly accepted founder of Hsing-I Chuan is General Yueh Fei 1103–1142. A famous anti-Jin general of the Sung Dynasty (960–1276), Yueh Fei was from Tangyin in the Honan province. His family was extremely poor and he worked with his father doing farm work by day and studied by night. He was fond of reading Master Zuo's 'Spring and Autumn Annals' and admired Sun Tzu's book *The Art of War*.

Legend has it that he was taught a divine art from his Taoist teacher Chou Ton (Zhou Tong) who was also a military leader and Chen Guang, a famous spearman of his time. Yueh Fei was known to be very faithful and loyal to his country. Before he was an adult Yueh could already draw a 300 Jin bow and was skilled with a spear, he could shoot left- and right-handed and his skills exceeded all others in the country. As a young man, he joined the Song army to fight against the Jin invaders. Because of his great skill in spear, bow and military tactics he rose through the ranks quickly to attain the rank of general. Always outnumbered, he was said to have fought over one hundred and twenty battles and never lost and from this it gave rise to the saying "It is easier to fight a mountain than to fight the army of General Yueh Fei". It is said that whilst fighting against foreign tribes, he passed on his knowledge of Hsing-I to his troops.

Due to political jealousy and Yueh Fei's success on the battlefield, he was put in prison by the emperor of the time and died at the age of thirty-nine. On 27 January 1142 on false charges Yueh Fei, his adopted son and his general assistant were executed; an act that was seen by the people as a great injustice. As his execution grew near he wrote on his deposition "One-day Heaven will vindicate me!"

Twenty years later, Xiao Zhong-Shen attained the throne and in order to calm the anger of the people had Yue Fei's body exhumed and re-buried with full and appropriate ceremonies in Xixialingluan in Hangzhou. Also, a lot of Yeuh Fei's writings were published, in particular his martial creations which include the Hsing-I manual which held the arts entire teachings. Other works included Yueh style connected boxing, Yueh style boxing ten sets, Yueh style spear and several other weapons manuals. The characteristics of his works are many hand techniques and fewer foot techniques all without embellishment. They always valued fighting and practical use. It is assumed that a student of Yueh Fei's was entrusted with these teachings, although between the dates of 1142 and 1602 the historical lineage of Hsing-I is blank, it resurfaces again with the emergence of Chi Lung-Feng. The factual link between Yeuh Fei and any other teachers prior to Chi Lung-Feng is not clear.

Chi Lung-Feng (aka Ji Jike) 1602–1680

About 500 years after Yueh Fei's death a man named Chi Lung-Feng who was born at the end of the Ming Dynasty visited a cave where he claims an eccentric hermit gave him instruction and a book from Yeuh Fei. Chi Lung-Feng was his official name and in some texts, this same person is referred to as Ji Jike. Born in 1602, Pudong County, Shansi Province, he liked martial arts and is said to have also studied at Shaolin temple for about ten years.

At an early age Chi already considered his fighting skills to be exceptional. However, he was never satisfied and felt there was more to the arts. Seeking a teacher with superior skills, Chi travelled extensively between 1630 and 1660 and finally located such a man, a Taoist hermit, living at the foot of the Chung Nan Mountains in the Shansi province. The Taoist hermit taught Chi the essence of the art he practiced and presented him with an instructional book on the subject. He told Chi that this was the same Hsing-I book written and handed down by General Yueh Fei. Chi studied and practiced enthusiastically day and night, until he was able to master all the movements. He made such great progress in his Hsing-I that no one was able to match his fighting skills. It is Chi Lung-Feng who is thought to have ascribed the source of Hsing-I Chuan to Yeuh Fei.

During his lifetime, he became a leader of the resistance for the Chinese people and fought against invading forces, mainly the Manchurians from the north who waged war with the Chinese forces for many years and further developed his martial skills in particular the spear where later in life he became known as 'Heavenly Spear'. Little more is written about Chi Lung-Feng's life and teachings other than later he retired to his home village, where he taught a great number of students. Two of Chi Lung-Feng's most famous students later founded their own schools. Ma Xueli started the Honan school and **Ts'ao Chi-Wu** founded the Shansi school.

Ts'ao Chi-Wu (aka Cao Jiwu) 1665 – Date of death unknown

Ts'ao Chi-Wu, a native of Shanghai learned Hsing-I directly from Chi Lung-Feng. It should be of note here that different historical sources differ on where Ts'ao originated from and Daxing and Honan are also quoted in some literature. From an early age, it is said he practiced Hsing-I under the tutorage of Chi Lung-Feng. Ts'ao practiced his Hsing-I every day and after twelve arduous years his art was refined and he became well known for his martial ability.

In 1693, he was placed first in the martial examinations in Shuntian district and a year later graduated first among all entrants in the highest-level military examinations and was selected by the emperor to become one of his personal bodyguards within the Forbidden City. Over the next seven years he followed the emperor into many battles and was regularly rewarded for his distinguished service. Later in life, he became the Commanding General of the Shansi province. Due to his military genius, troops under his command won a great many battles over the Muslim tribes.

At this point in the records there appears to be a difference of opinion as to Ts'ao's fate. Some sources suggest that Ts'ao died young at the age of thirty-nine after contracting hypothermia during relief operations with his troops after a great flood, however other sources suggest after retiring from the army he devoted himself to perfecting his Hsing-I and taught many students of which the Tai brothers, **Tai Lung-Pang** and Tai Ling-Pang were the most well-known. These two brothers practiced hard and learned quickly, becoming Ts'ao's best students.

Tai Lung-Pang (aka Dai Longbang) 1713–1802

Tai Lung-Pang was a native of Shansi province and became founder of the Northern school of Hsing-I boxing. From his youth, he loved martial arts and studied Chang style boxing. In 1726, at thirteen years old, he travelled to Chizhou where he met Ts'ao Chi-Wu and studied with him for over ten years and attained a high level of skill in Hsing-I. During his travels and training he met and exchanged ideas with another student of Ts'ao Chi-Wu called Ma Xueli who later became founder of the Honan school of Hsing-I. From this encounter, it is said that Tai wrote the *Treatise on Xinyi Six Harmonies Boxing* and from this were developed the 'Tuo' and 'Tai' animal forms taking them from ten to twelve in number and which are practiced in the Shansi lineage seen today. Tai Lung-Pang became the more famous of the two brothers and had many students and among them was his two nephews Tai Wen-Xiong and Tai Wen-Liang and more questionably **Li Lao-Nan**.

Li Lao-Nan (aka Li Feiyu, pen name Laoneng) approx. 1802/1809–1890

Originally from Shen County, Hebei Province from a young age he studied Hua style boxing. Later whilst travelling on business to Shansi Province, it was there that he made the acquaintance of the Tai family and seeing their skills, Li asked if he could study with them. In 1845, he moved to Chi County, Shansi Province and started learning Hsing-I at the relatively late age of thirty-seven. He practiced hard for ten years. Tai Lung-Pang or it is also said more probably Tai Wen-Xiong the nephew of Tai Lung-Pang (if the dates of birth and death are accurate) taught him all he knew of the art and due to his knowledge of Hsing-I, Li was never defeated in a boxing match.

It is claimed Li could beat his opponents from a great distance and could jump over eight feet in the air at any given moment. Some of Li's skills were said to be so incredible that one person referred to his style as 'divine boxing' and it was due to his teachings that Hsing-I became wide spread in many provinces of China. Li became the founder of Hebei style Hsing-I boxing.

In around 1856 Li was asked to take charge of house security for a wealthy landowner and it was at this point he began to take on students. Li Lao-Nan lived to be over eighty years of age. He also became referred to as the greatest Master in Hsing-I history. It is said Li systemised Hsing-I into an excellent training method and had a great many students who were all well known for their Hsing-I abilities. One of these students was **Liu Chi-Lan**.

Liu Chi-Lan (aka Liu Chilan) 1819–1889

Liu Chi-Lan was a native of Shen County, Hebei Province. From his youth, he was fond of fighting and the fighting arts. In his early years, he became skilled at many empty hand and weapons forms and became known as 'The Distinguished Gentleman with Sagely Hands'. Later he studied Hsing-I boxing and spent many years under the guidance of Li Lao-Nan. He attained a high level of skill. Although not as well-known as some of his classmates, Liu nevertheless was very good. He enjoyed teaching and taught openly, breaking with the tradition of secrecy within the arts and devoted his life to spreading his knowledge of Hsing-I. Liu felt that for Hsing-I to conform to Taoist principles, the mind must be mindless and the body bodiless.

Liu Chi-Lan and his also famed Hsing-I brother Guo Yun-Shen travelled together to Beijing, both won all their fights until they met Master Dong Hai-Chuan, the founder of Pa Kua Zhang. The three experimented with each other testing their skills and finally they concluded that Master Dong's skills were the better and agreed that Hsing-I and Pa Kua's principles were very similar but with different training methods. From this point on they became great friends and combined their knowledge. Since this time both Hsing-I and Pa Kua became thought of as members of the same family. Liu Chi-Lan had many famous disciples, **Li Tsun-I** being the foremost.

Li Tsun-I (aka Li Cunyi) 1847–1921

Li Tsun-I was a native of Shen County, Hebei Province. As a young man, his family was poor, making a living in the moving services. In his spare time, he practiced many arts and sought out teachers whenever he could on his travels. In midlife, he happened on Liu Chi-Lan and began his study of Hsing-I boxing and after this he furthered his study with Liu's Hsing-I brother, Guo Yun-Shen. Later he studied Pa Kua with Dong Hai-Chuan where he excelled and reached a high level in the art.

In 1894, he accepted a post in the Ching army as a martial arts instructor and attained the rank of Province Commander-in-Chief. After he left the army he set up the 'Wan Tong' bodyguard service where he made his living guarding convoys and taught many students. During this time, the eight allied armies occupied Beijing and to resist this insult Li lead his students in the boxer rebellion to fight against the foreign invaders. At the battle of Lao Long Kou, he inflicted heavy casualties where he fought at the head of his troops carrying a single blade and because of this his fame spread widely and he became known as 'Single Saber Li'.

In 1911 Li helped establish the Chinese martial arts assembly where he acted as Vice President and Chief Instructor. He led a team of more than ten of his students to attend the world martial arts competition in Beijing where Li himself famously defeated the Russian strongman Kangtaier. Later in life he gave up his bodyguard business and settled to teaching. Some of his famous students include Sun Lu-Tang the founder of Sun style Tai Chi, **Chang Chung-Feng** and **Shang Yun-Chang**.

Note: At this point the lineage splits into two branches.

Branch one:

Shang Yun-Chang (aka Shang Yun Xiang) 1864–1938

Shang Yun-Chang was born in Le Ling County, Shandong province. When young he studied Shaolin Gong Li Quan. At age twenty-one he met Master Li Tsun-I becoming his top student and an employee of his bodyguard service in Tainjin. From Master Li he learned Hsing-I Chuan and Pa Kua Zhang and specialised in the use of the spear. Later Shang learned some Pa Kua from the famous Cheng Ting-Hua and lived with the famous Hsing-I master Guo Yun-Shen. From Master Guo, Shang learned Ban Bu Peng Quan (Half Step Smashing Fist) and the skill of Dan Tian Fu Da (Dan Tien Belly Beating technique). He was a small but powerful man; outspoken and quick tempered, he fought often. A difficult teacher it was said he was 'hands on' and many of his students were injured during training, some seriously. Shang was a practically minded teacher and believed in training for actual combat. In over twenty-five years of teaching he trained over 100 students. One of his best students was **Liu Tsu-Yen**.

Liu Tsu-Yen (aka Liu Chi Yuan) Dates Unknown

Liu Tsu-Yen was a student of Shang Yun-Chang. Liu's teaching methods were very similar to his masters with direct hands on approach and because of this he was one of only a handful of students who stayed with Shang. After many years, Liu went to Shen Yang city, joining the warlord army there where he attained the rank of general and became a master of Hsing-I and Tai Chi. He also became the Chief Martial Arts Instructor for the North-Eastern Military Division. His best and most famous student was **Chiao Chang-Hung**.

Chiao Chang-Hung 1912–2001

Grand Master Chiao Chang-Hung was born to a family living at the foot of the 'Yi Wu Lu' Mountain in the District of Jing Zhou, Liaoning Province, in the North-Eastern region of China. The Family of Grand Master Chiao made regular contributions to a temple nearby named 'San Ching' Taoist Temple located at the top of 'Wu Lu Shan' mountain and had donated ten acres of land.

Grand Master Chiao was gifted in the Chinese martial arts. In his teenage years, he had picked up several traditional martial arts from the family's security guards who were skilled kung-fu fighters. He was taught Hsing-I and Tai Chi Chuan from his father's friend, General Liu Chi-Yuan who was the Chief Instructor to the military in North East military division, China. Later he learned Dragon style Pa-Kua from Yang Ju-Lin who was the top apprentice of the Pa-Kua master, Ma Wei-Chi.

As a youngster Chiao enjoyed roaming the mountains. One day, when he was sixteen, Chiao visited San Ching Temple and whilst walking around the compound he came to the backyard that was rather quiet, with a connection door securely closed. Spurred by curiosity, he climbed over the fenced wall and inside, he saw a Taoist devotee sitting in deep meditation seemingly oblivious to this intrusion. Chiao, with his youthful indifference, walked around the backyard and eventually came to scrutinise the Taoist. After a while, the Taoist opened his eyes and spoke to Chiao. In reply young and impulsive, he quickly boasted of his martial art expertise. The Taoist devotee suggested that he demonstrate some of his capabilities, which Chiao did with great enthusiasm. When he finished, the Taoist devotee said to him: "That was quite spectacular, probably not very useful." This reaction was not what Chiao expected. The Taoist devotee then extended his hand and put forward a finger in the form of a hook and said to him: "Now, if you can move me, I'll take back my words!" With all the effort he could gather, Chiao tried and tried but failed. In the end, he knelt on his knees and asked to be accepted as a student.

The Taoist, known as 'Lushan Daoren', told Chiao, "It is a fate that we meet. Your family has made many contributions to this temple in the past and they are greatly appreciated. If your father agrees, you may come and practice with me."

Subsequently Chiao spent two intensive years of learning in seclusion in San Ching Temple and began to learn the ancient art of Kung Fu called 'Hsiao Chiu Tien' or 'Little Nine Heaven'. This style consists of boxing, swordsmanship and Shih Shui Kung fu. Grand Master Chiao became the 33rd generation disciple and was the first non-devotee to be taught the complete arts of the system.

In his youth, Chiao studied at the Japanese Military Academy. However, he was expelled from the Academy for misconduct when he defeated his Japanese instructor with his Chinese sword during one of the practice sessions. He then went back to China and became an intelligence officer. Later during the Japanese war, he was arrested by the Japanese and carried the physical scars left by the torture he endured from his capture. Fortunately, he was rescued by his Japanese wife and was able to escape back to China.

During the 1950s, Chiao migrated with General Chiang Kai-Chek's government to Taiwan. He served as a government officer within the National Security Department. During that time, he helped to promote the art of kung-fu. Though various introductions and personal associations, he taught the art of Shih Shui to other kung-fu masters as well as government officials, generals and numerous students in Taiwan. He achieved the following positions and awards:

- One of only four people to be awarded the title of Grand Master by the government of Taiwan.
- Founder member of the Tai Chi Chuan Club now called the Tai Chi Chuan Association of Taiwan.
- Appointed Chief Instructor of the National Taiwan Kung-Fu Team.
- Appointed Head Referee for International Kung-Fu Tournaments.
- Advisor to the Chinese Kung-Fu Research Institute (Paris, France).
- The first Grand Master to teach the art of Shih Shui to the interested public.
- The only Grand Master to write and publish a book about the art of 'Shih Shui'.

In the late '70s, Grand Master Chiao decided to open up the teachings of the Chinese intellectual arts to the public. He only accepted students who showed sufficient spirit and commitment to learn the art. This dedication continues with his senior disciples who were chosen to spread the art. Master Carl Kao, Master Tan Ching-Yun of Taiwan and **Master James McNeil** of the United States were chosen to teach others, as well as spread the name of Shih Shui. The reason for his unique gift of knowledge was to pay homage to the loyal and generous body of people that represented the new-found land of Chinese Renaissance - Taiwan. Grand Master Chiao realised mastery in Hsing-I, Pa-Kua, Tai Chi and Little Nine Heaven Wu Tao. He was James McNeil's teacher in Hsing-I, Pa Kua and Little Nine Heaven Wu Tao until he passed away in August 2001 at the age of eighty-nine. In recognition of Grand Master Chiao's position as 33rd generation lineage holder of Little Nine Heaven Wu Tao, a documentary is to be made of his life and extraordinary level of skill and achievements, in his homeland of China.

Branch Two:

Chang Chung-Feng (aka Zhang Junfeng) 1902–1974

Chang Chung-Feng was a well-known Chinese martial artist who specialised in the internal styles of Pa Qua, Hsing-I and Tai Chi. Chang Chun-Feng was born around 1902 in Shandong Province. At the age of nine he moved to Tianjin to apprentice in the fruit wholesaling business. At the age of sixteen, Chang became interested in martial arts. He studied Gao Style Pa Qua with founder Gao Yi-Sheng. Because Chang was busy working all day, he studied with Gao privately in the early morning and at night. Gao often taught classes at Chang's home. Because Gao worked with Chang privately, his progress was fast. He improved rapidly and gained a reputation in Tianjin. Chang studied and later taught martial arts in Tianjin. During that time, Tianjin was the centre of internal martial arts activity. Chang also studied Hsing-I with Li Tsun-I and he also studied Tai Chi with Hao Wei-Zhen.

In 1948, with the political situation in Mainland China deteriorating rapidly, Chang moved to Taiwan. Financially, Chang had a difficult time making a living in Taiwan. Fortunately, people started to become interested in his martial arts skills. He practised martial arts in his spare time near the Round Mountain area in the northern part of Taipei.

The arts he was practising were unlike any that the Taiwanese were accustomed to seeing and he would frequently draw a crowd when he was training. Local martial artists began coming around to see what he could do. He easily defeated many who tried to test his skill and thereby began to acquire students.

In the late 1950s, after performing in a martial arts demonstration at the presidential building, Chang was invited by President Chiang Kai-Chek to teach him internal martial arts and Chi Kung. Shortly after Chang began teaching Chiang Kai-Chek, he was also invited to teach the staff at the Presidential Building, at the Air Force headquarters, at the Police Headquarters, at the Central Investigation Bureau, and the Intelligence Bureau. In 1961, he began training officers in the Department of Defense and taught a number of famous Generals. Chang had an extensive knowledge of bone setting, Traditional Chinese Medicine and Chinese herbs for traumatology. He knew that in the practice of martial arts, injuries were unavoidable and thought that students should have fundamental training in how to heal injuries.

Chang Chun-Feng died on the 16th day of the 5th lunar month in 1974. On the day Chang was buried there were more than 3000 people in attendance, many were high ranking government officials. One of his first and longest, most devoted practicing students in Taiwan was **Hung I-Hsuang**.

Hung I-Hsuang (aka Hung Yixiang) 1925–1993

Hung I-Hsuang was born in Taiwan and studied Shaolin Kung Fu until he was introduced to Chang Chung-Feng in 1948 by Master Chiao Chang-Hung, where he began his studies of the internal Chinese martial arts.

When Chang began teaching in the northern part of Taipei, his first group of core students included the three Hung brothers: Hung I-Hsuang, Hung I-Wen and Hung I-Mien . It is said that Hung I-Hsuang was the Hsing-I Chuan specialist, Hung I-Mien was the Pa Kua Zhang specialist, and Hung I-Wen specialised in Tai Chi Chuan.

After he had studied with Chang for several years, Hung often led classes for Chang. Because the internal martial arts were still very new in Taiwan, many curious people would come to test Chang's skill. Hung who was large for a Chinese said that Chang would often send him out to show the visitors what the internal styles were all about. Many martial artists in Taiwan remember Hung as being someone who was involved in many fights, both in and out of the martial arts studio and from this he gained a reputation for being a skilled fighter.

In the mid-1960s Hung I-Hsuang opened his own school under the name 'Tang Shou Tao'. Many of Hung's students dominated the full-contact tournaments in Taiwan. One student, Weng Hsien-Ming won the Taiwan full contact championships three years in a row. Another, Huang Hsi-I also usually won his full contact tournaments with knock-outs. Another, student of Hung I-Hsuang was Hsu Hong-Chi who became one of his most skilled in both martial arts and healing arts and went on to become internationally renowned.

Hsu Hong-Chi (aka Xu Hongji) 1934–1977

Hsu Hong-Chi was a Taiwanese martial artist who specialised in the internal Chinese art of Hsing-I Chuan. Hsu was born in Taipei, Taiwan in 1934 to a family of six brothers. In school, he was very athletic and participated in swimming, soccer and judo. He began his study of Shaolin Kung-Fu with his father at an early age. He also learned boxing and became a skilled street fighter. After studying the external styles of Shaolin for many years, he discovered the unique effectiveness of the internal martial arts and began training with Hung I-Hsuang, a master of all three of the classical Chinese internal arts. He studied and trained for many hours a day and became the number one student of Hung I-Hsuang.

After many years of training Hsu opened his own Hsing-I school. Hsu named his school 'Shen Long Tang Shou Tao' which translates as Spirit Dragon Chinese Hand Way. 'Shen Long Tang Shou Tao' is not a separate style of martial art, but rather a practical, step-by-step, systematic approach to learning internal martial arts and developing highly refined levels of skill. Although he incorporated elements learned from other teachers, Hsu's 'Shen Long Tang Shou Tao' curriculum was very similar to Hung's.

Hsu felt that if a person, no matter what their race or nationality, sincerely wanted to learn and was willing to work hard then he would teach them. In the late 1960s he began teaching American and Japanese students in Taiwan. This led to his falling out of grace with many of his fellow Chinese, including his teacher Hung I-Hsiang, even though Hsu was one of Hung's senior students at the time.

According to Master Hsu Hong-Chi when practicing Hsing-I the following rules should be adhered to:

A student of Hsing-I should be wise but ignorant because a wise man does not show his skill unless he must.

One should keep everything to himself and in a real fight. He should feel emptiness and act like no one is there.

When attacking, the hands and body should move together. The hands should be alive and the legs light.

If every strike and step is coordinated, one will not lose the upper hand to the opponent.

For many years, Hsu went to teach in Japan and several of his Japanese students opened schools there. He also went to the US several times and taught a number of long-term American students in Taiwan. One such student was **James McNeil**. Master Hsu Hong-Chi was James McNeil's teacher from 1978 until his death in 1984. In Taiwan, his best students were his son Hsu Chang-Wang and Carl Kao.

Simplified Shansi Lineage Chart for Master McNeil's School Of Hsing-I

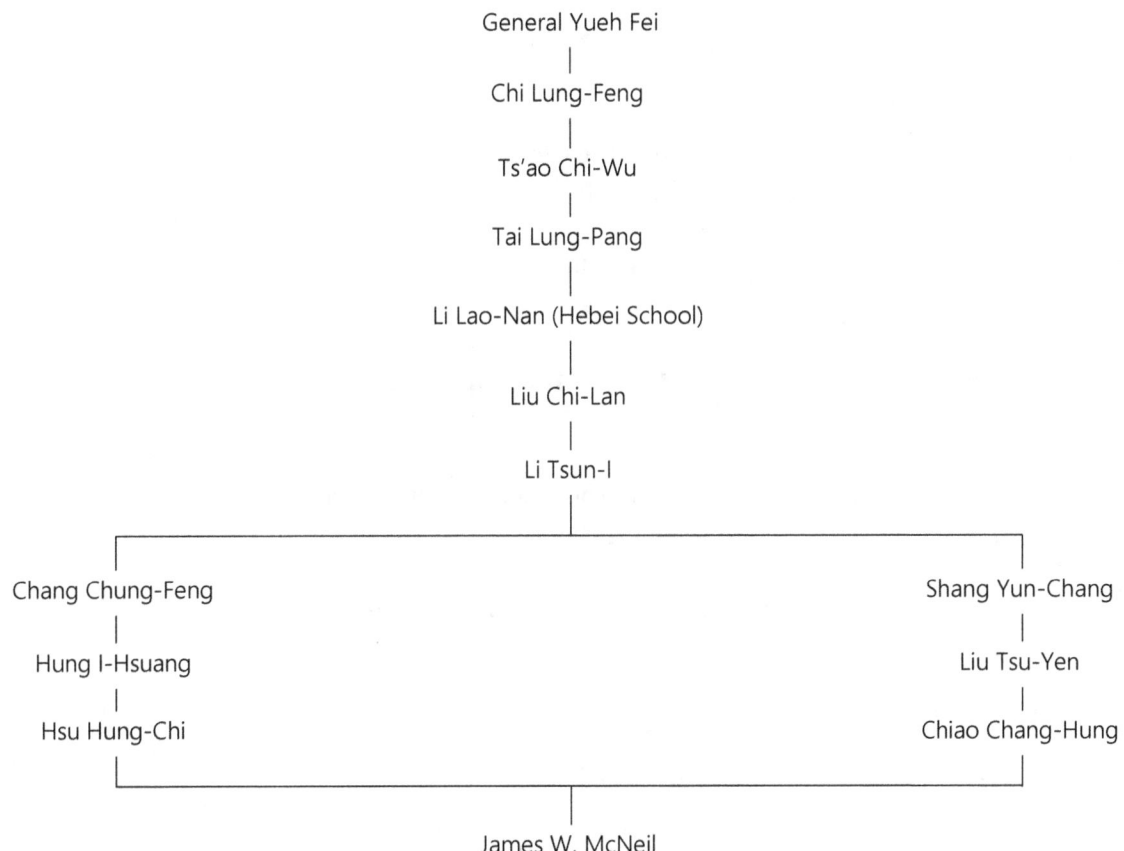

The Shansi System Hsing-I Lineage

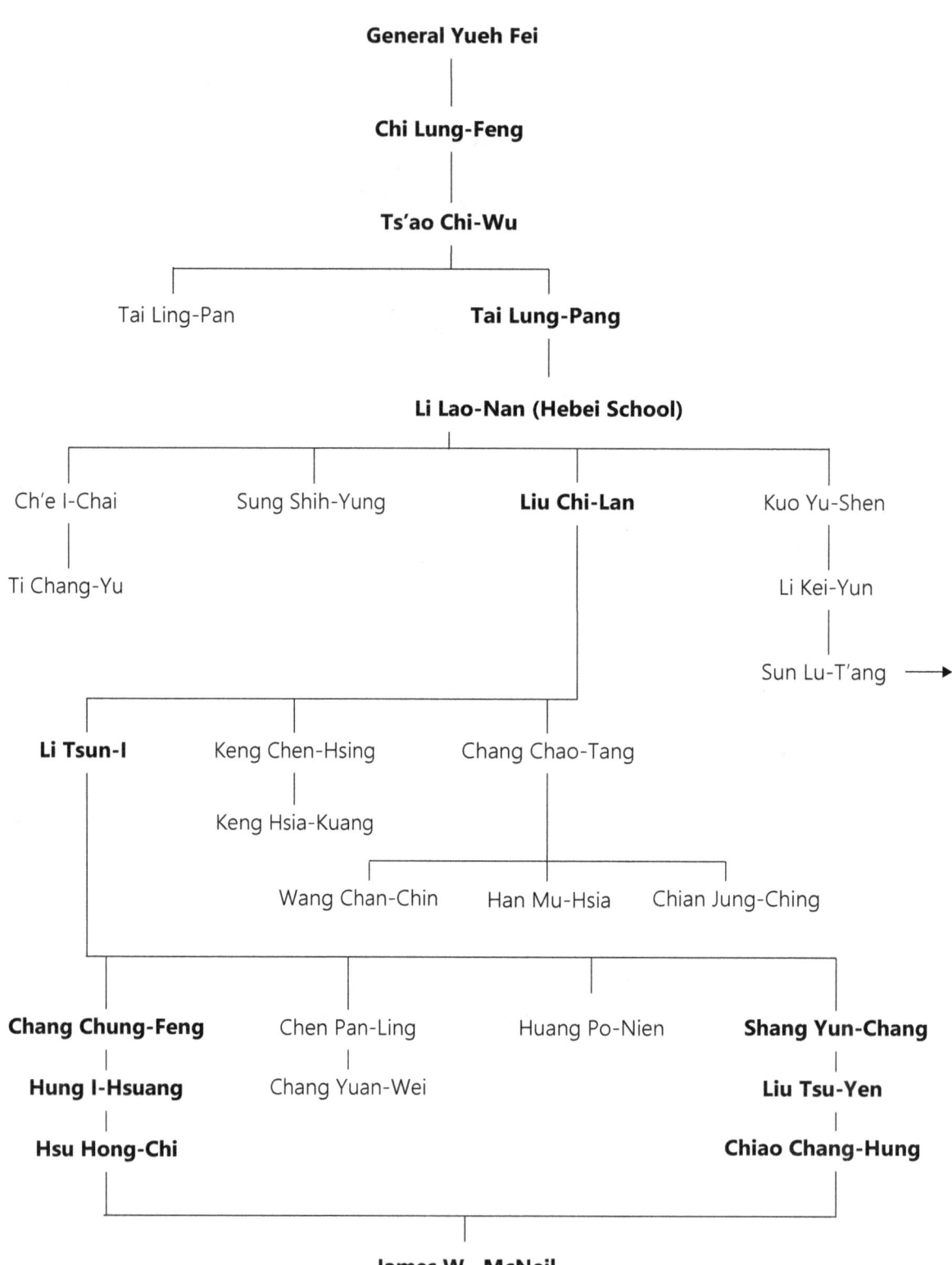

Chapter 3

The Connection between Hsing-I Chuan and the Tao

This is a detailed subject that could be discussed in a book of its own. Much has been written about the 'Tao' by Sages of the past and for readers who want more knowledge in this area, it is suggested they seek out specialist literature devoted to this subject. Here we have tried to give a brief overview with the aim of helping the Hsing-I practitioner see the connection between their practice of Hsing-I and its link to the Tao and classical Taoist philosophy. Throughout this book the use of the terms 'chi' and 'energy' are used interchangeably, as appropriate, to describe the same biological life-giving and universal force of nature.

So first let us look at the classical Taoist philosophy and examine how its understanding of the evolution of the universe underpins this internal art.

'Tao' and 'Wuji' Theory – the nature of existence!

Classical Taoist philosophy states:

'The Tao is the original creative force of the universe; it is both formless and infinite. The Tao contains the inexhaustible potential for all of life and if we were able to open our minds to this pure source, we would be able to comprehend the very nature of existence.'

The vastness of the Tao knows no limits and has always existed before anything else known to man. Contained within the Tao are a combination of the two poles known as Yin and Yang. Prior to the creation of all things known and unknown, Yin and Yang were not differentiated; they were merged into a single mass of energy. The Taoists name for this original pure mass of energy is 'Wuji' and its nature is total stillness.

Taoists believe that from this total state of stillness came forth a spontaneous natural form of movement, like a sudden vibration, rippling in a pond. This vibration manifested as a spiralling form of energy expanding from the centre of Wuji. Some in the west would compare this to the more modern theory of the 'Big Bang'. The Taoists refer to this manifestation of a ripple as 'Taiji' and its nature is movement.

Through the spiralling energy of Taiji, Yin and Yang were said to be created. At this point these names only represent extremes; of course, life and all material things around us are not made up of complete extremes. Between the colours of black and white there are numerous shades of grey. Everything that exists, both tangible and intangible in the universe are made up of a combination of these extremes, everything that contains Yin, must also contain Yang to varying degrees. Those varying degrees, when discussing energy, are made up from a multitude of individual vibrational frequencies and are what makes things different from one another.

Taoist Symbol of Wuji

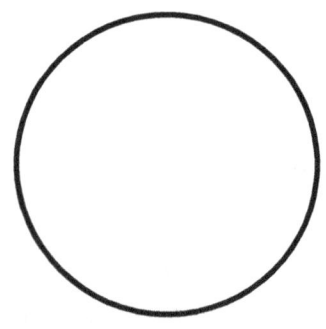

An example of varying frequencies of vibration found in material things would be visual colours; for instance, the colour blue, which vibrates at a different frequency from the colour red and that is how we can differentiate the two colours when we see them. A second example maybe body tissues where the heart vibrates at a different frequency from the kidney and that is why they look and function differently within the body. If all things vibrated at the same frequency, everything would be the same and nothing different would exist as we know it, both in the universe and the body. Everything would be a blank canvas and this is why Taoist philosophy depicts the state of Wuji as a blank white circle, which represents the nothingness state before creation. The circle represents the cyclical nature of the swirling mass of energy with no end and no beginning.

This subject of vibration and frequencies is currently at the forefront of physics theory and is being scientifically explored in detail. It is highly likely that in years to come the Taoist theories of old will prove correct in that all things are made from energy or chi, in the form of vibrations and that strings of energy combined in different ways are the foundation of all things, some we can sense and even things we cannot. Examples of things we can sense would be light, heat, some sounds and physical form. Although within some of these examples there are ranges that our human senses cannot knowingly detect, however this does not mean that because we cannot knowingly detect things they do not exist.

Hsing-I Chuan and Yin/Yang Theory

It is said that from the state of stillness came Yin and Yang. This is depicted as the classic Taoist symbol so well known today which shows the two extremes or poles interchanging with one another in a cyclical pattern. Within Hsing-I, the Yin/Yang theory is evident in all its forms and movements and its theory underpins the very essence of the art.

Alone, neither Yin nor Yang can form life, nor can one exist without the other. In the human body, Yin and Yang govern every limb, bone and gesture. When the two are harmonised, the body and its movements are strong and healthy. Without it, strength is scattered and the movements confused. It is for this reason that the theory and balance of Yin and Yang must be understood by the practitioner of Hsing-I.

Yin/Yang – Its Origins, Principles and their Effect on the Body

The concept of Yin/Yang is one of the underlying foundations of Chinese culture. Perhaps more than any other concept, it defines the Chinese way of life because they believe that everything, in every part of the universe conforms to the theory of Yin/Yang. Together they are thought of as complementary forces that interact and join together to form the universe. Yin cannot exist without Yang and vice versa. For example, night (Yin) cannot exist without day (Yang) as a comparative.

To be alive or be in good health depends on maintaining a state of balance and harmony between Yin and Yang, and in effect unifying one's mind and body. The study of Hsing-I can help the practitioner address this need for balance and regular practice regulates the chi flow within the body thereby balancing both Yin and Yang within. All the movements of Hsing-I have a balanced Yin/Yang aspect and this must be understood to gain the health benefits and martial effectiveness that this complete system offers.

The Symbol of Yin/Yang

The universally famous Taoist Yin/Yang symbol provides a visual representation of the basic mechanics of Taoist philosophy. The outer circle is a representation of the Tao and its cyclical nature. It symbolises the universe as a whole, self-sufficient unit, which contains both polar opposites of Yin and Yang.

Consequently, the circle is differentiated into two equal divisions, Yin being represented by the black division and Yang the white. The curved line down the middle shows the constant state of change between Yin and Yang as they create, control and transform into each other. Within each division is a small circle illustrating that within Yin there is always an element of Yang and vice versa.

Neither Yin nor Yang can ever truly dominate the opposite force, or at the very moment that one reaches the highest point of its power it transforms into the other. This is one reason why the symbol shows the two forces curled around each other, with a small circle of the other in the centre of each. The small contrasting circles enclosed within the larger divisions are also used to illustrate the belief that an element of Yang resides within Yin just as an element in Yin resides within Yang. Nothing is absolutely Yin or Yang.

In essence, the theory of Yin/Yang is based on the existence of two polar opposites that are neither mystical forces nor material objects. Rather they are terms used to describe the interaction of entities to each other and to the universe. They express the natural laws of change and the Chinese concept of everything being part of the whole.

阴 YIN   阳 YANG

The character of Yin originally meant "the shady side of a mountain". Yin is associated with qualities such as negative, cold, darkness, passive, downward, interior and inward. The original meaning of the character of Yang was "the sunny side of a mountain" and refers to positive, hot, light, active, upward, exterior and outward.

The human body is also a carefully balanced system that can be described using the Yin/Yang theory. Physical and functional aspects of the body can be described in comparison with their opposites. For example, the front of the body is considered Yin whilst the back is Yang. The lower body is Yin and the upper body is Yang, certain organs are classified as Yin organs and other organs are Yang. Body fluids and blood are classed as Yin while chi is classed as Yang. In TCM terms imbalances between Yin and Yang within the body are seen to be potential causes of disease and sickness.

The Fundamental Principles of Yin/Yang

Understanding the six fundamental principles of Yin/Yang even at a basic level helps the practitioner of Hsing-I understand why the forms, their alignments and breathing must be so precise in order for their practice to be effective in benefiting their health. While most things can be broadly segregated into either Yin or Yang, it is essential to remember that the energies of both Yin and Yang are always present in all things to varying degrees.

1. All things have two sides; they contain both Yin and Yang

Everything is made up of two opposites that combine to make the whole. Species may be divided into male and female, temperature into hot and cold, weight into heavy and light, direction into up and down, states into active or passive. These are all examples of Yin/Yang opposites but they serve to describe the same base states. For example, when practising Hsing-I the practitioner must know where the forward hand is in relation to the backward hand at all times. They can only know this if they have two sides or in this example, hands to make a comparison with. The forward hand must always balance the backward hand, stopping and starting their movements together.

2. Any Yin/Yang aspect can be infinitely divided into both Yin and Yang aspects

Each Yin/Yang category can be further subdivided into another Yin/Yang category. For example, the front of the body is considered Yin, the back Yang, this could be further subdivided so that the stomach is Yin (lower) and the chest is Yang (higher). Within any Yin/Yang aspect there are also elements of both Yin and Yang present. For example, when practising Hsing-I the two hands move together with one going forwards at the same time as the other going backwards. This is a physical analysis but within this physical movement the two hands must start and stop their movement at exactly the same time. This is a movement or energetic analysis. This is a further sub-analysis of the same hand technique using Yin/Yang principles of infinite division.

3. Yin and Yang mutually create each other

Although Yin and Yang are opposites, they cannot be separated from each other. They mutually depend on one another for their existence. How could you describe light if there was no dark for comparison? In Hsing-I, how could there be a forward hand if there were not a backward hand to compare it with. As one hand moves ahead of the other it creates a comparative rear hand. The rear hand equally pulls back during the same movement to create a forward hand.

4. Yin and Yang control and balance each other

Yin and Yang are like the balancing of a scale. If Yin is excessive then Yang will be deficient and vice versa. For example, if something is too cold there must be a lack of heat. If the room is excessively dark, then there is a deficiency of light. When Yang is deficient, Yin becomes excessive. An illness of heat in the body such as fever (excess Yang) may be due to insufficient Yin, as blood and fluids are dried up by the increased internal body heat. An example within Hsing-I practice would be; the hands and feet must move as one. If the hand issues forward without its corresponding foot the upper and lower aspects of the body will become unbalanced and there will be a lack of power in the technique through instability.

5. Yin and Yang transform into each other

Both Yin and Yang progress through a cycle of transformation, an example in this case could be the seasons, from one extreme (hot summer) through a period of moderation (autumn) to the other extreme (cold winter). They can either transform naturally and in harmony or change suddenly due to disharmony. For example, if you were to run as fast as possible for as long as possible, you will eventually collapse from exhaustion. This is a good example of extreme Yang suddenly changing into

Yin in the body. An example within Hsing-I practice would be; as the forward hand finishes its technique, issuing out its force to its maximum it then immediately starts to withdraw backwards eventually transforming itself into becoming the rear hand, only to start the cycle again. All the time the opposite hand is working reciprocally in unison to create maximum power within the technique.

6. Yin and Yang are relative
You can distinguish a Yin/Yang aspect but not separate them. Yin and Yang depend on each other for their definition. For example; to understand strength you must know what weakness is. Objects cannot be adequately described without using a Yin or Yang aspect. Within modern science today we know that mortality exists yet we cannot reason that immortality is possible. Taoist philosophy views immortality as an enlightened state and does not require science to prove it exists. If the state of mortality exists then surely there must be the state of immortality. If there is Yin there must be Yang to complement it. An example in Hsing-I practice would be; the left and right sides of the body or the upper and lower halves of the body. You can only analyse them in a technique if you have an opposing body part to refer it against. The theory of Hsing-I when practiced correctly seeks to ensure that both Yin and Yang are balanced at all times within the systems movements and techniques. This leads to chi flowing freely through the meridians and creates a healthy body alongside a powerful technique.

The Concept of the Yin/Yang Theory within the body

Yin and Yang fluctuates in cycles that occur both in the universe and the human body. At various times, energy must be stored and consumed. Energy is drawn inward and concentrated (Yin) and when sufficient energy has been accumulated, to allow a specific activity to be carried out, the energy is then expended (Yang). For example, one moment the heart is filling with blood (Yin), the next moment it is forcing blood into the circulatory system (Yang). One of the fundamental purposes, of Hsing-I is to ensure that the practitioner builds an abundant supply of free-flowing chi and stores it in their Tan Tien and joints ready for it to be utilised as required in its movements.

Consequently, when practising Hsing-I, if the balance between Yin and Yang are unequal, the production and movement of chi and blood will also become out of balance leading potentially to ill health and a body whose functions operate below their optimal performance levels.

In the following table are some universal Yin/Yang characteristics to help you see how all things can be thought of in this way.

YIN	YANG
Cold	Hot
Wet	Dry
Heavy	Light
Night	Day
Female	Male
Weakness	Strength
Internal	External
Blood	Chi
Blood itself	Circulation of blood
Perspiration/ Sweating	Production of heat/ energy
Contraction	Expansion
Backwards	Forwards
Earth	Heaven

The Creation of Heaven, Man and Earth

The Taoist Canon states: **"From 'Yin and Yang' came the emergence of 'Heaven and Earth."**

The above statement declares, that after the creation of the two poles came the emergence of the three energies. In Taoist philosophy, the three energies are represented in the universe as Heaven, Man and Earth. Heaven is Yang, above and white, Earth is Yin, below and black. In between like a conduit for the universal energy flowing between the two universal energies is Man, one of the many shades of grey that make up the structure of the universe.

The next stage in the process was the evolution of the four seasons; spring, summer, autumn and winter and then the five elemental energies; metal, water, wood, fire and earth which are seen as the material building blocks for supporting our life and the world we live in. Essentially, the Tao gave rise to the two poles of Yin and Yang, which in turn formed the 10,000 things, which implies the creation of everything we see, know and understand in our universe. On this subject, the great Taoist sage Lao Tzu in an excerpt from the *Tao Te Ching* Chapter One states:

The Tao that can be named is not the true Tao.
The name that can be spoken is not the true name.
That without name was the beginning of Heaven and Earth.
That which is named brought forth the ten thousand things.

To understand this except we see that if something has a name, then it actually becomes a tangible thing. Truly the Tao is a state of emptiness and pure nothing.

Therefore, in its true self it is nothing and cannot have a name as it does not exist. If we give it a name then it is not truly the Tao. The creation of Heaven and Earth came from the pure stillness of nothing and Taoists give it the name Tao simply so as we can talk about it in human terms. Once we have the formation of Heaven and Earth we now have tangible things to talk about and so they have names as do the ten thousand things of the physical world as we know it.

When practising Hsing-I, the body mirrors the universe. Scientists in the West refer to the universe as the macrocosm and Taoists view that the human body within is just like a miniature version of the universe, hence in the west it is referred to as the microcosm. When practicing the art of Hsing-I the practitioner aims to follow the same principles of creation within their bodies as that of the universe outlined previously.

On this subject Master McNeil states:

"Practising Hsing-I can be likened to the natural conception of an embryo. You start from emptiness (Wuji), and then receive the nourishment of the mother (Yin), and then spirit, chi and vigor (Yang), this balanced combination starts a child forming, which in turn starts movement (Taiji). Wuji which represents stillness separates into two polar opposites, Yin and Yang. When you have movement, you know you have life. This is the natural process of development."

'San Ti' Posture Training

To understand and explain the theoretical link between the Taoist theory of evolution and the practice of Hsing-I it is best to look at the first and most important training given to any serious Hsing-I practitioner. That of San Ti Posture training or Three Body Posture training as it is sometimes referred to in the West. This training is the very foundation of Hsing-I.

Regardless of a practitioner's level of experience, when they start their practice of Hsing-I it begins from Wuji posture, a state of emptiness, where there is no thought or intention. Before beginning practice the practitioner should be empty of mind, no spirit should be visible in the eyes or hands, and they should remain in a calm state with no reference of Yin and Yang. The body should be completely still both internally and externally.

Wuji Posture

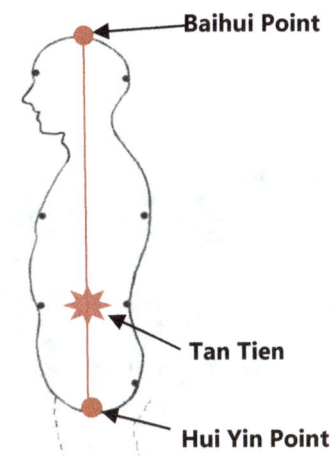

Out of the stillness of Wuji comes the intention to produce a movement, like a spontaneous vibration out of the stillness of the heart, spirit fills the body. The head presses up from the crown to the sky from within at the acupuncture point 'Baihui'. Brightness pierces the eyes, the tongue rises to touch the roof of the mouth and the acupuncture point between the genitals and anus called the 'Hui Yin' point gently lifts as the Tan Tien fills with chi. At this stage, external movement has been thought about but not yet begun, like a spiralling ripple of energy emitting from the centre of stillness, but not yet reached the surface of the body. These subtle movements are almost invisible to the eye but show the emergence of Taiji and the formation of Yin and Yang from Wuji within the body during Hsing-I practice. From the formation of Yin and Yang it is possible to generate all things.

This intention comes first, instinctively from the heart (emotionally) and must coincide with the conscious wisdom of the mind (brain). Next the mind activates and guides the chi, transforming the invisible, internal energetic functions to visible external movement. This complies with the Six Harmonies theory of Hsing-I, where the mind activates the chi in the joints, muscles and tissues, then physical movement occurs.

This whole process of energetic evolution within the microcosm of the body is clearly demonstrated as the practitioner opens and steps out into 'San Ti' posture which depicts all the fundamental theories of the body observed within Hsing-I practice and discussed in later chapters of this book.

Stepping into San Ti Posture

Wuji → Taiji → → → → → San Ti

3.1 → 3.2 → 3.3 → 3.4 → 3.5 → 3.6 → 3.7

Figure 3.1

Stepping into San Ti posture first starts from Wuji which is a relaxed posture facing straight ahead with both the head and the body. The hands are relaxed and placed naturally at the sides. The eyes look straight ahead and the feet are 45 degrees apart with the centre line directly down the middle. The knees are relaxed and straight.

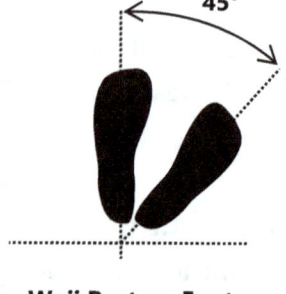

Wuji Posture Foot

Note: In some lineages of Hsing-I this Wuji posture starts with the feet at 90 degrees apart and changes to 45 degrees before stepping out into San Ti posture. Both methods are variations of the same theory.

Figure 3.2

From 'Wuji' posture the body initiates movement through mental intent which is the start of 'Taiji' and the production of Yin and Yang. Physically the body turns to an angle of 45 degrees to the right and the two hands move from the relaxed state at the sides of the body and come together with the back of the (R) hand placed on top of the palm of the (L) hand. The arms are naturally relaxed and curved with the hands held slightly off the body at the height of the 'Tan Tien'. The head and eyes remain facing straight ahead.

Figure 3.3

From the hands coming together at the 'Tan Tien' they simultaneously open to the sides with palms facing to heaven as if holding two bowls of water. The knees remain relaxed and straight. The arms remain curved and the head and eyes stay focused straight ahead.

Figure 3.4
The arms continue to raise and circle over the level of the top of the head and the palms of the hands turn over to face earth with the palm of the (R) hand resting on top of the back of the (L) hand. The head and eyes remain focused straight ahead.

Figure 3.5
As the hands press down to earth and the legs bend at the knees, sinking the body in time with the hands. The knees both bend subtly with the kneecaps moving slightly in the direction of the feet below them. The legs should remain close together and not part too much throughout this movement although this can vary between individuals and their natural body structures. At the point when the hands reach the level of the Tan Tien the knees should have ended their movement. This timing of upper and lower body must remain completely coordinated and should start and finish together. The eyes and head remain focused straight ahead and the feet remain at 45 degrees throughout.

Figure 3.6
Next, the feet remain rooted in the same position whilst the waist turns back to the left in effect facing the body straight ahead. At the same time, the (R) hand drives forward in the form of a fist to the height of the nose, with the (L) arm and fist following closely, hidden behind the elbow of the (R) arm. The eyes and head remain focused straight ahead and the feet remain at 45 degrees throughout.

Figure 3.7
Finally, as the (R) hand reaches the height of the nose the (L) hand punches directly up and over the top of the (R) arm in effect replacing it and then the (L) hand opens and presses subtly outwards and downwards in action. At the same time, the (R) hand pulls subtly back to the height of the Tan Tien opening and pressing its palm down to earth. As the (L) arm and hand move forward so does the (L) leg and foot, in effect opening the stance. The weighting should be 70/30% on the back foot at first to build leg strength but over time this can change to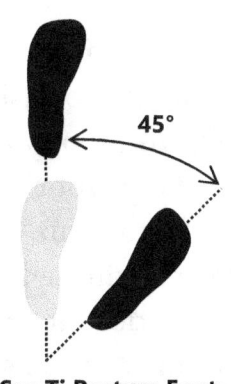
50/50% to gain increased agility as the practitioner becomes more experienced. The timing of both hands and feet must be perfect and all movements must start and finish together. The eyes and head remain focused straight ahead and the feet remain angled at 45 degrees apart throughout.

San Ti Posture Foot

Divisions of Three

When the body is placed in 'San Ti' posture it can be subdivided and analysed into further groups of three; the first division is the head, body and limbs. The second division is the limbs which can be divided by their respective joints. The hips, knees and ankles divide the legs. The shoulders, elbows and wrists divide the arms. Finally, the third division is the nose, the index finger of the forward hand and the big toe of the forward foot which should all line up like the crosshairs of a gunsight to make the most stable structure possible. This stance is the very core of Hsing-I practice and should be practiced diligently.

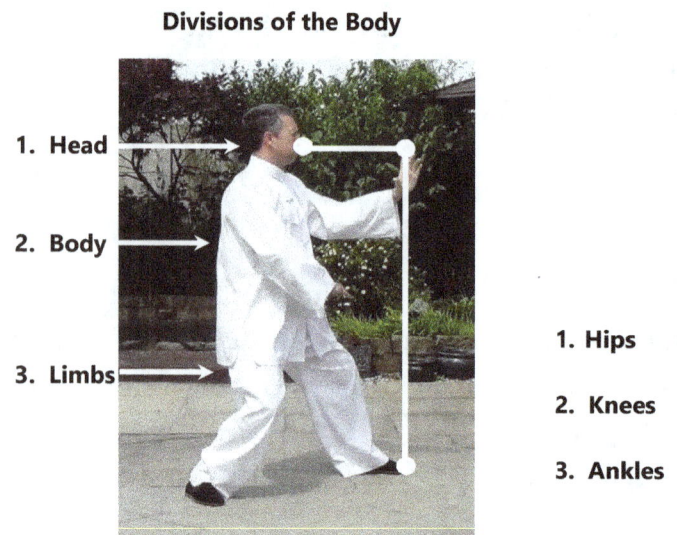

The reason San Ti posture is so important is that it gives rise to all theories pertaining to Hsing-I and from which all movements of Hsing-I can be created. Following on with the Taoist numerical theory of evolution, the three of San Ti creates the four, in the form of the chi directed to the four extremities of the body.

As the San Ti posture take its true form the spirit is raised within and the chi directed through the meridians to the extreme end points of the body. The four extremities are the tongue, teeth, nails and hair respectively. The tongue is the extremity of the muscles, teeth the bones, nails the tendons and hair the blood.

Taoist philosophy states ***"If one branch moves, hundreds of branches shake."***

When considering the four extremities this statement signifies that the movement of any of the four extremities leads to the movement of everything else as all is connected in the body as one. If the four extremities are vibrant and healthy, this then indicates that the mind is coordinated with the chi and the meridians are fully open allowing chi to flow freely to all areas of the body.

When the four extremities are energised with chi it is like holding a car ready to move by controlling the clutch and accelerator pedals. The correct exchange of energy through the feet to the pedals causes the car to move. In Hsing-I the body is held in San Ti posture in the same way, ready to move, but not yet moving. This state of readiness keeps the body alert inside and is termed 'spirited'. The practitioner is ready to move in any direction, at any second. All that is required is the heart and the mind to combine and the chi flow will be activated to create movement of the body.

Next in the evolutionary theory is the number five in the form of the Five Element Fists whose movements form the basic building blocks for Hsing-I practice. From this comes the 10,000 things in the form of the Six Harmonies, Seven Stars, Eight Fundamentals, Nine Essences, Twelve Animal forms and all other movements pertaining to Hsing-I. Most Hsing-I practice starts and returns through this San Ti posture and it is sometimes referred to as the 'Mother Form' as it gives birth to the many different postures inherent in the system. In summary, out of the nothingness that is Wuji to the creation of all potential Hsing-I movements and the eventual return to the nothingness of Wuji. Therefore, the practice of Hsing-I follows the full cycle and natural laws of the Tao.

Hsing-I Originates from Nature

As Hsing-I follows the natural laws of Tao it is therefore derived from nature. The Masters of old observed nature in the form of the universe and the natural elements it produced, they also observed in nature the animals and wildlife. In combining the spirit of nature with that of their own, the art of Hsing-I was thought to be developed.

In ancient China, there was a basic belief that the universe was made up from the five elemental energies of metal, water, wood, fire and earth and they saw these elements as the foundation of all material things. From this belief, the five element techniques were thought to be formed, which then formed the basic movements from which all other techniques are developed. If these are the basic theories from nature then it is only logical they should become the same basic theories of Hsing-I.

To survive in the harshness of nature, animals and other living species have mastered the ability to survive and protect themselves. For this reason, the spirit of each animal was closely observed and the essence and strength of each animal was absorbed into the movements of the twelve animal forms. Originally it is thought that ten animal forms were practiced and which are still practiced by some lineages today. However, later in Hsing-I's history a further two were added (Tuo and Tai forms) to make the twelve forms practiced today in some lineages, including the one contained in this book.

It should be noted that there is some contradiction and debate in the historical literature available as to how the Hsing-I forms evolved and there are two common disputed opinions within the Hsing-I community today, although neither can be factually proven. Some say that the animal forms were quite complex to learn and that the five elements techniques may have evolved later to simplify the complicated animal techniques with a view to creating an easier to assimilate training method within the Hsing-I system. Others suggest that the five elements forms were developed first and pre-existed the animal forms as a separate system and at some time in history they were combined. This may be supported by the fact that the five elements theory was fully developed and documented within ancient Taoist and Chinese medicine texts over 3000 years ago and provides the underlying theory to five elements practice in Hsing-I today. Therefore, it would seem logical that if Hsing-I was developed following the laws of Tao, then the building blocks of life in the form of the five elements would evolve first, followed by the 10,000 things in the form of the twelve animals. Whatever the truth is, today it is most common to learn the five element techniques first before going on to study the twelve animal forms, as the postures and the energy associated within the five element forms are further developed when studying the animal forms.

Chapter 4

The Internal Aspect of Hsing-I Chuan

"The internal aspect of the martial arts is a subject that is discussed by everyone who studies kung-fu, but is known and practiced by only a few. It is the power you cannot see and comes from within your body. The Chinese refer to the power that is stored and utilised within the body as 'chi' and developing your chi requires daily practice. The changes that take place within your body are gradual and are very subtle. It is not a visible change or something that is developed instantly but rather takes a great deal of patience and time to cultivate."
Master James McNeil

To understand why the practice of Hsing-I benefits the health it is important first to understand the importance of chi and blood within our bodies and the Chinese view of how the body operates. In truth, most Western, non-medically trained persons don't understand in any real detail how the body works from a Western medical perspective and therefore it would foolish to assume they would understand a medical framework that they have not even grown up with or been educated in.

When reading general literature concerning the internal arts about the benefits of practice to the body and its organs it must be remembered that this understanding is derived from a Taoist and therefore TCM perspective and not a Western medical one, unless stated otherwise. Sometimes the view points of the two systems are similar, but often they are vastly different.

For example, when it is said in Hsing-I that the practice of the element Fire benefits the heart, it is meaning from an energetic perspective and understanding the energetic functions of the heart based from TCM theory is key to understanding the benefits to the practitioner of practicing Fire form. If a person has weak vessel walls within the heart from a Western medical diagnosis, it may be more appropriate to practice Earth form as it is Earth element and the spleen organ that is seen to be responsible for the quality of the vessel walls within the body. Therefore, a practitioner needs a TCM diagnosis to determine which form is best to practice in relation to their health problems.

To understand the functions of the organs from a TCM perspective the practitioner needs to study the many well written translated texts available within Chinese medical literature or seek the advice of a qualified TCM doctor. The five elements chapter of this book will endeavour to explain a few of the main functions energetically related to each organ, but this is only a superficial analysis as a detailed review is beyond the scope of this book.

The remainder of this chapter will seek to explain how the body functions from a Taoist point of view and the structures and terminology involved so as the reader may gain a basic understanding from a Chinese based energetic perspective and relate this to their understanding and practice of Hsing-I.

Chi and Blood – The Key to Health and Life!

Health from the Taoist point of view is 'energy' which means 'movement' – movement of chi, blood and essence. As life depends on the free movement of chi, blood and essence, any obstruction or stagnation in the movement of these vital substances will cause illness or possibly death. Therefore, harmonious distribution and movement of these substances in the correct amounts are of great importance if one is to avoid ill health.

TCM literature states *"Like a dammed river, water can be flooding upstream (meaning too much energy) and downstream a drought can be experienced (meaning too little energy). Both can be problematic."*

To maintain this harmonious flow, the energetic action of chi is required to allow the blood to move and once blood moves, it can then mutually nourish chi and all the tissues of the body. This mutually dependent relationship then allows chi to further ensure movement of blood. So, from this it can be clearly understood that chi and blood are interdependent; one cannot function without the other, just as was discussed in the theory of Yin/Yang previously.

As the functioning body is in constant motion and change, the natural flow of chi and blood can be affected and influenced by many factors, such as physical injury, the weather and seasons, internal emotions and universal energies such as the movement of the stars, planets, sun and moon, to name but a few.

One way to understand chi is to think of the body, initially alive on one hand, then deceased on the other. What is the body's difference in the two states? Physically, nothing has changed. The body initially remains unchanged, except the heart stops beating and breathing is non-existent. What is missing from the body when dead may be defined as chi.

What is Chi?

Chi is seen to be a biological life-giving force, an energy that dictates the course and future of human life and everything that surrounds it. Without chi, life itself would be impossible because the whole process of life is based on chi. Long ago through the process of developing meditation and various life prolonging methods, Taoist sages discovered and documented an energy based circulation system within the body which they named the 'Jing Luo'. These pathways of chi were mapped by a line drawn between structures or acupuncture points to form clear routes throughout the body. In TCM these pathways are known as 'meridians'.

Diagram illustrating the meridian pathways

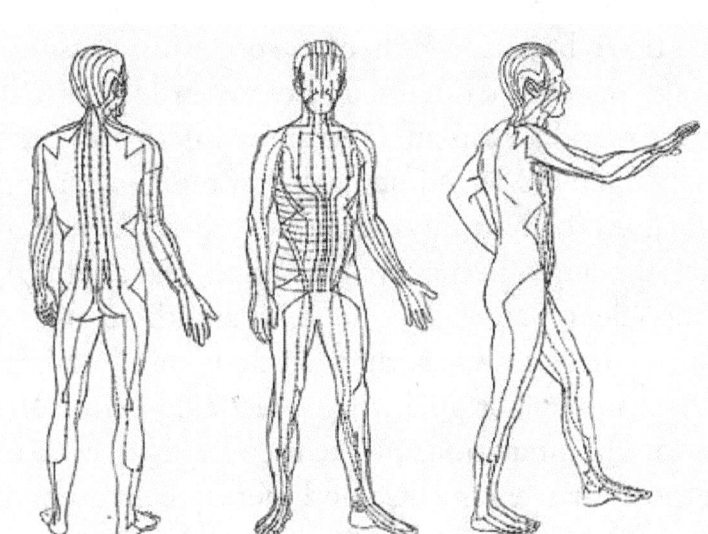

The Meridian Network (Jing Luo)

The Taoist Canon states:
"Meridians are channels through which life and death can be judged."
Meridians are pathways that carry chi to every cell around the entire body. They are not physical structures, such as nerve pathways or blood vessels. They are an independent system of energetic pathways. Chi flows in every tissue and cell of the body, but it is seen to be more concentrated in the pathways that make up the meridian network. Any tissue of the body that is devoid of chi will also be devoid of blood and this will lead to necrosis/tissue death.

A meridian is composed of a subtle energy field that includes pathways like those of arteries and nerves and it is for this reason it is said that meridians are pathways which allow chi to be circulated to various parts of the body. There are twelve main meridians relating to the organs and eight extraordinary meridians (sometimes called eight psychic meridians) which act as reservoirs to control and regulate the flow and quantity of chi within the twelve main organ meridians.

The eight extraordinary meridians are seen to be located deeper within the body than the twelve main organ meridians and are, therefore, better protected from harm. There are also several other major meridian networks which are directly related to Taoist theory and practice, some of which are mentioned in this book, however, further reading beyond this text is required for a more detailed analysis. Importantly, all the different categories of meridians are linked together to combine one systemic energy system to supply the whole body.

When discussing any one of the twelve main meridians, it is not only related to a specific organ from which its name is derived, but also originates from that organ. The acupuncture points directly affect the meridian, organ, or tissue, with which they are associated. This is because the chi of the organs and tissues are transported to the surface of the body via the meridians. Therefore, striking, needling, or massaging specific points on the meridian can affect both the interior and exterior of the body.

Today people living in modern times have lost much of their high-level abilities of sensitivity which allow them to see and feel the effects of the meridians at random. This is because they are taught in modern education that anything which cannot be seen or proven using scientific tests does not exist and therefore they switch off their natural perception to these senses as their wisdom mind or brain overrides their natural intuitive senses. A major goal when practicing Hsing-I and other internal arts should be to for the practitioner to rediscover their own natural abilities in sensing the chi of the human energy field and thereby help them to live closer to the natural path of Tao.

Listed next are the most commonly used TCM descriptions pertaining to the functions of the meridians within the body.

Functions of the Meridians

To transport and circulate chi, blood and fluids – meridians act to transport chi and stimulate the flow of blood, nourishing the tendons and bones and improve the function of joints.

To warm and nourish tissues – meridians allow chi and blood to circulate together through the body ensuring organs and tissues are energetically warmed and nourished, protecting them from attack by pathogens.

To transmit chi – during solo practice of Hsing-I forms or healing treatments such as acupuncture or massage, the functions of a meridian are regulated and the balance between Yin and Yang in the body is also restored. This is achieved by either conducting the flow of chi using metallic needles, encouraging the flow of chi using massage techniques or by stimulating the flow of chi by combining the breath with the mind and movement of tissues in correct alignment as when practicing Hsing-I. Conversely, in applying Hsing-I against an opponent, if an acupuncture point or meridian is struck accurately, damage to the chi flow can affect not only the local area but also potentially the internal organ associated with the damaged meridian. If the chi flow to the organ is affected this can have a global effect on the health of the body.

To transmit disease – the meridians are transmission routes for diseases. As meridians connect directly with their interior organs, they can reflect disorders of their related organs and vice versa. Therefore, an organ can affect a meridian and a meridian can affect an organ. The meridian network can also spread disease from one meridian to another, hence from one organ to another as all are either directly or indirectly connected.

To provide communication between the mind and body – the meridian network makes it possible to connect upper with lower and internal with external. It not only connects physical structures such as organs, tissues and orifices but it also links up all the other meridians so that they can communicate with each other via the mind on an energetic level.

Where does our chi come from?

Chi is a universal power. The chi of heaven is the chi of the universe. It controls and coordinates the movements of the celestial bodies (planets) and because of this it has considerable influence upon the chi of earth and man. Its influence is evident through the thermal energy of the sun and the gravitational pull of the moon upon the tides. Even small fluctuations in this energy have a dramatic effect on the earth and its climate.

The chi of man is as individual as our fingerprints; no two people are truly identical. It is our life energy and shapes our very personalities. Mankind, like all living things, relies on the chi of the earth for food and the chi of the heavens for a habitable climate.

The three sources of chi in the body:

1. 'Yuan Chi' gained from our parents and acquired (prenatal) prior to being born. This gift of chi from our parents is a fixed amount which is stored in the kidneys and can only be depleted throughout life. Therefore, we must seek to protect it by strengthening our postnatal chi levels using the methods 2 and 3 discussed next. If your parents were not in peak health at the time of your conception, then your acquired chi will be weaker than it could have been.

"To produce a racehorse, you don't breed sick animals."

2. 'Gu Chi' created from food which can affect the level and quality of our chi throughout life. Obviously, a good diet will strengthen the body's chi and a poor diet will weaken it. The better the quality of raw materials placed in the stomach, the better the quality of chi will be produced. This is a major issue for modern society today where in Western countries food is abundant but the quality is nutritionally very poor. This can be seen in the rise of many chronic illnesses such as diabetes and obesity in ever younger members of the population.

"If you put dirty fuel in a car, don't expect it to run at optimum performance."

3. 'Zhong Chi' created from breathing in the environment. When we breathe we take in air to nourish and feed the body. The quality of the air and of our breathing directly affects the quality of our chi and this can directly affect our health throughout life. Correct practice of Hsing-I and its associated breathing methods will therefore strengthen the body's postnatal chi and prevent its need to draw on prenatal chi reserves as we get older. The environment we live in the West is becoming increasingly polluted through industry and our careless lifestyles. This leads to poor quality air and these effects can be seen in the increase chronic respiratory disease such as asthma and allergies within the general population and the need for medications ever increasing even in children.

"Reduced oxygen levels in the air leads to poor combustion and reduced engine power."

On this subject Master McNeil states:

"When we do not look after our lifestyle, diet and breathing methods, the body can become weak and sick. It will naturally draw on the reserve of chi we acquired from our parents prior to being born and this will shorten our life span. To avoid this, we need to look after our diet and cultivate our breathing methods to preserve our chi levels and increase our longevity. The longer we live with a healthy body, the longer we have in this world to practice our Hsing-I and therefore have a greater chance of achieving immortality!"

In truth, you cannot physically put chi under the microscope. There is no scientifically acceptable apparatus or test yet that can accurately measure chi. However, it exists, just as the force of gravity exists, but is not visible. Like gravity, which causes objects to be attracted to larger bodies, chi is best examined by its various functions, not by its form.

Furthermore, Master McNeil states:

"Two hundred years ago nobody believed that electricity existed as you could not see or create it. It has always been there in the lay lines of the earth and the lightning of the universe, yet until science could create and harness it, electricity would have been seen as the stuff of nonsense and superstition. Chi is no different, many western medically trained doctors and scientists say the concept of chi is nonsense yet they cannot explain many things of how the body works. Until science can prove it, it will always be this way. It would seem that knowledge obtained from modern day education can limit us from being open minded in accepting what we don't understand. The truth is that it is up to science to understand what it does not know and not to ridicule what it cannot explain. Not too long-ago men of learning laughed at the notion that the earth might be round, but now we know it to be true and the people who foresaw this are now seen to be great and learned beings. We need to undo this way of restrictive thinking if we want to be free and progress in our return to the Tao."

In TCM the chi contained within our bodies is often referred to by different names depending on its particular function. These different names describe the same energetic substance of chi but serve to differentiate the many functions of chi within the complex human body. Listed next are the most commonly used names for the different types of chi and a useful flow diagram to help visualise how this one energetic substance can be used by the body to provide the energy source for all it needs.

Types of Chi in the Body

Gu Chi (Grain/Food Chi)
Gu Chi formation is the first stage in the transformation of food. Food is first 'rotted and ripened' by the stomach and then sent to the spleen to make Gu Chi. Next Gu Chi is split into two parts, one is sent from the spleen and stomach to the lungs where it combines with air to form Zhong Chi and the remaining part is sent to the heart where it is transformed into blood.

Wei Chi (Protective Chi)
Wei Chi travels both inside and outside the channels. It flows primarily in the superficial layers of the body and its functions are to protect the body from attack by exogenous pathogenic influences (coming from outside e.g. Wind, Cold, Heat, Dampness) and to warm, moisten and aid in nourishing skin and muscles.

Ying Chi (Nutritive Chi)

Ying Chi nourishes the internal organs and the whole body. It is closely related to blood, and flows with blood in the vessels as well in the channels. Ying Chi is highly concentrated for two hours in each channel, moving through all twelve channels in a twenty-four-hour period. During these periods, the specific organs are nourished and maintained by the Ying Chi.

Yuan Chi (Original/Ancestral Chi)

Yuan Chi has its root in the kidneys. It is the foundation of all the Yin and Yang energies of the body. Yuan Chi, like Prenatal Jing, is hereditary, fixed in quantity, but nourished throughout life by Postnatal Jing. It is the dynamic force that motivates the functional activity of the internal organs and is the foundation of vitality. It circulates all over the body in the channels, relying on the transporting system of the San Jiao (Triple Burner).

Zheng Chi (True/Upright Chi)

Zheng Chi is transformed by Zhong Chi with the help of Yuan Chi. Zheng Chi is the final stage in the transformation and refinement of Chi. It is the chi that circulates in the channels and nourishes the organs. Zheng Chi has two different forms relating to its functions, Ying Chi and Wei Chi.

Zhong Chi (Gathering Chi)

The spleen sends Gu Chi up to the Lungs, where it combines with air and transforms into Zhong Chi. Zhong Chi nourishes the heart and lungs and forms the basis for the involuntary functions of heartbeat and respiration. It assists the Lungs in controlling chi and respiration and the heart's function of governing the blood and blood vessels.

Simplified Chi Diagram for the Body

What are the functions of Chi in the body?

Chi is the source of all movement within the body
A very strong activating force, chi is the source of all movement yet also accompanies all movement, together with all its physiological and metabolic activities. All bodily activities rely on the movement of chi, which includes obvious activities such as walking or running, but also includes involuntary movements such as breathing and the heartbeat, willed action such as eating and speaking, mental action such as thinking and dreaming and the development, growth and life process of birth and aging. Chi is in constant motion and has four primary directions: ascending, descending, entering and exiting. When practicing Hsing-I these natural directions of chi flow should be adhered to in the natural smooth flow from one posture to another in the forms.

Chi serves to protect the body
'Wei Chi' is the name given to the type and action of chi that protects the superficial part of the body and resists the invasion of outside pathological influences such as bacteria or viruses (for example flu) into the body. 'Wei Chi' operates to actively fight off those external pathological influences and permeates from the skin all over the body. When the body is strong and healthy it will be better able to fight off illness and this can be achieved through the regular practice of Hsing-I.

Chi is responsible for all actions of transformation in the body
When food and water are ingested, it is the action of chi that transforms them into vital fluids such as blood, sweat, tears and urine. These vital fluids are generated after food and drink are digested. They are subsequently distributed to essential parts of the body. These changes depend on the harmonious transformative function of chi. Chi is the driving force behind all chemical reactions within the body and therefore the ability to refine and transform substances such as hormones to keep the body healthy.

Chi governs the holding or retention of the body's substances and organs
Chi governs retention of the body's substances by preventing excessive loss of various fluids such as sweat, saliva and urine. It also means that chi maintains all the organs in their proper place and keeps body fluids in their normal pathways, preventing excessive loss; such as would occur with bleeding or excess blood leaking out of the blood vessels. This function also prevents the occurrence of prolapses of bodily parts or organs. A sure sign of deterioration and aging of the body is prolapsed organs and varicose veins where tissues and fluids are no longer able to withstand the effects of gravity on earth. If Hsing-I is practiced correctly, chi will remain abundant and

circulate in the body for longer. If the skill level is high and the connection between heaven and earth can be established, the negative, yin effects of gravity on earth can be held back and balanced out by the positive, yang energy of heaven.

Chi warms the body

Chi is responsible for keeping the different parts of the body at the correct temperature (homeostasis), especially after injury or against a hostile environment. Continual fluctuations in the production of heat are required to balance the impact of a constantly changing temperature within the body. Thus, the body is able to maintain a stable temperature in cooler environments; conversely it causes us to sweat when we overheat. This is critical to health as only a small degree of variation is tolerated in the body's core temperature before life is threatened.

Chi has both Yin and Yang aspects that must be balanced and coordinated within the body. For example, when the body is too hot, chi is responsible for controlling the mechanism of sweating. When the body is too cold, chi is responsible for controlling the mechanism of shivering. These are the body's methods of regulating homeostasis and maintaining life. A smooth distribution of chi is essential for the body to operate efficiently. Therefore Hsing-I concerns itself with maintaining the proper balance of Yin and Yang in practice of its forms by building up the levels of chi within the Tan Tien and helping to circulate it appropriately.

On this subject Master McNeil states:

"All movements must complement each other, when exiting there must be equal entering, when rising this must be accompanied by equal falling, left must compliment right and vice versa. To be efficient the body must be united in all that it does both internally and externally. To maintain a strong and healthy body, a person must learn how to keep chi circulating smoothly. Daily practice of Hsing-I is required to increase the amount of chi in the meridians and to build up an abundant store of chi for future use; it also improves the quality of the chi. When chi is abundant within the body, one enjoys good health. Disease and depression vanish, youth is maintained and longevity increases. By practicing Hsing-I and its exercises correctly every day, you will strengthen the chi of the internal organs and reduce stress on your nervous system and improve the efficiency of your chi flow. Regular practice will greatly improve your overall health both mentally and physically."

San Ti Posture – Hsing-I Chuan's 'Standing Exercise'

To start to build up the chi levels required to practice the internal arts, most systems have developed a method of standing meditation. There are many different standing exercises in the internal arts and the following 'San Ti' standing exercise is common to Hsing-I. It is one of the best and is used to build up a strong foundation to progress Hsing-I training from.

This practice is classed as a form of 'Nei-Kung' which unlike 'Chi-Kung' does not have any externally visible movement. 'Nei-Kung' is practice that involves circulating the energy within you, using the mind to guide the chi whilst remaining still. Standing still and concentrating the mind allows the body to relax and find its natural posture in tune with the natural force of gravity. When the body is relaxed and the mind focused, the chi can gather and flow smoothly to all areas without obstruction caused by physical and mental tensions. When the chi is flowing smoothly the body will become strong and healthy.

It was common for Hsing-I teachers of the past to make their students practice this San Ti standing posture for up to a year, for hours at a time, before they could move onto the movements of the elements and animal forms. This method served three main purposes and created a strong base to develop from. Physically it improved strength and posture and energetically it improved the chi levels stored within the Tan Tien. It also tested the mental strength and patience of the student prior to learning more of the art. It was a good test of loyalty and worthiness so often lacking in students today.

Exercise One. 'San Ti' Standing Posture Training

Right side San Ti posture   **Left side San Ti posture**

When starting this practice first you should concentrate yourself on attaining the correct physical structure and alignment of the body. It is not sufficient to be almost correct, you have to aim for perfection in your stance, weighting, angles of feet and other joints. This is the foundation of your training and it must be strong to support the training in years to follow. You should practice standing for equal lengths of time on both left- and right-side postures. At first you should start at about five minutes on either side and build this up to a minimum of twenty minutes daily. Of course, the longer you stand the stronger your foundation will become.

Failure to work on this basic area of training can lead to weakness and problems in your practice later. Many students lack the discipline to practice standing as they get bored and often don't see the benefits immediately.

At first you should stand completely still for set lengths of time and you can use a clock to obtain your goals. As you get more proficient at the exercise you can forget time and just stand as long as you want too. You will be surprised how when you settle into this aspect of training time just passes, especially if you don't focus on it and standing upwards of an hour can seem like only minutes. This feeling is a good sign of progress.

On the physical level at first you must concentrate on maintaining correct posture. Keep your weight 70% on the back foot and 30% on the front to develop the leg strength needed in Hsing-I Chuan forms. You will feel aches and pains in different parts of your body, also burning sensations in your muscles and tendons. This is all perfectly natural as your body is adapting to this new posture and in a relatively short period of time these sensations should pass and standing training will become more enjoyable. It is important not to give up when the physical pain is there, do not put your arms down or stand up out of your stance. Just acknowledge the pain or sensation and let it pass until you have reached your goal for the session.

Concentrate at first on the clock and make your goal, this will help you pass through the physical barriers. TCM theory views the pain and sensations experienced in this early stage of practice as chi trying to force its way through blocked areas in the body. When you stand in a posture that is new to your body the muscles will soon tire and then tense or cramp up. When this tension is present in the body the flow of chi is impeded and the result is pain. As your body becomes used to the posture and relaxes the chi will flow more smoothly through these areas and the symptoms will reduce. Furthermore, as your body relaxes so will your structure and bones and it is not unusual to hear clicking and cracking sounds as the natural tensions built up in your body over years of stress and poor posture which have been held in your muscles and tissues naturally find their true alignment.

This method of training is relatively safe as you are standing still and therefore not likely to injure yourself through poorly coordinated movements. By the time you start the first movements of your training your body structures should have naturally strengthened, stretched and aligned without too much external force being exerted through them. Using this method, the natural force of gravity provided by the Tao has helped you to prepare for the training to come.

This stage of training usually lasts about six to twelve weeks if practiced regularly. Obtaining natural alignment depends on what your stress and posture were like before you started training. When you can stand for twenty minutes or more virtually pain free you are ready to start the second level of this exercise which involves correct breathing and is discussed later in this chapter.

Note: No matter how experienced you are at Hsing-I this form of training should continue throughout and standing in San Ti posture should be always a part of your daily practice.

'Breathing' – The key to a healthy life!

On this subject Master McNeil states:

"Because all other functions depend on it, breathing is considered the most important function of the body. We all can exist for some time without eating and a shorter time without water but without air, our existence is measured in minutes. Our first breath leads us into life and our last takes us back to the Way! We go to various health clubs to tone our external bodies so that we may look good but we seldom think about toning our inner organs using proper breathing exercises. Correct breathing keeps the body healthy and free of disease."

Illustrated below are the three most common types of breathing seen in people today.

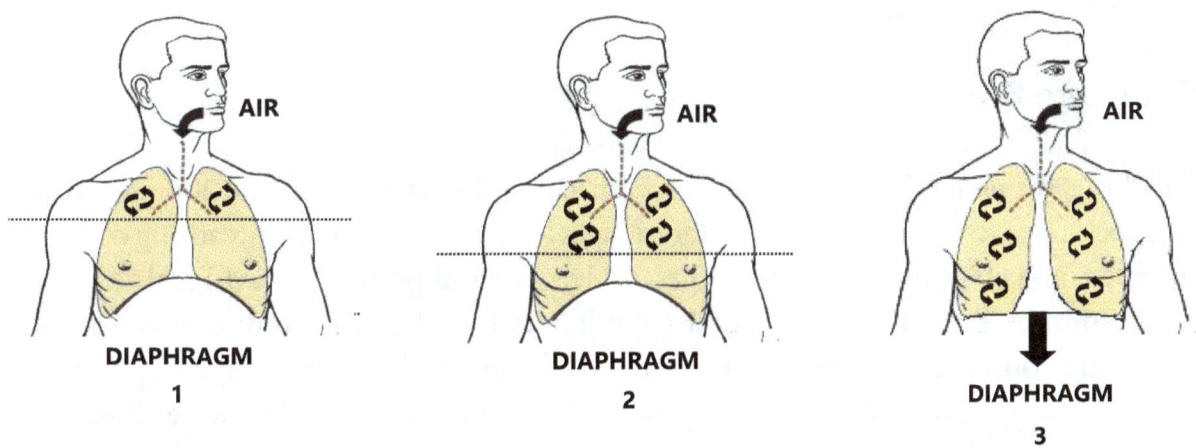

1. **Upper Breathing**, in which only the top one third of the lungs are being used.
2. **Middle Breathing**, in which only the top two thirds of the lungs are being used. Here the diaphragm is only partially being used efficiently.
3. **Complete Breathing**, in which the total lung capacity is being used and the diaphragm is utilised to its maximum efficiency.

Further to this Master McNeil states:

"We are all meant to breathe in this third way, as we did as infants. Only with complete breathing can all stagnant air be moved from the bottom of our lungs and be replaced with fresh air. Using this complete breathing technique, one will keep healthy and free of disease."

Most people breathe only using the first or at best second breathing method; this may be due to the fact that in Western society we see body image as so important. Modern media portrays the body image to be desired as slim and people hold their stomachs in and puff their chests out, thinking this to be more visibly attractive. Over time this becomes their normal posture and their muscles and soft tissue structure adapt until they know no other way.

Another reason some people may utilise the upper or middle breathing methods are those who suffer respiratory problems where lung tissue may have been damaged due to disease, resulting in limited ability to access all the sections of lung tissue for oxygen exchange. In this case they breathe very shallow or when necessary try to breathe more deeply to utilise deeper tissues, but as this method is born out of necessity rather than training it does not use the diaphragm as efficiently as when using the trained method which teaches the mind to guide the breath to sink to the Tan Tien.

As small children, we didn't worry about self-image and breathed freely as in the way we were born, using the 'Complete Breathing' method. The third method of Complete Breathing, which is utilised in the practice of Hsing-I is a deliberate and controlled Taoist health cultivation practice.

'Complete Breathing'

Breathing is one of the most important aspects of Taoist practice and integral to the progress of a practitioner of Hsing-I. Taoist sages long ago realised that breathing correctly was the connection between the energetic (Heaven) and physical (Earth) realms.

Complete Breathing is a natural technique which has a profound effect on our health and consciousness. Benefits range from relaxing the body mentally and physically to connecting spiritually with the original natural energies of the Universe. Breathing serves a multitude of purposes in the body, but the main purposes are as follows:

1. Maximising oxygen intake to the body

Oxygen is taken into the body through the lungs and distributed to every cell in the body via the bloodstream. Complete breathing helps maximise the efficiency of this process. The body and the brain requires a large amount of oxygen to function and so to improve our physical and mental capacity, our breathing must be efficient to meet this demand. When the chi rises clearly to the brain and is abundant the mind will be clear and actions appropriate.

2. Improving the rate of carbon dioxide removal from the body

If there is any excess of carbon dioxide detected within the body a person can quickly become ill. To combat this problem our breathing will naturally speed up to expel this toxic waste from our blood stream. This will result in an increased respiratory rate. When breathing quickly the body doesn't have time to breathe deeply to the bottom of the lungs and this results in breathing in the upper section of the lungs only which is counterproductive as it means carbon dioxide will remain in the lower part of the lungs for much longer. When this happens, the brain responds to the carbon dioxide levels still being too high and speeds up the respiratory rate further, which can create a sense of panic and stress in a person. This leads to a negative cycle that over time is not good for the tissues of the body. Using complete breathing, we breathe smoother and longer using the whole of the lungs and cleaning out all the carbon dioxide and the person remains calm and relaxed and the body remains healthy.

3. Balancing our emotions

From a Taoist perspective, emotions are nothing more than an energetic manifestation of a state of our consciousness. Complete breathing allows a person to calm their emotional imbalances and regulate them to some degree. It is easy to see how people experience a shift in breathing patterns when experiencing strong emotions. For example, anger produces short rasping breaths, sadness makes people sigh a lot, drawing in long breaths and fear makes us hold or stagnate our breath. It is important to understand our emotions can affect our breathing and vice versa. Adverse emotions therefore can cause damage to our health through the creation of stress internally which physically leads to an inefficient breathing pattern.

4. Increasing our postnatal chi levels to support our prenatal chi.

As previously mentioned, postnatal chi is the energy we take into our body from the environment after we are born. This energy is taken mainly from our food and air and mixed within the body. As well as oxygen, our breathing enables us to draw in chi from our environment, absorbing natural energy from the sun, moon, trees and plants, etc. Complete breathing allows us to maximise this and benefit our health.

5. Balancing the natural internal pressures of the body

The body is divided into two main chambers; the chest cavity and the abdominal cavity. Complete breathing causes the diaphragm to move up and down which alternates the physical and energetic pressure of these two cavities. This alternating air pressure between the two cavities causes the organs to be gently squeezed and released as we breathe. This serves as an internal massage, which helps to maintain the longevity of the organs by improving chi flow to them. Breathing too forcefully can cause too much pressure, which can be detrimental to the organs.

6. Re-establishing the link between man and the original energy of the universe
At the highest level of complete breathing, the practitioner aims to reconnect to the two great vibrational energies of the universe. This energy is in the form of Yin energy of Earth and Yang energy of Heaven which, according to Taoist philosophy, gave birth to life. By increasing our oxygen intake given to us by the Earth, we can refine this along with our Jing and build up our levels of chi internally. When the levels of chi are sufficient we can refine the Chi to Shen which resonates more closely with the energy of Heaven. When a practitioner can do this in their practice, they will have attained a high level of skill in Hsing-I and become closer to the Tao.

Exercise Two – Correct Breathing in San Ti Standing Posture

When you have been practicing standing San Ti posture training as described previously in Exercise One and can maintain a good posture for twenty minutes or more without having to adjust yourself, you can now start to concentrate on breathing to enhance the effectiveness of the exercise. At this point this exercise is now classified as 'Nei Kung' as the mind now works in harmony with the breath and guides the chi. Of course, you are breathing the same as in Exercise One previously, but the difference was that your focus was not on the breath or the chi, but rather the physical posture. Now the posture is correct you can concentrate the mind on the flow of chi and the exercise becomes a form of standing meditation.

Over time this exercise will help you to become relaxed, focused, centred and solid which are all prerequisites for a strong Hsing-I foundation. The lessons you learn in this training will all be carried forward into the moving forms you practice later in your training.

When practicing Exercise Two of San Ti standing posture training you should adopt the method of complete breathing. First you place your tongue against the roof of your mouth, your teeth are lightly together without any conscious pressure of the jaw and you breathe naturally, inhaling and exhaling only through your nose. As you breathe in your abdomen should expand outwards from the centre of the lower Tan Tien. As you breathe out your abdomen should return to its natural state.

When practising this method, you concentrate on the expansion of the abdomen physically and this practice is the first level of breathing which is closely linked to the method of refining Jing (physical) or seminal essence, to Chi (energy) within Hsing-I training. With regular practice, this complete method of breathing will become more natural and then you can develop the method further by starting to use your mind to focus and guide the breath to the lower Tan Tien.

On this subject Master McNeil states:

"Over time practicing this way you will re-program the brain to use this breathing method at all times as you did before you were born and were forming in

the foetus. You instinctively breathed this natural way as you knew no other way. Remember, when you were in the foetus and surrounded by fluid you breathed and acquired nourishment through your umbilical cord and used your Tan Tien naturally as a pump mechanism to make this process happen. Immediately after you were born and the umbilical cord was severed you then started to breathe through your mouth and nose, but your body still efficiently used this abdominal method to breathe efficiently, as you grow your body and mind grows further away from the Tao and what was natural and your ego starts to affect the way you breathe and present yourself. The development of the ego is detrimental to your health and wellbeing."

When the complete breathing method has been successfully embedded into the San Ti posture exercise you can then progress to guiding the flow of chi with the mind as you no longer need to concentrate directly on posture and breathing.

Now as you inhale, the breath should be guided by the mind up the centre of your spine to the brain and the top of the head. Physically your abdomen expands in time with the in breath just the same, the difference is that now you concentrate on the flow of chi up the spine, rather than the expansion of the abdomen. At the same time, you should be aware that your head is gently lifted from the crown as though suspended by a piece of cotton at the acupuncture point Baihui. This process lightly opens the spinal column and surrounding structures allowing a smooth flow of energy to the brain. Simultaneously you should be aware that the acupuncture point Hui Yin between your genitals and anus is slightly lifted, often termed 'sucked up' during the in breath.

As you exhale the mind follows the flow of chi naturally down the front of the body from the top of the head back to the point Hui Yin, which also relaxes back to its normal state. This practice is the second level of breathing and is linked to the stage of refining Chi (energy) to Shen (spiritual essence) within Hsing-I training.

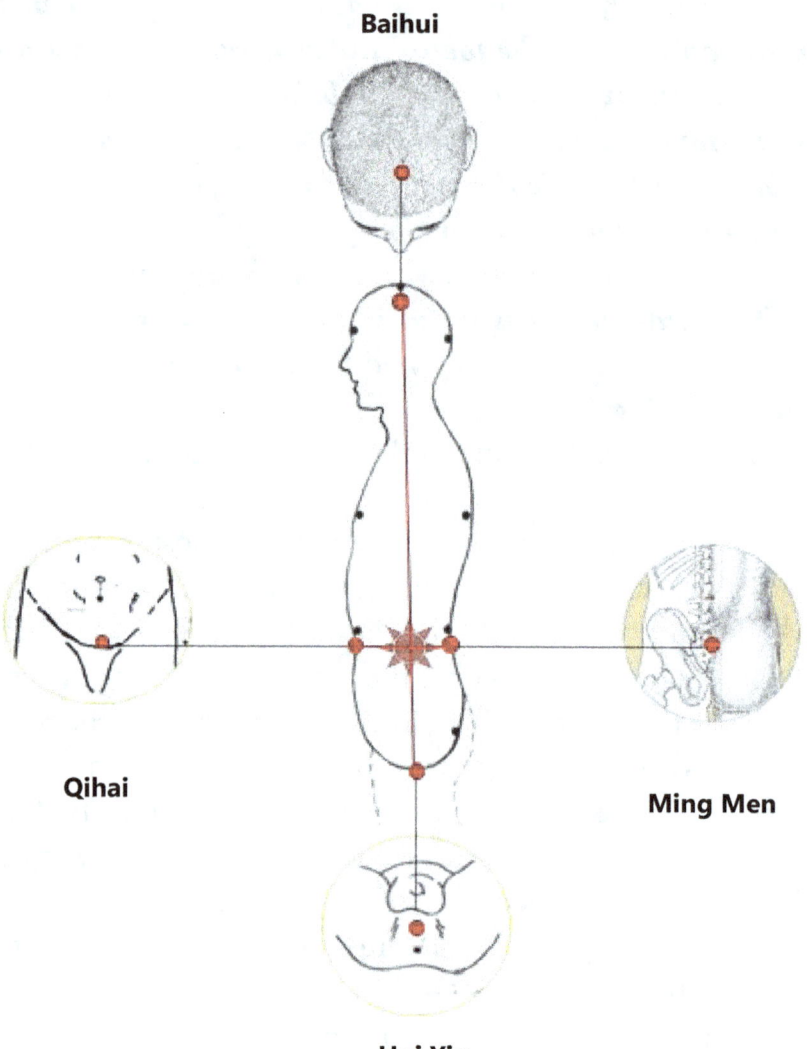

In Taoist philosophy, this method of connecting the two points is referred to as 'Man connecting with Heaven and Earth' and closely follows the principles of creation discussed earlier in this book. When this method of breathing is practiced correctly the 'Little Nine Heaven Circulation' is opened which naturally stimulates the chi flow connecting and balancing Yin and Yang in the body via the Ren and Du meridians. Located along the Ren and Du meridians are nine major energy points or 'gates' as they are referred to in Taoist practice. These nine gates are called the 'Nine Heavens' and must be opened sequentially to achieve good health and longevity.

The Little Nine Heaven Circulation Diagram

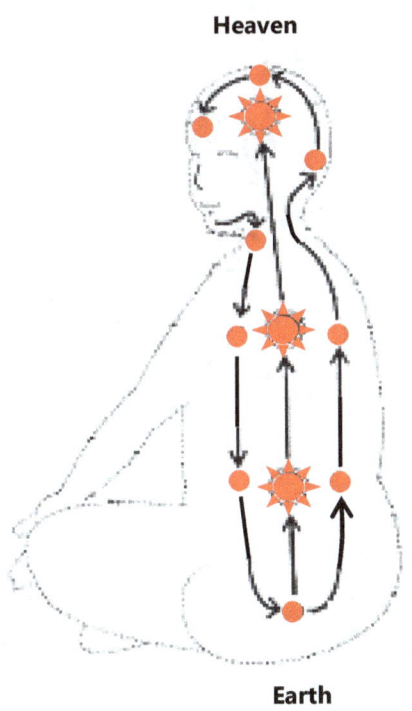

Finally, when the first two levels of breathing have been achieved, the third and final level is to practise levels one and two with no conscious thought whilst practising San Ti posture and then apply this to all Hsing-I forms and movements. This stage in training is linked to refining "Shen"(spiritual essence) back into emptiness, or pre-natal awareness as it was before you were born and you were part of the emptiness that is Tao. When you can practise and apply your Hsing-I in this empty state you have reached the highest level of practice. If the practitioner can reach this third level it is said they will have connected with the original energy of Heaven and Earth. Their body will be healthy and vibrant and they will be mentally calm and clear. Taoists believe that at this level the person will naturally understand the meaning of life!

Chapter 5

The Three Principle Stages of Hsing-I Chuan Training

If the practitioner trains correctly, absorbs and combines all the theories that are attributed to Hsing-I into their training, their body and mind will naturally move through the following three principle stages of development. It is in this development that patience is required as there is no time limit as to how long each stage will take an individual. It is a natural process and cannot be forced; however, it can be influenced by regular practice and a knowledgeable teacher.

On this subject Master McNeil says:

"These are the stages of progression involved in changing your mind and body back to what they were before birth by practicing Hsing-I. The Chinese believe that a child's mind is like a blank tape. After years of problems and troubles, the tape must be wiped clean. This is the objective of Hsing-I. It is common knowledge that most children heal faster, are generally better, fitter and more flexible than older people. Returning to this condition will make you physically and mentally healthy and help to prolong your life."

The progress of Hsing-I training can be monitored through the following three distinct stages of improvement. These stages are defined by a practitioners increase in technical ability. They also show a marked advancement in the body's physical and energetic development. These stages were first thought to be categorised and documented by Master Guo Yun-Shen (1820–1901) who was a famous student of Li Lao-Nan.

Stage of Development	Physical Development	Energetic Development
1 Visible strength	Modify bones	Refine Jing to Chi
2 Invisible strength	Modify muscles	Refine Chi to Shen
3 Refined inner strength	Modify the spinal cord	Refine Shen back into emptiness

Stage 1

Refine Jing (physical/seminal essence) to chi (energy) – modify bones – visible strength

To achieve this first stage of visible strength, the main objective is to become competent in all the basic postures and movements of the forms. The practitioner must study the hand and foot techniques and learn to combine them to move as one unit. The application and execution of techniques must be accurate. On executing the half-step method, a clear sound should be noted when the back foot strikes the ground which is timed exactly as the hands strike. Improvement of strength, speed and flexibility should also be accomplished. Movements must flow smoothly; balance and breath must be relaxed and controlled. To attain this, they must practice slowly at first in order to integrate all the different aspects of each movement with the timing of the breath.

The first level of the complete breathing method should be practiced, where the practitioner focuses their mind on expanding and relaxing the lower Tan Tien. Jing energy comes from our parents prior to birth and is supplemented through our life by the food we eat and the air we breathe. Within TCM it is believed that this Jing energy is stored in the body via the kidneys and when utilised, physically takes the form of natural body fluids. With time and practice, Jing energy will be more efficiently transformed, as when the external body becomes more coordinated so does the internal aspects such as the mind, organs and bodily functions.

Practice at this level will increase the naturally released energy in the formation and secretion of bodily fluids which are then moved mentally via the will of the mind and physically by the relaxation and contraction of muscles and tissues which in turn allows a smoother flow of Jing from different parts of the body to the Tan Tien. With correct focus on the breath and the lower Tan Tien, Jing will naturally be transformed into chi.

Before considering any further stages of refinement it is worth grasping the following concept. Chi is the same substance as Jing, just vibrating at a higher frequency. Shen is also the same substance of energy as Jing and chi just vibrating at a higher frequency than chi. Jing vibrates more closely to the frequency of Earth energy and the physical realm, which is why it presents as a physical substance. When Jing is transformed it then vibrates at a higher frequency becoming chi and this is in tune with the energetic realm. These processes of energy refinement are all going on naturally in the body all the time otherwise it wouldn't be alive. A useful example to visualise this concept would be ice changing to water. Just add a little energy to the ice in the form of heat and it will change to water. The substance is still the same, just in a different form.

When practicing Hsing-I, the practitioner is looking to improve the quality of this energy refinement to a higher, more efficient level, thus becoming mentally aware and sensitive to its process. When this stage is achieved the practitioners health will benefit from improved internal efficiency and function.

The classic literature of Hsing-I states:

"When the practitioner is proficient in the hard, physical skills of Hsing-I, the bones will harden like steel and the body will refine the physical essence of Jing into Chi within the Tan Tien."

Stage 2

Refine Chi to Shen (spiritual essence) – modify muscles – invisible strength

When training at the second stage of invisible strength, the practitioner's movements should become smooth and rounded. The techniques should flow and appear unbroken in their transition from one to another. All the body segments (head, shoulders, elbows, hands, knees, hips and feet) should be totally coordinated, even when changing direction. It should become more difficult for the opponent to sense their intentions.

To achieve this, the 'Six Harmonies' of Hsing-I must be mastered. Training must emphasise increased flexibility and agility. The change of form from slow to fast and high to low should appear uninterrupted. When the movements stop, the power and intent should continue to issue out from the technique. When executing the half-step method, the sound of the rear foot should change from loud to soft. Movements within the forms should become smaller and softer. Training looks as though the power has diminished, but actually it has increased through becoming relaxed, flexible and having total coordination, both physically and energetically. Coordination of movements with the breath should be fully integrated. The second level of complete breathing should be used where the mind should consciously lead the breath and chi during practice.

Internally the increased quantity of chi developed from transformed Jing nourishes and continues to modify the muscles and tendons, helping to further strengthen them and improve their flexibility. Also, the ability to combine the heart and mind with the physical body helps develop the Shen (spirit) in practice. Correct practice of the physical movements combined with breath and mind allows the opening of the body's network of energy pathways (meridians) strengthening its flow making it more spontaneous and unimpeded. This process takes place at the middle Tan Tien in the centre of the practitioner's chest.

When the middle Tan Tien is sufficiently full of chi it can refine or vibrate at a higher, more efficient frequency which in effect converts the chi to Shen. A useful example to help visualise this would be water turning to steam. Again, it is the same substance as was originally ice, but with increased energy in the form of heat, the cycle continues and changes the water to steam which naturally rises to the sky, just as Chi converts to Shen and rises in the body to the upper Tan Tien located in the head.

Stage 3

Refine Shen back into emptiness (prenatal awareness)– modify spinal cord – refined inner strength

In this final third stage, that of refined inner strength; the highest level of practice, the previous two stages must be completely mastered. The heart and mind must be as one and combine completely with physical movement. This stage is when all unites and becomes completely natural. No conscious thought is required to act.

To observe, the movements and execution of techniques looks easy and effortless. The body is light as a feather and the heart is empty. There should be no excessive emotions and the strikes should issue forth whenever they are required. The practitioner's applications of form should always be the right one for the situation, no mistakes, it is as though the mind works without conscious thought.

The classic literature of Hsing-I states:

"The body moves as though it is on fire. All is united with the breath. At this stage, the practitioner fights an opponent as though no one is there!"

Internally as the body refines Jing to Chi to Shen efficiently, no thought must be given to this process, it just happens naturally and the body becomes as it was before birth. From here the energy pathway up the centre of the body (thrusting meridian) can be accessed, known as 'modifying the spinal cord' to refine the Shen to the brain where it is said the process of enlightenment can be achieved. An example here would be the body refining steam from the ice and water. Steam naturally rises to the sky, as does Shen to the brain and potentially out to the universe. When the internal refinement of energy is complete, it is also said that the practitioner has connected with the pure Yin of Earth and Yang of Heaven energies. At this level, the practitioner is said to be at one with Tao!

The following summarises the energetic process that evolves during the long-term practice of Hsing-I. The three Tan Tien's are seen in Taoist practice as the areas of the body where each refinement of energy takes place. These areas are closely related to the three stages of training in Hsing-I. First the Jing is refined in the lower Tan Tien just below the naval. As this substance is refined it naturally rises within the body via the 'Thrusting' meridian which is the meridian that connects the three Tan Tien's through the centre of the body.

As the second stage of training is complete the refinement of chi takes place at the middle Tan Tien which is located in the centre of the body at the level of the heart. As this stage is completed the Jing transforms to Chi and Shen rising to the upper Tan Tien which resides just behind the centre of the eyebrows within the brain. Taoists refer to this area as the 'Ni Wan Palace'.

As the third stage of training is complete, the Thrusting meridian is fully open connecting the three Tan Tien's and the ability to link with the pure energy of the

Heavens is possible. Here the Shen vibrates at the frequency closest to that of Yang or Heaven and with correct instruction from a knowledgeable teacher, this area can be opened to communicate with the great energies of the universe and it is said Immortality can be achieved.

The Three Tan Tien's

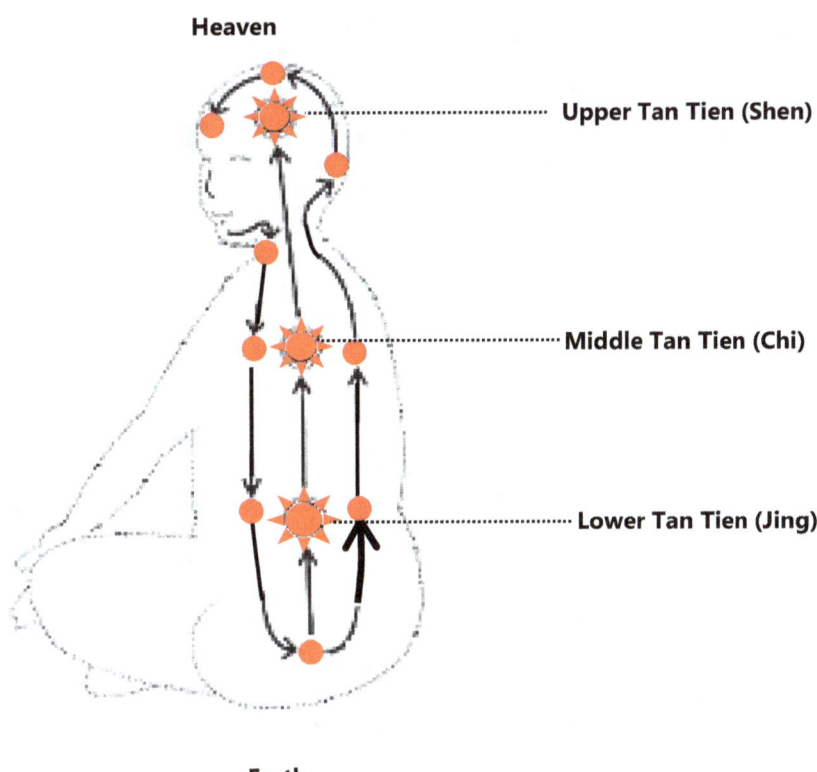

Chapter 6

The Two Levels of Practice in Hsing-I Chuan

Introduction

On the Two Levels of Practice Master McNeil states:

"When the Two Levels of Practice have been achieved the practitioner will have developed both physically and mentally. As the skill level increases the confidence within is balanced by the ability on the outside. When practising with a partner or fighting, the need to show visible strength and dominance over the opponent is no longer required as the ego is dissolved and inside the spirit is calm. Many people when practising show arrogance to their partner and this ego will only get in the way of true learning and development of sensitivity. Remember always respect your opponent and even your enemy, if you can beat them without embarrassing them then you will have truly defeated them, not just in the moment, they will also respect you forever.

When practising at the highest level it is possible to defeat the attack simply by subtly moving, off balancing and controlling the opponent without physically showing any obvious visible movement or even the need to strike. As the opponent tries to move or attack they are immediately countered and their energy dissolved to a point where it works against them. This skill requires excellent sensitivity developed through regular practice. When applied correctly the challenger feels the technique very subtly and knows that he cannot defend against it."

The first level of practice can be divided into three areas:

1. Understanding the way of power.

To understand the way of power the practitioner must be centred, balanced and have developed total body coordination in their movements. Before the internal energy or chi can be cultivated and combined, the external body must have complete harmony mechanically. This perfect alignment of all the body segments throughout all physical movements allows the body to have efficient production of Jing, which is the basic raw material for producing chi.

2. Cultivating the chi naturally.

To cultivate the chi naturally the practitioner must have developed the skill of combining the breath with mental intent and be able to gather the chi from inside the body and also its external environment, collecting and holding it in the Tan Tien. Perfect alignment of the body, both physically and energetically, allows the chi to be gathered efficiently. When gathered, chi must be held in its place in the Tan Tien and circulated appropriately during practice to any given action. In Taoist practice the gathering of the energies within the body and holding them in place is referred to as collecting the three herbs, flowers or treasures.

3. Defeating an opponent in 'No Sign'.

When using their skill, even though the body has visible physical form, the practitioner's intent must be concealed within the physical form. This way the opponent cannot easily see their attack. They must be able to flow from one technique to another without showing their true intentions and react to whatever situation arises. At this level, the movements should be light and soft to conceal their inherent power and ability.

On this subject Master McNeil states: *"He knew and I knew! This is an example of beating someone in 'no sign'."*

Classical Hsing-I literature states *"You will not be hit because you will never be there! When you hit, all will be as one and you will have the power of a mountain!"*

When a practitioner can combine the chi with the power successfully in all techniques they will have the ability to defeat an opponent in 'no sign' and they will have balanced the energies of both Yin and Yang in their body. At this point, the first level of practice in Hsing-I will be complete.

The second level of practice can be divided into three areas:

1. Learning how to dissolve power.

When the body and mind move as one in complete harmony the body will become extremely sensitive to all around it. The practitioner will strike, advance and retreat with no apparent force. Not only will the body issue power effectively but the ability to absorb and dissolve power will also be developed. This in effect allows the practitioner to use an opponent's own energy against them by moving subtly and changing alignment. By sensing an opponent's moves it becomes possible to use their energy and redirect it to cause them injury or putting them at a disadvantage. This skill allows the combined power of the practitioner to be heightened with that of their opponents' and can lead to feats of seemingly impossible strength, throwing people great distances, and causing devastating internal injuries.

2. Learning how to change the marrow in the body.

The practitioner's ability to be able to completely relax the body during practice and in stressful situations is now natural. The chi within the body is abundant in the Tan Tien and now flows smoothly to all organs and extremities. The marrow in the bones is full and this leads to the natural increased production of more red blood cells. This process improves the quality of the blood and nourishes all the cells and tissues having a beneficial effect on the health of the whole body.

In the classical literature pertaining to the internal arts the mention of a practice as 'having an effect on the bones and marrow' literally means 'deep in the core of the body', as the bones are seen as the deepest most hard to reach tissues in the body. If the body is pure and healthy from the bones then this means it is healthy from deep within and your inner strength will be great. If the practice of Hsing-I can affect bone level then it is at a high level.

3. Achieving a state of spiritual emptiness.

Finally, the goal of Hsing-I practice is to regain the energetic state of body pre-birth. All skills and sensations that are felt in the body during life are acquired post-birth. When the practitioner reaches the level that no conscious thought is required to act and that all movements and actions, including thoughts are appropriate to the given situation, then the body will feel light and empty in all that it does.

Only now does the practitioner become the conduit that connects the great energies of both Heaven and Earth and will again be at one with the Tao. This level of spiritual emptiness and awareness will affect the body, not only in practice, but in all levels of its being. It is said that a person who has achieved this level will experience a change in their demeanour, ego, attitude towards themselves and others and this profound change will be for the greater good.

When this second level of practice in Hsing-I is complete, the practitioner will become a master of themselves. Hsing-I is born from ancient Taoist practice and has the ultimate goal of a return to a spiritually empty state. Like Taoist meditation, which goes from inaction to action, Hsing-I uses action to inaction as its method of training.

Chapter 7

Hsing-I Chuan and the Taoist Five Elements Theory

The Five Fists or 'Wu Chuan' of Hsing-I are derived from the concept of the Five Elements or 'Wu Hsing' (Wu Xing) which were developed from the ancient Taoist theories connected to the evolution of the universe. These Five Fists are the most basic, fundamental techniques in Hsing-I practise and form the cornerstone from which a practitioner's Hsing-I is developed. 'Wu Hsing', commonly translated in the West as the Five Elements, is comprised of Metal, Water, Wood, Fire and Earth. 'Wu' means five, however, 'Hsing', unfortunately, does not simply translate as 'element'; instead 'Hsing' variably describes a movement, phase or process. Therefore, the Five Elements should not be thought of as physical substances but rather as movements of energy in a specific way. Each element is also associated with a particular organ within the body and the correct practice of the appropriate Five Element form will benefit the relevant organs' energetic function. The aim of this chapter is to discuss the theories of the Five Elements from both a Taoist universal aspect, TCM and Hsing-I perspective. Pictures showing the sequence of physical movements and self-defence applications of each element will be discussed later in Part Two of this book, 'The Practice of Hsing-I Chuan'.

Before discussing Hsing-I and its relationship with the Five Element Theory, it is useful to understand how the Taoist theory of evolution developed the Five Element Theory in the beginning.

History and Development of Five Elements Theory

The first known recorded reference of the five elements theory dates back to the warring states period (475–221 BCE). It was developed after the theory of Yin/Yang and this is why the principles of Yin and Yang are so evident within the theory of the five elements. It is also said that the Five Element Theory was developed by the Taoist Yin/Yang School of philosophy in ancient times. Its influences were obvious in a wide variety of applications within China, including medicine, martial arts, astrology, the natural sciences, the calendar, music and even politics.

The ancient Taoist philosophers were highly esteemed and the rulers of the time feared them because they professed to be able to interpret nature, in the light of the universal laws and subsequently, draw political conclusions from the findings. They also claimed they could predict the succession of rulers by referring to the various cycles of the five elements. Each emperor of the time was associated with a certain element and every ceremony held by the emperor had to conform to all aspects of their corresponding element, including colour, season and numbers. A classic example of this can be seen in the year 2600 BCE when Huang Ti, the Yellow Emperor, succeeded Shen Nung, the Red Emperor. This association between rulers and elements suggests the Five Element Theory was well established over 4500 years ago in truth.

Apart from its political involvement, the theory of the five elements was also used to classify the different phases of nature; such as the five seasons which was useful when understanding the weather for planting and harvesting of crops and even predicting the right moment to do battle during times of war.

Ancient sages recognised that the five elements were the basic substances or the building blocks that are essential for life. These basic substances are natural energies that cannot be dispensed with and they constitute every object or thing in existence. Taoists believe that everything on earth belongs to at least one of the categories of the five elements. They are qualities of nature, each separate; yet still retain the capacity to either transform into one another or alternatively nourish or generate each other.

The Five Elements in the Universe

Taoist philosophy states: ***"From the endless energy source of the Tao sprang forth the building blocks of the Universe as we know it. Out of the void spontaneously came matter and space or Yin and Yang. This energy formed cycles and patterns that can be observed in all things, which are commonly known as the laws of nature. They cannot be broken for they are universal laws and are at one with the Tao."***

One such energetic cycle attributed to the universal laws is that of the five elements, each element symbiotic to the other. They create a special kind of endless rhythm that dictates the forces of life energy; one which allows the universe to be mirrored into the 'small universe' of the body, and vice versa. When this rhythm is in harmony and balanced, it is possible for us to live and function at our most efficient capacity in a universe that is created for our needs.

The cycles of the five elements can be seen clearly in nature and have been well documented within classical Chinese literature over many centuries. Presented next are some of the obvious universal cycles that affect the lives of all living creatures on earth with commentary on them and their links with the five elements.

When a practitioner of Hsing-I understands how the five element cycle affects the way they live, they can then appreciate how this same theory affects their own internal energetic functioning. The seasons, days, earthly directions and organ chi flow all affect a person's ability to live a healthy life and without balance the planet would be a hostile environment to survive and the body would soon become ill with disease. Living out of harmony with the five elements will lead to poor quality of life and a reduced overall lifespan.

Therefore, regularly practising Hsing-I offers a method which helps to balance the internal energies of the organs and creates a healthy body from which the practitioner can enjoy their life. The Five Element Theory provides a framework to analyse the energies of the universe alongside the energies within the body. In doing so, the practitioner can recognise and adjust their practise and lifestyle, when needed, to keep the body as healthy as possible throughout its life cycle.

The Five Elements and the Seasons

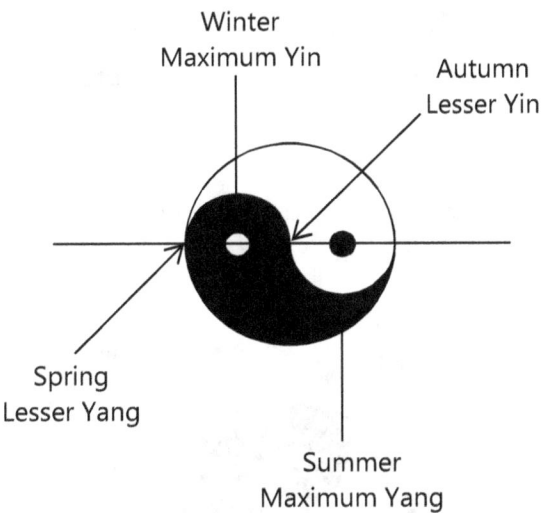

Spring (Wood): Regarded as the beginning of the new cycle of life, spring energy describes movement, expansion, and birth of all living things. It is the season when plants germinate and bring forth new shoots, all around is green in colour, animals emerge from hibernation and life begins anew. The natural quality of spring is wind, like the gentle wind of nature moving through the world, stirring, and changing all around it. Energetically the season of spring is Lesser Yang but Yang energy is starting to increase and Yin energy is in decline.

Summer (Fire): This is the season when growth is at its peak and nature is in full bloom. The sun is high in the sky and warm and the colour representing the heat of summer is red. Crops soak up the energy of the sun and reach their peak of ripeness. It is the energy of summer, which begins at the spring equinox when the days and nights are of equal length. Energetically the season of summer is Maximum Yang, when Yang energy of day dominates over Yin energy of night and the length of each day increases.

Late Summer (Earth): This is the time when summer appears to linger until autumn arrives. It is the period of slow transformation where the yellow colour of element earth is like the golden colour of ripe fruit. Earth is a period of neutrality that occurs between summer and autumn. Late summer is sometimes called Indian summer, when the days continue to become increasingly humid.

Autumn (Metal): Autumn is the season when the Yang energies of nature are in decline. Dryness is the predominating quality of autumn, much like the withering of trees and shrivelling up of plants seen in nature. It is related to the reaping of the harvest. Animals prepare for the coming cold months ahead. The colour is white as nature drops its leaves and the canvas left behind is blank. Energetically, autumn is a time of Lesser Yin and we can see Yin energy increasing and Yang energy decreasing.

Winter (Water): Winter is the season for storage, hibernation, rest and contraction. It is the time for restoring energies to prepare for the coming of the next cycle. The days shorten and the blackness of night is dominant, therefore the colour of winter is black. Winter energy is cold like water and the quality of coldness is mostly felt during this season. Therefore, energetically winter is essentially Maximum Yin.

The Five Elements and the Daily Cycle

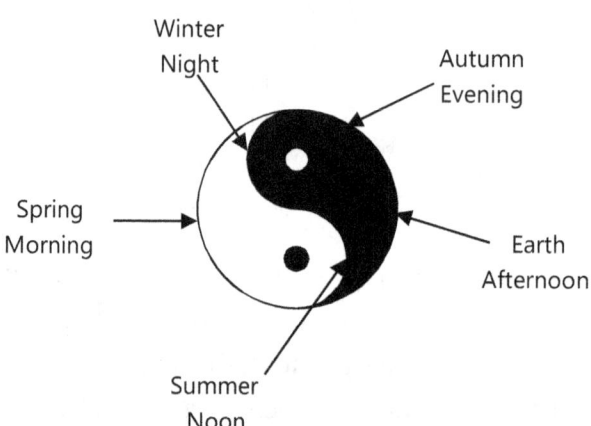

WOOD – Morning/Spring: When the rising warmth of the sun stirs the day to begin, it is the spring time of day when all arise from rest. This rise is very much like wind rustling through the trees, urging the day into activity, movement and change. Hence, morning relates to Wood energy.

FIRE – Noon/Summer: The summer time of day is when everything is at its peak. It is the period of day that relates to the energy of heat when the sun is high and daylight is at its maximum. Hence, noon relates to Fire energy.

EARTH – Afternoon: The Earth time of day is when the heat of day has passed its peak, but lingers on before dusk arrives. The Earth element activates its energy of dampness and humidity, that of thickness and slowness. Hence, afternoon relates to Earth energy.

METAL – Evening/Autumn: This is the autumn time of day when the coolness of evening begins to dominate and nature's energies prepare for the long night ahead gathering its energy inwards. Hence, evening relates to Metal energy.

WATER – Night/Winter: The winter time of the daily cycle is night, when its quality is coldness, everything sleeps and the world appears dark, as if dead. Hence, night relates to Water energy.

The Five Elements and the Compass Directions

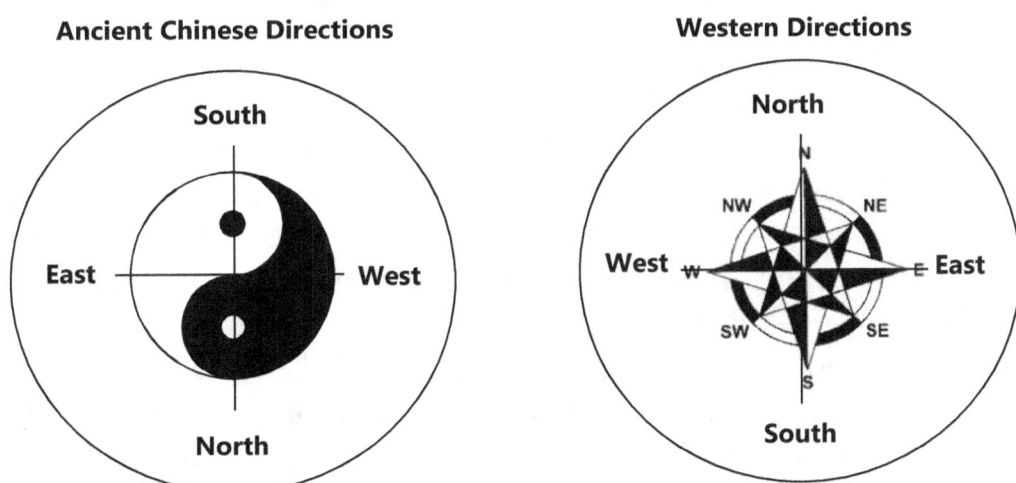

When ancient Chinese literature refers to the compass and its directions, sages of the time placed south at the top as this reflects the element Fire and the rising Yang energy associated with it. Therefore, the direction of north is placed at the bottom which reflects water and the sinking Yin energy. Yang energy is on top as is heaven and Yin energy is on the bottom as is earth. As the directions of north and south are reversed so are the directions of east and west and the compass directions are viewed from a five-element perspective (like the diagram above).

East/Wood: The compass direction east is wood energy. East correlates with the ascent of the rising sun like the ascending energetic nature of wood.

South/Fire: According to the location of China on the world map, south is hot; like the upward flaring nature of fire, therefore, south relates to fire energy.

West/Metal: The compass direction west is metal energy. West correlates with the descent of the setting sun like the descending energetic nature of metal.

North/Water: According to the location of China on the world map, north is cold, like the cold nature of water, thus the north corresponds to water.

Centre/Earth: The centre relates to earth and its energy and keeps everything centred, just as man is in the middle of heaven and earth. "Earth is the mother of all things." Earth designates balance and neutrality and therefore, places itself in the centre with no allegiance to any particular direction.

So, it can be said that the five element theory is a cycle of energetic phases that arise out of the observation of the natural cycles of the universe which created the cycles of the four seasons and their relationship to the many natural cycles found on earth. These cycles are listed in the table below for easy reference.

Five Elements	Seasons	Environmental Factors	Growth and Development	Colours	Times of Day	Orientations
Wood	Spring	Wind	Germination	Green	Morning	East
Fire	Summer	Heat	Growth	Red	Noon	South
Earth	Late Summer	Dampness	Transformation	Yellow	Afternoon	Centre
Metal	Autumn	Dryness	Reaping	White	Evening	West
Water	Winter	Cold	Storage	Black	Night	North

Key to understanding disharmony within the body is the understanding of the energetic characteristics of the five types of organ chi involved, how they are seen to operate within the body and their general functions. When this is understood the many different symptoms the body reveals when showing signs of physical illness or energetic disharmony, can be swiftly analysed and appropriate action taken to restore balance, before the problem becomes deeply rooted and difficult to cure. Each chi can be attached to one of the five elements and subsequently, a yin and yang classified organ. Next are some simple descriptions of the energetic characteristics of the five elements, this will help a practitioner understand why the chi of each element is seen to act as it does, not only in the universe but within their body also.

The Energetic Characteristics of the Five Elements

Wood: The nature of Wood energy is characterised as 'straight growing', spreading out freely and unobstructed. It is also said that "Wood is to be simultaneously crooked and straight," like a crooked branch growing straight out of a tree trunk. Wood is the energy of expansion and growth where all is movement, activity and change. Within the body, the liver is the major organ associated with Wood energy because the liver energy has a similar ascending nature within the body.

Fire: The nature of Fire energy is to burn and rise; it is hot and flares upwards. Therefore, Fire symbolises anything that is hot and has a pattern of flaring up. Fire designates functions that have reached a maximum state of activity, prior to their decline. Within the body the heart is the major organ associated with Fire energy because the

Yang energy of the heart brings about warmth and stimulates flaring up of emotions.

Earth: The nature of Earth energy supports the promotion of the nourishing process when one state transforms into another. Earth energy uses its neutrality to slowly smooth out the process of change between each of the other elements. Within the body, the spleen is the major organ and stomach the minor organ that are associated with the element of earth as they are located in the centre of the body. In TCM they are responsible for controlling digestion and transportation of energy derived from food in the stomach to nourish and support the other organs and body tissues.

In another version, thought to be older, of the five elements diagram (see below), Earth is placed in the centre and operates as a buffer between the other elements, helping them to move from one to the other in a smooth transition.

"Classic of Categories" (1624) states: *"**Earth pertains to the centre and its influence manifests for 18 days at the end of each of the four seasons. It does not pertain to any season on its own.**"*

The Ancient Five Element Diagram

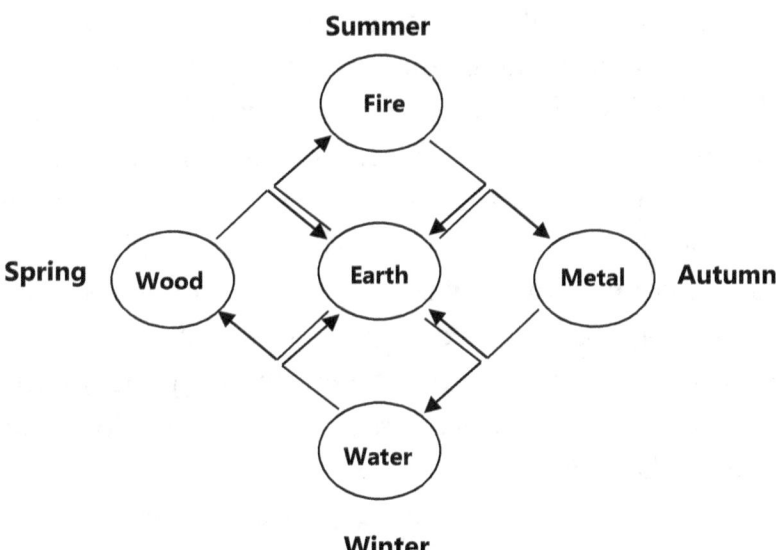

Metal: The nature of Metal energy is characterised by its capacity to be remoulded, modified and to yield. Metal represents functions in a declining stage where all around is falling away, not dead, just preparing for winter. Therefore, its natural energy is that of descending. Within the body the lung is the major organ associated with Metal as its energy naturally descends within the body drawing in air to be transformed into chi.

Water: The nature of Water energy is to moisten and flow filling any space it can occupy. Water represents functions that have reached a maximal state of rest, hence are about to change the direction of their activity. Within the body, the kidneys are the major organ seen to represent Water because their energetic function is to regulate and control the circulation of water within the body.

The Five Element Theory and the Human Body

The human body is the product of the energies of Heaven and Earth, drawn from the Tao by the interaction of Yin and Yang; it is governed by the laws of nature and contains within it the energies of the five elements. Not only do the five elements directly relate to each organ and tissue of the human body, they also relate to human emotions and actions. It is through this relationship that the practice of Hsing-I can have a positive effect on the health of the practitioner.

As previously stated, each element is associated with specific organs and their meridians. This connection comes from the nature of the chi associated with each organ and its action within the body. The link between element and organ can be better understood by knowing the TCM functions for each organ and what each organs chi does within the body.

For example, Lung Chi descends, bringing air into the body; as does the energy of autumn; drawing withering plants back into earth ready for winter. Therefore, the lungs can be associated with metal element in their general function of descending energy within the body. Five Element Theory, however complex, starts by observing the energetic nature of a bodily process and then categorises it by linking it to a similar energetic process found in nature. Of course, the theory is much more complex than a simple example and detailed study of TCM texts is required to gain a thorough understanding of the connection between each element and its associated organs.

Not only are the organs classified by an individual element but they are also subclassified into a Yin or Yang category depending on their function. Each of the five elements has a Yin and Yang organ assigned to it. Yin organs are called 'Zang' and Yang organs are called 'Fu'.

The 'Zang' organs are considered to be solid and protective in their structure. They concern themselves primarily with the filling and storing of blood (Yin) which serves to provide nutrition for the body. These organs are considered more important in function and are said to be deeper in the body than their 'Fu' partners and this depth helps to protect them as any disharmony or disease takes longer to penetrate to their level and affect them. Therefore, when they are affected the symptoms and prognosis tends to be more serious.

In contrast, their partnered 'Fu' organs are considered to be hollow organs, whose functions are to move all other bodily substances than blood such as food, urine, faeces, bile, etc. through the body and are associated more closely with the moving Yang function of chi. The Fu organs are said to be more superficial in the body and are more easily affected by illness and disease as any pathogens invading the body from outside arrive at these organs first. As these organs do not directly concern themselves with blood, the symptoms from disease here are viewed as less serious in nature as they have not penetrated deep into the body yet. Therefore, if a pathogen attacks the body it will invade from the surface (skin level) and if left untreated will begin to penetrate deeper into the body, like a flowing river with many tributaries, passing through the meridian network and eventually arriving at the organs. First it will affect the Fu and then eventually it will reach the Zang organs. With each stage of progression, the effects of the pathogen become more serious to the body's health and more difficult to treat from a TCM perspective.

When considering the classification of the organs to their respective elements each of the elements has a pair of organs assigned to it; however, there is an exception, as there are five elements and twelve organs, the element Fire is designated two pairs; a pair of Fire princes, which are heart (Zang), and small intestine (Fu) and a pair of Fire ministers which are Pericardium (Zang) and Three Heater (Fu). Classical Chinese medical literature refers to the body like a royal palace. Within this palace the organs act as the royal court. Zang organs are referred to as members of the royal family, hence they are named 'princes' and have important positions acting as commanders within the body. 'Fu' organs are referred to as 'ministers' as they are responsible for administration within the palace and are less important in their title. The minister's role is to see things get efficiently done within the palace.

Another confusing issue for the Western mind to understand is the Chinese names for organs when they have been translated into English. Sometimes a direct equivalent cannot be found. This may be misleading and the problem is with the translation, not the organ per se. For example, the Three Heater organ, which is a process rather than a physical structure, yet in TCM it is classed as an organ as all organs are thought of in terms of their energetic functions rather than their physical structures. The function of the Three Heater organ is like a thermostat on a heating system and acts to regulate the three body levels (upper, middle and lower Jiao's) and the organs contained within them, seeing that all the body's functions run smoothly in conjunction with one another. Therefore, it is important to 'think the way the Chinese masters think' when applying this theory to Hsing-I practise.

Regardless of its differences with Western medicine it must be pointed out that the organ system in TCM is viewed as a combined unit which requires all organs to function together to provide maximum health. Prime consideration is given to their energetic functions rather than their physical states. It is the normal cyclic flow of chi through the organs in the body that keeps it in good health, allowing a person to live and enjoy life. When the balance in the normal flow of chi is interrupted, for example by stress, overwork, injury or improper diet then illness, disease or even death may occur.

Below is an easy reference table showing the five elements and their relationship with the organs. It also shows the tissues of the body that the organs are directly linked to via its meridians and even more importantly, the human emotions attached to each element. The body and mind are considered as one in Taoist philosophy just as they are in Hsing-I.

Five Elements	Zang/Yin Organs	Fu/Yang Organs	Five Sense Organs	Five Tissues	Five Emotions
Wood	Liver	Gall Bladder	Eyes	Tendons	Anger
Fire	Heart/ Pericardium	Small Intestine/ Three Heater	Tongue	Vessels	Joy
Earth	Spleen	Stomach	Mouth	Muscle	Worry
Metal	Lung	Colon	Nose	Skin and Hair	Grief
Water	Kidney	Bladder	Ear	Bone	Fright and Fear

Now the relationship between the five elements, nature and the body has been discussed, the next area to understand is the Five Element Model itself and the different cycles it follows within the human body. By understanding these cycles, the practitioner can better understand the energetic state of health within their own body and how best to rebalance it through the correct practice of their Hsing-I.

The Five Element Cycles

According to the Five Element Theory there are two cyclical patterns which are generated through the normal flow of chi within the body. They are the 'Creative' or 'Generating' cycle which is called the 'Sheng' cycle in Chinese, and the 'Destructive' or 'Control' cycle which is called the 'Ke' cycle in Chinese. The Generating cycle allows one element to be nourished and to grow, whereas the Control cycle keeps another element in check, restricting it from growing too fast and thereby keeping it in balance.

When discussing the body in relation to its health it makes more sense to use the terms 'Generating' and 'Controlling' as these more accurately explain what is happening to the chi circulation within the body during its natural functions, however, when discussing Hsing-I as a martial art, the terms 'Creative' and 'Destructive' are more appropriate as they describe better the action of the chi in the martial technique. Therefore, in this book the terms used will switch as appropriate to the subject being discussed, but both terms mean the same thing.

Both the 'Generating' and 'Controlling' cycles represent the normal flow of chi within the body throughout its natural twenty-four-hour daily cycle. Each of the twelve organs has a strong flow of chi through its meridian for two hours of each day where the organ in question nourishes itself. Therefore, it takes the body twenty-four hours to fully circulate its chi around all the twelve organs in any one day, allowing them to rejuvenate themselves ready for the next cycle.

The following chart shows the order of chi flow through the organs over a 24-hour period.

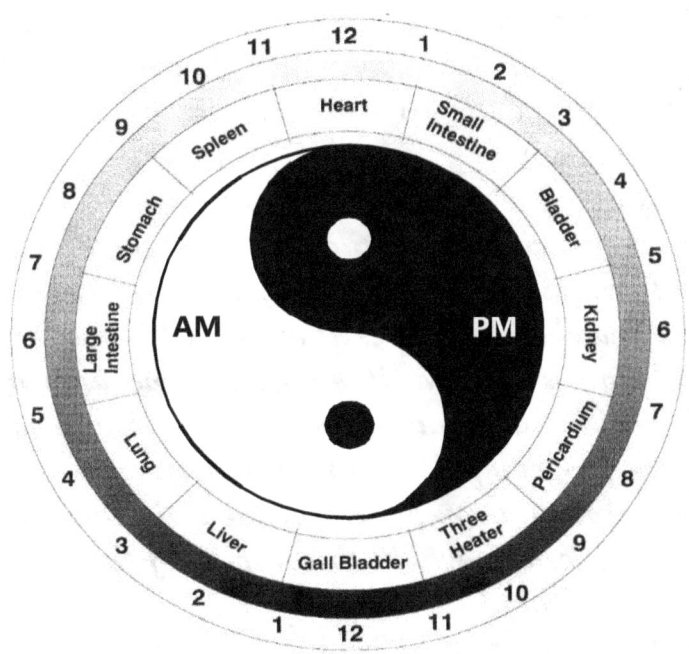

The 'Sheng' or 'Generating' Cycle

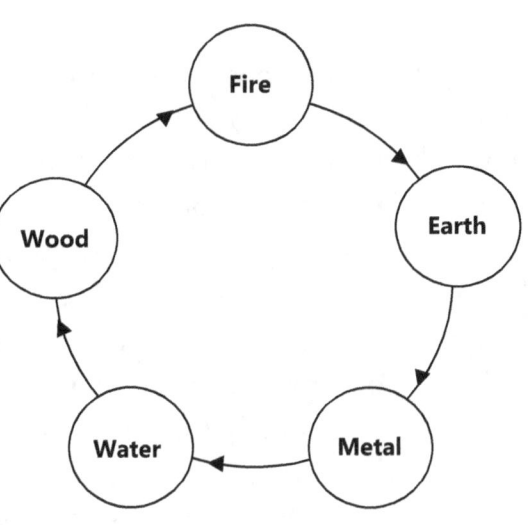

The Generating Energy Cycle is predominant during the day in harmony with the Yang energy of the day promoting activity, growth and generation. It is the Generating or nourishing cycle which is referred to as the 'Mother–Child relationship'. This 'Mother nourishing Child' cycle ensures continual growth and generation. It means that each element generates another and is also generated by one. Thus, wood generates fire, fire generates earth, earth generates metal, metal generates water and water generates wood, starting the cycle anew.

The Chinese Medicine classic literature states:

'Wood burns to create Fire.'
'When Fire has finished burning, ashes are left behind to form Earth.'
'Earth allows the formation and mining of Metals.' (The Metals found in Earth)
'When Metals are heated, they become liquid.' (Hence like Water)
'Water provides nourishing growth for plants and trees, Wood.'

Like the mother who feeds the child, when each element is fed and strengthened, and provided there is no obstruction or stagnation in the flow of chi, it will automatically feed the next element in the cycle, hence it is called the 'Generating Cycle'. Each element can be a 'Child', yet the 'Mother' of another. For example, Wood is generated by Water, and it generates Fire. Therefore, Wood is the 'Child' of water and the 'Mother' of fire.

On this subject Master McNeil comments:

"According to the principal of mutual creation, metal creates water, water creates wood, wood creates fire, fire creates Earth, and Earth creates metal. In nature, the geologic and chemical forces at work within the Earth serve to create metal. Metal itself becomes liquid as it melts when encountering sufficient heat. Water, combined with the nutrients of the Earth, creates wood. Wood, in turn creates fire, with the proper application of friction and heat. When wood is reduced to ashes it becomes a component of the soil, thus creating Earth. This cycle of creation can be seen clearly in the practise of the Five Element Linking Chain form of Hsing-I Chuan."

Note: The Five Element Linking Chain form will be shown in the second part of this book.

The 'Ke' or 'Controlling' Cycle

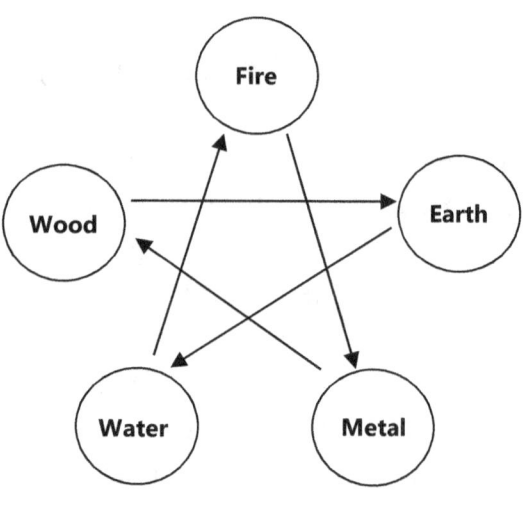

The Controlling Cycle is predominant during the night, in harmony with the Yin energy of night which promotes rest and nourishment from the day's activity and growth. Therefore, this is a time of control and restriction where the body can rest and rejuvenate itself. The Controlling Cycle moves two steps forward in time, in other words it is two steps forward in sequence, to form the 'Grandmother to Grandchild' Cycle.

The Controlling Cycle is the restrictive cycle which maintains balance and equilibrium in the body. This is necessary to ensure a peaceful and unobstructed flow of chi is maintained throughout the body. Therefore, Wood controls Earth, Earth controls Water, Water controls Fire, Fire controls Metal and Metal controls Wood. In this sequence, each of the elements is responsible for controlling another element, but in turn is being controlled by another. For example, Wood controls Earth, but is subsequently controlled by Metal. This Controlling sequence ensures that a balance is maintained among the five elements. The creative cycle if left unchecked can over-nourish and cause things to grow too quickly. Therefore, the Controlling cycle controls growth within healthy limits.

The Chinese medicine classic literature states:

'Wood controls or destroys Earth by covering it with plants, breaking up the soil and depleting its minerals.'

'Earth controls or destroys Water, by damming and blocking it.'

'Water controls or destroys Fire, by cooling and extinguishing it.'

'Fire controls or destroys Metal by heating and melting it.'

'Metal controls or destroys Wood by chopping and cutting it down.'

On this subject Master McNeil, further comments:

"The principal of mutual destruction holds that metal, in the form of tools, such as saws and axes, can destroy wood. The element of water overcomes fire. Wood can overcome Earth by depleting the minerals and nutrients that make it fertile. Fire consumes wood and Earth traps and soaks up water in depressions or dams. This destructive cycle can be seen clearly in the practice of the 'Two Man Fighting form' of Hsing-I Chuan."

Note: The Five Element Two Man Fighting form will be shown in the second part of this book.

The Interrelationship Between the Generating and Controlling Cycles

The interrelationship between the Generating and Controlling Cycles ensures that self-regulation of growth and development is maintained at all times. They are inseparable and must work together to maintain the health of the body. For example: Wood controls Earth, but Earth generates Metal, which controls Wood. Wood controls Earth, but on the other hand Wood generates Fire which in turn generates Earth.

In the Generating and Controlling energy flows, neither the promotion of growth nor the control of growth can be dispensed with. Without promotion of growth there would be no birth and development. Without control, there would be excessive growth that could be detrimental in the future or cause immediate harm. Hence, it can be said that in line with Taoist Yin/Yang and Five Element theory, the Sheng and Ke cycles are both in cooperation and in opposition to each other to ensure a relative balance is maintained for normal growth and development.

On the subject of Hsing-I and Five Elements practice, Master McNeil states:

"By following the natural cycles of the five element theories and applying a little logic, one can see that metal defeats wood, as an axe bites into a tree trunk, eventually felling the mighty tree. Wood will defeat Earth, as wood in the form of trees grows and covers our mother Earth. Earth will then conquer water, as Earth muddies the water and subsequently turns water itself into Earth. Water will destroy fire because this element can overcome the fiercest conflagration. Finally, fire will overcome metal as the heat of the blacksmith's forge melts iron.

The creative and destructive natures of the five elements work toward a common end. The Tao of the creative is used in building up body fitness, increasing power, strength and energy. The Tao of the destructive is used in fighting and self-defence. Putting the two natures of the five elements together, if practiced hard and learned well, will teach one how to change their reaction to an attack when facing an opponent."

The following easy reference table illustrates the organs involved in the five element cycles and highlights the 'mother/child' and grandmother/grandchild' relationships.

Organ	Element	Mother	Child	Grandchild
Liver	Wood	Kidney	Heart	Spleen
Heart	Fire	Liver	Spleen	Lung
Spleen	Earth	Heart	Lung	Kidney
Lung	Metal	Spleen	Kidney	Liver
Kidney	Water	Lung	Liver	Heart

Following is a table of correspondences relating to the five elements that is common to most TCM and classical Chinese literature texts and shows in more detail the association between some common categories both within the universe and the body, however, there is an infinite number of categories which could be put into this table, these are just a few examples.

The Five Element Table of Correspondences

	Wood	Fire	Earth	Metal	Water
Yin Organs	Liver	Heart	Spleen	Lung	Kidney
Yang Organs	Gall Bladder	Small Intestine	Stomach	Large Intestine	Bladder
Sense Organs	Eyes	Tongue	Mouth	Nose	Ears
Tissues	Sinews/Tendons	Vessels/Arteries	Muscles	Skin	Bones
Body Fluids	Tears	Sweat	Mouth Fluids	Nose Running	Saliva
Body Segments	Neck	Chest	Spine	Back	Waist
Extremities	Nails	Complexion	Breast	Breath	Hair
Emotions	Anger	Joy	Pensiveness/Worry	Sadness	Fear
Sounds	Shouting	Laughing	Singing	Crying	Groaning
Smell	Pungent	Burned	Fragrant	Rancid	Rotten
Taste	Sour	Bitter	Sweet	Acrid	Salty
Movements	Walk	Look	Sit	Lay Down	Stand
Seasons	Spring	Summer	Late Summer	Autumn	Winter
Stage of Development	Birth	Growth	Transformation	Harvest	Storage
Climates	Wind	Heat	Dampness	Dryness	Cold
Directions	East	South	Centre	West	North
Colours	Green	Red	Yellow	White	Black
Numbers	8	7	5	9	6
Planets	Jupiter	Mars	Saturn	Venus	Mercury
Animals	Fish	Birds	Human	Mammals	Shell covered
Domestic Animals	Sheep	Fowl	Ox	Dog	Pig
Grains	Wheat	Beans	Rice	Hemp/Corn	Millet
Meat/Poultry	Chicken	Lamb	Beef	Horse	Pork
Fruit and Nuts	Plum	Apricot	Date	Peach	Chestnut
Yin/Yang	Lesser Yang	Utmost Yang	Centre	Lesser Yin	Utmost Yin

Hsing-I Chuan and its Relationship to Five Elements Theory

Now we have looked at the Five Element Theory from a Taoist and TCM perspective, let us discuss how this same theory has influenced the development of Hsing-I. The five elements forms of Hsing-I were said to be developed by observing and imitating the essential energetic qualities of the natural forces of nature. For instance, Water always seeks its own level of adaptation, flowing and accumulating or sinking in. Fire, being less dense than water, rises. Wood can be made into a variety of shapes, either curved or straight, it can be strong yet very supple. Metal can be forged, melted, refined and made pliable or unyielding. Earth is the source of nourishment and can generate all the other elements. In Hsing-I theory, the basis of the complementary relationships between the five elements is defined by the principles of mutual creation and mutual destruction.

Understanding the natural cycles of the body also helps the practitioner to train in the correct element in the correct environment and at the right times of day in order to benefit the chi flow of the body. Further to this, understanding how chi flow can be disrupted allows the knowledgeable practitioner to avoid damaging their chi built up through their practice.

On this subject Master McNeil comments:

"By practicing the Five Elements Forms every day, one learns to condition the mind and body and also improve their fighting ability. The inner organs of the body will be conditioned due to proper breathing and posture and the chi will travel smoothly to the different organs, massaging and strengthening them in the process.

The best time to practice Hsing-I this way is early in the morning or late in the evening as this is when the air is at its purist and the pollution of the day is gone. Try to avoid busy built up places where there is traffic as this affects air quality and poisons the body if deeply inhaled. Try to practise near to trees and plants as they are natural suppliers of oxygen.

Do not eat or drink anything for one hour after training as this creates confusion in the body and scatters the chi that you have built up during practice. If you eat and drink straight away the body will divert its energy to dealing with this process instead of naturally circulating all its resources derived from practice to nourish the organs.

Take a bath or shower before practicing Hsing-I, not immediately afterwards. Bathing immediately after practice will wash away the chi that permeates your body at the superficial level; this is called your 'Wei Chi' and serves to protect you from external illness. Also, the shock to your system of anything extreme such as a hot or cold drink or a hot or cold water during bathing will scatter the chi within, preventing it from nourishing the organs effectively.

After practice it is a good idea to wrap up and sit or stand quietly and breathe naturally for a while and allow your body to circulate the chi you have built up during practice. Let it return to normal activity slowly over 20 minutes or more, practicing this way greatly benefits your health."

The Five Element Fists of Hsing-I Chuan

Before looking at each individual element relating to Hsing-I practice lets first take heed of some valuable advice from Master McNeil which he constantly emphasises during teaching of his students:

"Let it be noted that just because the five elements are referred to as basic techniques, this does not infer that they are not important or do not require time and skill to master. These techniques are some of the first to be learned but refinement of them continues for a lifetime. Just as all things are formed of the five elements so are all movements of Hsing-I derived out of the five element fists. Perfection of these techniques should remain a constant goal throughout a student's lifetime and should never be undervalued."

Below is an easy reference table listing the five element Hsing-I fists, Chinese names and the specific intent of the chi alongside the minds image within each technique.

Western Name	Chinese Name	Intent of Chi	Mind Image
Metal Fist	Pi Chuan	Splitting	Like an axe falling
Water Fist	Tzuan Chuan	Drilling	Like lightning
Wood Fist	Peng Chuan	Crushing	Like shooting an arrow
Fire Fist	Pao Chuan	Pounding	Like firing a cannon
Earth Fist	Heng Chuan	Crossing	Round like a marble

When practising any form in Hsing-I it can be basically broken down into three areas of advancement depending on the practitioner's level of skill. Initially the beginner works on each area separately but as they gain experience the body and mind will coordinate and eventually combine all the areas with no thought to them required.

1. **Physical/Structure** – What a practitioner is physically doing with their body in every movement of the form.
2. **Energetic/Breath** – How they breathe during every move of the form.
3. **Mind/Intent** – What their mind is focused on during every move of the form.

In the remainder of this chapter, each of the five elements will be discussed using the three areas of advancement as a guide. Each element will also be accompanied by a poem composed by Master Hsu Hong-Chi and given to his teacher, Master McNeil. In past times education was poor and literacy among the common people was limited, so the theories of Hsing-I were often passed on through the generations in the form of a poem composed by the master of the time and which could be remembered by their students in its oral form. This tradition of not writing down the secrets of the system also protected the knowledge from undeserving people as it could not be easily bought or stolen.

Following on, each element will then be discussed in relation to the health aspects of training. An explanation of how the method of breathing can be adapted to focus on the health benefits as opposed to martial application. Also, a TCM description of common signs of illness relating to each organ is provided to help a practitioner recognise simple imbalances in their own energetic system. Finally, there is a meridian diagram for each appropriate organ showing its direction of chi flow and a list of its main energetic and physiological functions it performs in the body.

Note: Remember these functions relate to the energetic system of the body and correlate with TCM theory; therefore, they may differ considerably from the Western medical understanding of how the body operates. The functions listed also contain mental/emotional level correspondences of each organ as the physical and emotional body cannot be separated in Taoist theory.

Metal Fist Form (Pi Chuan)

The first of the five element fists is Metal or 'Pi Chuan' as it is called in Chinese. It is very closely linked to the 'Three body posture' or San Ti, discussed earlier in this book and so it is logical to develop this basic standing posture into the first movement or 'form' as they are referred to in practice.

The character 'Pi' in Chinese describes the action of 'splitting' or 'chopping' in nature. The main problem with directly translating any character from Chinese to English is that there isn't always a single word in the English language that can accurately describe all the variations and meanings that can come from a single Chinese character. Because of this problem, often translations can be taken too literally by some practitioners and this can lead to conflicts on what a character really represents. It is at this time a knowledgeable teacher in Hsing-I can help the student to understand the true meaning of the character in its relation to the physical movement from a Hsing-I context.

Intent of the Mind

Within the form of Metal, the energy of the movement travels forward and down, like swinging an axe at an object out and in front of you. Visualisation of this 'axe splitting' action and timing it with the out breath on striking is important in developing this technique as it is this mental process that links the mind to the chi and keeps the physical movement smooth and flowing in its application.

Physical Action of the Body

When practising Metal Form; raise the hands up towards the mouth as fists, twisting and driving forward with the front hand, rising to the eyes of the opponent, the rear hand follows closely behind as though the two were connected. As the chi (breath) sinks to the Tan Tien so do the elbows. The hands open revealing the 'Tigers Mouth', dropping like an axe and tearing apart as they fall. As the front hand makes this forward splitting motion, the back hand pulls back and down with equal force to the area of the Tan Tien.

Note: This combined movement of both hands moving in opposite directions is referred to as 'Tearing' in Hsing-I, as its action is as though the practitioner is tearing a piece of paper with their hands.

The forward, attacking hand is always referred to as the Yang hand as this is moving forward, issuing out energy. The rear, defensive hand is always referred to as the Yin hand as this is moving backward drawing energy in to the joints and back to the Tan Tien. The rear hand is protective of the body's centre. Both Yin and Yang hands must work in total coordination for the technique to be effective.

As the practitioner steps forward toward their opponent, they lead with their forward foot and follow quickly with their back foot to regain their original stance. The timing of this step should be in time with the strike and this stepping action is known in Hsing-I as the 'half-step' method. The three points are; the tip of the nose, the tip of the front foot and the tip of the forward fist/index finger and these should be aligned at all times; just as in the practice of San Ti posture. By keeping the little finger side of the hand twisted upward, even when it is a closed fist, means to coil the energy through the forearm, making it strong and in effect, rotates the fist to its maximum torque without bending the wrist or distorting the body when striking.

Poem by Master Hsu Hong-Chi

'Pi Chuan'

"From underneath the chin, the two closely-spaced fists thrust forward to the level of the eyebrows. The right hand is forward, followed by the left. As the arms cross, the left hand goes forward. The heart unites, and the chi descends to the Tan Tien as the body begins to move. Place the left foot forward as the hands separate. The 'Hu Kou' (Tigers Mouth) opens with all the fingers held in a crescent. The front

hand pushes to a point between the eyebrows and the heart. The rear hand stays below the level of the armpit. Hands, nose and feet all form the three-point set. In Pi Chuan, Keep the little fingers turned up as the hands thrust upward. Sink the feet and hands together. The tongue is kept at the roof of the mouth. In advancing and in changing styles, the rear palm sinks downward."

The Health Aspects of Practising Hsing-I Five Elements Forms

When discussing health from a TCM perspective it is often the Yin organs that are considered to be the most important and often treated ahead of the Yang organs. With this in mind, most symptom descriptions in classic Chinese literature discuss and relate all energetic imbalances to an appropriate Yin organ rather than its Yang partner. For example; when suffering constipation, the large intestine (Metal elements Yang organ), maybe seen initially as the organ with an imbalance. However, very often it is a Yin organ that is directly responsible, such as the lungs' descending energy not helping to move waste in the right direction out of the body. However, it could also be diagnosed that the liver organ (Wood element) is not providing the smooth flow of chi and blood through the large intestine, causing it to become sluggish. In order to diagnose accurately the cause of the symptom, a detailed TCM assessment of the whole body, both mentally and physically, is required to highlight the root of the problem, as to truly cure a problem, you must treat the root cause.

Furthermore, when treating an energetic imbalance using TCM, there are many different modalities which may be used. Diet and lifestyle are of key importance to a healthy body and treating with herbs and acupuncture are often seen as a last resort when a person is relying on doctors to help cure them. If a practitioner is sensitive to their own body's energy by practising their Hsing-I regularly, they should first aim to redress the imbalance through their practice and diet, in order to solve the problem, before doctors are required. When discussing diet and foods that are good or bad for different ailments, TCM considers all the foods by their energetic qualities and, therefore, eating energetically warming foods will benefit cold conditions and vice versa. Diet from this viewpoint can be as equally a complex method as Chinese Medicine itself and there are a lot of well written books available on Chinese diet for those wishing to study this area in more detail.

Finally, when practising any of the five element forms with a view to helping an ailment of the body, the practitioner first needs to understand which organ or element is causing the problem. As with the previous example, if the problem is constipation you may need to practise Wood form rather than Metal form, to help a problem with the large intestine. It is advised at first to keep things simple and practice the element and place the intent on the organ you think is most likely to improve the situation. If the symptom does not improve or it gets worse, then seek out a more detailed consultation with a knowledgeable teacher or TCM doctor to confirm whether your diagnosis is correct.

The Health Aspects of Training Metal Form

With regards to health, Metal is associated with the lungs (Yin) and large intestine (Yang) organs. Metal energy is descending in nature and so is the energy of the lungs taking in air and the large intestine which expels waste down and out of the body. Correct practice of Metal form combined with the correct method of breathing and visualisation of energy will greatly enhance the smooth flow of chi and blood through these organs and their respective meridians. Remember *'The mind moves the chi and the chi moves the blood'*, therefore, focusing the mind on an organ function can enhance its performance.

Regulating the lungs by using the 'complete breathing' method during practice will help supply higher levels of oxygen to the body and its tissues via the blood and in turn allow for increased chi production in the Tan Tien. The physical movements of Metal form serve to massage the related organs and meridians and encourage any blockages and stagnations to resolve and reopen. When this is combined with correct posture throughout practice it allows the organs to relax in their correct space and receive increased nourishment of chi and blood allowing them to function more efficiently.

When the body is out of balance and the energy through the Metal organs is not smooth then physical symptoms may arise. Next are a few of the general types of disorders that may be encountered which relate to affected chi flow in the Metal organs. Remember these are just generalisations and every person is different therefore their individual symptoms may vary.

Chinese Medicine classical literature states:

"If you have Lung or Large Intestine problems your nose will usually bother you and your skin will usually turn white. You will have a running nose and cough a lot. Try to avoid living in the West because it's climate not beneficial to your lungs. Don't eat rice, horse meat or peaches. Your back will be very tight and don't lie down too often. You might also feel mournful or sad."

Commentary of the Classical Literature

The skin is referred to as the third lung in the body and it is in effect a breathable membrane allowing sweat and chi to pass through it at appropriate times. This chi flow around the skin is referred to as 'Wei Chi' and is commanded by the lungs. It is responsible for the body's defence against pathogens from outside. If you have weak Lung Chi you will catch colds more often. If the lungs do not have the strength of chi to control the pores then the open pores will be a source of entrance to the meridians for any pathogens. Problems with Lung Chi can often be reflected in the skin and this can be seen in people who suffer asthma (lung) who also often have eczema (skin) problems.

The skin may generally look white or grey like metal as this reflects poor circulation of Lung Chi on the surface of the body which normally warms the skin and gives it its natural colour. The emotion of the lungs is sadness and grief, this can be seen in people who sigh a lot when sad and feel the need to keep taking in deep breaths as they are unable to use their lungs efficiently to sink their chi.

Poor lung function results in weak respiratory muscles and may affect the general strength and mobility of the back, as breathing requires efficient use of the trunks musculature to be effective. Also, Lung Chi is responsible for descending fluids down into the body. Poor function here will lead to build up of fluids on the chest and this will be made worse for lying down as gravity is no longer effectively helping the body descend fluids.

It is the lungs' partner, the large intestine, whose meridian runs directly to the nose and it is this link to the lungs, via their association of the Metal element that provides the answer to the symptom that the more superficial Yang organ is affected before the deeper Yin organ is penetrated. Often a runny nose precedes the chesty cough in a common cold.

Living in a climate and eating a diet that supports these energetic weaknesses will also make the symptoms worse. This is why the classic literature tells us to avoid certain foods and climates energetically relevant to each element. Likewise, living in a beneficial climate and eating the right foods energetically will help redress any energetic imbalances.

To help heal the lungs or large intestine energy flow, the practitioner should practice the Metal form of Hsing-I. The method by which they practice the form changes slightly when they practice purely for health. This is mainly in their breathing pattern, intent and visualisation, but the physical aspect of the form remains the same, it is just practiced slower.

The Practice of Metal Form for Health

Start in Pi-Chuan stance. Stare at the index finger of the forward hand and breathe slowly from the lower stomach/Tan Tien, using the complete breathing method. Inhale and exhale three to five times thinking only of the lungs or large intestine, inhaling and filling the organ with clear (pure) chi, exhaling and breathing out dirty, Turbid Chi. Then step forward as in Metal form and repeat the process on the opposite side. Continue this process for a minimum of 20 minutes each day and always finish the form in the correct way. Over time any symptoms should subside and the practitioner's health should regain its strength.

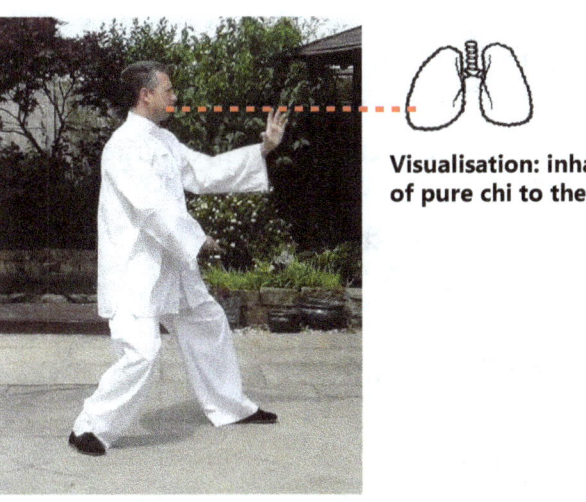

Visualisation: inhalation of pure chi to the lungs

Main Organ functions of Metal Element
Lungs:

Organ Meridians of Metal Element

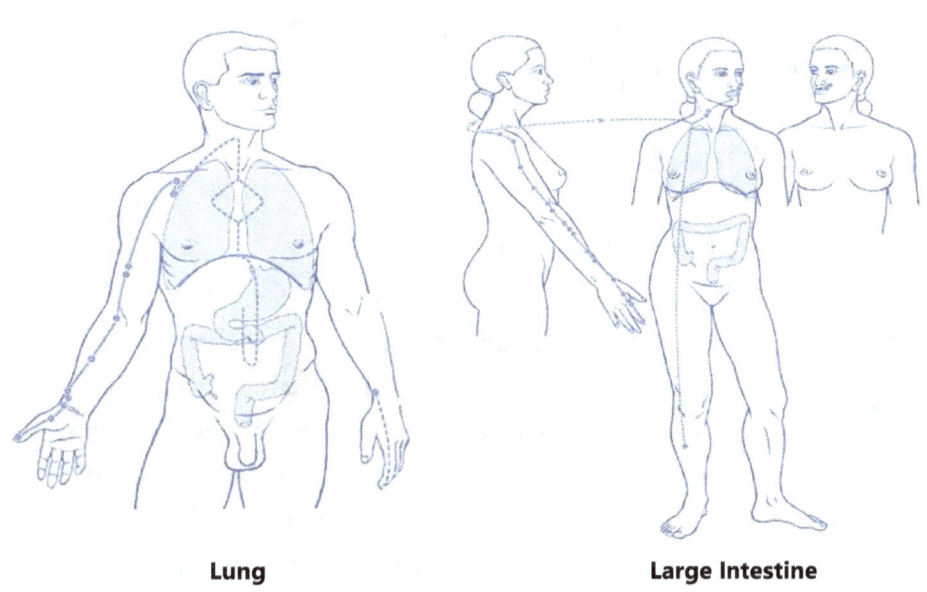

Lung **Large Intestine**

The lungs govern chi and respiration and are responsible for inhaling air into the body. They are the main organ involved in connecting the internal environment of the body and the external environment and for this reason they are closely linked with the skin and body hair. The lungs inhale pure chi and exhale dirty chi, they also descend and disperse chi and fluids around the bodily tissues and in particular they distribute defensive Wei Chi around the skin to protect the body from external pathogens. The lungs descending responsibilities are also used to send fluids down to the lower organs such as the kidneys and bladder for filtering and excretion from the body.

The lungs are said to be the house of the corporeal soul, called the 'Po' in Chinese philosophy. The 'Po' is seen to be the most physical earthly part of the human soul and therefore is Yin in nature. The 'Po' on an emotional level is directly affected by the emotions of sadness and when affected has a profound effect on breathing.

The main TCM energetic functions of the lungs are to:
- govern chi and influence bodily fluids
- govern respiration
- control dispersing and descending of chi
- regulate water passages
- control skin and body hair
- house the 'Po'/corporeal soul

Large intestine:
Very little is said about the actions of the large intestines within TCM, but its main energetic and physical functions are listed below.

The main TCM energetic functions of large intestines are to:
- receive food and drink from the small intestines
- absorb nutrients and expel waste in the form of stools

Water Fist Form (Tzuan Chuan)

Intent of the Mind
The second form which is that of Water is called 'Tzuan Chuan' in Chinese. The word 'Tzuan' means to 'drill' or 'push through'. Waters energy therefore is to twist like a drill-bit and force its way through to its target. Water flows forward but can also force upwards like a spring or rush downwards like the twisting rapids of a river. It will find its way through any gaps in that which seeks to contain it. Water's intent is like a streak of lightning through the clouds of a storm and it is that visualisation the practitioner should seek when applying the energy of Water form.

Water can be extremely powerful in the form of a raging torrent or a tsunami, destroying all in its path. The nature of Water is soft and liquid and yet it can easily destroy hard rock, pounding it to sand, it can also move buildings from their foundations especially if it can get under them. It is for this reason Water energy comes from deep in the Tan Tien and issues forth twisting upwards almost unseen along the centre line, destabilising all that it makes contact with. The flow of the technique should be smooth like water and able to flow in any direction, finding its own level.

Physical Action of the Body

When practising Water form, the front hand grabs, pulling quickly downwards and back past the centreline, protecting the Tan Tien. At the same time, the rear hand forms a fist and drills sharply up the centreline and out to the height of the face in effect becoming the Yang, forward hand. The elbows are kept tight to the body for protection and the feet move the whole body as one. The forward drilling fist should finish in a palm up position. This means maximum rotation of the attacking forearm without affecting the alignment of the head and body. Throughout the changes of movement in the form, the head should remain smooth and level, like water.

As the practitioner steps forward into their opponent they should lead with their forward foot and follow quickly with the back foot to regain their original stance. The movement of the feet must be in time with the hands and as the rear foot 'half-steps' up to complete the footwork the hand strike must be completed simultaneously. It is important to focus the eyes on the lead hand and this will in turn focus the spirit and guide the chi through the whole technique.

Poem by Master Hsu Hong-Chi

'Tzuan Chuan'

"The forehand hand 'Yin palm' presses down. The rear hand 'Yang fist' thrusts up. The fist strikes to the level of the eyebrows. Elbows embrace the heart as the rear foot moves. Gaze at the forward hand. Stop the movement of hands and feet, Styles change like flowing water. Front foot steps first, back foot follow steps. Rear hand faces down, the elbows sink. Step by step, keep the three-point set. Forward hand strikes the nose. Your little finger turns upward. Protect the heart with the elbows. Tzuan Chuan strikes the nose upon advancing. Forward hand presses down, then turns up as you step forward."

The Health Aspects of Training Water Form

When the movements of Water form are smooth, then the chi will flow unhindered and the kidneys and bladder will be sufficiently nourished. When practiced correctly, chi can reach all parts of the body like water finds all available space in its flow. The kidneys command water and fluids within the body and therefore when water is controlled so it will cool and keep Fire (internal body heat) under control. In effect, this is Yin balancing Yang within and this harmony is crucial to the body's health. This balance of Fire and Water keeps the balance between the mind and the body calm and stops internal disharmony from arising. From a TCM perspective any sudden, inappropriate outbursts of emotions are viewed to be imbalances of chi which create internal heat rising or 'Rising Yang' in the body.

Chinese Medicine classical literature states:

"If you have a kidney or bladder problem, keep in mind that these organs are associated with your urine and the water will go to your ears as the kidney channel opens into the ears. This will make the inner eardrum wet, so it will be hard to hear and you will begin having ear problems. You may feel cold through to the bones when others do not. Try to avoid living in the North because it is cold and wet. You should not eat beans, pork or chestnuts. If you stand too long your body will feel uncomfortable and your bones and waist will hurt. You might also feel fearful most of the time."

Physically the practice of Water form massages the meridians of the kidney and bladder and also the organs themselves. The postures of the form help stretch and relax the musculature of the legs and back allowing for improved physical mobility and circulation of chi and blood. Internally the kidney meridians open into the ears and often chronic problems that affect the hearing can be directly related to the quality of the Kidney Chi. Kidney energy is directly linked to growth and development of the body and nourishes the bones; therefore, weakness of Kidney Chi can cause or be related to weak or under developed bones.

The body normally has two kidneys, in TCM one relates to Kidney Yin (water) and the other Kidney Yang (fire). Kidney Yang is known as the 'Fire of Ming Men' and is responsible for warming the body from within. Any deterioration in this function will lead to feeling cold from the bones deep within. 'Fear' is the emotion of the kidneys and a weakness in Kidney Chi will show as 'weak-kneed' and the urge to urinate uncontrollable as the bones and bladder are directly linked to kidney energy. This leads to popular sayings of 'shaking with fear' and 'cold to the bones', often heard.

Kidney problems will be made worse when living in a cold climate, from damp or wet conditions and for eating a cold diet such as raw food. Likewise, living in a warm, dry climate and eating the correct (warming) foods will help to redress an energetic imbalance.

To help improve the Kidneys or Bladder chi flow, the practitioner should practice the Water form of Hsing-I. The method by which they practice the form changes slightly when they practice purely for health. This is mainly in their breathing pattern, intent and visualisation, but the physical aspect of the form remains the same, it is just practiced slower.

The Practice of Water Form for Health

Start by opening into Pi Chuan stance. Step into the first posture of the Water form. Stare at the index finger of the forward hand and breathe slowly from the lower stomach/Tan Tien, using the complete breathing method. Inhale and exhale three to five times thinking only of the kidneys or bladder, inhaling and mentally filling the organ with clear chi, exhaling and breathing out dirty, Turbid Chi. Then step forward as in Water form and repeat the process on the opposite side. Continue this process for a minimum of twenty minutes each day and always finish the form in the correct way. Over time any symptoms should subside and the practitioner's health should regain its strength

Visualisation: inhalation of pure chi to the kidneys

Organ functions of Water Element
Kidneys:

Organ Meridians of Water Element

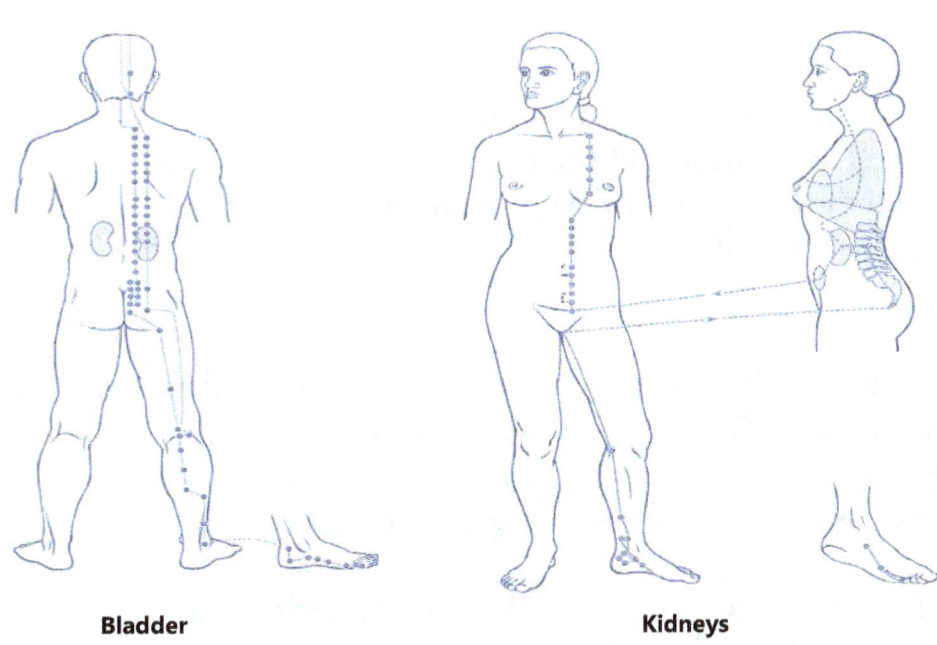

Bladder **Kidneys**

The kidneys are referred to as the 'root of life' as they are seen to store the essence derived from the parents at the time of conception. Because of this they are the foundation of Yin and Yang energies for all the other organs of the body. When any organ becomes deficient in chi it will turn to the kidneys and draw from the ancestral Jing stored there. If this happens too frequently the body will age and deteriorate more quickly than normal.

The essence stored in the kidneys is the organic foundation of marrow. Marrow in TCM does not correspond to that of Western medicine. The Taoists see the marrow as a common substance within the matrix of bones that further fills up the spinal column and the brain or Celestial Stem in Chinese. For this reason, the kidneys, spinal column and brain are all closely related.

The kidneys are viewed as a controller of the gates that allow flow of water and fluids in the body in the lower Jiao and because of its close link to the bladder they are seen to be the commander in charge of quality and quantity urination. As the major organ in the lower Jiao they help draw chi down from the descending chi of the lungs and anchoring it within the body.

The kidneys are also seen to be the residence of the will power or 'Zhi' as it is referred to in Chinese philosophy. If the kidneys are strong and healthy so is the will power and the mind will be able to set and focus on goals achieving things in a single-minded way. Of course, if the kidneys are weak then the opposite is true.

The main TCM energetic functions of the kidneys are to:
- be the storehouse of essence (Jing)
- govern birth, growth, reproduction and development
- be responsible for the production of marrow, filling the brain and control the bones
- govern water
- control the reception of chi into the body
- manifest in the quality of head hair
- control the lower two orifices (genitals and anus)
- house the Zhi/will power

Bladder:
The bladder generally has a larger sphere of activity in TCM than Western medicine, not only does it store urine but its chi also helps transform fluids ready for production into urine. On a mental level disharmony of Bladder Chi is said to evoke negative emotions such as jealousy and holding long standing grudges.

The main TCM energetic functions of the Bladder are to:
remove water by chi transformation

Wood Fist Form (Peng Chuan)

Intent of the Mind

The third element form is 'Wood' or 'Peng Chuan' as it is called in Chinese. The energetic characteristic of Wood is to expand, extending straight out and forward like an arrow being shot from a bow. The intent of Wood form is that it will pass through anything, crushing all that lies in its path until it reaches its target. At the same time as it extends forward it also retracts back in the opposite direction. Therefore, naturally corresponding to the theory of Yin and Yang and most clearly of all the elements demonstrates the 'tearing' technique in its movements.

When you drive forward in Wood form you must project your spirit and energy as far through the strike as possible, in effect visualising beyond the target itself and into the distance. Focus your sight on the horizon. The 'Hui Yin point' (between the genitals and anus), should be sucked up throughout the technique to help raise chi to the head. This should avoid any 'swaying in the wind' and 'loosing of the roots' thereby keeping the body stable through execution of the technique. The energy of Wood holds tremendous power, if the roots of a tree get into buildings and walls they can easily force them off their foundations, the energy just keeps pushing and expanding until it overwhelms all before it.

Physical Action of the Body

When practising Wood form, the 'Three Tips' formed by the nose, front foot and forward hand should remain aligned. Wood fist is aligned with the eye of the fist facing towards heaven and when it strikes it shoots straight from the hip out to either the height of the Tan Tien or solar plexus. There should be no drawing back of the fist, prior to it striking; it should travel in the straightest possible path to its target, crushing all before it.

The technique is strengthened by the equal force of the withdrawing hand and these two must combine stopping and starting their movements exactly in time with one another. The ending of the strike should be in time with the half-stepping of the rear foot.

The feet and body must also move as one using the half-step method, which keeps the whole technique rooted like a tree and solid to the ground when it delivers is power. The tongue touches the roof of the mouth allowing the breath to sink to the Tan Tien and clear chi to rise to the head, keeping the back and neck straight. By raising chi to the head, it should keep the body straight like the trunk of a great oak tree, helping it to remain level throughout movement.

Poem by Master Hsu Hong-Chi

'Peng Chuan'

"'Peng Chuan' starts with the three-point set. The 'Hui Yin' point up as high as the heart. The front hand "Yang fist" stays under the armpit. Step out with one foot, follow-step with the other. Shaped like a "T", the two feet are firm. Your body turns, while the eyes look straight. Keep the back straight when stepping. Toe out the foot when you move forward. Hands and feet move swiftly as one. One foot moves, the other follows naturally. Keep the tongue at the roof of the mouth. The arms are curved, not straight. Punch to the armpits when you advance, quick and firm. The rear foot always follow-steps."

The Health Aspects of Training Wood Form

When the movements of Wood form are smooth and coordinated, the chi flows smoothly through the liver and gall bladder organs and their associated meridians. This is of key importance to health as the main function of the Liver in TCM is to control smooth flow of chi and blood through all the meridians and to all the organs and tissues of the body. Therefore, if the Liver Chi is not abundant all the body's functions may be affected.

Chinese Medicine classical literature states:

"If you have gall bladder or liver problems you will have tight tendons. The nails will also be affected and can show how long you have had this problem. The whites of the eyes will also have turned a little green and your neck will become very tight. As the liver channel opens into the eyes, the vision maybe affected and it may become blurred or have floating black spots in it. When you have a liver problem, you are afraid of the breeze, in particular an east wind, you become angry easily, tears will come often and your body will have a grasping or twitching action. Like the wind your symptoms may move around from one part of the body to another for no apparent reason. This concept describes disorders in the body such as shaking of the limbs, convulsions or itchiness that migrates over the skin, where the meridians are said to be invaded by wind. Try not to live in the eastern part of the country. With a liver problem one shouldn't eat wheat, chicken or plums and don't walk too much."

The liver is responsible for nourishment of tendons and its energy opens via internal meridians into the eyes. Strong Liver Chi has an impact on the spirit as the eyes are seen to be the windows to the soul. In accordance with this, the spirit in the eyes reflects the condition of the liver organ and that of chi and blood flow within the body; therefore, any problems with vision will reflect on the strength of Liver Chi.

The liver is also seen as the storehouse for blood, so any deficiency here will lead to a drying out of the body through lack of nourishment generally. If blood and chi are abundant then the tendons will be strong and supple and the technique powerful. If the liver is deficient then the tendons and tissues will be dry and be prone to injury.

If Liver Chi is smooth, the emotions will be harmonious and stable. This does not mean that a person will be devoid of emotions, just that they will be appropriate to the given circumstance. The nails are seen as the extremities of the tendons and their quality reflects the quality of the Liver Chi and blood within your body at any given time. If the nails are brittle or crack easily this shows a lack of nourishment from the liver. If the superficial extremities show signs of weakness then it is highly likely the deeper internal tissues will be affected also. Musculature around the neck may tighten as the meridians of the gall bladder pass directly through this area and as the liver's Yang organ partner; problems in one organ may show symptoms in its partner.

To help heal the liver or gall bladder chi flow, the practitioner should practice the Wood form of Hsing-I. The method by which they practice the form changes slightly when they practice purely for health. This is mainly in their breathing pattern, intent and visualisation, but the physical aspect of the form remains the same, it is just practiced slower.

The Practice of Wood Form for Health

Start by opening into your Pi-Chuan stance. Step into the first closed wood posture and then into the second open wood posture of the Wood form. From the open Wood posture stare into the distance beyond the fist of the forward hand and breathe slowly from your lower stomach/Tan Tien, using the complete breathing method. Inhale and exhale three to five times thinking only of your liver or gall bladder, inhaling and filling it with clear chi, exhaling and breathing out dirty, Turbid Chi. Then step forward as in Wood form and repeat the process on the opposite side. Continue this process for a minimum of twenty minutes each day and always finish the form in the correct way. Over time any symptoms should subside and the practitioner's health should regain its strength.

Visualisation: inhalation of pure chi to the liver

Organ functions of Wood Element
Liver:

Organ Meridians of Wood Element

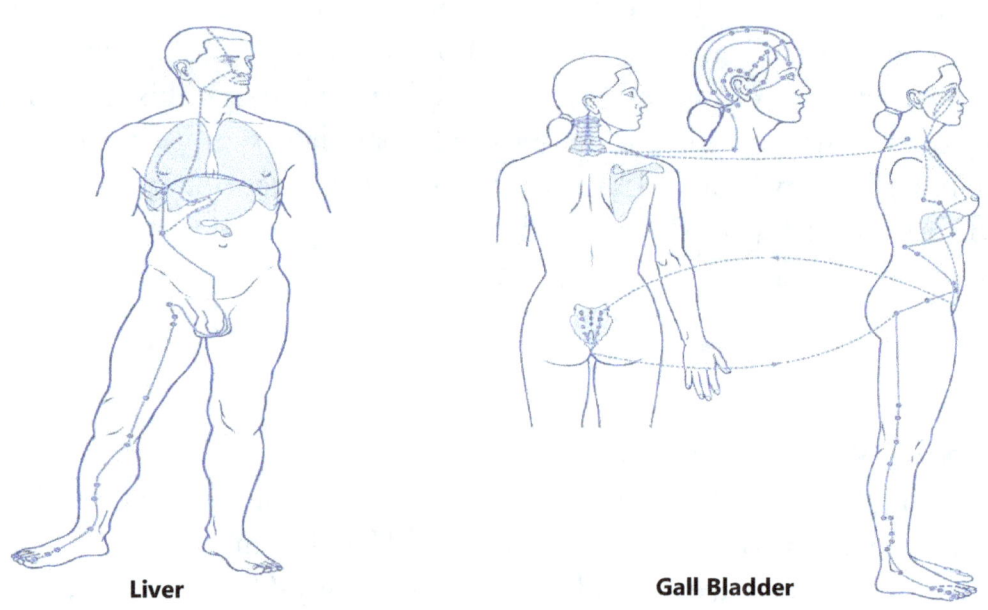

Liver **Gall Bladder**

The liver has the most important function of storing the blood and ensuring the smooth flow of chi and blood to all areas and activities of the body. It is like a general who oversees the storing and distribution of supplies to his troops all through the army. When flow is smooth and blood is abundant the extremities of the nails will be pink and healthy and the tendons will be relaxed and supple.

The ethereal soul is called the 'Hun' in Chinese philosophy and is said to reside in the liver. The Hun is like the spirit of the body and is Yang in nature, closer to the energy of heaven. It is said to be responsible for the ability to plan our lives and any weakness in Liver Chi may lead to a lack of direction in life and mental confusion. If liver blood is weak then the Hun may rise unanchored and leave the body especially at night during sleep and result in strange dreams or poor sleep patterns.

The main TCM energetic functions of the liver are to:
- store the blood
- ensure smooth flow of chi and blood
- control the tendons
- manifest in the nails
- house the Hun/ethereal soul

Gall Bladder:
The gall bladder organ is special within the Fu organs as it is the only one that does not deal with moving of food and drink. Its responsibility is to store a refined pure substance of bile received from the liver and its function within TCM is very similar to that in Western medicine. The smooth flow and production of bile helps with the digestive process within the body. Courage and initiative are said to be closely linked with the gall bladder and psychologically the ability to drive forward, make changes and seize the initiative are strong and decisive if Gall Bladder Chi is healthy.

The main TCM energetic functions of the Gall Bladder are to:
- store and excrete bile
- control mental judgment
- control the sinews

Fire Fist Form (Pao Chuan)

Intent of the Mind
The fourth element is Fire or 'Pao Chuan' as it is called in Chinese. The energy of Fire form is like that of a cannon firing. The energetic pathway is therefore strong, fast and aggressive, moving straight out and rising naturally as it goes like the trajectory of a cannon ball. It is very destructive and the mind should mirror this in its intent to attack and pound the opponent's body with no fear like a cannon battering down the gates of a beleaguered city.

Because the energy is related to the heart, its nature is to remain calm, but when striking with this technique the energy explodes suddenly and then returns calm again, just like a cannon firing. This sudden release of total Yang energy associated with fire can be lethal.

Fire should be visualised like flames coming in to contact with a tree, where it engulfs it and climbs up passing its energy through it furiously reducing all before it to ashes. Fire can move quickly, leaping from one object to another and this should be depicted in the mind when applying this technique. Initially calm and smouldering, but at the first opportunity it should erupt fast and furious, ready to step and change depending on the situation. The chi should be released on the strike like a dragon breathing fire.

Physical Action of the Body
When practicing the form of Fire, the practitioner draws in tightly the arms, sinking the elbows to protect the ribs. At the same time, they must sink the breath to fill

the Tan Tien. Both hands are Yang in nature forming fists, palm up at the Tan Tien level. The body turns to 45 degrees and is in 'cat stance'. The forward hand fires out, upwards, forwards and then slightly backwards with the forearm rotating as it moves. This has the effect of producing a tearing action in combination with the rear striking hand and clears the way for the rear striking hand which pounds like a cannon ball striking the target at the height of the solar plexus. The energy of the heart is released via the breath on the strike. When contact is made the rear hand and arm should not be fully extended, rather it should extend into and through the target on contact. At the point of contact the fist should be facing 'eye' up like that of Wood fist. The feet and body must also move as one using the 'half-step' method, which keeps the whole technique rooted. The 'Three Points' remain aligned throughout the technique to allow maximum power to be achieved.

Poem by Master Hsu Hong-Chi

'Pao Chuan'

"The elbows tightly embrace the body as you lift the foot. The "Yang fist" must be firm. The chi falls to the Tan Tien as styles change. Keep the Three-point set in place. Fists explode outward, up as high as the heart. The Hui Yin and elbows are kept downward. In Pao Chuan, the lead foot is on its toes, then steps out and drops as the fists thrust up. Step out diagonally with hands and feet coordinated. The rear foot follow-steps."

The Health Aspects of Training Fire Form

When the energy flow from Fire element is smooth and unhindered the body will feel at ease and relaxed. The emotions will be calm and there will be no build-up of excess heat within the body. By practicing Fire form correctly, the energy released through the breath of each technique allowing the body to release its tensions and unblock any stagnations of energy within. These blockages can be caused from both physical and emotional stresses as both can lead to disharmony in chi flow and create a build-up of internal heat. As the heart is the commander of the emotional mind, both control and calmness here are the key to good health. A calm emotional mind allows clear chi to be raised to the head and the mind to act logically and naturally.

Chinese Medicine classical literature states:

"If you have a heart or small intestine problem your tongue will be solidified or will be tight. Your chest will be tight and you will give the impression that you are very happy (Joy) and may talk incessantly. Your face will turn red or flushed and your body odour will have a burning smell. You will have a fondness for bitter foods and you will be afraid of heat. You will laugh a lot and your body will sweat. Try not to live in the south because it is too hot and not beneficial for your heart. Don't eat corn, lamb or apricots. Don't stare too much."

Any disharmony of chi flow affecting the heart can lead to the state of confusion and an inability to act appropriately. The heart meridian opens directly to the tongue via its internal meridian network and therefore the condition of heart energy can be reflected in the tongue, particularly the tip. This is often seen in people who have suffered heart attack, who are often are left with a short, stiff and deviated tongue that is purple in colour which reflects the stagnation of chi and blood within the heart meridian.

Emotions when not calm can often appear excessive or inappropriate to the circumstance. Too much joy is seen as a person that keeps laughing when something is not really funny. Too much heat or heart fire can be reflected in a person appearing very red in the face and manic in their behaviour, talking or shouting a lot, it is as though they are on fire from within. Alcohol is seen as heating energetically and too much can show these manic symptoms when a person is drunk. As fire energy naturally rises, so does fire energy in the body rising to the head producing many kinds of mental symptoms. This heat can also dry up the body internally in effect drying up blood and leaving symptoms of dryness in tissues and an unquenchable thirst. A classic cause of extreme fire would be sunstroke.

The spirit is said to be housed in the heart and reflected in the eyes. It is then logical that staring with the eyes for long periods will unsettle the spirit within as it cannot remain calm and settled if the mind is distracted by looking at physical objects all the time.

To help heal the heart or small intestine chi flow, the practitioner should practice the Fire form of Hsing-I. The method by which they practice the form changes slightly when they practice purely for health. This is mainly in their breathing pattern, intent and visualisation, but the physical aspect of the form remains the same, it is just practiced slower.

The Practice of Fire Form for Health
Start by opening into Pi-Chuan stance. Make the first posture of the Fire form and then step out and strike into the second posture, softly and controlled with perfect timing. Look directly out into the distance beyond the fist of the rear striking hand but focus on nothing intentionally. Breathe slowly from your lower stomach (Tan Tien) using the complete breathing method. Inhale and exhale three to five times thinking only of the organ you want to benefit. This could be the Heart or the Small Intestine. Concentrate on the appropriate organ inhaling and filling it with clear chi, exhaling and breathing out dirty, Turbid Chi. Then step forward as in Fire form and repeat the process on the opposite side. Continue this process for a minimum of twenty minutes each day and always finish the form in the correct way. Over time your symptoms should subside as your health recovers its strength.

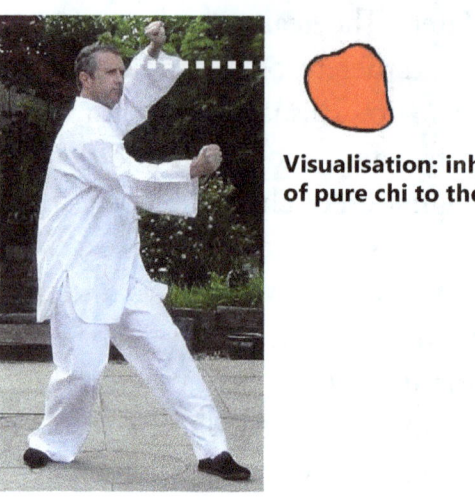

Visualisation: inhalation of pure chi to the heart

Organ functions of Fire Element
Heart:

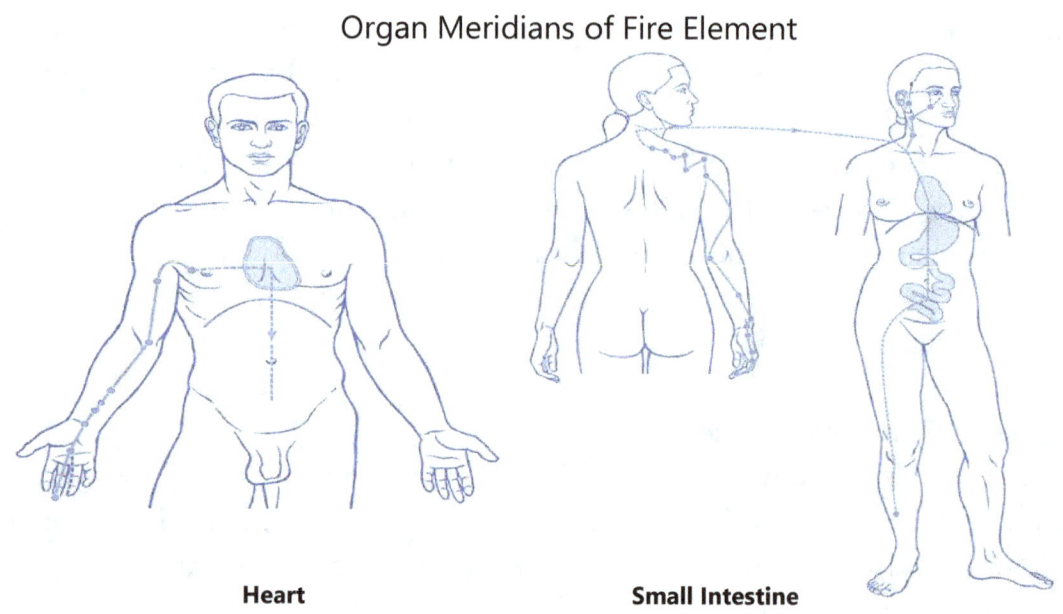

Organ Meridians of Fire Element

Heart **Small Intestine**

The heart is said to be the ruler of all the internal organs as it governs the blood and is the residence of the Shen or emotional mind. Similar to Western medicine the heart is seen to be responsible for the circulation of blood. If the Heart Chi is weak then so is the blood flow and the general health of the person will be weak too. If the blood vessels are strong this will be reflected in a strong, regular and healthy pulse.

Importantly it is the link to the mind or spirit, 'Shen' in Chinese. If Heart Chi is weak, the Shen will be restless and many types of mental symptoms may arise. Thought and logic will be affected emotional outbursts in particular anger may manifest.

Note: There are five Shen which are the spirits associated with each of the body's five yin organs (heart, kidney, spleen, liver and lungs). Each of these spirits has a connection with a yin organ and its associated element. When considering the five Shen there is seen to be a spiritual hierarchy: Shen, the spirit of the Heart is the Emperor, with different aspects of its power, like ministers, residing as the different spirits of the other organs. When these spirits function as faithful emissaries of the heart's Shen, communication between the organs is balanced and harmonious, resulting in a mentally healthy body.

The main TCM energetic functions of the heart are to:
- govern the blood
- control the blood vessels
- manifest in the complexion
- house the Shen/mind

Small Intestine:
The main role of the small intestines is to separate clean usable chi from foods and drink and transport on the dirty part to the large intestines and bladder for further refining and excretion.

The main TCM energetic functions of the small intestines are to:
- control receiving and transforming of energy from food and drink
- separate fluids and nutrients from food and drink

Pericardium:
The main TCM energetic functions of the Pericardium are:

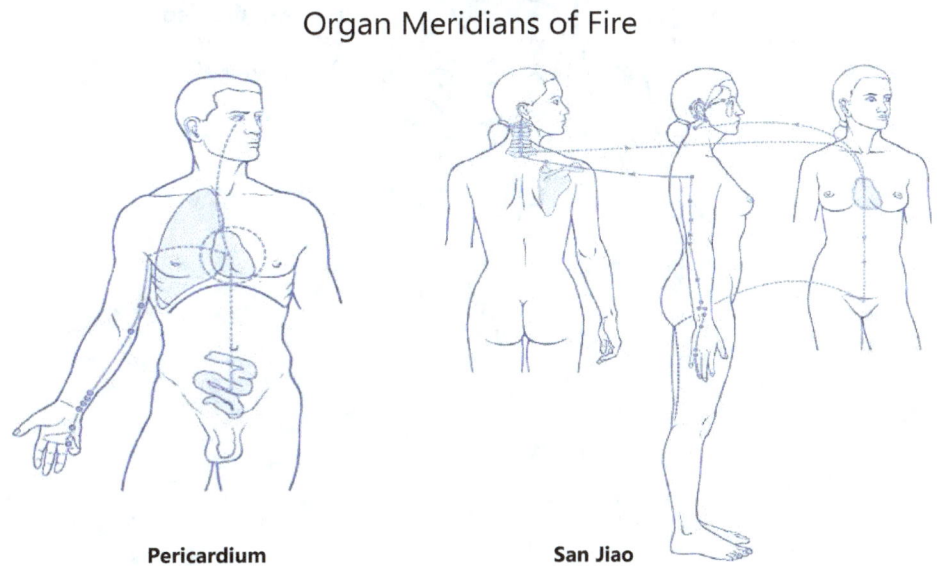

Organ Meridians of Fire

Pericardium   **San Jiao**

The pericardium's function is closely linked to the heart and as its protective covering. It is directly responsible for stopping outside pathogens from attacking and affecting the hearts energetic function.

San Jiao:
The main TCM energetic functions of the San Jiao are:

This view point relating to the 'San Jiao' is derived from the 'Classic of Difficulties' and the 'Spiritual Axis' which describe the body as being split into three divisions, the 'upper burner' (Jiao), 'middle burner' and 'lower burner' (see diagram below). The upper burner contains the heart, lungs, pericardium, throat and head. The middle burner contains the stomach, spleen and gall bladder. The lower burner contains the liver, kidneys, intestines and bladder. The functions of the San Jiao are to combine the energetic functions of all the organs situated in the different divisions and see that they all work in harmony with one another. Even though individual organs are seen to have their own roles within the body they must all combine with one another to keep the body healthy.

San Jiao Divisions of the Body

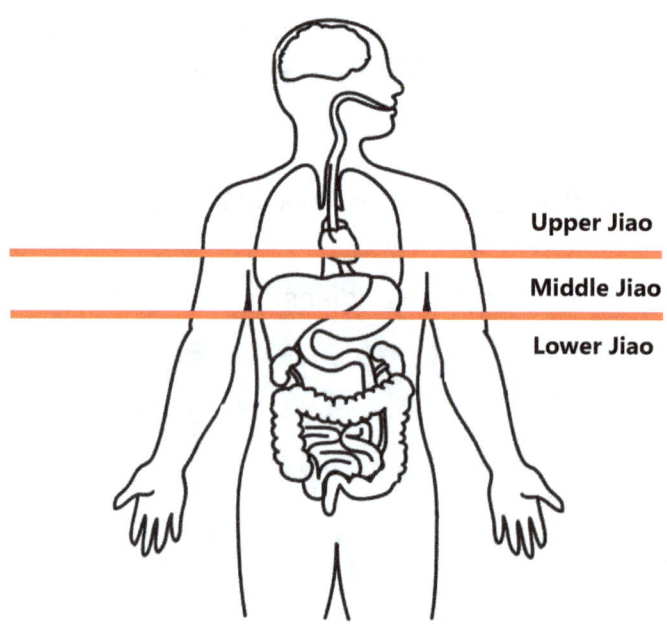

Earth Fist Form (Heng Chuan)

Intent of the mind

The fifth and final element is Earth or 'Heng Chuan' as it is called in Chinese. The word 'Heng' means to cross or movement rolling in a sideways fashion. The energy of Earth is to move in a sideways motion whilst driving out into the target. Specific to Earth form, when the arms strike out and pull back, they also cross over as they move.

The energy of Earth form also has a drilling action similar to Water, an evident tearing action of the two arms working together similar to Wood, its footwork is the same as Fire and it drives outwards with feet at 45 degrees similar to Metal stance, albeit in a sideways fashion. Therefore, it is evident that Earth form has a deep connection energetically with all the elements as its energy is in a way a combination of them. The role of Earth is the neutral energy supporting all the other elements and this combination of the elements is reflected in the technique of the Earth form.

As with all Hsing-I movements it is aggressive and powerful like an earthquake, destroying all before it, moving round and attacking from all sides. It is probably the reason Masters of old taught this element last, as skill of the first four is required to perform and understand Earth form well.

On this subject Master McNeil says:

"If you study a person's Earth form closely it will reveal their level of skill in Hsing-I Chuan."

Physical Action of the Body

When practicing Earth form the fist of the front hand faces palm up, keeping the forearm tightly coiled giving its tendons the strength of tightly twisted rope. The palm of the rear fist faces palm down and sits directly under the elbow of the front arm. The feet are placed in 'cat stance' with the body turned at 45 degrees. When the practitioner moves, they drive out, pushing off the rear foot and the body moves as one using the 'half-step' method. As they move their feet the hands to must follow, the rear fist moves tightly up the underside of the forward arm 'wiping off' and twisting as it goes, coiling the strength of the tendons rolling over like a marble and driving up and out into its target. Exhale forcefully like rumble of an earthquake on the strike. At the same time, the opposite hand pulls sharply back to the same side hip, giving supporting 'tearing' power to the technique. This movement issues its power sideways from the centre and therefore it is necessary to remain solid and centred for the stance to remain effective.

Keeping the tongue on the roof of the mouth allows the chi to sink with the breath and circulate correctly. This helps the practitioner to sink their centre and keep them grounded. In the first posture, the practitioner must align the 'Three Points'. As they drive out into the second posture the body is straight in the spine but twisted from the waist to produce a sideways strike. At the end of the second posture the 'Three Points' of the nose, rear attacking fist and rear foot are all aligned. The whole crossing action of the two arms must remain close and tight to the body to protect the centre at all times. The two arms roll and rub over one another as they exchange positions; this is called 'wiping off' in Hsing-I as one arm literally wipes the other off as they move against one another.

Poem by Master Hsu Hong-Chi

'Heng Chuan'

"Forehand 'Yang fist', rear hand Yin. The rear hand is kept just below the elbow. Lift up the lead foot as the fists begin to move. With the body firm, the chi is settled. The tongue curls up and the air is inhaled. Half-turn the body, while the hands and feet move. The rear hand twists, then thrusts upward. The fist, nose and feet are linked together in one line. In Heng Chuan always keep the rear fist Yin and the forward fist Yang. Your elbows protect the heart. The left and right arms thrust out like bows. Hands and feet sink together. Keep the tongue at the roof of the mouth as the air is exhaled."

The Health Aspects of Training Earth Form

When the energy flow from the Earth element is harmonious, the spleen and stomach will be nourished. The twisting action of the body whilst practicing Earth form will help chi to gather at the body's centre and in turn nourish all the muscles of the body. When Earth Chi is strong it will nourish all the other energy systems of the body, just as Mother Earth provides for all that live on it.

In TCM the function of the stomach is to break down the grains to create chi and then the spleen supports this process by transporting and transforming the newly created chi to other areas of the body. Therefore, practise of Earth form helps rotate the body, physically massaging the stomach and spleen organs and their meridians, helping them in this digestive and transporting process.

Chinese Medicine classical literature states:

"If you have spleen or stomach problems your lips will turn yellow. This problem also produces a fragrant smell in the body odor and you will enjoy eating sweets. The tightness will be around your spinal cord and you will always be afraid. If you have sickness in the spleen your joints will be damp and your underarms will be wet at all times. Try not to live in the middle of the country. You will also probably vomit a lot. You should not eat sweet things, millet, beef or dates and don't sit too long in one spot."

The internal meridians of the stomach and spleen open into the mouth and their health are reflected in the lips. Any discoloration of the lips shows disharmony in the Earth organs. Sweet foods damage the spleen and stomach as seen in diabetes and regulation of sweet foods is paramount to good health. The spleen also commands the muscles and a weakness here can be seen in muscle wasting or atrophy as commonly seen in diabetes.

When Spleen Chi is weak it will not transport and transform chi effectively, therefore, the chi and fluids in the body will stagnate and pool, just like a stream that is blocked and becomes stagnant. This causes swelling of tissues and joints, particularly in the legs where the effects of gravity cause the stagnated fluid to collect at the body's lowest point. Remember water always sinks to find its own level and that too is true of the body. In TCM this problem is referred to as internal damp as there is too much stagnant fluid in the body. When fluid sits in the joints it stops them moving freely and they become stiff and painful. Eating too many sweet or fried foods which are viewed to be energetically damp forming will over time damage the Earth organs as will living in a damp environment. When there is too much fluid in the body this also gives the kidneys a problem as their role is to command the water passages and keep them open. If Kidney Chi is then depleted from having to deal with too much fluid then the emotion of fear and being afraid will prevail. This is a classic example of how a problem in one element can affect another as all are linked by a continuous cycle.

To help heal the Spleen or Stomach Chi flow, the practitioner should practice the Earth form of Hsing-I. The method by which they practice the form changes slightly when they practice purely for health. This is mainly in their breathing pattern, intent and visualisation, but the physical aspect of the form remains the same, it is just practiced slower.

The Practice of Earth Form for Health

Start by opening into Pi-Chuan stance. Step into the first posture of the Earth form and then into the second posture. Stare into the distance beyond the fist of the forward hand and breathe slowly from your lower stomach/Tan Tien, using the complete breathing method. Inhale and exhale three to five times thinking only of your spleen or stomach, inhaling and filling it with clear chi, exhaling and breathing out the Turbid Chi. Then step forward as in Earth form and repeat the process on the opposite side. Continue this process for a minimum of twenty minutes each day and always finish the form in the correct way. Over time your symptoms should subside as your health recovers its strength.

Visualisation: inhalation of pure chi to the spleen

Organ functions of Earth Element
Earth:

Organ meridians of Earth Element

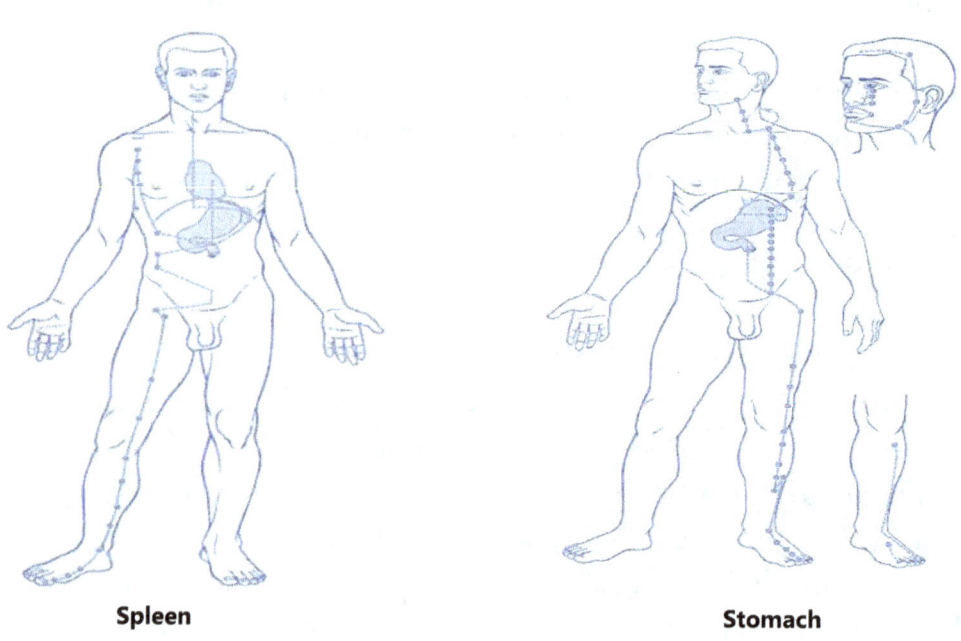

Spleen   Stomach

The spleen's main function is to assist the stomach in rotting and ripening of foods in order to extract the essence required to produce chi and blood. In this process, the spleen and stomach act to transform and transport the essence in the form of chi and carry it upwards to combine with the air of the lungs. When combined these two types of chi 'Gu' and 'Zhong' respectively transfer to the heart where it can be circulated around the body. The stomach and spleen together form the Earth element and are the main source of post-heaven chi in the body. This process is crucial to be efficient in order for the body to avoid depleting pre-heaven chi which is stored in the kidneys.

Energetically, Stomach Chi helps descend food and drink, allowing it to be rotted and its fluids/essence extracted before being passed on down to the intestines for further refinement and eventual excretion from the body. Therefore, the stomach is seen to be the origin of bodily fluids. The Spleen Chi in contrast helps transport the pure essence that is obtained from the food and raises it back up to the upper Jiao to be transformed into blood for distribution to the body. The quality of the muscles in their strength energetically and their physical bulk are directly linked to the energy transported to them from the stomach via the spleen. A weak spleen will manifest in wasted muscles (atrophy). The lips will show discolouration if the Spleen and Stomach Chi is not healthy.

Finally, the spleen is said to house the 'Yi' (spirit) which is the source of thought and therefore the maintains the capacity for studying, thinking, focusing and memorising. It is closely linked with the health of Spleen Chi. Worry is the emotion of the spleen and weakness of Spleen Chi will result in excessive overthinking and worrying which will affect the stomach manifesting in the symptoms of sickness and poor digestive functioning. Of all the organ partnerships, these two are most closely related.

The main TCM energetic functions of the spleen are to:
- govern transportation and transformation of chi
- control the blood
- control the muscles and the four limbs
- manifest in the lips
- control rising of pure chi
- house the 'Yi' spirit/ thought

Stomach:

The main TCM energetic functions of the stomach are to:
- control the rotting and ripening of food
- control the transportation of food essences
- control the descending of chi
- be the origin of bodily fluids

Hsing-I Chuan Five Element Diagram

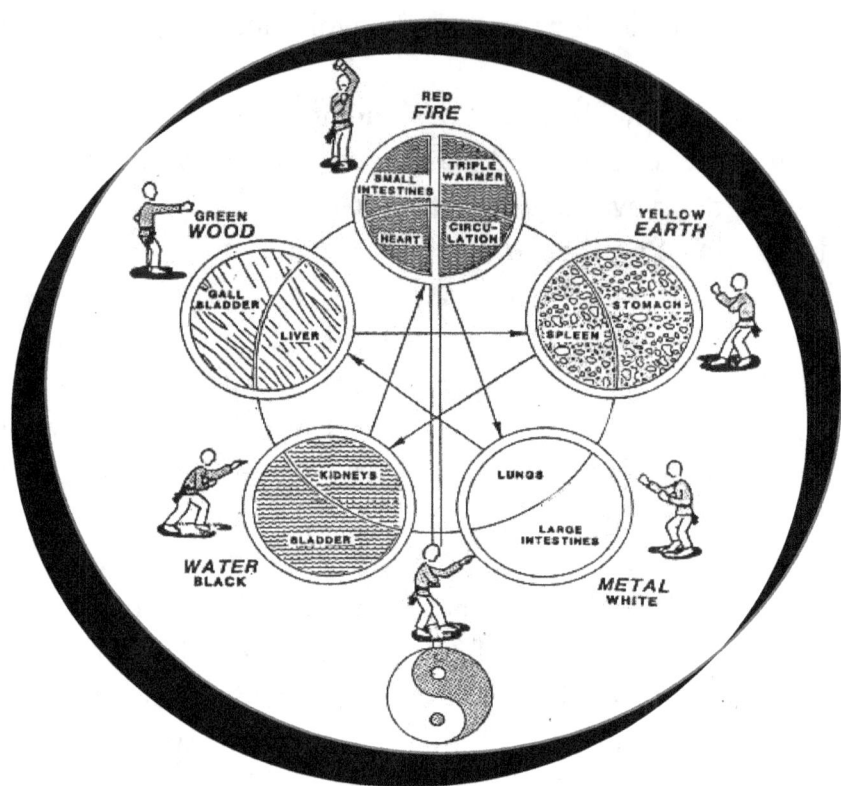

The Hsing-I Five Element diagram depicts the creative and destructive sequences of Hsing-I movements and of the five element energies according to the laws of the Tao. The chart begins at the bottom of the diagram where there is a symbol of Yin/Yang. This shows the split of energies coming from the one that is Tao in creating the form of two poles each containing a piece of the other. The black circle that surrounds the Yin/Yang symbol also represents the Tao, encircling Yin and Yang and from which they were both created. This complete circle also shows there is no natural beginning or end to the Tao.

Emerging next from the symbol of Yin/Yang is Man in the form of San Ti posture. Remember from the previous Chapter 3, the sequence of creation from the Tao. From the one of the Tao (stillness), came the two of Yin/Yang (movement). Next from the two came the three of San Ti posture. The diagram now shows the creation of Heaven, Man and Earth which is reflected in the opening posture of Hsing-I. Within the movement and creation of San Ti posture the energy fills all four extremities of the body and when this sequence is complete the movements of the five elements can be created. From these five movements come all the movements of Hsing-I.

Continuing out from the head of the Man in San Ti posture is drawn a straight line up to the element of Fire. This line passes through the man's centre and out through the top of his head, connecting the two important points of Hui Yin and Baihui and emphasises the connection between Heaven, Man and Earth and the cycle of the five elements.

The heart is the prince of the Fire element and controls the emotional mind where all thought and intention originates. Therefore, the Fire element is the starting point internally for physical movement to externally manifest from. This conforms to the Taoist laws surrounding the natural movements of the five element energies and the law of creation which is shown in the reference table below.

The Taoist Law of Creation

Elements	Fire	Earth	Metal	Water	Wood
Movements	Expansion	Division	Contraction	Sink down	Shoot forward

The Taoist law of creation indicates that within nature the energetic order of movement first expands, then divides, then contracts to the centre, then sinks down before shooting forwards and expanding again. This cycle is constantly in motion with no beginning or end. The link to Fire being first in this sequence here shows that from the nothing of the Tao comes the spontaneous spiral of energy expanding outwards as it goes and therefore expansion (Fire) was seen as the first in the sequence as it came from nothing. This law of creation can be observed by simply watching the growth of a plant, first it grows shoots and expands into a plant dividing into stems and branches, eventually it seeds and divides and then shrivels or contracts sinking back down to the earth ready to start the process all over again. Clever analysis can see this energetic process in all things. Most analysis of the creative cycle usually start with wood, but from the first cycle in the creation of the Universe, the energy was seen to be a spontaneous expansion with nothing preceding it, in essence it was the starting point of what is now a never-ending cycle.

In nature, it is the shooting forward of Wood that provides the energy for expansion and some styles of Hsing-I teach Wood form first to reflect this process. The lineage shown in this book starts with Metal form due to its natural connection with San Ti and follows the natural generating cycle to water and so forth. In effect, it doesn't matter which element you start from as truly there is no start point, just a continuation from one element to another. This is reflected in practice where all elements pass from Wuji to Taiji and then to San Ti and finish in the reverse way passing back to Wuji, in readiness to start again.

So, the diagram of the five elements presented is a complex one and within it is stored a lot of useful information in practicing Hsing-I. It also shows the various connections of the Creative (circle) and Destructive (star) cycles and the organs relating to each element all of which have been discussed earlier in this chapter. Finally, it shows the appropriate Hsing-I posture for each element and the order to practice them finally ending back with the Tao. When following the Sheng Cycle (circle) the practitioners posture naturally moves from one into another following the correct order of the Tao. Following the Ke Cycle (star) the practitioner is shown which technique can defeat which when fighting.

Chapter 8

The 'Six Styles of the Body' Theory of Hsing-I Chuan

The theory concerning the 'Six Styles of the Body' originates from the classic literature pertaining to Hsing-I and is a common feature to most pure lineages. When the Six Styles of the Body are unified into one posture and embedded in the practitioner's forms, the result is an extremely powerful fighting style which is very practical for self-defence.

The posture of 'San Ti' is where this theory is first trained and once a solid foundation has been established the knowledge and skills learned can be transferred into postures of different forms. When the theory and structures of the Six Styles are correctly embedded in all areas of practice it will allow the smooth flow of chi through the meridians to nourish the organs and extremities creating a strong and healthy body. Furthermore, this theory will help the practitioner to understand how to utilise the power stored at the Tan Tien, as when the correct mechanics born from this practice are combined with the mind and the breath, the chi can flow naturally from the Tan Tien through the technique.

The six styles of the body are:

1. Chicken Legs

70%   30%

Chicken Step

In the style of 'Chicken Legs' the characteristic should be light and powerful, which creates mobility and speed in all directions at any given moment. This posture classically keeps the knees bent in keeping with the other main theories of the Eight Fundamentals and Nine Essences theories. The 'Chicken Legs' allow the body to become grounded and centred with the bent legs allowing chi to be stored in the joints like a coiled spring ready to explode as required. The rear leg stores the energy and contains 70% of the bodyweight. The forward leg remains light and can move swiftly to attack or defend and holds 30% of the bodyweight. This posture keeps the body and head level throughout movements allowing balance, strength and power to be maintained at all times.

2. Dragon Body

Three Divisions of the Dragon Body

Three Subdivisions of the Limbs

The 'Dragon Body' can be best understood by viewing from the side. It shows the body to be split into three divisions and uses three major joints to show these divides. First are ankles to knees. Second are knees to hips and third are hips to head. The characteristic of the 'Dragon Body' is strength and its ability to extend, shrink and twist by folding its bones.

The legend of the dragon purports it to have the ability to fly up to the heavens and dive quickly down to the water. In Hsing-I this ability is observed by using the different body sections to fold and expand by flexing and extending the combination of joints, this also allows the body to rise and fall in a controlled manner. This same principle can be subdivided into the arms, where the three joints are the shoulders, elbows and wrists and they too along with the body and legs can reflect the abilities of the 'Dragon Body' when practicing Hsing-I.

3. Eagle Claws

The energy of the 'Eagles Claws' are mirrored in the hands and fingers of all open hand postures in Hsing-I. The hands should remain alive and ready to strike or grasp, not too tense but not too relaxed either. The characteristic of the eagle is to be skilled at sudden diving and grasping of its prey with complete accuracy and this spirit should be mastered in Hsing-I.

4. Bear Shoulders

The 'Bears Shoulders' are strong and powerful, they should be held slightly forward but level as they store power ready for both attack and defence. They work together in combination and transfer power through the arms to the hands as necessary. The characteristics of the bear are shown in its strength when it stands up on its hind legs to dominate its prey, the bear has a strong stance where the power of the shoulders can be transferred to the hands to deliver fast and powerful hand strikes. These characteristics whilst integrated in all postures are best demonstrated in the twelve animal form 'Eagle/Bear'.

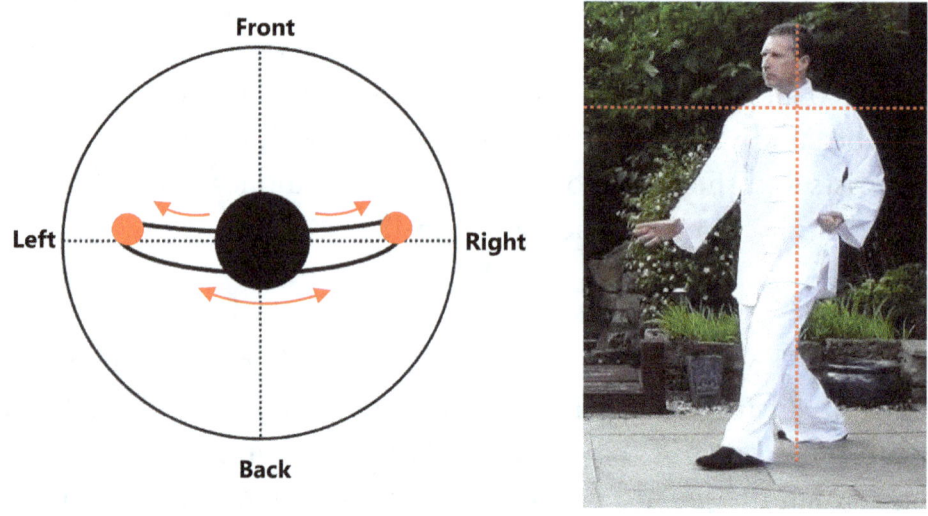

Bears shoulders straight back, level and drawn forward

5. Tiger Embrace

The theory of 'Tiger Embrace' is shown clearly in Tiger form where the two arms embrace the chest and reflect the rounded and slightly retracted image of the tiger stalking menacingly from its cave. They are ready to extend and strike or grasp and retreat at any given moment. The tigers attribute is that it is fearless and can attack at will, even when moving backwards it still looks to attack, this is reflected in the arms abilities to grasp and pull or shoot forward to strike when moving in any direction. Like the tiger, the practitioner never truly retreats in Hsing-I and they constantly look for the opportunity to attack even when moving backwards.

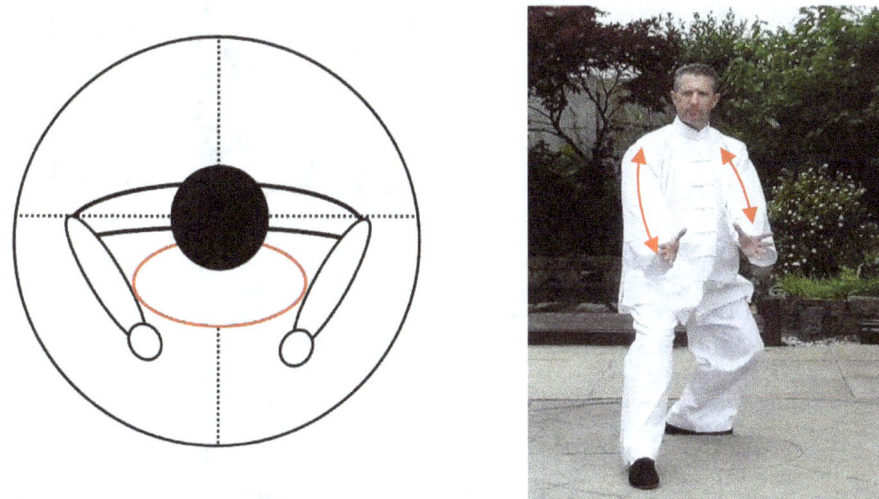

Tigers embrace retracted and rounded form

6. Thunder and Roaring

In connection with the previous five externally viewed styles of the body, the sixth style combines the internal manifestation of the breath sinking, with the eruption of chi out from the Tan Tien with any given technique. This takes the form of 'Thunder and Roaring' in Hsing-I and is heard as a natural sound emitting from the Tan Tien on striking. This actual sound varies from person to person, but should always be natural and spontaneous coming from deep within. It is likened to the rumble of a volcano as it omits its power and destruction.

When correctly combined with any strike this technique harnesses the power of the chi from the body, greatly increasing its effects. As in nature, from the 'Thunder and Roaring' should follow the lightening in the form of a strike so fast, it should hardly be seen, only felt.

On the subject of the 'Six Styles' theory Master McNeil comments:

"No matter how it is changed, a style cannot pull away from its origins. In Hsing-I, we use light and powerfully mobile 'Chicken Legs' and the indomitable strength of the 'Dragon Body'. This is combined with the engulfing, crushing force of 'Bear Shoulders' and the gripping, rending slash of the 'Eagle Claws'. The body's movements should be agile like a monkey; it should not lean forward or backward, but must always be centred to facilitate for quick and balanced movement. The expulsion of breath is as the sound of 'Thunder and Roaring' from within as the chi fills the body and begs release. When viewed from the front, the body should look as if it were facing to the side. From the side, it should seem to face the front. This is an extremely subtle compromise in body placement and can only be learned from a competent teacher. When first training the 'Six Styles' from 'San Ti' posture the front leg should be light, the back leg solid. The legs should be neither straight nor bent. If kept too straight or bent too much, you will be unstable. The force of the hand should be in the wrist and its power should be transmitted to the fingers. The back should be straight and the shoulders should drop. Because if the shoulders are too high they become stiff and cannot move quickly into a full and devastating attack."

Chapter 9

The Six Harmonies Theory of Hsing-I Chuan

To understand the very core of Hsing-I practice, the theory of the 'Six Harmonies' must be fully understood. This theory demonstrates how both the internal and external aspects of practice must be completely and seamlessly combined to produce the extraordinary power that Hsing-I is famed for. To accomplish this the practitioner must train hard, paying close attention to the structural alignment of all postures and learn how to combine them with the breath and the mind to ultimately harness the power of the chi within them. Their practice should be led by the mind and this way they will mobilise the muscles and circulate their chi to a higher level of efficiency.

The 'Six Harmonies' are split into three external and three internal pairings of which one is Yin and the other Yang in nature. Accomplishing unity in these pairings coordinates the body to move as one and balances the circulation of chi in accordance with the laws of Tao. It should be remembered though, that even though this theory splits aspects up into individual component parts, in practice the body should be viewed as one complete entity. Understanding this should be a major goal in a practitioner's training.

THE SIX EXTERNAL HARMONIES OF HSING – I

1	2
SHOULDER (YANG)	HIPS (YIN)
THE SHOULDER MATCHES THE OPPOSITE HIP	

3	4
ELBOW (YANG)	KNEE (YIN)
THE ELBOWS AND KNEES MOVE AS ONE TO PRODUCE MORE POWER	

5	6
HAND (YANG)	FEET (YIN)
THE HANDS AND FEET MOVE TOGETHER FOR GREATER SPEED AND POWER	

The Six External Harmonies

'The shoulder matches the opposite hip'

When the two shoulders are relaxed and drawn in like a bow and the hips are drawn in by tightening of the buttocks and tilting upward of the pelvis, the joints will be loaded with energy. The mind should focus on the point GB 21 (Jian Jing) of the shoulder and point GB 30 (Huantiao) on the opposite hip. These points should move in sequence with each other. Then it is said that the shoulders and hips are harmonised.

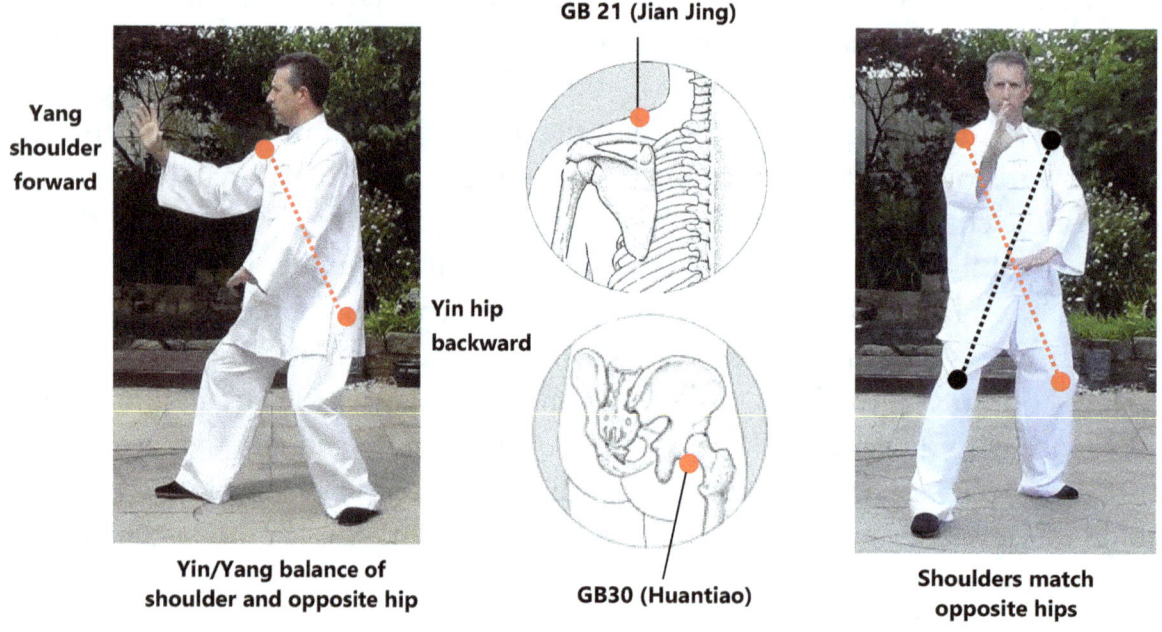

'The elbows and knees move as one'

When the elbows are dropped and the knees are aligned and bowed, both are ready to transfer their energy. The elbows should move directly with the knees as they are the same mid-joints of their respective limbs. The mind should focus on LI 11 (QuChi) point on the elbow and the point GB 34 (Langlingquan) on the opposite knee. When this is done correctly the elbows and knees are said to be harmonised.

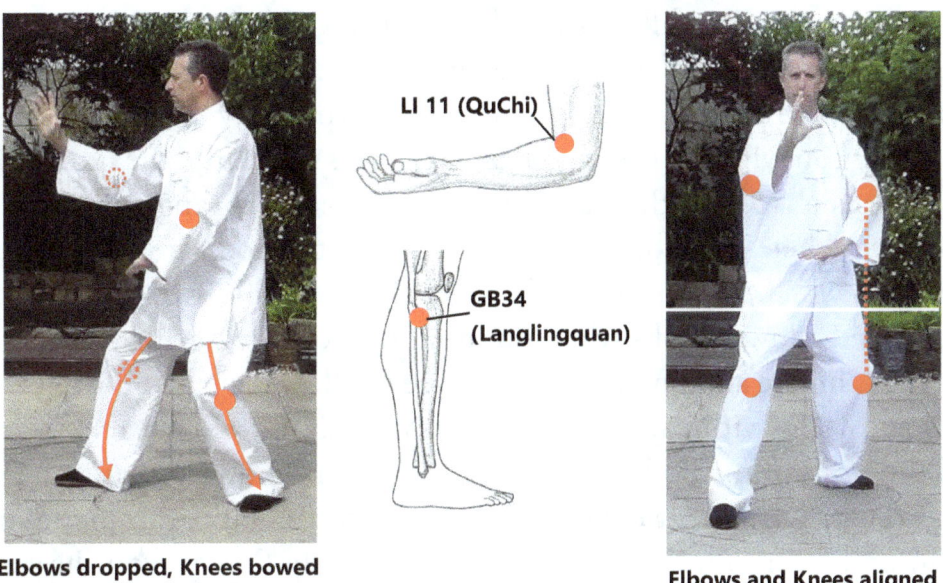

'The hands and feet move together'

The hands must be spirited and ready to grab and the feet must be rooted, sinking into the earth. The hands must move exactly in time with the feet as they are the same distal joints of their respective limbs. The mind should focus on acupuncture point P 8 (Lao Gong) on the palm of the hand and the acupuncture point Kid 1 (Yong Quan) on the sole of the opposite foot. When the hands and feet are coordinated in this way they are said to be harmonised.

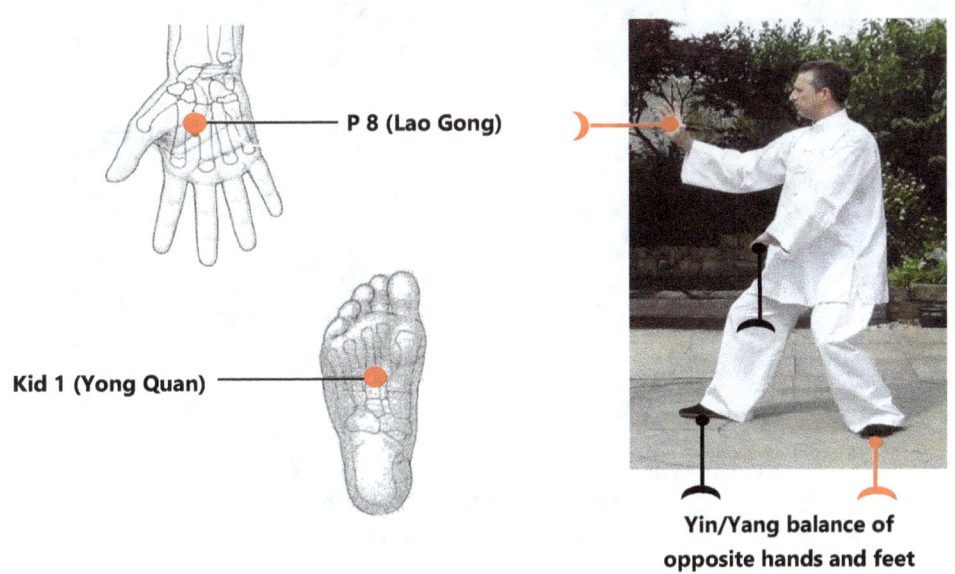

Yin and Yang Aspects of the Six External Harmonies

To understand how the different body parts are divided into their Yin/Yang components it is first useful to consider how the Chinese view the body and its energy in relation to the universe. When viewing the body as a whole, the head is yang in comparison with the feet which are Yin. This is because the head is above the feet, just as heaven is above the earth in nature. Heaven is Yang and earth is Yin in relation to each other. Therefore, the upper limbs of the body are Yang in relation to the lower limbs which are Yin simply because the upper limbs are higher and closer to heaven than the lower limbs when standing in the Chinese anatomical position.

From the Chinese anatomical position (see chi flow diagram) it can be observed that the flow of chi within the Zang organ meridians, which are Yin in nature, moves up the front of the body (Yin) from earth (Yin) drawn towards the direction of heaven (Yang). Likewise, the flow of chi through the Fu organ meridians which are Yang in nature, moves down the back of the body (Yang) from heaven (Yang) drawn down towards the energy of earth (Yin).

Therefore, when the cycle of chi within the body flows through its natural course, from one organ meridian to another, it naturally passes up and down the body from top to bottom as it continues to move from a Yin meridian to a Yang meridian in a continuous twenty-four-hour cycle.

Chinese Anatomical Position
Chi Flow Diagram

THE SIX INTERNAL HARMONIES OF HSING – I

1	2
YIN	YANG
THE HEART MATCHES THE MIND	

3	4
YIN	YANG
THE MIND MATCHES THE CHI	

5	6
YIN	YANG
THE CHI MATCHES THE STRENGTH	

The Six Internal Harmonies

'The Heart matches the Mind'
The heart and the mind are the origin of all physical actions. When the heart (emotional mind) matches with the mind/brain (wisdom mind) and both are concentrated together, the movements initiated will be spontaneous and appropriate. It is said if you want to win in a fight; the heart must first turn cold in order to execute the action without hesitation.

'The Mind matches the Chi'
When the mind matches the chi, movement can be initiated. When this process is smooth and natural so will be the resulting technique. Chi can be directed anywhere in the body by the concentration of the mind and therefore any part of the body maybe mobilised by the concentration of the mind.

'The Chi matches the Strength'
When the chi matches the strength, the appropriate amount of force and energy will be efficiently mobilised to the muscles. Therefore, the correct power and technique will be utilised to create a successful outcome to any situation.

'Yin and Yang aspects of the Six Internal Harmonies'
In relation to Yin and Yang the heart represents the energetic and therefore emotional aspect rather than the physical structure itself. The heart is said to be the 'seat of all emotions' and is a Yin organ closely related to the production and nourishment of blood, just as the earth nourishes life. The mind which is housed in the brain or 'Ni-Wan Palace' (an area located in the brain approximately two inches behind the acupuncture point Yin Tang) and is closer to heaven than the heart and therefore is more Yang in nature.

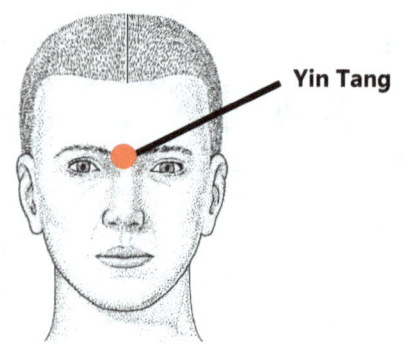

In addition to this, the heart is Yin where it is nurturing the emotional intention to act. It is the wisdom mind that is Yang when it actually actions the intent to physically act. It is this comparison between emotional and physical levels that also shows the harmony between Yin and Yang in this process.

Another point of note is that chi is usually seen as Yang in nature as its functions are warming and moving within the body. But in this theory the energy of chi is being compared with the physical structures of the muscles and the concept of strength. When considered in this way chi is seen to be deeper in the body and nourishing to the muscles therefore chi is showing its Yin, energetic qualities. The muscles are more superficial in the body than chi and concern themselves here with strength and movement which is more physical and Yang in nature. Therefore, the laws of Yin and Yang state that 'within Yin there is always Yang and vice versa'. It just depends from which viewpoint you are looking from.

Chapter 10

The Seven Stars of Hsing-I Chuan

When applying Hsing-I in self-defence, a strike must follow a prescribed chain of movement. No matter which one or combination of the Seven Stars are being used to strike with, they must all assist each other in the generation and transfer of power from one joint to another until the strike makes contact and maximum power is transferred to the opponent. The chain of power begins with the foot and follows through to every joint, ending finally at the part of the body that is striking.

When utilised correctly the generation of energy created by the Seven Stars can be likened to the cracking of a bull tail whip, where the handle of the whip generates the power which is subsequently transferred along the tail like a wave of energy until it is emitted from the end so fast and powerful that a loud 'cracking' sound is heard as the speed and power of the whip's tail is faster than the speed of sound.

This sequence of movement creates the theory of the 'Seven Stars of Hsing-I'. The Seven Stars are the head, shoulders, elbows, hands, hips, knees and feet; all of which can be used as a single striking entity or in combination with each other. They are the weapons of the human body that can attack with great power. With these rules comes the means by which one can successfully deliver an attack.

On the subject of the Seven Stars, Master McNeil states:

*"**When striking, use all of one's inner power is to move the hands and legs together. Fists are as cannons, pounding like cannon balls. The body expands and contracts as required, like a dragon, storing chi in its joints as it does so. In the face of an attacker you should look alive and deadly. Move as if you have flames running all over your body'. If you want your attack to be successful, you must move first!"*

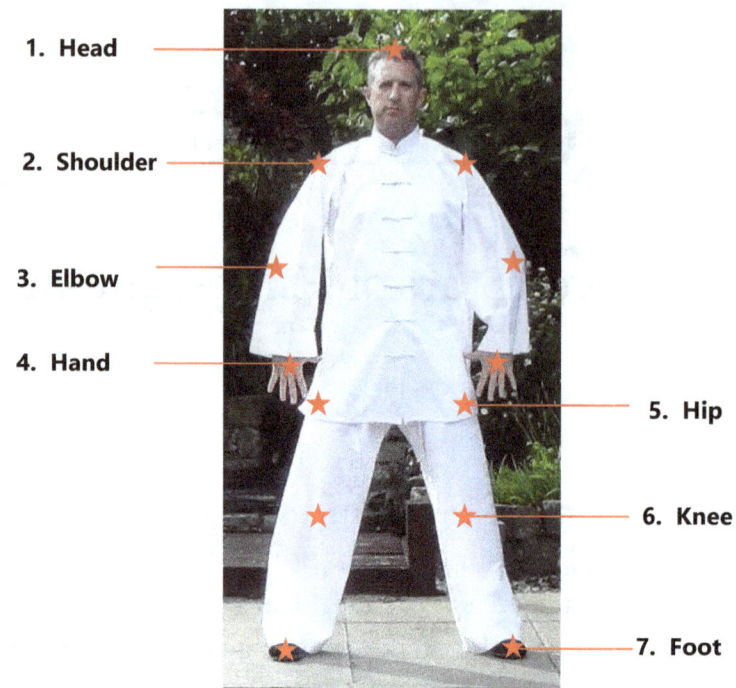

1. Head
2. Shoulder
3. Elbow
4. Hand
5. Hip
6. Knee
7. Foot

1. Head Hit

To strike with the head the practitioner must step forward and the whole body moves as one. The feet are aligned under the body along the centreline, so that when they strike with the head the body remains centred and balanced. The 'step in' should occupy their opponents centre line with the whole body and take his space leaving it difficult to defend. When the centreline is attacked it can open up many vital points!

2. Shoulder Hit

To effectively use a shoulder, which is the root section of the arm, the practitioner must step in close to their opponent and their body must be rooted and centred to produce power. The use of either right or left shoulder depends on the situation. As one shoulder strikes (Yang), the opposite shoulder should retreat (Yin) with equal spirit, getting ready to store chi for the next strike.

3. Elbow Hit

When attacking with an elbow strike it is important to keep the elbow down along the centreline and coordinated with both the knees and feet. This allows the strike to remain hidden and the body balanced as the power is transferred to the opponent. By keeping the strike hidden the opponent cannot see what strike is coming next. This puts the attacker in an advantageous situation. Structurally the elbow is the mid-section of the upper limb and is strong and sharp in nature. When delivered correctly the elbow can cause great damage!

4. Hand Hit

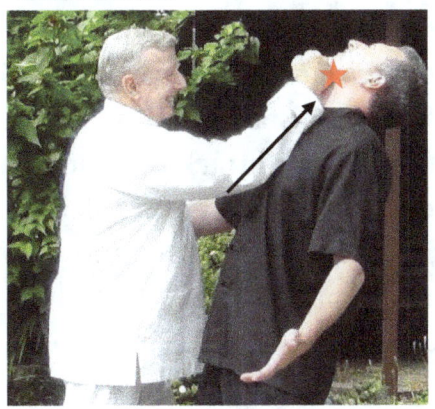

Moving out from the chest, the hands should be like a powerful tiger catching a delicate lamb. The strength in the hands should be interchangeable and the elbows should be lowered to protect the body, ready to explode with power. The hands are the distal section of the upper limb. The back hand is Yin, protecting and storing power for the next technique. The front hand is Yang, attacking and exploding forward to deliver its energy to the opponent. Both hands must work equally together and the strike must hit in time with the feet. The mind must be focused on the target and this will lead the chi into the technique, strengthening the muscles and maximising the strikes effectiveness.

5. Hip Hit

Yin or Yang, left or right depends on the situation. The practitioner must be rooted whilst moving the feet and be quick as lightning when attacking with the hips. The hips are the root section of the lower limbs and in order to move the hips must be relaxed and mobile. When this is correct the body can move swiftly in any direction. The forward or striking hip is Yang and the rear or chi storing hip is Yin, both must be coordinated equally to maintain balance and centre throughout the hip hit technique. The practitioner must be close in order to hit with the hips and the body must hit as one unit. If they arrive as one in their technique the power through the hips will knock an opponent clean over!

6. Knee Hit

Like the elbow, the knee is the mid-section of the lower limb and is strong and solid in nature. Knee strikes against any vital point can be fatal. Always hold the hands up in front to balance the body. Never lean back when striking with the knee, use the folding of the bones method seen in the 'Dragons Body' to draw in the opponent and deliver maximum power whilst remaining centred and solid throughout delivery of the strike. Use the hands to distract the opponent prior to delivering the strike!

7. Foot Hit

Steps are firm; strength comes from one foot rooted to the ground. Kick only with full powered shots to vital areas. The feet are the distal sections of the lower limbs, when the decision to attack is made the practitioner should not hesitate, they should kick forward powerfully from the standing foot and aim to plant their striking foot directly into their opponents centre line, this way they will be at a disadvantage and the practitioner can press home any attack. The feet should be fast and accurate at all times as the feet are the foundations of Hsing-I!

Chapter 11

The Eight Fundamentals Theory of Hsing-I Chuan

The Eight Fundamentals, sometimes termed the 'Eight Words' of Hsing–I provide the practitioner with a visualisation of the correct posture and alignment that needs to be mastered in all techniques. Each word contains three key points; this makes a total of twenty-four key points to be observed throughout practice. Whilst they may be looked at individually when studying them, their true strength is realised when they are combined as one.

Externally attaining the correct alignment is crucial to progression in Hsing-I training as not only does it make the structure of each posture strong physically, from the foundations upwards, it also allows the practitioner to issue and dissolve power efficiently when fighting. Internally it allows the structures within the body (meridians, vessels, bones and organs), to sit in their correct position which allows chi and blood to manifest and flow smoothly which is the key to good health.

The most obvious place to observe the Eight Fundamentals in practice is within 'San Ti' posture where they can be developed at first in standing practice and then later, absorbed into all movements of a practitioners Hsing-I practice. Only when these points are totally embedded can a practitioner expected to benefit from them in terms of health and martial abilities.

1. San Ding – The Three Press-Ups

Head
The head is the headquarters of the body. When the head lifts up, the chi can travel along the back of the body to the top of the head; this is beneficial to one's health. In keeping the head upright, the neck should remain feeling slightly stretched but not tense and not too relaxed. When moving, the head must remain still and not sway around. Do not tense the face or jaw muscles as this tension will transfer into the whole posture of the body. Internally the mind should be focused on mentally raising the chi, in effect pressing it up to the top of the head.

Tongue

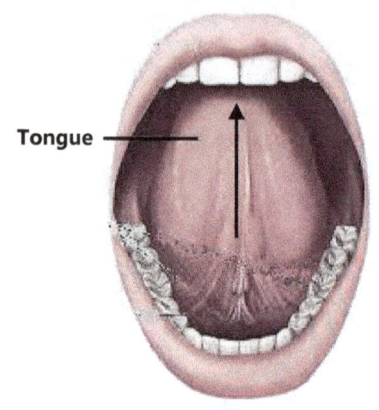

When pressed upwards against the palate in a relaxed manner, the tongue will help the chi move down to the Tan Tien. The tongue works as a type of switch with saliva as the conductor and connects the two meridians of Du and Ren to complete the full circuit of chi known as the 'Little Nine Heaven' circulation. Physically this placement of the tongue keeps the mouth in a condition which helps control thirst and in a fight, it also keeps the tongue from being bitten if you are hit.

Palm

When pressed outward in the proper position, the palm will help the chi to extend to each part of the body and helps strengthen the fingers and arms. The index finger of the forward hand should be stretched up to lead the chi to the extremities of the hands. Whilst this skill can be discussed in theory the novice practitioner needs the attention of a knowledgeable teacher to truly master this feeling. There is a very subtle skill in keeping the hands curved yet pressing in the right directions at all times. No part of the hand should be too relaxed or too tense, this feeling is referred to as 'spirited' or 'alive' when practising.

2. San Kao – The Three Suppresses

Shoulder

The shoulders suppress which means to slightly sink inwards and downwards, so that the front of the chest will feel empty and strength will flow down to the elbows. It is like the tensioning of two ends of a bow, storing energy ready to expand and strike out through the arms when required. This posture relaxes the chest which allows for more efficient breathing via the Tan Tien.

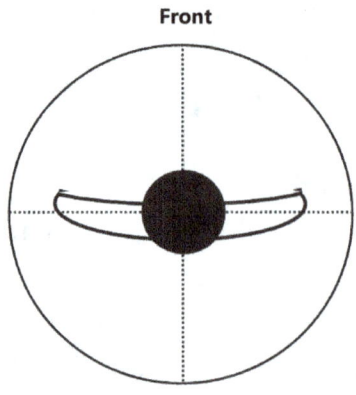

Hands

The hands and feet work as one unit. Suppress the hands with the upper arms, but be relaxed. The hands, arms, back, waist and feet are all closely linked. The backs of the hands and feet are suppressed which makes them stronger, the hands are poised to grab in attack and the feet are poised to grab at the ground to make the body more stable and rooted.

Teeth

The teeth and chin suppress downward, so that the ligaments and bones of the jaw feel tight. This strengthens the bones in the body and makes the jaw strong and stable to protect the head and neck in a fight.

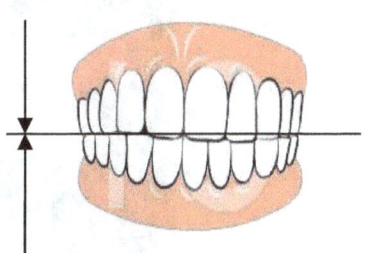

3. San Yuan – The Three Rounds

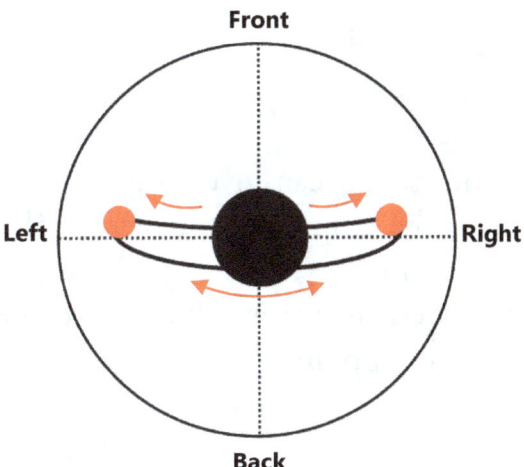

Back

The back is slightly rounded in conjunction with the suppressed shoulders, so that one is relaxed and ready. This gives the posture of the 'Bears Shoulders' and allows power to be easily transferred through the waist and into the arms.

Chest
The chest is rounded in a concave and empty way so as to combine with the back and shoulders. This posture will give full strength when power is needed and permits smooth, relaxed breathing. This emptying of the chest also brings in the elbows to protect the ribs and heart.

Hands
The hands will be rounded and relaxed so as chi may be felt. The round is in the 'Tigers Mouth' of the hand and all the fingers, so as power maybe utilised in grabbing and seizing the opponent. The rounded posture of all the joints in the hands allows for smooth flow of chi and blood which is paramount to good health.

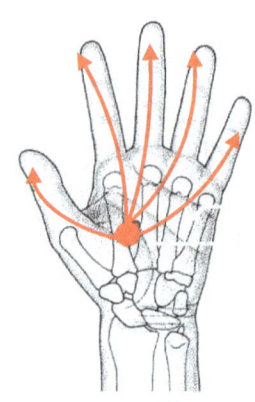

4. San Min – The Three Sensitives

Eyes
The eyes are sensitive windows that can give away one's feelings, when facing an opponent, it is important to be confident and fierce. The eyes pass information to the mind and must be alert for the mind to make a quick analysis of any given situation. When the eyes are alert the spirit will be raised and the body alive to react and keep the hands ahead of an opponent's.

Heart
The TCM concept is that the heart controls the mind, so the quality of the practitioner's Heart Chi can either help or destroy them. One should be alert and quick to respond, always maintain a fierce attitude in life and death situations. The heart is the seat of the emotional mind and can affect the nature of the response to any given situation. These heart driven decisions can often override the wisdom mind (brain) and a balance between the two is the key to success in Hsing-I training.

Hands

The hands are sensitive so they will quickly respond to situations. If the practitioner learns to 'feel' and 'listen' with their hands they will eventually become like the eyes. Correct posture of the hands and fingers combined with the correct amount of spirit allows the hands to move as lightning in attack or defence. Too much power and strength held in the hands is wasteful and they will soon tire and become weak. If the hands are held too tensely they will potentially lose a beat in movement time because they have to relax slightly in order to move them, in effect, slowing them down.

5. San Bao – The Three Holdings

Tan Tien

The Tan Tien must be filled with chi; this is the reservoir of life energy and the main supply for the whole body. The practitioners focus should be on directing the breath to the Tan Tien in order to sink the chi. Concentration on the Tan Tien keeps the chi strong and in its correct place, from here the body can be supplied as required for any given circumstance.

Breath

Holding and directing of the breath will bring many health benefits. Correct breathing allows the efficient fuel for chi to be created and for the body to function at its optimum. Controlling the breath will keep the mind and emotions calm and this will help the practitioner respond more appropriately to any situation. Physiologically, controlling the oxygen and carbon dioxide exchange allows the body to remain calm and functional especially in stressful situations.

Arms

Holding the arms in a proper way will build strength and endurance which creates a stable platform to fight from. They will allow for protection of vulnerable points such as the ribs which protects the organs and the armpits which provide easy access to tendons nerves and vessels. Correct posture here also allows for smooth flow of chi to the extremities keeping them healthy and functional.

6. San Chui – The Three Sinkings

Chi

The sinking of chi to the Tan Tien helps the body become strong and transcend physical limitations; it keeps the body centred which is a prerequisite to developing power in all techniques. It also helps the body overcome many illnesses. This is achieved by the mind leading the breath and chi to the Tan Tien. Combined with the correct posture outlined in the Eight Fundamentals the chi can flow freely to all the extremities which is good for the health.

Shoulders

The sinking of the shoulders can bring about both relaxation and power. This is done in conjunction with the suppressing of the shoulders. When the shoulders are suppressed the chest empties and the elbows point down which allows chi to flow freely through the arms to the hands giving them strength and power.

Elbows

The sinking of the elbows will provide protection to the ribs and armpits. It also places the arms in the correct position for chi to be abundant to the hands and power to issue forth.

7. San Qu – The Three Curves

Elbows

The elbows curve and will be full of energy. The correct angle will allow a full flow of chi through the joint. Like the drawing of a bow to store energy prior to firing an arrow the gentle curves throughout the body's structure allow this same process to happen and the joints can store energy ready to release in the case of an attack.

Wrists

The wrists curve and will allow chi to flow naturally. This position when held correctly will greatly increase the strength of the wrist, palm and fingers.

Knees

The knees curve and the cycle of power is fulfilled. Just like the elbows in the upper limbs, the knees have a similar role in the lower limbs where they can be used to store energy and can emit power when required to explode in any direction. The knees also play a pivotal role in keeping the body at a constant height throughout all movement, like the suspension of a car providing a smooth and level ride on a bumpy road.

Note: In all the curves, one should be stretched and extended, but one should have the flexibility to recoil without tension.

8. San Ting – The Three Straightenings

Neck

With the neck straightened, the head is upright and energy will flow to the top of the head. In practise the neck must remain relaxed and supple, not stiff. The neck is a continuum of the spine and follows the same rules as the spine discussed below.

Spine

With the spine straightened, chi will flow throughout the body. If the lower back is bent in any way the practitioner will become weak and will lose their centre, this means they will have no base to issue their power from. Never lean forward, backwards or to the sides as this will offset the centre making the body weak. Do not be stiff, be relaxed and supple yet always remain straight and centred.

Knees

With the knees straightened and firmly rooted, one will surely feel the power of the chi. Here straightness refers to reaching outward with the advanced leg. When looking at the leg from the angle of the foot below it should look aligned in a

Hsing-I Chuan | The Practice of Heart and Mind Boxing

straight and linear fashion. The Chinese say that "The leg is straight, yet bent." Even though it is aligned straight with the foot, if viewed from the side angle the knees are always slightly flexed and the leg appears bent.

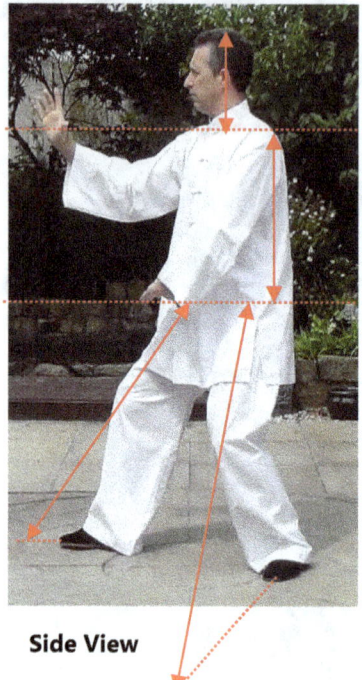

Side View

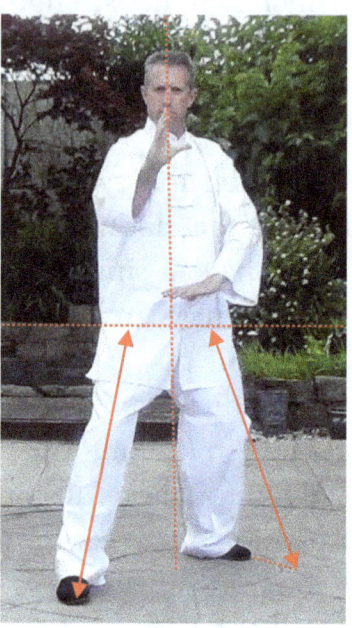

Front View

Chapter 12

The Nine Essences Theory of Hsing-I Chuan

These Nine Essences are derived from the Hsing-I classic literature and further add to the Eight Fundamentals in obtaining the correct posture, weighting and alignment of the body in Hsing-I practice. All these points can be clearly observed in San Ti posture and once they are fully understood should be seamlessly integrated into all the movements and forms of Hsing-I. The pictures and descriptions in this chapter are all described from right stance San Ti posture, but the same theory applies to left side posture also.

1. Tongue

The chi will be weak if the tongue is not rolled to the roof of the mouth. Chi sinks to the Tan Tien when the eyes are lowered and the mind focused. The muscles of the face are immoveable like iron and when chi is successfully lowered to the Tan Tien the extremities and the inner organs will be strengthened.

2. Body

The body should be straight, never leaning forward, backward, left or right. This keeps the body centred and balanced at all times. It should remain spirited and alert to all situations at all times. The body should be turned slightly to give protection from its centre. Within the body, the spine should feel slightly stretched from either end, although it should maintain its natural curvature throughout. Correct posture here allows the chi to flow naturally and is of great benefit to nourish the organs within as they can sit comfortably in their correct space.

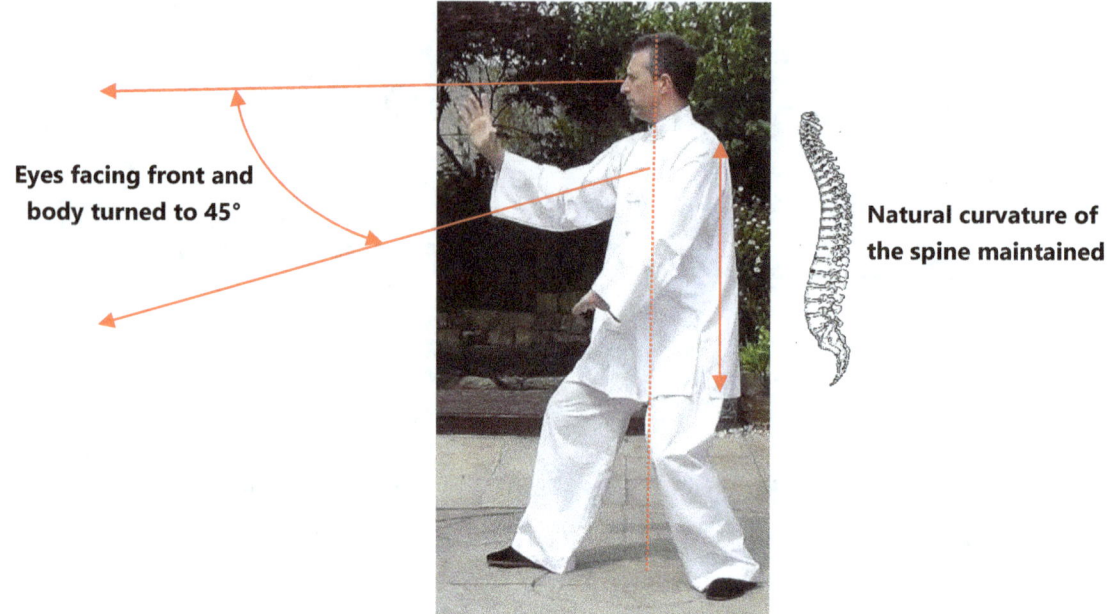

3. Shoulders

The shoulders should be level, but dropped downward and remain relaxed. Let the shoulders move together in a natural flow, as one leads the other follows. It is through the shoulders that the strength in the body is transferred to the hands.

4. Arms

The right arm is stretched forward. The left arm is held to protect the ribs with the elbow pointing down. The arms should be bent, but not contracted, stretched but not stiff. Too contracted, they cannot reach far and are easily trapped. Too straight, they cannot be powerful and are easily captured. This way as the forward arm attacks, the rear arm can protect.

5. Hands

The left hand is held at the Tan Tien. The right hand is held at chest level. The left hand is relaxed, but never dead. The right hand should have strength and be alive. Both hands are held palms downward. Strength in each hand should be even and spirited, ready to respond in attack or defence. The hands should carefully guard the space in front and protect the body's centre line at all times. The hands should appear open and full, this allows the chi to flow smoothly at all times.

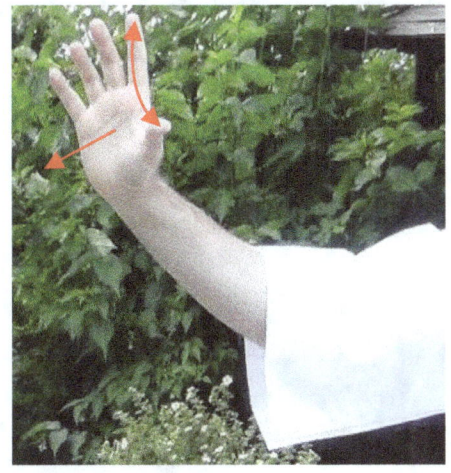

6. Fingers

Each finger is separated, shaped as hooks. The index finger and thumb forms a crescent which is called the 'Tigers Mouth'. The fingers are held with strength, but are not forced. If the hand is held too tense it will prevent chi flowing smoothly and this will reduce its strength.

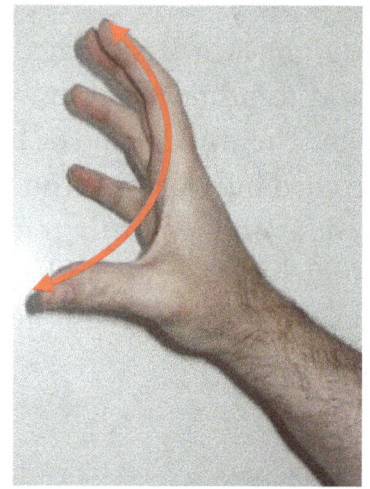

Tigers Mouth

7. Hips

The hips should be level and tilted slightly forward; this should be combined with the raising of the Hui Yin point so that the chi can be moved correctly to the limbs and up to the head. This posture should lead to a feeling of fullness in the waist area and allow for efficient transfer of power from the lower body to the upper body in practice. If this is ignored the chi flow will stagnate and it will be scattered inefficiently throughout the body resulting in poor health benefits and reduced power in technique.

Hui Yin Point

8. Legs

The right leg is to the front, left leg behind. Be straight but not stiff. Be bent slightly, yet straight overall. The Chinese say this is "Being straight, but not straight. Bent but not bent like a chicken." This is known as 'Chicken Legs' in Hsing-I. This slight curve in the legs allows for strengthening the posture and making the stance strong and rooted like a tree. The knees should always align with the toes and never turn inwards or outwards as this will lead to potential injury of the ligaments and tendons in practice. The energy stored in the knees can be utilised to move or kick with speed and power in any direction. The body's weight can be distributed to varying degrees using the legs and usually in the beginning it is 70% on the back leg and 30% on the front to build strength and endurance in the legs, however this can become more evenly weighted as the practitioner becomes more experienced and centred.

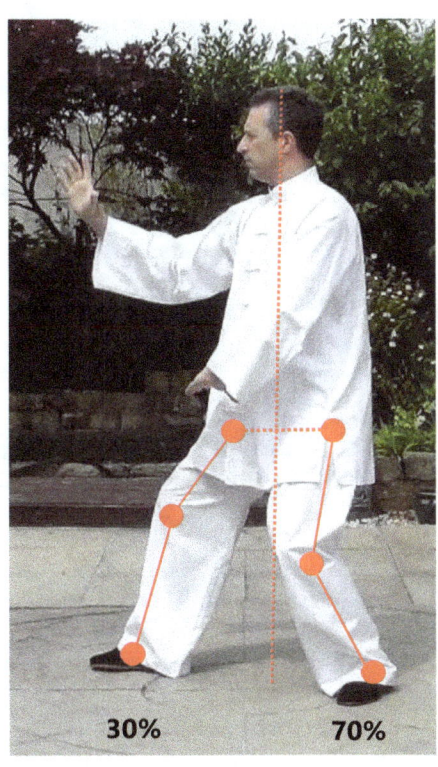

9. Feet

The front foot should be orientated straight with all toes pointing forward, never to the sides. The left backward foot is positioned at a 45 degrees sideward stance. The distance between the feet depends on the individual and is determined by their natural leg length. Toes should be firm almost like gripping the ground, not too tense but alive, mirroring the action of the hands. The weight should be settled evenly across the whole of the foot and not biased through either the heel or the ball of the foot.

Chapter 13

The Twelve Animals Theory of Hsing-I Chuan

Introduction

In the practice of the Twelve Animal Forms of Hsing-I Chuan it is important to note that the spirit or energetic (Hsing) characteristics of each individual animal is more important than the form itself physically looking like an animal, which is common in other animal-related martial arts styles. Different lineages have different movements relating to each animal and this is not to say that any one is better than another, what is important is that the spirit reflected in the movements is appropriate to the animal portrayed and in this way the connection to the animal can be clearly understood. It is this common thread that connects all the lineages of Hsing-I to make them one family regardless of their variation in forms.

Some lineages also give the forms different names. For example, 'Tow' is seen by some as a mythical animal, some say it is an alligator, lizard, turtle or tortoise, but again it is the energetic movements of such animals and how they interact with nature that should be analysed to see their similarities to one another. The truth is that 'Tow' could reflect any one of the animals in the example and it is how the form has been developed by the lineage and teachers within that lineage which has shaped its physical movements. It is best not to argue about such discrepancies in both the classical and current literature as all have valid points, just look at each form's energy and learn to use it, and your Hsing-I will progress. The twelve animals presented in this chapter are from the Shansi lineage as passed from the teachers listed in the history section of this book.

Understanding how each animal applies itself in attack and defence is the key to becoming skilled in the use of these techniques for self-defence. Each animal technique also has its benefits on the health within the body as we are again looking at moving chi in a specific way with each form and if practiced correctly, the smooth flow of chi developed from each animal form will have a profound benefit to the chi of the body and its associated organs. If practiced incorrectly of course the chi flow may be impeded and this can lead to ill health developing within the body.

Therefore, competent instruction is required and attention to detail when practicing any Hsing-I forms in order to obtain the health benefits contained within them.

This chapter will discuss each animal in turn, describing its spirit (energetic) qualities and what each animal contributes to the body in terms of its health. There is no particular order to learning the Twelve Animal Forms and it varies from teacher to teacher on their preference. The actual forms themselves and their application in self-defence will be shown in the second part of this book.

1. Dragon – Lung Hsing

Dragon or 'Lung' as it is called in Chinese is a mythical animal and revered by the ancient Taoists for its abilities to reflect the incredible powers of nature. Its energetic attributes are to fold its bones or shrink itself and expand again, transforming itself at any given moment. It is said to live and swim in the seas and lakes and because of this it pertains to Yin and the element of Water. As the dragon belongs to water in nature it has the ability to control fire within and breathe it out to disperse it as required. The dragon also has the ability to fly and soar up to the heavens; therefore, it connects the energies of heaven and earth with its very spirit.

Dragon heads the list of the Twelve Animal Forms and its practice serves to train the body for rising and falling, contracting, expanding and stretching, retracting and extending the arms and hands and changing kicks while jumping. It is arguably the most physically demanding of the animal forms and serves to increase stamina and strengthen the muscles, tendons and bones required for combat.

When moving the Dragon form of Hsing-I incorporates rising and falling whilst travelling forwards in a straight line and its characteristics are to be tight and compact through its movements. When rising, jumping and changing the practitioner must be light and explosive but also on falling and landing they must be solid, balanced and coordinated.

As already stated Dragon pertains to Water, however there is an obvious influence of other elements within this form. Wood element can be seen with its straight, retracting and extending of both body and arms. The body when viewed from the side shows its ability to fold its bones and tendons in all segments. Also evident is the element of Metal and its energetic descending nature has a strong influence in the forms continuous changing of hand techniques which replicate the rising and falling of the dragon flying between ocean and sky. The intent of the chi within Dragon form is rising and falling and this is replicated in the combination of Woods ascending and Metals descending energetic natures. According to the five elements creative cycle the element of Water is positioned between these two elements and therefore is the mother of Wood and the child of Metal. All three elements are inseparably linked in the Dragon form.

When discussing Dragon form in relation to chi and health its practice is seen to reduce Yang fire in the body to a minimum. This is because the dragon is seen to be Yin in nature. When the Yin Water Chi naturally descends via the central pathway of Yin, the Ren meridian, it calms the rising fire of Yang within the body. On a physical level, the constant transformative powers of the dragon are reflected in the constant rising and falling, expanding and contracting, retracting and extending of the tendons, muscles and bones which promotes the flow of chi and blood around the body keeping it healthy.

The Dragon form must be performed in a controlled, harmonious but vigorous way to benefit the body and keep the internal Fire controlled. If this form is performed in an erratic and unbalanced way the chi flow will be impeded and injury both externally and internally may ensue. If the internal Fire is not controlled it may rise and consume Yin within, drying out the body and depriving the organs and tissues of nourishment from blood and fluids, ultimately upsetting the body's natural balance of Yin and Yang.

As the dragon is a mythical animal it is logical to think that ancient Taoists themselves have developed its characteristics and spiritual attributes. This suggests that the dragon is truly a reflection of man himself, conforming to the evolutionary theory of Heaven, Man and Earth where the dragon like man forms the connection between the energies of heaven and earth.

The dragon is thought of as a noble beast and the primary leader of all animals and with this in mind its character also reflects man at his most noble. As a species, humans are unique in that they have the brain and ability to create and manage complexity. This makes them arguably different from all other animals in their environment. Therefore, the spirit of the dragon is said to represent what is great and positive in the human spirit and is reflected in man's ability to think and strategise their actions and act for the greater good. When applied correctly in training, the spirit of the Dragon will have a positive influence on all the practitioners' forms and actions.

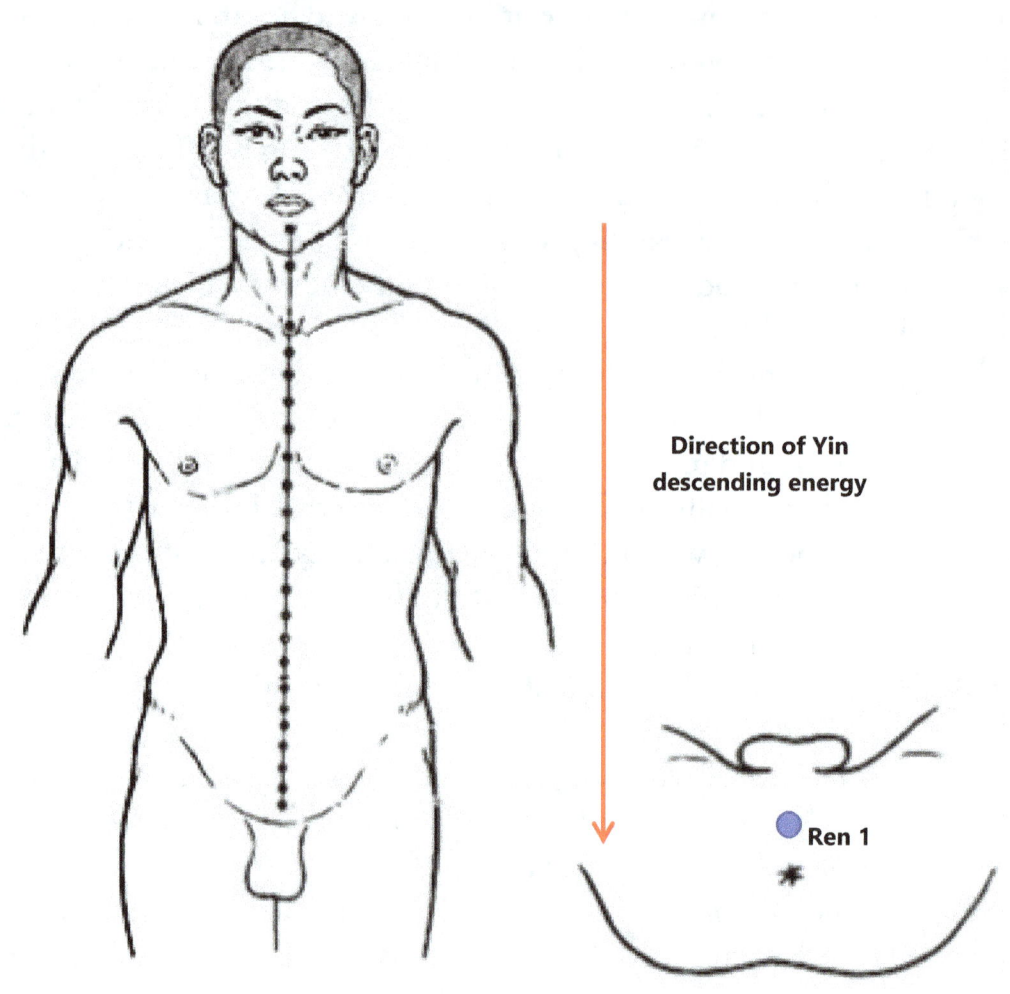

Ren Meridian Central Pathway of Yin

2. Tiger – Hu Hsing

The Tiger or 'Hu', as it is called in Chinese, is considered to be the king of all the animals. Sadly, once quite common the Chinese tiger is almost extinct in its natural habitat today. In the practice of Hsing-I the tiger spirit represents a form of internal strength developed from the Tan-Tien. It has a fierce external appearance and a great internal softness. The different hand and finger postures of Tiger form seek to represent the paws, claws, jaws and teeth of the tiger in application. Practice of this form can give one great power and confidence as in nature, the spirit of the tiger is fearless and ferocious in its attack. When it moves, it is with great speed, power and confidence and when it attacks nothing can stop it!

When fighting, the tiger pounces forward, leaping on its prey, using the rear legs as a stable base to push from. This method allows it to pounce large distances to close large distances, taking down animals much larger than itself. The intent of the chi in Tiger form is pounding, clawing, seizing, crushing, shaking and turning over, imitating the tiger's instinct to dominate and drag its catch to the ground. Like the Fire element to which it pertains, tiger's footwork is the same, driving forward from the front foot and pushing off the back foot.

When attacking using the Tiger form, the arms can push forward and down creating great internal pressure on the organs as they are forced down into the pelvic cavity or they can drive forward and upwards pushing the opponent back and off balance, either way it is a devastating technique when applied correctly.

Within this lineage there are five different forms of Tiger. All have the same footwork but a different hand form representing the different striking methods of the tiger in attack. The hand positions of clawing, pushing and striking can vary depending on the technique being performed but the powerful Yang energetic qualities of the tiger remain the same whatever the application. The whole body must move as one when executing any Tiger technique and the chi must issue forth from within. This leads to the saying "The wind follows the tiger" as in the wild the tiger will often attack from concealment and from different angles and heights which is similar to how the wind will change and blow from all directions without warning.

The tiger is seen to be Yang in nature and its energy starts at the Hui Yin point between the genitals and rises like smoke from a fire up to the top of the head via the Du meridian to point Bahui to nourish the brain. This rising chi flow follows the natural central pathway of Yang and when it is combined with the descending Yin energy of the Dragon form mentioned previously it completes the circuit of chi, known as the 'Little Nine Heaven Circulation'. Within Taoist internal practice this is often referred to as Dragon and Tiger copulating, which means the two working intimately together to produce a balanced flow of Yin and Yang within the body.

When practiced correctly, the Tiger form strengthens the quality of flow of chi to the organs and purifies breathing. The first posture of the form naturally opens the chest allowing the lungs within to expand to their maximum drawing clear air and chi down to the Tan Tien. On the second posture, with correct mental intent, the chi can be driven up the Du meridian and this ascending action helps to naturally clear Turbid Chi and stagnant air fully from the lungs. Therefore, the Tiger form efficiently exercises the respiratory system, in particular the respiratory muscles, and helps the body generate chi more efficiently.

If the Tiger form is practiced erratically the chi of the body will become stagnated and all the meridians and organs may be affected as the Yang energy of the Du meridian is the source of chi for all the meridians. If there isn't enough air drawn into the lungs, then there won't be enough raw material (oxygen) to help increase the formation of chi and fill the Tan Tien. If this is the case then there will be a natural deficiency of chi in the body and over time it will become weak and lethargic.

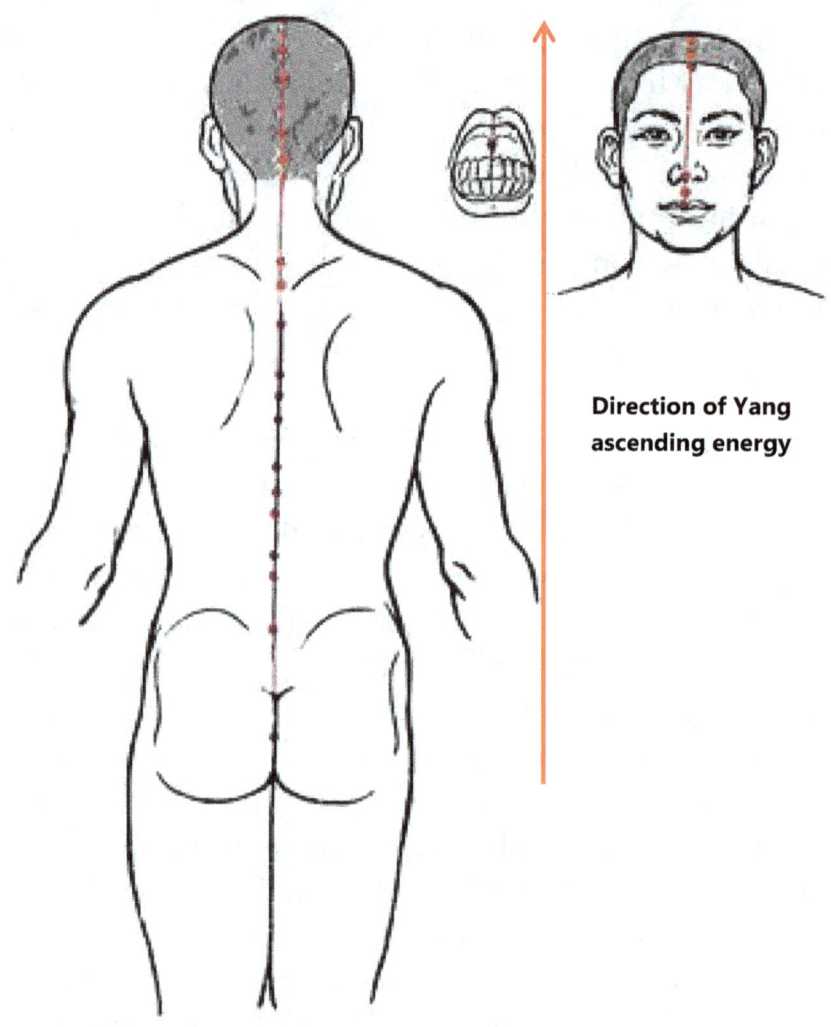

Du Meridian Central Pathway of Yang

3. Monkey – Hou Hsing

The Monkey, or 'Hou' as it is called in Chinese, is common to most Chinese regions. It is lively, active, resourceful and intelligent and is thought to be one of the smartest of the animals, showing the ability to weigh options, especially when being confronted by something physically more powerful than itself. The monkey has the ability to climb, jump and swing from tree to tree making it strong and athletic for its size. Its nature is free, confident and agile especially in its own mountain environment. Chinese legend says that one particularly crafty monkey even outwitted the gods by taking a peach from their table and in eating it, achieving immortality becoming known as 'The Monkey King.'

Monkeys use their agile hands and feet for many purposes and when they fix their intent on something, especially food, they will usually find a way to get what they want. When threatened the monkey will often back off at first, cleverly weighing up his options, then, when the time is right, it will attack vulnerable points with speed and accuracy from different levels, before quickly retreating to a safe distance again. If a monkey is cornered or frightened, it will use a fast slapping defence against its aggressor.

The spirit of the monkey can be seen in the Hsing-I form and it is one of the more complex forms to learn. This is because the attack has to be powerful, light, fast and accurate but also has to come from a stable base and this combination of skills can be difficult to master. It is for this reason it is often taught towards the end of the Twelve Animal Forms. Within the form there are crossing steps, twists and opposing hand/foot combinations in both a forwards and backwards motion which seek to replicate the complexities of the monkey spirit.

To gain competency in the Monkey form the practitioner needs to be clever and cunning and look for opportunities to apply the technique. Over time, if practiced correctly, they will develop a lightness in their body and footwork, whilst still retaining the stability and balance to issue power effectively through the fast, multiple slaps inherent in the Monkey form. When fighting, do not underestimate the power of a slap; if trained correctly and targeted to the right areas a trained slap can be fatal.

The complex variation of energies displayed in Monkey form are seen in the varied pathways in which its techniques manifest themselves and is only limited by the practitioner's ability to apply it. The intent of the chi in Monkey form is opening, closing, evading, climbing, falling, offering, grabbing, springing, slapping and deceiving.

The energetic character of the monkey pertains to the element Fire and therefore, the heart organ. The heart is the seat of the emotions and houses the spirit within the body so when practiced correctly the cleverness and stability required of the Monkey form will benefit the mind by keeping the emotions focused, stable and balanced. If the Heart Chi is balanced then the spirit will flourish and sit comfortably within, leaving the practitioner feeling calm, quiet and controlled whatever the situation.

If practiced erratically the mind will become confused and unbalanced. If the Heart Chi is not balanced it will not anchor down the spirit within but will rise instead and become chaotic in the head. This symptom is known as 'the monkey mind' and its mischievousness, another characteristic of the monkey, will lead the practitioner astray in their training and cause them to panic when fighting.

4. Horse – Ma Hsing

The Horse, or 'Ma' as it is called in Chinese, is a fast and powerful animal full of life and energy; it has great stamina and a strong heart. While engaged in fighting, a horse will rise up on its hind legs and strike repeatedly with its front hooves, mimicking the way it gallops and utilising this natural action to defend itself. In the application of this form, the movement of the upper and lower parts of the body must be balanced properly. This will show the strong and powerful characteristics of the Horse form.

When the horse stands on its rear legs it raises its height to be more dominant in attack. It attacks with speed, striking out forward, up or down depending on its situation. Its centre remains over the back legs and, therefore, requires excellent balance and stability to execute its attacks efficiently. If a horse sees a gap in a fence or wall it will instinctively bolt straight through it and with this mindset when applying the strategy of Horse form in a fighting situation the practitioner should be constantly on the lookout for a gap in their opponent's defence. If a gap is spotted they should aim to penetrate straight through it in attack!

When practicing Horse form in Hsing-I, the weight must remain heavily over the back foot and use this loading of the power to drive straight forward from the ground, channelling this energy up through the body and out through the arms into the opponent. It is important to stay balanced and solid throughout both the first and second postures of the form.

Horse form pertains to the element Fire and has similar twisting and turning actions of the forearms throughout its movements as practiced in Fire form. This torque through the arms gives the muscles and tendons increased strength in application. The intent of the chi in Horse form is driving forward, leaping and trampling. Speed in manoeuvring and a keen sense of anticipation are key to its successful application. These are all energies that can be seen in the Horse form and in the strategy used to apply it in self-defence.

The character of the horse is that of a loyal animal, honourable and pious in its actions. This represents the consciousness within the body and connects with the emotions. This connection with the emotional mind means it aligns with the heart organ. When practiced correctly with smooth and harmonious movements, Horse form will strengthen the chi of the heart. This in turn will keep the emotions calm, reducing anger within, which can easily arise under stressful situations such as fighting. By keeping the emotions calm, the breathing pattern also will remain calm and this will help keep the brain supplied with clear chi, rich in oxygen allowing the practitioner to think clearly and act honourably. When executed correctly the Horse form will appear assured, confident and be successful in its attack. If practiced erratically, the breathing pattern will become erratic and the mind confused. This will lead to anger and frustration in the technique and the practitioner will act rashly and be easily defeated.

5. Tortoise – Tuo Hsing

The Tortoise, or 'Tuo' (Tow) as this form is called in Chinese, is a powerful animal, especially when in its natural habitat of water. Within the different lineages of Hsing-I this animal form alludes to many different names. In this lineage, it is referred to as Tortoise but this is more of a literary translation as when spoken, the word 'Tuo' sounds similar to 'Totle' which can easily be taken to mean 'Turtle' or 'Tortoise'. In fact, when researched in more detail the animal 'Tuo' was deemed to be a mythical one, similar to a crocodile but also part dragon. This is because to the Chinese in ancient times the crocodile, which is thought to have evolved and survived over the last 100 million years, was classed in the same category of species along with the turtle and dragon.

This classification pertaining to Tuo came from Chinese legend, where it was said that the father of all dragons produced nine sons. All the sons looked entirely different from their father and each was said to have its own habitat and special powers. Tuo was one of them, and he lived in water, resembling the crocodile. According to legend the Tuo animal was said to have possessed magical powers and seemingly impossible skills in both the water and on the land.

The similarity of Tuo form to the crocodile fits well, as the crocodile would be well known to the ancient Chinese population where they were commonly found throughout large areas of China. Today they are more commonly found in areas surrounding the Yangtze River which passes through Hubei province, one of the cradles of Hsing-I development. When the form of Tuo is considered from an energetic perspective it is easy to envisage the characteristics of the crocodile or a similar mythical animal in its movements and applications. Therefore, the lineage in this book refers to this animal as Tuo rather than a more recognisable Western name in order to try and avoid any ambiguity between other animals and lineages. Regardless of which translation is used for this animal, the common denominator is that all the main Hsing-I lineages call this animal Tuo regardless of how they choose to translate it.

When training in the form of Tuo it is particularly important to coordinate the movements of the upper and lower parts of the body. The whole body must be lively and resilient, with the emphasis placed on turning the waist, which constitutes the centre of movement for the whole body. This movement at the waist is similar to that of the crocodile or similar reptile when moving on both land and water, twisting from side to side as it goes.

The general characteristics of the Tuo are its ability to be totally still and wait for the moment to strike; it can also move very quickly for short distances and strike from different angles. It has a strong body which it uses to great effect when it rapidly rotates itself after taking hold of its prey thrashing and twisting, taking it down under the water to its death.

Therefore, the intent of the chi in this form is dividing, rolling, thrashing, twisting and springing and this can be seen in the twisting, rotating, striking, throwing or taking down of the opponent in the many practical applications of Tuo when fighting.

When practicing Tuo form, the back must remain straight and all the joints must move smoothly and remain supple. When the body is turned from side to side the waist should be strong, flexible and lead the movement. The footwork should turn from side to side similar to that of the crocodile, the waist must turn and the hands must crossover in time with the feet. All movements should start together and end together from stillness to movement and back to total stillness again.

The emphasis on the turning of the waist and the crossing and rolling of the arms shows its close link to the element of Earth and, therefore Tuo pertains to the spleen and stomach organs. Correct practice of this form will enhance the production of chi from the stomach to the Tan Tien. It will also help the spleen to transport and transform chi around the body and in particular, help raising clear chi to the head allowing clear and concise thought. It will also help with digestive problems by massaging the organs and their meridians in the body's middle and lower Jiao's respectively.

The muscles whose quality is governed by the spleen will also be nourished and movement of the body will be strong, supple and smooth. When the energy between the inside of the body and the movements on the outside of the body is completely balanced it is said "The practitioner will be able to float in complete stillness on top of the water just like the magical ability of the Tuo."

If practiced erratically this form may injure the digestive process, wasting of the muscles maybe seen and organs maybe prone to prolapse due to the spleen not raising the chi efficiently and holding up the structures of the body. Thought may also become clouded and body and head may feel heavy and lethargic. Movement will become disjointed and this will affect balance and flexibility.

6. Cock – Gi Hsing

The Cock (Rooster) form, or 'Gi' as it is called in Chinese, has a combined series of movements imitating the attributes of the cock. The cockerel is born with a naturally competitive nature, ideal for fighting. It will fight bravely and its spirit never gives in, it is persistent and will often fight to the death. When fighting, the cock has the ability to stand on one leg and shake its wings and feathers, making it seem much larger than it is. It uses its spurs and beak to deadly accuracy and will protect its female brood at all costs. It can appear arrogant and 'cocky' as it struts around but this should not be taken lightly as it is intelligent in using its attributes to best advantage.

The intent of the chi in Cock form is advancing, retreating, rising, lowering, grabbing, pulling, pecking and stamping, using the various movements of its wings and feet, along with changes of the body, to bring about a state of confusion in one's opponent. The cock sometimes fights standing on one leg and some movements within the form imitate this characteristic. Cock form trains agility and coordination through the combination of body, hand and footwork. In practice, the form must be confident, fast, accurate and well balanced.

On the physical level, Cock form pertains to the element Wood and the influence of this element can be clearly seen in some of the movements with straight line forward attacks and open and closed footwork consistent with Wood form. On an energetic level, it aligns to the liver and gall bladder organs. Correct practice of Cock form strengthens the liver function and therefore, has a positive effect on the smooth flow of chi from the Tan Tien and circulation of blood throughout the whole body, as this is a major responsibility of the liver organ in TCM. It is said that Cock also pertains to the wind as this is the climate associated to Wood element. Externally the wind can be seen in the way with the speed that the cockerel can move when fighting. Internally the wind refers to the breath and correct practice will enhance the respiratory function and improve its capacity. When Cock form rises to one leg the mental intent raises clear chi from the ground or foot to the top of the head and on falling then drops the chi from the head, dispersing it around the whole body to nourish all tissues. In effect, these actions connect the upper body with the lower in its spread of chi.

Finally, if Cock form is practiced erratically, the raising of pure chi to the head will be affected and therefore thought, vision, hearing and poorly coordinated limb function will occur due to disharmony in the upper and lower segments creating an imbalance between Yin and Yang within the practitioner.

7. Phoenix – Tai Hsing

The Phoenix or 'Tai' as it is called in Chinese is a mythical bird of Taoist legend and is thought to be a sign of good luck. Some lineages have different names for Tai such as ostrich, flycatcher or various hawks, to name a few, though some are not even native birds to China which makes them a strange choice as a translation. However, this is no different than saying it is mythical bird in the fact that how does anyone truly know what it looks like or fights like ?

The important thing to understand is the spirit and energetic actions of the animal is what the practitioner is trying to emulate. Legendary stories and depictions of old from China help create mental and physical images of the Tai bird and, just like the Dragon and Tuo mentioned earlier. The attributes of the animal in question can be deemed and recreated from this information.

In ancient legend, the Tai bird is represented by the sign of two birds, one female and one male. Entwined together, they die engulfed in flames and from the flames the phoenix rises from their ashes with its mighty wings lifting it skyward. When the phoenix flaps its wings, it emphasises its form and intention and the power generated from the flapping of the wings is said to be able to knock anything over that gets in its path. Its attributes are that it is strong, fast and agile in flight soaring high towards the heavens and then diving down towards the earth and swooping up again.

Within the Phoenix form the practitioner seeks to imitate this movement of the wings with their arms and fists. The footwork used is the same as Fire form allowing the phoenix to rise from the ashes and this action provides a strong and stable base to issue power from. Simultaneously the arms raise together towards the skies and cross like the intertwining wings of the phoenix, protecting the head and body, blocking all in its path. It uses the power of the circling of the arms to deflect any oncoming attack rather than meeting it head on, opening a gap in the attacker's defence before swooping down to attack a vulnerable opening. The key to gaining complete power in this technique is to combine the energy of the lower body with the upper body like a wave from the ground travelling through the legs and body and out through the arms.

The intent of the chi within the Phoenix form is to rise and fall in an instant; circle, roll over, cover, fly through and change from curved to straight. It pertains to the elements of both Water and Fire as it is a balance of these two elements within the body that lead to a balance of Yin and Yang respectively. Within the body it represents the kidneys which in TCM theory are the root of Yin and Yang and the foundation of prenatal life. The left kidney represents Yin/Water and is responsible for cooling the body via the water metabolism; the right kidney represents Yang/Fire and is responsible for maintaining the fire of 'Ming Men' or the gate of life and its function is to warm the body.

Practice of the Phoenix form promotes circulation of the Du (Yang) meridian upwards and Ren (Yin) meridian downwards and strengthens the kidneys. When the form flies upwards, if combined with the correct breath and intent of the mind, the chi will follow and likewise, as the form swoops down, so will the chi. When Phoenix form is practiced correctly the Ren and Du circulation will be smooth and the 'Little Nine Heaven circulation' will be complete. These two meridians provide and store chi for all other organs and their associated meridians so a smooth flow in their circulation will benefit the whole body. If practiced erratically, fire and water will fail to control one another and the body may become too hot or cold internally. If this imbalance remains for long, the Yin/Yang balance of all the organs will be affected and illness and disease will ensue.

8. Sparrow-Hawk – Yao Hsing

The 'Sparrow-Hawk', or 'Yao' as it is called in Chinese, is a bird of prey that looks similar to the eagle but is much smaller. In nature, it shows its strengths when it dives and twists through the air and back to the ground with great speed and agility to catch its prey. It can fly through the trees with great accuracy weaving and rolling through the foliage, but when it spots its target with sharp eyes, it can pierce through the forest canopy with great accuracy, flying fast, hard and straight, giving its prey no chance of escape.

When practicing this form, the practitioner should seek to imitate the open claws of the sparrow-hawk. In transition between the postures, the arms cross over close to the body emulating the folding of the wings of the sparrow-hawk in flight when it passes through the branches and prepares to dive and seize its prey. The overall movement of the form emphasises twisting from the ground and feet, up through the body and this energy continues to twist and issue forth through the arms and hands.

In application, the eyes and spirit must be alert throughout this form looking for an opportunity to pierce through the opponent's guard going straight for the vital points, stunning and taking them to the ground to finish the attack. This strategy mimics the sharp penetrating abilities of the sparrow-hawk in attacking its prey in mid-air and stunning it before taking it to the ground for the kill. The technique should be fast and agile with perfect timing required of the whole body in a real fighting application. This makes the Sparrow-Hawk one of the more complicated of the animals to master.

The intent of the chi in Sparrow-Hawk form is to turn, roll over, penetrate, sink, rise, fall, seize, contract and expand. The physical rotating nature of the form links it closely with the element of Earth and, therefore, it pertains closely to the centre of the body and the Tan Tien. Correct practise of the Sparrow-Hawk form fills the Tan-Tien with chi; it further exercises the hypogastric area between the navel and pubic bone, greatly benefitting the deep abdominal muscles and the lower Jiao organs of the digestive system (large intestine and small intestine and bladder), which are heavily involved in the process of extracting essence from foods and liquids and processing them into chi. Further to this the organs of the lower Jiao are responsible for the expelling of toxic waste from the body keeping it healthy. The rotation of the whole body in this technique also benefits all the meridians of the twelve organs by massaging them internally and, therefore, has a benefit on the whole body.

Erratic practise of this form can lead to digestive problems and general weakness of energy throughout the body, as the extraction of chi from food and fluids becomes impaired. When energy to the lower Jiao is insufficient it stagnates, becoming blocked rather like a grid in a drainage system. When the grid becomes blocked the waste builds up and the body becomes toxic leading to ill health and disease.

9. Swallow – Yen Hsing

The 'Swallow', or 'Yen' as it is called in Chinese, is a very small bird with long and powerful wings. It can fly at a very high rate of speed skimming across the water and is very light and swift. The swallow is not a bird which one normally thinks as a fighter but when attacked, it can intimidate intruders by swooping down upon them and catching them off guard. When fighting, the swallow constantly changes its angles and height of attack, making it very difficult to anticipate and defend against. The intent of the chi in Swallow form is rising, falling, forwards, backwards, circling, rolling, crossing over, swooping, catching and skimming.

When practicing Swallow form, the movements are more varied and subtle than some of the other animal forms. This makes it more challenging to learn and is usually studied towards the end of the animal forms as skill in the other forms helps prepare the body for the more physically demanding aspects of the Swallow form.

The form imitates the swooping and skimming action of the swallow in flight. For example: if someone attacks high at the head the practitioner can dive down and catch the opponent's leg, pulling it out from under them. The form requires impeccable timing and flexibility but also stamina and strength to execute the moves swiftly with the coordination and balance of the swallow. Within the form there are quick circling movements, attack and defence techniques at different heights and subtle interchanging hand and footwork which links the individual postures of the form. In practicing this form, the practitioner will learn that by moving the head and shoulders back just a little they are able to evade a blow and swiftly counter attack. All the movements must flow as smoothly as the swallow skimming the surface of the water to be effective in a fighting application.

Internally, the challenging nature of this form stimulates the brain and will keep the body full of spirit. Swallow form pertains to the element of Water and the organ of the kidneys. When practiced correctly, the upward postures of the form draw the Water energy of the kidney naturally upwards to help the body keep the Fire energy of the heart under control. This is in accordance with the Tao, in balancing Yin and Yang in the body.

The physical movements of rising and falling within the form help the upper and lower body unite and this is good for the circulation of chi, keeping the body strong and free from stagnation. The physical demands of falling and swooping, crossing over and rising help strengthen the tissues, muscles and tendons and keep them supple. Further to this when the physical structures are nourished through repetitive relaxation and contraction the chi will flow smoothly, keeping the body healthy and free from injury.

If practiced erratically, movements will look clumsy, uncoordinated and injury may occur due to lack of flexibility and control of the joints. Internally the Water energy of the kidney will not cool efficiently and, therefore, allow Fire energy to flare out of control. This internal fire will affect the emotional mind housed in the heart and create confusion in the wisdom mind housed in the brain leading to poor decision making. If the body's Water energy does not flow smoothly then it will stagnate and cause chi flow stagnation to all organs via the meridians which will lead to illness and poor health.

10. Snake – Sher Hsing

The 'Snake', or 'Sher' as it is called in Chinese, is a legless reptile, which can move quickly and silently. It is common in all areas of China and is represented by many different species. In nature, it has the ability to conceal itself and attack suddenly with devastating accuracy. The snake is a very sensitive reptile sensing the energy around by flicking out its tongue.

Due to the snake's length and flexibility it is able to attack animals with either its head, its body and tail or both simultaneously. In attack, the snake can move from side to side making it hard to predict. Some snakes can strike fast with a venomous and deadly bite, others have long strong powerful muscles in their bodies which they can use to wrap around their prey and literally constrict the life from them.

Snake form is one of the earlier animals to be learned in most Hsing-I lineages and is a simple form to practice and understand as a lot of its applications are obvious. However, as with all Hsing-I's forms often the simpler they appear the harder they are to master. Within Snake form there are many subtleties to be understood in particular, the skill of sensitivity when controlling and coiling against an opponent. Learning touch, feeling, sensitivity and technique are key skills to master and they are only developed over many years of regular practice.

When practicing snake form, the practitioner seeks to imitate the spirit and physical attributes of the snake. The intent of the chi is to rise, fall, extend, contract, constrict, coil and shoot forward. These energetic qualities are demonstrated in the Snake form when rising and extending in the first posture with the arm and hand blocking high, only then to coil, contract and fall, moving smoothly, quickly and silently striking out and forward into the second posture to complete the attack.

In the application of Snake form, the practitioner aims to control and coil around their opponent and create opportunities to take them to the ground in many ways. They also learn to constrict their opponent's movements and finish the attack with either a devastating strike to a vital point or by choking them unconscious. The movement and particularly, the footwork, must be agile and quick allowing the change of angle in attack to be undetected. Throughout all applications the upper and lower body must remain coordinated and solid to effectively apply the different types of energy contained within the varied applications of the Snake form.

It is said that practice of the Snake form in Hsing-I has the effect of rubbing positive and negative energies together meaning the Yin and Yang energies of the body being harmonised. Within the body the Snake form pertains to the element of Water and is, therefore, related to the kidney organs. The kidney organs represent both Yin and Yang and are the source of fire and water within our bodies. The rising and falling of the Snake form when combined with the intent of the rising and falling of the chi has a cause and effect of Yang rising upwards and Yin flowing downwards, naturally rubbing together. This means working together to form a balanced cycle of energy throughout the body's meridians allowing the chi of all the channels to remain abundant and the body vibrant.

When practiced erratically, the natural flow of Yin and Yang will be interrupted and the body will become unbalanced. This will lead to clumsy, uncoordinated movements externally and slow illogical decision making internally. Fire chi will become restricted, affecting it from rising naturally to the head by Water chi which due to the Water element associated to Snake form has a propensity to become the more dominant force.

11. Eagle/Bear – Ying/Xiong Hsing

The 'Eagle/Bear', or 'Ying/Xiong' as it translates in Chinese, is the combination of the Eagle and Bear styles. The form features the integration of the accuracy and boldness of an eagle in seizing its prey, with the vigor and uprightness of the bear defending itself. Some lineages of Hsing-I separate these styles and practice them as individual animal forms. Others, including this one, practice the two animals as one combined form.

Classic Hsing-I literature suggests that this form may have developed from watching an eagle and a bear in confrontation, however, as interesting as this concept sounds it has not been factually proven. Some literature also suggests that the form 'Eagle/Bear' should be 'Bear/Eagle' and states that "the 'Bear Eagle' is actually one animal in the form of a bird of prey found in China and that some aspects of its character mimic that of a bear as well as an eagle when it fights". This may also be true but the question then is why do some schools separate the characteristic of one bird into two separate animal forms? Furthermore, if they are practicing a form that is thought of as a bird but in truth they are thinking that it fights like a bear, then truly they are fighting like a bear and not like a bird. Regardless of the belief of any lineage, school or teacher, the simple fact is that when practicing this form, the practitioner seeks to emulate the energetic spirit of the eagle and the bear which have different qualities associated with them. In some lineages of Hsing-I, the Eagle and Bear forms are practised as separate animal forms, however, in the system of Hsing-I shown in this book, Master Hsu Hong Chi, combined both Eagle and Bear forms to create a single form.

When practising the Eagle/Bear form from this lineage, the first posture seeks to show the spirit of the Eagle and the second posture represents the spirit of the Bear. In executing both postures of the form, the practitioner must keep the head, neck and body straight, which is referred to as 'standing upright like a bear'. For ease of description it is best to split the form into two separate movements and discuss the Eagle posture first. The attributes of the eagle are that it effortlessly circles in the sky and has very sharp vision. The intent of the chi within the Eagle form is splitting, seizing, pinching, circling, shooting forward, rising and falling. When its prey is spotted the eagle dives with speed and accuracy, hitting with power and using its sharp claws to grasp the prey, giving it no chance of escape.

In the first posture, the practitioner must circle and be agile with their footwork, keeping it light and balanced throughout. The spirit must be raised and the eyes sharp looking for an opportunity to strike. The arms must move quickly, striking through the guard and penetrating deep into the vital areas of the opponent, seizing or grasping them and pulling and tearing to control and create maximum damage to the target point.

The method of the Eagle can be used as a standalone technique in fighting or it can be immediately followed by the second posture of the Bear. From the grasping controlling aspect of the Eagle follows the raw power, strength and stability of the Bear to finish off the attack. The attributes of the bear are strength, stability, size and a dominating spirit and belief that nothing can stop its attack.

The intent of the chi in Bear form is striking, pounding, slashing, rising, falling, crushing, rooting and moving relentlessly forward. The practitioner's arms must have the strength to overturn the arm of their attacker and the hands must drop like the heavy pounding of the bear's paws. To gain the power of the bear in their attack, their feet must be rooted and solid with the ground. The back must remain straight and then the power can be passed through the legs and waist into the shoulders; this way they will generate full body power in their strike. Once in attack, they must move forward dominating their opponent, pounding, blocking and striking with each swipe of the hands. The body should remain erect throughout and the hands and feet must move in perfect harmony. When combining the two postures as one form, the transition from one style to another must be seamless and the head should remain level at all times.

The combined practice of Eagle/Bear form aids in the circulation of breath and balance of Yin and Yang energies within the body. The Eagle is said to be Yang on the outside and Yin on the inside. It is very aggressive and active externally in attack, but at the same time, internally it is calm, clearsighted and calculated, using skill to win its fights. Eagle is the yin posture of the combined Eagle/Bear form as the movements are predominantly drawing energy inward and then shooting out, clawing inwards aggressively and thus require calculation and skill to apply when fighting.

This is a direct opposite of the Bear, which is said to be Yin on the outside; slower, heavier, and generally less agile in attack than the eagle. When attacking, the Bear's Yang energy suddenly burst forth from within like a rage rising inside and from this observation it is said to be Yang on the inside. Its movement is arguably more forceful than skilled, overwhelming its prey with sheer power and strength rather than precision. This means that the solo practice of Eagle/Bear as a combined form perfectly harmonises the balance of Yin and Yang energies within the body.

Internally, the very Yin nature of circling and drawing in of the Eagle form in the first posture, combined with the in-breath down to the Tan Tien and raising chi to the head, gives the clear acute vision attributed to the eagle. The Yang nature of Bear form then follows this, with the opening of the chest and the downward strike in time with the expelling of the breath. When practiced correctly the form of Eagle/Bear reflects a perfect balance of Yin and Yang within the body. The sequence of movements harmonises the breath and benefits the respiratory system.

When practiced erratically, the Yin and Yang energies become unbalanced which leads to unclear thinking and uncoordinated movements of the limbs. If Yang becomes dominant, heat will develop within and this will agitate the emotional mind. If Yin dominates, the body will become heavy, lethargic and weak and the wisdom mind will become unclear. If the breath is not harmonised, production of chi will be inefficient and the health will decline.

12. Fighting Chicken – Dou Gi Hsing

The Fighting Chicken, or 'Dou Gi' as it is called in Chinese, has great physical power and courage for fighting. Today we think of the chicken as a domesticated bird as over the years the natural fighting spirit has been bred out of it and it is often kept in controlled environments for use as part of the food chain. The wild chicken though is a vastly different character and can be extremely brave when protecting its young. In a fight, chickens; both male and female, will often fight to the death and although not the best animal in flight, the chicken is brave and spirited. Its natural habitat is in the forests on ground level and due to its highly coloured feathers, it is a standout target. Because of this it needs to use its natural attributes to defend itself against often much more dominant attackers.

The main attributes of the fighting chicken are its claws, spurs, beak and wings. It is also incredibly fast, agile and can dive and weave, bobbing its head to evade oncoming attacks. To strike back the chicken needs to be brave enough to stay in range of the attack, evading the blows and then be able to counter, therefore, it must be very surefooted and balanced when under intense pressure in a life or death situation.

In the practice of Fighting Chicken form, the 'Chicken Step Method' is of paramount importance as this footwork can be utilised effectively in combination with any other of the elements or animal forms, allowing the practitioner to generate increased power on the strike when combined with the swift change of feet in time with the hands. Furthermore, this footwork makes the practitioner very light and agile when fighting, allowing them to change foot, deceive or stamp on the opponent and still be in range to counter. The arms remain close in to the body throughout the form to protect the ribs and heart and rise and fall like the furious flapping of the wings, to get inside an opponent's attack and allow for a strike at their vital points. The hands form the posture of the chicken's beak and can attack eyes and soft targets with great effect. On the turn the arms fly out like flapping wings to block or strike in any direction, the body can drop, duck and fly back up in a blink of an eye, such is the agility of the chicken. The intent of the chi in the Chicken form is forwards, backwards, expand, contract, shake, drill, peck, pluck, rise and fall.

As the chicken is in the same animal category as the cock it therefore pertains to Wood element and it links closely to the liver and gall bladder organs. Correct practice of Chicken form strengthens the liver energy and, therefore, has a positive effect on the smooth flow of chi from the Tan Tien and circulation of blood throughout the whole body, as this is a major responsibility of the liver organ in TCM. Chicken form also benefits respiration and breathing in the body and regular practice will enhance the respiratory function. When Chicken form rises and falls during the turn it raises clear chi from the heels to the top of the head and on falling the chi then drops from the head, dispersing it around the whole body to nourish all tissues. In effect Chicken form connects the upper body with the lower in its spread of chi.

When Chicken form is practiced erratically, the head will lack the pure ascending chi associated with the liver and Wood element and thought, vision, hearing, dizziness, headaches and poorly coordinated limb function may occur as the upper and lower segments of the body are in disharmony. Smooth flow of chi and blood may also be generally affected leading potentially to ill health and disease.

Chapter 14

Fighting Theory of Hsing-I Chuan

General Yue Fei

There are many different articles which have been written about the fighting tactics used to apply the techniques of Hsing-I. Most have been translated from the 'Ten Important Theses' thought to be written by General Yue Fei and which have been passed down through the various lineages over time. These Ten Theses form the basis from which most Hsing-I articles and documents have been written by subsequent masters over the centuries and cover all aspects of the art.

When studying other commentaries on these Ten Theses the reader may find some variation in their translations, often some copies tend to repeat themselves and this is probably due to the way they have been passed down and preserved over the centuries. Different masters and lineages have remembered and recorded them differently and created slight variations in the written documents we read today. However, in essence they all still contain the same information which is the foundation of classical Hsing-I Chuan theory.

The tenth thesis is titled 'Jiao Shou Lun' which translates as 'The Thesis of Fighting'. It is a few pages in length when written in Chinese characters and lengths of the commentaries vary by the individual translators. Below is a summarised content of this tenth thesis which is written in its translated form in bold type and combined with a commentary relevant to the content of this book which is written in standard text directly underneath the relevant section of the thesis. Master McNeil has also written a commentary in support of this chapter based from his own experiences in applying Hsing-I in fighting situations.

The remaining nine theses themselves are not printed in this book as they are already well documented in the general Hsing-I literature already available. If a practitioner wants to study the 'Ten Important Theses of Yue Fei' for themselves then they should obtain a copy accompanied by a well written commentary.

'The Theses of Fighting' by General Yeuh Fei

"When attacking, the hands must move together as one, the feet must take root and be solid. When striking, the chi must come from the very core, the bones of the body".

Regardless of whether you are in a real fighting situation or practising, when you initiate an attack your whole body must be coordinated. Your feet must be stable and rooted to the ground in order to provide a solid platform from which to issue power. Both hands must work together – one attacking and issuing energy out and the other defending and withdrawing in readiness for the next strike. Both hands must work in unison thereby complying with the laws of Yin and Yang. The marrow situated deep within the bones is the source for chi and blood. When you attack your mental and physical intent should raise and direct your chi from the marrow and through the strike, in effect coming from your very core. The marrow reflects the depth of this intent and as coming from your very core, described in the theses. When this is achieved your attack will issue chi efficiently. It will be true and cannot be stopped.

"When striking, the mind leads the chi and throughout, the body remains relaxed. At the point of contact with the opponent, the fist should tighten up".

When the skill level is sufficient the mind and body will be relaxed even in stressful situations. When the body is physically relaxed the chi can flow smoothly within the meridians, this allows the heart and mind to remain clear and focused. When the heart and mind are clear there will be no panic which causes the chi to scatter. Only then can the heart and mind harmonise as they guide the chi and initiate an appropriate action to any situation. When attacking the body must remain relaxed so the chi can reach its target without hindrance of tense muscle and tissue. Any tension of the body structure will slow the technique down and reduce its power as it will be working antagonistically against the direction of the attack. Only when the attack hits its target should the fist or part of the body that is striking tighten up as this transfers added strength to the point of the strike and reduces the potential for self-injury. This level of skill is only accomplished after many years of practice and competence in all techniques has been achieved.

"When advancing forward, feel the ground with the heels first. When using the fists, curl in the fingers to make them strong. When grasping an opponent, use chi. When entering or exiting in a confrontation, let the heart command. Keep the elbows lowered and the hands positioned correctly. The action of the fist is initiated in the heart and activated by the body. When one branch moves, hundreds of branches follow. When the hand grabs, it is through the action of the whole body. Regardless of the striking method, all must follow each other. Use the front gate to attack; this is the method".

When moving in a fighting situation your feet should step carefully. Footwork and feeling are the key to a successful outcome in a fighting situation as it sets you up to attack and helps you evade in defence. If you lose your footing at a crucial moment you may easily lose the fight. If your footwork is not stable you will not issue maximum power on your strike. By stepping carefully placing the heel first it allows you to feel the ground below before placing your whole bodyweight through the foot. This keeps you agile and allows you the opportunity to change step or direction as quickly as is required. Remember when fighting the situation is in constant change and you must react to your opponent's step as well as dictate your own.

When you draw in the fist, curl your fingers in tightly, drawing in the little finger of each hand first, with each finger following in succession. This method will make the tightest possible fist and reduce the possibility of self-injury when you strike an opponent. In making a fist in this way it will also coil your forearm muscles making the whole arm and technique stronger. This coiling method is like the tensioning of steel wire where the individual strands of wire are placed together and twisted tightly. The energy stored within the wires combined twisted strands binds them and increases their strength. This same effect happens in the body with the energy of chi binding together the muscles and tissues to increase their strength.

When you grab an opponent, you must do so with intention. You not only grab with your hand but with your mind and whole body also. When you can combine the mind with your chi and transfer this effectively into your technique it will have tremendous effect on your opponent. Remember in Hsing-I it is said all movements on the outside are initiated first from the emotional mind on the inside. The emotional mind is housed in the heart. Therefore, whether you are advancing, retreating, attacking or defending all your intentions must come straight from the heart.

At all times, the elbows should be lowered to protect vital areas of the body. This position also helps them store chi effectively within the joints for attack. The hands must also be alive and ready to respond to the constant changing situations in a fight. When this is done, they are in their correct position!

When a movement is initiated in Hsing-I the whole body must move as one unit. This skill is highlighted in the perfection of the 'Six Harmonies'. This coordination of both mind and movement is reinforced in the saying "When one branch moves, hundreds of branches follow."

When attacking your opponent, it is beneficial to "Occupy their front door!" This means to step directly into their centreline. This is often achieved by continually driving your front foot in attack directly between the opponent's feet using the half-step method most. Continually achieving this objective will give you the advantage and put your opponent under a constant threat. When practicing Hsing-I forms this is why it is important to constantly move forward in a straight line using the half-step method.

"The bones must be aligned to create strength. The hands must be fast and must not be delayed. Follow up from striking to be successful. The heart must remain cold and the eyes focussed. When hands and feet are alive, they are threatening. The practitioner must be brave and fierce in combat, like a wild animal. The face remains still, the mind's intent is venomous. Use the intelligence of the scholar, move the body like thunder and lightning".

The three sections of the body (head, torso, legs) must be in harmony. This is the 'Body of the Dragon' and its ability to fold and expand the bones must be mastered in all the techniques of Hsing-I. When the three sections are aligned the strength will be realised and the technique will be true.

When the spirit is alert the eyes will see with the acute vision of the eagle. This will allow the opportunity to see the opening and strike ahead of your opponent. To do this the hands must be faster than your opponents and your feet more agile. As soon as you strike you must be ready to strike again and press home your advantage. This way the opponent will remain on the back foot.

All your techniques must be initiated from a cold heart and this way any emotions will not get in the way of decision making. A moment's hesitation or self-doubt and the advantage may be lost. When the heart is cold, action will be fast and the chi will be directed straight to the target. Inside the mind remains calm and your intent will not be given away as your face shows only stillness. To utilise your skill you must think with the logic and brain of a learned scholar, not act like a mindless drunk and strike unannounced like thunder erupting from a storm.

"Observe your adversary and how their body moves. When their feet move to the east, be alert to danger attacking from the west. When the top is empty, the bottom must be full. Strategy must be used to create openings in order to be

victorious. When rising, expect falling and vice versa. One always follows the other. Turn like a tiger in the wild. When not moving like a scholar, employ the skills of the dragon and tiger. If the distance is far, do not strike. When attacking from the right, intercept with the right and vice versa. This is the quickest method. At long range, use the foot. At close range, use the elbow or knee".

When you are fighting you must carefully analyse your opponent's strategy and gauge your own. This is thinking like a scholar. There is a constant need to weigh up their strengths and weaknesses in an instant. To do this well you must watch how they move and where they place their feet as this is their foundation from which they will attack. The setting of the feet can often give away the impending technique, although this can be disguised if their skill level is high. The angle or shape of the posture can also show the opponents intent, which direction they may attack from and what type of technique they may use. If the lower body is centred and solid it allows for an attack from the upper body to be delivered effectively but limits attacks using the legs. If the weighting is light on one foot and heavy on one foot then kicking attacks are useful but the upper body is less powerful as it has a poor foundation to issue power from.

When an opponent is rising you can expect them to fall immediately after and vice versa. This may seem obvious but in the stressful situation of a fight, seeing and anticipating this can provide you with an opportunity to strike and win the fight. You must keep moving and searching for the opening with the vigour and intent of the tiger searching the mountain for prey and rise and fall with the skill of the dragon soaring between heaven and earth. This way your opponent will find it difficult to attack as you are never static. These observations are constantly changing and you must be agile and sharp to see and act upon them successfully. Only practice and experience will allow you to achieve this level of skill.

Another important aspect in fighting strategy is distancing! You must know the tactical distance between yourself and your opponent at all times. This way you are always aware of whether you are in range to attack yourself and what type of technique will be best suited at different distances. If you are close, you can switch a fist to an elbow or even a shoulder strike. If you are too close to kick you can change to a knee or hip strike.

You must always try to take the shortest route to the target and therefore beat your opponent to the strike. By intercepting a strike from the right with your right you will create the opening to beat your opponent to the mark and this is also true of the same technique on the opposite side. This is a common practice in the strategy of Hsing-I and is what gives rise to the reputation of it being a very fast art. It is not that it is particularly faster than any other system for striking; it is that it is very efficient in its use of straight line technique over the shortest distance that makes it so effective. Knowing 'distance' allows you to set up for a successful strike. It is also important to know if your opponent is in range to strike you and with what type of technique, therefore you can also defend effectively when you understand distance.

"To defeat the opponent be vigilant of the ground. The feet must always be agile and the hands quick. The heart must remain neutral and the spirit will be calm. The eyes must remain focussed. If all are as one, you will be victorious. A successful strike can be initiated from less than an inch and from over ten feet".

When fighting you not only have to be aware of your opponent, but also of the environment that you are fighting in, you must quickly calculate the ground you are fighting on, is it flat, uneven, wet, dry, icy, muddy or even changeable in different areas? How much room do you have? What objects or other people are around you? These are just a few of many variables that could affect the outcome of your fight. You must be light on your feet and fast with the hands, meaning ready to change to any situation, trying to manipulate not only your opponent but also your environment to your advantage. Remember these theses came from a general thinking about tactics for his whole army. In the past, many battles were fought unprepared and some famous ones have been lost due to the geography and weather not best suited for troops to fight upon.

To effectively analyse all this information your mind must be clear even under pressure. To achieve this, you must remain calm inside and the emotions of the heart must remain in check. When all is calm and balanced inside the clear chi will rise to the head and the spirit will show in the eyes. This means your thoughts will be clear, alert and agile to respond to all possibilities.

When your body is aligned and balanced correctly you will have the ability to fight effectively at any distance. When the structure is correct you will be able to issue power from any of the Seven Stars appropriate to the distance you are fighting at.

"When the body moves, it is like a building collapsing. When the feet are planted firmly on the ground, they grow deep roots. When the hands issue forward, it is like a cannon ball firing. Like a snake, when the head is attacked, the tail will respond and vice versa. When moving forward, be vigilant of behind. When moving backwards, be vigilant of the front. When the forward hand and foot move, the rear follows in support".

This paragraph refers to the wave of energy that passes through the body when all its parts are connected and its movements are in harmony. The roots or feet always stay stable by keeping the body centred as do the foundations of the wall, but when the energy of the wall collapses and transfers to any object in its way it has a devastating effect. It is not just the weight of one brick, but of all the bricks falling with combined weight and velocity that makes it so powerful. This is the same of the body in Hsing-I when all its parts are combined and moving as one, you have whole body power and not just that of a fist.

The rising of the hands is like the pounding of the cannon, shooting its ball up and out. This depicts both the mental and physical intent of the energy in a rising attack. You should visualise your technique up, out, into and through your opponent like a cannonball blasting through the walls of a castle. To issue this type of power the cannon requires a very stable platform and this should be the same in your posture.

To stay one step ahead of your opponent in a fight you must be constantly alert. Like the snake waiting to strike, it fixes its attentions on its prey. If you are alert you can respond to any situation. When attacked at the head you can evade and strike with your feet. Remember to exploit your opponent's weakness. If they attack with the upper body, then their lower body is vulnerable to counter and vice versa. This principle is the same when moving forward in attack. If your intention is focused on the forward direction then your rear is vulnerable. A skilled practitioner always knows exactly where they are and has all-round perception; even when they are focused on one direction they still maintain an awareness of what is around them.

Remember when fighting there maybe others involved and you must be aware of others attacking you from any direction. When General Yue Fei wrote these theses, this was especially true as battle was often chaos all around and attacks could come from multiple directions with weapons of many different ranges.

When moving in any direction the hands and feet must closely follow each other. This allows the body to stay constantly aligned and centred regardless of which direction it moves. Furthermore, it allows for continuation of attack and the ability to press home a victory with continuous strikes when the opportunity arises.

"When the heart and spirit are unified, you will be confident in battle and not be defeated. If you cannot read your opponent, you will be afraid to move. When you control your opponent, you move first and command the fight. If you are outmanoeuvred by your opponent, you will be controlled. Think of advancing and never retreating, this is the mindset".

As the principle behind the very core of Hsing-I practice the heart must make decisions first and fast to be the victor in combat. There can be no hesitation once the opening in the enemy has been detected. Any delay may result in lost opportunity and even a lost battle. To make decisions as a general in an army or as an individual in a fight requires calm logical thinking, even under pressure and absolute bravery in commitment to attack. Any hesitation will result in lack of troop confidence or in the case of an individual a weak half-hearted attack which is easy to counter. Remember when you attack you are often at your most vulnerable to a counter strike, so you must always attack with spirit and total commitment.

Where possible understand your opponent and be calculated in your attack. If you can read their intentions then you can better anticipate their moves. This will allow you to attack first and strike decisively and to win the fight. As with most Hsing-I strategy the aim is to be brave, decisive and press forward wherever possible, striking in the shortest most effective way. This will keep your opponent at a constant disadvantage and scatter any thoughts of counter strike.

"The three sections must be clear and the tips must be aligned. The six harmonies must come together and be commanded by the heart. Practice diligently, day and night. Over time, all will become natural. These are sincere words and not meaningless talk".

Whenever you fight or practise the rules are the same. The three sections of the 'Dragon Body' must be aligned in every technique and every application. The 'Three Tips' of the hands, the feet and the nose must also remain constant. If this is done correctly your techniques will have the ability to defeat your opponent whatever their strength.

The four extremities are the tongue, teeth, nails and hair. When in a fight and the chi fills the whole body, these extremes become energised to their full potential. When this happens, the body will take on a frightening appearance to your opponent. It is said that the hair will stand on end filling with blood giving a larger than life appearance. The teeth will clench together strengthening the bones and make the face look fierce. The tongue will touch the roof of the mouth allowing the chi to circulate efficiently and the nails will curl with the fingers making the tendons strong and the strike powerful. This effect is natural like a wild animal making the most of its assets to appear more powerful against its attacker.

If you remain calm and controlled in your actions, this natural bodily reaction in a fight can be used to your advantage by intimidating your opponent by your physical presence alone.

The heart must lead all movement and the physical body must be totally aligned and integrated with the intent of the chi. This skill can only be achieved by constant practice, so force yourself at every minute available if you truly want to master Hsing-I Chuan. This is the only way!

On the subject of fighting theory Master McNeil states:

"During regular practice, one should act as if facing a top opponent. However, in a real fight, one cultivates emptiness of mind through meditation and reacts like an echo. When attacking, step forward, constantly oriented to the centre gate. The hand and body move together. The hand should be alive and flexible, the leg light and ready to move. One should move left, right or back using one's nose as the cross hairs. Attacking is attacking and retreating is retreating. One can efficiently block or strike while retreating or advancing. Every step and strike should be coordinated. In this way, one will not lose the advantage.

Combining the heart and body with the will creates reactions that become natural and automatic, rather than stiff or contrived. As the mind begins to absorb the techniques, their usage becomes more instinctive. Often, if the heart is fearful, hesitation will result.

The most important point is learning to utilise the breath. When the breathing is correct this relaxes the body and mind, producing movements that are natural and flowing. If the breathing is erratic all actions become unnatural and ultimately, the mind or will cannot move the body efficiently. The road to achieving this level of skill is neither smooth nor easy, but with perseverance and an experienced teacher one can make significant progress.

When chi is held in the lower abdomen or Tan-Tien, the body will be harmonious and stable. When chi erupts from the Tan-Tien, power is produced to work the forge of the will. The power is held within until it is used and is self-regenerating. Every movement contains the theory of 'Yin/Yang' or 'True Not True'. Every move must be creative and destructive and also combine long and short. It is important not to over-emphasise the hard, explosive aspects of Hsing-I. All of its spirit is in the Tan-Tien. All power and energy are conserved inside until needed; yet this power will never be fully tapped. One's attack or defence follows the heart and mind. The posture should be gentle and the power should be in harmony with hard and soft.

Hsing-I is considered a defensive style where the opponent is allowed to make the first move and is then drawn into the counterattack. However, this can also be combined with our modern-day street fighting theories, which allow for attacking first in a multiple-attacker situation.

The defensive theory gives birth to the theories of 'Touch-Go-Kiss' and 'True-Not-True' or changing a technique as the opponent moves. As the opponent attacks, one must take the first step to deflect or 'touch' the strike away. At the same time, you 'go' or penetrate deeply into the opponent, close enough to 'kiss' or defeat him, by using any of the Seven Stars techniques.

The 'True-Not-True' theory reflects the ability to change quickly from one technique to another even in mid strike in order to adapt to changes in the opponent's intention. This requires speed and delicate sensitivity to incoming force and above all, regular practice. Furthermore, when applying any techniques in a fight you must first understand mathematics. With this I mean the distance between yourself and your opponent at all times!

Hsing-I is also considered a soft style, which means that receiving and manipulating the opponent is just as important as striking. The opponent's force is used against him and allows one to pull him into a vortex of destruction. Every vital spot is a target in one furious barrage. When the circle is completed the maximum power will be transferred. Because of the inherent danger in this system, to defeat someone is not the most important aspect. It is balancing a respect for all life with respect for your own."

Methods to developing fighting skills in Hsing-I Chuan

When learning Hsing-I Chuan, the basic method of practice which builds up to the level of ability required to fight is the same as the other classical Chinese internal martial arts. Primarily it is the practice of forms, which teaches the novice practitioner the basic movements of the system and provides them with a strong foundation to build from. It strengthens the body and allows the mind to synchronise with the physical movements until constant practise makes them almost a reflex action, just like riding a bike. At first, we are all unstable but after much practise eventually we can ride, balanced, without thinking, even with no hands. The body no longer must think about what it does, it just does it. This is the goal of constant forms practice.

The forms are designed to teach you balance, timing, coordination, strength, power, stability, rooting and how to use the body and mind as one. You must be able to perform the forms flawlessly in any direction and in any amount of space without a moment's pause between movements, before you can assume competency. They must become a part of your very being. Only when a high level of form competence has been achieved can you think seriously about applying it to fight with.

It is important to have a good level of ability to be safe and effective in application of techniques as Hsing-I which is a soft, or internal, martial art and therefore, requires structure, timing and utilisation of chi to be effective. These skills cannot be acquired in a short time.

Over time, when a suitable level of technical competence in a form has been achieved, the intermediate level practitioner progresses to single partner applications. Each individual movement of each form must be analysed and understood and then practised on prearranged attacks from your partner. Often you start with the simplest most obvious application first, practicing this way builds up confidence in a technique with reduced risk of being injured.

There are many different fighting applications for each technique and you are only limited by your ability and imagination in applying them. Any single application must be practised using both sides of the body and from different heights, speeds and angles of attack to determine its usefulness in different situations. You should also practise with people of different heights and skill levels as this too will benefit your development. When practicing with a partner, remember to be respectful. If you are with a partner who is more skilful than yourself, do not be resentful of this. Let their skill help teach you and learn from your errors.

Within the art of Hsing-I Chuan there are also two-man forms specifically designed to help you develop your techniques against a partner who also applies prearranged techniques. This method allows combinations of techniques to be applied in a continuous cycle, allowing the body to develop muscle memory and reflex response to given situations. The speed and intensity of the two-man forms can be increased to develop the mind to react under increased pressure, yet still remain in a relatively safe environment of learning.

With practise over time, the level of competence will increase and so will the confidence and control of each technique. The next stage for the advanced practitioner is to practise with a partner; random, single and eventually multiple attacks, where you have to apply an appropriate counter-technique with no prearranged warning of what strike will come. When you can apply techniques at this level and at full speed you will have reached a high level of competency and can develop your training to suit your needs.

A further point on training for fighting is conditioning. It is one thing to practice your skills in thin air, but when you actually hit an object the feeling is totally different. Therefore, as a partner would soon tire of being hit several times it is good practice to train your techniques on punch bags or striking dummies to get a true feel for what it takes to maintain perfect alignment structurally when you hit something. Also, it pays dividends to strengthen your hands, body and feet so as they can withstand the punishment they will receive in a real fight.

Finally, the only way you can test your true ability to fight is when you fight for real. The more you fight the better you will become. As it is not advocated to go out looking for trouble, the best way is to arrange friendly sparring sessions using gloves, pads and protective equipment to allow for a more real fighting experience or go into open competitions with people of different martial styles and with whom you are unfamiliar. This is never quite the same as controlling yourself in a real life and death situation, but it will give you a feel of the emotions that build up in a fight situation and help you learn to control them and keep the heart calm and the head clear under pressure so as you can deliver the techniques inherent in Hsing-I cleanly and effectively.

Part 2

The Practice of Hsing-I Chuan

Chapter 15

Hand Techniques of Hsing-I Chuan

Introduction

Hand techniques are one of the most fundamental methods common to all martial arts systems and they can be used in application of both defence and attack. There are several commonly used hand postures within the Hsing-I forms that allow a wide variety of hand techniques to be applied during fighting. Hand postures can be broadly placed into two categories; firstly; open palm (Zhang) and secondly; closed fist (Chuan) varieties. When they are formed and applied correctly they can be used to deliver devastating strikes to an opponent. The hands must be sensitive and have 'feeling'. They can be used to strike, grasp, pinch, block and control an opponent to gain an advantage.

When discussing hand techniques, the hand is viewed the final link in the kinetic energy chain. It is the hand which will deliver the power generated through the combination of correct body alignment and coordination of breath. When a technique is executed correctly the power is generated from the ground directly to the opponent and therefore, it needs to be perfectly positioned for each individual technique to be effective and the hand to avoid injury. If the hand posture is incorrect on contact with the opponent injury may result; not only to the many small bones and joints of the hand, but also to the joints directly supporting the technique, such as the wrist and elbow.

The practice of Hsing-I trains the hands using internal methods which combine physical, breath and mental intent (Jing, Chi and Shen). If the training is carried out correctly the associated trauma caused to the hands from the impact of training and rigors of general daily life should be negated. To execute the techniques correctly and maximise their effectiveness, the following important points should be considered:

- Correct focus on executing the technique
- Total coordination of the whole body through the technique
- Correct application of opposing Yin/Yang forces through the technique

- Accuracy of the technique
- Correct balance when executing the technique
- Speed of the technique's delivery
- Correct breathing and relaxation throughout the technique
- Correct calculation of distance to the target
- Correct stance relevant to execute the technique
- Correct hand posture and sufficient conditioning of the hand to execute the strike effectively

Before analysing some of the more common hand postures used in Hsing-I, the practitioner should first understand the anatomy of the hand and its complexity both physically and energetically. The number of bones, muscles and joints make it very dexterous and sensitive and, therefore, it is the primary method of the Seven Stars for the practitioner to use in application of techniques. Because of its complexity, the hand is also vulnerable to injury if techniques are not applied correctly and it should be trained and conditioned appropriately to each individual technique and method of application. Injuries to the hands from incorrect training and poor application of technique can result in fractured bones, torn tendons, dislocated joints, ruptured ligaments, injury to nerves resulting in reduced or total loss of function. Any physical trauma to the hand also damages the meridians which affects the natural flow of chi through the tissues. Reduced chi flow through the damaged area can affect the hands ability to heal and recover from the trauma of an injury.

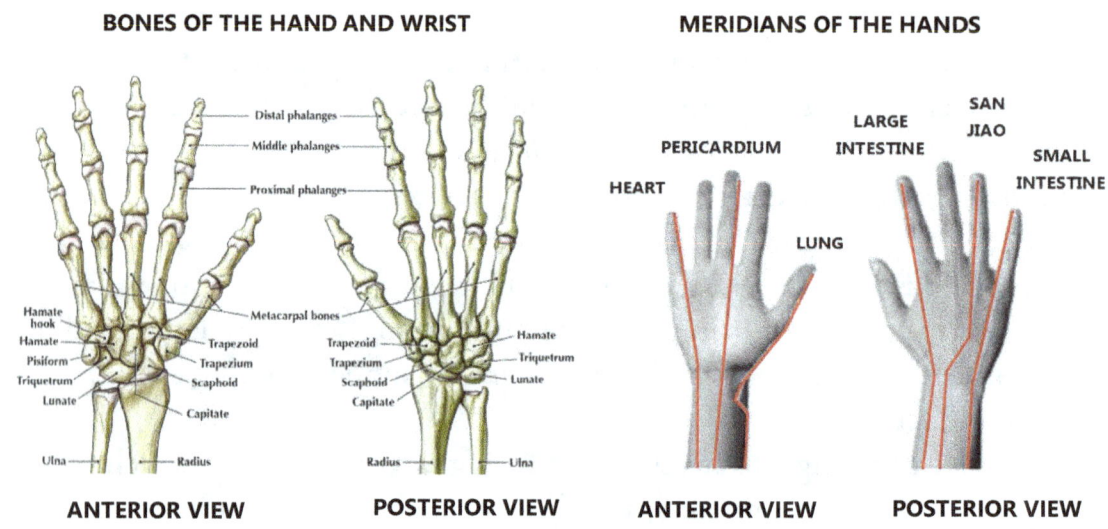

Anatomy of the Human Hand

The human hand is made up of twenty-eight bones, muscles, tendons and has a high density of nerve endings compared to other parts of the body, giving them great sensitivity. The fingers have three bones, known as the phalanges. The bone at the tip of any finger is the distal phalange, the bone in the middle part of any finger is known as middle phalange and the bone at the bottom end of every finger is known as proximal phalange. Each finger is connected to the base of the wrist by a bone known as the metacarpus. Collectively, these connecting bones are known as metacarpals. The metacarpals have a base of eight bones known as trapezoid, trapezium, capitate, scaphoid, lunate, pisiform, triquetrum and hamate. The hand ends at the wrist and is connected by two bones, the larger one is known as radius and the relatively slimmer one is known as ulna. All the individual bones are connected by ligaments and controlled by the actions of the muscles attached to them.

From a Taoist energetic perspective, correct hand position combined with breath and mental intent for each technique promotes the smooth flow of chi and blood through the joints and to the most distal areas of the meridians contained within the hands. When the flow of chi is smooth and continuous it keeps the hand looking and feeling youthful, with good circulation keeping the hands adept, warm, bones strong, skin nourished and nails healthy, well into old age! When chi flow to the extremities is strong this reflects the strength of chi within the whole body. Further to this, when training has reached a high level, the chi developed within the practitioner's body can be directed to penetrate the opponent on impact and increase the overall effectiveness of the strike. This type of internal energy strike is what Hsing-I is famous for and its results can be deadly on impact. Six of the twelve main meridians are found in the hands. The three organ meridians on the Yin (palm side) are the heart, pericardium and lung. The three organ meridians on the Yang (dorsal side) are the large intestine, triple heater and small intestine.

The following diagrams show the hand in both open and closed form with appropriate labelling to areas used to anatomically describe the hand from a martial arts perspective. These terms are used to help the reader better understand the shape of each hand posture and the striking area used when executing the techniques described in the remainder of this chapter.

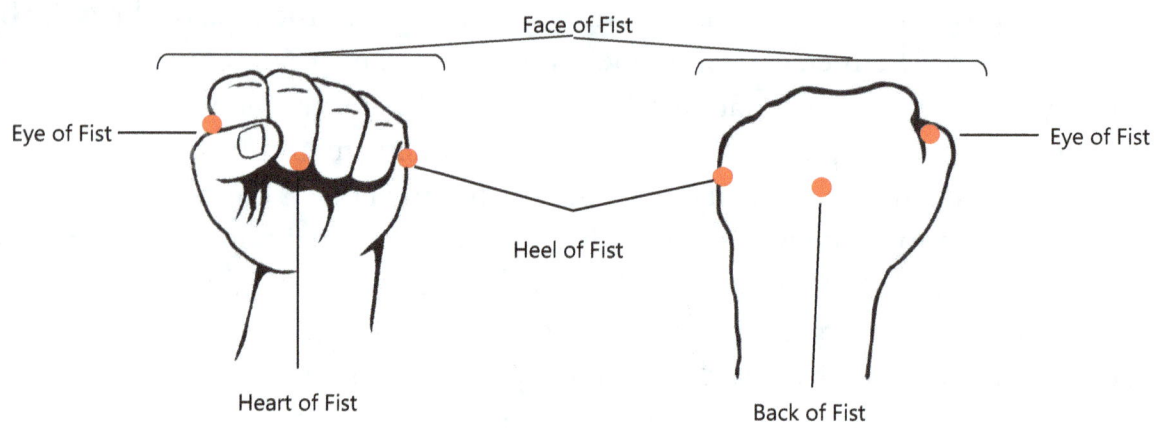

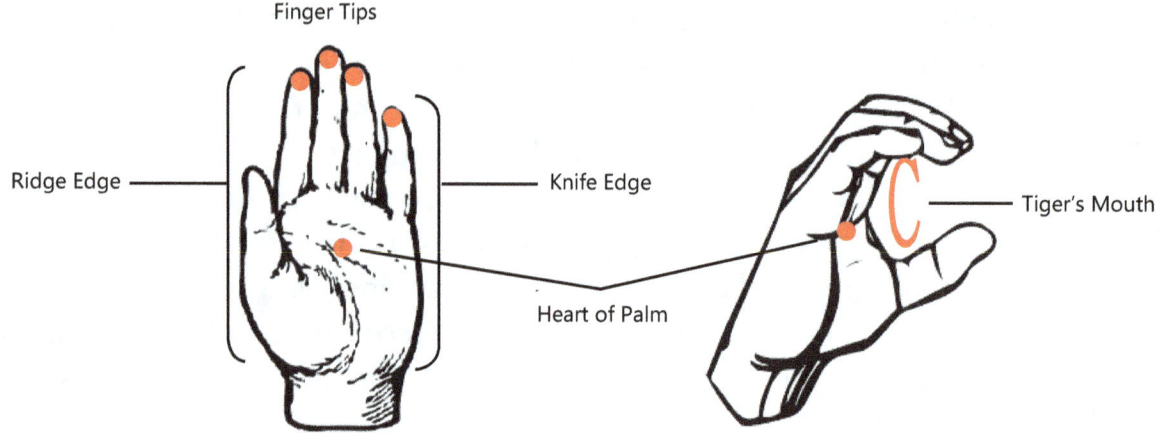

Hand Postures and Techniques

The following section of this chapter shows some of the most commonly used hand postures in this lineage of Hsing-I and some simple applications appropriate to them. With regards to applications, the variation for each hand technique is limitless and the examples shown in this chapter give the reader just a few of the many possible applications.

1. Round Palm

Fig 15-1a

Metal form depicts best the 'Round Palm' which is sometimes called the 'Hsing-I Palm'. This open hand posture is most common to Hsing-I practice and can attack or defend at any given moment. It is the general default fighting hand posture of the Hsing-I practitioner.

The arrow marked **'a'** represents the circular area formed by the index finger and thumb and is commonly termed the 'Tigers Mouth'.

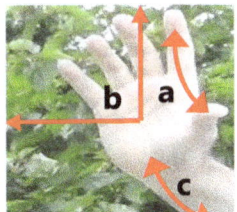
Fig 15-1b

The arrow marked **'b'** shows the centre (heart) of the palm pressing outwards with the four fingers extending upwards which keeps the hand spirited and alert to changing requirements in combat.

The arrow marked **'c'** shows the wrist slightly curved allowing smooth flow of chi to the hands extremities.

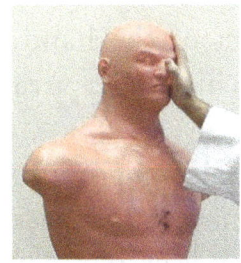
Fig 15-1c

In the example shown in figure 15-1c the round palm striking method is used against the jaw and temporomandibular joint of the face.

As well as a palm strike this hand posture can be easily transformed to grab, seize or pinch an opponent, making it the ideal hand posture to be utilised as a guard posture of which all other hand techniques can be formed.

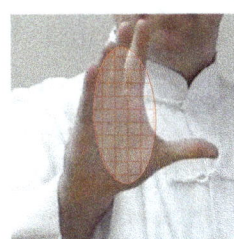
Fig 15-1d

Figure 15-1d highlights the area of the hand utilised when striking an opponent with the round palm technique.

Fig 15-1e

Fighting Application:
Black attacks White with a (R) punch to the mid-section. White counters with a (R) crescent palm block and grab to Black's (R) arm and attacks using (L) round palm strike to Black's jaw.

2. Palm Strike

Fig 15-2a

Monkey form best illustrates the power and effectiveness of the 'Palm Strike' method, however variations of this technique are used extensively within many of the forms of this lineage of Hsing-I. This hand position can be used to block or attack at a wide variety of angles and when applied correctly can cause deep internal injuries to an opponent. Importantly this type of strike reduces the chance of serious injury to the practitioner due to the anatomy of the striking area of the hand being naturally well protected. The palm area is ideal for striking large area targets but is particularly suitable for hard bony targets like the skull, chest or arms.

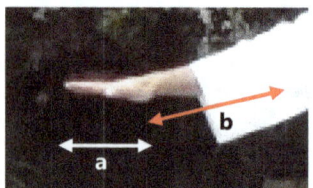

Fig 15-2b

The arrow marked 'a' shows the palm strike, with the palmer aspect of the hand parallel to the ground, formed by the four fingers held closely together and projected forwards supporting each other. The fingers are further reinforced by the thumb pressing against the ridge aspect of the hand. This hand position gives a strong and specific target area from which to block or strike.

The arrow marked 'b' shows the angle of the wrist as straight. This alignment allows the practitioner to deliver a powerful palm strike to an appropriate target area. This straight wrist angle also allows smooth flow of chi to the hands extremities which adds to the potential power of the technique.

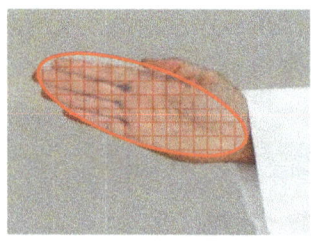

Fig 15-2c

Figure 15-2c highlights the palm strike position turned sideways to show the striking area which covers the total area of the palm and four fingers of the hand combined. This type of strike can be effective by a novice practitioner but to apply the internal power that this method is famed for the advanced practitioner must condition the striking area suitably and learn to apply the mechanics of whole body power and correct breathing in its application.

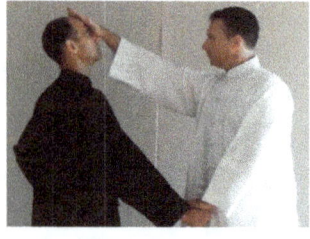

Fig 15-2d

Fighting Application

Figure 15-2d shows a fighting application using the palm strike technique. Black attacks White with a (R) punch to the mid-section. White counters with a (L) covering palm block to Black's attack and simultaneously counter strikes in a straight line using a (R) palm strike to Black's nose and forehead along the centreline.

3. Knife Hand

Fig 15-3a

The 'Knife Hand' strike is one of the most common striking methods in all systems of kung-fu and it is no different in this lineage of Hsing-I. The image of this hand position is a classic icon in all methods of martial arts and can be used both in attacking strikes and in defensive blocking techniques. The knife area of the hand can be applied with the palm facing towards the mid-line of the practitioner in a forward plane. It can also be turned palm up or down and used in a sideways plane to equal good effect. This area of the hand is less prone to potential injury as the area of impact is mainly absorbed by the hypothenar eminence and lateral aspect of the little finger. To use this technique effectively one must condition the striking area suitably to avoid potential injury.

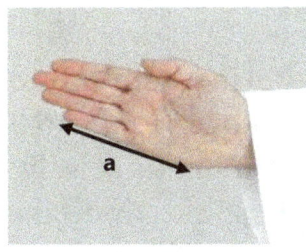

Fig 15-3b

The arrow marked 'a' shows the knife face of the hand which is facing downwards towards the earth and formed by the four fingers being held closely together with the thumb pressed firmly across the lateral side of the index finger to provide support to the four fingers on impact. In this forward plane, the practitioner would strike from top to bottom using the knife edge of the hand to strike the target area on their opponent. The wrist is also straight allowing a strong alignment and a smooth flow of chi to the hands extremities which adds to the power of the technique when applied correctly.

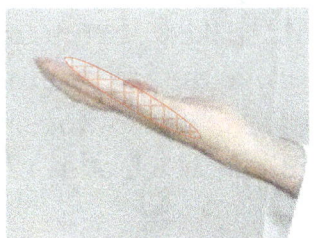

Fig 15-3c

Figure 15-3c highlights the knife edge of the hand which is the area across the lateral aspect of the hand formed by the lateral aspects of the hypothenar eminence and the little finger. This area is used to strike or block the selected target area of the opponent.

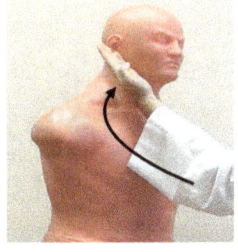

Fig 15-3d

Fighting Application: 1

Figure 15-3d shows a fighting application using the knife hand technique in a sideways plane, where the strike is executed from inside to outside, aimed at the lateral aspect of the opponent's neck.

Hsing-I Chuan | The Practice of Heart and Mind Boxing

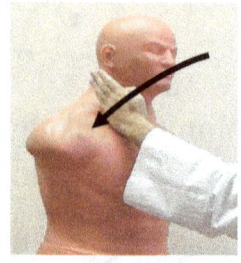

Fig 15-3e

Fighting Application: 2
Figure 15-3e shows a fighting application using the knife hand technique in a forward plane, where the strike is executed from top to bottom aimed at the opponent's clavicle.

4. Ridge Hand

Fig 15-4a

The 'Ridge Hand' method is trained in several forms in this lineage of Hsing-I. This hand position is used both in striking and in blocking and can be applied from various angles. In application, the 'ridge' area of the hand can be used with the palm facing towards or away from the practitioner in a sideways plane and can operate both from inside to outside (I/O) or outside to inside (O/I) depending on the situation. It can also be inverted to strike in a forward plane from top to bottom as shown in figure 15-4a. This area of the hand is more prone to potential injury as the area of impact is mainly absorbed by the adducted thumb (first MTP joint) and lateral aspect of the index finger. To use this technique effectively the practitioner must condition the striking area suitably to avoid any possible injury.

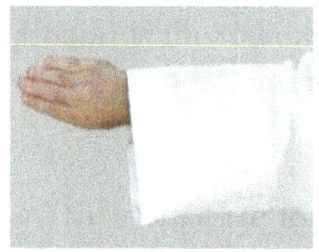

Fig 15-4b

Figure 15-4b shows the inverted ridge face of the hand which is facing downwards and formed by the four fingers being held closely together with the thumb tucked firmly across the palm area to avoid potential injury on impact. In this forward plane, the practitioner would strike from top to bottom using the ridge of the hand to strike the target area on their opponent. The wrist is also straight allowing a strong alignment and a smooth flow of chi to the hands extremities which adds to the potential power of the technique.

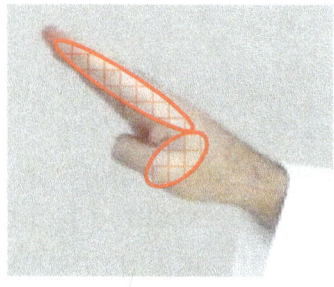

Fig 15-4c

Figure 15-4c highlights the ridge face of the hand which is the area across the lateral aspect of the hand, formed by the lateral aspects of the thumb and index finger.

In this sideways plane, the practitioner would strike or block from outside/in (O/I) with the palm facing down or vice versa if the palm starting position was facing up.

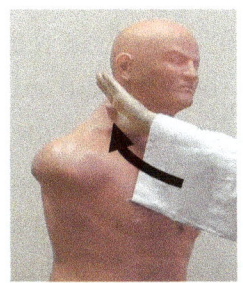

Fig 15-4d

Fighting Application: 1

Figure 15-4d highlights the target area of the ridge hand technique striking an appropriate target on the side of the neck. This area contains vulnerable structures such as the sternocleidomastoid muscle and the carotid artery.

Fig 15-4e

Fighting Application: 2

Figure 15-4e shows a fighting application using the ridge hand technique to defend from O/I in a sideways plane. Black attacks White with a (R) punch to the face. White counters with a (R) O/I ridge hand block to Black's (R) arm attack and simultaneously prepares to counter strike using (L) hand to an appropriate target.

5. Spear Hand

Fig 15-5a

The 'Spear Hand' striking method is trained prominently in Water form, Cock form and Ba-Shi Chuan of the combined forms within this lineage of Hsing-I. This method is most commonly used in a straight-line direction from mid or close range to the opponent and used with the palmer aspect of the hand facing upwards towards heaven. It is essentially the opposing technique of the 'Finger Thrust' technique. This hand position can be used to great effect at any suitable target usually between groin and head height.

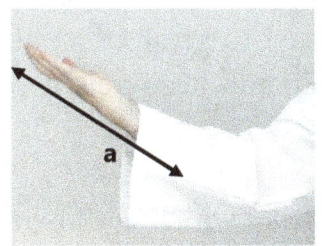

Fig 15-5b

Figure 15-5b shows the spear hand strike facing forwards with the palm up and formed by the four fingers held closely together and projected forwards supporting each other. The fingers are further reinforced by the thumb pressing against the ridge aspect of the hand. This hand position gives a strong and specific target area at the ends of the four projected fingers which is ideal for targeting specific pressure points or soft targets like the throat, armpit, and groin.

The arrow marked 'a' shows the wrist straight allowing a strong alignment to deliver a powerful spear hand strike. This straight wrist angle also allows smooth flow of chi to the hands extremities which adds to the potential power of the technique.

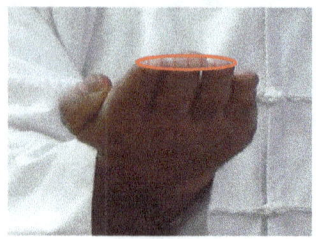

Fig 15-5c

Figure 15-5c highlights the spear hand striking position which is the combined area created by the three distal ends of the second, third and fourth digits combined. When striking using this method the middle finger is usually slightly bent bringing its tip in line with the two supporting fingers either side. This creates a more uniform striking area and avoids potential injury to the lone protruding middle finger. To use this technique effectively the practitioner must condition the striking area appropriately to avoid possible injury.

Fig 15-5d

Fighting Application:
Figure 15-5d shows a fighting application using the spear hand technique.

Black attacks White with a (R) punch to the midsection. White counters with a (L) crescent palm block to Black's (R) arm attack and simultaneously counter strikes in a straight line using (R) spear hand strike to Black's throat on the centreline.

6. Finger Thrust

Fig 15-6a

The 'Finger Thrust' striking method is trained in Ba Shi Chuan of the combined forms within this lineage of Hsing-I. (See (R) hand in figure 15-6a.)

This method is most commonly used in a straight line direction from mid or close range to the opponent and used with the palmer aspect of the hand facing downwards towards earth. It is essentially the opposing technique of the spear hand which has the palmer aspect of the hand facing upwards. This hand position can be used to great effect at any suitable target usually between groin and head height.

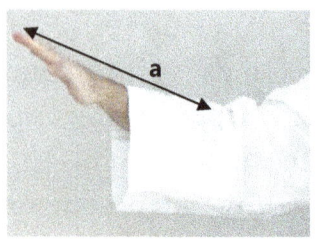

Fig 15-6b

Figure 15-6b shows the finger thrust strike which is shown facing forwards and formed by the four fingers held closely together and projected forwards supporting each other. The fingers are further reinforced by the thumb pressing against the ridge aspect of the hand. This hand position gives a strong and specific target area at the ends of the four projected fingers which is ideal for targeting specific pressure points or soft targets like the throat, armpit, groin and eyes.

The arrow marked 'a' shows the wrist straight allowing a strong alignment to deliver a powerful finger thrust strike to an appropriate target area. This straight wrist angle also allows smooth flow of chi to the hands extremities which adds to the power of the technique.

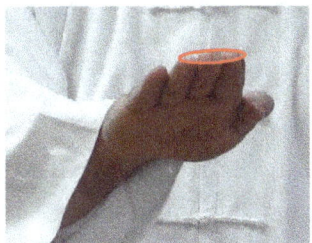

Fig 15-6c

Figure 15-6c highlights the finger thrust striking position which is the combined area created by the three distal ends of the second, third and fourth digits combined. When striking using this method the middle finger is slightly bent bringing its tip in line with the two supporting fingers either side. This creates a more uniform striking area and avoids injury to the lone protruding middle finger. To use this technique effectively the practitioner must condition the striking area suitably to avoid possible injury.

Fig 15-6d

Fighting Application:
Figure 15-6d shows a fighting application using the finger thrusting technique.

Black attacks White with a (R) punch to the mid-section. White counters with a (L) covering palm block to Black's (R) arm attack and simultaneously counter strikes in a straight line using (R) finger thrust method to Black's eyes on the centreline.

7. Crescent Palm

Fig 15-7a

The Horse form clearly illustrates the power and effectiveness of the 'Crescent Palm' block, however variations of this technique are used extensively within many of the forms of this lineage of Hsing-I. This hand position can be used to block or strike at a wide variety of angles and when applied correctly can cause significant injury to an opponent. This method therefore even though it is considered a defensive block can also be applied to cause injury to an opponent making it also an offensive technique. Importantly this type of block is efficient as it uses the whole area of the palmer aspect of the hand to cover its target and is less likely to miss in its application.

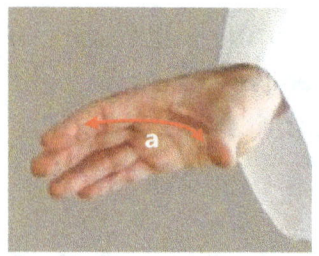

Fig 15-7b

The arrow marked 'a' in figure 15-7b shows the crescent palm block with the palmer aspect of the hand parallel to the earth and formed by the four fingers held closely together and projected forwards supporting each other. The thumb is held abducted away from the hands midline forming an arch similar to that of the 'Tigers Mouth' which creates a natural arch from which to block, grab and control an opponent. The crescent palm is ideal for targeting larger area targets but is particularly suitable for hard bony targets like the upper or lower arm and elbow and wrist joints.

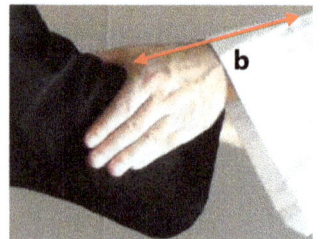

Fig 15-7c

The arrow marked 'b' in figure 15-7c shows the wrist straight allowing a strong alignment to deliver an effective crescent palm block to an attacking limb. Care should be taken with the exposed thumb as this could be injured if the technique was inaccurate. This straight wrist angle also allows smooth flow of chi to the hands extremities which adds to the effectiveness of the technique.

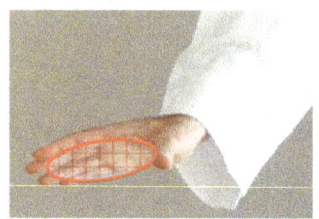

Fig 15-7d

Figure 15-7d highlights the crescent palm block position which is the total area of the palm and four fingers of the hand combined with the thumb abducted to create the crescent, vice like structure this hand posture gets its name from.

Fig 15-7e

Fighting Application:
Figure 15-7e shows a fighting application using the crescent palm blocking technique.
    Black attacks White with a (R) punch to the midsection. White counters with a (L) crescent palm block to Black's (R) arm attack, controlling it and simultaneously prepares to counter attack with the (R) hand to an appropriate target.

8. Sword Finger

Fig 15-8a

The 'Sword Finger' striking method is trained in Cock form and Twelve Red Hammers of the combined forms within this lineage of Hsing-I. A variation is also used in Tiger form where the two extended fingers are used to tear in a hooking motion in application. This hand position can be used to great effect especially when accurately 'poking' a vulnerable point on an opponent.

This method is most commonly used in a straight line direction from mid or close range to the opponent and can be used traditionally with the knife edge of the hand facing earth as shown in figure 15-8a but also with the palmer aspect of the hand facing earth with the index and middle fingers held in the same position, as in Cock form.

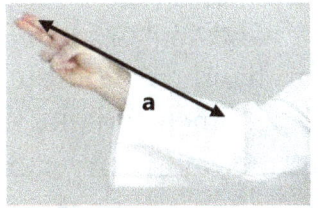

Fig 15-8b

Figure 15-8b shows the sword finger strike which is facing forwards and formed by the index and middle fingers held closely together and projected forwards supporting each other. The ring and little finger are held flexed and firmly protected from injury by the thumb pressing on the distal phalanges of the fourth and fifth fingers. This hand position gives a strong and specific target area at the ends of the two projected fingers which is ideal for targeting specific pressure points or soft targets like the eyes and areas on the throat.

The arrow marked 'a' shows the wrist straight allowing a strong alignment to deliver a powerful sword finger strike. This straight wrist angle also allows smooth flow of chi to the hands extremities which adds to the power of the technique

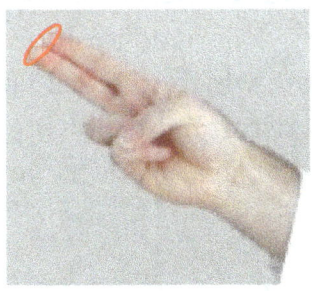

Fig 15-8c

Figure 15-8c shows the sword finger strike position which is the pointed area created by the fully extended distal ends of the index and middle fingers combined. To use this technique effectively the practitioner must condition the striking area suitably to avoid possible injury.

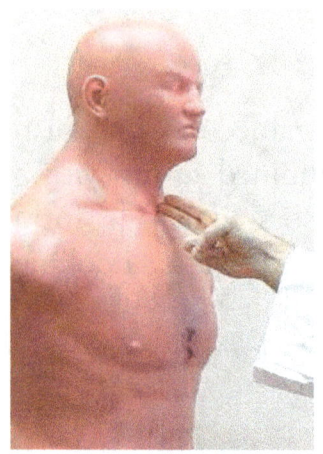

Fig 15-8d

Fighting Application:
Figure 15-8d highlights a common target area for the sword finger technique. In this example, the vulnerable structures of the larynx and trachea contained within the central throat cavity.

9. Eagles Claw

Fig 15-9a

The Eagle/Bear and Sparrow Hawk forms alongside the combined forms of Lien Wan and Twelve Red Hammers clearly illustrate the technique of the 'Eagle Claw' hand technique in this lineage of Hsing-I. This hand position can be used to block and grasp or attack, pierce, pinch and pluck at both mid and close range. When this method is targeted accurately it can cause significant injury to an opponent.

Fig 15-9b

The eagle claw method, which is shown with the palmer aspect of the hand turned upwards and formed by the thumb and index fingers held in a gripping pincer like posture. The fingers of the third, fourth and fifth digits are flexed tightly into the palm of the hand to avoid injury. This hand position gives a strong and specific target area from which to block or strike. The arrow marked '**a**' shows the wrist straight allowing a strong alignment to deliver the eagle claw strike to an appropriate target area.

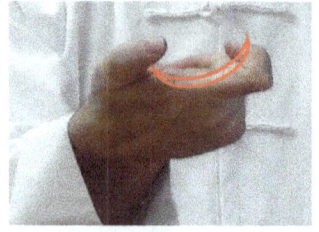

Fig 15-9c

Figure 15-9c shows the eagle claw striking area which is the area between the thumb and index finger of the hand. This technique is ideal for targeting specific structures such as tendons, blood vessels and pressure points and must be applied swiftly and accurately to be effective.

Fig 15-9d

Fighting Application:
Figure 15-9d shows a fighting application using the eagle claw strike technique.

Black attacks White with a (R) punch to the midsection. White counters with a (L) covering palm block to Black's (R) arm attack and simultaneously counter strikes in a straight line, upward motion using (R) eagle claw striking technique to the larynx on the anterior aspect of the throat.

10. Reverse Punch

Fig 15-10a

The Ba Bu Da preliminary exercises trains the 'Reverse Punch' method in this lineage of Hsing-I. This hand position is a basic fist position which can attack and deliver a forceful punch to the opponent especially when combined with total combined body power developed through correct practice.

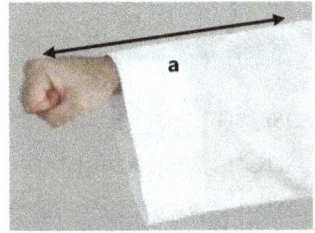

Fig 15-10b

Figure 15-10b shows the centre or 'eye' of the fist facing towards the centreline of the practitioner and formed by the clenched index and middle fingers being held firmly in position by the thumb pressing along the middle phalanges of the two fingers.

The arrow marked 'a' shows the wrist straight allowing a strong alignment to deliver a powerful punch. This straight wrist angle also allows smooth flow of chi to the hands extremities which adds to the power of the technique.

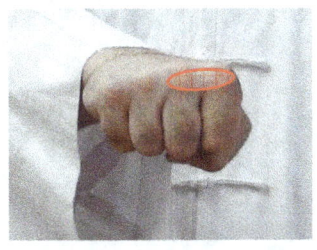

Fig 15-10c

Figure 15-10c shows the face of the fist which is the full flat area created by the four proximal phalanges when the fingers are tightly clenched. The area of the second and third metacarpal phalangeal joints or 'knuckles' are used to strike the selected target area of the opponent. This target area focusses the energy of the technique into a smaller area making it more effective.

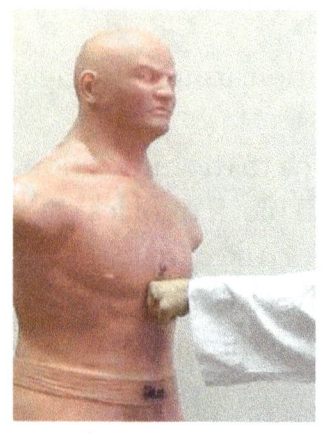

Fig 15-10d

Fighting Application:
Figure 15-10d highlights a common target area for the reverse punch technique. In this example, the solar plexus.

11. Straight Punch

Fig 15-11a

The Wood element form demonstrates clearly the 'Straight Punch' method, however this technique is used extensively within many of the forms of this lineage of Hsing-I. This hand position is the most commonly used fist technique which can attack with lightening precision when used in a straight-line direction from mid or close range to the opponent.

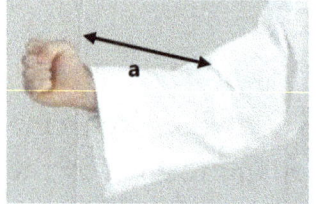

Fig 15-11b

Figure 15-11b shows the 'eye' of the fist facing upwards and formed by the clenched index and middle fingers being held firmly in position by the thumb pressing along the middle phalanges of the second and third digits.

The arrow marked 'a' shows the wrist straight with the elbow pointing downwards allowing a strong alignment to deliver a powerful punch. This straight wrist angle also allows smooth flow of chi to the hands extremities which adds to the power of the technique.

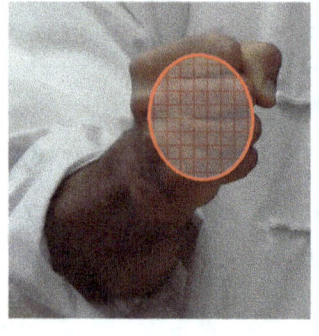

Fig 15-11c

Figure 15-11c highlights the 'face' of the fist which is the full flat area created by the four proximal phalanges when the fingers are tightly clenched. This area is used to strike the selected target area of the opponent.

Fig 15-11d

Fighting Application:

Figure 15-11d shows a fighting application using the straight punch technique.

Black attacks White with a (R) punch to the face. White counters with a (L) covering palm block to Black's (R) arm attack and simultaneously counter strikes using (R) straight punch to Black's jaw.

12. Back Fist

Fig 15-12a

The 'Back Fist' method is trained extensively within many of the forms of this lineage of Hsing-I. This hand position is used both in striking and in blocking and can be used to great effect especially when accurately targeting an appropriate structure on an opponent. This fist technique can be used in a straight line direction from mid or close range to the opponent whilst moving forwards, backwards and on turning to change the angle of attack.

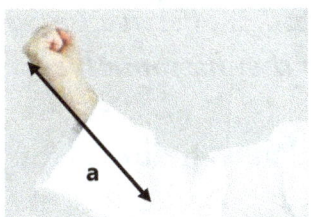

Fig 15-12b

Figure 15-12b shows the back (dorsal) face of the fist which is facing downwards and formed by the clenched index and middle fingers being held firmly in position by the thumb pressing along the middle phalanges of the two fingers. The 'eye' of the fist is facing laterally away from the practitioners centreline. The arrow marked '**a**' shows the wrist straight allowing a strong alignment to deliver a powerful back fist strike. This straight wrist angle also allows smooth flow of chi to the hands extremities which adds to the power of the technique.

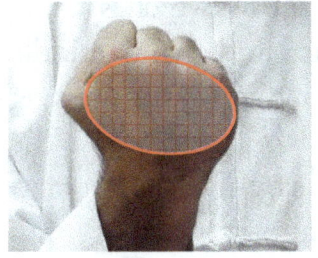

Fig 15-12c

Figure 15-12c highlights the 'back' of the fist which is the full flat area across the dorsal face of the hand when held as a fist. This area is used to strike the selected target area of the opponent.

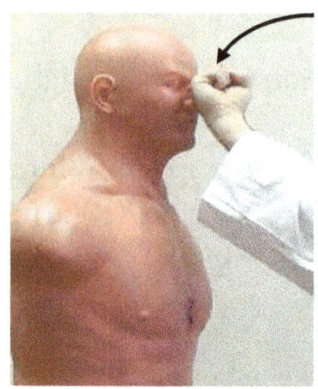

Fig 15-12d

Figure 15-12d highlights a common target area for the back fist. In this example, the bridge of the nose.

13. Hammer Fist

Fig 15-13a

The 'Hammer Fist' method is trained in several forms of this lineage of Hsing-I. This hand position is used both in striking and in blocking and can be applied from both a top to bottom action in a forward plane or from O/I in a sideways plane of motion. This fist technique can be used from mid or close range to the opponent. This area of the hand is very effective on striking and is less likely to be injured on impact if it is well conditioned making it an ideal technique for both the novice and experienced Hsing-I practitioner alike.

On discussing this technique Master McNeil says: ***"When you observe an infant you will often see them naturally hit an object or the ground with this area of their hand. The infant instinctively knows that this area of the hand is effective but is naturally well protected and they will hurt themselves less when they hit something."***

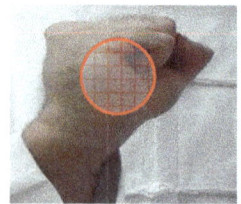

Fig 15-13b

Figure 15-13b shows the 'heel' of the fist which is the area across the base of the hand when held as a fist. This area is used to strike the selected target area of the opponent.

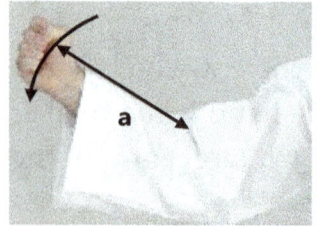

Fig 15-13c

Figure 15-13c shows the hammer face of the fist which is facing downwards and formed by the clenched index and middle fingers being held firmly in position by the thumb pressing along the middle phalanges of the second and third digits. The 'eye' of the fist is facing upwards toward heaven. In this forward plane, the practitioner would strike from top to bottom using the heel of the fist to strike the target area on their opponent.

The arrow marked 'a' shows the wrist is also straight allowing a strong alignment to deliver a powerful hammer fist strike and also allows smooth flow of chi to the hands extremities which adds to the power of the technique.

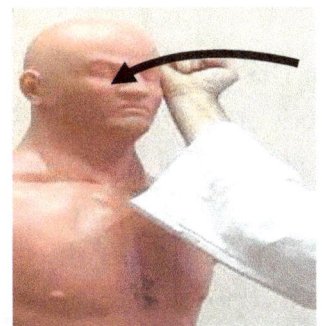

Fig 15-13d

Fighting Application: 1

Figure 15-13d highlights a common target area of the hammer fist technique making striking contact with the temple in an O/I sideways plane.

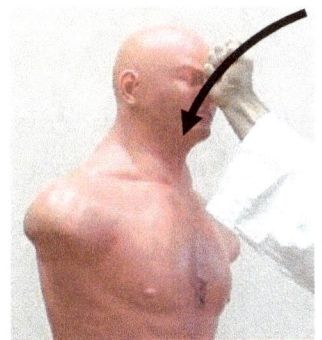

Fig 15-13e

Fighting Application: 2

Figure 15-13e highlights another common target area of the hammer fist technique making striking contact with the nose in a forward plane from top to bottom.

14. Phoenix Eye Fist

Fig 15-14a

The 'Phoenix Eye Fist' method is trained traditionally in Wood form, Chu Chi Chuan and predominantly in the Phoenix form of Master Hsu within this lineage of Hsing-I. This hand position can be used to great effect especially when accurately targeting an appropriate point on an opponent. This fist technique can be used from mid or close range to the opponent and can be especially useful when evading or sidestepping an opponent and striking from an angle.

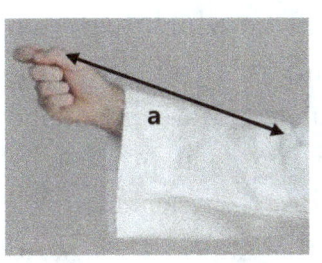

Fig 15-14b

Figure 15-14b shows the phoenix eye of the fist which is shown facing forwards and formed by the clenched middle, ring and little fingers, leaving the index finger protruding bent at the first inter phalangeal joint. This leaves the index finger mid-joint as the small but effective target area being held supported in position by the thumb pressing along the distal phalange of the index finger.

The arrow marked **'a'** shows the wrist straight allowing a strong alignment to deliver a powerful strike; however, the wrist angle can vary with this technique allowing the pointed striking area to penetrate more difficult to access targets such as pressure points.

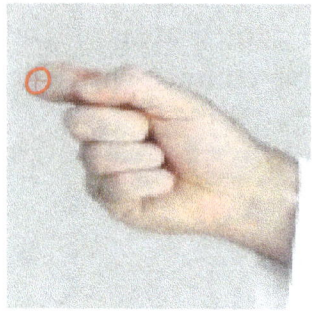

Fig 15-14c

Figure 15-14c shows the phoenix eye of the fist which is the pointed area created by the fully flexed index finger. The target area selected is usually a small anatomical cavity or pressure point or a vulnerable structure such as a single rib bone. To use this technique effectively the practitioner must condition the striking area suitably to avoid potential injury.

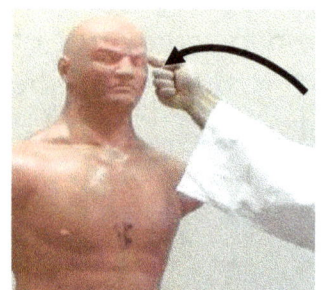

Fig 15-14d

Fighting Application:
Figure 15-14d highlights the target area of the phoenix eye technique making striking contact with an appropriate target, in this example the temple pressure point (Tai Yang) on the side of the head.

15. Leopard Fist

Fig 15-15a

The 'Leopard Fist' striking method is shown prominently in Cock form within this lineage of Hsing-I. This method is most commonly used in a straight line direction from mid or close range to the opponent and used with the palmer aspect of the hand facing downwards. This hand position can be used to great effect at any suitable target usually between groin and head height.

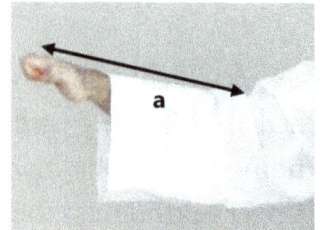

Fig 15-15b

Figure 15-15b shows the leopard fist strike which is shown facing forwards with the palm down and formed by the four fingers held closely together, hinged at the mid-phalangeal joints and projected forwards supporting each other. The fully flexed fingers are further reinforced by the thumb pressing against the ridge aspect of the hand. This hand position gives a strong and specific target area at the ends of the four projected phalange joints which is ideal for targeting specific soft targets like the throat.

The arrow marked '**a**' shows the wrist straight providing the perfect alignment to deliver a powerful leopard fist strike and provides the optimal wrist position to allow a smooth flow of chi to the hand.

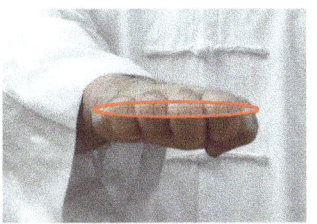

Fig 15-15c

Figure 15-15c shows the leopard fist striking position which is the combined area created by the ends of the flexed mid-phalangeal joints of the four fingers combined. To use this technique effectively the practitioner must condition the striking area suitably to avoid potential injury.

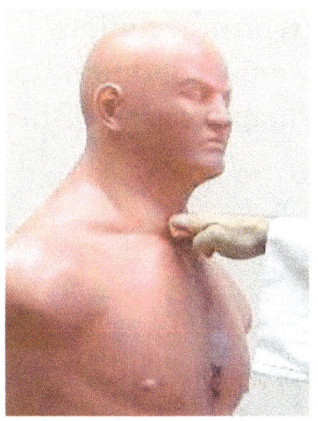

Fig 15-15d

Fighting Application:
Figure 15-15d highlights the target area of the leopard fist technique striking an appropriate target, in this example the central area of the throat.

16. Cranes Beak

Fig 15-16a

The Swallow and Fighting Chicken forms best illustrates the technique of the 'Cranes Beak' strike in this lineage of Hsing-I, although this hand posture is sometimes referred to as 'hook' method in other styles of Hsing-I. This hand position can be used to block or attack at both mid and close range. When this technique is targeted accurately it can cause significant injury to an opponent.

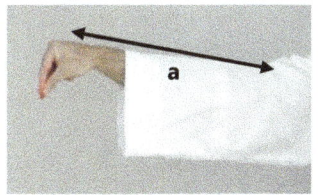

Fig 15-16b

Figure 15-16b shows the cranes beak method with the palmer aspect of the hand parallel to the earth and formed by the index and middle fingers held fully extended and closely together. Their metacarpal phalangeal (MCP) joints are flexed at 90 degrees and both fingers support each other.

These two fingers are further reinforced by the pad of the thumb pressing firmly up against the distal pads of the first two fingers. The ring and little fingers are flexed tightly into the palm of the hand to avoid injury. This hand position gives a specific target area from which to block or strike.

This technique is ideal for targeting specific structures such as the ribs or sternum but can also be effective in blocking an opponent's attack and hooking and controlling their technique.

The arrow marked '**a**' shows the wrist straight allowing a strong alignment to deliver a strike and also allows smooth flow of chi to the hands extremities which adds to the effectiveness of the technique.

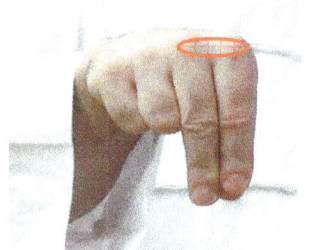

Fig 15-16c

Figure 15-16c shows the cranes beak striking area which is the area of the knuckles formed by the flexed first and second finger MCP joints combined. For this type of technique to be effective offensively the practitioner must condition the striking area suitably and be accurate in application of the technique.

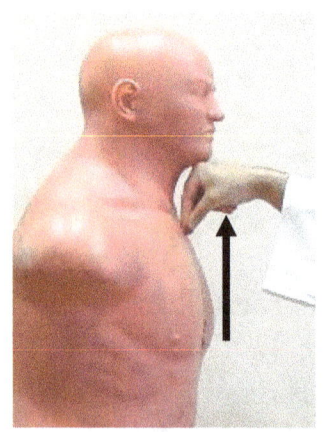

Fig 15-16d

Fighting Application:

Figure 15-16d highlights a common target area of the cranes beak strike technique. In this example, an upwards strike along the centreline to the underside of the opponent's mandible.

Chapter 16

Foot Techniques of Hsing-I Chuan

Introduction

Foot techniques are arguably the second most utilised skill of the Seven Stars in the application of Hsing-I and should never be under estimated as they form the practitioners direct connection with the earth and provides the power, stability and balance required to execute both the offensive and defensive foot techniques found within the system. There are several commonly used foot techniques within the Hsing-I forms that allow for a variety of applications during fighting. Different areas of the foot can also be utilised to strike or block and the techniques are usually simple and efficient in their delivery. The feet can be used to strike, stomp, trap, block, sweep and unbalance an opponent in order to gain an advantage when fighting.

When considering foot techniques, the foot can be used to either block or strike and is viewed as the final link of the kinetic energy chain when kicking. It is the foot which will deliver the power generated through the combination of correct body alignment and coordination of breath, directly to the opponent. The opposite foot that remains firmly rooted to the ground as the technique is executed is viewed as the first link of the kinetic energy chain. As the foot is a weight-bearing part of the human anatomy it is generally more robust through its development and use over the lifetime of the practitioner and can, as a rule, withstand more trauma and impact than its counterpart; the hand. The foot is also often protected via footwear which makes it less vulnerable to injury, as opposed to other striking areas of the body. However, even though its structure is generally better suited to increased stresses, its overall construction and complexity is very similar to the hand and, therefore, has potential for injury should it be utilised incorrectly. The same ten important points to consider when developing hand techniques (See Chapter 15 previous) also apply to the execution of foot techniques described later in this chapter.

Before looking at some of the common foot postures used in this lineage of Hsing-I, first the practitioner should understand the anatomy of the foot both physically and energetically. The number of bones, muscles and joints make it very mobile and crucial to the practitioner's ability to move and kick efficiently. Because of its complexity the foot can also be vulnerable to injury if techniques are not applied correctly. Injuries to the feet from incorrect training or technique application can result in fractured bones, torn tendons, dislocated joints, ruptured ligaments and injury to nerves resulting in reduced or total loss of function of any affected body part. Any physical trauma to the foot can also damage the meridians which affects the natural flow of chi through the tissues.

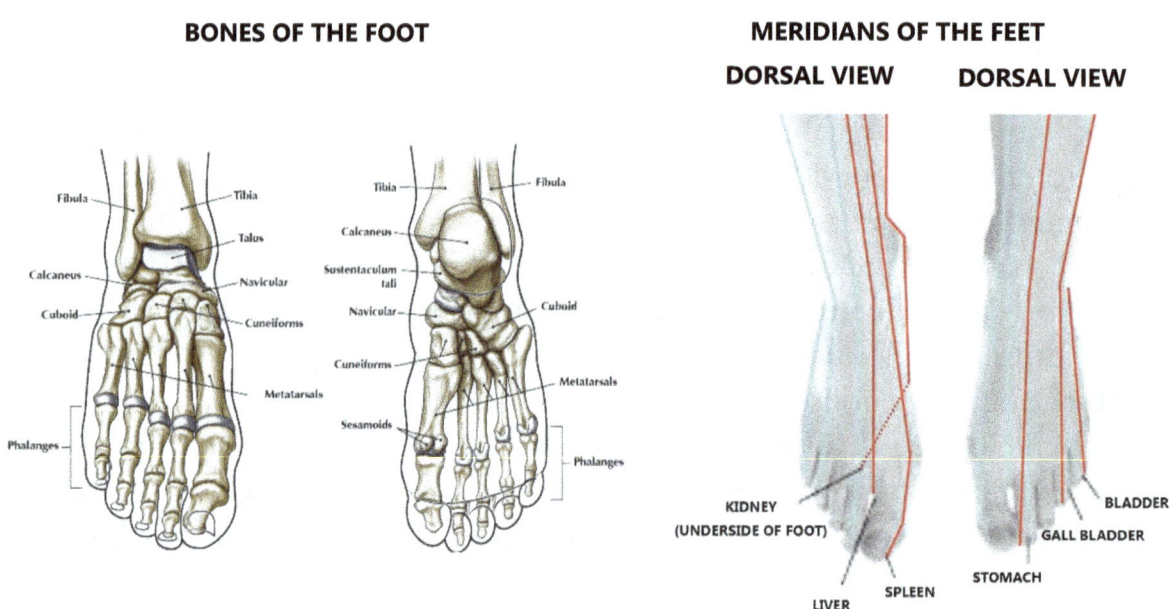

Anatomy of the Human Foot

The foot's shape, along with the body's natural balance-keeping systems, makes humans capable of walking, running and countless other complex activities. Its structure contains twenty-six bones and more than one hundred tendons, ligaments, and muscles that move thirty-three joints. The structure of the foot is similar to that of the hand, but because the foot bears more weight, it is generally stronger but this strength is gained at the expense of dexterity.

The largest bone of the foot, the calcaneus, forms what is commonly referred to as the heel of the foot. It slopes upward to meet the tarsal bones, which point downward along with the remaining bones of the feet. Below the juncture of these bones are the three arches of the foot, that makes walking easier and more efficient for the body. These arches are created by the angles of the bones and strengthened by the tendons that connect the muscles, and the ligaments that connect the bones. The bones of the foot are organised into rows named tarsal bones, metatarsal bones, and phalanges. These make up the toes and broad section of the foot. All the bones of the foot are connected by ligaments and mobilised by the attachments of muscles and their tendons.

Many of the muscles that affect larger foot movements are located below the knee in the lower leg. However, the foot itself has a web of muscles that can perform specific articulations that help maintain balance as a person moves. Incorrect position and function of the feet can lead to problems that affect the feet and spine. Therefore, attention to detail in correct body alignment when practising Hsing-I and in executing its postures, is crucial to both health and ultimately, an effective technique.

From a Taoist energetic perspective, correct foot position combined with correct breathing and mental intent for each technique, promotes the smooth flow of chi and blood through the joints and to the most distal areas of the meridians contained within the feet. This is excellent to keep the bones strong and the feet feeling youthful, mobile and with good circulation the feet will be warm, the skin nourished and nails healthy. When the chi flow to the extremities is strong this reflects the strength of chi within the whole body. Six of the twelve main meridians are found in the feet. The three organ meridians on the Yin (plantar side) are the kidney, spleen and bladder. The three organ meridians on the Yang (dorsal side) are the liver, stomach and gall bladder.

The following diagrams show the foot with appropriate labelling to areas used to anatomically describe the foot from a martial arts perspective. These terms are used to help the reader better understand each foot posture and the striking area to be used when executing the techniques described in the remainder of this chapter.

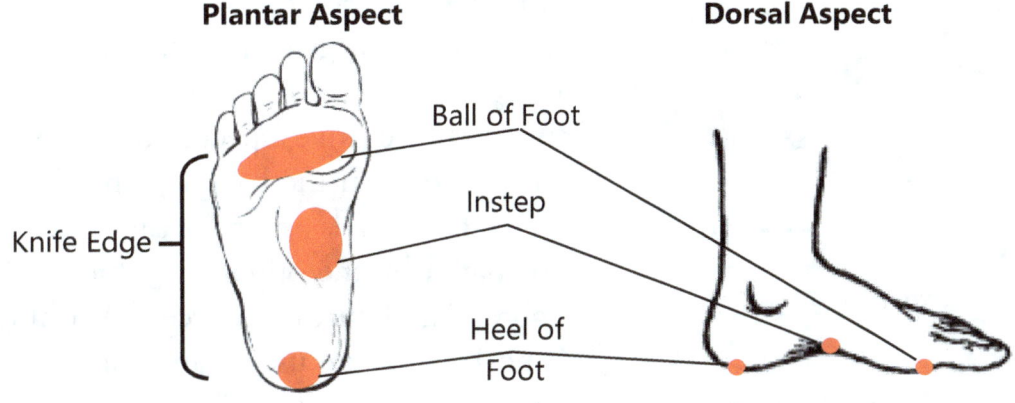

The following section of this chapter shows some of the most commonly used foot techniques in Hsing-I practice and some basic fighting applications appropriate to them. With regards to fighting applications, the variation for each foot technique is limitless and the ones shown give the reader just some of the many possible applications.

1. Straight Leg Kick

Front Leg Option

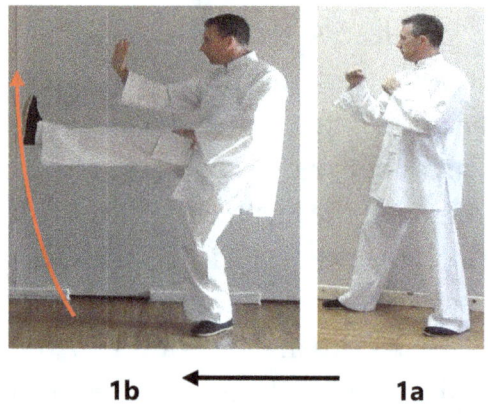

Figure 16-1a-1b

The front straight leg kick (SLK) technique is a commonly used kick within the Hsing-I system and is trained in countless forms. It allows the practitioner to deliver a kick from close range to an opponent without them seeing it coming. This technique is extremely difficult to defend against when delivered with speed and accuracy. It is effective on centreline targets, particularly groin attacks.

Back Leg Option

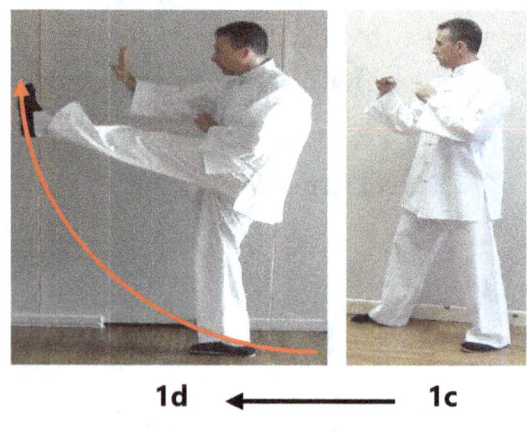

Figure 16-1c-1d

The back SLK technique is similar to the front SLK discussed previously, however, it is delivered from the rear standing leg rather than the forward leg. This allows the practitioner to generate increased power through the speed and distance the kick travels. The negative aspect to this is that as it is delivered from the back leg and therefore the technique is more easily seen and anticipated by the opponent which reduces is potential chances of success. Within this Hsing-I system it is used mainly on centreline targets, particularly groin and knee strikes and occasionally strikes to areas higher, such as the Tan Tien or solar plexus level.

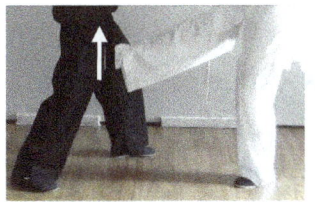 

Figure 16-1e-1f

In application, both techniques attack in the same way. Figure 16-1e and 1f shows the striking foot attacking with a toe up position which is useful in targeting the 'Huin' pressure point on an opponent.

Figure 16-1g-1h

Figure 16-1g and 1h shows the foot plantar flexed (toes pointing forwards), which is useful in targeting the groin area and further extends the reach of the technique. The same technique can be applied even if the opponent is close where straight front leg is raised, making contact with the shin or even knee to the opponent's groin.

Figure 16-1i

Fighting Application:
Figure 16-1i shows an appropriate fighting application using the straight leg kick technique.
Black attacks White with an attempt to grab double handed to White's body. White anticipates the attack and blocks with his (L) hand and simultaneously kicks to Black's groin with a (R) front SLK.

2. 45-Degree Kick (Rising)

Figure 16-2a-2b

This kicking technique is trained in Dragon form and Wood form from this Hsing-I lineage and has an energy that rises from the ground up and forwards into the opponent. In application this technique can be delivered from the front or back leg depending on the distance and angle to the target area.

It is effective particularly on low targets such as the knee and can be used from different angles of attack to hit the side or back of the knee joint and effectively break an opponent's balance or stance. The rear of the knee is particularly vulnerable with its tendons and soft tissues being easily damaged. The patella (knee cap) is also a useful target as the rising angle of this techniques delivery can displace the patella off its normal tracking line on the femur which will leave the knee joint immediately immobilised and unable to function. Further to this it can be used in a defensive nature to block an oncoming kick or sweep technique from an opponent. This type of block kick can also cause damage to an opponent's foot, ankle or knee joint if timed correctly.

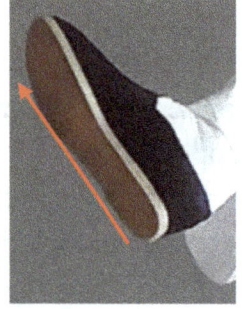

Figure 16-2c and 2d shows the striking foot attacking with a 45-degree foot position which is useful in attacking or blocking an opponent. The heel or whole sole of the foot can be used to make contact with the opponent.

Figure 16-2c-2d

Figure 16-2e highlights the target area for a 45 degree rising kick technique making striking contact with an appropriate target, in this case the inside of the knee targeting the medial ligament across the joint line.

Figure 16-2e

Fighting Application:
Figure 16-2f shows an appropriate fighting application using the 45-degree rising kick technique. Black attacks White with a (R) punch to the mid-section. White counters with a (R) I/O circle block to Black's (R) arm attack and simultaneously counter strikes using (R) leg 45-degree rising kick aimed at displacing Black's (R) patella.

Figure 16-2f

3. 45-Degree Kick (Falling)

The '45-degree Falling Kick' technique is a second variation and application of the same 45 degree rising kick discussed previously. Sometimes referred to as a 'Stomping' kick the difference being the intention of the energy which drops (stomps) down towards the ground from a raised position.

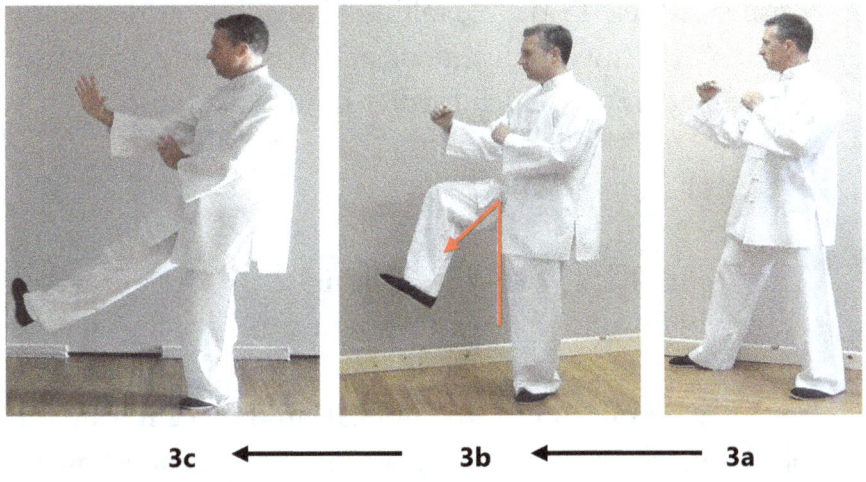

Figure 16-3a-3b-3c

In application this technique can be delivered from the front or back leg depending on the distance and angle to the target area. It is effective particularly on low targets such as the knee and can be used from different angles of attack to hit the side or back of the knee joint and effectively break an opponent's balance or stance. The rear of the knee is particularly vulnerable with its tendons and soft tissues being easily damaged. The ankle and foot are also often targeted to injure the bones and joints, but also to trap the opponent's foot to the ground in order to upset their balance and ability to move. Further to this it can be used in a defensive nature to block and stomp down an oncoming kick or sweep technique from an opponent.

Figure 16-3d

Figure 16-3d shows the striking foot attacking downward and outward with a 45-degree foot position which is useful in attacking or blocking an opponent's intended attack. The heel or whole sole of the foot can be used to make contact with the opponent. The angle of the foot provides a larger surface area to make the technique more likely to hit its target area and be more successful.

Figure 16-3e

Fighting Application:
Figure 16-3e shows a fighting application using the 45-degree falling kick technique.

Black attacks White with a (R) punch to the midsection. White counters with a (R) I/O circle block to Black's (R) arm attack and simultaneously counter strikes using (R) leg 45-degree falling kick aimed at damaging Black's (R) medial ligament and jarring the knee into hyperextension, which further injures the joint.

4. Side Kick

Figure 16-4a

Figure 16-4b

The 'Side Kick' (16-4a) technique is demonstrated clearly in 'Swallow' form (See figure 16-4b) and has an energy that thrusts out sideways from the practitioner towards the opponent. In application this technique can be delivered from the front or back leg depending on the distance and angle to the target area. It is effective on low and mid height target areas such as the knee, Tan Tien, ribs, solar plexus and generally considered a long range technique in the Hsing-I arsenal. The power of this technique when delivered with speed and accuracy can be devastating, breaking bones, immobilising joints and causing internal injuries to organs.

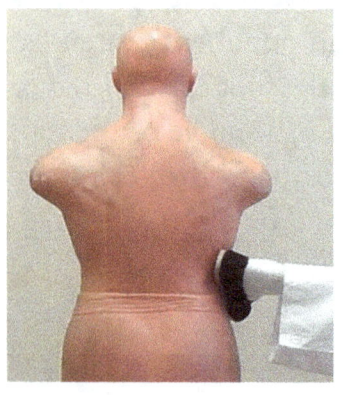

Figure 16-4c

Figure 16-4c shows the striking foot attacking with a slight downward angle allowing the heel and lateral edge of the foot to make contact with the target area, in this case the opponent's ribs. The angle of the foot provides a large surface area to make the technique more likely to hit its target area and be more successful.

Figure 16-4d

Fighting Application:
Figure 16-4d shows a fighting application using the side kick technique.
Black attacks White with a (R) punch to the midsection. White counters with a (R) block and grab to Black's (R) arm attack and counter strikes using (R) side kick to Black's ribs.

5. Heel Kick

Figure 16-5a

The 'Heel Kick' technique is a variation of the straight leg kick, where the toes are sharply pulled backwards dorsiflexing the foot allowing the heel to make contact with the target on impact. This technique has an energetic quality that thrusts outwards and forwards from the practitioner towards the opponent. In application this technique can be delivered from the front or back leg depending on the distance and angle to the target area. It is effective on mid height target areas such as the groin, Tan Tien, ribs, solar plexus and generally considered a long range technique in the Hsing-I arsenal. The power of this technique when delivered with speed and accuracy can be devastating as the energy is focused into the smaller heel area. This technique can easily break bones, immobilise joints and cause internal injuries to organs.

Figure 16-5b highlights a common target area for a heel kick technique in this example the Tan Tien.

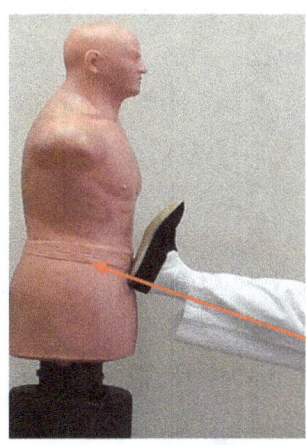

5b

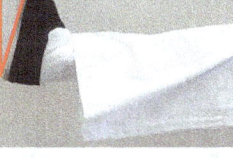

5c

Figure 16-5c shows the striking foot attacking with a slight forward thrusting of the heel.

Figure 16-5b-5c

Figure 16-5d

Fighting Application:

Figure 16-5d shows a fighting application using the heel kick technique.

Black attacks White with a (R) punch to the midsection. White counters with a (R) block to Black's (R) arm attack and simultaneously counter strikes using (R) heel kick to Black's Tan Tien.

6. Back Kick

Figure 16-6a

The 'Back Kick' technique is one of the most powerful but difficult to apply methods, requiring excellent timing and balance alongside anticipation of the opponent's movement in delivery.

Figure 16-6a shows the fully extended back kick executed from a long range to its intended target.

Figure 16-6b

Figure 16-6b shows a close range example of the back kick taken from the 'Swallow' form in the Hsing-I lineage. This type of kick is sometimes referred to as the 'Donkey' or 'Mule' kick due to the way it is delivered.

On striking using either method the toes are pulled backwards dorsiflexing the foot allowing the heel to make contact with the target on impact. This technique has an energy that thrusts out backwards and upwards from the practitioner towards the opponent.

In application, this technique can be delivered from the front or back leg depending on the distance and angle to the target area. It is effective on mid height target areas such as the groin, Tan Tien, ribs, solar plexus, various organs and can be delivered from mid to long range distance to the opponent. The power of this technique when delivered with speed and accuracy can be devastating as the energy is focused into the smaller heel area. This technique can easily break bones, immobilise joints and causing internal injuries to organs.

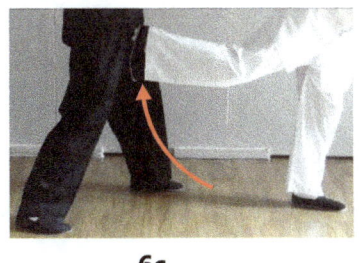 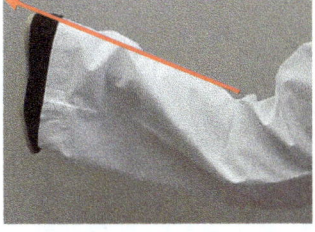

6c   **6d**

Figure 16-6c and 6d shows the striking foot attacking with a slight forward thrusting of the heel, allowing it to make contact with the target area, in this case the opponent's groin area.

Figure 16-6c-6d

Fighting Application:

Figure 16-6e

Figure 16-6e shows a fighting application using the back kick technique.

Black attacks White with a (L) punch to the midsection. White counters by leaning out of range of Black's attack and simultaneously counter striking with a midrange (R) back kick to Black's Tan Tien area.

Chapter 17

Stepping Methods of Hsing-I Chuan

Introduction

Footwork is probably one of the most important aspects of Hsing-I training. It does not matter how experienced the practitioner is, this aspect should never be overlooked and should be thoroughly understood in every movement of every form. While it is true that a high percentage of applications are performed from the hands in Hsing-I, it is the footwork and stepping methods that prepare the practitioner to be successful in their application of a technique.

If the stepping method is incorrect, the stance and balance of the practitioner will be affected. This will lead to an unstable platform from which to deliver strikes with any of the Seven Stars. Constant practise of the forms different stepping methods and attention down to the smallest detail will lead to a strong foundation from which a novice practitioner can progress to an advanced level.

Stepping methods in Hsing-I should be relaxed and look natural, transitioning from one move to the next without hesitation. It is ultimately the footwork and the ability to step correctly that will allow the practitioner to attack or defend successfully in confrontation. To achieve this level of proficiency is not easy and requires time and patience when training.

The following chapter shows some of the most common stepping methods employed in this system of Hsing-I and guidance to their practice. When practising the different stepping methods, remember that all practitioners are different. They are human beings, not machines, therefore, the size of steps and placement of feet will be individual to each practitioner. It takes time for some practitioners to develop the strength and flexibility required of the lower limbs to achieve the correct foot placements and this should be achieved slowly and without injury. The stepping methods shown can be employed alongside any combination of hand techniques from this system and so it is for this reason the reader is shown only the lower body section in the picture sequences that follow.

1. Half-Step Method

The 'Half-Step' method, sometimes referred to as the 'Follow-Step' method is the most commonly used stepping method in the Hsing-I system. It is taught from the very beginning of a practitioner's training and should become as natural as walking down the street. This method allows the practitioner to press forward into an opponent in a straight linear direction. As the practitioner moves forward they immediately follow up with their rear foot to recreate the original stance which is loaded with its weight at approximately 70% in the back foot to allow forward lunging power. Keeping the weight on the back foot and the front foot lighter allows increased multidirectional mobility and reduced vulnerability to attack from front leg sweeping techniques of an opponent.

This method can be applied by stepping through, in effect changing from one foot to the other (see figures 17-1a to 1e), which covers a larger distance. It can also be applied by remaining on the same side and stepping forward with the lead foot, half-stepping up with the rear foot and then repeating this process, in effect moving forward without changing stances. This can be useful when pressing into an opponent and they don't yield backwards; therefore, the practitioner can keep moving into them in small increments, keeping them under pressure and pressing home an advantage.

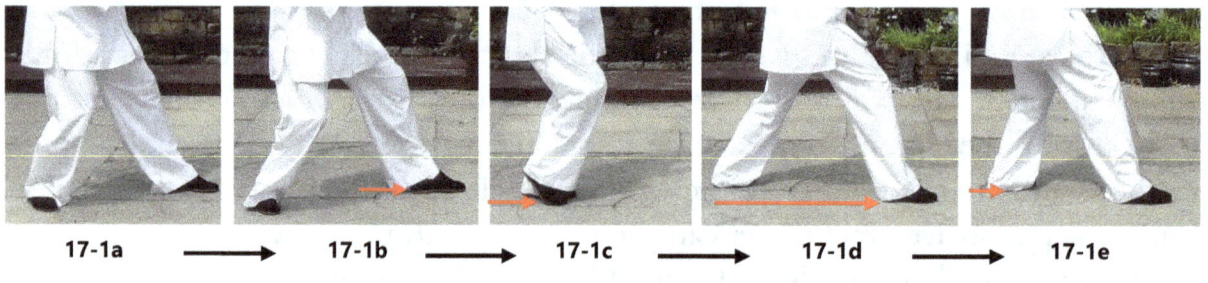

Figure 17-1

Figure 17-1a
Pi Chuan (L) stance with the power loaded into the (R) rear foot.
Figure 17-1b
From the (L) stance the practitioner takes a small step forward with (L) foot.
Figure 17-1c
Next the practitioner steps forward off the back (R) foot, transferring the weight and power into the (L) foot while passing closely to the inside of the (L) foot.
Figure 17-1d
The practitioners (R) foot continues forward and out in front, now becoming the lead foot, with the weight and power transferring into the (R) foot.
Figure 17-1e
As soon as the (R) foot is firmly planted in front of the practitioner it is immediately followed up by the (L) rear foot to half the distance between the two feet and

allowing the weight to transfer and sink into the (L) rear foot, ready for the step to be repeated. The practitioner is now in Pi Chuan (R) stance.

2. Chicken-Step Method

The 'Chicken-Step' method is an effective stepping method of the Hsing-I system made famous by Li Cheng of Honan province who was the nephew of Master Chang Chih-Cheng. Li became very proficient at Hsing-I and had plenty of opportunity to apply his skills as he worked as a bodyguard for supply convoys. It was said he would often be seen practising his chicken-step in his free time by chasing horses or mules in the convoys.

This method is borne out of the Pi Chuan stance where the weight is loaded into the rear foot and allows the practitioner to rapidly change feet, either on the spot or moving forwards. The stomping action of the foot can be used by an experienced practitioner to generate increased transference of chi into an attacking technique and allows for a quick change of feet which can confuse an opponent. The stomping action of the foot can also be applied directly as a method of attack when executed directly onto an opponent's ankle or foot. When practising the chicken-step method, the head should never 'bob' up and down, but should remain still throughout. When performed correctly the chicken-step method should be executed with such speed that the opponent has no time to react.

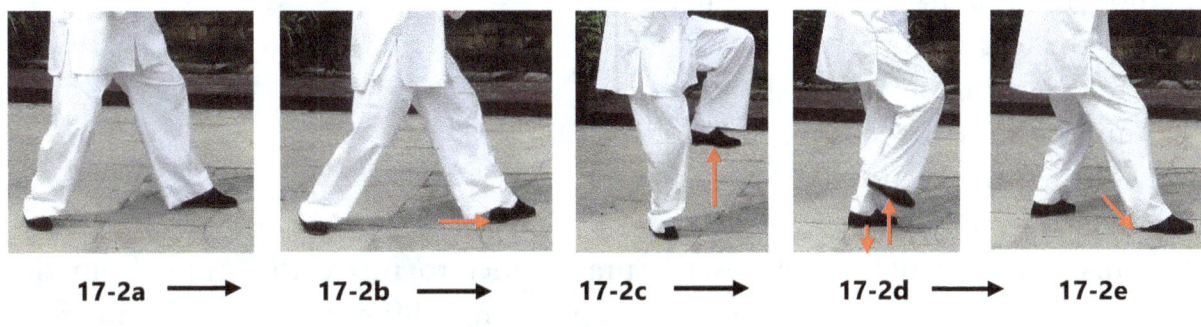

Figure 17-2

Figure 17-2a
Pi Chuan (L) stance with the power loaded into the (R) rear foot.

Figure 17-2b
In this forward stepping example of the chicken-step the practitioner takes a small step forwards with the front (L) foot, being mindful to keep the weight still loaded into the rear (R) foot and the forward foot relatively light.

Figure 17-2c
The practitioner rapidly raises the (L) foot from the hip, raising the knee and thigh parallel to the ground. The trunk of the body must remain still and head level throughout.

Figure 17-2d

The (L) foot is stomped firmly to the ground and as soon as contact is made the opposite (R) foot is raised, in effect transferring the weight and power from the (R) foot to the (L) foot.

Note: At no time should both feet be off the ground at the same time. This is 'jumping' and leaves the practitioner disconnected from the ground and therefore vulnerable to attack and completely unstable.

Figure 17-2e

When the (L) foot is planted solidly to the ground the raised (R) foot can then be placed forwards to complete the chicken-step technique and place the practitioner in Pi Chuan (R) stance.

3. 45-degree Hook-Step Method

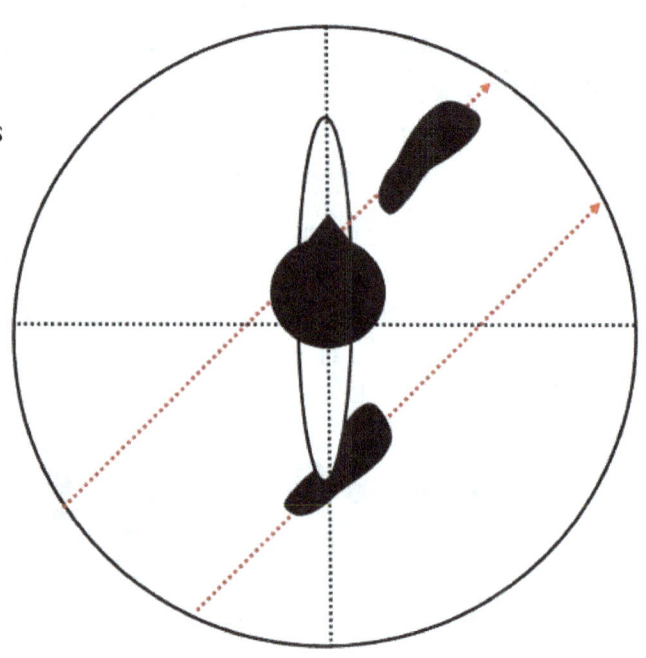

The '45-degree Hook-Step' method is from this lineage of Hsing-I. Sometimes it is referred to as 'saw tooth' or 'zig-zag' stepping, however in essence they are all similar descriptions for the same method. The main reason for this stepping method is to allow the practitioner to keep the feet moving forwards and close to the centreline whilst allowing the upper body to change angle, away from the centreline of an opponent's attack.

This stepping method allows the practitioner to rotate the trunk from the normal 45-degree angle seen in Pi Chuan position to 90 degrees which is in effect side on to the opponent's attack. By keeping both feet at the 45-degree angle to the centreline this allows the upper body to evade an oncoming straight line attack without losing the centreline advantage to the opponent. See diagram opposite.

Note: The sequence of pictures below (see figures 17-3a to 3b) are shown from head on as this is the clearest way to show the angles of the steps employed in this method.

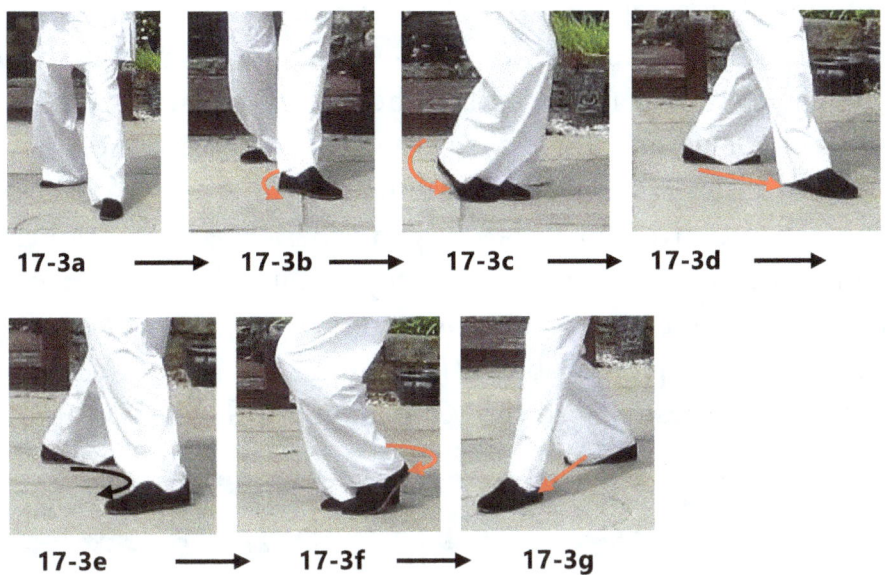

Figure 17-3

Figure 17-3a

The practitioner starts in (L) Pi Chuan stance.

Figure 17-3b

The practitioner begins with the weight held in the rear (R) foot. Next, they step forward with the (L) foot, hook stepping at 45-degrees to the outside of the centreline.

Figure 17-3c

Transferring the weight into the (L) foot, the (R) rear foot is brought up alongside the (L) foot but remaining weightless as it passes alongside the inside of the (L) foot.

Figure 17-3d

The (R) foot passes through the inside of the (L) foot and is placed facing outwards at a 45-degree angle to the centreline, mirroring the angle of the opposite foot. As soon as the (R) foot is planted on the ground the (L) foot is brought a half-step forward, but remaining behind the (R) foot just as in the half-step method discussed previously to re-establish the weighting on the rear foot.

Figure 17-3e, 3f and 3g

Repeats the same movements on the opposite side which leaves the practitioner in the starting position as shown in figure 17-3a above.

4. 45-degree Half-Step Method

The '45-degree Half-Step' method is simply a variation of the half-step method discussed previously and utilises the same angles of the feet with the forward foot pointing straight ahead and the rear foot placed at a 45-degree angle, just as with Pi Chuan stance. It is initially learned by the practitioner in the Five Elements forms of Fire and Earth, and further trained throughout several of the Twelve Animals and

Combination forms. This stepping method allows the practitioner to step out of the direct straight line of attack and counter attack from a more favourable angle.

This stepping method can also be useful when a practitioner is physically weaker than their opponent or potentially less experienced. Instead of meeting the attack head on, the practitioner can side step and redirect the linear force of the opponent's attack away from their centre. Further to this an experienced practitioner can easily unbalance an opponent and open up a new range of target areas to attack which are not normally available from a head on position.

Note: The sequence of pictures below (see figures 17-4a to 4f) are shown from head on as this is the clearest way to show the angles of the steps employed in this method.

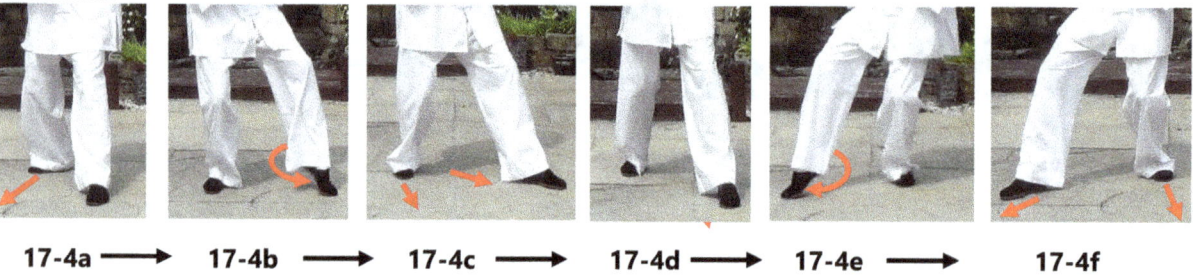

17-4a ➔ 17-4b ➔ 17-4c ➔ 17-4d ➔ 17-4e ➔ 17-4f

Figure 17-4

Figure 17-4a
Starting in (L) Pi Chuan stance. Transfer the weight into the (L) foot and then step forward with the rear (R) foot at an angle of 45-degrees to the centreline.

Figure 17-4b
Next transfer the weight back into the rear (R) foot as the practitioner turns to the left bringing the (L) foot onto its ball and into (L) cat stance.

Figure 17-4c
From (L) cat stance position the practitioner takes a small step forward with the lightly weighted (L) foot at an angle of 45 degrees to the centreline and then follows up with the (R) foot by using the half-step method, thereby returning the balance of weight into the rear (R) foot.

Figure 17-4d, 4e, 4f
Next the practitioner takes a small step forwards with the (R) foot back down the original centreline of the starting position and repeats the same sequence of movements on the opposite right side.

Note: The practitioner always takes a step straight forward before turning to the 45-degree angle and this is in keeping with the constant forward pressing theories seen in the application of most Hsing-I techniques.

5. Shock-Step Method

The 'Shock-Step' method is utilised when a practitioner must move backwards from an opponent's attack. This is useful when the practitioner is looking to counter an attack and yet remain able to deliver an attack of their own. An opponent is most vulnerable when they are fully committed to an attack and an experienced practitioner can use this moment to draw in the opponent and then simultaneously unleash a counter strike of their own.

The method is referred to as 'shock-stepping', as when the practitioner steps back they stop dead in their tracks, creating a shock-like wave of energy from the ground back up to their hands. This is achieved by planting their rear stepping foot firmly into the ground providing them with a firm foundation and platform to counterstrike. At the same time moving back from the opponent in time with their attack allows the practitioner to negate the incoming attacks flow of energy. As the opponent is committed to their own strike, they literally impale themselves on the shock-step and counterstrike like a train hitting the buffers at the end of the line. If the retreating platform is stable, this self-inflicted force increases the total power of the counterstrike, making it potentially devastating.

The pictures below are shown from right to left as this is the clearest way to show the sequence of the steps employed in this method.

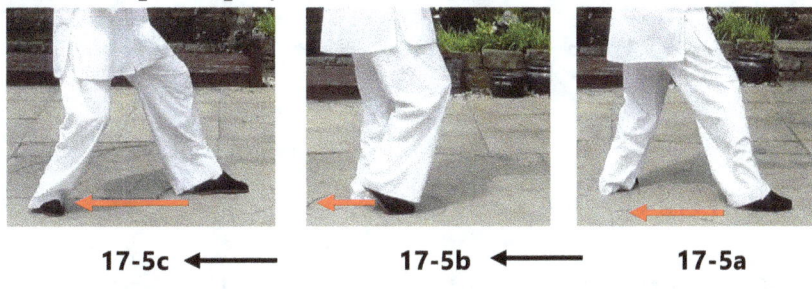

Figure 17-5

Figure 17-5a
Starting at the far right of the sequence above and moving backwards, the practitioner starts in Pi Chuan (R) stance.

Figure 17-5b
Maintaining the weight firmly into the (L) rear foot, the (R) foot is drawn backwards, passing closely by the inside of the (L) foot.

Figure 17-5c
On passing behind the (L) foot, the (R) foot then plants itself hard against the floor at a 45-degree angle consistent with the same alignment of the Pi Chuan starting position only this time in (L) Pi Chuan stance.

Note: This movement sequence must be smooth and perfectly timed with the opponents attack to be truly effective. There is no half-step with this method.

Hsing-I Chuan | The Practice of Heart and Mind Boxing

6. Hook-Step Method

The 'Hook-Step' method is trained in Tuo form of the Twelve Animal forms in this lineage of Hsing-I. This method is very useful in stepping around, behind or even onto the foot of an opponent. This initial step is then followed up immediately by the rear foot in effect turning the practitioner sideways facing to their opponent. This obviously allows the practitioner to evade an oncoming, frontal attack and change the angles in favour of their own counter attack.

The hook-step can also be used to hook the foot around an opponent's ankle or foot and create an opportunity to sweep, trip and even trap at the knee or ankle. When executed correctly this can unbalance an opponent and leave them vulnerable to attack.

Note: The sequence of pictures below (See figures 17-6a to 6e) are shown from head on as this is the clearest way to show the angles of the steps employed in this method.

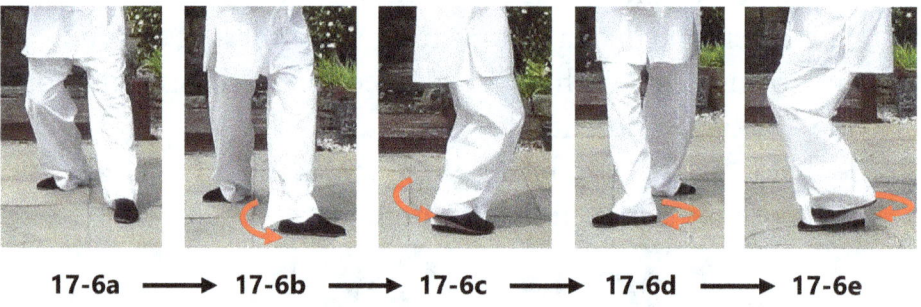

Figure 17-6

Figure 17-6a
The practitioner starts in (L) Pi Chuan stance.

Figure 17-6b
Stepping forwards with the (L) foot, the practitioner hooks the (L) foot outwards away from their own centreline to an angle of 90 degrees from the starting position in figure 16-6a above. At the same time, the (R) foot drives forwards in the same direction to support the (L) foots advance.

Figure 17-6c
As the weight is transferred into the (L) foot the (R) foot now follows through and turns to 90 degrees in sync with the whole body and rests slightly off the ground with the legs pressed lightly together.

Figure 17-6d
Stepping forwards with the (R) foot, the practitioner hooks the (R) foot outwards away from their own centreline to an angle of 90 degrees from the centreline.

Figure 17-6e
At the same time, the (L) foot drives forwards in the same direction to support the advance of the (R) foot. From this position, the same hook-step and follow up step

can be repeated to the opposite side in effect turning the practitioner through 180 degrees with each step taken.

Note: The hook-step method can be practiced stepping either forwards or backwards as in Tuo form allowing it to be trained for use in both attack and counter attack situations.

7. Close the Gap Step Method

The 'Close the Gap' stepping method is first trained in Wood form of the Five Elements and later in several of the Combination forms in this lineage of Hsing-I. It is commonly used to advance steadily into an opponent often in time with their movements allowing the practitioner to keep a favourable fighting distance to attack from. In practical application, this stepping method can be used forwards or backwards, it can close and open the feet on the same side or switch from side to side depending on the situation.

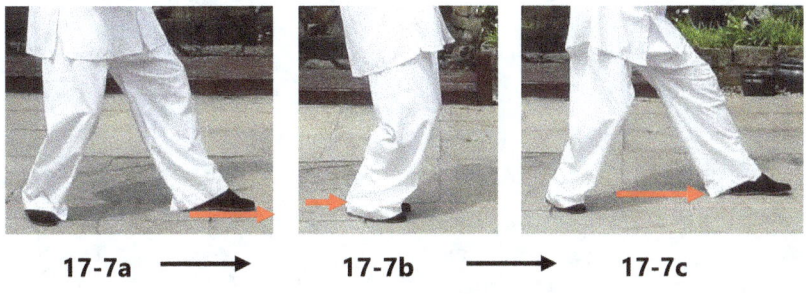

17-7a ⟶   17-7b ⟶   17-7c

Figure 17-7

Figure 17-7a
The practitioner starts in (L) Pi Chuan stance with weight set in the rear (R) foot.
Figure 17-7b
Next the practitioner takes a small step forward with the (L) foot and then follows immediately with the (R) foot, transferring the weight into the (L) foot whilst the (R) foot steps up bringing it to rest solidly planted into the ground with the insteps of both feet interlocked. As the feet come together the weight should be transferred back into the (R) foot.
Figure 17-7c
Next the (L) foot can then step forward followed up by a half-step with the (R) foot behind, returning the practitioner to the same starting position as figure 17-7a above.

Note: The half-step following up of the rear foot is not always used or necessary in this stepping method. In Wood form, it is used but in some movements contained within the Combined forms and when moving backwards it is not. In applications, the use of a half-step helps with delivery of power and brings the stance back to its original form but it is only used if the distance of the step to an opponent requires it.

8. Crescent-Step Method

The 'Crescent-Step' method is trained within the Eight Preparatory forms (Ba Bu Da) in this lineage of Hsing-I. Its method trains the practitioner to advance forwards whilst also allowing them to step inside or outside the opponents forward leg and take control of their centre. This stepping method can leave the opponent vulnerable to a sweep from the outside or the inside and can be used forwards or backwards and serves to move the practitioners forward foot into a more favourable position to dominate the fighting situation. Its method keeps the practitioner centrally weighted making it generally more stable at the expense of mobility.

The half-step of the rear foot is used in the sequence of the forms, but not always used or necessary in application of the forms techniques against an opponent. As with all use of the half-step method in Hsing-I applications, the stepping up of the rear foot helps with power delivery and brings the stance back to its original form but is only used if the distance of the step towards the opponent requires it.

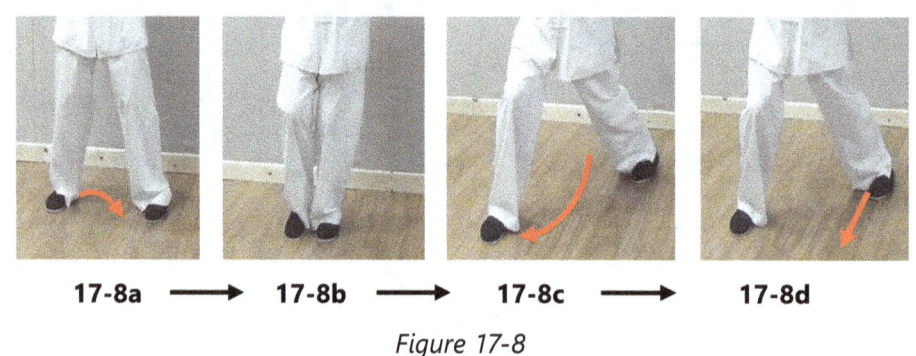

Figure 17-8

Figure 17-8a, 8b
The practitioner starts in a high horse stance with the weight set equally between both feet. From this position, the (R) foot moves inwards to the centreline and the opposite foot, transferring the weight across to the (L) foot.

Figure 17-8c
Next the practitioner steps forward with the (R) foot in an arcing pattern from inside out (I/O) planting it firmly on the ground in a (R) bow stance opening up the stance to its original width with feet at approximately shoulders width apart.

Figure 17-8d
From figure 17-8c the (L) rear foot can then follow up with a half-step placing the practitioner into a (R) forward stance with the weight set centrally between both feet. When this stepping method is completed both feet face forwards, as though placed on tram lines making it different from the usual 45-degree rear foot found in most of the Hsing-I stepping methods and stances previously described. From the finish position shown in figure 17-8d the practitioner then takes a small step

forwards with the (R) foot and then steps through with the (L) foot in an arcing pattern repeating the sequence on the opposite side as previously described in figures 17-8a to 8d.

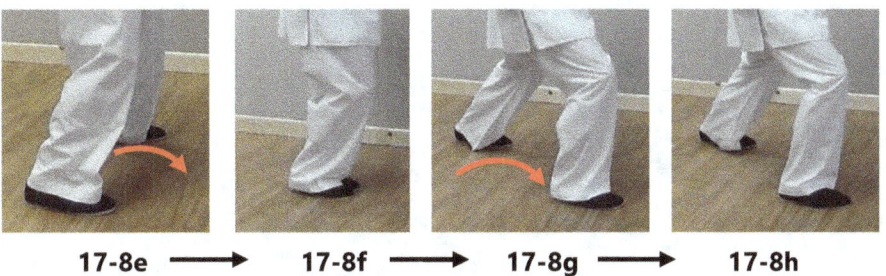

Figure 17-8e, 8f, 8g, 8h

For visual reference figures 17-8e to 8h shows the same right sided stepping sequence as figures 17-8a to 8d previously from a side angle view.

Chapter 18

Stances of Hsing-I Chuan

Introduction

'Stance' refers to the position of the lower limbs and feet when in a fixed stationary position. In order to achieve a high level of skill a practitioner's stances must be correct to allow the muscles and tendons to relax, thereby enhancing the natural flow of chi and blood to the lower limbs, keeping them strong and healthy.

The correct stance in Hsing-I practice is the foundation to all movements. Movement is dependent on balance and balance is dependent on stance. It is difficult to perform efficient movement without balance. Whether a technique is successful or not depends on efficient movement. Therefore, the most important function of any stance is to achieve balance, despite a moving centre of gravity and maintain it whilst leading a movement to its next stance.

The centre of gravity originates from the gravity of earth. Therefore, the wider the stance, the more stable and safely balanced the practitioner is when their base is equidistant from both sides of the centre of gravity (figure 18-0a). If the stance is shorter and the centre of gravity is not equidistant from each side (figure 18-0b) then the more unstable the practitioner is and the easier it will be to uproot them and move them off balance.

Figure 18-0

However, whilst a low, wide equal stance may make a strong foundation to strike from, it is less manoeuvrable as it is rooted firmly to the ground at both feet. A higher, narrower off centred stance is generally a weaker platform to strike from but much more mobile, allowing the practitioner to move, evade and attack which maybe more useful in a given situation.

Within this lineage there are a wide variation of stances which utilise centre, balance, weighting, height and distance of base to allow for increased or decreased mobility relevant to the technique being delivered. The appropriate stance is always a deliberation between stability and mobility and this choice ultimately affects the success of an application of technique. The varied stances of the system are routinely practiced throughout the forms making them second nature to the experienced practitioner.

1. Pi Chuan Stance

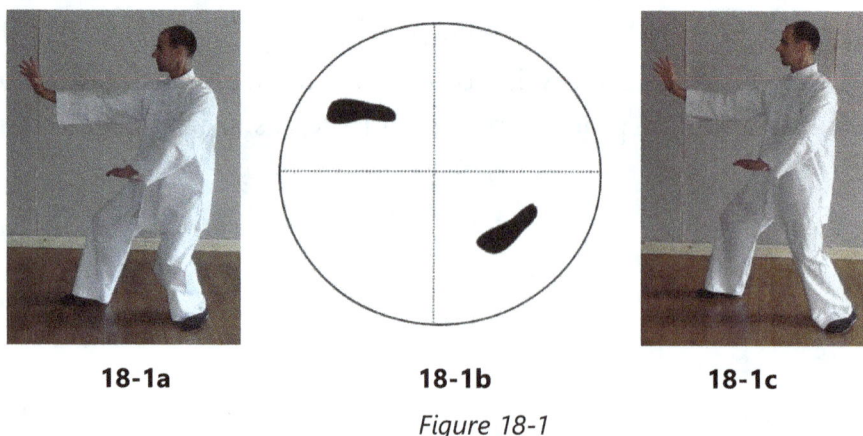

Figure 18-1

'Pi Chuan' stance is the most commonly practised stance in the Hsing-I system. Initially it is trained with a distribution of 70% of the weight into the back leg/foot (See figure 18-1a). The forward foot, with 30% of the weight, points directly straight ahead towards the opponent with the rear foot pointing at 45 degrees (See figure

18-1b). The knees are aligned directly with the foot, which allows the practitioner to develop strong muscles and tendons suitable for the application of Hsing-I in practise. This weighting also allows for good mobility and stores chi in the rear leg ready to power the body forward as required.

As a practitioner becomes more experienced and the lower limbs are well developed through training, the stance can then be practised from a 50:50 weighting (See figure 18-1c). This stance creates a more stable base to deliver power from while retaining a suitable amount of mobility and is characteristic of the Shanxi lineage. An experienced practitioner who is able to manipulate their opponent in practise is confident enough to reduce their need for mobility in order to have a stronger centre from which they can overwhelm and dominate their opponent.

2. Cross Stance

18-2a   18-2b

Figure 18-2

The 'Cross' stance can be practised at various heights and distances of base depending on the given situation. This stance is sometimes referred to as 'T' stance due to the 'T' shaped alignment of the feet. The method allows for the simple crossing over of the feet without getting them tangled, where the forward foot is placed at 90 degrees and takes 70% or more of the body weight initially before weighting back to 50:50 on completion of the stance. This stance can advance directly at the opponent, retreat tactically, drawing in an opponent or side step away from an opponent's centreline of attack, allowing for a more favourable angle to be created for the practitioner to counter attack.

The placing of the front foot at 90 degrees can be used to cross over and stamp down on an opponent's foot which can cause considerable injury to the small bones and joints. It also prevents the opponent from withdrawing as the practitioner delivers their attack. This trapping of the opponent's foot in attack is a strong characteristic of the Hsing-I fighting method. Figure 18-2a shows a cross stance withdrawing away from an attack while simultaneously blocking with the rear hand using a crescent palm block. This technique is demonstrated from Swallow form.

3. Bow Stance

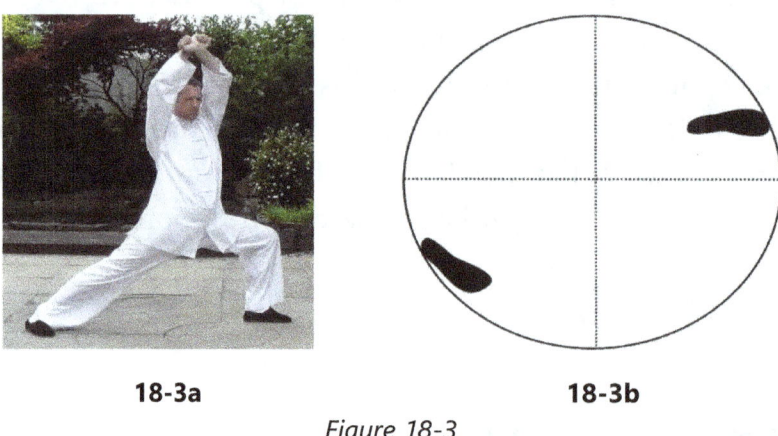

18-3a   **18-3b**

Figure 18-3

In 'Bow' stance, the feet are placed widely apart making it a stable stance in a forward direction facing an opponent. The forward leg is bent at the knee between 70 and 90 degrees, like a bow holding 70% or more of the weight. The rear leg is held straight but never totally locked at the knee, storing 30% or less of the weight. There are several variations of the bow stance used in Hsing-I which utilises different weight, height and base distributions and allows the stance to be applied to different techniques both offensively and defensively.

Figure 18-3a shows a 90-degree front leg variation of the bow stance with a straight facing front foot. This is combined with a high double-handed cross block used to an overhead attack from the front. This technique is practised in several of the combined forms of Hsing-I.

4. Pigeon Toe Stance

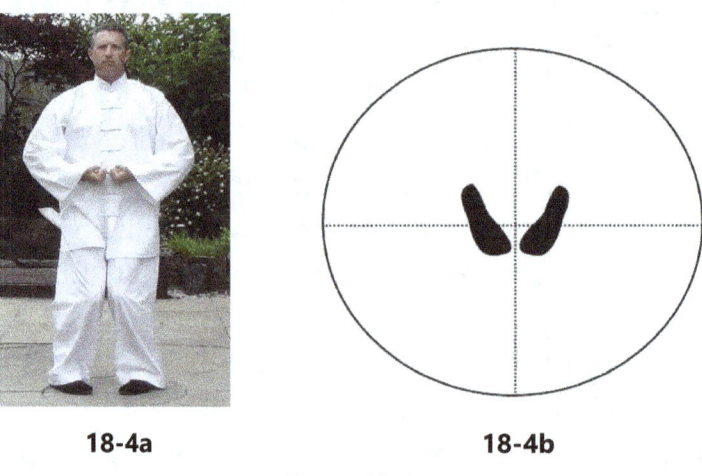

18-4a   **18-4b**

Figure 18-4

'Pigeon Toe' stance is a narrow stance which reduces the overall stability of the practitioner, however, its weighting makes it very mobile and is usually applied when turning and changing direction quickly. The weight is 50:50 and transferred through the heels of the feet alternately as the practitioner changes direction (figure 18-4a).

The feet are hooked inwards to 45 degrees (figure 18-4b) as they turn and can be utilised to hook behind an opponent's ankle, sweeping them off balance. Furthermore, the angle of the knees pointing together can also be used to apply pressure to the opponent's lower limb. When the foot is anchored correctly behind the opponent's foot and pressure through the practitioner's stance is applied this method can take an opponent to the ground. This turned in angle of the knees also serves to guard against any groin attack on turning into or away from the opponent. This stance is shown clearly in the turn during practice of Metal and Wood forms of the Five Elements.

5. Horse Stance

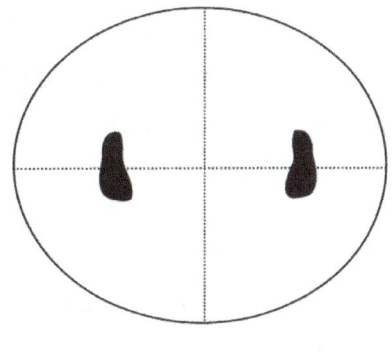

18-5a   18-5b

Figure 18-5

In 'Horse' stance, the feet are placed equal distance apart from the centreline as if straddling a horse. Both knees are bent between 45 and 90 degrees parallel to the ground. Variations of this stance are common to almost all styles of kung-fu and forms the core practice for leg strength training and formation of a foundation to practise basic techniques from. The very fact that almost all styles of kung-fu train this stance shows its importance in practice. There are a few variations of the stance which usually involves changes to foot positions and angle of the knees.

Horse stance is very stable from side to side due to its linear base of support and its centre of gravity, but not so practical in fighting applications where it is less than advisable to stand directly opposite your opponent revealing your own centreline face on. When pressure is applied from front to back in this stance it is more easily uprooted. It is for this reason the Hsing-I practitioner favours Pi Chuan stance in application.

Figure 18-5a above shows a horse stance with a 45 degree knee bend and 50/50% weighting. The feet face straight forwards with the knees flexed directly over but not beyond the toes. This stance restricts undue stress on the knee ligaments, limiting chance of injury during training and allows a smooth flow of chi through the joints keeping them strong and healthy.

6. Cat Stance

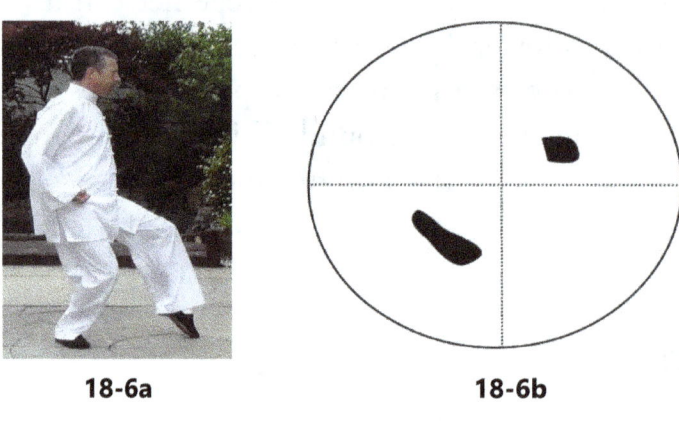

18-6a 18-6b

Figure 18-6

'Cat' stance is a narrow and mobile stance (See figure 18-6a). The weighting is held heavily in the rear leg at approximately 90:10 ratio. It is for this reason the stance is sometimes called 'sitting' stance due to the fact the practitioner sits into their rear leg. In Hsing-I this stance is the backbone of the chicken-step method which allows for quick mobile feet and legs changing from left to right stance in an instant. This can confuse an opponent and create a new angle or target of attack for the experienced practitioner.

The lightly weighted front foot allows for reduced vulnerability to sweeps at the front leg and also the ability to attack or block with the foot from close range, which is the preferred range of the Hsing-I fighter.

This stance is demonstrated in numerous forms throughout the Hsing-I system and is often used as a transition stance when changing from one posture to another. It is most frequently trained in Fire and Earth forms of the Five Elements.

7. Single Leg Stance

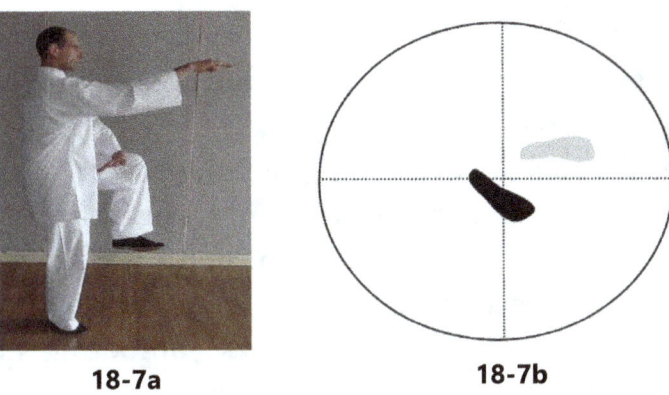

Figure 18-7

'Single Leg' stance uses a very narrow base of support, reducing the stability and foundation of the practitioner to the minimum. As its name suggests, the weighting is 100% on one leg. The effectiveness of this stance should not be underestimated as it allows the feet to be very mobile and is often used to spin or turn quickly out of the attack line of an opponent and counter attack at speed. It also allows the practitioner to raise and lower their form in order to attack or evade from different heights.

Variations of this stance can have the raised knee between 20 and 90 degrees. The foot can also be angled with the toe pointing towards the ground utilising the full power of the gastrocnemius and hamstring muscles to drive home a knee strike or dorsi-flexed holding the sole parallel to the ground enabling the practitioner to stomp hard to the opponent's foot or block an oncoming kick as shown in figure 18-7a. This stance can be used in training to develop a practitioners balance and sense of centre, helping to create internal awareness and creation of a strong root. It is mainly practised in Cock and Tuo of the Twelve Animal forms.

8. Drop Stance

Figure 18-8

'Drop' stance can be a difficult stance to train for the novice practitioner. It requires flexibility in the back, hips, knees and ankles, alongside appropriate leg strength, to hold an approximate 90% weighting in the rear leg (See figure 18-8a). Both feet should remain planted to the ground and the rear knee should remain in line with the rear foot in order to avoid injury.

Practise, time and patience allows most practitioners to achieve this stance to an acceptable level, however, as a practitioner gets older or if the novice is older before starting training, the stance can be modified and still be effective in its application.

This stance allows the practitioner to change heights rapidly when fighting and can be used to drop and grab an opponent's lower leg uprooting them. It is also useful to evade high-kicking attacks such as roundhouse kicks. To execute this technique as a fighting application the practitioner requires courage and timing alongside balance and speed to stay in range of an attack, relying solely on their technique to evade and counter it.

This stance is practised in Swallow form and is usually trained later in the Hsing-I system, to allow for the practitioner to build up appropriate leg strength and flexibility before starting to train this stance.

9. Dragon Stance

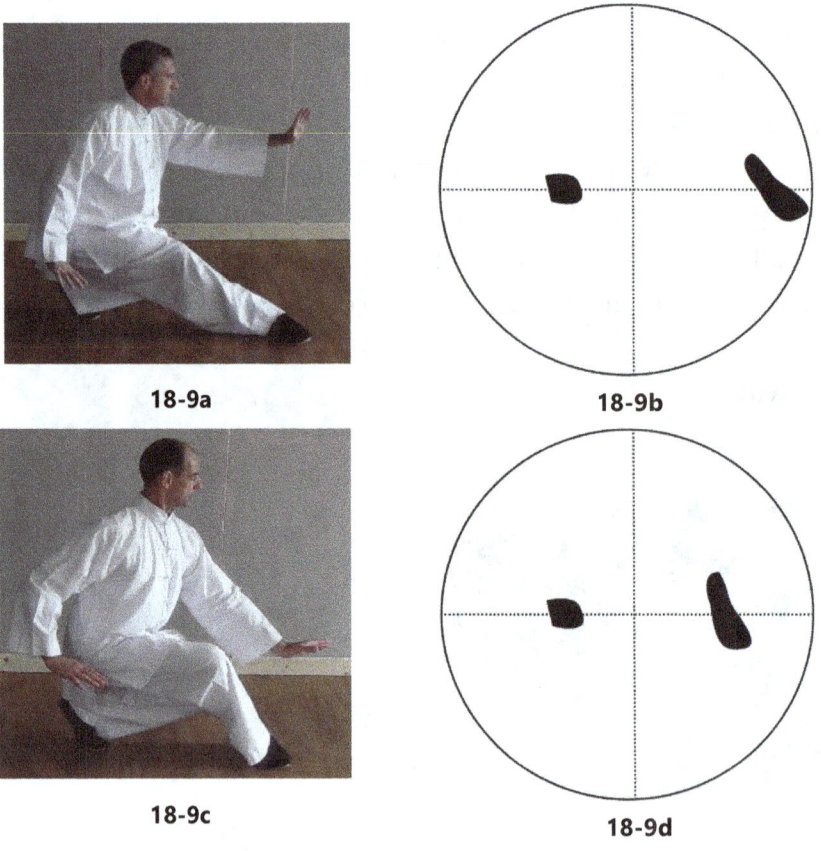

Figure 18-9

'Dragon' stance takes its name from the animal form it is practised in most frequently. It is a low stance with the weighting heavily on the rear leg (See figure 18-9a). In this stance, the front foot is placed flat to the ground at a 45-degree angle outside the centreline and the rear foot kept balanced on the ball of the foot. This is another stance that is difficult to achieve for the novice. There are variations to this stance that can be made to accommodate any practitioner who cannot achieve this stance by raising the height to standing or by changing the weighting to 50:50 and shortening the distance between the feet. This variation is often referred to as 'cross-sitting' stance (See figure 18-9c).

In application, the 45-degree forward foot can be used to trap an opponent's foot or kick to the knee. On lowering and pressing forward to the ground this stance can be used to press an opponent's knee into hyperextension and force them to the ground.

Dragon stance is also practised in Wood of the Five Elements forms and practise of this stance improves balance and leg strength, which also serves to strengthen the whole body, helping to develop the muscles, tendons and bones suitable for the rigorous demands of self-defence. The aerobic demands of the posture in the rising and falling also help to move chi and blood throughout the body, keeping it internally healthy.

10. Bow Stance with 45 Degree Foot

18-10a   18-10b   18-10c

Figure 18-10

A variation of the Bow stance discussed earlier is that of Water form (See figure 18-10a). The weighting of this stance is similar, with approximately 60% on the front leg and 40% on the back leg (See figure 18-10b). The main characteristic is the change in angle of the front foot which is placed at a 45-degree angle in opposition to the rear foot which is at 45 degrees in the opposite direction (See figure 18-10c).

In application, this stance allows the practitioner to press forward into the opponent and use the angle of the forward foot to trap or stomp on the opponents corresponding forward foot. The 45-degree angle helps to avoid missing the target foot as the sideways foot is wider than the forward facing foot, which could easily slip off the target area. Regardless of the angle of the foot employed in any bow stance the knee above the foot must always follow the same direction and angle as the foot below to avoid injury. Further to this, the 45-degree angle gives a more stable base to drill the Water form hand technique forward into its target area.

Chapter 19

Opening and Closing Method of Hsing-I Forms

Introduction

The method of opening into 'San Ti' (Pi Chuan) posture prior to starting almost all the forms of this lineage is also common to most lineages of Hsing-I Chuan. Once the practitioner can open into or return to (L) Pi Chuan posture correctly they can start or finish most of the forms from the system. It is therefore important to study these sequences to open and close the forms which are discussed in later chapters of this book correctly.

The opening method leads the practitioner to a left sided Pi Chuan stance and likewise the closing method returns through a left sided Pi Chuan stance. Traditionally Hsing-I starts, turns and finishes on the left side, which means when the left foot is forwards in a given posture. This is carried out in accordance with the Taoist belief that the energy of the heavens revolves around the earth to the left and therefore the practitioner should adhere to this principle starting, turning and finishing always to the left, as this is in balance with the natural law of the universe.

Opening and closing of forms is crucially important as this sequence of movements sets the tone, both mentally and physically for the whole form being practiced. It is the point when the practitioner focuses their intent and spirit on the movements of the form and then subsequently returns them back to their normal pre-Hsing-I mindset. As with all movement in Hsing-I the sequence has martial application and learning to be gained from it and should not just be considered as a simple method to start and finish the forms. The reason an opening and closing method exists in all forms tells the practitioner that it must be important or why keep practicing it!

Note: There are several forms in this lineage that do not use (L) Pi Chuan to start and finish their sequences, however these forms do start from and finish to the left side. When these forms are shown in this book the appropriate start and finish sequence will be shown and described as part of the sequence.

1. Opening Method

Figure 19-1

Figure 19-1a

All forms of Hsing-I are started from 'Wuji' or neutral posture. The feet are together with the left front foot facing forward down the centreline and the right rear foot angled at 45 degrees to the front foot with heels touching. The legs and body are straight with the arms and hands relaxed at the sides of the body.

Figure 19-1b

Opening a form into (L) Pi Chuan posture the practitioner first starts with their feet together, the (L) foot pointing straight forward and the (R) foot at a 45-degree angle. The heels are touching and the knees are relaxed and straight. The hands move from the sides of the body and the dominant hand rests in its opposite's palm, facing upward with the tips of the thumbs touching. The arms are naturally relaxed and curved with the hands held slightly off the body at the height of the Tan Tien. The eyes are looking straight ahead.

Figure 19-1c, 1d

The hands smoothly open, raised in a symmetrical arc to the sides, palms up as the practitioner inhales. The knees remain relaxed and straight. The arms remain curved and the head and eyes stay focused straight ahead. The arms and hands continue to raise and circle over the level of the top of the head.

Figure 19-1e

Upon reaching the highest point above the head, the hands come together, facing palms down with the thumbs and index fingers touching.

1f → 1g → 1h → 1i → 1j →

Figure 19-1f, 1g

Both the hands press down to the height of the Tan Tien as the practitioner exhales, the legs bend at the knees, sinking the body in time with the hands. The knees both bend subtly with the knee caps moving slightly in the direction of the feet below them. The legs should remain close together throughout this movement. At the point when the hands reach the level of the Tan Tien the knees should have ended their movement. This timing of upper and lower body must remain completely coordinated and should start and finish together.

Figure 19-1h

Next, the feet remain rooted and in the same position whilst the waist and body turn back to the left in effect facing the upper body straight ahead. At the same time, the practitioner inhales as the (R) hand drives forward in the form of a fist, punching outwards to the height of the nose, with the (L) fist held closely at the (R) elbow.

Figure 19-1i, 1j

Finally, the practitioner exhales as the (R) hand has reached the height of the nose the (L) hand punches directly up and over the top of the (R) arm in effect replacing it and then the (L) hand opens and presses subtly outwards and downwards in front. At the same time, the (R) hand pulls subtly backwards and down to the height of the Tan Tien opening and pressing palm down. As the (L) arm and hand move forward so does the (L) leg and foot, in effect opening the stance. The body turns back to 45 degrees from the centreline of the form. The weighting should be 70:30 on the back foot. The timing of both hands and feet must be perfect and all movements must start and finish together. The eyes and head remain focused straight ahead throughout this sequence. The practitioner is now in (L) Pi Chuan posture and ready to commence the chosen form.

Note: There is no half-step with the rear foot on this opening movement.

2. Closing Method

Figure 19-2

From (L) Pi Chuan stance the practitioner can finish any form correctly. This process is simply a reverse sequence of the opening method described above.

Figure 19-2a

The practitioner starts the closing method in (L) Pi Chuan.

Figure 19-2b

First take a small step forward with the (L) foot, keeping it facing toes forward. Follow this by bringing up the back (R) foot to place its heel next to the heel of the (L) foot. The back foot remains at 45 degrees to the front foot. The knees remain bent, keeping the practitioner consistent with the height of the previous posture. At the same time both hands come together with the dominant hand resting in its opposite's palm, facing palms upward with the tips of the thumbs touching. The arms are naturally relaxed and curved with the hands held slightly off the body at the height of the 'Tan Tien'. The eyes are looking straight ahead.

Figure 19-2c, 2d, 2e

The feet remain in the same position with the legs close together and the knees held bent. The hands smoothly open, raised in a symmetrical arc to the sides, palms up as the practitioner inhales. The arms remain curved and continue to raise and circle over the level of the top of the head.

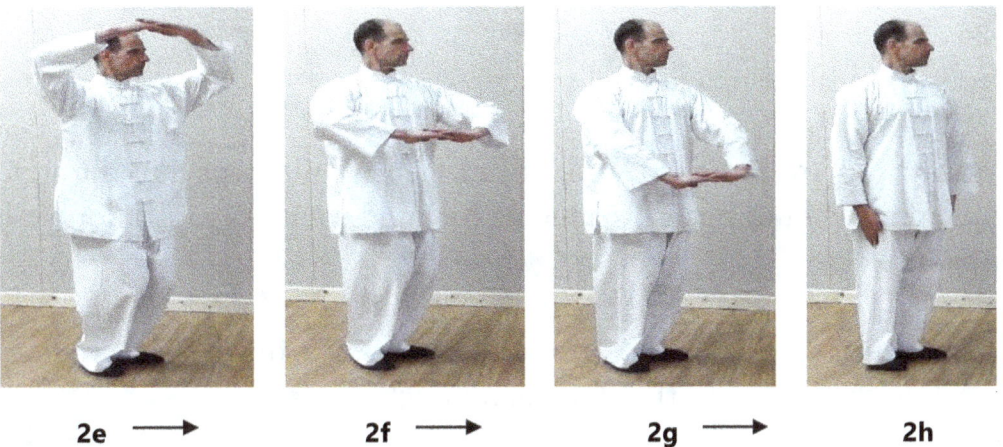

2e → 2f → 2g → 2h

Figure 19-2f, 2g

Both the hands press, palms down to the height of the Tan Tien as the practitioner exhales, the legs straighten at the knees, raising the body back to its full height in time with the hands. The legs should remain close together throughout this movement. At the point when the hands reach the level of the Tan Tien the knees should have ended their movement. This timing of upper and lower body must remain completely coordinated and should start and finish together. The eyes and head remain focused straight ahead throughout.

Figure 19-2h

Finally, all forms of Hsing-I are finished by returning to the empty state of Wuji posture. The feet are together with the left front foot facing forward down the centreline and the right rear foot angled at 45 degrees to the front foot with heels touching. The legs and body are straight with the arms and hands returning to a relaxed position at the sides of the body.

This completes the 'opening' and 'closing' methods for use in this lineage of Hsing-I. Following are two simple examples of possible fighting applications that can be derived from the 'open' and 'close' sequence of movements.

3. Open and Close Sequence - Fighting Applications:

Opening Form - Movements: 1g, 1h and 1i

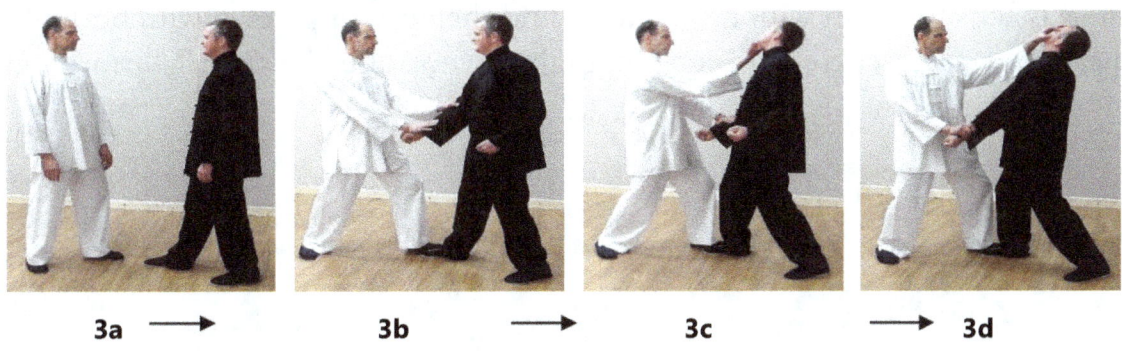

3a → 3b → 3c → 3d

App 19-3a
White faces off to Black in a neutral stance.
App 19-3b
Black throws a (R) low punch to White's Tan Tien. White steps into the attack with his (L) foot, directly onto Black's advancing foot and counters with a double-handed crescent palm block.
App 19-3c
On taking control of Black's (R) arm White presses it down and simultaneously strikes Black to the jaw using (R) Pi Chuan punch.
App 19-3d
Before Black can react, White then cover blocks Black's attempted (L) punch and strikes with a (L) Pi Chuan palm to Black's jaw.

Closing Form Movements:

Application 1 - Movement 2g

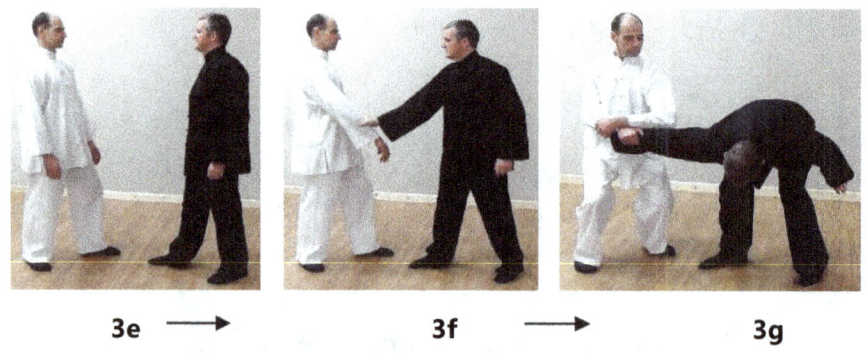

Figure 19-3e
White faces off to Black in a neutral stance.
Figure 19-3f
Black steps in (R) and cross grabs to White's (R) wrist.
Figure 19-3g
White steps to the outside of Black's attack with his (L) foot and counters by circling around Black's (R) wrist with his (L) hand and then pressing down with both hands to perform a small circle wrist lock and taking control of Black's (R) arm, forcing him towards the ground.

Application 2 - Movements 2b, 2c, 2d, 2e, 2f and 2g

3h → 3i → 3j → 3k

Figure 19-3h
White faces off to Black in a neutral stance.

Figure 19-3i
Black steps in (L) and throws a (L) low punch to White's ribs. White steps to the outside of the attack with his (R) foot and counters with a (R) spear hand block to the inside of Black's attacking arm.

Figure 19-3j
White then circles his (L) arm under Black's attacking arm and around his (L) shoulder.

Figure 19-3k
Next, White presses down on Black's shoulder with his (R) hand and simultaneously anchors Black's (L) wrist against his own shoulder creating a lock of both the joints of the elbow and shoulder and forces Black to the ground.

Chapter 20

Preparatory Forms – Ba Bu Da

Introduction

'Ba Bu Da' or 'Eight Step Hit' when translated into English language is a sequence of eight separate forms which are usually taught to the practitioner of Hsing-I at the start of their training, hence referring to them as preparatory forms. This reference should not however detract from them their importance in the development of the practitioner whatever their level of skill.

These forms were taught through Master Hsu's 'Tang Shou Tao' lineage and the essence of their movements are drawn from both Hsing-I and Ba Gua. Their simple yet profound movements serve to teach the fundamental concepts of internal body mechanics. Each form trains the practitioner to become centred and solid throughout each movement and teaches how to connect the individual body segments from the feet through to the hands effectively.

Most importantly, the connection of movement from the feet through to the hands must come through activation of the waist and hips. After the initial step forwards in each movement sequence the feet then remain static and the lower limbs rooted whilst the upper body remains fluid and flexible as it executes the hand techniques. To generate maximum power within each individual technique each form utilises the movement of the waist in a relaxed and efficient manner. When this concept is thoroughly understood the experienced practitioner can apply this knowledge to all their techniques and learn to generate the power Hsing-I is renowned for.

Even though these forms may appear simple and are taught early on in training the lessons to be learned are most valuable and it requires the input of a knowledgeable teacher to truly understand and perfect the subtleties hidden within these forms.

The direction of the all the individual forms is to move forwards in a straight line, repeating itself on both left and right sides as it advances. The form then turns 180 degrees and repeats its movements in the opposite direction before turning again to finish facing the direction the practitioner originally started in accordance with traditional Hsing-I practice.

The eight forms of Ba Bu Da all open, turn and close in the same manner and these methods will be discussed first. This will then be followed by each of the eight individual forms. After each form has been explained there will be a few examples of possible fighting applications for some of the movements, however it should be noted that there are many possible fighting applications for each of the movements and the examples shown are simply to give the reader an understanding of how they may be applied.

1. Ba Bu Da Opening Form

Figure 20-1

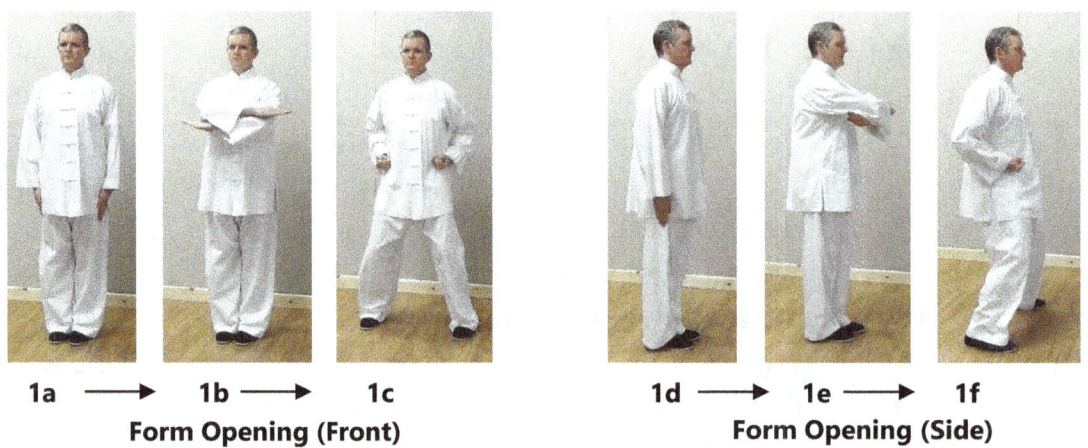

1a → 1b → 1c   1d → 1e → 1f
Form Opening (Front)   **Form Opening (Side)**

Shown in the pictures above are the sequence of movements used to open each of the eight Ba Bu Da forms. The same sequence is shown both from the front and the side view to help the reader better understand this opening method.

(Figure 20-1a/1d) Start in Wuji posture with feet together and hands held relaxed at the sides of the body.

(Figure 20-1b/1e) Next, hands cross over in front of the body with the (R) hand on top at solar plexus height.

(Figure 20-1c/1f) Next, each hand closes as a fist as it pulls back across to its respective side, drawing down to the level of the iliac crests, above the hips with the fists facing palm up. At the same time as the hands draw to the sides of the body, the practitioner then steps out to the left side with the (L) foot into a high horse stance. In this stance, the feet are shoulder width apart and face straight ahead. The knees should be flexed so as the practitioner cannot see their own toes if they were to look down.

2. Ba Bu Da Turning Form

Figure 20-2

2a → 2b → 2c

Turning on the left

Shown in the pictures above are the sequence of movements used to turn 180 degrees for each of the eight Ba Bu Da forms. All the eight forms turn using the same movements. Usually each form turns when the practitioner has their (L) foot forward however it is prudent to practice the turns on both the left and right side to be effective in fighting applications. The movements for turning on the right side are a mirror image of the ones shown above.

(Figure 20-2a) Turning from a left sided 'Box' stance, the practitioner looks 90 degrees to the right and chops out directly to the side with the (R) hand, using a knife hand strike with the palm facing down to earth. The opposite (L) hand remains held at the (L) hip as a fist with the palm facing up to heaven.

Note: The term 'Box' stance is more commonly used in the description of Tai Chi practice, however the same principle stance is also used in the Ba Bu Da forms. Box stance describes a stance where the feet are both facing forwards and of equal distance apart in both length and width. This is as though the feet are placed on opposite corners of a square or box. The body is centrally weighted between both feet and this stance provides a solid base from which to turn the waist and develop power from.

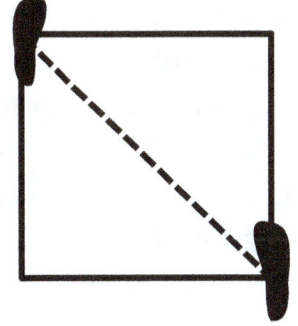

Box Stance Diagram

(Figure 20-2b) Next, the practitioner spins 180 degrees on their (R) foot with the (R) hand held out to the side in the static knife hand position. As the body turns the (L) foot follows in a circle sweeping motion lifting upwards with the sole of the (L) foot facing the inside of the (R) leg at knee height. The opposite (L) hand remains held at the (L) hip as a fist with the palm facing up to heaven.

(Figure 20-2c) To complete the turn sequence the (R) hand closes as a fist as it pulls back across to its respective (R) side, drawing down to the level of the iliac crests, above the hips with the fists facing palm up. At the same time as the hand draws to the hip the practitioner steps out to the left side with the (L) foot into a high horse stance. This returns the practitioner to the starting open stance position ready to begin the form again.

3. Ba Bu Da Closing Form

Figure 20-3

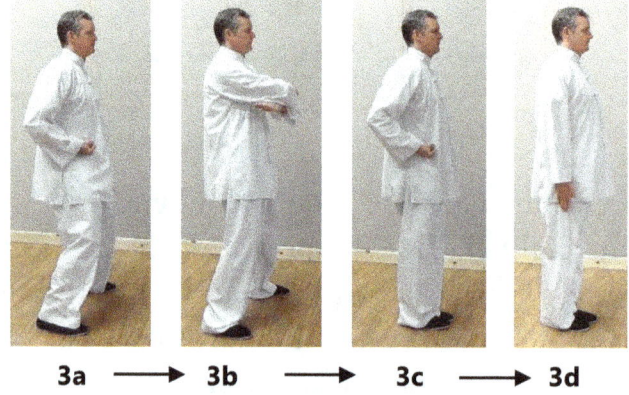

Figures 20-3a-3d show the sequence of movements used to close each of the eight Ba Bu Da forms. The sequences of movements are simply a reversal of the opening movements which return the practitioner from the final turn of the form back to Wuji posture.

(Figure 20-3) When the practitioner has completed the 180-degree turning movement of the form and is now facing the way they originally began the form, both hands held as fists above their respective hips and stood in a high horse stance they are then ready to finish the form.

(Figure 20-3) Next the hands open and cross over in front of the body with the (R) hand on top at solar plexus height.

(Figure 20-3) Next, each hand closes as a fist as it pulls back across to its respective side, drawing down to the level of the iliac crests with the fists facing palm up. At the same time as the hands draw to the hips the practitioner draws in the (L) foot next to the (R) foot straightening their knees to stand up at their full height with both feet facing straight ahead.

(Figure 20-3) In order to complete the closing sequence, the practitioner lowers and opens their hands placing them facing fingers down at their sides returning them back to Wuji posture.

4. Ba Bu Da Form 1

Figure 20-4

To open the form into high horse stance opening posture Figure 20-4a) below use the opening method explained previously.

(Figure 20-4a) Starting from high horse stance opening posture.

(Figure 20-4b) Step forwards with the (R) foot using the crescent step method and at the same time the (R) fist reverse punches straight out to solar plexus height along the centre line.

(Figure 20-4c) Both feet remain static in a centrally weighted box stance with the feet facing forwards approximately shoulder width apart. The (L) fist reverse punches straight out to solar plexus height along the centre line and at the same time the (R) fist is drawn back to the (R) hip with the palm facing up.

(Figure 20-4d and e) Without further moving the feet, the sequence of (R) and (L) reverse punches is repeated.

Note: This makes a total of four reverse punches from the opening step of the form which leaves the practitioner with their (R) foot forward and their (L) hand punching out. Only on the opening step of the form or on the first step after turning does the practitioner perform four reverse punches. On every other step moving forwards there are only three reverse punches executed which always ends each stepping sequence with the opposite hand and foot extended.

4f → 4g → 4h → 4i

(Figure 20-4f and 4g) Take a small step forwards with the (R) foot and then step through with the (L) foot using the crescent step method and following up with the (R) rear foot half-step into a (L) box stance. At the same time, the (R) fist reverse punches straight out to solar plexus height along the centre line, whilst the (L) fist reciprocally withdraws to the (L) hip facing palm up.

(Figure 20-4h and 4i) Without further moving the feet, the sequence of (L) and (R) reverse punches is repeated.

Note: This makes a total of three reverse punches from the (L) box stance of the form which ends with the practitioner having their (L) foot forward and their (R) hand punching out.

This stepping sequence of one crescent step combined with three reverse punches can then be continually repeated in a straight line moving forwards until the practitioner opts to turn. When turning the (L) foot is usually the forward foot and the turning sequence discussed at the start of this chapter is performed. After turning 180 degrees, the practitioner then repeats the form in the opposite direction turning again to finally face the way the form originally started. From there they can continue to repeat the form or end their practice using the 'closing' method discussed earlier in this chapter.

Ba Bu Da Form 1 Fighting Application:

4j → 4k → 4l

(Figure 20-4j) White faces off to Black in a neutral stance.
(Figure 20-4k) Black throws a (R) straight punch to White's ribs, White counters by crescent stepping directly into Black's attack with a straight, reverse punch using it to deflect Black's attack and at the same time strike to Black's ribs.
(Figure 20-4l) White immediately withdraws his (L) striking hand down Black's retreating (R) arm grabbing it at the wrist and at the same time delivers a second reverse punch down the centre line to Black's solar plexus.

5. Ba Bu Da Form 2

Figure 20-5
To open the form into high horse stance opening posture (Figure 20-5a) below use the opening method explained previously.

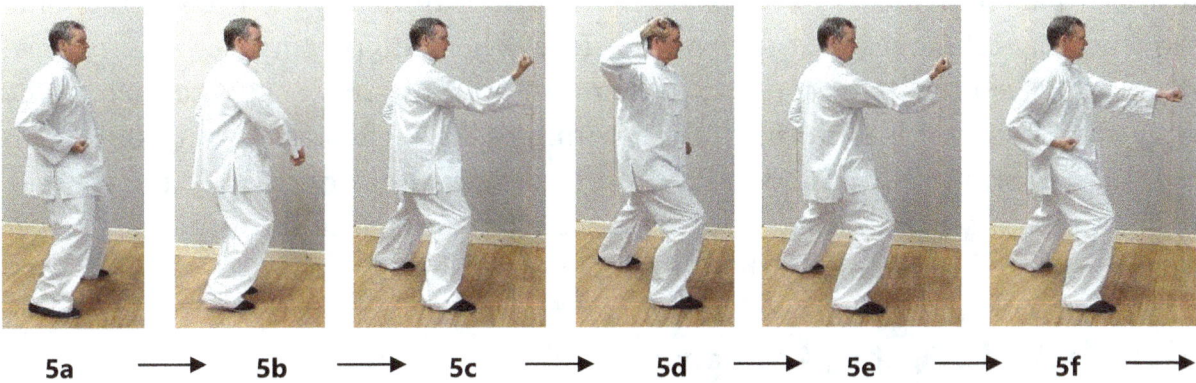

(Figure 20-5a) Starting from high horse stance opening posture.
(Figure 20-5b) Step inwards with the (R) foot using the crescent step method and at the same time the (R) arm circle blocks at Tan Tien level across the centreline.
(Figure 20-5c) Continue to step forwards with the (R) foot using the crescent step method ending in a (R) box stance. At the same time, the (R) arm circles upwards and over striking with a back fist to nose height along the centreline.
(Figure 20-5d) Both feet then remain static in a centrally weighted box stance with the feet facing forwards approximately shoulder width apart. The (R) arm is raised as a high block at head height like the block employed in 'Pao Chuan' of the Five Elements forms. The (L) hand remains held throughout at the (L) hip as a fist facing palm up.
(Figure 20-5e) Without further moving the feet the high blocking (R) hand is circled forwards and downwards along the centreline executing a back-fist strike to nose height along the centreline. The (L) hand remains held throughout at the (L) hip as a fist facing palm up.
(Figure 20-5f) Without further moving the feet the (R) hand is circled downwards along the centreline and then backwards coming to rest at the (R) hip as a fist with the palm facing up. At the same time, the (L) hand reciprocally executes a reverse punch to solar plexus height along the centreline.

Hsing-I Chuan | The Practice of Heart and Mind Boxing

(Figure 20-5g to 20-5k) Take a small step forwards with the (R) foot and then step through with the (L) foot using the crescent step method, following up with the (R) rear foot half-step into a (L) box stance. The hands and arms then repeat the same sequence of techniques on the opposite side. When the practitioner opts to turn the (L) foot is usually the forward foot and the turning sequence discussed at the start of this chapter is performed. After turning 180 degrees, the practitioner then repeats the form in the opposite direction turning again to finally face the way the form originally started. From there they can continue to repeat the form or end their practice using the 'closing' method discussed earlier in this chapter.

Ba Bu Da Form 2 Fighting Application:

(Figure 20-5l) White faces off to Black in a neutral stance.
(Figure 20-5m) Black throws a (L) straight punch to White's mid-section. White counters by crescent stepping (L) and executes a low circle block to defend against the punch with the (L) arm whilst simultaneously covering the attacking fist with a (R) open palm.
(Figure 20-5n) White immediately controls Black's (L) striking arm and circles upwards to execute a back-fist strike to Black's face.
(Figure 20-5o) In response Black attempts a (R) roundhouse punch at White's head. White keeps control of Black's (L) arm and draws back his own (L) arm to block the oncoming punch.
(Figure 20-5p) The (L) high block technique then sets White up to strike with the (L) back fist again to Black's face.
(Figure 20-5q) White continues the attack by drawing back his (L) hand to control Black's extended (R) arm and simultaneously delivers a (R) reverse punch to Black's Tan Tien.

6. Ba Bu Da Form 3

To open the form into high horse stance opening posture (Figure 20-6a) below use the opening method explained previously.

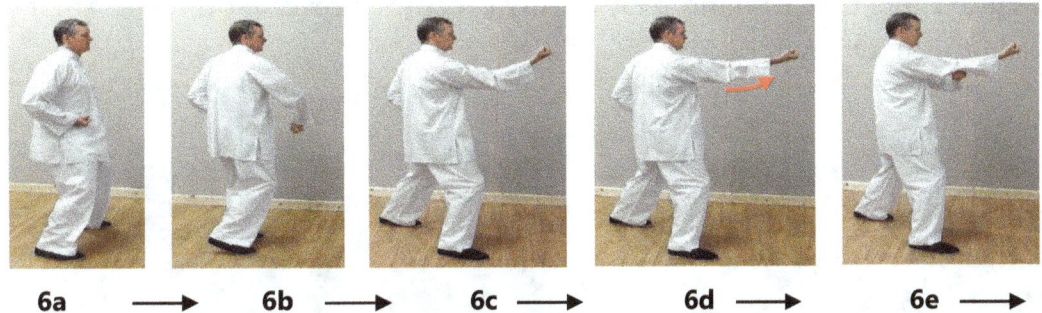

(Figure 20-6a) Starting from high horse stance opening posture.
(Figure 20-6b) Step inwards with the (R) foot using the crescent step method and at the same time the (R) arm circle blocks at Tan Tien level across the centreline.
(Figure 20-6c) Continue to step forwards with the (R) foot using the crescent step method ending in a (R) box stance. At the same time, the (R) arm circles upwards and over, striking with a back fist to nose height along the centreline.
(Figure 20-6d) Both feet then remain static in a centrally weighted box stance with the feet facing forwards approximately shoulder width apart. From the back fist position the (R) fist drives straight out, forwards and upwards along the centreline.
(Figure 20-6e) Both feet remain static. The (L) fist then moves from the (L) hip to be placed directly under the (R) elbow facing palm down.

6f → 6g → 6h → 6i →

(Figure 20-6f) Without further moving the feet the (L) hand wipes off up the underside of the outstretched (R) arm, executing a (L) Heng Chuan punch as in Earth element form.

(Figure 20-6g) Both feet remain static. The (R) fist then moves from the (R) hip to be placed directly under the (L) elbow facing palm down.

(Figure 20-6h) Without further moving the feet the (R) hand wipes off up the underside of the outstretched (L) arm, executing a (R) Heng Chuan punch as in Earth element form.

Note: This is a reverse Heng Chuan as the same hand and foot are forward at the completion of the strike.

(Figure 20-6i) Without further moving the feet the (R) hand withdraws downwards along the centreline coming to rest at the (R) hip as a fist with the palm facing up. At the same time, the (L) hand reciprocally executes a reverse punch to solar plexus height along the centreline.

6j → 6k → 6l → 6m →

6n → 6o → 6p → 6q

(Figure 20-6j-6q) Take a small step forwards with the (R) foot and then step through with the (L) foot using the crescent step method following up with the (R) rear foot half-step into a (L) box stance. The hands and arms then repeat the same sequence of techniques on the opposite side. When the practitioner opts to turn the (L) foot is usually the forward foot and the turning sequence discussed at the start of this chapter is performed. After turning 180 degrees, the practitioner then repeats the form in the opposite direction turning again to finally face the way the form originally started. From there they can continue to repeat the form or end their practice using the 'closing' method discussed earlier in this chapter.

Ba Bu Da Form 3 Fighting Application:

(Figure 20-6r) White faces off to Black in a neutral stance.
(Figure 20-6s) Black throws a (L) straight punch to White's midsection. White counters by crescent stepping (L) and circle blocking the punch with the (L) arm whilst simultaneously covering the attacking fist with a (R) open palm.
(Figure 20-6t) White immediately controls Black's (R) striking arm and circles upwards to execute a back-fist strike to Black's face.
(Figure 20-6u) In response, Black leans backwards to put himself out of range of the back-fist strike. To counter White uses the same (L) hand to strike out forward, directly from the previous back-fist attack and execute an (L) upper cut strike to Black's jaw.
(Figure 20-6v) In trying to recover, Black grabs out at White's (L) extended arm and White immediately reacts by wiping off the grab from the underside with his (R) arm.
(Figure 20-6w) White continues from the wipe off technique with a (R) Heng Chuan punch to Black's face.
(Figure 20-6x) To finish, White draws back his (R) hand to cover any attempt at a counterstrike and delivers a (L) reverse punch to Black's Tan Tien.

7. Ba Bu Da Form 4

Figure 20-7
To open the form into high horse stance opening posture (Figure 20-7a) below use the opening method explained previously.

7a → 7b → 7c → 7d → 7e →

(Figure 20-7a) Starting from high horse stance opening posture.
(Figure 20-7b) Step inwards with the (R) foot using the crescent step method and at the same time the (R) arm strikes downwards and inwards towards the centreline using a spear hand technique with the palm facing up to Tan Tien level.
(Figure 20-7c, 7d) Continue to step forwards with the (R) foot using the crescent step method ending in a (R) box stance. At the same time, the (R) arm circles in an anti-clockwise direction upwards with an open hand across the face and over to strike with a crescent palm technique at Tan Tien level.
(Figure 20-7e) Both feet then remain static in a centrally weighted box stance with the feet facing forwards approximately shoulder width apart. From the crescent palm position the (R) hand forms a fist and circle blocks back upwards in an clockwise direction to face height.

7f → 7g → 7h → 7i → 7j →

(Figure 20-7f) Without further moving the feet the (R) hand withdraws downwards along the centreline coming to rest at the (R) hip as a fist with the palm facing up. At the same time, the (L) hand reciprocally executes a reverse punch to solar plexus height along the centreline.
(Figure 20-7g) Both feet remain static. The (L) fist then turns face up by rotating the (L) arm backwards and then forwards in a small circular action at the shoulder to execute an (L) uppercut technique.

(Figure 20-7h) Both feet remain static. The (R) fist then moves from the (R) hip to be placed directly under the (L) elbow facing palm down.

(Figure 20-7i) Without further moving the feet the (R) hand wipes off up the underside of the outstretched (L) arm, executing a (R) Heng Chuan punch as in Earth element form.

Note: This is a reverse Heng Chuan as the same hand and foot are forward at the completion of the strike.

(Figure 20-7j) Without further moving the feet the (R) hand withdraws downwards along the centreline coming to rest at the (R) hip as a fist with the palm facing up. At the same time, the (L) hand reciprocally executes a reverse punch to solar plexus height along the centreline.

(Figure 20-7k to 7s) Take a small step forwards with the (R) foot and then step through with the (L) foot using the crescent step method. The (R) foot follows using the half-step method and the practitioner ends in a (L) box stance. At the same time, the hands and arms then repeat the same sequence of techniques on the opposite side. When the practitioner opts to turn the (L) foot is usually the forward foot and the turning sequence discussed at the start of this chapter is performed. After turning 180 degrees, the practitioner then repeats the form in the opposite direction turning again to finally face the way the form originally started. From there they can continue to repeat the form or end their practice using the 'closing' method discussed earlier in this chapter.

Ba Bu Da Form 4 Fighting Application:

(Figure 20-7t) White faces off to Black in a neutral stance.
(Figure 20-7u) Black throws a (R) straight punch to White's midsection. White counters by crescent stepping (L) and blocking the punch with the (L) arm.
(Figure 20-7v, 7w and 7x) White immediately controls Black's (R) striking arm with his (R) hand and circles his (L) hand upwards to execute a palm strike to Black's face.
(Figure 20-7y) In response, Black attempts to strike low with his (L) hand to White's ribs. To counter White continues to use his (L) hand to circle down and block the oncoming punch with an open palm block.
(Figure 20-7z) To finish, White circles back his (L) hand to strike Black's jaw with a reverse hammer fist technique.

Note: The reverse hammer fist method uses the 'eye' of the fist to strike rather than the 'heel' normally used in this technique.

8. Ba Bu Da Form 5

Figure 20-8
To open the form into high horse stance opening posture (Figure 20-8a) below use the opening method explained previously.

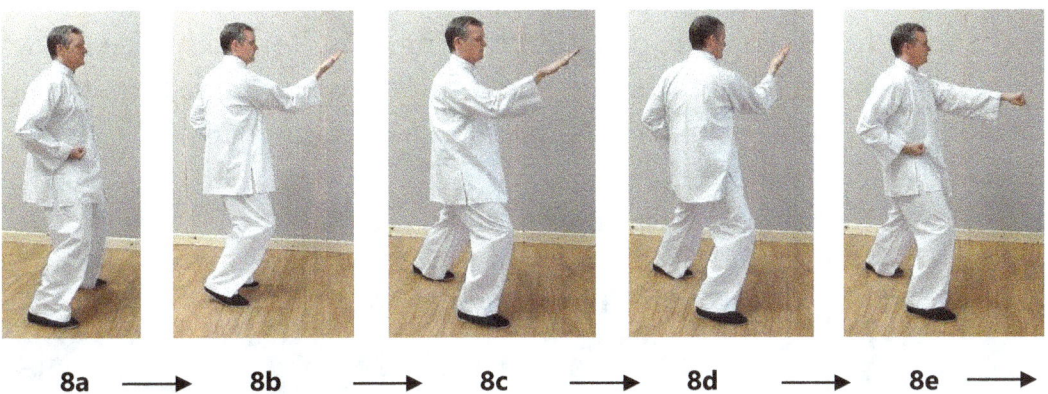

8a → 8b → 8c → 8d → 8e →

(Figure 20-8a) Starting from high horse stance opening posture.

(Figure 20-8b) Step inwards with the (R) foot using the crescent step method and at the same time the (R) arm strikes forwards and upwards towards the centreline, using a spear hand technique with the palm facing up to eye level.

(Figure 20-8c) Continue to step forwards with the (R) foot using the crescent step method ending in a (R) box stance. At the same time, the (R) arm strikes outwards and sideways away from the centre line. The (R) hand turns over to execute a knife hand strike to neck height with the palm facing down.

(Figure 20-8d) Both feet then remain static in a centrally weighted box stance with the feet facing forwards approximately shoulder width apart. At the same time, the (R) arm strikes inwards back towards the centreline. The (R) hand turns over to execute a knife hand strike to neck height with the palm facing up.

(Figure 20-8e) Without further moving the feet the (R) hand withdraws downwards along the centreline coming to rest at the (R) hip as a fist with the palm facing up. At the same time, the (L) hand reciprocally executes a reverse punch to solar plexus height along the centreline.

8f → 8g → 8h → 8i

(Figure 20-8f to 8i) Take a small step forwards with the (R) foot and then step through with the (L) foot using the crescent step method following up with the (R) rear foot half-step into a (L) box stance. The hands and arms then repeat the same sequence of techniques on the opposite side. When the practitioner opts to turn the (L) foot is usually the forward foot and the turning sequence discussed at the start of this chapter is performed. After turning 180 degrees, the practitioner then repeats the form in the opposite direction turning again to finally face the way the form originally started. From there they can continue to repeat the form or end their practice using the 'closing' method discussed earlier in this chapter.

Ba Bu Da Form 5 Fighting Application:

(Figure 20-8j) White faces off to Black in a neutral stance.
(Figure 20-8k) Black throws a (R) straight punch to White's face. White counters by crescent stepping (R) and cover blocking the punch from I/O with the (R) arm.
(Figure 20-8l) White continues immediately from the blocking technique to strike out along the line of Black's (R) extended arm attacking the neck of Black.
(Figure 20-8m) To finish, White draws back his (R) hand to cover any attempt at a counterstrike and delivers a (L) reverse punch to Black's Tan Tien.

9. Ba Bu Da Form 6

Figure 20-9
To open the form into high horse stance opening posture (Figure 20-9a) below use the opening method explained previously.

(Figure 20-9a) Starting from high horse stance opening posture.
(Figure 20-9b) Step inwards with the (R) foot using the crescent step method ending in a (R) box stance. At the same, time both arms strike simultaneously forwards as fists with palms facing up to head height.

(Figure 20-9c) Without further moving the feet the (L) fist then moves backwards down the line of the (R) forearm to be placed directly under the (R) elbow facing palm down.

(Figure 20-9d) Without further moving the feet the (L) hand wipes off up the underside of the outstretched (R) arm, executing a (L) Heng Chuan punch as in Earth element form.

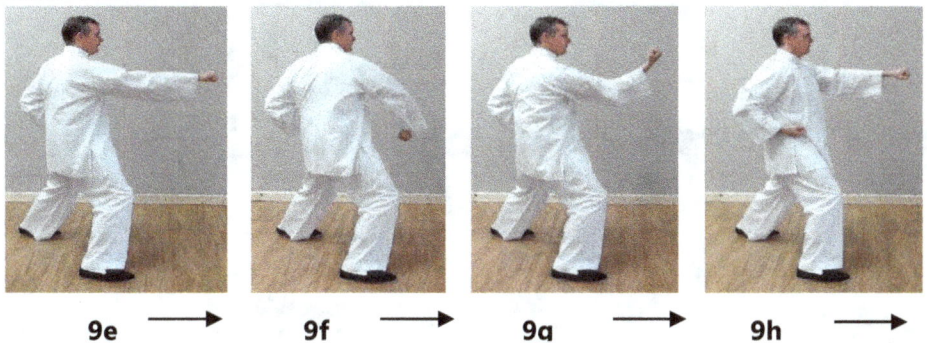

(Figure 20-9e) Without further moving the feet the (L) hand withdraws downwards along the centreline coming to rest at the (L) hip as a fist with the palm facing up. At the same time, the (R) hand reciprocally executes a reverse punch to solar plexus height along the centreline.

(Figure 20-9f) Without further moving the feet the (R) arm circle blocks at Tan Tien level across the centreline.

(Figure 20-9g) Without further moving the feet the (R) arm circles upwards and over to strike with a back fist to nose height along the centreline.

(Figure 20-9h) Without further moving the feet the (R) hand is circled downwards along the centreline and then backwards coming to rest at the (R) hip as a fist with the palm facing up. At the same time, the (L) hand reciprocally executes a reverse punch to solar plexus height along the centreline.

(Figure 20-9i to 9o) Take a small step forwards with the (R) foot and then step through with the (L) foot using the crescent step method following up with the (R) rear foot half-step into a (L) box stance. The hands and arms then repeat the same sequence of techniques on the opposite side. When the practitioner opts to turn the (L) foot is usually the forward foot and the turning sequence discussed at the start of this chapter is performed. After turning 180 degrees, the practitioner then repeats the form in the opposite direction turning again to finally face the way the form originally started. From there they can continue to repeat the form or end their practice using the 'closing' method discussed earlier in this chapter.

Ba Bu Da Form 6 Fighting Application:

(Figure 20-9p) White faces off to Black in a neutral stance.
(Figure 20-9q) Black grabs out with his (R) hand to White's chest. White counters by crescent stepping (R) and simultaneously breaking the grab of the attacking hand with a (L) I/O block.
(Figure 20-9r) Black then simultaneously executes a (R) uppercut to Black's solar plexus.
(Figure 20-9s) Attempting to recover, Black grabs out at White's (R) extended arm and White immediately reacts by wiping off the grab from the underside with his (R) arm.
(Figure 20-9t) White continues from wipe off technique with a (L) Heng Chuan punch to Black's jaw.
(Figure 20-9u) To finish, White draws back his (L) hand to cover any attempt at a counterstrike and delivers a (R) reverse punch to Black's ribs.

10. Ba Bu Da Form 7

Figure 20-10
To open the form into high horse stance opening posture (Figure 20-10a) below use the opening method explained previously.

10a → 10b → 10c → 10d →

(Figure 20-10a) Starting from high horse stance opening posture.
(Figure 20-10b) Step inwards with the (R) foot using the crescent step method and at the same time the (R) arm strikes forwards and upwards towards the centreline, using a spear hand technique with the palm facing up to eye level. The (L) hand opens and moves from the (L) hip to be placed directly under the (R) elbow with palm facing down.
(Figure 20-10c) Step forwards with the (R) foot using the crescent step method ending in a (R) box stance. At the same time, the body turns 90 degrees to the left with the (L) hand wiping off along the underside of the extended (R) forearm and blocks to the (L) side with a knife hand block at head height. The (R) hand simultaneously draws back to the (R) hip as a fist facing palm up.
(Figure 20-10d) As the body turns fully to face 90 degrees left of the starting position both feet also turn to 90 degrees to maintain the correct box stance alignment. At the same time, the (R) hand blocks with an O/I block at head height and the extended (L) hand reciprocally withdraws as a fist to the (L) hip.

10e → 10f → 10g →

(Figure 20-10e) Next the practitioner takes a sideways half-step to the right with both feet and simultaneously executes a double elbow strike with both elbows to mid-rib level.

Note: The 'sideways half-step' method is the same as the half-step method, only that the practitioner is turned sideways on to their opponent when they use it. The forward foot moves out first and is followed by the rear foot to readjust the feet to a stable sideways box stance.

(Figure 20-10f) The practitioner then turns both the body and the feet 90 degrees back to the right remaining in a (R) box stance to face the original direction of the form. At the same time, the (R) arm circles upwards and over striking with a back-fist to nose height along the centreline.

(Figure 20-10g) Without further moving the feet the (R) hand is circled downwards along the centreline and then backwards coming to rest at the (R) hip as a fist with the palm facing up. At the same time, the (L) hand reciprocally executes a reverse punch to solar plexus height along the centreline.

(Figure 20-10h to 10m) Take a small step forwards with the (R) foot and then step through with the (L) foot using the crescent step method following up with the (R) rear foot half-step into a (L) box stance. The hands and arms then repeat the same sequence of techniques on the opposite side. When the practitioner opts to turn the (L) foot is usually the forward foot and the turning sequence discussed at the start of this chapter is performed. After turning 180 degrees, the practitioner then repeats the form in the opposite direction turning again to finally face the way the form originally started. From there they can continue to repeat the form or end their practice using the 'closing' method discussed earlier in this chapter.

Ba Bu Da Form 7 Fighting Application:

10n → 10o → 10p → 10q

(Figure 20-10n) White faces off to Black in a neutral stance.
(Figure 20-10o) Black throws a (R) straight punch to White's face. White counters by sidestepping (R) to the outside of Black's attack and simultaneously blocking the strike with a (R) I/O open hand block.
(Figure 20-10p) White continues from the blocking technique, taking control of Black's extended arm with his (R) hand and executes a (L) O/I block to the back of Black's extended (R) elbow causing a hyperextension injury to the joint.
(Figure 20-10q) To finish, White executes a (L) elbow strike to Black's ribs.

11. Ba Bu Da Form 8

Figure 20-11

   Note: Ba Bu Da Form 8 is almost identical to form 7 discussed previously apart from an additional two moves added before the final technique of each sequence. To open the form into high horse stance opening posture (Figure 20-11a) below use the opening method explained previously.

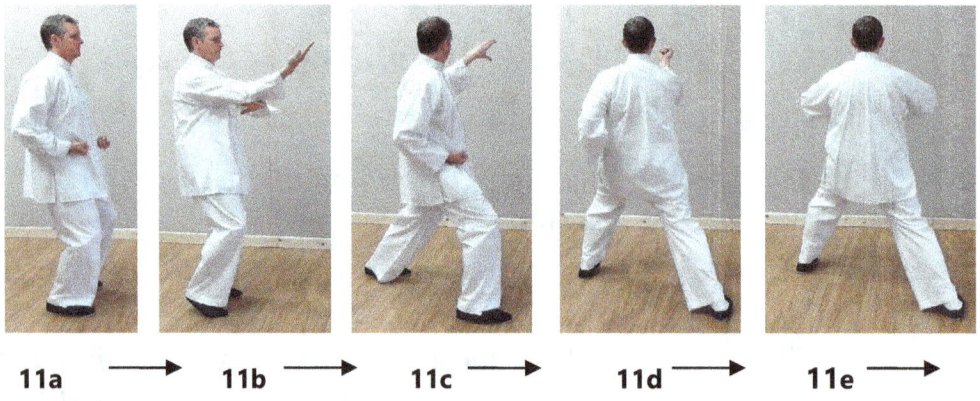

11a → 11b → 11c → 11d → 11e →

(Figure 20-11a) Starting from high horse stance opening posture.
(Figure 20-11b) Step inwards with the (R) foot using the crescent step method and at the same time the (R) arm strikes forwards and upwards towards the centreline,

using a spear hand technique with the palm facing up to eye level. The (L) hand opens and moves from the (L) hip to be placed directly under the (R) elbow with palm facing down.

(Figure 20-11c) Step forwards with the (R) foot using the crescent step method ending in a (R) box stance. At the same time, the body turns 90 degrees to the left with the (L) hand wiping off along the underside of the extended (R) forearm and blocks to the (L) side with a knife hand block at head height. The (R) hand simultaneously draws back to the (R) hip as a fist facing palm up.

(Figure 20-11d) As the body turns fully to face 90 degrees left of the starting position both feet also turn to 90 degrees to maintain the correct box stance alignment. At the same time, the (R) hand blocks with an O/I block at head height and the extended (L) hand reciprocally withdraws as a fist to the (L) hip.

(Figure 20-11e) Next the practitioner takes a sideways half-step to the right with both feet and simultaneously executes a double elbow strike with both elbows to mid-rib level.

11f → 11g → 11h → 11i →

(Figure 20-11f) The practitioner then turns both the body and the feet 90 degrees back to the right remaining in a (R) box stance to face the original direction of the form. At the same time, the (R) arm circles upwards and over striking with a backfist to nose height along the centreline.

(Figure 20-11g) Without further moving the feet the (R) arm is flexed to execute a (R) elbow strike to mid-rib level and the (L) hand reciprocally moves as an open palm target for the (R) elbow strike. (See figure 11o for a mirror image of this position)

(Figure 20-11h) Without further moving the feet the (R) flexed arm fully extends executing a knife hand strike with the palm facing down to neck height. Simultaneously the (L) hand withdraws as a fist to the (L) hip.

(Figure 20-11i Without further moving the feet the extended (R) hand is withdrawn downwards along the centreline coming to rest at the (R) hip as a fist with the palm facing up. At the same time, the (L) hand reciprocally executes a reverse punch to solar plexus height along the centreline.

(Figure 20-11j to 11q) Take a small step forwards with the (R) foot and then step through with the (L) foot using the crescent step method following up with the (R) rear foot half-step into a (L) box stance. The hands and arms then repeat the same sequence of techniques on the opposite side. When the practitioner opts to turn the (L) foot is usually the forward foot and the turning sequence discussed at the start of this chapter is performed. After turning 180 degrees, the practitioner then repeats the form in the opposite direction turning again to finally face the way the form originally started.

From this position, the practitioner can continue to repeat the form or end their practice using the 'closing' method discussed earlier in this chapter.

Ba Bu Da Form 8 Fighting Application:

(Figure 20-11r) White faces off to Black in a neutral stance.

(Figure 20-11s) Black throws a (R) straight punch to White's face. White counters by (R) crescent stepping to the outside of Black's attack and simultaneously blocking the strike with a (R) I/O open hand block.

(Figure 20-11t) White continues from the blocking technique by turning 90 degrees to the side into a (R) box stance, taking control of Black's extended arm with his (R) hand and executes a (L) elbow strike to Black's jaw.

(Figure 20-11u) White continues from the elbow strike by extending his (L) arm across Black's neck, forcing him off balance and simultaneously executing a knife hand strike to the throat.

(Figure 20-11v) To finish, White draws back his (L) hand to keep Black off balance and delivers a (R) reverse punch to Black's ribs.

Chapter 21

Five Element Fist Forms – Wu Chuan

Introduction

The 'Wu Chuan Forms', or 'Five Fists' when translated into English, are trained initially as a sequence of five separate forms. Each individual form has the energetic characteristic of an element which is why they are commonly referred to as the 'Five Element Forms' in practice. These forms are usually taught to the practitioner of Hsing-I in the early stages of their training. The Five Element forms become the basic building blocks for understanding and ultimately perfecting the complete Hsing-I system.

The Five Element Forms discussed in this chapter derive from both Master Hsu's and Grand Master Chiao's respective lineages and they will be referenced appropriately as each form is discussed. As both Masters taught variations of the Shansi lineage of Hsing-I it is of no surprise that the Five Element Forms practiced are almost the same. The differences on a physical level are noted on some of the methods of turning, however the main difference between the two methods of practice is found in the energetic or chi level of practice where the intent of each techniques delivery is considerably different. To understand these subtle differences again requires the explanation from an experienced and knowledgeable teacher of each method. No method is necessarily better than the other, just a different way of practicing each form. Each individual form complies with the Taoist theory of Yin/Yang and understanding this principle is key to truly mastering the subtleties hidden within them.

After each of the five forms have been individually learned they can then be combined and practiced as one complete form and also trained with a partner as a two-man fighting form. All the forms mentioned above are discussed in this chapter.

The direction for each individual form is to move up and down in a straight line, repeating itself on both left and right sides as it advances. The form then turns 180 degrees and repeats its movements in the opposite direction before turning again to finish facing the direction the practitioner originally started in accordance with traditional Hsing-I practice.

The Five Element Forms almost all open and close in the same manner and these methods are discussed in detail in Chapter 19 of this book. After each form has been explained there will be a few examples of some possible fighting applications for some of the movements, however it should be noted that there are many possible fighting applications for each of the movements and the examples shown are simply to give the reader a basic understanding of how they may be applied.

1. Metal Form – Pi Chuan

Grand Master Chiao

To open the form into (L) Pi Chuan (figure 21-1.1) use the opening method shown in Chapter 19 previously.

(Figure 21-1.1) Starting from (L) Pi Chuan posture.

(Figure 21-1.2) Draw in the (L) hand making a fist facing palm down. At the same time, make a fist with the (R) hand facing palm down so as both fists are drawn in to the Tan Tien simultaneously.

(Figure 21-1.3) Step forwards with the (L) foot and at the same time the (L) fist punches straight out to nose height followed closely by the (R) fist which is kept close to the (L) elbow.

(Figure 21.-1.4) Step through with the (R) foot and follow up with the (L) foot using the half-step method. At the same time as stepping execute a (R) punch straight up to nose height following the line of the previous (L) punch and as soon as the (R) punch reaches its full extension open the hands dropping the (L) hand down to the mid-section, protecting the Tan Tien and the (R) hand chops forward and down the centreline in a splitting action. At the end of this sequence the practitioner should now be in (R) Pi Chuan posture.

(Figures 21-1.5, 1.6 and 1.7) Repeats the same sequence on the opposite side returning the practitioner to (L) Pi Chuan posture.

Note: At this point the sequence can be performed repeatedly forward in a straight line until the practitioner chooses to turn and change direction. Traditionally Hsing-I practitioners turn their forms on the (L) side; however, it is prudent to practise turns on both sides from a fighting application purpose.

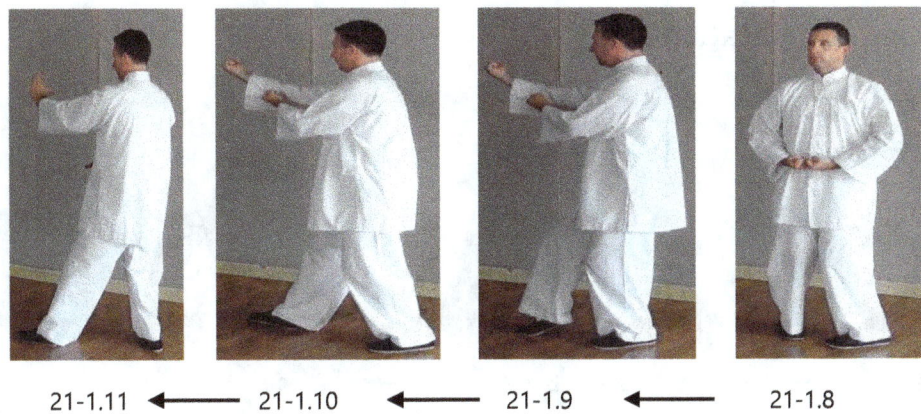

21-1.11 ← 21-1.10 ← 21-1.9 ← 21-1.8

(Figure 21-1.8) In a (L) turn, the practitioner turns 90 degrees clockwise from (L) Pi Chuan posture into pigeon toe stance and at the same time brings both hands as fists facing palms up to Tan Tien level.

(Figures 21-1.9 and 1.10) The practitioner continues to turn clockwise a further 90 degrees to face the way they came from. Step out with the (R) foot, punching out with the (R) fist to nose height, keeping the (L) fist close to the (R) elbow.

(Figure 21-1.11) Step through with the (L) foot and follow up with the (R) foot using the half-step method. At the same time (L) punch straight up the line of the (R) arm to nose height and open the hands pressing down and out into (L) Pi Chuan posture again.

Note: Now the practitioner follows the same steps back again as many times as they wish. At any time when they are in (L) Pi Chuan posture they may turn using the same method described previously.

21-1.12 → 21-1.13 → 21-1.14 → 21-1.15

Figures 21-1.12, 1.13, 1.14 and 1.15) In this example the practitioner turns immediately from (L) Pi Chuan, 180 degrees and returns to the original starting position as shown in Figure 21-1.15.

To finish the form correctly the practitioner uses the closing method described in Chapter 19 previously.

Metal Form Fighting Applications:

Metal Form – Application 1

1a → 1b → 1c → 1d

(Figure 1a) White faces off to Black in a neutral stance.
(Figure 1b) Black throws a (R) straight punch to White's face, White counters stepping directly into Black's attack with a (R) straight punch using it to deflect Black's attack and at the same time strike to Black's face.
(Figure 1c) White immediately withdraws his (R) hand down Black's retreating (R) arm grabbing it at the wrist and at the same time delivers a splitting palm strike to Black's jaw.
(Figure 1d) White keeps control of Black's (R) arm and steps through with his (L) foot, sinking his body and uses Metals chopping action to take Black to the ground with an arm bar technique.

Metal Form – Application 2

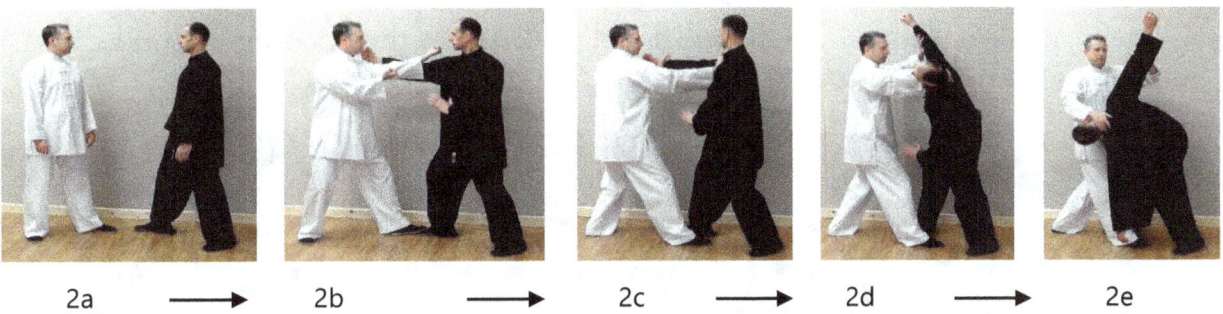

2a → 2b → 2c → 2d → 2e

(Figure 2a) White faces off to Black in a neutral stance.

(Figure 2b) Black throws a (R) straight punch to White's face, White counters stepping directly into the inside of Black's attack utilising a straight punch to deflect and at the same time strike to Black's face.

(Figure 2c) White immediately steps forward with his (R) foot into Black's centreline and withdraws his (L) striking hand down Black's retreating (R) arm grabbing it at the wrist and at the same time delivers a (R) splitting palm strike to Black's (R) shoulder joint.

(Figure 2d) White keeps control of Black's (R) arm and simultaneously slides his (R) hand behind Black's neck pressing downwards, whilst pushing Black's (R) arm upwards.

(Figure 2e) White keeps control of Black's neck and rotates Black off balance using his extended (R) arm as a lever to potentially dislocate the shoulder joint and take Black to the ground.

2. Water Form – Tsuan Chuan

Master Hsu

The method of turning shown in this sequence of Water form is from Master Chiao's lineage and the difference between the two methods is on the turn at each end of the form. The turn for Master Hsu's version of the form is shown separately. All other movements of the form are the same from both teachers.

To open the form into (L) Pi Chuan (figure 21-2.1) use the opening method shown in Chapter 19 previously.

21-2.1 → 21-2.2 → 21-2.3 → 21-2.4 →

21-2.5 → 21-2.6

(Figure 21-2.1) Starting from (L) Pi Chuan posture.

(Figure 21-2.2) The (L) hand is up and the (R) hand is down. The (L) hand twists counter-clockwise with the palm up to throat height and the fingers come together to form spear hand. The (R) hand remains palm down protecting the Tan Tien. At the same time, the (L) foot steps forward into a 45-degree bow stance carrying the 60% of the weight in the forward leg with the toes pointed outward at a 45-degree angle. The (R) foot remains in its previous position.

(Figure 21-2.3) The (L) hand twists clockwise into a fist as the (R) hand also forms a fist. Both (R) hand and (R) foot step forward in unison. The (R) hand punches out and up to nose level, while the (L) hand pulls down in front of the navel. The rising (R) fist follows a path inside that of the dropping (L) hand, which is held in a fist (palm down). The (R) foot has stepped through to a forward position and the (L) foot follows using the half-step method. This returns the stance to a 70:30 weighting on the back foot as in Pi Chuan stance. This posture is (R) Tsuan Chuan.

(Figures 21-2.4 and 2.5) Repeat the same sequence as figures 21-2.2 and 2.3 on the opposite side. In figure 21-2.5 the end posture is (L) Tsuan Chuan.

Note: At this point the sequence can be performed repeatedly forward in a straight line until the practitioner chooses to turn and change direction. Traditionally Hsing-I practitioners turn their forms on the (L) side, however it is prudent to practise turns on both sides from a fighting application purpose.

(Figure 21-2.6) In a (L) turn the practitioner turns quickly through 180 degrees to face the direction they came from. Transferring the weight from the rear (R) foot into the forward (L) foot allows the practitioner to pivot round and return to Pi Chuan stance with the weighting with the power stored now in the rear (L) leg.

21-2.11 ← 21-2.10 ← 21-2.9 ← 21-2.8 ← 21.2.7

21-2.13 ← 21-2.12 ←

(Figure 21-2.7) Now facing the opposite direction in Pi Chuan (R) stance, the hands simultaneously block with the (R) hand blocking high at face height using the ridge hand and the (L) hand blocking low using the knife edge of the hand.

(Figure 21-2.8) The (R) hand twists clockwise into a fist facing palm down at the same time the (L) hand also forms a fist facing palm down.

(Figure 21-2.9) Both (L) hand and (L) foot step forward in unison. The (L) hand punches out and up to nose level, while the (R) hand pulls down in front of the navel. The (L) foot has stepped through to a forward position and the (R) foot follows using the half-step method. This returns the stance to a 70:30 weighting on the (R) rear foot.

(Figures 21-2.10, 2.11, 2.12 and 2.13) The practitioner can then follow the same steps back again as many times as they wish, at any time when they are in (L) Tsuan Chuan posture they may turn using the same method described previously in figures 21-2.7 and 2.8.

Hsing-I Chuan | The Practice of Heart and Mind Boxing

(Figures 21-2.14, 2.15 and 2.16) In this example the practitioner turns 180 degrees from a (L) Tsuan Chuan (figure 21-2.13) and steps through into another (L) Tsuan Chuan.

(Figures 21-2.17, 2.18, 2.19, 2.20 and 2.21) From this position the practitioner simply steps forward with the (L) foot, at the same time bringing the palms and feet together and closes the form in the same manner as if finishing from Pi Chuan form.

Master Hsu's Water Turn Method

From far right to left

(Figure 21-2.22) When the practitioner is in a (L) Tsuan Chuan posture the turn method can be initiated.

Note: Traditionally Hsing-I practitioners turn their forms on the (L) side, however it is prudent to practise turns on both sides from a fighting application purpose.

(Figure 21-2.23) In a (L) turn the practitioner takes a small step forward with the (L) foot whilst transferring the weight from the rear (R) foot into the forward (L) foot. This allows the practitioner to pivot round 180 degrees. At the same time, the (R) hand which was held as a fist at the hip previously (figure 21-2.22) spirals open at the (R) hip and prepares to drive forward as a spear hand along the centreline.

(Figure 21-2.24) Now facing the opposite direction the (R) spear hand rises upwards along the centreline to throat height. At the same time, the (R) foot steps forward into a 45-degree bow stance carrying approximately 60% of the weight in the forward leg with the toes pointed outward at a 45-degree angle. The (L) hand reciprocally pulls down protecting the Tan Tien and comes to rest level with the (L) hip as a fist facing palm down.

(Figure 21-2.25) Both (L) hand and (L) foot step forward in unison. The (L) hand punches out and up to nose level, while the (R) hand pulls down in front of the navel. The (L) foot has stepped through to a forward position and the (R) foot follows using the half-step method. This returns the stance to a 70:30 weighting on the (R) rear foot.

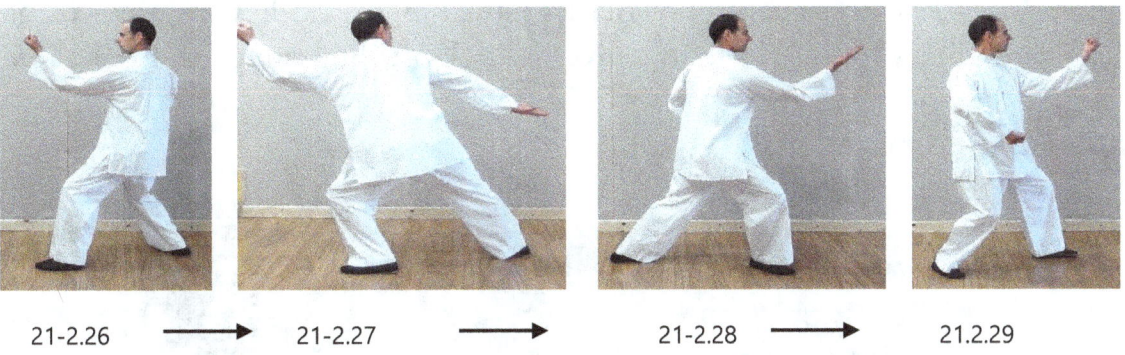

21-2.26 → 21-2.27 → 21-2.28 → 21.2.29

From far left to right

(Figures 21-2.26, 2.27, 2.28 and 2.29) The following sequence shows the same turn method from the opposite direction. In-between the turn sequences the practitioner can then follow Water form with as many repetitions as they wish and at any time when they are in (L) Tsuan Chuan posture they may turn using the same method described previously in figures 21-2.22 to 2.25).

Note: To finish the form from (L) Tsuan Chuan the practitioner simply steps forward with the (L) foot, at the same time bringing the palms and feet together and closes the form in the same manner as shown previously in figures 21-2.17 to 2.21.

Water Form Fighting Applications:

Water Form – Application 1

3a → 3b → 3c → 3d

(Figure 3a) White faces off to Black in a neutral stance.
(Figure 3b) Black attempts a (R) straight punch to White's midsection. White blocks the punch with a (L) open palm block and counters by stepping directly into Black's centreline delivering a spear hand strike to Black's throat.
(Figure 3c) White immediately withdraws his (R) hand down Black's retreating chest grabbing his clothes at the neck line.
(Figure 3d) White keeps control of Black's retreat by his clothes and steps through Black's centreline with his (L) foot, delivering a (L) drilling punch to Black's jaw.

Water Form – Application 2

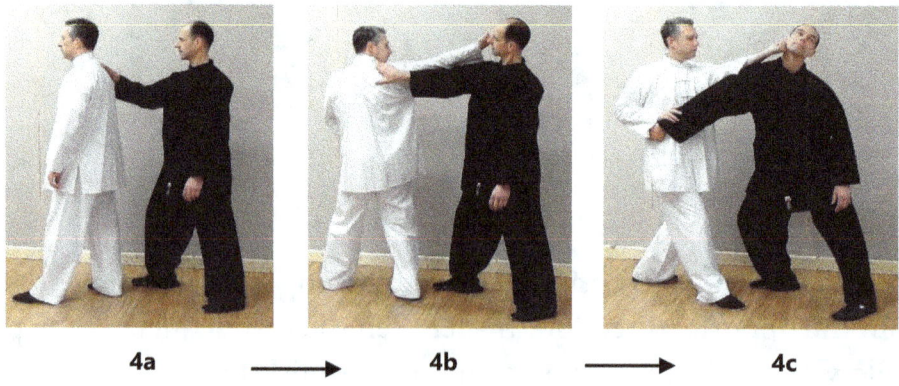

4a → 4b → 4c

(Figure 4a) Black approaches White from behind and attempts to grab his (R) shoulder.
(Figure 4b) White spins quickly clockwise and executes a (R) straight arm ridge hand strike to the outside of Black's extended (R) arm to dislodge his grip and simultaneously strike Black to the temple area of the head.
(Figure 4c) White then continues to turn 180 degrees to face Black and whilst taking control of Black's (R) arm, White then half-steps forward into Black's centreline to deliver a (L) drilling punch to Black's jaw.

3. Wood Form - Peng Chuan

Master Hsu

To open the form into (L) Pi Chuan (figure 21-3.1) use the opening method shown in Chapter 19 previously.

21-3.1 → 21-3.2 → 21-3.3 → 21.3.4 → 21-3.5 →

→ 21-3.6 → 21-3.7

(Figure 21-3.1) Starting from (L) Pi Chuan posture.
(Figure 21-3.2) From (L) Pi Chuan the (R) hand forms a fist and then punches straight out approximately to the height of the solar plexus. Simultaneously, the (L) hand forms a fist and pulls back to the (L) side of the waist. As the (R) hand punches, the (L) foot takes a step forward followed closely by the (R) foot which steps forward, alongside the (L) foot, ending tight alongside the instep, about one inch behind the left toe. This posture is called 'closed' Wood due to the closed position of the feet in this posture.

(Figure 21-3.3) Next, the (L) fist punches, coming out toward the centreline of the body in front of the solar plexus and brushing over the (R) arm, which is simultaneously drawing back to the (R) side of the waist. In this step, the (L) foot moves out and the (R) foot follows using the half-step method. This posture is called 'open' Wood due to the open position of the feet in this posture.

(Figures 21-3.4 and 3.5) Repeats the sequence of (figures 21-3.2 and 3.3) above.

Note: At this point the sequence can be performed repeatedly forward in a straight line until the practitioner chooses to turn and change direction. Traditionally Hsing-I practitioners turn their forms on the (L) side as demonstrated in this sequence.

(Figure 21-3.6) The turn can be initiated when the practitioner is in the open Wood position as in figure 21-3.5 above. Without moving the feet, the practitioner punches straight out with the (R) fist and at the same time withdraws the (L) fist.

(Figure 21-3.7) The practitioner then turns 90 degrees clockwise into pigeon toe stance and draws both fists into the Tan Tien with palms facing up.

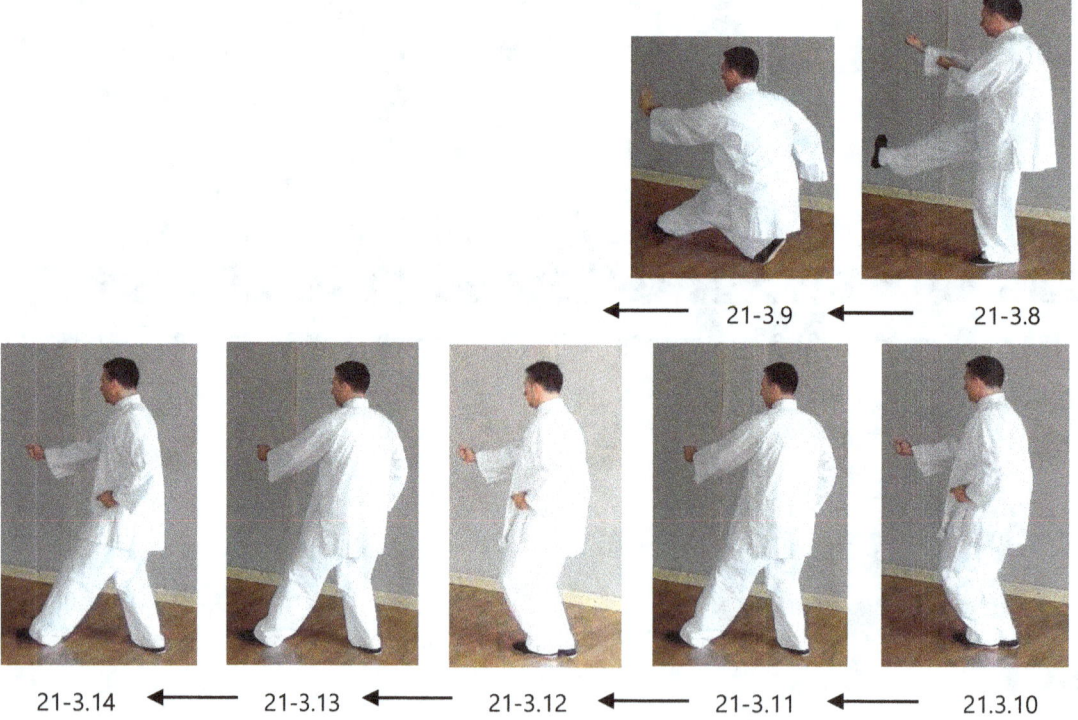

(Figure 21-3.8) The practitioner then continues to turn a further 90 degrees clockwise in effect returning along the same direction they came. The (R) foot kicks out using the 45-degree rising kick to knee height and at the same time the (R) arm punches straight out to face height with the (L) fist held closely at the (R) elbow.

(Figure 21-3.9) From the kicking position the body then drops straight to the ground into dragon stance. As the body drops the (L) hand punches forward up the line of the (R) arm as in Metal form and the two hands open and change positions with the (L) hand pressing out and forwards and the (R) hand pressing palm down and held at the (R) waist.

Note: This low posture requires strength and balance in the (L) leg as the (R) kicking leg should not touch the ground before the dragon stance is complete. Also of note is that the forward hand is held stretched out and the rear hand is pulled back to the waist. This is consistent with reverse Metal posture as the opposite hands and feet are forward.

(Figure 21-3.10) Next, the (R) foot takes a small step forwards followed by the (L) foot raising the practitioner smoothly back to the closed Wood position discussed previously. At the same time as stepping the (R) hand makes a fist and punches forwards, whilst the (L) hand forms a fist and withdraws to the (L) waist.

(Figures 21-3.11, 3.12 and 3.13) Follows the same continued sequence of open and closed Wood repetitions.

(Figure 21-3.14) When in (L) open Wood the practitioner initiates the turn with a (R) straight punch as in previous turn shown in figure 21-3.6.

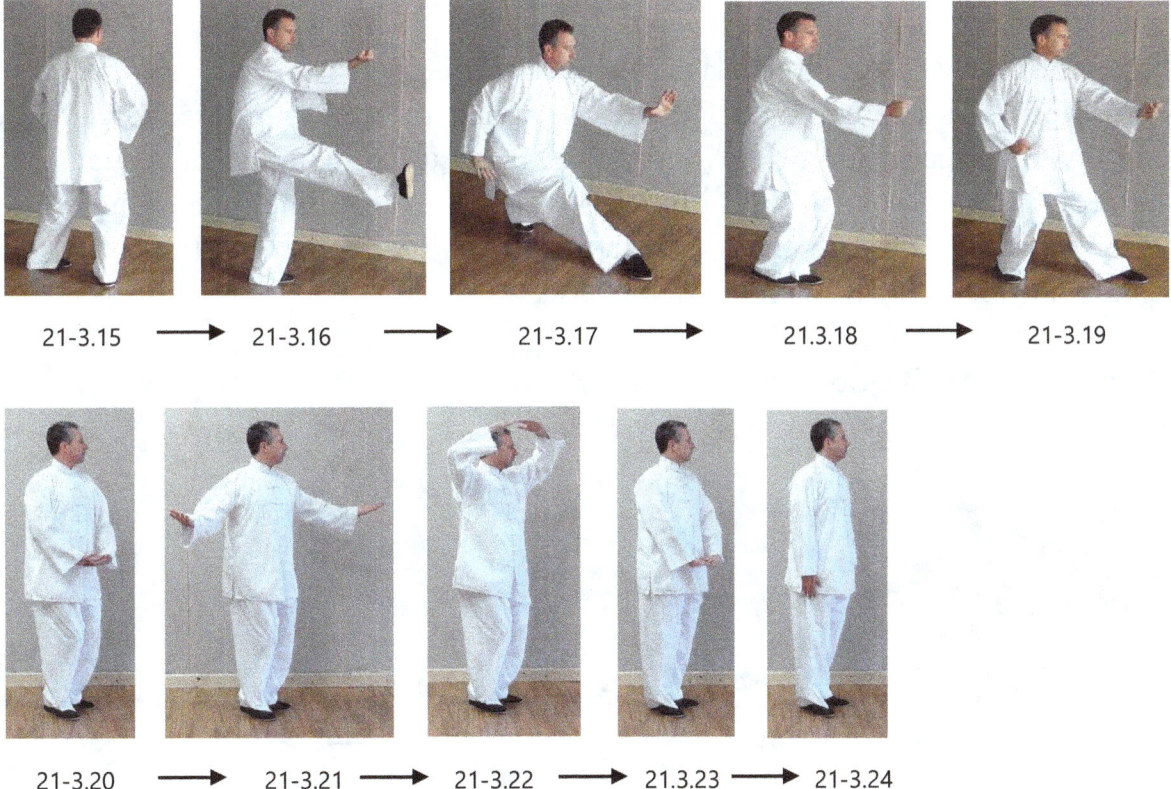

(Figures 21-3.15, 3.16 and 3.17) Repeats the same turn sequence as discussed previously but from the opposite direction.

(Figures 21-3.18 and 19) The practitioner steps forwards into closed and then open Wood postures respectively.

(Figures 21-3.20 to 3.24) From (L) open Wood (figure 21-3.19) the form can be finished by simply stepping forward with the (L) foot and bringing both feet and palms together and finishing in the same manner as from Pi Chuan form.

Note: Wood Form does not step into (L) Pi Chuan to close. As it is already on the (L) side in its open Wood posture, it simply steps up with the forward (L) foot to close.

Wood Form Fighting Applications:

Wood Form – Application 1

5a → 5b

(Figure 5a) White faces off to Black in a neutral stance.
(Figure 5b) Black attempts a (R) straight punch to White's midsection. White counters the punch with a (L) Wood punch using its straight line of trajectory to intercept Black's attack and beat him to the target. At the same time as punching, White steps forward into Black's centre and stands directly on Black's (R) foot making it difficult for Black to evade the attack.

Wood Form – Application 2

6a → 6b → 6c → 6d

(Figure 6a) White faces off to Black in a neutral stance.
(Figure 6b) Black attempts a (L) straight punch to White's face. White steps into Black's centre and blocks the punch with a (L) straight punch to Black's face.
(Figure 6c) White immediately withdraws his (L) striking hand down Black's retreating arm grabbing him at the wrist and at the same time grabs Black's arm above the elbow joint with his (R) hand, twisting it into an elbow lock.
(Figure 6d) White keeps control of Black's arm using the elbow lock and at the same

time executes a 45-degree rising kick to Black's (L) knee to dislocate the patella.

4. Fire Form – Pao Chuan

Grand Master Chiao

To open the form into (L) Pi Chuan (figure 21-4.1) use the opening method shown in Chapter 19 previously.

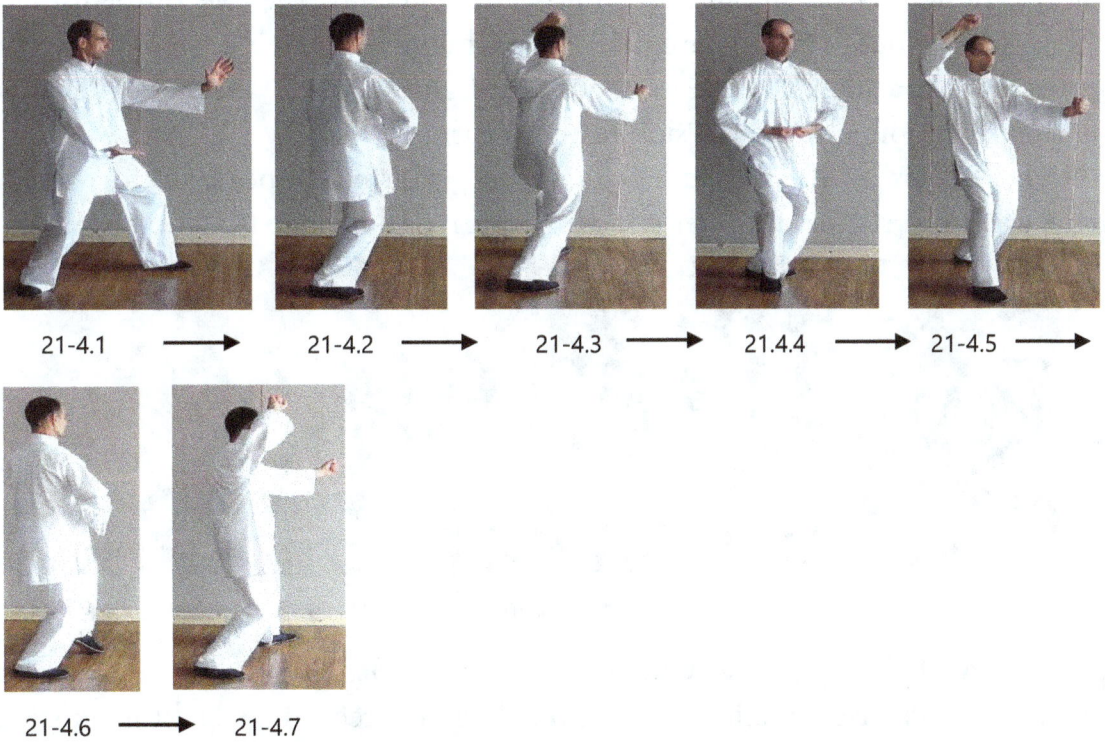

(Figure 21-4.1) Starting from (L) Pi Chuan posture.
(Figure 21-4.2) Step out at a 45-degree angle with the (R) foot. The (L) foot follows, while at the same time the hands close into fists, facing palm up and draw into the Tan Tien (see figure 21-4.4 for front view). Now the body faces 45 degrees outward

from the original starting centreline in a cat stance weighted heavily on the (R) rear leg. The (L) foot is resting lightly on the ball and toes.

(Figure 21-4.3) Step forwards at the 45-degree angle to the left, pushing off the rear (R) foot and leading with the forward (L) foot, using the half-step method. At the same time, block upward with the (L) arm just above eye level, keeping the elbow pointing down and the forearm retained at 45 degrees. Simultaneously the (R) fist punches straight out to the midsection, keeping the 'eye' of the fist facing upwards throughout. This posture is (L) Pao Chuan.

(Figure 21-4.4) Next, step forward down the direction of the original centreline of the form with the (L) foot and turn inward to a 45-degree angle. At the same time, both hands close into fists and are drawn in together at the Tan Tien. Now the body faces 45 degrees inward from the original centreline at the start of the form (see figure 21-4.1) in a (R) cat stance weighted heavily on the (L) rear leg. The (R) foot is resting lightly on the ball and toes.

(Figure 21-4.5) Next, step forwards at 45 degrees to the right, pushing off the rear (L) leg and leading with the forward (R) foot, using the half-step method. At the same time, block upward with the (R) arm just above the level of the eyes, keeping the elbow pointing down and the forearm retained at 45 degrees. Simultaneously the (L) fist punches straight out to the midsection, keeping the 'eye' of the fist facing upwards throughout. This posture is (R) Pao Chuan.

(Figures 21-4.6 and 4.7) Repeats sequence (figures 21-4.2 and 4.3) previous to bring the practitioner to the (L) side ready to turn.

Note: At this point the sequence can be performed repeatedly forward in a straight line until the practitioner chooses to turn and change direction.

21-4.12 ← 21-4.11 ← 21-4.10 ← 21-4.9 ← 21.4.8

(Figure 21-4.8) From (L) Pao Chuan (figure 21-4.7) the (L) front foot is turned inwards in a clockwise direction approximately 45 degrees, the weight is transferred from the (R) foot to the (L) foot and at the same time the hands are brought in towards the Tan Tien as fists facing palm down in mid turn.

(Figure 21-4.9) The practitioner continues to turn in a clockwise direction a further 180 degrees ending the pivot in (R) cat stance with the fists drawn fully in to the body at Tan Tien level with the palms now turned face up as shown clearly in figure 21-4.4 previous.

(Figure 21-4.10) From here the practitioner drives forward into (R) Pao Chuan as described in figure 21-4.5 previously, using the half-step method.
(Figures 21-4.11 and 4.12) Continues the sequence stepping forwards into (L) Pao Chuan ready to turn.

(Figures 21-4.13, 4.14 and 4.15) Repeats the turn sequence and ends with the practitioner in (R) Pao Chuan. (See figures 21-4.8, 4.9 and 4.10 described previous.)
(Figures 21-4.16 and 4.17) Next, the practitioner turns to face the original centreline stepping forward with the (R) foot and punching forwards with the (R) fist simultaneously. The (L) fist is held at the (R) elbow as in Pi Chuan and the practitioner steps forward with the (L) foot into (L) Pi Chuan posture. To finish the form correctly from (L) Pi Chuan the practitioner uses the closing method described in Chapter 19 previous.

Fire Form Fighting Applications:

Fire Form – Application 1

(Figure 7a) White faces off to Black in a neutral stance.
(Figure 7b) Black attempts a (R) roundhouse punch to White's face. White steps inside Black's attack blocking with the (L) arm and simultaneously strikes Black's solar plexus with the (R) fist using Pao Chuan (L).
(Figure 7c) To fight back, Black throws a second (L) roundhouse punch at White's head. White instinctively switches into (R) Pao Chuan and executes a second (L)

Pao Chuan strike to the solar plexus.

Fire Form - Application 2

(Figure 8a) White faces off to Black in a neutral stance.
(Figure 8b) Black attempts a (R) roundhouse punch to White's face. White steps inside Black's attack blocking with the (L) arm and simultaneously strikes Black's solar plexus with the (R) fist using (L) Pao Chuan.
(Figure 8c) White then steps to the outside of Black and switches the (L) Pao Chuan into a lateral rotation shoulder lock, potentially dislocating Black's (R) shoulder joint and taking him to the ground.

5. Earth Form – Heng Chuan

Grand Master Chiao

To open the form into (L) Pi Chuan (figure 21-5.1) use the opening method shown in Chapter 19 previously.

Master James McNeil & Andrew Jackson

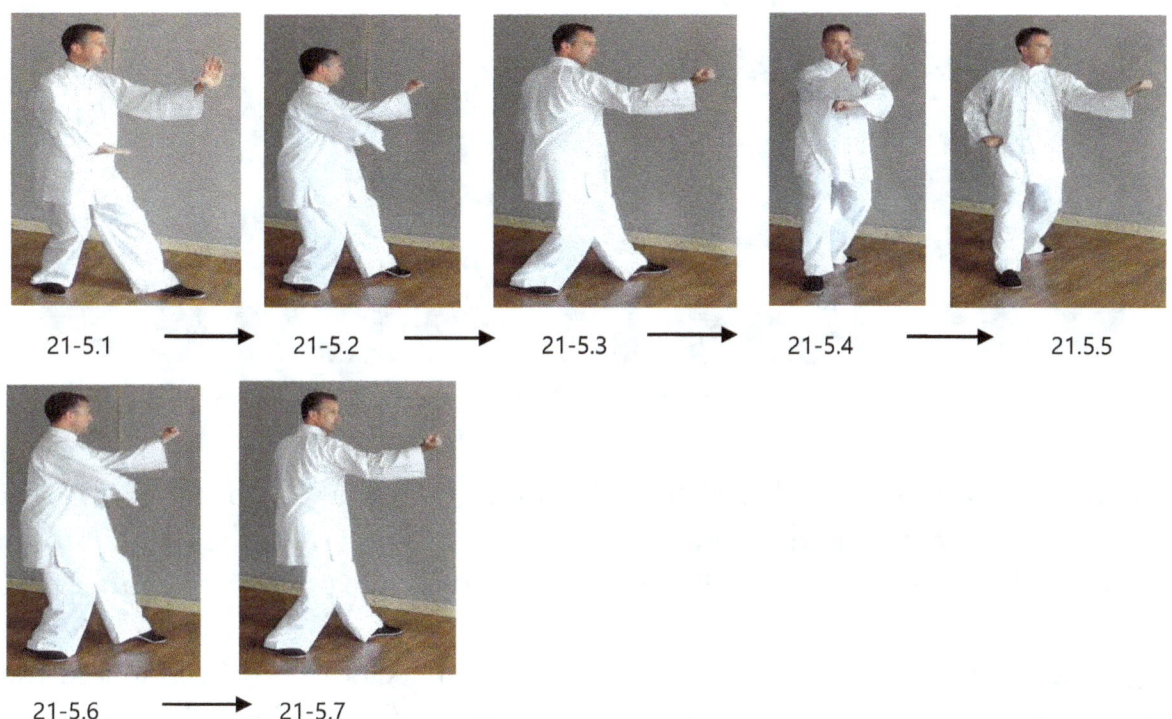

(Figure 21-5.1) Starting from (L) Pi Chuan posture.

(Figure 21-5.2) Begin by stepping out with the (R) foot at a 45-degree angle. Next turn the body outward 45 degrees, counter clockwise to the left into a (L) cat stance. The right foot is flat, the left foot is on its ball and toes. At the same time, the (L) hand holds its position and makes a fist facing palm up. The (R) hand makes a fist and moves directly under the (L) elbow facing palm down.

Note: The footwork of Earth form is the same as the footwork in Fire form.

(Figure 21-5.3) Now step out left as the (R) fist wipes off up the underside of the (L) forearm, beginning contact at the (L) elbow. The (R) fist circles clockwise and punches outward, at the height of the ribs, palm up. At the same time, the (L) fist twists palm down, pulling back to the waist and then rests just in front of the Tan Tien. The (R) foot follows the left using the half-step method. This posture is (L) Heng Chuan.

(Figure 21-5.4) Next, step forward with the (L) foot and turn inward 45 degrees into (R) cat stance. Leave the (R) fist in the same position as the (L) fist moves directly under the (R) elbow facing palm down.

(Figure 21-5.5) Step out to a 45-degree angle with the (R) foot, as the (L) foot follows in a half-step. Simultaneously, the (L) fist rubs the underside of the (R) forearm beginning contact at the elbow and strikes outward at rib level. As the (R) fist drops to the Tan Tien it twists to face palm down. This posture is (R) Heng Chuan.

(Figures 21-5.6 and 5.7) Repeats sequence of figures 21-5.2 and 21-5.3 previously to bring the practitioner to the (L) side ready to turn.

Note: At this point the sequence can be performed repeatedly forward in a straight line until the practitioner chooses to turn and change direction.

21-5.12 ← 21-5.11 ← 21-5.10 ← 21-5.9 ← 21.5.8

(Figure 21-5.8) From (L) Heng Chuan (figure 25-5.7) the (L) front foot is turned inwards approximately 45 degrees, the weight is transferred from the (R) foot to the (L) foot and at the same time the hands remain in the same position as figure 21-5.7 throughout.

(Figure 21-5.9) The practitioner continues to turn in a clockwise direction a further 180 degrees ending the pivot in (R) cat stance with the (R) hand remaining held as a fist at nose level. As the turn is completed the (L) fist is positioned under the (R) elbow facing palm down. This hand position is shown clearly in figure 21-5.4 previous.

(Figure 21-5.10) From here the practitioner drives forward into (R) Heng Chuan as described in figure 21-5.5 previously.

(Figures 21-5.11 and 5.12) Continues the sequence stepping forwards into (L) Heng Chuan ready to turn.

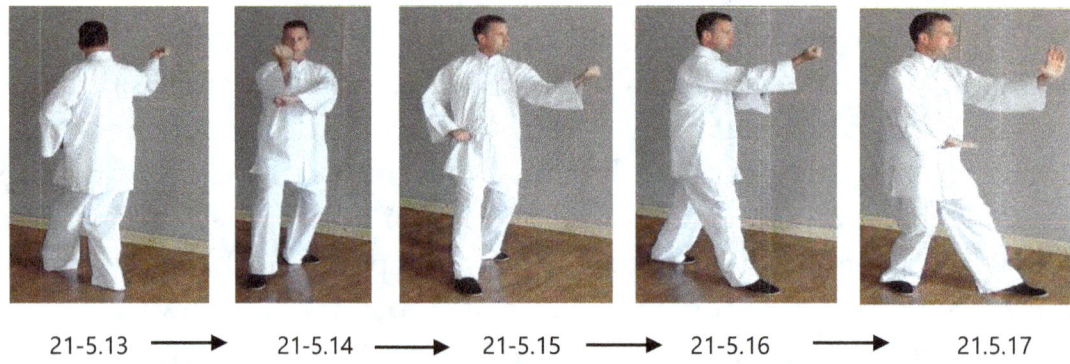

21-5.13 → 21-5.14 → 21-5.15 → 21-5.16 → 21.5.17

(Figures 21-5.13, 5.14 and 5.15) Repeats the turn sequence and ends with the practitioner in (R) Heng Chuan. See figures 21-5.8, 5.9 and 5.10 described previous.

(Figures 21-5.16 and 5.17) Next the practitioner turns to face the original centreline stepping forward with the (R) foot and punching forwards with the (R) fist simultaneously. The (L) fist is held at the (R) elbow as in Pi Chuan and the practitioner steps forward with the (L) foot into (L) Pi Chuan posture. To finish the form correctly from (L) Pi Chuan the practitioner uses the closing method described in Chapter 19 previously.

Earth Form Fighting Applications:

Earth Form – Application 1

9a → 9b → 9c

(Figure 9a) White faces off to Black in a neutral stance.
(Figure 9b) Black attempts a (R) straight punch to White's face. White steps to the outside, 45 degrees from the centreline of Black's attack, blocking with the (R) arm at the rear of Black's elbow joint.
(Figure 9c) From this change of angle White opens Black's intercostal region and strikes Black's ribs with the (L) fist using (R) Heng Chuan.

Earth Form – Application 2

10a → 10b → 10c

(Figure 10a) White faces off to Black in a neutral stance.
(Figure 10b) Black attempts a (R) straight punch to White's face. White steps to the outside, 45 degrees from the centreline of Black's attack, blocking with the (R) arm at the rear of Black's elbow joint.
(Figure 10c) From this change of angle, White drives forward with the (R) foot using the half-step method and grabs Black's (R) arm/wrist and simultaneously uses the (L) arm to execute Heng Chuan (R) driving the punch under Black's arm striking the chin. White's (L) shoulder also strikes into Black's (R) armpit. This technique can also be used to create a lever effect that can dislocate the opponent's shoulder or break the elbow, if applied correctly.

6. Five Element Chain Form – Wu Hsing

When the Five Element forms have been thoroughly practiced individually, they can then be practiced in a combined form called 'Wu Hsing' or 'Five Element Chain'. This is the beginning of the novice practitioner developing the ability to change from one posture to another seamlessly. This form follows the order of the 'Sheng' or 'Creative' cycle of the Five Element Cycle discussed previously in Chapter 7 of this book.

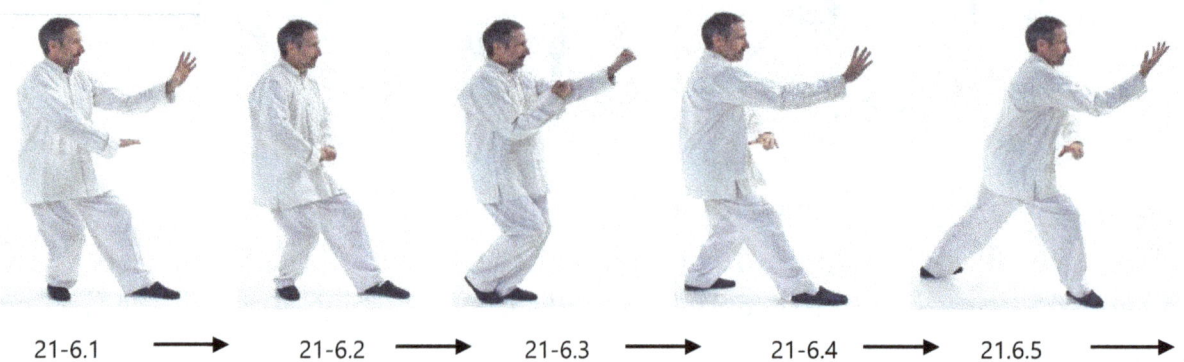

21-6.1 → 21-6.2 → 21-6.3 → 21-6.4 → 21.6.5 →

To open the form into (L) Pi Chuan (figure 21-6.1) use the opening method shown in Chapter 19 previously.
(Figure 21-6.1) Starting from (L) Pi Chuan posture.
(Figure 21-6.2) Draw in the (L) hand making a fist facing palm down. At the same time, make a fist with the (R) hand so as both fists are drawn in to the Tan Tien simultaneously.
(Figure 21-6.3) Step forwards with the (L) foot and at the same time the (L) fist punches straight out to nose height followed closely by the (R) fist which is kept close to the (L) elbow.
(Figure 21-6.4) Step through with the (R) foot and follow up with the (L) foot using the half-step method. At the same time as stepping execute a (R) punch straight up to nose height following the line of the previous (L) punch and as soon as the (R) punch reaches its full extension open the hands dropping the (L) hand down to the midsection, protecting the Tan Tien and the (R) hand chops forward and down the centreline in a splitting action. At the end of this sequence the practitioner should now be in (R) Pi Chuan posture.
(Figure 21-6.5) Moving from Pi Chuan (R). The (R) hand twists counter-clockwise with the palm up to throat height and the fingers come together to form a spear hand posture. The (L) hand remains palm down protecting the Tan Tien. At the same time, the (R) foot steps forward carrying most of the weight with the toes pointed outward at a 45-degree angle. The (R) foot remains in its previous position.

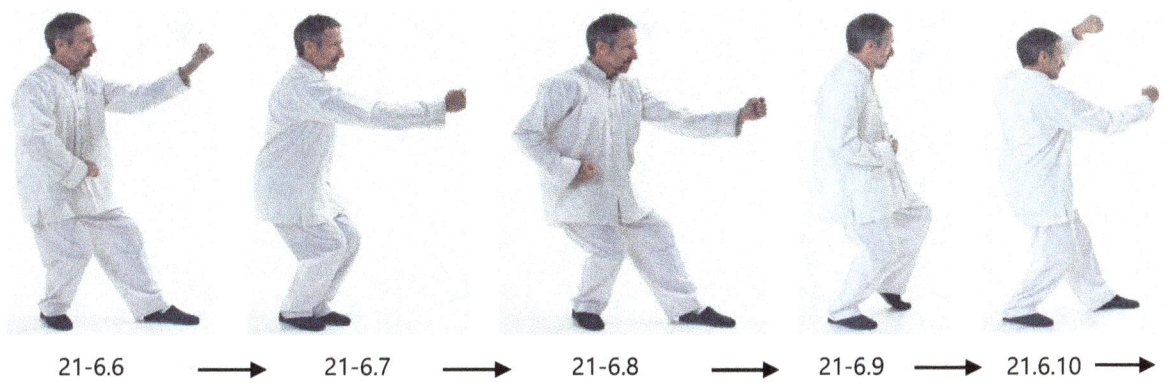

21-6.6 → 21-6.7 → 21-6.8 → 21-6.9 → 21.6.10 →

(Figure 21-6.6) The (R) hand twists clockwise into a fist as the (L) hand also forms a fist. Both (L) hand and (L) foot step forward in unison. The (L) hand punches out and up to nose level, while the (R) hand pulls down in front of the navel. The rising (L) fist follows a path inside that of the dropping (R) hand, which is held in a fist facing palm down. The (L) foot has stepped through to a forward position and the (R) foot follows using the half-step method. This returns the stance to a 70:30 weighting on the back foot. This posture is (L) Tsuan Chuan.

(Figure 21-6.7) From (L) Tsuan Chuan the (R) hand forms a fist and then punches straight out approximately to the height of the solar plexus. Simultaneously, the (L) hand forms a fist and pulls back to the (L) side of the waist. As the (R) hand punches, the (L) foot takes a step forward followed closely by the (R) foot which steps forward, alongside the (L) foot, ending tight alongside the instep, about one inch behind the left toe.

(Figure 21-6.8) Next, the (L) fist punches, coming out toward the centreline of the body in front of the solar plexus and brushing over the (R) arm, which is simultaneously drawing back to the (R) side of the waist. In this step, the (L) foot moves out and the (R) foot follows using the half-step method.

(Figure 21-6.9) Step out at a 45-degree angle with the (R) foot. The (L) foot follows, while at the same time the hands close into fists, facing palm up and draw into the Tan Tien. Now the body faces 45 degrees outward (anti-clockwise) from the starting centreline shown in picture figure 21-6.1. The practitioner is in a cat stance with the weight on the (R) leg. The (L) foot is resting lightly on the ball and toes.

(Figure 21-6.10) Step forwards at the 45-degree angle to the left, pushing off the rear (R) foot and leading with the forward (L) foot, using the half-step method. At the same time, block upward with the (L) arm just above the level of the eyes, keeping the elbow pointing down and the forearm retained at 45 degrees. Simultaneously the (R) fist punches straight out to the midsection, keeping the 'eye' of the fist facing upwards throughout. This posture is (L) Pao Chuan.

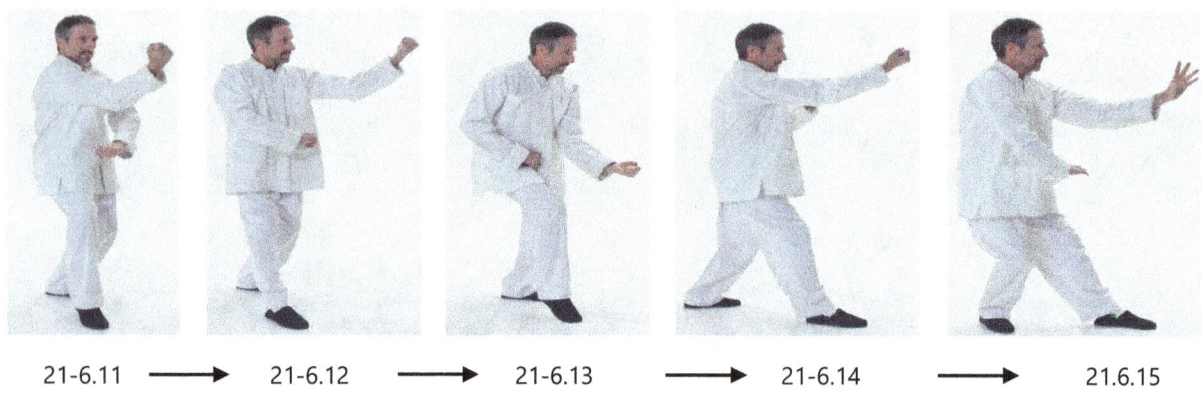

21-6.11 → 21-6.12 → 21-6.13 → 21-6.14 → 21.6.15

(Figure 21-6.11) Next, step forward with the (L) foot and turn inward 45 degrees into (R) cat stance. The (L) arm blocks as a fist, palm down and the (R) fist punches upward to nose height.

(Figure 21-6.12) Step out to a 45-degree angle with the (R) foot, as the (L) follows in a half-step. Simultaneously, the (L) fist rubs the underside of the (R) forearm beginning contact at the elbow and strikes outward at nose level. As the (R) fist drops to the Tan Tien and twists to face palm down. This posture is (R) Heng Chuan.

(Figure 21-6.13) The (L) arm circles clockwise, blocking down the centreline to waist height, while the (R) fist simultaneously moves towards the inside of the (L) elbow.

(Figure 21-6.14) Step forwards with the (R) foot and at the same time the (R) fist punches straight out to nose height followed closely by the (L) fist which is kept close to the (R) elbow.

(Figure 21-6.15) Step through with the (L) foot and follow up with the (R) foot using the half-step method. At the same time as stepping execute a (L) punch straight up to nose height following the line of the previous (R) punch and as soon as the (L) punch reaches its full extension open the hands dropping the (R) hand down to the mid-section, protecting the Tan Tien and the (L) hand chops forward and down the centreline in a splitting action. At the end of this sequence the practitioner should now be in (L) Pi Chuan posture.

← 21-6.18 ← 21-6.17 ← 21.6.16

(Figure 21-6.16) In a (L) turn the practitioner turns 90 degrees clockwise from (L) Pi Chuan posture into pigeon toe stance and at the same time brings both hands as fists facing palms up to Tan Tien level.

(Figure 21-6.17) The practitioner continues to turn clockwise a further 90 degrees to face the way they came from. Stepping out with the (R) foot and punching out with the (R) fist to nose height, keeping the (L) fist close to the (R) elbow.

(Figure 21-6.18) Step through with the (L) foot and follow up with the (R) foot using the half-step method. At the same time (L) punch straight up the line of the (R) arm to nose height and open the hands pressing down and out into (L) Pi Chuan posture again.

(Figures 21-6.19 to 6.35) Below repeats the same steps (figures 21-6.1 to 6.18) back again, returning the practitioner to their original starting point, (L) Pi Chuan.

→ 21-6.34   → 21.6.35

To finish the form correctly from (L) Pi Chuan the practitioner uses the closing method described in Chapter 19 previously.

Note: This sequence of Five Element movements can be repeated as many times as a practitioner wishes before opting to finish the form. Further this sequence forms the first half of the Five Element Linking Chain form (Wu Hsing Lien Wan). From (L) Pi Chuan shown in figure 21-6.35 the practitioner may opt to move straight into the Linking Chain (Lien Wan) section of the form shown in the Combined Forms Chapter 22 of this book.

7. Two Man Five Element Fighting Form/Wu Hsing I Er Ren

The Two Man Fighting Form is the final development sequence of the practitioner's empty hand Five Element training. This form follows the order and theory of the 'Ke' or 'Destructive' cycle in the Five Element Cycle discussed earlier in Chapter 7 of this book. It introduces the practitioner to the concept of using the individual element postures and applying them in a controlled contact sequence. This form allows the practitioner to develop their footwork, stance, reaction speed, distance, timing and physical conditioning against an opponent.

The principle reason for this two-man form is to train the five element techniques whilst being placed under pressure by an opponent. This training allows the practitioner to understand each of the techniques' applications and their variations both physically and strategically. It further develops the ability to enter and close on an opponent which is key to applying a technique, gaining the advantage, and controlling the opponent's movements effectively. Training of this form is used as a precursor to free fighting using the Hsing-I method.

The form generally moves in a circular direction consistent with the flow of the five-element model of creation as each practitioner creates the next creative element of the sequence in between the techniques of their opponent. Within this circular direction of the form is that of the star, depicting the destructive cycle of the five-element model, where each practitioner cuts across their opponent's attack using the appropriate element technique to counter attack their opponent. In the reality of practise, the form is never a perfect circle or star with in it and its true shape varies on the size of the steps of the two practitioners and the adjustments they must make to accommodate each other's technique. As two practitioners are never the same, neither will be the actual shape of the form.

In the following sequence of pictures, two practitioners compete with each other. In figure 21-7.1 below the practitioner on the left side, dressed in White is referred to as 'White', while the practitioner on the right side, dressed in Black is referred to as 'Black'.

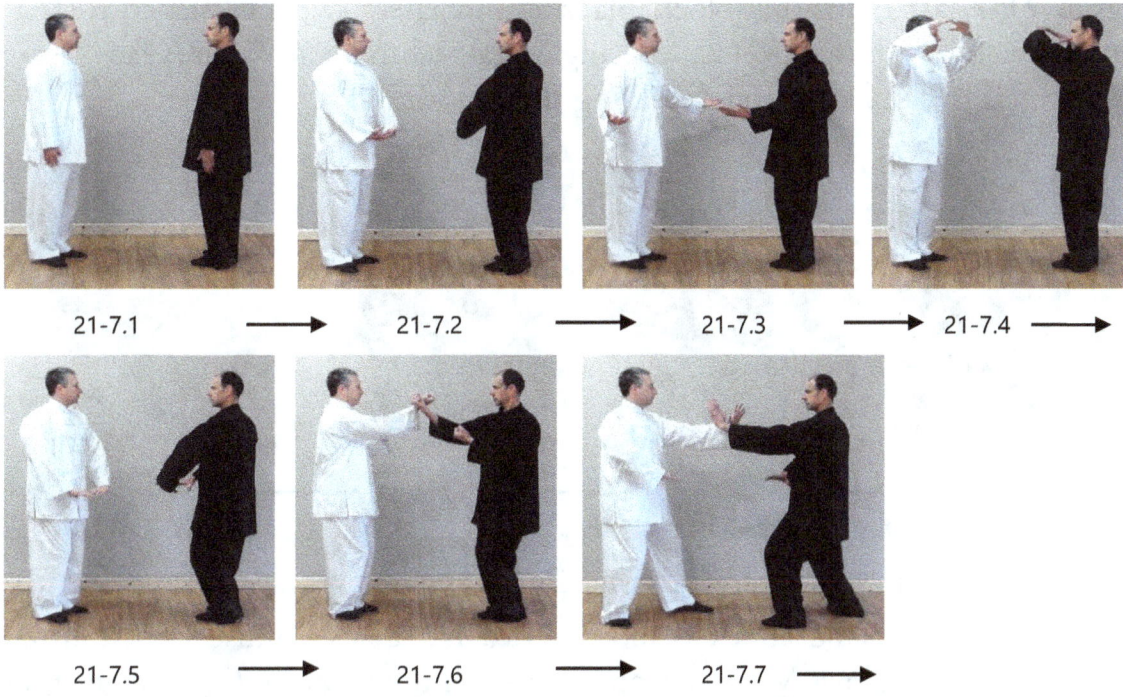

21-7.1 → 21-7.2 → 21-7.3 → 21-7.4 →

21-7.5 → 21-7.6 → 21-7.7 →

(Figure 21-7.1) Both practitioners begin by standing opposite each other in the Wuji posture.

(Figures 21-7.2, 7.3, 7.4, 7.5, 7.6 and 7.7) Both practitioners open their posture simultaneously into (L) Pi Chuan posture, facing directly into their opponents centreline. (See opening method in Chapter 19 of this book.)

Note: Traditionally the practitioner who takes control of the centreline first, attacks first and initiates the start of the sequence. In this example, it is White who initiates their attack first and therefore Black who retreats and defends first.

21-7.8 → 21-7.9 → 21-7.10 →

(Figure 21-7.8) First, White moves forward with their left foot and punches with their (R) fist to midsection, using the Wood punch technique. Simultaneously, Black draws backward and blocks the punch, using a (L) open crescent palm block.

(Figure 21-7.9) White then moves ahead with their left foot while punching with their (L) fist against the face of Black, using a (L) Wood punch technique. Simultaneously, Black cross steps to the outside away from the line of attack and turns their (L) fist upward to block the attack.

(Figure 21-7.10) From this block Black immediately switches stance to (R) Pi Chuan, striking with their (R) hand using Metal technique to White's face.

   Note: This is called, **Metal defeating the Wood.**

21-7.11 → 21-7.12 → 21-7.13 → 21-7.14 →

(Figure 21-7.11) During this time, White turns their (L) wrist upward with speed so that Black's (R) hand attack is blocked, leaving Black's midsection, centreline unprotected. This allows White an opening to simultaneously (R) straight punch Black's solar plexus using (L) Fire technique.

   Note: This is called, **Fire defeating Metal.**

(Figure 21-7.12) Now, when White attacks using Fire technique, Black steps back to the centreline with their (L) foot and blocks the strike using a (L) open palm block. Black then (R) punches White using Water technique at jaw height, drilling up the centreline.

   Note: This is called, **Water defeating Fire.**

(Figure 21-7.13 and 7.14) White then drives their (L) foot outwards at an angle of 45 degrees to Blacks centreline, keeping their weight heavily loaded into the rear (R) leg. White simultaneously blocks downwards with their (L) arm, striking the (R) forearm of Black to counter the attack. At the same time White (R) punches using Earth's crossing fist technique to Black's open ribs.

   Note: This is called, **Earth conquers Water.**

21-7.15 → 21-7.16 →

(Figure 21-7.15 and 7.16) To evade White's attack, Black withdraws their body and simultaneously blocks White's punch with a (R) covering block and simultaneously delivers a (L) Wood punch directly at Black's (R) ribs. In counter, White shock steps backwards with his (R) foot, covers Blacks Wood punch using an (R) crescent palm block and simultaneously attacks with a (L) Wood punch of their own to Black's midsection. This sequence creates a stalemate in techniques as both practitioners counter each other's movements at the same time.

Note: This is called, **Wood conquering Earth.**

At this point in the form the sequence of the five elements are complete and the practitioners reverse roles, in effect White becomes Black and vice versa. From here the sequence begins again with Black now attacking White first. Both practitioners continue the same sequence until a stalemate is reached again.

21-7.17 → 21-7.18 → 21-7.19 → 21-7.20 →

21-7.21 → 21-7.22 → 21-7.23 → 21-7.24 →

(Figures 21-7.17 to 7.24) Repeats the cycle again until both practitioners have each completed one further cycle of the form and are now again in a stalemate position.

Note: This cycle can be continuously repeated until one practitioner defeats the other by landing a blow or both the practitioners decide to end the form in a stalemate.

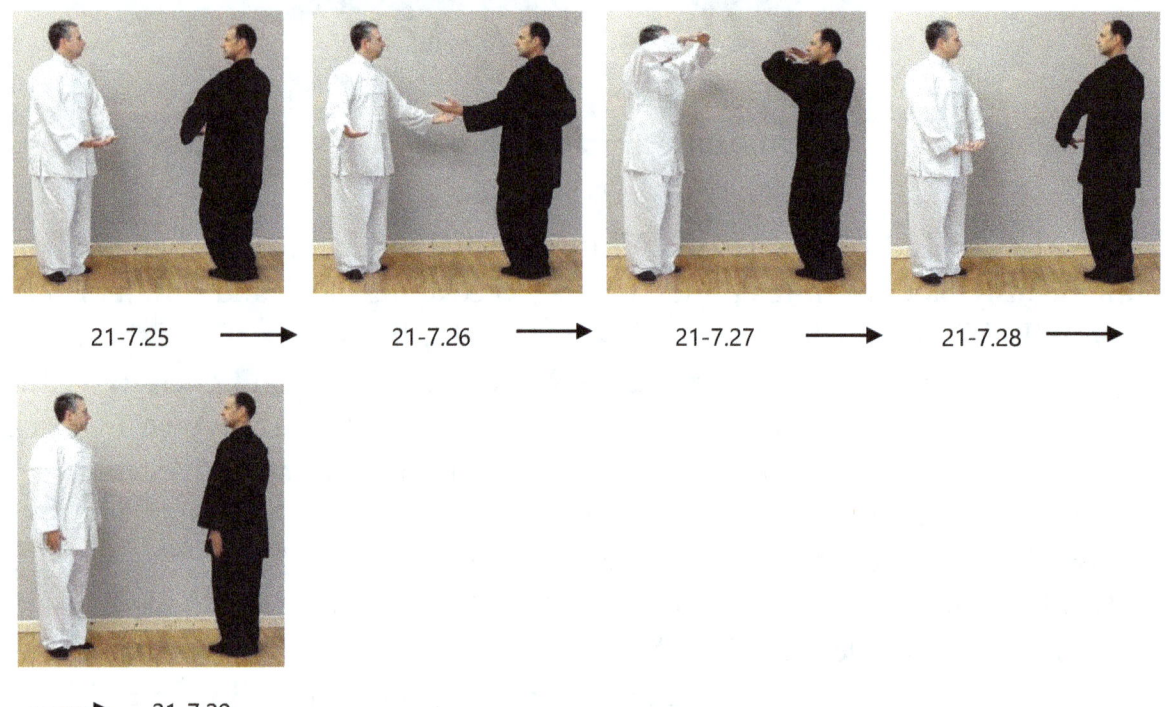

(Figures 21-7.25, 7.26, 7.27, 7.28 and 7.29) When both White and Black are in a stalemate as shown in figure 21-7.24 both can then take a step backwards away from each other and finish the form using the closing method discussed in Chapter 19 of this book. This sequence returns both practitioners in Wuji posture facing each other as they began.

Chapter 22

Combined Forms of Hsing-I Chuan

1. Linking Chain Form – Lien Wan

The first of the five combined forms taught in this system is 'Lien Hwan'. This form is connected to the Five Elements Linked Form (see Chapter 21) when practised in its entirety. First 'Wu Hsing' is performed and then without finishing the practitioner moves straight into 'Lien Hwan'. When practiced this way the form is referred to as 'Wu Hsing Lien Hwan' or 'Five Element Linking Chain Form'. This is a traditional form common to most lineages of Hsing-I although its pattern can vary from style to style.

Direction: Most of the movements in this form are practised in a straight line, with each movement stepping forwards from the last. However, in movements (Figures 22-1.3, 1.4 and 1.5) below the sequence takes a step backwards. Also in movements (Figures 22-1.8 and 1.9) below the sequence turns to and steps out to a 45-degree angle before returning to the original line of the form. The form then turns 180 degrees and repeats its movements in the opposite direction before turning again to finish where the practitioner originally started.

Figure 22-1

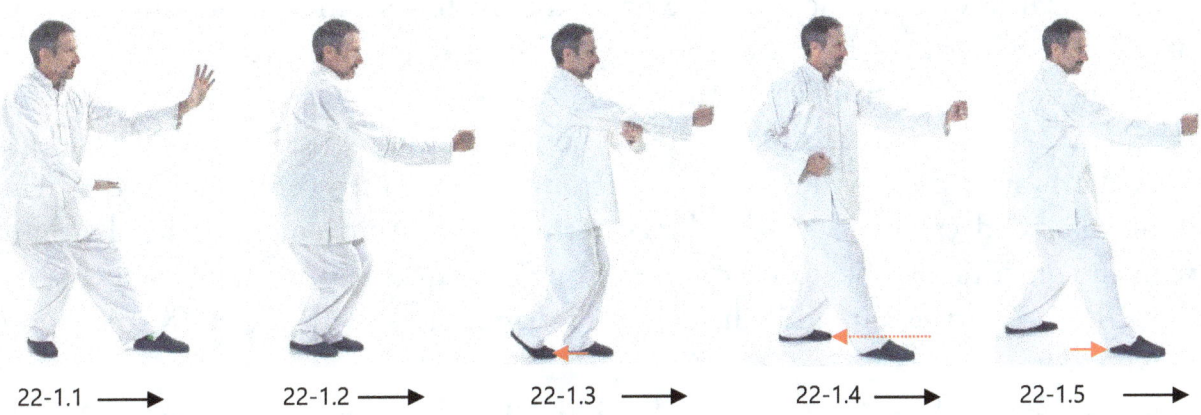

22-1.1 →   22-1.2 →   22-1.3 →   22-1.4 →   22-1.5 →

Note: To open the form into (L) Pi Chuan (Figure 22-1.1) use the opening method shown previously in Chapter 19.

(Figure 22-1.1) Starting from (L) Pi Chuan posture.

(Figure 22-1.2) Step forward with the (L) foot and then bring up the (R) foot to the (L) instep into closed Wood posture. At the same time, punch forward using Peng Chuan technique with the (R) hand down the centreline at the height of the solar plexus.

(Figure 22-1.3) Step backwards with the (R) foot, placing it on the ball and toes and at the same time the (L) fist moves underneath the (R) elbow facing palm up.

(Figure 22-1.4) Next, step back with the (L) foot and press the (R) foot flat to the ground. The practitioner is now in (R) Pi Chuan stance. At the same time as stepping back the (L) fist wipes off up the underside of the (R) forearm and executes a (L) Peng Chuan punch straight down the centreline at solar plexus level. The (R) fist reciprocally draws back to the (R) hip.

(Figure 22-1.5) Next, take a small step forward with the (R) foot, opening the stance and at the same time execute a (R) Peng Chuan punch at solar plexus level. The (L) fist draws back to the (L) hip. This is now open Wood posture.

(Figure 22-1.6) Step forward with (L) foot into (L) bow stance and at the same time the hands execute a low double-handed cross block, directly out and in front of the centreline at the height of the groin. The body is turned to 45 degrees from the straight forward line of the form.

(Figure 22-1.7) Continue to hold the (L) bow stance and 45-degree body position. Raise both arms directly up, out and in front of the body's centreline into a high double handed cross block. This block terminates its movement at head height with the practitioner able to see clearly through the underside of their own crossed arms. Both forearms should be held at a 45-degree angle with the elbows pointing downwards.

(Figure 22-1.8) The forward facing (L) foot turns inwards to 45 degrees and the (R) rear foot is brought up and 'dropped' with force to the ground alongside the

(L) foot. The practitioner now faces totally 45 degrees to the straight forward line of direction of the form. At the same time as the (R) foot is dropped to the floor, the high crossed fists circle outward and down, in time with one another and the (R) fist strikes the (L) palm, precisely as the (R) foot strikes the ground. The back remains straight and the eyes look forward throughout the sequence.

(Figure 22-1.9) Step out at the 45-degree angle to the forward line of the form and perform (R) Pao Chuan technique.

(Figure 22-1.10) Keep the (L) rear foot rooted to the ground as the (R) forward foot sweeps in a circular motion to the inside, turning the body straight back in line with the forward line of the form. The (R) foot hook sweeps and at the same time the (R) arm blocks across the body at face height. The block and sweep must be executed together, starting and finishing at the same time. The (L) fist simultaneously pulls back to the (L) hip.

22-1.11 →   22-1.12 →   22-1.13 →   22-1.14 →   22-1.15 →

(Figure 22-1.11) Next, the (R) foot is drawn backwards into the instep of the (L) foot, at the same time the (R) fist starts to draw backwards and down as the (L) fist punches upwards to nose height in the line of the withdrawing (R) arm, as in Pi Chuan technique.

(Figure 22-1.12) The (R) foot continues to take a large step backwards, planting itself solidly on the ground with the foot at a 45-degree angle. The (L) foot is also drawn back due to the large back step movement of the opposing foot and drawn onto the ball of its foot, facing forwards. At the same time, the (R) fist continues to pull back and down to the (R) hip and the (L) hand opens from a fist, pulling downwards and backwards in time with the opposing hand.

(Figure 22-1.13) Step forwards with the (L) foot and follow with the (R) foot using the half-step method. Block down with the (R) hand using an open palm at the height of the Tan Tien, whilst simultaneously striking forward down the centreline at the height of the throat using a (L) eagle claw hand technique.

(Figure 22-1.14) Step forward again using the half-step method, however remain on the (L) side by pushing of the (R) rear foot and taking a step forward with the

(L) foot at the same time. As the practitioner pushes off the (R) foot they must not step through and past the (L) foot. This means the practitioner moves forward, but remains in a (L) Pi Chuan stance. Block down with the (L) hand using an open palm at the height of the Tan Tien, whilst simultaneously striking forward down the centreline at the height of the throat using a (R) eagle claw hand technique.

(Figure 22-1.15) Take a small step forward with the (L) foot and bring the (R) foot up alongside the (L) foot. At the same time both hands block out in front of the body using crescent palm block hand techniques. Both hands should be held in line with each other, with the (R) hand slightly above and ahead of the (L) hand.

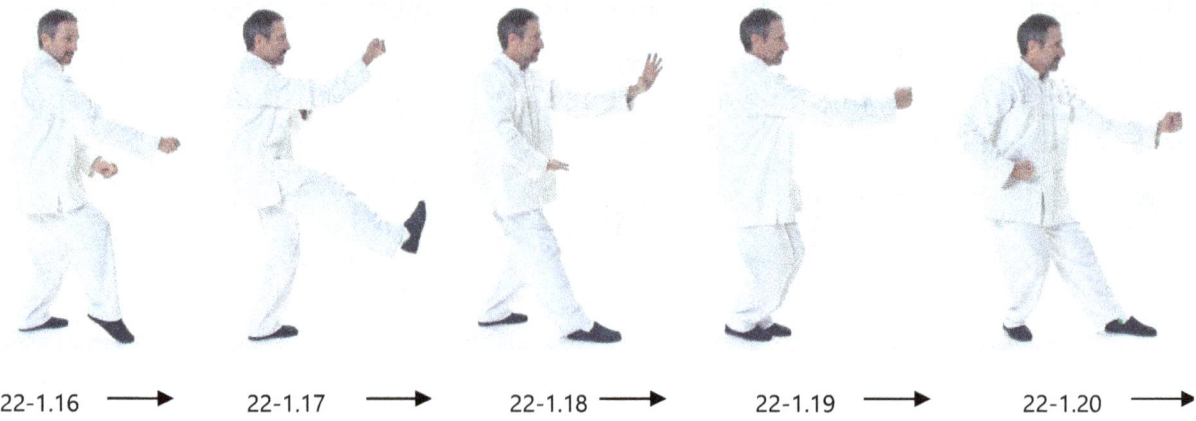

22-1.16 → 22-1.17 → 22-1.18 → 22-1.19 → 22-1.20 →

(Figure 22-1.16) Continue to step through and forward with the (R) foot, whilst at the same time the two hands held in front 'grasp' into fists in the same arm position as (figure 22-1.15) previous.

(Figure 22-1.17) As the (R) foot moves forward it raises and kicks out forwards at knee height, using 45 degree rising kick technique. Simultaneously the two fists twist to face palms up and drive upwards and forwards to nose height with the (R) fist leading and the (L) fist held at the (R) elbow.

(Figure 22-1.18) Before the (R) kicking foot touches the ground, the (L) rear foot pushes forward allowing the practitioner to take a forward, lunging step with the lead (R) foot and this is backed up using the half-step method, in effect putting the practitioner in a (R) Pi Chuan stance. At the same time, the (L) hand punches up the (R) forearm performing a Pi Chuan hand technique. This movement places the practitioner with (R) foot and opposing (L) hand forward. This is called (R) reverse Pi Chuan posture.

(Figure 22-1.19) From (R) reverse Pi Chuan, take a small step forward with the (R) foot and then step straight through with the (L) foot into closed Wood posture. The (L) foot is forwards with the (R) foot tucked into the instep. The (R) hand executes a Peng Chuan punch to solar plexus height, whilst the (L) hand pulls back to the (L) hip.

(Figure 22-1.20) From closed Wood step straight forward in to open Wood posture.

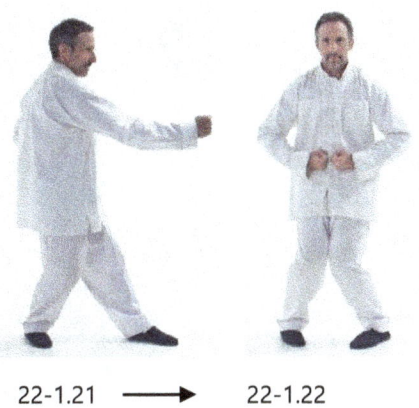

(Figures 22-1.21, 1.22, 1.23 and 1.24) From open Wood then execute the Wood turn sequence to turn the form 180 degrees from the starting direction.

(Figures 22-1.25 to 1.51) The remaining sequence below repeats the same movements in the opposite direction. After movement (figure 1.45) the practitioner turns 180 degrees again to face the direction they started. They then continue the opening sequence of the form to movement (figure 1.51) below.

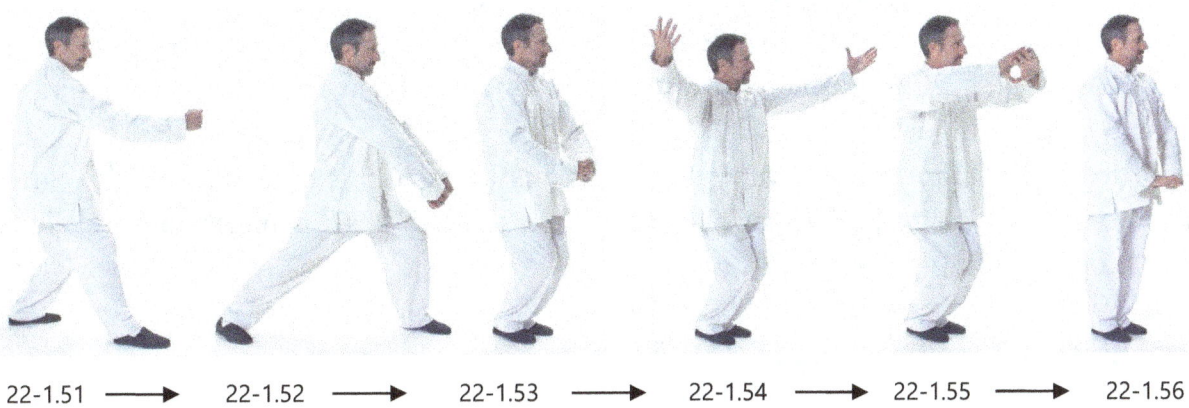

22-1.51 → 22-1.52 → 22-1.53 → 22-1.54 → 22-1.55 → 22-1.56

(Figure 22-1.51) Open Wood posture.

(Figure 22-1.52) From open Wood posture take a large step forward with the (L) foot into (L) bow stance. Keep the body facing straight on in line with the front foot. At the same time both hands block as fists over the (L) knee. Keep the back straight and the head held upright.

(Figure 22-1.53) Take a small step forwards with the (L) foot, placing it with toes straight ahead. Bring up the back (R) foot, placing it at 45 degrees with the heels together. Bring both hands together at the height of the Tan Tien and keep the knees bent retaining the height of the previous movement.

(Figure 22-1.54, 1.55 and 1.56) Both hands open and rise in a symmetrical arc at opposing sides of the body, coming together at the height of the head. Without stopping the palms press down to the height of the Tan Tien and simultaneously the knees straighten returning the practitioner to their natural height prior to starting the form.

Lien Hwan - Fighting Applications:

Application 1 – movements 22-1.3, 1.4, 1.5

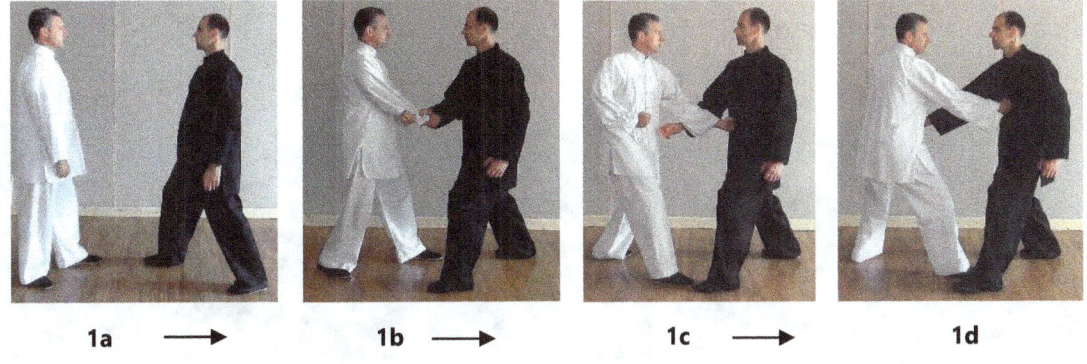

1a → 1b → 1c → 1d

(Figure 1a) White faces off to Black in a neutral stance.

(Figure 1b) Black cross grabs White's (R) arm with his (R) hand.
(Figure 1c) White counters by stepping directly into Black's attack and executes a (L) Peng Chuan punch using it to break Black's grip and at the same time strike to Black's Tan Tien.
(Figure 1d) White immediately withdraws his (L) striking hand and at the same time delivers a second (R) Peng Chuan punch to Black's solar plexus before Black has time to react.

Application 2 – movements 22-1.6, 1.7

(Figure 2a) White faces off to Black in a neutral stance.
(Figure 2b) Black steps in and attacks White with a low (L) punch to the Tan Tien. White counters by stepping forward into (L) bow stance and blocking Black's punch with a (R) low block.
(Figure 2c) Black immediately throws a (R) straight punch to White's face. White remains in (L) bow stance and evades by raising his (R) arm to block to the outside of Black's attack.
(Figure 2d) Black is now open to his outside and from here White can counter attack using Heng Chuan by grabbing Black's (R) arm and anchoring it whilst at the same time driving through with an elbow locking/breaking technique.

Application 3 – movement 22-1.8

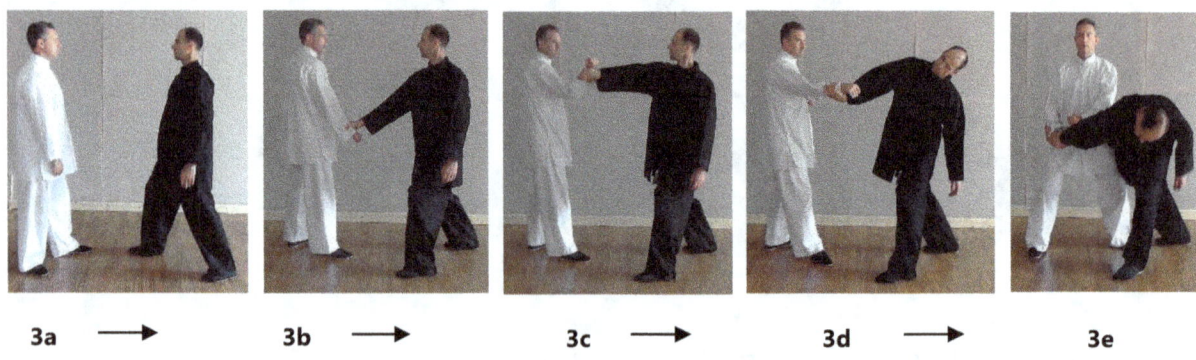

(Figure 3a) White faces off to Black in a neutral stance.
(Figure 3b) Black steps in (L) and cross grabs White's (R) wrist.
(Figure 3c) White immediately steps towards Black and at the same time turns his (R) arm upwards, to turn Black's grabbing (R) arm and elbow up into a vulnerable position. This action also protects White by making it difficult for Black to punch effectively with this free (L) hand.
(Figure 3d) White continues to circle around Black's wrist with his (R) hand and grabs, taking control of Black's arm, forcing him off balance.
(Figure 3e) White now controls Black's arm and immediately steps forwards with his (L) foot into horse stance, forcing Black completely off balance. From here the option to strike the back of Black's (R) elbow or control Black with an elbow lock technique presents itself.

Application 4 – movements 22-1.10, 1.11, 1.12

(Figure 4a) White faces off to Black in a neutral stance.
(Figure 4b) Black steps in (L) and throws a (L) straight punch to White's face. Black counters with an O/I (R) circle block to Black's punch. At the same time, White circle sweeps with a (R) hooked foot behind Black's (L) foot to off balance him.
(Figure 4c) Black attempts a second (R) punch to White's face. White uses his (R) hand to circle block from O/I to counter the strike. Black's hands are now crossed in front of him making it difficult to attack.
(Figure 4d) White seizes the initiative and grabs the (R) wrist with his (R) hand and steps back with his (R) foot, pulling Black with his momentum towards the ground where White can now control him using an elbow lock technique.

Application 5 – movement 22-1.13

5a → 5b

(**Figure 5a**) White faces off to Black in a neutral stance.
(**Figure 5b**) Black steps in (R) and throws a (R) low punch to White's Tan Tien. White steps into the attack with his (R) foot and counters with a (L) crescent palm block and at the same time strikes using the eagle claw technique directly through the centreline to Black's throat.

Application 6 – movements 22-1.15, 1.16, 1.17

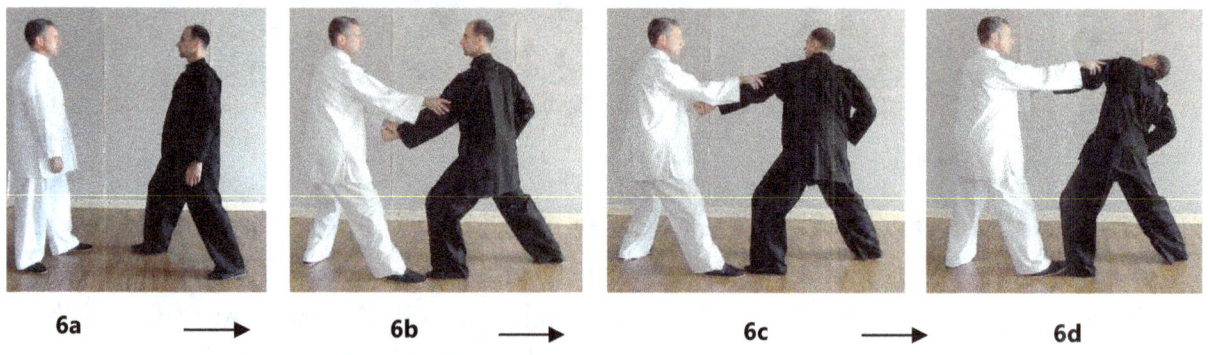

6a → 6b → 6c → 6d

(**Figure 6a**) White faces off to Black in a neutral stance.
(**Figure 6b**) Black steps in (L) and throws a (L) low punch to White's Tan Tien. White steps into the attack with his (R) foot and counters with a double handed crescent palm block, grabbing and taking control of Black's (L) arm.
(**Figure 6c**) On taking control of Black's (L) arm White twists it, locking it at the elbow and wrist simultaneously in a clockwise direction, this turns the elbow up and the shoulder into internal rotation.
(**Figure 6d**) White then steps in (R) and places his foot on Black's forward (L) foot to stop him from retreating. At the same time, White drives Black's own (L) shoulder into his own jaw by using his locked arm to knock him unconscious.

Application 7 - movement 22-1.52

7a → 7b → 7c

(Figure 7a) White is unexpectedly grabbed from behind by Black using a 'bear hug' technique.

(Figure 7b) White steps forward with his (R) foot to counter the momentum of the attack. White sinks his centre to stabilise himself and at the same time drops his shoulders and rotates his arms outwards symmetrically to pull Black off balance and break his grip.

(Figure 7c) Whilst Black lets go to try and regain his balance, White takes the initiative and rotates to his (L) driving his (L) elbow deep into Black's open (L) rib cage and knocking him off balance.

2. Eight Form Fist Form – Ba Shih Chuan

The second of the five combined forms taught in the system is 'Ba Shih Chuan'. This is another traditional form common to many lineages of Hsing-I, although its pattern can vary from style to style. Thought to have been developed originally by General Yue Fei, it was Tai Lung-Pang (1713–1802) who is first documented to have taught and passed on the form within the Shansi lineage. Traditionally this form is said to correspond to the spirits and energies of a selection of eight of the Five Elements and Twelve Animals, hence its name. In no particular order these energies are Water, Wood, Fire, Earth, Horse, Chicken, Sparrow-Hawk and Swallow. Remember that the actual postures of these forms are not always directly represented in the form, but the energetic actions and spirit associated to them can be demonstrated and applied to different postures practiced within the form.

Direction: Most of the movements in this form are practiced in a straight line, with each movement stepping forwards from the last. However, in movement (Figure 22-2.10) below the sequence takes a step backwards. Also in movements (Figures 22-2.22 and 2.23) below the sequence turns to and steps out to a 45-degree angle before returning to the original line of the form. The form then turns 180 degrees and repeats its movements in the opposite direction before turning again to finish where the practitioner originally started.

Figure 22-2

22-2.1 → 22-2.2 → 22-2.3 → 22-2.4 → 22-2.5 →

Note: Ba Shih Chuan starts from its own unique opening posture.

(Figure 22-2.1) Starting from (L) opening posture, the hands are held symmetrically as fists, with palms facing up at the height of the Tan Tien. The front foot faces forwards and the back foot is places at 45 degrees with the heels touching.

(Figure 22-2.2) Step forward with the (L) foot, lowering the body into a horse stance and at the same time the (R) knife hand strikes in a circular motion from outside to inside down the centreline at the height of the Tan Tien. The (L) fist is brought alongside the inside of the (R) elbow.

(Figure 22-2.3) Next, keep the feet rooted to the ground and sink the body down fully by flexing both knees to the angle of 90 degrees. At the same time keep the back straight and perform a (L) Peng Chuan punch down the direct line of the extended (R) arm aimed at the height of the groin. At the same time, the (R) hand pulls back as a fist to the (R) hip.

(Figure 22-2.4) Continue to step forward into a low cross stance with the (R) foot. This stepping action raises the height of the practitioner slightly as they move forward. At the same time as stepping execute a (R) Peng Chuan punch straight down the centreline at groin level. The (L) fist reciprocally draws back to the (L) hip.

(Figure 22-2.5) Next, step forward into (L) Pi Chuan stance using the half-step method. This step forward brings the practitioner up to their full height. At the same time execute a (L) Peng Chuan punch at Tan Tien level. The (R) fist draws back to the (R) hip. This is open Wood posture.

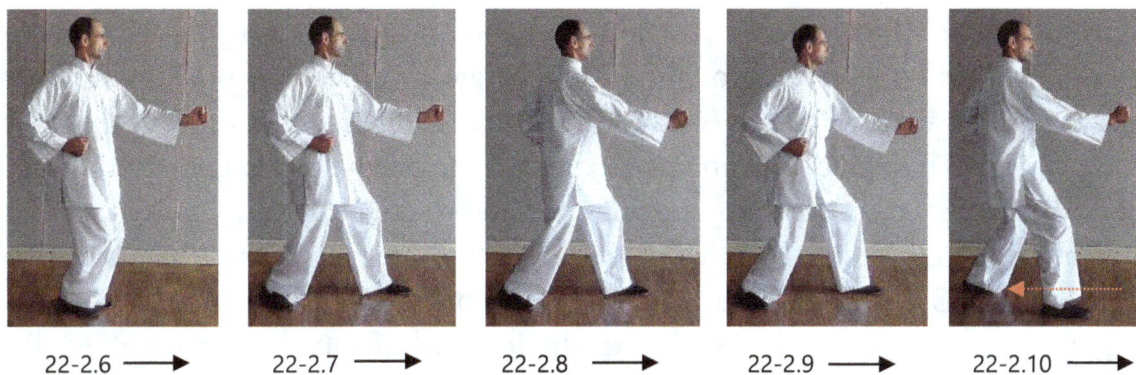

22-2.6 → 22-2.7 → 22-2.8 → 22-2.9 → 22-2.10 →

(Figure 22-2.6) Step up with rear (R) foot into closed Wood stance and keep the hands held in the previous (L) Peng Chuan position.

(Figure 22-2.7) Continue to step out forwards with the (L) foot returning to open Wood posture and at the same time keep the hands held in the previous (L) Peng Chuan position.

   Note: 22-2. 6 and 2.7 combined steps make up the 'close the gap' stepping method (see Chapter 17).

(Figure 22-2.8) Still in (L) open Wood posture the practitioner executes a (R) Peng Chuan punch at Tan Tien level.

   Note: This posture is called reverse open Wood as the stance is open and the punch is on the opposite side to the forward foot.

(Figure 22-2.9) Do not move forward and remain in (L) open Wood posture. Execute a (L) Peng Chuan punch at Tan Tien level. This is now returned to (L) open Wood posture.

(Figure 22-2.10) Next the practitioner steps backwards with the (L) foot, planting it solidly into the ground and transferring the weight into the now rear (L) leg. At the same time, they execute a (R) Peng Chuan punch at Tan Tien level. This is now to (R) open Wood posture.

   Note: This backward step whilst punching is called 'shock stepping' (see Chapter 17).

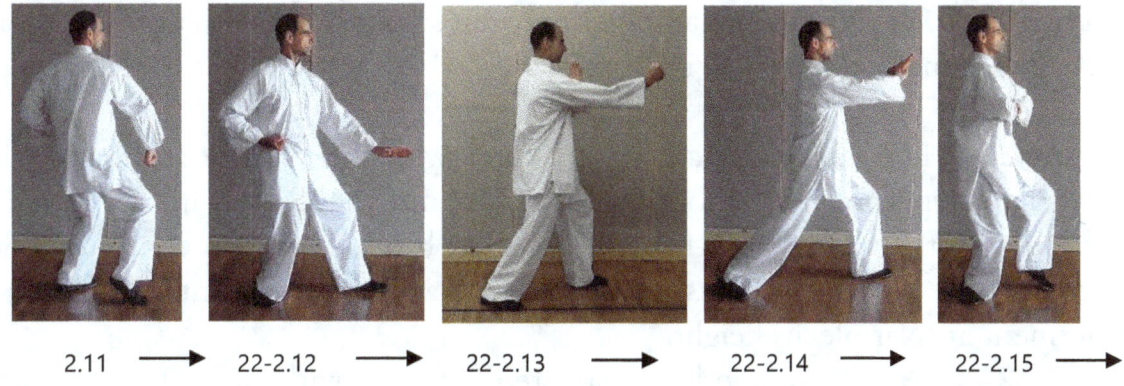

2.11 → 22-2.12 → 22-2.13 → 22-2.14 → 22-2.15 →

(Figure 22-2.11) Next, the (R) foot is drawn back into (R) cat stance and at the same time the (R) fist circle blocks low from outside to inside to protect the centreline at Tan Tien level. The (L) fist remains at the (L) hip throughout.

311

(Figure 22-2.12) Both feet then rapidly exchange positions using the chicken step method. The head stays level throughout this change of stance. The practitioner is now in (L) Pi Chuan stance. Simultaneously with the feet the hands change, with the (R) fist circling round as if to grab with an open hand and the drawing in to the (R) hip as a fist again. The (L) fist comes forward opening the hand to crescent palm block at Tan Tien height along the centreline. Both hands must start and finish their movements together.

(Figure 22-2.13) Step forwards with the (L) foot and follow with the (R) foot using the half-step method. Punch straight forward at face height with (R) Peng Chuan whilst covering the centreline with the (L) hand using an open palm block at shoulder height.

(Figure 22-2.14) Step forward with the (L) foot again into (L) bow stance. Keep the rear (R) foot static throughout. Slide the (L) open palm down the inside of the extended (R) arm and execute a double, crossed block with open hands at throat height.

(Figure 22-2.15) Draw in the (L) foot into (L) cat stance and at the same time both hands circle down and continue circling until they face palms up, drawing in the arms and hands together along the centreline. As the (R) hand draws in it becomes a fist facing palm up and comes to rest in the open palm of the (L) hand resting against the chest at solar plexus height.

22-2.16 ⟶   22-2.17 ⟶   22-2.18 ⟶   22-2.19 ⟶   22-2.20 ⟶

(Figure 22-2.16) From (L) cat stance previous step forward with the (L) foot using the half-step method into (L) Pi Chuan stance, whilst at the same time executing (L) horse posture.

(Figure 22-2.17) Take a small step forwards with the (L) foot and back this up with a half-step with the rear foot. At the same time, the (R) rear fist strikes straight down the centreline as a back-fist strike to nose height and then continuing down to contact the 'eye' of the outstretched (L) fist as its target point, terminating its movement at solar plexus height.

(Figure 22-2.18) Take another small step forwards with the (L) foot and then execute a (R) rear straight leg kick along the centreline. At the same time, the (R) fist pulls back to the (R) hip. The (L) fist punches out in time with the kick using Peng Chuan technique.

(Figure 22-2.19) Next, step straight forward with a half-step in to (R) open Wood posture. At the same time execute a (R) Peng Chuan punch to Tan Tien height.

(Figure 22-2.20) Step forward with (L) foot into (L) bow stance and at the same time execute a low double-handed cross block, directly out and in front of the centreline at the height of the groin. The body is turned to 45 degrees from the straight forward line of the form.

22-2.21 → 22-2.22 → 22-2.23 → 22-2.24 → 22-2.25 →

(Figure 22-2.21) Continue to hold the (L) bow stance and 45-degree body position. Raise both arms directly up, out and in front of the body's centreline into a high double-handed cross block. This block terminates its movement at head height with the practitioner able to see clearly through the underside of their own crossed arms. Both forearms should be held at a 45-degree angle with the elbows pointing downwards.

(Figure 22-2.22) The forward facing (L) foot turns inwards to 45 degrees and the (R) rear foot is brought up and dropped with force to the ground alongside the (L) foot. The practitioner now faces totally 45 degrees to the straight forward line of direction of the form. At the same time as the (R) foot is dropped to the floor, the high crossed fists circle outward and down, in time with one another and the (R) fist strikes the (L) palm, precisely as the (R) foot strikes the ground. The back remains straight and the eyes look forwards throughout the sequence.

(Figure 22-2.23) Step out at the 45-degree angle to the forward line of the form into (R) Pi Chuan stance. At the same time, the (R) hand opens and forms a spear hand, striking with the drilling energy of Tsuan Chuan upwards along the centreline to throat height. The (L) hand forms a crescent palm hand and blocks downwards along the centreline to the height of the Tan Tien. Both hands must start and finish their movements together.

(Figure 22-2.24) Next, step forward with the (L) foot into (L) Pi Chuan stance. The (L) hand strikes out forwards with a knife hand strike with the palm facing down aimed at mid-rib height. The (R) hand pulls back to the height of the (R) temple as an open hand in opposition to the (L) hand.

(Figure 22-2.25) Next, take a small step forward with the (L) foot and at the same time the (L) hand turns upwards and executes a spear hand finger strike upwards along the centreline to throat height. The (R) hand also forms a spear hand posture with the palm down and executes a finger thrusting strike downwards along the centreline to the height of the groin. Both hands must start and finish their movements together.

22-2.26 → 22-2.27

(Figures 22-2.26 and 2.27) Follow on by stepping forward using the chicken step method to change feet to (R) foot forward ending in (R) Pi Chuan stance. At the same time, the (L) hand blocks palm upwards at the height of the head and is closely followed by the (R) palm blocking up in a rolling, circular motion which changes the hands positions. The (L) hand terminates at the height of the forehead, along the left side of the centreline. The (R) hand thrusts out forwards with a knife hand strike with the palm facing down aimed at mid-rib height. Both hands and feet must start and finish their movements together.

Note: The energy associated with this movement is the same as that developed in Swallow form.

← 22-2.32   ← 22-2.31   ← 22-2.30   ← 22-2.29   ← 22-2.28

(Figure 22-2.28) The practitioner then transfers their weight from the (L) rear leg (figure 22-2.27) into the (R) leg and steps behind themselves with the (L) leg, allowing them to turn 180 degrees and lower into a horse stance, with the back held straight. The practitioner now faces the direction they came from. At the same time the (R) arm circles round low, crossing the centreline at the height of the waist and blocks using the knife edge of the hand. The (L) arm crosses the centreline and the (L) hand comes to rest as a fist at the inside of the (R) elbow.

Note: The crossing over action of the arms during the sequence of the turn is the same as the 'crossing' energy developed in Heng Chuan form.

(Figures 22-2.29 to 2.55) Repeats the same sequence in the opposite direction. At **(Figure 22-2.54)** the practitioner turns 180 degrees again to face the direction they started.

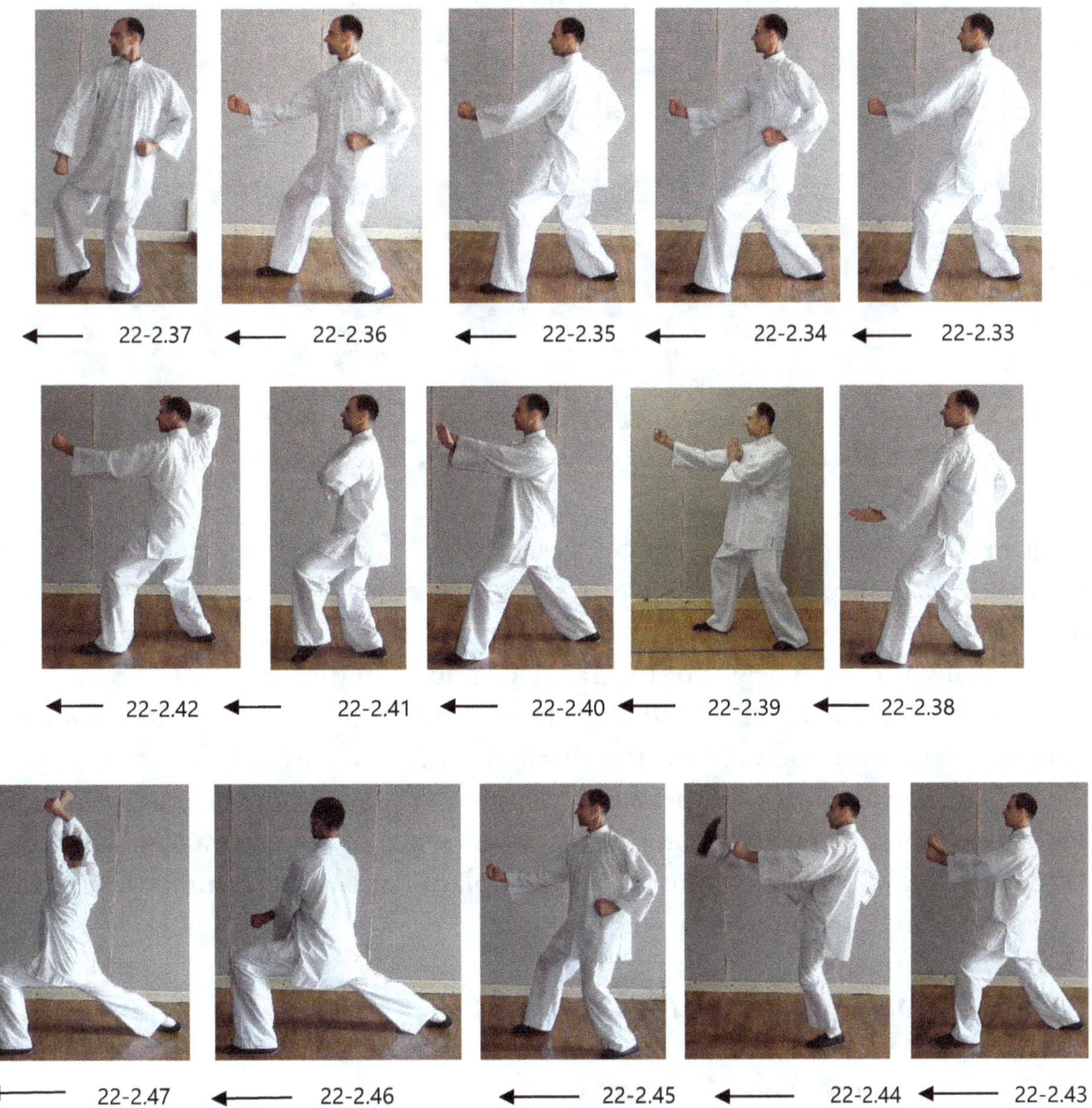

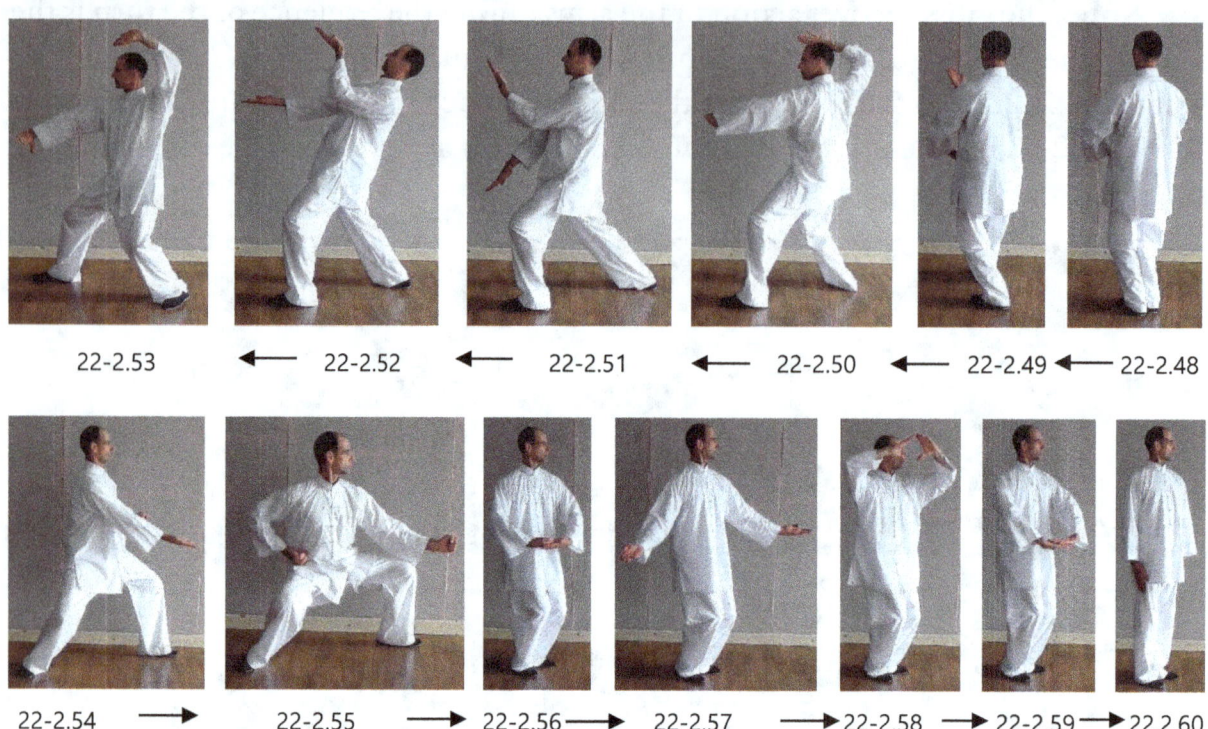

(Figure 22-2.56) From horse stance (see Figure 22-2.55) take a small step forwards with the (L) foot, placing it with toes straight ahead. Bring up the back (R) foot, placing it at 45 degrees with their heels together. Bring both hands together with palms facing up at the height of the Tan Tien and keep the knees bent.

(Figures 22-2.57, 2.58 and 2.59) Both hands open and rise in a symmetrical arc at opposing sides of the body, coming together at the height of the head. Without stopping, the palms press down to the height of the Tan Tien and simultaneously the knees straighten returning the practitioner to their natural height prior to starting the form.

(Figure 22-2.60) Before finishing the form, place both hands symmetrically at the sides of the body and return to Wuji posture.

Ba Shih Chuan – Fighting Applications:

Application 1 – movements 22-2.2 and 2.3

(Figure 1a) White faces off to Black in a neutral stance.
(Figure 1b) Black attacks White with a low (R) punch to the Tan Tien. White counters Black by blocking the punch at the elbow with a (R) O/I circle block, using the knife edge of the hand.
(Figure 1c) White then attacks Black's open centreline by stepping in with the (L) foot and executing a (L) Peng Chuan punch to the Tan Tien.

Application 2 – movement 22-2.4

2a → 2b

(Figure 2a) White faces off to Black in a neutral stance.
(Figure 2b) Black throws a (L) roundhouse punch to White's head. White counters and blocks the punch with a (R) open palm block whilst at the same time stepping into (R) cross stance, directly onto Black's (L) foot to stop him retreating and delivers a (L) Peng Chuan punch to Black's Tan Tien.

Application 3 – movements 22-2.11 and 2.12

3a → 3b → 3c → 3d

(Figure 3a) Black cross grabs White's (R) wrist with his (R) hand.
(Figure 3b) White immediately draws in his foot and circle blocks low with his (R) arm to open up Black's grip.
(Figure 3c) White counters by stepping directly into Black's centreline and at the same time twists upwards his own (R) arm into Tsuan Chuan posture. This twisting manoeuvre turns Black's (R) arm over leaving the elbow pointing up and vulnerable to attack.

Hsing-I Chuan | The Practice of Heart and Mind Boxing

(Figure 3d) White then circles his (R) hand around Black's wrist, breaking his grip and taking control of Black's (R) arm. Next White steps forward into (L) Pi Chuan stance and applies an elbow lock to Black with his (L) hand taking him to the ground.

Application 4 – movement 22-2.13

4a → 4b

(Figure 4a) White faces off to Black in a neutral stance.
(Figure 4b) Black throws a (R) straight punch to White's face. White steps forward, past the outside of Black with his (L) foot and simultaneously cover blocks the punch with a (L) open palm block. At the same time, he delivers a (R) Peng Chuan punch directly into Black's jaw.

Application 5 – movement 22-2.14

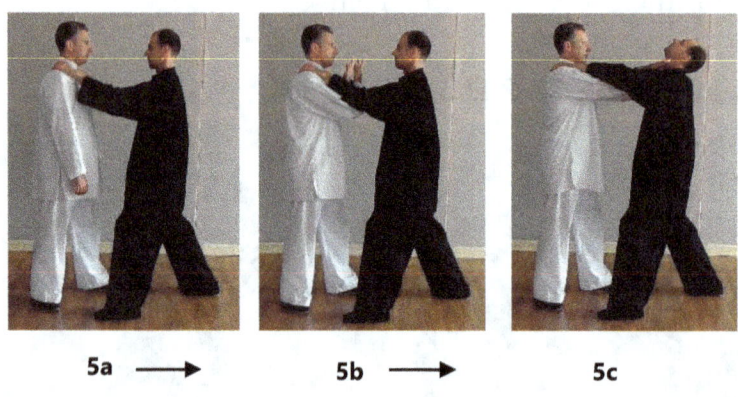

5a → 5b → 5c

(Figure 5a) Black grabs White around the throat with both hands.
(Figure 5b) White counters by cross blocking his hands inside Black's arms to loosen the grip.
(Figure 5c) As soon as White contacts with Black's arms and loosens the grip he then drives both his hands forward, down the inside line of Black's arms to deliver a double knife hand strike to Black's throat.

Application 6 – movement 22-2.15

6a → 6b → 6c → 6d

(Figure 6a) Black grabs White's jacket with his (R) hand at chest level.
(Figure 6b) White counters by cross grabbing with his (R) hand, Black's (R) wrist over the top of his arm.
(Figure 6c) White takes control of Black's (R) wrist and twists it counter-clockwise to break the grip, applying a wrist lock and turning the arm over into a vulnerable, extended position.
(Figure 6d) White then steps directly into Black in the line of his (R) extended arm, forcing him off balance and breaks the (R) wrist using his own chest.

Application 7 – movement 22-2.16

7a → 7b

(Figure 7a) White faces off to Black in a neutral stance.
(Figure 7b) Black throws a (R) straight punch to White's face. White counters by blocking the punch with his (R) hand and simultaneously stepping directly into Black's attack with his (L) foot, executing a (L) Peng Chuan punch to break Black's ribs.

Application 8 – movement 22-2.17

8a → 8b → 8c →

(Figure 8a) Black (R) hand cross grabs White's jacket at chest height.
(Figure 8b) White counters by cross grabbing with his (L) hand, Black's (R) wrist over the top of his arm.
(Figure 8c) White takes control of Black's (R) wrist and twists it clockwise to break the grip and off-balance Black. White then immediately delivers a (R) back fist strike to Black's nose.

Application 9 – movement 22-2.18

9a → 9b → 9c → 9d

(Figure 9a) Black cross grabs White's (R) arm with his (R) hand.
(Figure 9b) White counters by stepping directly into Black's centreline and at the same time twists upwards his own (R) arm into Tsuan Chuan posture. This twisting manoeuvre turns Black's (R) arm over leaving the elbow pointing up and vulnerable to attack.
(Figure 9c) White then circles his (R) hand around Black's wrist, breaking his grip and taking control of Black's (R) arm. Next White delivers a (R) straight leg kick to Black's groin.
(Figure 9d) As soon as White's (R) foot plants to the ground he delivers a (L) Peng Chuan punch to Black's ribs.

Application 10 – movement 22-2.23

10a → 10b

(Figure 10a) White faces off to Black in a neutral stance.
(Figure 10b) Black attempts a low (R) punch to White's Tan Tien. White counters by stepping directly into Black's centreline and blocks the punch using a (L) open palm block. At the same time, he executes a (R) spear hand thrust directly at Black's throat.

3. Basic Beginning Form – Chu Chi Chuan

The third of the five combined forms taught in the system is 'Chu Chi Chuan'. This traditional form of Hsing-I introduces the concept of using techniques previously learned whilst stepping backwards as well as forwards, which is generally more common to the practice of Hsing-I. Chu Chi Chuan starts to train the practitioner to move in different directions and maintain alignment of posture whilst still being able to deliver an effective technique. The back-stepping method used in this form, called 'shock stepping' can and should be practiced with all Hsing-I postures, making the practitioner more adaptable to the variables encountered when fighting.

Direction: The movements in this form are practised forwards and backwards in a straight line. However, in this form the practitioner moves mainly forwards with each step in the first half of the form and then moves backwards with each step in the second half of the form. Finally, the form finishes taking a step forward to end facing the same direction as when starting.

Figure 22-3
To open the form into (L) Pi Chuan (Figure 22-3.1) use the opening method shown in Chapter 19 previous.

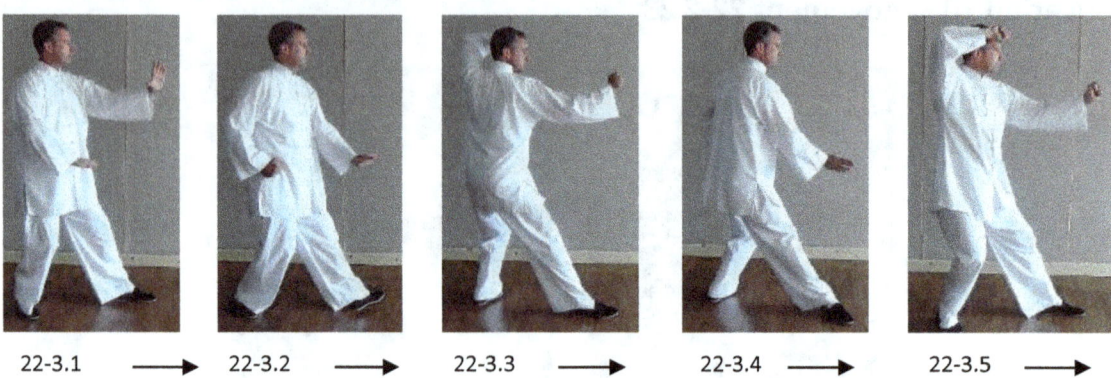

22-3.1 → 22-3.2 → 22-3.3 → 22-3.4 → 22-3.5 →

(Figure 22-3.1) Starting from (L) Pi Chuan posture.

(Figure 22-3.2) Step forward with the (L) foot and block down to the centreline at Tan Tien level with the (L) hand as a crescent palm block. At the same time, the (R) hand draws back to the (R) hip as a fist facing 'eye' up.

(Figure 22-3.3) Step forwards with the (R) foot and follow up with the (L) foot using the half-step method. At the same time, the (R) hand punches straight up the centreline to nose height using Peng Chuan technique. The (L) hand simultaneously draws upwards and backwards in opposition as a fist and ends its movement in line with the (L) temple. This is (R) horse posture.

(Figure 22-3.4 and 3.5) The next movements (Figures 22-3.4 and 3.5) repeat the sequence of movements (Figures 22-3.2 and 3.3) on the opposite side. This sequence ends with the practitioner in (L) horse posture (Figure 22-3.5).

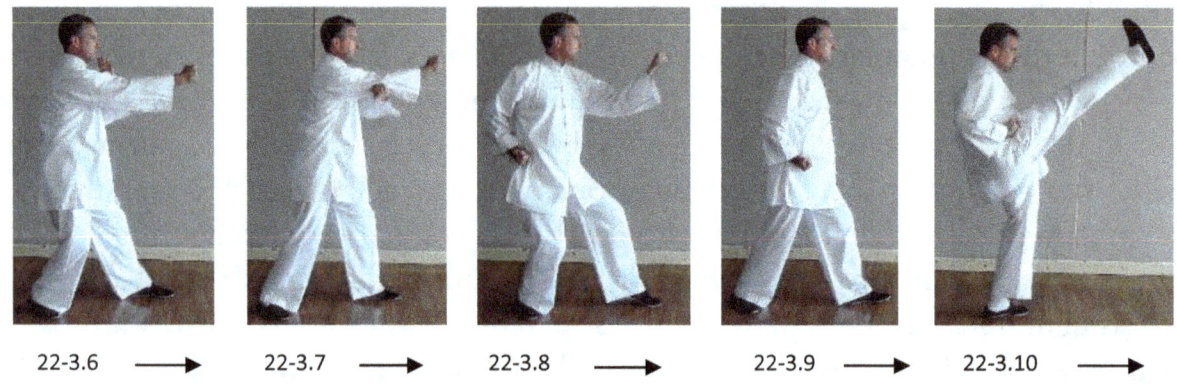

22-3.6 → 22-3.7 → 22-3.8 → 22-3.9 → 22-3.10 →

(Figure 22-3.6) Next step forwards with the (L) foot and follow with the (R) foot using the half-step method. Punch straight forward at face height with (R) Peng Chuan whilst covering the centreline with the (L) hand using an open palm block at shoulder height.

(Figure 22-3.7) Next, take a large step backwards with the (R) foot and place the (L) fist facing palm down, under the (R) elbow.

(Figure 22-3.8) Transfer the weight back into the rear (R) leg and draw the (L) leg into (L) cat stance. Wipe the (L) hand off the underside of the (R) forearm drawing the (R) hand as a fist to the (R) hip, facing palm up. At the same time punch out with the (L) hand as in Heng Chuan technique.

(Figure 22-3.9) Step forwards with the (L) foot and draw the (L) fist to the (L) hip, mirroring the opposite hand.

(Figure 22-3.10) Execute a rear straight leg kick with the (R) foot straight down the centreline. The hands remain as fists held at hip height.

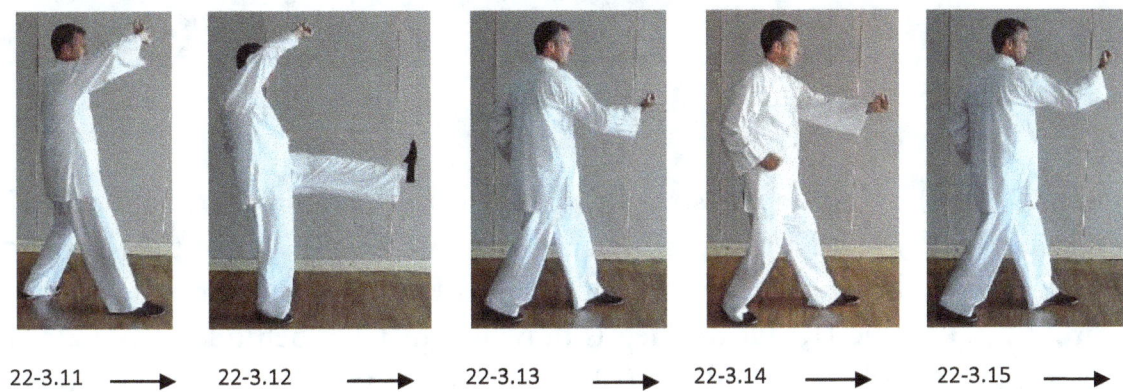

22-3.11 → 22-3.12 → 22-3.13 → 22-3.14 → 22-3.15 →

(Figure 22-3.11) Next, the (R) foot is placed in front from the previous kick and the (L) foot follows up using the half-step method. At the same time both hands circle up from the hips in time and strike in front of the head at temple height. The (L) hand is held palm open and the (R) hand forms a phoenix eye fist and strikes the centre of the (L) open palm.

(Figure 22-3.12) Take a small step forwards with the (R) foot and then execute a rear straight leg kick with the (L) foot straight down the centreline. At the same time, the (L) hand draws back to the (L) hip as a fist and the (R) hand executes a (R) high block with the forearm held at a 45-degree angle with the elbow pointing down.

(Figures 22-3.13 and 3.14) As the (L) foot lands it is placed firmly on the ground in front and the (R) foot follows up using the half-step method. At the same time, the (R) hand strikes down the centreline as a back fist, terminating its movement at the (R) hip. As the (R) hand reaches the (R) hip the (L) hand punches straight out at Tan Tien height using Peng Chuan technique. This is now (L) open Wood posture.

(Figure 22-3.15) Next, take a small step forwards with the (L) foot as the (R) hand simultaneously punches forwards to nose height along the centreline.

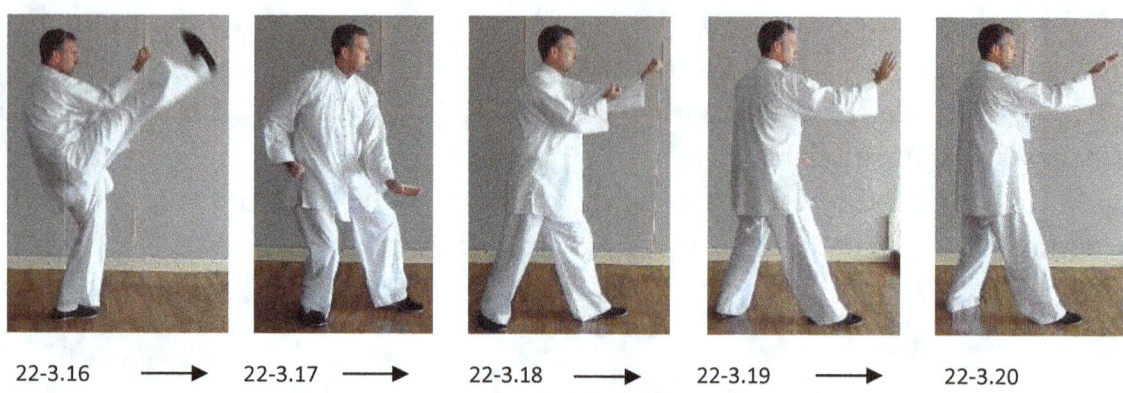

22-3.16 → 22-3.17 → 22-3.18 → 22-3.19 → 22-3.20

(Figure 22-3.16) Execute a rear straight leg kick with the (R) foot straight down the centreline. The (R) hand remain as a fist held at nose height, whilst the (L) hand is placed as a fist at the inside of the (R) elbow as in Pi Chuan technique.

(Figure 22-3.17) The (R) kicking leg is drawn right back behind the practitioner at the end of the technique and the (L) foot is drawn into (L) cat stance, in effect moving the practitioner backwards. At the same time, the practitioner punches up the (R) arm with the (L) fist as in Pi Chuan technique [not clearly shown] and then draws the (R) hand back to the (R) hip as a fist. The (L) hand blocks down the centreline at groin height as an open crescent palm in time with the opposing (R) hand.

(Figure 22-3.18) Next, take a small step forwards with the (L) foot as the (L) hand simultaneously punches forwards to nose height along the centreline. The (R) hand is drawn to the inside of the (L) elbow as in Pi Chuan technique.

(Figure 22-3.19) Step through with the (R) foot and follow up with the (L) foot using the half-step method. At the same time as stepping execute a (R) punch straight up to nose height following the line of the previous (L) punch and as soon as the (R) punch reaches its full extension open the hands dropping the (L) hand down to the mid-section, protecting the Tan Tien and the (R) hand chops forward and down the centreline in a splitting action. At the end of this sequence the practitioner should now be in (R) Pi Chuan posture.

(Figure 22-3.20) The feet remain planted in Pi Chuan stance as the (R) hand turns to face palm up in a spear hand posture. Simultaneously the (L) hand turns palm up also as a spear hand and is held closely to the inside of the (R) elbow.

← 22-3.25   ← 22-3.24   ← 22-3.23   ← 22-3.22   ← 22-3.21

(Figure 22-3.21) Step back with the (R) leg into Pi Chuan (L) stance using the shock step method. At the same time perform Pi Chuan hand technique but with open hands instead of the usual fists. This is now (L) Pi Chuan posture.

Note: In this form, when moving forwards and applying Pi Chuan use the normal method. When moving backwards using Pi Chuan, the hands remain open throughout the movement and do not make fists at any time.

(Figure 22-3.22) Next with the feet remaining in (L) Pi Chuan stance, punch straight forward at face height with (R) hand Peng Chuan whilst covering the centreline with the (L) hand using an open palm block at shoulder height.

(Figure 22-3.23) Keep the feet static in (L) Pi Chuan stance. Chop down the line of the extended (R) arm with the (L) hand using the knife hand edge, palm down to strike at neck height along the centreline. At the same time the (R) fist pulls back along the centreline as an open hand to shoulder height facing palm down.

(Figure 22-3.24) Keep the feet static in (L) Pi Chuan stance. Chop forward using a knife hand strike along the centreline, to neck height with the knife edge of the hand facing palm up. At the same time, the (L) hand draws back palm up to the inside of the (R) elbow.

(Figure 22-3.25) Step back with the (L) foot into (R) Pi Chuan stance. At the same time slide the (L) hand up the inside of the (R) forearm along the centreline to face height and then part the two arms into the shape of a 'V' with both palms of the hands facing upwards.

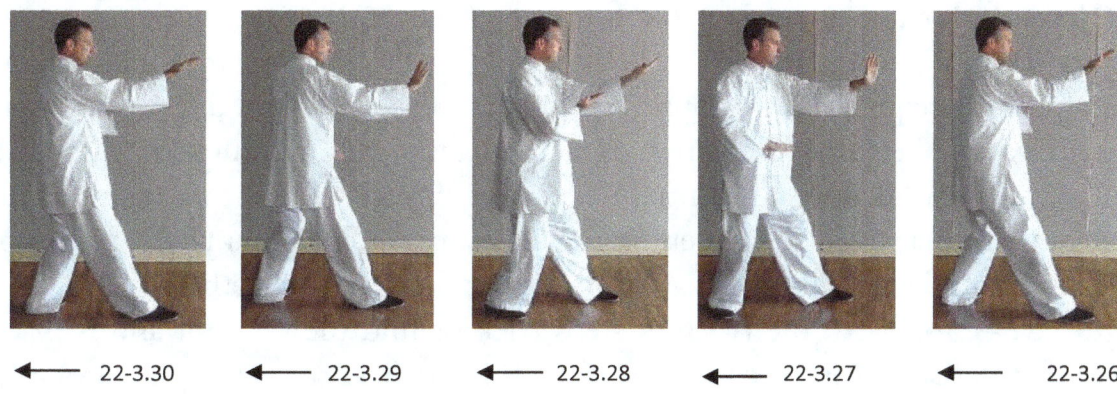

← 22-3.30   ← 22-3.29   ← 22-3.28   ← 22-3.27   ← 22-3.26

(Figure 22-3.26) The feet remain planted in (R) Pi Chuan stance as the (R) hand turns to face palm up in a spear hand position. Simultaneously the (L) hand turns palm up as a spear hand and is held closely to the inside of the (R) elbow.

(Figure 22-3.27) Step back with the (R) leg into Pi Chuan (L) stance using the shock step method. At the same time perform Pi Chuan hand technique but with open hands instead of the usual fists. This is now (L) Pi Chuan posture.

(Figure 22-3.28) The feet remain planted in (L) Pi Chuan stance as the (L) hand turns to face palm up in a spear hand position. Simultaneously the (R) hand turns palm up as a spear hand and is held closely to the inside of the (L) elbow.

(Figure 22-3.29) Step back with the (L) leg into Pi Chuan (R) stance using the shock step method. At the same time perform Pi Chuan hand technique but with open hands instead of the usual fists. This is now (R) Pi Chuan posture.

(Figure 22-3.30) Repeat sequence shown in (figure 22-3.26) previously.

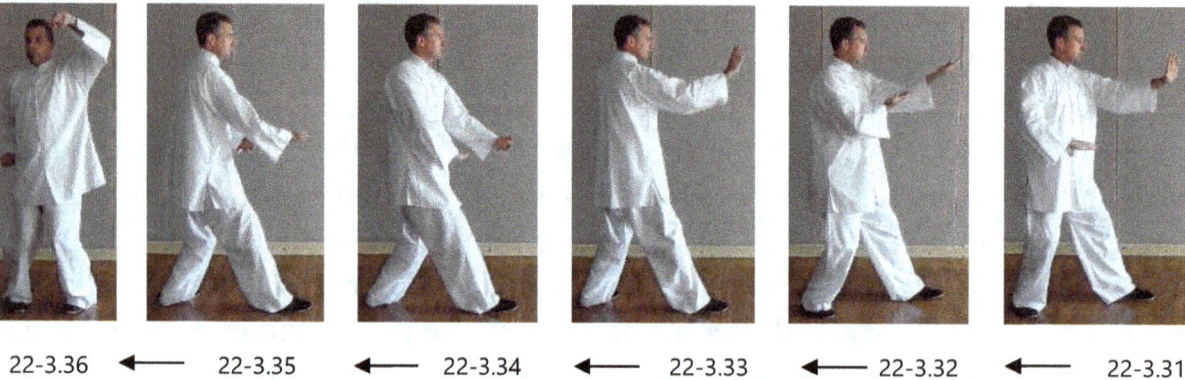

22-3.36 ← 22-3.35 ← 22-3.34 ← 22-3.33 ← 22-3.32 ← 22-3.31

(Figure 22-3.31) Repeat sequence shown in (figure 22-3.27) previously.
(Figure 22-3.32) Repeat sequence shown in (figure 22-3.28) previously.
(Figure 22-3.33) Repeat sequence shown in (figure 22-3.29) previously.
(Figure 22-3.34) The feet remain planted in (R) Pi Chuan stance as the (R) hand draws back to the centreline at the height of the Tan Tien facing palm down. Simultaneously the (L) hand moves forward along the centreline, passing directly underneath the retreating (R) hand, terminating its movement at the height of the Tan Tien facing palm up.

Note: Both hands must start and finish their movement together.

(Figure 22-3.35) The feet remain planted in (R) Pi Chuan stance. Both hands then repeat the sequence in the opposite direction. The (L) hand draws back to the centreline at the height of the Tan Tien facing palm down. Simultaneously the (R) hand moves forward along the centreline, passing directly underneath the retreating (L) hand, terminating its movement at the height of the Tan Tien facing palm up.

Note: Both hands must start and finish their movement together.

(Figure 22-3.36) Next, the (R) foot steps back behind the (L) foot and is placed alongside the (L) foot in pigeon-toe stance. This in effect turns the practitioner 90 degrees in a clockwise direction. At the same time, the (R) hand draws back to the (R) hip as a fist facing palm up. Simultaneously the (L) hand circles upwards and forming a phoenix eye fist. This strike terminates its movement at temple height in front of the practitioner.

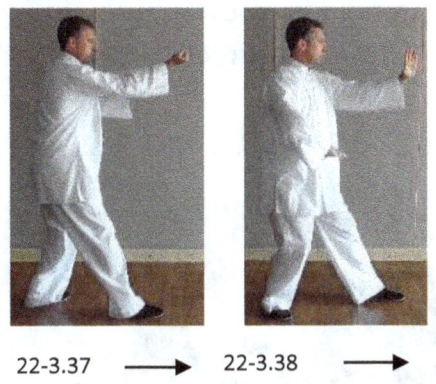

22-3.37 → 22-3.38 →

(Figure 22-3.37) Next, turn back 90 degrees anti-clockwise to the original starting line of the form. Take a small step forwards with the (R) foot as the (R) hand simultaneously punches forwards to nose height along the centreline. The (L) hand is drawn to the inside of the (R) elbow as in Pi Chuan technique.

(Figure 22-3.38) Step through with the (L) foot and follow up with the (R) foot using the half-step method. At the same time as stepping execute a (L) punch straight up to nose height following the line of the previous (R) punch and as soon as the (L) punch reaches its full extension open the hands dropping the (R) hand down to the mid-section, protecting the Tan Tien and the (L) hand chops forward and down the centreline in a splitting action. At the end of this sequence the practitioner should now be in (L) Pi Chuan posture.

Note: To finish the form correctly the practitioner uses the closing method described in Chapter 19 of this book.

Chu Chi Chuan – Fighting Applications:

Application 1 – movements 22-3.2 and 3.3

1a → 1b → 1c

(Figure 1a) White faces off to Black in a neutral stance.
(Figure 1b) Black throws a low (R) straight punch to White's Tan Tien. White steps forward, stepping directly onto the (R) foot of Black with his (L) foot and simultaneously cover blocks the punch with a (L) crescent palm block.
(Figure 1c) White then counters by forward stepping directly down Black's centreline and delivers a (R) Peng Chuan punch directly into Black's jaw.

Application 2 – movements 22-3.7, 3.8, 3.9, 3.10, 3.11

(Figure 2a) Black (R) cross grabs White's (R) wrist.
(Figure 2b and 2c) White counters by stepping backwards with his (R) foot and simultaneously wiping off Black's gripping hand with his (L) hand.
(Figure 2d) Black is now wide open to attack and White delivers a (R) rear straight leg kick to Black's groin.
(Figure 2e) White finishes by stepping into Black's centreline and strikes his (L) temple with a (R) phoenix eye fist strike.

Application 3 – movements 22-3.12, 3.13, 3.14

(Figure 3a) Black throws a (R) straight punch to White's face.
(Figure 3b and 3c) White counters by using a (R) high block and simultaneously drives a (R) rear straight leg kick to Black's open groin.
(Figure 3d) White then draws down his (R) blocking arm, bringing Black's (R) arm with it and delivers a (R) back fist to Black's nose.

(Figure 3e) White finishes by stepping into Black's centreline and strikes his (L) side ribs with a (L) Peng Chuan punch.

Application 4 – movements 22-3.16, 3.17

4a → 4b → 4c → 4d

(Figure 4a) White faces off to Black in a neutral stance.
(Figure 4b) Black throws a (R) straight punch to White's face. White counters by using (R) Pi Chuan to block and simultaneously executes a (R) rear straight leg kick to the outside of Black's forward (R) leg.
(Figure 4c) White then draws back his (R) kicking leg behind Black's (R) leg whilst simultaneously using his (R) blocking arm to come across Black's chest.
(Figure 4d) White finishes by sweeping back through Black's (R) leg taking him off balance and down to the ground. To enhance the effect of the leg sweep White also uses his (R) forearm across Black's chest to create a scissor effect between Black's upper and lower body.

Application 5 – movements 22-3.23, 22-3.24

5a → 5b → 5c → 5d

(Figure 5a) White faces off to Black in a neutral stance.
(Figure 5b) Black throws a (L) straight punch to White's face. White counters by using (R) O/I knife hand block.
(Figure 5c) White then draws back and down with his (R) blocking hand and

prepares to counterstrike Black's neck.
(Figure 5d) White finishes by taking control of Black's attacking (L) arm, pressing it down and immediately attacks with a horizontal (L) knife hand strike to Black's neck.

Application 6 – movements 22-3.23, 3.24

(Figure 6a) White faces off to Black in a neutral stance.
(Figure 6b) Black throws a (L) straight punch to White's face. White counters by using (R) O/I knife hand block.
(Figure 6c) White then draws back and down with his (R) blocking hand and prepares to counter strike Black's neck with his (L) hand.
(Figure 6d) Before White can attack, Black throws a second (R) punch to White's face. White uses his prepared (L) hand to block the punch with a (L) horizontal knife hand block.
(Figure 6e) White then finishes by taking control of Black's attacking (R) arm and immediately attacks with a horizontal (R) knife hand strike to Black's neck.

Application 7 – movement 22-3.25

(Figure 7a) Black lunges forward with both hands to grab White around the throat. White anticipates and steps back slightly whilst simultaneously blocking Black's arms with a double I/O open hand block.

(Figure 7b) White then takes control, pushing Black's arms down and away from his throat.

(Figure 7c) White then steps in with his (R) foot down Black's centreline, head butting Black to the bridge of the nose.

Application 8 – movement 22-3.34

8a → 8b → 8c

(Figure 8a) White faces off to Black in a neutral stance.

(Figure 8b) Black attacks White with a low straight punch to the Tan Tien. White anticipates the attack and blocks using a (R) crescent palm block. At the same time White strikes the back of Black's (R) elbow, jarring it into hyper extension.

(Figure 8c) White then steps in with his (L) foot directly onto Black's forward (R) foot to stop him from retreating and applies leverage to Black's locked (R) arm and taking control of the situation.

4. Three Gate Fist Form – San Guan Chuan

The fourth combined form taught in the system is 'San Guan Chuan'. This form is thought to be one of the older and rarer forms taught in Hsing-I. There is very little information currently written in any of the available translated historical literature or orally passed down through the Masters of the lineage that conclusively explains the reason for this form's name. When loosely translated it is called 'Three Gate Fist' which may have some reference to the three main energy centres contained within the body from a Taoist viewpoint, other translations include 'Dual or Piercing Hand Fist' which may draw reference to the nature of the hand techniques developed within the form. However, until further evidence is brought to light as to the correct translation of the forms name any factual statements about its true meaning would be fictional guesswork and so for now it sadly remains a mystery lost in time.

San Guan Chuan is less commonly seen within Hsing-I lineages practiced today. When viewed it appears smooth and fluid in its nature with the practitioner making quick transitions with the feet and hands whilst moving forward both with

Hsing-I Chuan | The Practice of Heart and Mind Boxing

and without the traditional half-step method. The hand positions are varied and sometimes in opposition to their corresponding feet. Some techniques are like the energies of the Five Elements and the Twelve Animals but with different hand postures and reversed feet to the traditional forms. This variation of movements is useful in training the practitioner to adapt their traditional postures, creating a myriad of applications and to become more flexible when using them in varied fighting scenarios.

Direction: Most of the movements in this form are practised in a straight line, with each movement stepping forwards from the last. However, in movements (figures 22-4.8 and 4.25) below the sequence takes a step backwards. The form then turns 180 degrees and repeats its movements in the opposite direction before turning again to finish where the practitioner originally started.

Figure 22-4

22-4.1 → 22-4.2 → 22-4.3 → 22-4.4 →

Note: San Guan Chuan starts from a neutral Wuji opening posture which is different from the normal opening method. The form steps out straight into its first posture, without any formal opening sequence. However, it does close in the normal sequence from (L) Pi Chuan as discussed in Chapter 19 of this book.

(Figure 22-4.1) Starting from Wuji posture, the hands are held open and straight alongside the body. The front (L) foot faces forwards and the back foot is places at 45 degrees with the heels touching.

(Figure 22-4.2) Step forward with the (R) foot, placed at 45 degrees to the centreline of the form. At the same time, the (R) hand punches straight up the centreline in a drilling motion the same as Tsuan Chuan to the height of the nose. The (L) hand blocks down the centreline at the height of the Tan Tien as an open palm.

(Figure 22-4.3, 4.4) Next, step through with the (L) foot and keep the (R) foot rooted to the ground with the foot angled at 45 degrees. At the same time the (L) open hand circles forwards, upwards and backwards around the (R) fist and comes to rest guarding the centreline at solar plexus height. Simultaneously the (R) hand moves in the opposite direction and draws backwards, inwards and downwards in a circular motion and then punches straight forward as a fist using Peng Chuan to solar plexus height.

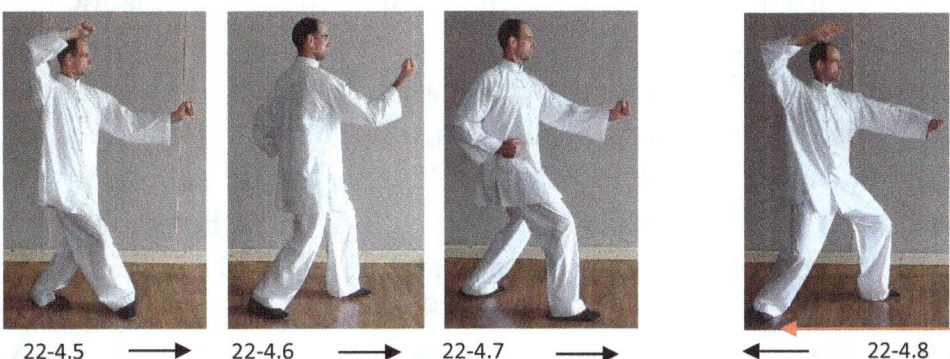

22-4.5 → 22-4.6 → 22-4.7 → ← 22-4.8

(Figure 22-4.5) Step forwards with the (R) foot at an angle of 90 degrees to the centreline of the form into (R) cross stance with the (L) foot planted on the ball of the foot. The (L) hand punches straight down the centreline to the height of the solar plexus and the (R) hand draws back to the side of the (R) temple as in horse form.

Note: This posture is a called a 'reverse' posture as the opposing hand and foot are forward.

(Figure 22-4.6) Next, step forward into (L) Pi Chuan stance without using the half-step method. At the same time execute a (R) back fist strike to nose level. The (L) fist draws back to the (L) hip with the 'eye' of the fist facing upwards as in Peng Chuan.

(Figure 22-4.7) Next, step forward into (R) Pi Chuan stance without using the half-step method. At the same time execute a (L) Peng Chuan punch to Tan Tien level. The (R) fist draws back to the (R) hip with the 'eye' of the fist facing upwards as in Peng Chuan. This is reverse open Wood posture.

(Figure 22-4.8) Next, step backwards using the shock step method into (L) Pi Chuan stance. At the same time execute a (L) open palm knife hand strike to rib level. The (R) hand opens and draws back in opposition to the height of the (R) temple with the palm of the hand facing outwards. This posture is the same as horse form but with open hands.

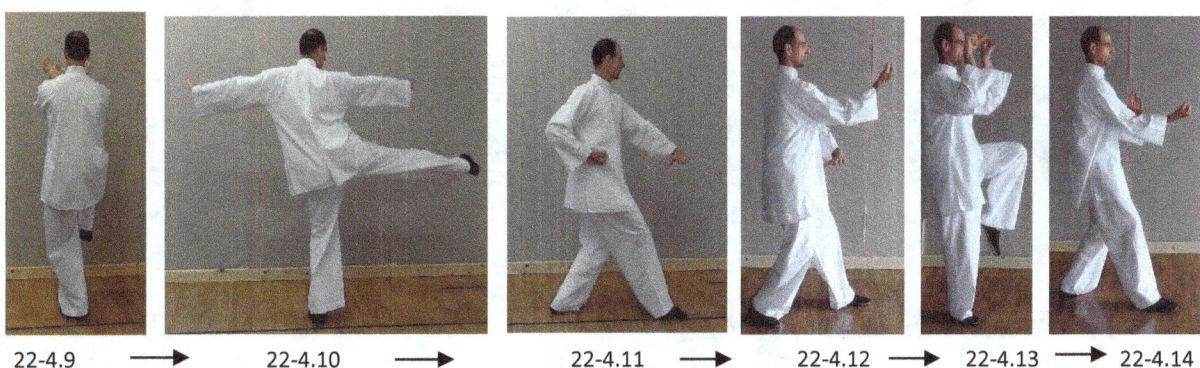

22-4.9 → 22-4.10 → 22-4.11 → 22-4.12 → 22-4.13 → 22-4.14

(Figure 22-4.9) Next, the practitioner turns 90 degrees anti-clockwise and the (R) foot is raised and drawn back into (L) single leg stance and at the same time both the hands are drawn across the body as open palms in a double handed cross block at the height of the head.

(Figure 22-4.10) The (R) foot then executes a (R) leg side kick to midsection height straight along the centreline. Simultaneously the (R) hand thrusts forwards, palm facing outwards in time and in line with the kick. The (L) hand reciprocally thrusts backward to counter balance the technique with its palm facing backwards. Both arms should appear symmetrical at the end of this kicking technique. (This is kick is from Swallow form).

(Figure 22-4.11) Step forwards with the (R) foot placing it at 45-degree angle. Keep the (L) foot rooted to the ground. At the same time, the (L) hand blocks with an open palm down the centreline at the height of the Tan Tien. The (R) hand draws back to the (R) hip as a fist facing palm up. (This posture is Bear form.)

(Figure 22-4.12) Step forward with the (L) foot and the (R) follows using the half-step method into (L) Pi Chuan stance. The (L) hand completes its palm block down the centreline as the (R) hand drills forwards and upwards along the centreline to the height of the face. (This posture is Chicken form.)

(Figure 22-4.13) Next, the (L) foot is raised and drawn back into (R) single leg stance and at the same time both the hands are drawn into the side of the head in cranes beak postures to the height of their corresponding temples. The elbows are held close to the body to protect the ribs as in Fighting Chicken form.

(Figure 22-4.14) Both feet then rapidly exchange positions using the chicken step method. The head stays level throughout this change of stance. The practitioner is now in (R) Pi Chuan stance. Simultaneously with the feet the hands change, with the (R) hand circling downwards and then upwards as an upper cut to the solar plexus height and the (L) hand blocking down to the centreline with an open palm ending in line with the inside of the (R) elbow. Both hands must start and finish their movements together.

22-4.15 → 22-4.16 → 22-4.17   ← 22-4.18

(Figure 22-4.15) Next, the (R) foot is drawn back into (R) cat stance and at the same time the (R) fist circle blocks low from outside to inside to protect the centreline at Tan Tien level. The (L) fist draws back to the (L) hip with palm facing upwards.

(Figure 22-4.16) Both feet then rapidly exchange positions using the chicken step method. The head stays level throughout this change of stance. The practitioner is now in (L) Pi Chuan stance. Simultaneously with the feet the hands change, with the (R) fist circling round as if to grab with an open hand and the drawing in to the (R) hip as a fist again. The (L) fist comes forward, opening the hand to crescent palm block at Tan Tien height along the centreline. Both hands must start and finish their movements together.

(Figure 22-4.17) Step forward with the (L) foot to an angle of 45 degrees. The (R) foot stays rooted throughout. The (L) hand strikes out with an open palm along the centreline at the height of the solar plexus. At the same time, the (R) hand blocks high with an open hand to protect the head, with the elbow pointing down to an angle of 45 degrees. This is (L) Pao Chuan posture but with open hands.

(Figure 22-4.18) The practitioner then turns to the right 90 degrees, turning the (L) foot round into pigeon toe stance. At the same time, the (L) hand blocks palm downwards along the centreline to the height of the Tan Tien. The (R) hand draws in as a fist at the Tan Tien facing palm down.

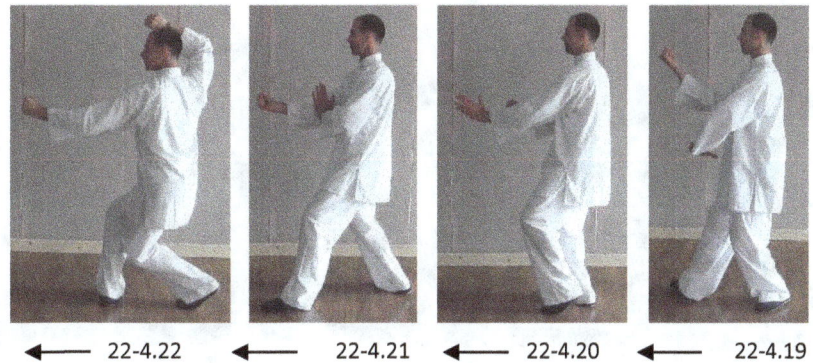

← 22-4.22   ← 22-4.21   ← 22-4.20   ← 22-4.19

(Figure 22-4.19) Continuing the turn the practitioner turns a further 90 degrees to the right to face the direction from which they came and step forward with the (R) foot, placed at 45 degrees to the centreline of the form. At the same time, the (R) hand punches straight up the centreline in a drilling motion the same as Tsuan Chuan to the height of the nose. The (L) hand completes its block down the centreline at the height of the Tan Tien as an open palm.

(Figure 22-4.19 to 36) Repeats the same sequence in the opposite direction. At movement (Figure 22-4.35) the practitioner turns 180 degrees again to face the direction they started.

(Figure 22-4.36) From the turn the practitioner faces the direction from which they originally started the form. The (R) foot is placed at 45 degrees to the centreline of the form. At the same time, the (R) hand punches straight up the centreline in a drilling motion the same as Tsuan Chuan to the height of the nose. The (L) hand completes its block down the centreline at the height of the Tan Tien as an open palm.

(Figure 22-4.37) Next, take a small step forwards with the (R) foot as the (R) hand simultaneously punches forwards to nose height along the centreline. The (L) hand is drawn to the inside of the (R) elbow as in Pi Chuan technique.

(Figure 22-4.38) Step through with the (L) foot and follow up with the (R) foot using the half-step method. At the same time as stepping execute a (L) punch straight up to nose height following the line of the previous (R) punch and as soon as the (L) punch reaches its full extension open the hands dropping the (R) hand down to the mid-section, protecting the Tan Tien and the (L) hand chops forward and down the centreline in a splitting action. At the end of this sequence the practitioner should now be in (L) Pi Chuan posture.

Note: To finish the form correctly the practitioner uses the closing method described in Chapter 19 of this book.

San Guan Chuan Fighting Applications:

Application 1 – movement 22-4.1

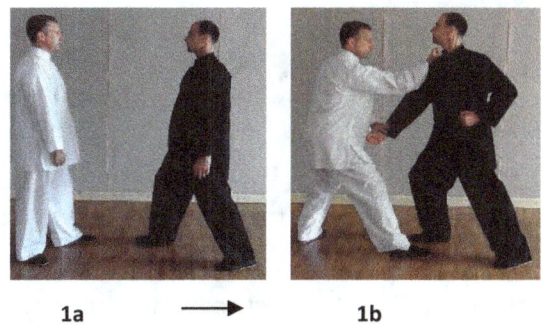

1a → 1b

(Figure 1a) White faces off to Black in a neutral stance.
(Figure 1b) Black throws a (R) low punch to White's Tan Tien. White counters by using (L) open palm block and at the same time steps in to Black's centreline with his (R) foot and drills a (R) Tsuan Chuan punch straight up into Black's jaw.

Application 2 – movements 22-4.2, 4.3 and 4.4

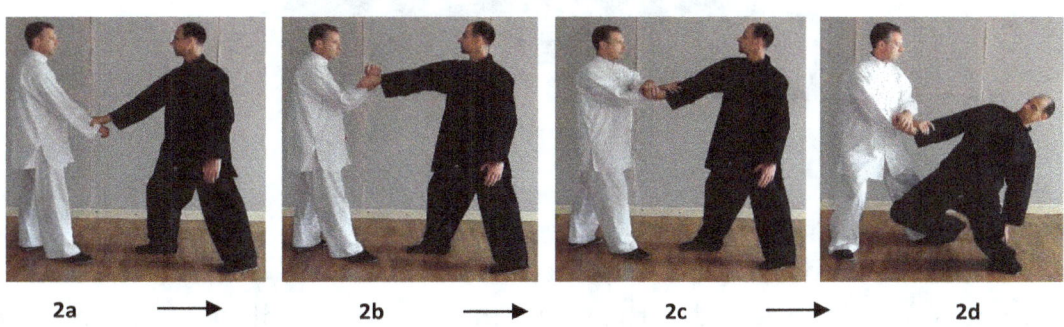

2a → 2b → 2c → 2d

(Figure 2a) Black (R) cross grabs White's (R) wrist.
(Figure 2b) White counters by stepping in with his (R) foot and raising his (R) hand using an I/O circle block technique. This raises and turns over Black's (R) arm and elbow into a vulnerable position.
(Figure 2c) White then opens his (R) hand and circles around Black's wrist taking control of his arm. To stop Black evading the small circle wrist lock, White also secures Black's (R) grabbing hand by trapping it with his (L) hand at the same time as pressure is applied to the wrist against the natural direction of the joint.

(Figure 2d) Finally, with the wrist lock complete White applies pressure against the joint and then controls Black to the ground to neutralise the threat.

Application 3 – movement 22-4.5

3a → 3b

(Figure 3a) White faces off to Black in a neutral stance.
(Figure 3b) Black throws a (R) straight punch to White's face. White counters by using (R) open palm block to guide Black's punch to the side of the head and at the same time cross steps in with his (R) foot, stamping directly down onto Black's foot and executes a (L) Peng Chuan punch to Black's open ribs.

Application 4 – movement 22-4.6

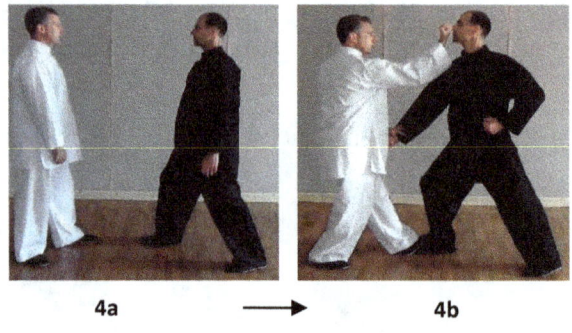

4a → 4b

(Figure 4a) White faces off to Black in a neutral stance.
(Figure 4b) Black throws a (R) low punch to White's Tan Tien. White counters by using (L) open palm block and at the same time steps onto Black's (R) foot with his (R) foot and delivers a (R) back fist to Black's nose.

Application 5 – movements 22-4.13 and 4.14

5a → 5b → 5c → 5d

(Figure 5a) White faces off to Black in a neutral stance.
(Figure 5b) Black throws a (R) straight punch to White's face. White steps with his (L) foot to the outside of Black's forward foot and counters by using (R) cranes beak block to deflect the strike to the side of his head.
(Figure 5c and 5d) White then raises his (L) foot and rapidly executes the chicken step method to change his feet and step in with his (R) foot along Black's centreline. At the same time, White circles round with his (R) arm and delivers an uppercut to Black's solar plexus.

Application 6 – movement 22-4.17

6a → 6b → 6c

(Figure 6a) White faces off to Black in a neutral stance.
(Figure 6b) Black throws a (R) roundhouse punch to White's face. White anticipates by stepping to 45 degrees to the outside of Black's (R) foot, in effect stepping into the attack to cut it off.
(Figure 6c) White then executes (L) Pao Chuan technique but with an open palm block and strike to Black's solar plexus rather than the traditional fist.

5. Twelve Red Hammers Form – Sher Er Hong Chewi

The final and arguably most advanced form of the five 'Combined' forms taught in the system is 'Sher Er Hong Chewi'. This form combines the different energies of the Five Element Fists and the Twelve Animals to make a whole. Most traditional lineages have a form that replicates this combination of techniques appropriate to their system. All the movements contain the principles of Yin and Yang, rise and fall, expansion and contraction in line with Hsing-I theory. Supposedly this is the Twelve Animals forms combined as one, but when closely analysed, it contains a myriad of postures and sequences from all the forms contained in the system. The form seeks to take the strong points from each of Hsing-I's postures and develop them through repetitive practice. This form's practice offers variety compared to practising just one form at a time. As this form contains movements and skills learned throughout the whole system it is logical that it is the last empty hand form to be taught when learning Hsing-I.

Direction: Most of the movements in this form are practiced in a straight line, with each movement stepping forwards from the last. However, in movements (figures 5.53 and 5.54) below the sequence takes a step backwards. Also in movements (figures 5.15 to 5.20 and 5.38 to 5.44 and 5.56 to 5.64) the sequence turns and steps out to 45-degree angles before returning to the original line of the form. This form is the longest empty hand form in the system and it turns the practitioner 180 degrees six times before finally finishing in the same direction that it started.

Figure 22-5
To open the form into (L) Pi Chuan (Figure 22-5.1) use the opening method shown in Chapter 19 previously.

22-5.1 → 22-5.2 → 22-5.3 → 22-5.4 → 22-5.5

(Figure 22-5.1) Starting from (L) Pi Chuan posture.
(Figure 22-5.2) Step forward with the (L) foot and block down to the centreline at Tan Tien level with the (L) hand as a crescent palm block. At the same time, the (R) hand draws back to the (R) hip as a fist facing 'eye' up.

(Figure 22-5.3) Step forwards with the (R) foot and follow up with the (L) foot using the half-step method. At the same time, the (R) hand punches straight up the centreline to nose height using Peng Chuan technique. The (L) hand simultaneously draws upwards and backwards in opposition as a fist and ends its movement in line with the (L) temple. This is (R) horse posture.

(Figure 22-5.4 and 5.5) Movements (figures 22-5.4 and 5.5) repeat the sequence of movements (figures 22-5.2 and 22-5.3) on the opposite side. This ends in movement (**Figure 22-5.5**) with the practitioner in (L) horse posture.

⬅ 22-5.10   ⬅ 22-5.9   ⬅ 22-5.8   ⬅ 22-5.7   ⬅ 22-5.6

(Figure 22-5.6) Next, the practitioner turns 180 degrees by sliding the (L) foot backwards behind the rear (R) foot. At the same time, the (L) forward arm drops down to (L) hip level, twisting the arm as it moves in a clockwise drilling action. The (R) hand simultaneously drops as a fist facing palm down along the centreline at solar plexus height.

(Figure 22-5.7) As the body fully turns to face the opposite direction the (L) foot, steps out into (L) cat stance and the (L) arm begins to drill upwards from the hip in a counter clockwise direction along the centreline. The (R) fist continues to protect the centreline with its fist twisting to face palm up.

(Figure 22-5.8) The practitioner's weight then transfers into the (L) foot which is planted fully to the ground. The (R) foot is drawn up alongside the (L) foot. At the same time, the (R) hand is brought to the inside of the (L) elbow facing palm up. The (L) hand continues to drill and punches straight up the centreline to nose height using Pi Chuan technique.

(Figure 22-5.9) The (R) hand then punches up the line of the extended (L) arm as the (R) foot, steps through and turns the practitioner to face 90 degrees left of the centreline of the form in a horse stance. At the same time both hands open symmetrically at the sides of the body with both palms facing downwards.

(Figure 22-5.10) As the practitioner fully sinks at their knees into horse stance the hands continue to press downwards blocking at the height of the hips in time with one another. The practitioner remains facing 90 degrees to the left of the centreline of the form.

Hsing-I Chuan | The Practice of Heart and Mind Boxing

22-5.11 → 22-5.12 → 22-5.13 → 22-5.14 → 22-5.15 →

(Figure 22-5.11) Step forward with the (L) foot and block down to the centreline at Tan Tien level with the (L) hand as a crescent palm block. At the same time, the (R) hand draws back to the (R) hip as a fist facing 'eye' up.

(Figure 22-5.12) Step forwards with the (R) foot and follow up with the (L) foot using the half-step method. At the same time, the (R) hand punches straight up the centreline to nose height using Peng Chuan technique. The (L) hand simultaneously draws upwards and backwards in opposition as a fist and ends its movement in line with the (L) temple. This is (R) horse posture.

(Figure 22-5.13) Step forward with the (L) foot using the half-step method. The (R) hand circle blocks downwards, from inside to outside across the centreline at Tan Tien height. The (L) hand simultaneously punches straight out at solar plexus height using Peng Chuan technique.

(Figure 22-5.14) Next repeat the previous movement on the opposite side. Step forward with the (R) foot using the half-step method. The (L) hand circle blocks downwards, from inside to outside across the centreline at Tan Tien height. The (R) hand simultaneously punches straight out at solar plexus height using Peng Chuan technique.

(Figure 22-5.15) Keeping the feet firmly planted to the ground, the body then rotates at the waist 45 degrees to the left. Both hands are drawn as fists facing palms forwards to the height of their corresponding temples. The elbows are held pointing downwards in front of the body with the forearms in line with the fists above.

22-5.16 → 22-5.17 → 22-5.18 → 22-5.19 → 22-5.20 →

(Figure 22-5.16) Next, the (R) foot is raised and drawn back into (L) single leg stance and at the same time both the arms circle forwards and strike with the fists retaining their palm out position at head height.

(Figure 22-5.17) Both feet then rapidly exchange positions using the chicken step method. The head stays level throughout this change of stance. The practitioner is now in (L) Pi Chuan stance at an angle of 45 degrees to the original straight line of the form. Simultaneously with the feet the hands complete their circular striking motion the same way as described in figure 22-5.16 previously. Both hands must start and finish their movements together.

Note: The emphasis of the circular arm strike should be to attack with both the elbows and the fists simultaneously.

(Figure 22-5.18) The body is then turned to face 45 degrees to the right of the original centreline of the form. The weight is transferred into the (R) foot and the (L) foot is raised. Both hands are drawn down to the height of the Tan Tien as fists facing palms downwards.

(Figure 22-5.19) Next, the (L) foot continues to rise until it is drawn back into (R) single leg stance and at the same time both the arms circle forwards and strike with the fists retaining their palm out position at head height.

(Figure 22-5.20) Both feet then rapidly exchange positions using the chicken step method. The head stays level throughout this change of stance. The practitioner is now in (R) Pi Chuan stance at an angle of 45 degrees to the original straight line of the form. Simultaneously with the feet the hands complete their circular striking motion. Both hands must start and finish their movements together.

Note: The sequence of movements described in movements (figures 22-5.15, 5.16, and 5.17) are repeated in movements (figures 22-5.18, 5.19 and 5.20) on the opposite side.

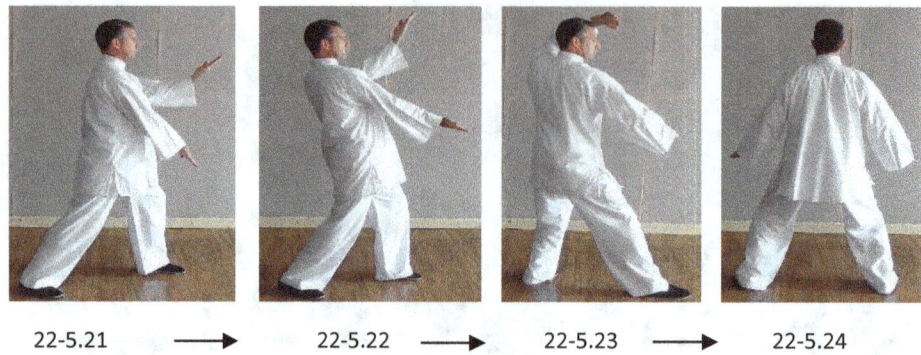

22-5.21 → 22-5.22 → 22-5.23 → 22-5.24

(Figure 22-5.21) Next, the (R) foot is raised and drawn back into (L) single leg stance both feet then rapidly exchange positions using the chicken step method. The head stays level throughout this change of stance. At the same time, the (L) hand turns upwards and executes a spear hand, finger strike upwards along the centreline to throat height. The (R) hand also forms a spear hand posture and thrusts downwards along the centreline to the height of the groin. Both hands must start and finish their movements together.

(Figures 22-5.22 and 5.23) Follow on by stepping forward using the chicken step method to change feet to (R) foot forward ending in (R) Pi Chuan stance. At the same time, the (L) hand blocks palm upwards at the height of the head and is closely followed by the (R) palm blocking up in a 'rolling' circular motion which changes the hands positions. The (L) hand terminates at the height of the forehead, along the left side of the centreline. The (R) hand thrusts out forwards with a knife hand strike with the palm facing down aimed at ribs height. Both hands and feet must start and finish their movements together.

(Figure 22-5.24) The practitioner then turns to their left by 90 degrees into horse stance. At the same time both hands open symmetrically at the sides of the body with both palms facing downwards. As the practitioner fully sinks into horse stance both the hands continue to press downwards blocking at the height of the hips in time with one another.

(Figures 22-5.25 to 5.47) Repeats the same sequence of movements in the opposite direction as (figures 22-5.2 to 5.23) described previously.

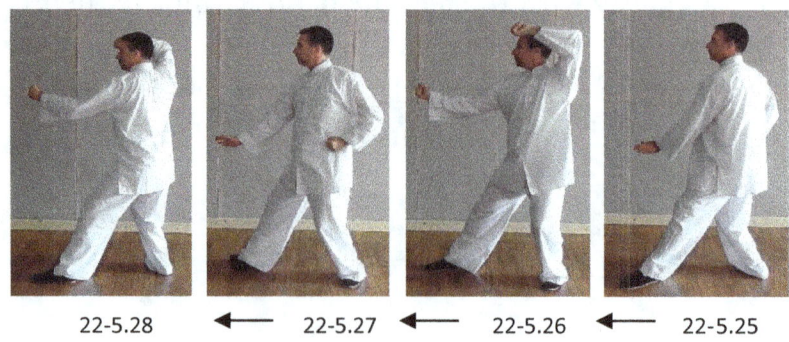

22-5.28 ← 22-5.27 ← 22-5.26 ← 22-5.25

Master James McNeil & Andrew Jackson

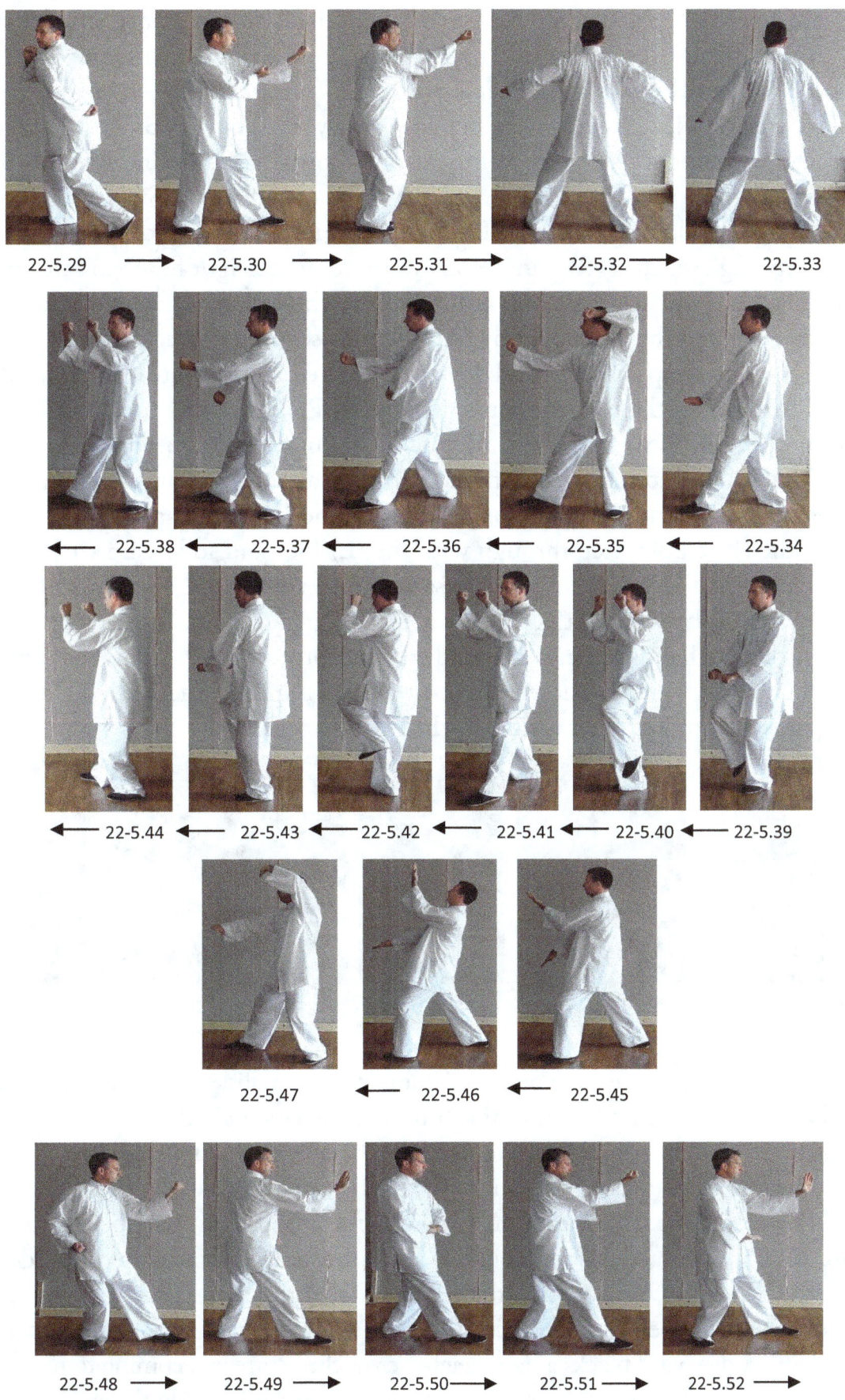

345

(Figure 22-5.48) Next, turn 180 degrees into (L) Pi Chuan stance. At the same time, the (L) hand executes a back-fist strike at nose height, whilst the (R) hand pulls back to the (R) hip as a fist facing palm up.

(Figure 22-5.49) Next, take a small step forwards with the (L) foot as the (L) hand simultaneously punches forwards to nose height along the centreline. The (R) hand is drawn to the inside of the (L) elbow as in Pi Chuan technique. Step through with the (R) foot and follow up with the (L) foot using the half-step method. At the same time as stepping execute a (R) punch straight up to nose height following the line of the previous (L) punch and as soon as the (R) punch reaches its full extension open the hands dropping the (L) hand down to the mid-section, protecting the Tan Tien and the (R) hand chops forward and down the centreline in a splitting action. At the end of this sequence the practitioner is now in (R) Pi Chuan posture.

(Figures 22-5.50, 5.51 and 5.52) Repeat Pi Chuan technique on the opposite side. Take a small step forwards with the (R) foot as the (R) hand simultaneously punches forwards to nose height along the centreline. The (L) hand is drawn to the inside of the (R) elbow. Step through with the (L) foot and follow up with the (R) foot using the half-step method. At the same time execute a (L) punch straight up to nose height and as soon as the (L) punch reaches its full extension open the hands dropping the (R) hand down to the mid-section, protecting the Tan Tien and the (L) hand chops forward and down the centreline in a splitting action. At the end of this sequence the practitioner is now in (L) Pi Chuan posture.

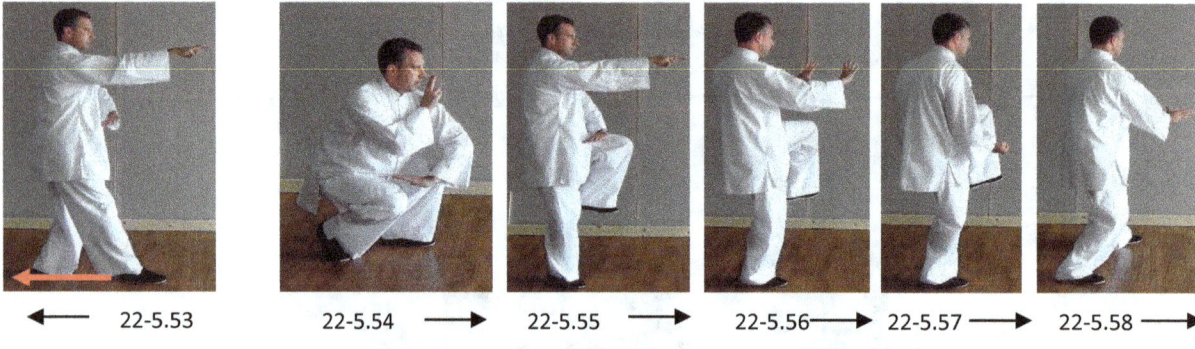

⟵ 22-5.53   22-5.54 ⟶   22-5.55 ⟶   22-5.56 ⟶   22-5.57 ⟶   22-5.58 ⟶

(Figure 22-5.53) From the previous (L) Pi Chuan posture slide the (L) foot backwards using the shock step method. At the same time, the (L) hand blocks down the centreline as an open palm facing downwards to Tan Tien height. Simultaneously the (R) hand strikes upwards and out along the centreline to the height of the eyes using the sword finger hand technique with the palm facing downwards. This is (R) Cock form.

(Figure 22-5.54) Next, hook sweep round with the forward (R) foot and turn 360 degrees to the left in a counter clock wise direction. As the body turns, both knees flex lowering the height of the practitioner like a 'cork screw' into the ground. At the same time as sweeping the (R) hand, ridge hand blocks at face height across the centreline, coming to rest firmly against the (L) shoulder. The (L) hand remains protecting the Tan Tien throughout.

(Figure 22-5.55) From the lowered position in movement (figure 22-5.54) the practitioner stands straight up on the (R) leg into (R) single leg stance. The (L) hand guards the Tan Tien and centreline, whilst the (R) hand thrusts straight out to the height of the throat using the sword finger hand technique with the palm facing downwards.
(Figure 22-5.56) Turn the body 45 degrees to the left with the (R) foot remaining firmly planted to the ground and the (L) foot raised with the (L) knee flexed to 90 degrees. At the same time both hands reach out forwards and grab at chest height.
(Figure 22-5.57) Both hands grasp into fists facing palm down and then circle over to face palm up. As the arms circle over, both the fists pass under the height of the raised (L) knee.
(Figure 22-5.58) Step out to an angle of 45 degrees to the left of the centreline of the form with (L) foot and follow with the (R) foot using the half-step method into (L) Pi Chuan stance. At the same time both hands open and push forward together in time with the body to the height of the waist. This is (L) Tiger Form.

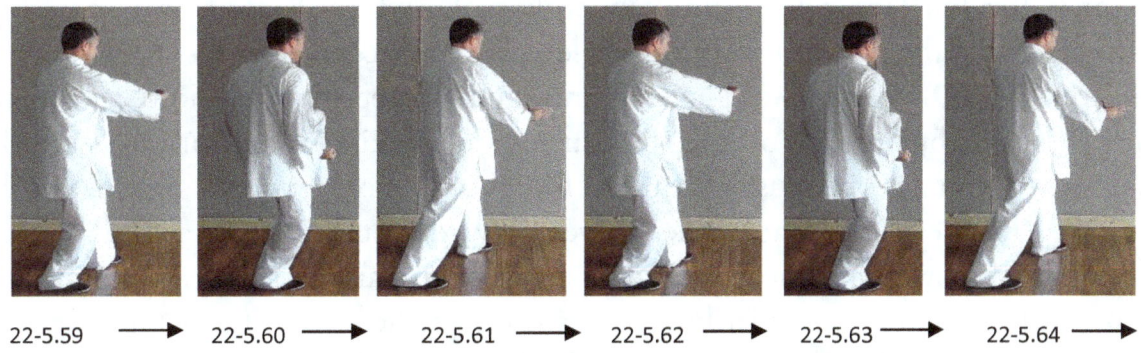

22-5.59 → 22-5.60 → 22-5.61 → 22-5.62 → 22-5.63 → 22-5.64 →

(Figures 22-5.59 to 5.64) From (L) Tiger form the open hands grasp palms down back into fists the same as movement (figure 22-5.56) described previously. The feet remain in (L) Pi Chuan stance. Next, repeat the same sequence of (L) Tiger Form as described in (figures 22-5.56, 5.57 and 5.58) previously a further two times on the same spot, remaining at an angle of 45 degrees to the left of the straight line of the form.

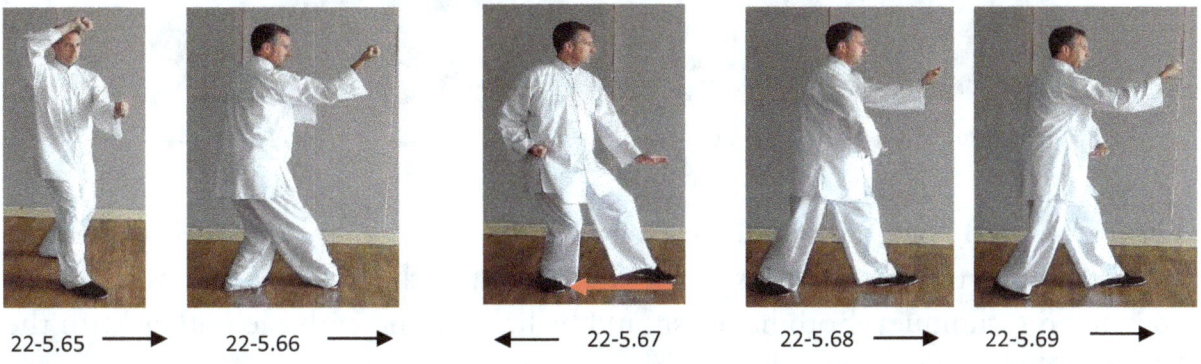

22-5.65 → 22-5.66 → ← 22-5.67 22-5.68 → 22-5.69 →

(Figure 22-5.65) From (L) Tiger Form then turn 90 degrees to the right and step out at the 45-degree angle to the right of the centreline of the form and execute (R) Pao Chuan technique.

(Figure 22-5.66) Keep the (L) rear foot rooted to the ground as the (R) forward foot sweeps in a circular motion to the inside, turning the body straight back in line with the forward line of the form. The (R) foot hook sweeps and at the same time the (R) fist blocks from O/I across the body at face height. The block and sweep must be executed together, starting and finishing at the same time. The (L) fist turns to face palm up at the inside of the (R) elbow.

(Figure 22-5.67) The (R) foot takes a step backwards, planting itself solidly on the ground with the foot at a 45-degree angle. The (L) foot is also drawn back due to the large back step movement of the opposing foot and drawn onto the ball of its foot, facing forwards. At the same time, the (R) fist continues to pull back and down to the (R) hip and the (L) hand opens from a fist, pulling downwards and backwards as a crescent palm block in time with the opposing hand.

(Figure 22-5.68) Step forwards with the (L) foot and follow with the (R) foot using the half-step method. Block down with the (R) hand using an open palm at the height of the Tan Tien, whilst simultaneously striking forward down the centreline at the height of the throat using a (L) eagle claw hand technique.

(Figure 22-5.69) Step forward again using the half-step method, however remain on the (L) side by pushing off the (R) rear foot and taking a step forward with the (L) foot at the same time. Push off the (R) foot, but do not step through and past the (L) foot. This means the practitioner moves forward, but remains in a (L) Pi Chuan stance. Block down with the (L) hand using an open palm at the height of the Tan Tien, whilst simultaneously striking forward down the centreline at the height of the throat using a (R) eagle claw hand technique.

22-5.70 → 22-5.71 → 22-5.72 → 22-5.73 →

(Figure 22-5.70) Take a small step forward with the (L) foot, placing it at 45 degrees and at the same time both hands block out in front of the body using crescent palm block hand techniques. Both hands should be held in line with each other, with the (R) hand slightly above and ahead of the (L) hand.

(Figure 22-5.71) Continue to step through and forward with the (R) foot, whilst at the same time the two hands held in front 'grasp' into fists in the same arm position as movement (figure 22-5.70) previously.

(Figure 22-5.72) As the (R) foot, steps through it raises and kicks out forwards at knee height, using 45-degree rising kick technique. Simultaneously the two fists twist to face palms up and punch upwards and forwards to nose height with the (R) fist leading and the (L) fist held at the (R) elbow.

(Figure 22-5.73) Before the (R) kicking foot touches the ground, the (L) rear foot pushes forward allowing the practitioner to take a big step with the lead (R) foot and this is backed up using the half-step method, in effect putting the practitioner in a (R) Pi Chuan stance. At the same time, the (L) hand punches up the (R) forearm performing a Pi Chuan hand technique. This movement places the practitioner with (R) foot and opposing (L) hand forward. This is called (R) reverse Pi Chuan posture.

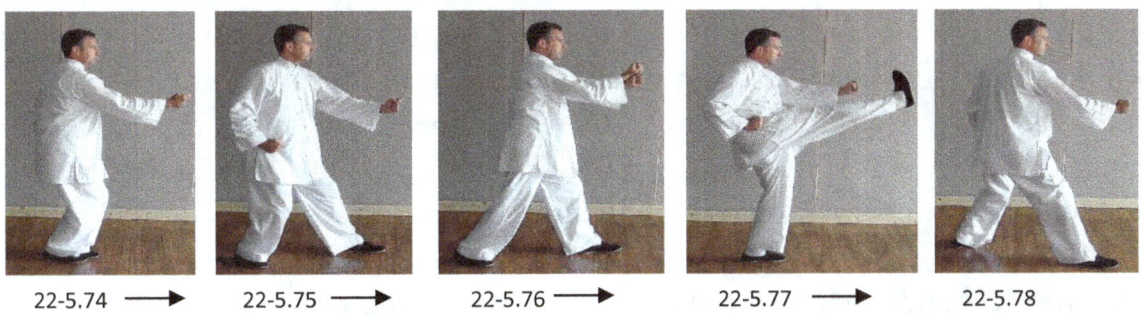

22-5.74 → 22-5.75 → 22-5.76 → 22-5.77 → 22-5.78

(Figure 22-5.74) From (R) reverse Pi Chuan, take a small step forward with the (R) foot and then step straight through with the (L) foot into closed Wood posture. The (L) foot is forwards with the (R) foot tucked into the instep. The (R) hand executes a Peng Chuan punch to solar plexus height, whilst the (L) hand pulls back to the (L) hip.

(Figure 22-5.75) From closed Wood step straight forward in to (L) open Wood posture.

(Figure 22-5.76) Take a small step forwards with the (L) foot and back this up with a half-step with the rear foot. At the same time, the (R) rear fist strikes straight down the centreline as a back-fist strike to nose height and makes contact with the 'eye' of the outstretched (L) fist as its target point, terminating its movement at solar plexus height.

(Figure 22-5.77) Take another small step forwards with the (L) foot and then execute a (R) rear straight leg kick along the centreline. At the same time, the (R) fist pulls back to the (R) hip. The (L) fist punches out in time with the kick using Peng Chuan technique.

(Figure 22-5.78) As the (R) foot completes its kick it descends towards the ground, but before it touches the ground it steps straight forward and is followed by the (R) foot using the half-step method into (R) open Wood posture. At the same time execute a (R) Peng Chuan punch to Tan Tien height.

| ← 22-5.83 | ← 22-5.82 | ← 22-5.81 | ← 22-5.80 | ← 22-5.79 |

(Figure 22-5.79) Next, the (L) rear foot, steps across, behind the (R) forward foot and the practitioner turns 180 degrees, shifting the weight forward into (L) bow stance. At the same time, the (R) hand opens and strikes using a palm strike in time with the turn of the body, up the centreline to the height of the groin. The (L) hand opens and moves from the (L) hip to the centreline at the height of the Tan Tien facing its palm towards the body. As both hands complete their movements, the inside of the (R) forearm should come to rest firmly against the palm of the (L) hand. **(Figure 22-5.80)** Step forward with the (R) foot into (R) cross stance. At the same time, the (R) hand circles up and over the head coming to rest above the rear heel of the (L) foot as a crescent palm block behind the practitioner. The (L) hand simultaneously circles downwards to the height of the groin and then up 'warding off' to the height of the Tan Tien. As the (L) hand wards off the palm turns to face palm out, away from the body.

Note: Movements (figures 22-5.79 and 22-5.80) described above are Swallow Form. **(Figures 22-5.81 to 5.84)** Next, repeat the same sequence of Swallow Form a further two times moving forwards along the straight line of the form.

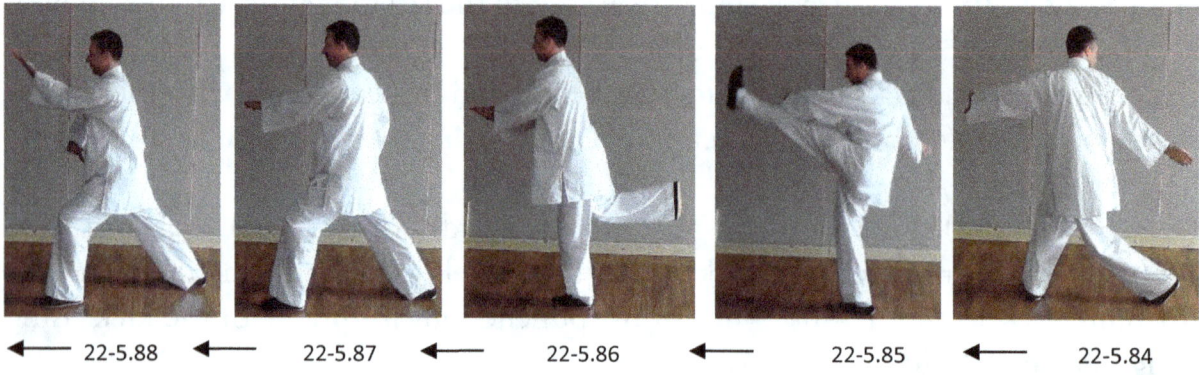

| ← 22-5.88 | ← 22-5.87 | ← 22-5.86 | ← 22-5.85 | ← 22-5.84 |

(Figure 22-5.85) With the (R) forward foot planted firmly on the ground, execute a (L) rear straight leg kick down the centreline. The (L) hand holds its forward ward off position and the rear (R) hand moves forward in time with the body's momentum, with the palm open.

(Figure 22-5.86) The (L) kicking foot should be brought to the ground under control and is planted firmly alongside the inside of the standing (R) foot. As soon as the (L) foot is planted the (R) foot executes a back-heel kick technique behind the practitioner to groin height. At the same time, the (L) forward hand turns to face palm down and the rear (R) hand circles straight up the centreline facing palm up coming to rest by 'slapping' firmly against the palm of the opposite hand.

(Figure 22-5.87) The (R) kicking foot should be brought to the ground under control and is planted firmly alongside the inside of the standing (L) foot. As soon as the (R) foot is planted the (L) foot, steps forwards into (L) bow stance. At the same time, the (L) forward hand strikes out along the centreline with a leopard fist to Tan Tien height and the rear (R) hand draws back in opposition to the (R) hip as a fist facing palm upwards.

(Figure 22-5.88) Take a small step forwards with the (L) foot and place it at 45 degrees to the centreline of the form. The (R) foot stays firmly planted to the ground. At the same time, the (L) hand drills palm upwards as a spear hand to throat height. The (R) hand blocks down the centreline with palm down protecting the Tan Tien. This is the first posture of Tsuan Chuan.

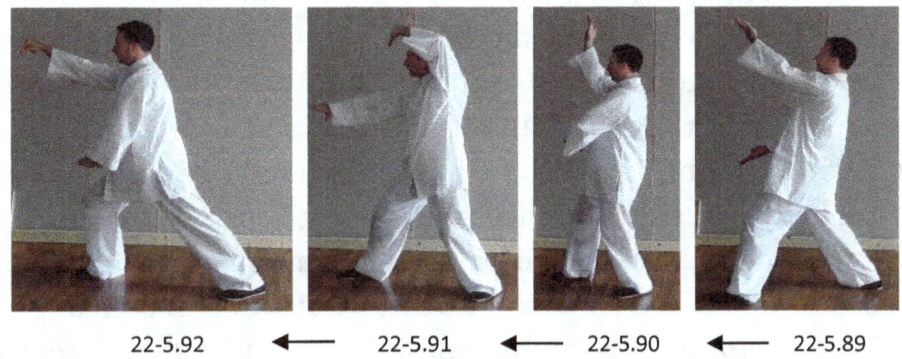

22-5.92 ← 22-5.91 ← 22-5.90 ← 22-5.89

(Figures 22-5.89 to 5.91) Follow on by stepping forward using chicken step method to change feet to (R) foot forward ending in (R) Pi Chuan stance. At the same time, the (L) hand blocks palm upwards at the height of the head and is closely followed by the (R) palm blocking up in a 'rolling' circular motion which changes the hands positions. The (L) hand terminates at the height of the forehead, along the left side of the centreline. The (R) hand thrusts out forwards with a knife hand strike with the palm facing down aimed at ribs height. Both hands and feet must start and finish their movements together.

(Figure 22-5.92) Take a small step forwards with the (R) foot into (R) bow stance. At the same time, the (R) hand forms a cranes beak and strikes directly up the centreline to jaw height. The (L) hand blocks down the centreline with an open palm to protect the Tan Tien.

22-5.93   22-5.94   22-5.95   22-5.96   22-5.97

(Figure 22-5.93) Next slide the rear (L) foot backwards and turn the body 180 degrees. At the same time flex the (R) knee and lower the body into (L) drop stance. At the same time, the (L) hand follows the line if the (L) leg and scoops round with the palm in a 'hooking' action as close to ground level as the flexibility of the practitioner allows. The (R) hand remains as a cranes beak and lowers only in time with the body.

(Figure 22-5.94) Staying as low as possible transfer the weight forwards into the (L) foot and cross step forwards with the (R) foot into (R) cross stance. At the same time, the (R) rear hand strikes downwards along the centreline of the form as a spear hand with palm facing away from the body. In opposition, the (L) hand blocks upwards as a spear hand to protect the head with its palm facing towards the body. Both hands and feet must start and finish their movements together.

(Figure 22-5.95) From the low cross step position stand straight up into (R) single leg stance. The body is turned completely to 90 degrees from the centreline of the form and the (L) raised knee should be flexed to an angle of 90 degrees. As the practitioner stands up the (R) hand also extends straight up as high as possible with the palm facing away from the body. In opposition, the (L) hand presses palm down, inside the raised (L) knee, to the height of the Tan Tien to protect the centreline.

(Figure 22-5.96) Next, with the (R) foot firmly planted the practitioner rotates the upper body and raised (L) leg 90 degrees to the left to face the natural centreline of the form. At the same time, the (R) hand simultaneously punches forwards to nose height along the centreline. The (L) hand is drawn to the inside of the (R) elbow as in Pi Chuan technique.

(Figure 22-5.97) Step down and through with the (L) foot and follow up with the (R) foot using the half-step method. At the same time as stepping execute a (L) punch straight up to nose height following the line of the previous (R) punch and as soon as the (L) punch reaches its full extension open the hands dropping the (R) hand down to the mid-section, protecting the Tan Tien and the (L) hand chops forward and down the centreline in a splitting action. At the end of this sequence the practitioner is now in (L) Pi Chuan posture.

Note: To finish the form correctly the practitioner uses the closing method described in Chapter 19 of this book.

Sher Er Hong Chewi – Fighting Applications:

Note: Only a small number of applications are shown for this form as it mainly consists of movements trained in all the other forms which are shown with applications in other chapters of this book.

Application 1 – movements 22-5.6, 5.7, 5.8, 5.9 and 5.10

1a → 1b → 1c → 1d → 1e → 1f

(Figure 1a) Black controls White by pinning White's (R) arm using a single 'arm bar' joint locking technique.

(Figure 1b) As White feels the pressure of his arm pinned against his back, he backs up a step to stop Black moving him forwards. This momentary pause causes Black to stop his forward momentum.

(Figure 1c) White immediately uses this pause to take a step forwards and away from Black before he can adjust his balance and stance. This creates a space to manoeuvre between the two.

(Figure 1d) White can now turn around and at the same time rotate his (R) shoulder and arm upwards, to break Black's grabbing (R) arm and force his elbow up into a vulnerable position. This action also protects White by making it difficult for Black to punch effectively with this free (L) hand.

(Figure 1e) White quickly steps across and in front of Black with his (L) foot and at the same time takes a hold of Black's (R) wrist with his (L) hand and applies pressure to Black's (R) extended elbow with his (L) hand.

(Figure 1f) White completes the movement by sinking into a horse stance and taking Black off balance and down to the ground.

Application 2 – movement 22-5.14

2a → 2b

(Figure 2a) White faces off to Black in a neutral stance.
(Figure 2b) Black throws a (R) low punch to White's Tan Tien. White counters by using (L) I/O forearm block and at the same time steps into Black's centreline and delivers a (R) Peng Chuan punch to Black's solar plexus.

Application 3 – movement 22-5.16 and 5.17

3a → 3b

(Figure 3a) White faces off to Black in a neutral stance.
(Figure 3b) Black throws a (L) straight punch to White's face. White counters by stepping to the outside with his rear (L) foot to avoid the punch and create a more favourable angle for attack. At the same time, he covers the incoming strike with his (L) forearm and simultaneously strikes down with his (R) elbow into Black's extended elbow joint line. As the elbow strike knocks down the (R) arm, White continues with the momentum of his attack, further striking Black's (L) temple with the palmer aspect of his (R) fist.

Application 4 – movement 22-5.21

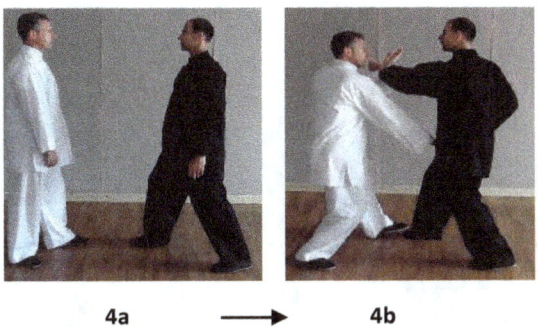

4a → 4b

(Figure 4a) White faces off to Black in a neutral stance.
(Figure 4b) Black throws a (R) straight punch to White's face. White counters by using (L) spear hand block to the outside and at the same time steps onto Black's (R) foot with his (R) foot and delivers a (R) finger thrust strike to Black's groin.

Chapter 23

The Twelve Animals Forms

Dragon Form

1. Dragon Form – Lung Hsing

Introduction

Grand Master Chiao

Dragon form is a challenging sequence of movements which combines the energies of Metal and Wood in conjunction with challenging stances, stepping methods, kicks and jumps which serve to condition the practitioner in both body and mind. This form also improves balance, stamina and endurance of the practitioner if practised regularly.

As previously stated in Chapter 13 of this book this lineage has two different methods of Dragon form. One form originates from Master Chiao and the other from Master Hsu. No one method is better than another. The movement pattern for both versions of the forms are the same except for the 'stepping kick' method utilised by Master Chiao and the 'jumping kick' method utilised by Master Hsu. When using either method the number of stepping or jumping kicks in each direction of the form is an odd number (e.g. 1, 3, 5, 7, 9 etc.). The space of the training area dictates the amount of kicks executed. Usually it is three kicks and then one kick before the practitioner turns and repeats the same number again in the opposite direction as described in method one below.

The direction for each individual form is to move up and down in a straight line. The form opens and moves forwards, then turns 180 degrees and continues its movements in the opposite direction before turning again, 180 degrees to finish facing the same direction the practitioner originally started in accordance with traditional Hsing-I practice.

Dragon Form – Method One (Master Chiao)

To open the form into (L) Pi Chuan (figure 23-1-1.1) use the opening method shown in Chapter 19 previously.

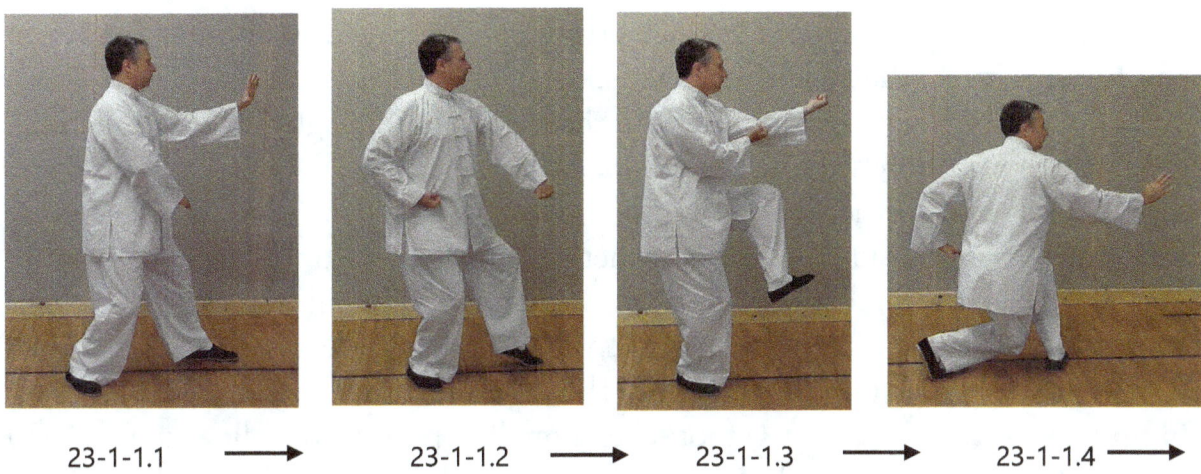

23-1-1.1 → 23-1-1.2 → 23-1-1.3 → 23-1-1.4 →

(Figure 23-1-1.1) Starting from (L) opening Metal posture.

(Figure 23-1-1.2) Next, the (L) hand forms a fist and circle blocks low across the centreline. The (R) hand also forms a fist and pulls back to the (R) hip. At the same time, the forward (L) foot draws inwards onto its toes placing the practitioner into a (L) cat stance.

(Figure 23-1-1.3) Next, the (L) foot rises upwards and kicks using the 45-degree stomping kick to knee height and at the same time the (L) arm punches straight out to face height with the (R) fist held closely at the (L) elbow.

(Figure 23-1-1.4) From the kicking position the body then drops straight down to the ground into dragon stance. As the body drops the (R) hand punches forward up the line of the (L) arm as in Metal form and the two hands open and change positions with the (R) hand pressing out and forwards and the (L) hand pressing palm down and held at the (L) waist.

Note: The forward hand is held stretched out and the rear hand is pulled back to the waist. This is consistent with reverse Metal posture as the opposite hands and feet are forward.

23-1-1.5 → 23-1-1.6 → 23-1-1.7 → 23-1-1.8 →

(Figure 23-1-1.5) Next, the (L) foot takes a small step forwards followed by the (R) foot swiftly executing a straight leg kick. This raises the practitioner quickly back to their full height. As the kick is delivered along the centreline the (R) hand forms a fist and punches straight out in time with the kick to head height. At the same time, the (L) fist is held closely at the (R) elbow, as in Metal form.

(Figure 23-1-1.6) As the (R) kicking foot firmly lands on the ground, the (L) rear foot pushes forward using the half-step method, in effect putting the practitioner in a (R) Pi Chuan stance. At the same time, the (L) hand punches up the (R) forearm performing a Pi Chuan hand technique. This movement places the practitioner with (R) foot and opposing (L) hand forward. This is called (R) reverse Pi Chuan posture.

(Figure 23-1-1.7) Next, the (R) foot takes a small step forwards followed by the (L) foot swiftly executing a straight leg kick. This raises the practitioner quickly back to their full height. As the kick is delivered along the centreline the (L) hand forms a fist and punches straight out in time with the kick to head height. At the same time, the (R) fist is held closely at the (L) elbow, as in Metal form.

(Figure 23-1-1.8) As the (L) kicking foot firmly lands on the ground, the (R) rear foot pushes forward using the half-step method, in effect putting the practitioner in a (L) Pi Chuan stance. At the same time, the (R) hand punches up the (L) forearm performing a Pi Chuan hand technique. This movement places the practitioner with (L) foot and opposing (R) hand forward. This is called (L) reverse Pi Chuan posture.

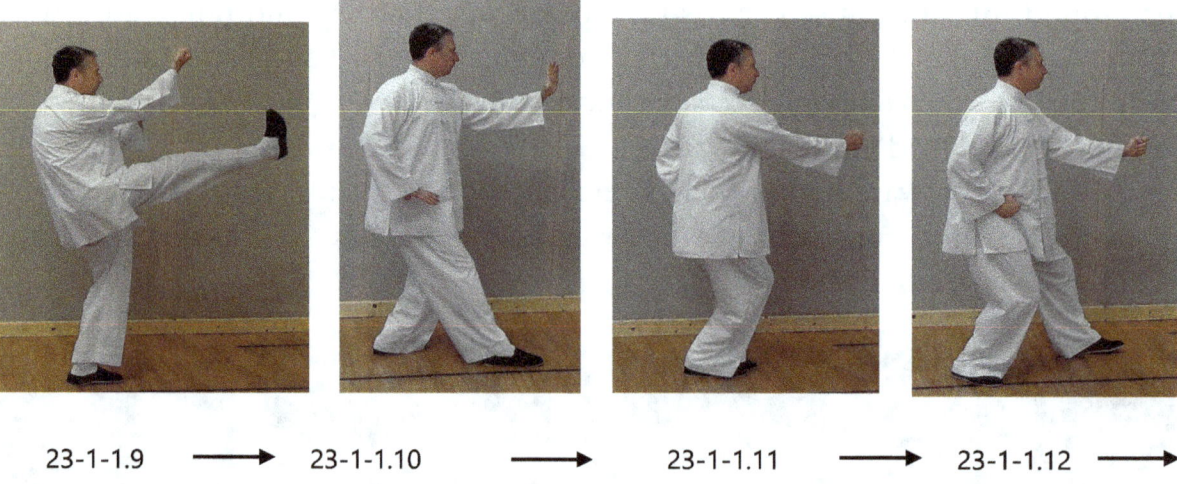

23-1-1.9 → 23-1-1.10 → 23-1-1.11 → 23-1-1.12 →

(Figure 23-1-1.9) Next, the (L) foot takes a small step forwards followed by the (R) foot swiftly executing a straight leg kick. This raises the practitioner quickly back to their full height. As the kick is delivered along the centreline the (R) hand forms a fist and punches straight out in time with the kick to head height. At the same time, the (L) fist is held closely at the (R) elbow, as in Metal form.

(Figure 23-1-1.10) As the (R) kicking foot firmly lands on the ground, the (L) rear foot pushes forward using the half-step method, in effect putting the practitioner in a (R) Pi Chuan stance. At the same time, the (L) hand punches up the (R) forearm performing a Pi Chuan hand technique. This movement places the practitioner with (R) foot and opposing (L) hand forward. This is called (R) reverse Pi Chuan posture.

Note: This completes the first sequence of three kicks.

(Figure 23-1-1.11) From (R) reverse Pi Chuan, take a small step forward with the (R) foot and then step straight through with the (L) foot into closed Wood posture. The (L) foot is forwards with the (R) foot tucked into the instep. The (R) hand executes a Peng Chuan punch to solar plexus height, whilst the (L) hand pulls back to the (L) hip.

(Figure 23-1-1.12) Next, the (L) foot steps out and the (R) foot follows using the half-step method. This places the practitioner into 'open' Wood posture. At the same time, the (L) hand executes a Peng Chuan punch to solar plexus height, whilst the (R) hand pulls back to the (L) hip.

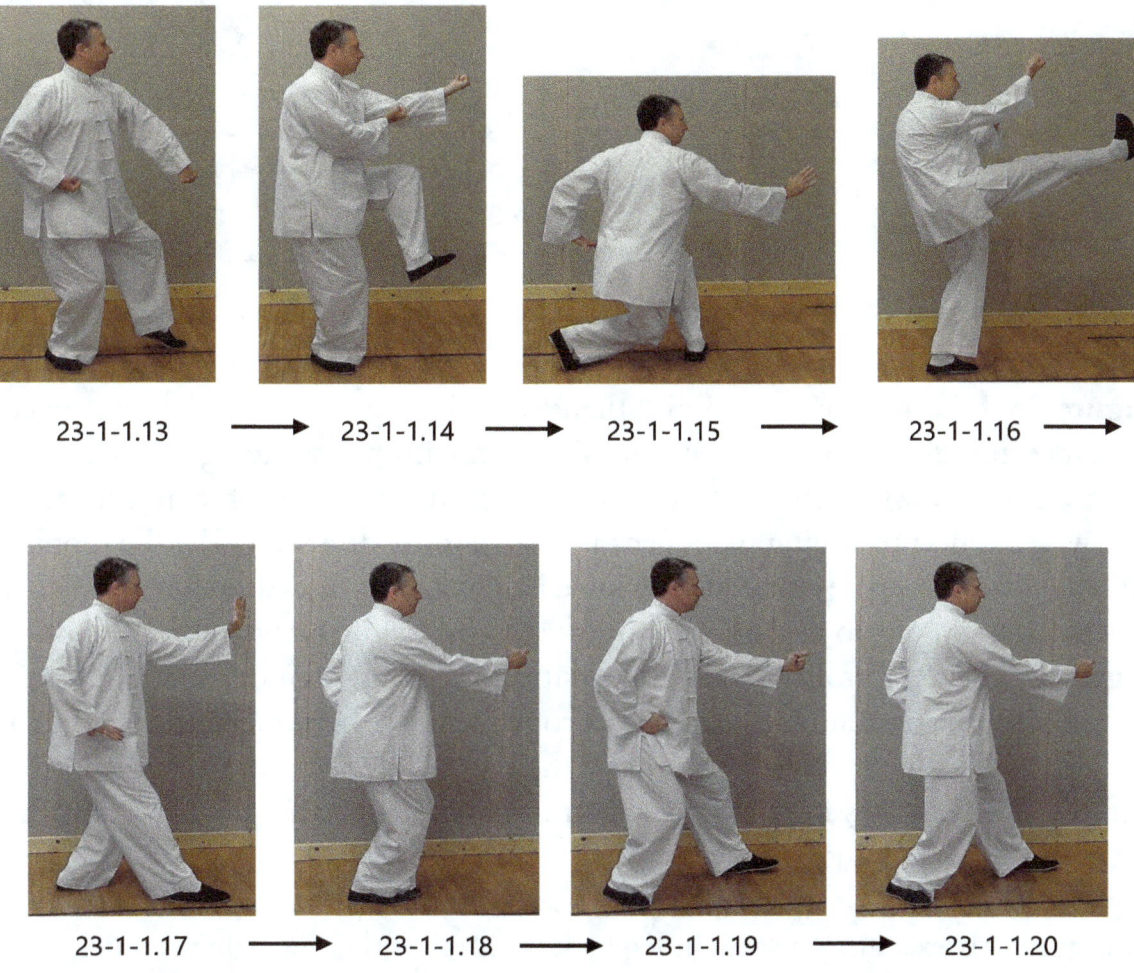

(Figures 23-1-1.13 to 1.17) Repeats the sequence of (figures 23-1-1.2 to 1.6) above.

Note: This completes the first sequence of one kick.

(Figure 23-1-1.18) From (R) reverse Pi Chuan, take a small step forward with the (R) foot and then step straight through with the (L) foot into closed Wood posture. The (L) foot is forwards with the (R) foot tucked into the instep. The (R) hand executes a Peng Chuan punch to solar plexus height, whilst the (L) hand pulls back to the (L) hip.

(Figure 23-1-1.19) Next, the (L) foot, steps out and the (R) foot follows using the half-step method. This places the practitioner into open Wood posture. At the same time, the (L) hand executes a Peng Chuan punch to solar plexus height, whilst the (R) hand pulls back to the (L) hip.

(Figure 23-1-1.20) The 180-degree turn can now be initiated when the practitioner is in the open Wood position. Without moving the feet, the practitioner punches straight out with the (R) fist and at the same time withdraws the (L) fist to the (L) hip.

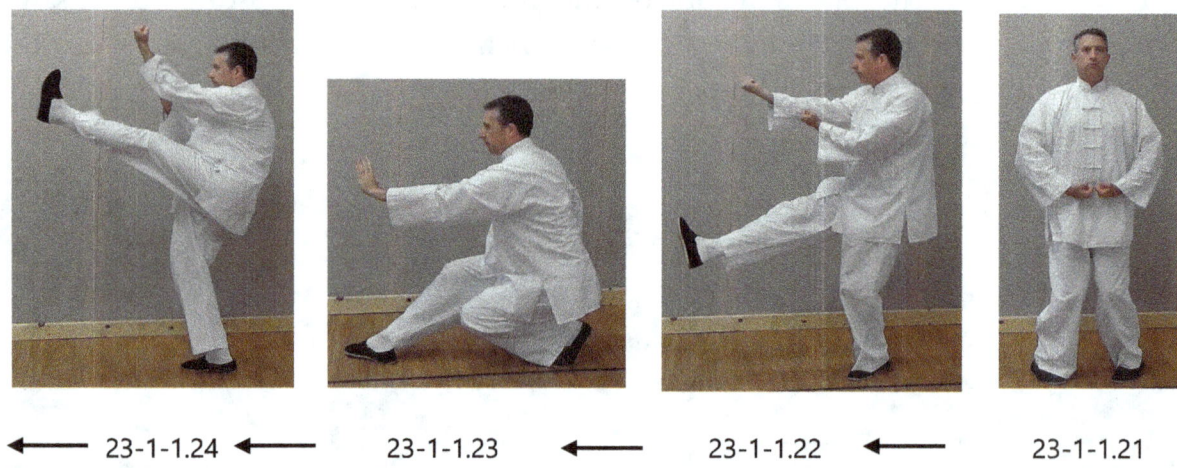

← 23-1-1.24 ← 23-1-1.23 ← 23-1-1.22 ← 23-1-1.21

(Figure 23-1-1.21) The practitioner then turns 90 degrees clockwise into pigeon-toe stance and draws both fists into the Tan Tien with palms facing up.

(Figure 23-1-1.22) The practitioner then continues to turn a further 90 degrees clockwise in effect returning them back in the opposite direction. The (R) foot kicks out using the 45-degree rising kick to knee height and at the same time the (R) arm punches straight out to face height with the (L) fist held closely at the (R) elbow.

(Figure 23-1-1.23) From the kicking position the body then drops straight to the ground into dragon stance. As the body drops the (L) hand punches forward up the line of the (R) arm as in Metal form and the two hands open and change positions with the (L) hand pressing out and forwards and the (R) hand pressing palm down and held at the (R) waist.

(Figure 23-1-1.24) Next, the (R) foot takes a small step forwards followed by the (L) foot swiftly executing a straight leg kick. This raises the practitioner quickly back to their full height. As the kick is delivered along the centreline the (L) hand forms a fist and punches straight out in time with the kick to head height. At the same time, the (R) fist is held closely at the (L) elbow, as in Metal form.

← 23-1-1.28　　← 23-1-1.27　　← 23-1-1.26　　← 23-1-1.25

(Figure 23-1-1.25) As the (L) kicking foot firmly lands on the ground, the (R) rear foot pushes forward using the half-step method, in effect putting the practitioner in a (L) Pi Chuan stance. At the same time, the (R) hand punches up the (L) forearm performing a Pi Chuan hand technique. This movement places the practitioner with (L) foot and opposing (R) hand forward. This is called (L) reverse Pi Chuan posture.
(Figure 23-1-1.26) Next, the (L) foot takes a small step forwards followed by the (R) foot swiftly executing a straight leg kick. This raises the practitioner quickly back to their full height. As the kick is delivered along the centreline the (R) hand forms a fist and punches straight out in time with the kick to head height. At the same time, the (L) fist is held closely at the (R) elbow, as in Metal form.
(Figure 23-1-1.27) As the (R) kicking foot firmly lands on the ground, the (L) rear foot pushes forward using the half-step method, in effect putting the practitioner in a (R) Pi Chuan stance. At the same time, the (L) hand punches up the (R) forearm performing a Pi Chuan hand technique. This movement places the practitioner with (R) foot and opposing (L) hand forward. This is called (R) reverse Pi Chuan posture.
(Figure 23-1-1.28) Next, the (R) foot takes a small step forwards followed by the (L) foot swiftly executing a straight leg kick. This raises the practitioner quickly back to their full height. As the kick is delivered along the centreline the (L) hand forms a fist and punches straight out in time with the kick to head height. At the same time, the (R) fist is held closely at the (L) elbow, as in Metal form.

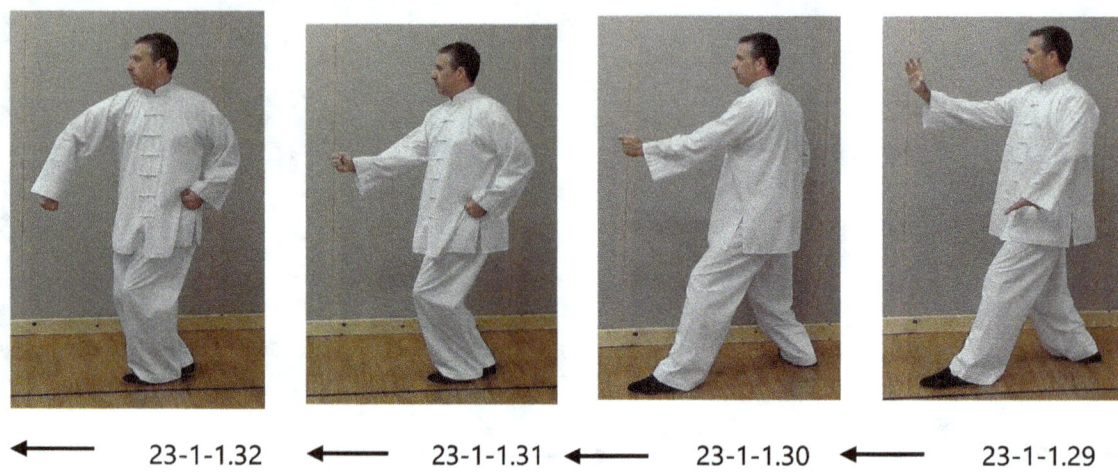

← 23-1-1.32   ← 23-1-1.31   ← 23-1-1.30   ← 23-1-1.29

(Figure 23-1-1.29) As the (L) kicking foot firmly lands on the ground, the (R) rear foot pushes forward using the half-step method, in effect putting the practitioner in a (L) Pi Chuan stance. At the same time, the (R) hand punches up the (L) forearm performing a Pi Chuan hand technique. This movement places the practitioner with (L) foot and opposing (R) hand forward. This is called (L) reverse Pi Chuan posture.

Note: This completes the second sequence of three kicks.

(Figure 23-1-1.30) Next, the (L) foot takes a step forwards and the (R) foot follows using the half-step method. This posture places the practitioner into 'open' Wood posture. At the same time, the (L) hand executes a Peng Chuan punch to solar plexus height, whilst the (R) hand pulls back to the (L) hip.

(Figure 23-1-1.31) Next, from an open Wood posture, take a small step forward with the (L) foot and then step up with the (R) foot into closed Wood posture. At the same time, the (R) hand executes a Peng Chuan punch to solar plexus height, whilst the (L) hand pulls back to the (L) hip.

(Figure 23-1-1.32) Next, the (R) hand circle blocks low across the centreline. The (L) hand reciprocally pulls back to the (L) hip. Both feet remain held in the closed Wood position throughout.

← 23-1-1.36   ← 23-1-1.35   ← 23-1-1.34   ← 23-1-1.33

(Figure 23-1-1.33) Next, the (R) foot kicks out using the 45-degree rising kick to knee height and at the same time the (R) arm punches straight out to face height with the (L) fist held closely at the (R) elbow.

(Figure 23-1-1.34) From the kicking position the body then drops straight to the ground into dragon stance. As the body drops the (L) hand punches forward up the line of the (R) arm as in Metal form and the two hands open and change positions with the (L) hand pressing out and forwards and the (R) hand pressing palm down and held at the (R) waist.

(Figure 23-1-1.35) Next, the (R) foot takes a small step forwards followed by the (L) foot swiftly executing a straight leg kick. This raises the practitioner quickly back to their full height. As the kick is delivered along the centreline the (L) hand forms a fist and punches straight out in time with the kick to head height. At the same time, the (R) fist is held closely at the (L) elbow, as in Metal form.

(Figure 23-1-1.36) As the (L) kicking foot firmly lands on the ground, the (R) rear foot pushes forward using the half-step method, in effect putting the practitioner in a (L) Pi Chuan stance. At the same time, the (R) hand punches up the (L) forearm performing a Pi Chuan hand technique. This movement places the practitioner with (L) foot and opposing (R) hand forward. This is called (L) reverse Pi Chuan posture.

Note: This completes the second sequence of single kick.

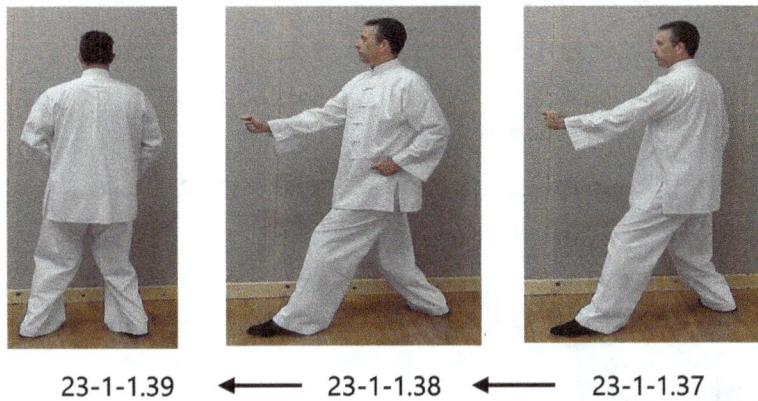

23-1-1.39 ← 23-1-1.38 ← 23-1-1.37

(Figure 23-1-1.37) Next, the (L) foot takes a step forwards and the (R) foot follows using the half-step method. This posture places the practitioner into 'open' Wood posture. At the same time, the (L) hand executes a Peng Chuan punch to solar plexus height, whilst the (R) hand pulls back to the (R) hip.

(Figure 23-1-1.38) Next. The practitioner takes a step forwards with the (L) foot and follows up with the rear (R) foot using the half-step method, leaving them remaining in (L) Pi Chuan stance. At the same time, the (R) hand executes a Peng Chuan punch to solar plexus height, whilst the (L) hand pulls back to the (L) hip. This posture is reverse open Wood as opposite hands and feet are forward.

(Figure 23-1-1.39) The practitioner then turns 90 degrees clockwise into pigeon toe stance and draws both fists into the Tan Tien with palms facing up.

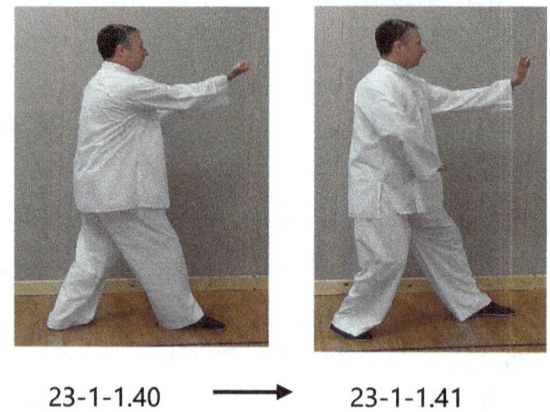

23-1-1.40 → 23-1-1.41

(Figure 23-1-1.40) The practitioner then continues to turn a further 90 degrees clockwise in effect returning them back along the same direction they started the form. Taking a small step forwards with the (R) foot as the (R) hand simultaneously punches forwards to nose height along the centreline. The (L) hand is drawn to the inside of the (R) elbow as in Pi Chuan technique.

(Figure 23-1-1.41) Step through with the (L) foot and follow up with the (R) foot using the half-step method. At the same time as stepping execute a (L) punch straight up to nose height following the line of the previous (R) punch and as soon as the (L) punch reaches its full extension open the hands dropping the (R) hand down to the mid-section, protecting the Tan Tien and the (L) hand chops forward and down the centreline in a splitting action. At the end of this sequence the practitioner should now be in (L) Pi Chuan posture.

Note: To finish the form correctly the practitioner uses the closing method described in Chapter 19 of this book.

Dragon Form – Method Two (Master Hsu)

Master Hsu's method of Dragon form is extremely strenuous on the legs, and therefore, requires good leg strength and agile balance to perform it correctly. A practitioner learning this form must take care not to injure themselves through poor technique. It is, however, an excellent method of building leg strength and its athletic nature serves to condition the whole body when trained correctly. It is said that some of the old Masters could perform up to three switching kicks of the legs on a single jump before landing perfectly in a low dragon stance each time.

23-1-2.1 → 23-1-2.2 → 23-1-2.3 → 23-1-2.4 → 23-1-2.5 → 23-1-2.6

When practising Master Hsu's method of Dragon form the sequence of movements are identical to Master Chiao's method discussed in detail previously, so they need not be described again here. The only difference in the two methods is that instead of the practitioner executing a straight leg kick and moving forward a step each time, when practising Master Hsu's method, the practitioner executes a jumping kick from the low dragon stance posture and swaps his feet in mid-air, landing again in a low dragon posture on the opposite side. The jumping kick switches the feet but does not move forward, therefore, the practitioner effectively remains in the same spot whilst performing the jump kick techniques. See the demonstrated example in figures 23-1-2.1 to 23-1-2.6 above.

Following is a brief directional description of Master Hsu's method of Dragon form. First the practitioner opens the form into (L) Pi Chuan posture and then drops into a low dragon stance. Next, the practitioner executes three jumping kicks on the spot, springing up like an uncoiling dragon before moving into open and closed Wood postures. Next, they execute a single jumping kick before passing through open and close Wood posture to turn 180 degrees. Next, they drop into a low dragon stance and execute three jumping kicks before passing through open and closed Wood postures. Next, they execute a single jumping leg kick and pass through open and reverse Wood posture, finally they turn though 180 degrees and finish the form using metal form method.

Dragon Form – Fighting Applications:

Application 1 – Movements 23-1-1.2 to 1.4

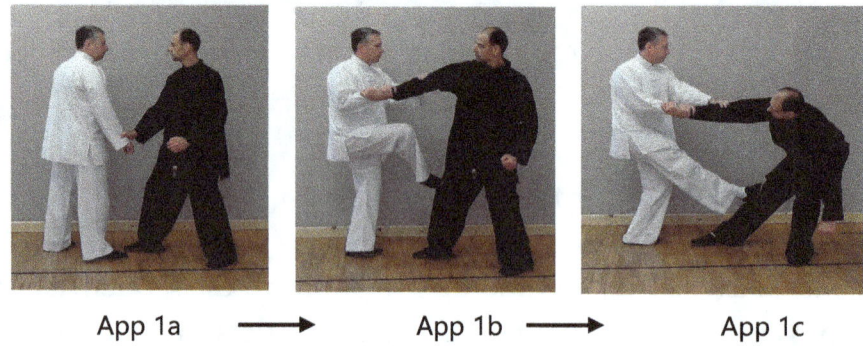

App 1a → App 1b → App 1c

(Figure 1a) Black cross grabs White's (R) wrist.
(Figure 1b) White immediately circles his (R) hand around Black's grabbing wrist and rotates Black's arm into an elbow lock by pressing against Black's extended elbow with his (L) rear hand.
(Figure 1c) White keeps control of Black's arm using the elbow lock and at the same time executes a (R) 45-degree stomping kick to the outside joint line of Black's (R) knee to break his balance and force him to the ground.

Application 2 – Movements 23-1-1.5 and 1.6

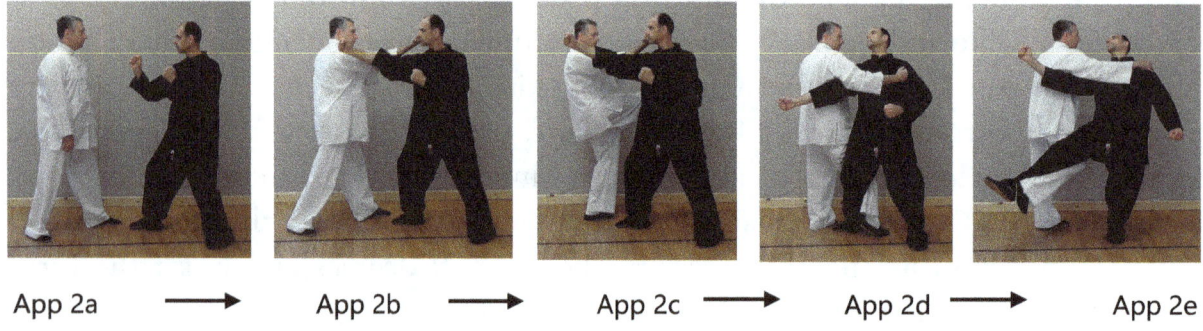

App 2a → App 2b → App 2c → App 2d → App 2e

(Figure 2a) White faces off to Black in a neutral stance.
(Figure 2b) Black throws a high (R) straight punch to White's face. White steps to the outside of Black's attack and blocks the punch by cover blocking Black's elbow and delivering a (R) Metal punch at Black's face.
(Figure 2c) White then feints, as though to step past Black to the outside but instead swings his (R) leg upwards as a straight leg kick.
(Figure 2d and 2e) As White's (R) leg swing passes by the outside of Black he then utilises the downward back swing of the kick as a sweeping technique taking away Black's standing (R) leg. White also uses his outstretched (R) arm to press across Black's chest to complete the manoeuvre.

Tiger Form

2. Tiger Form – Hu Hsing

Introduction

Grand Master Chiao

The tiger is often considered to be the king of all animals. As previously stated in Chapter 13 of this book this lineage has five different methods of Tiger form. No one method is better than another. The differences between the different methods just allow for a wider variation of fighting applications to be derived from their postures.

All the five Tiger form methods use the same movement pattern and so Method One will be discussed in more detail showing the complete form sequence and the remaining four methods will be discussed in a more abbreviated form sufficient for the reader to understand the subtle differences between each method.

The direction for each individual form is to move up and down in a straight line, repeating itself on both left and right sides as it advances. The form then turns 180 degrees and repeats its movements in the opposite direction before turning again to finish facing the direction the practitioner originally started in accordance with traditional Hsing-I practice.

Method One

Method One Hand Posture

The hand posture for the first method of Tiger form discussed below is a double-handed 'tigers claw' which is formed by the thumb and all four fingers equally flexed with spirit held in the hands which allows for a strong tearing action in application.

Tiger Form – Method One

To open the form into (L) Pi Chuan (Figure 23-2-1.1) use the opening method shown in Chapter 19 previously.

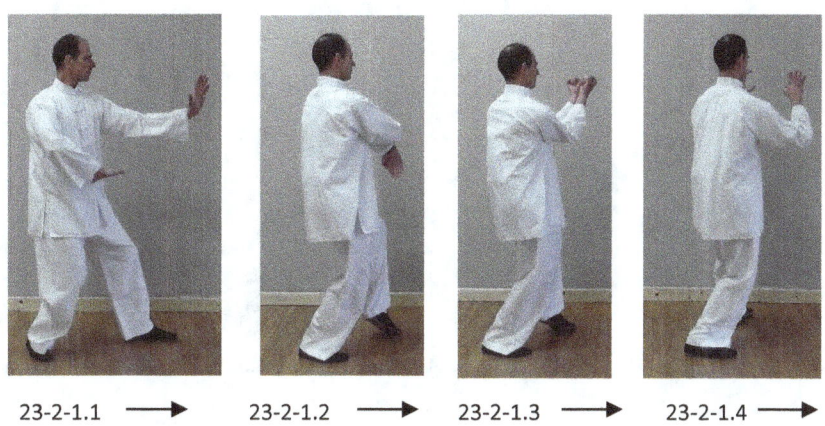

23-2-1.1 → 23-2-1.2 → 23-2-1.3 → 23-2-1.4 →

(Figure 23-2-1.1) Starting from (L) Pi Chuan posture.

(Figure 23-2-1.2) Step forward with the (R) foot and turn the body to the left at a 45-degree angle and step out forwards with the (L) foot placing it on the ball of the foot into (L) cat stance. At the same time cross over both arms in front of the body at Tan Tien height with hands above the hips, held open and palms facing down.

(Figure 23-2-1.3) Whilst holding the (L) cat stance, the practitioner then pulls both hands equally apart across the body in a 'tearing' action and closes the hands at their corresponding hips to form fists. The two arms then drive upwards and outwards at an angle of 45 degrees to the body, punching as a double-handed strike to nose height.

(Figure 23-2-1.4) Next the practitioner pushes forward from the back (R) foot and steps forward with the front (L) foot. The back foot follows up using the half-step method into a (L) Pi Chuan stance. At the same time both hands open with palms facing outwards to form the 'tigers claw' posture and simultaneously tear downwards in perfect timing with the rear foot half-step striking the ground. This is (L) Tiger posture.

Note: The downward tearing action of the hands in time with the stepping of the feet creates a whole body movement from which the technique derives its power. This tearing action is not just executed with arm strength alone. Perfection of this timing is crucial to the effectiveness of all the tiger form methods in any fighting application.

Hsing-I Chuan | The Practice of Heart and Mind Boxing

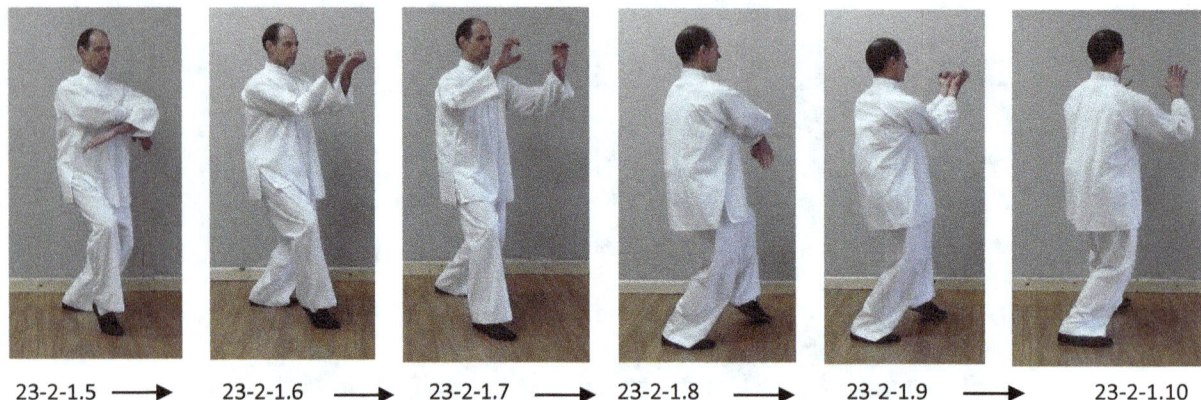

23-2-1.5 → 23-2-1.6 → 23-2-1.7 → 23-2-1.8 → 23-2-1.9 → 23-2-1.10

(Figures 23-2-1.5 to 1.7) The practitioner then steps forward along the centreline of the form with their (L) foot and turns their body 45 degrees to the right and steps into a (R) cat stance. From this position, they then repeat the same sequence of movements discussed in (Figures 23-2-1.2 to 1.4) previously which finishes with the practitioner in (R) Tiger posture. (Figure 23-2-1.7)

(Figures 23-2-1.8 to 1.10) At this point the same sequence of movements can be performed repeatedly forward in a straight line until the practitioner chooses to turn and change direction. Traditionally Hsing-I practitioners turn their forms on the (L) side; however, it is prudent to practice turns on both sides from a fighting application purpose.

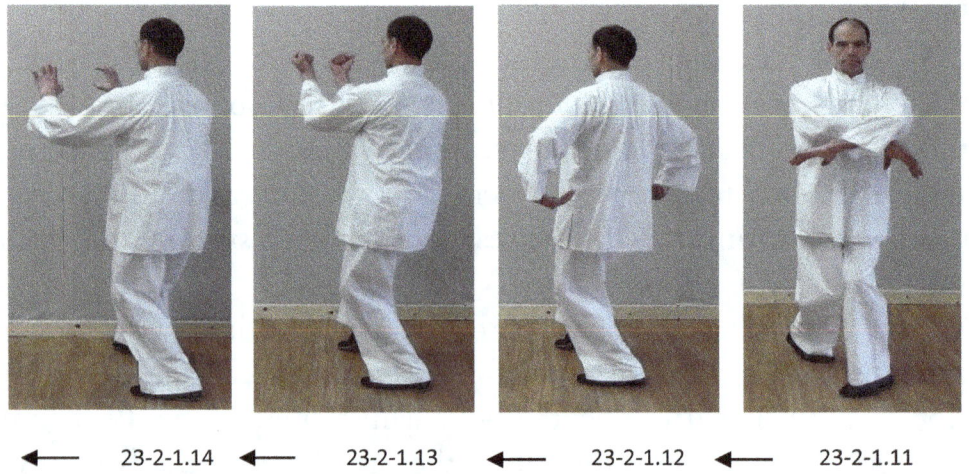

← 23-2-1.14 ← 23-2-1.13 ← 23-2-1.12 ← 23-2-1.11

(Figure 23-2-1.11) From (L) Tiger posture (figure 23-2-1.10) the (L) front foot is turned inwards in a clockwise direction approximately 45 degrees, the weight is transferred from the (R) foot to the (L) foot and at the same time both arms cross over the body at the height of the Tan Tien with the hands held above the hips.

(Figure 23-2-1.12) The practitioner continues to turn in a clockwise direction a further 180 degrees ending the pivot in (R) cat stance. At the same time both the hands pull equally apart across the body in a pulling action in preparation to form fists.

(Figure 23-2-1.13) Whilst remaining in a (R) cat stance, the hands form fists and both arms then drive upwards and outwards at an angle of 45 degrees to the body punching as a double-handed strike to nose height.

(Figure 23-2-1.14) Next the practitioner pushes forward from the back (L) foot and steps forward with the front (R) foot. The back foot follows up using the half-step method into a (R) Pi Chuan stance. At the same time both hands open with palms facing outwards to form the 'tigers claw' posture and simultaneously tear downwards in perfect timing with the rear foot half-step striking the ground. This is (R) Tiger posture.

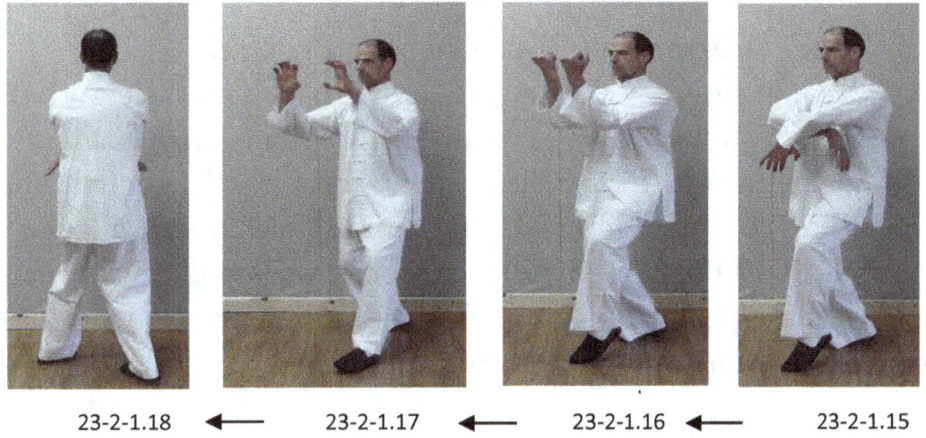

23-2-1.18 ← 23-2-1.17 ← 23-2-1.16 ← 23-2-1.15

(Figures 23-2-1.15 to 1.17) Continues the sequence stepping forwards into (L) Tiger posture ready to turn.

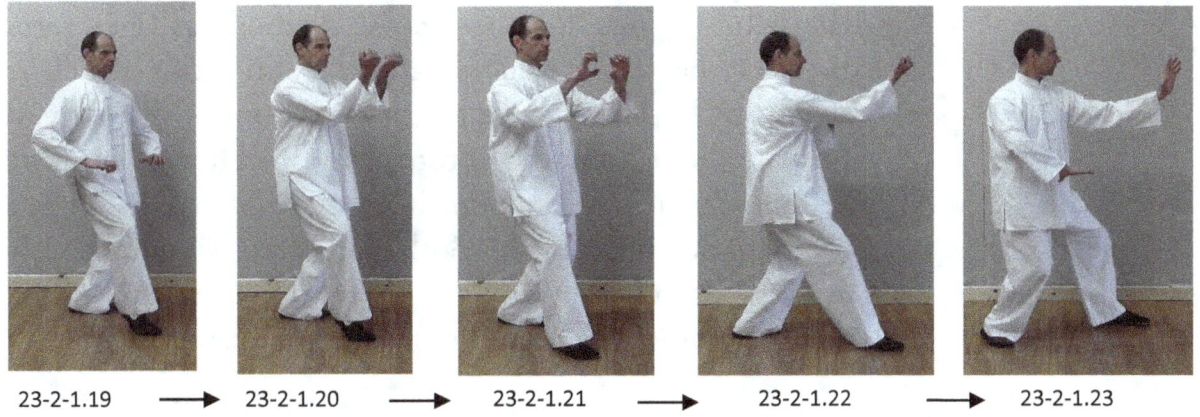

23-2-1.19 → 23-2-1.20 → 23-2-1.21 → 23-2-1.22 → 23-2-1.23

(Figures 23-2-1.18 to 1.21) Repeats the turn sequence and ends with the practitioner in (R) Tiger posture.

(Figures 23-2-1.22 and 1.23) Next, the practitioner turns to face the original centreline stepping forward with the (R) foot and punching forwards with the (R) fist simultaneously. The (L) fist is held at the (R) elbow as in Pi Chuan and the practitioner steps forward with the (L) foot into (L) Pi Chuan posture. To finish the form correctly from (L) Pi Chuan the practitioner uses the closing method described in Chapter 19 previous.

Method One Fighting Application:

1a → 1b → 1c

(Figure 1a) White's faces off with Black in a neutral stance.
(Figure 1b) Black throws a (R) straight punch to White's face. White counters by stepping across to the outside with the (L) rear foot, at the same time White simultaneously blocks and strikes Black to the face with a (R) straight punch.
(Figure 1c) Whites continues immediately from the blocking technique to control Black's arm with his (R) hand and half-steps forward to strike Black's face with his (L) palm and then claw down on Black's (L) ear. Both hands tear apart in opposition to one another on execution of this technique.

Method Two

Method Two Hand Posture

The hand posture for the second method of Tiger form discussed next is a double-handed palm strike which is formed by both the hands held out in front of the body in line with the centreline. The top hand has its fingers pointing upwards to heaven and the bottom hand has its fingers pointing down to earth. Both hands are simultaneously striking out in the form but in application they can be used independently of one another to block and strike.

Tiger Form – Method Two

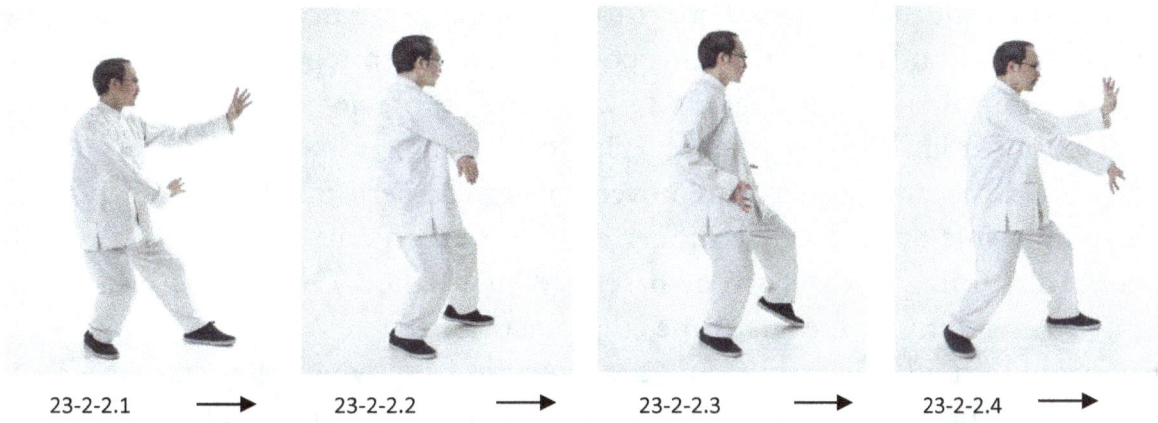

23-2-2.1 → 23-2-2.2 → 23-2-2.3 → 23-2-2.4 →

To open the form into (L) Pi Chuan (Figure 23-2-2.1) use the opening method shown in Chapter 19 previously.

(Figure 23-2-2.1) Starting from (L) Pi Chuan posture.

(Figure 23-2-2.2) Step forward with the (R) foot and turn the body to the left at a 45-degree angle and step out forwards with the (L) foot placing it on the ball of the foot into (L) cat stance. At the same time cross over both arms in front of the body at Tan Tien height with hands above the hips, held open and palms facing down.

(Figure 23-2-2.3) Whilst holding the (L) cat stance, the practitioner then pulls both hands equally apart across the body in a 'tearing' action and turns the hands to face palms outwards at their corresponding hips.

(Figure 23-2-2.4) Next the practitioner pushes forward from the back (R) foot and steps forward with the front (L) foot. The back foot follows up using the half-step method into a (L) Pi Chuan stance. At the same time both arms strike forwards with the (L) hand on top, at solar plexus height and the (R) hand directly underneath it at the height of the Tan Tien. The striking of both hands must be in perfect timing with the rear foot half-step striking the ground.

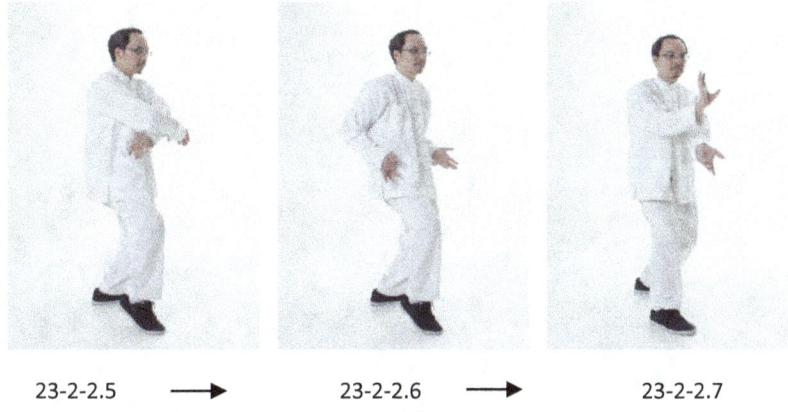

23-2-2.5 → 23-2-2.6 → 23-2-2.7

(Figures 23-2-2.5 to 2.7) The practitioner then steps forward along the centreline of the form with their (L) foot and turns their body 45 degrees to the right and steps into a (R) cat stance. From this position, they then repeat the same sequence of movements discussed in (Figures 23-2-2.2 to 2.4) previously which finishes with the practitioner in (R) Tiger posture. (Figure 23-2-2.7)

At this point the same sequence of movements can be performed repeatedly forward in a straight line until the practitioner chooses to turn and change direction. The method of turning is the same as described in Method One at the start of this chapter. After turning the first time, the practitioner repeats the movements and turns again to finish the form facing the direction from which they started. From a (R) Tiger posture the practitioner steps through into (L) Pi Chuan and finishes the form in the manner discussed in chapter 19 of this book.

Tiger Form – Method Two Fighting Application:

(Figure 2a) White faces off with Black in a neutral stance.
(Figure 2b) Black throws a (R) straight punch to White's Tan Tien. White counters by stepping inside Black's attack and blocking with a (L) open palm to the inside of Black's (R) arm and opening him up to a counterstrike.
(Figure 2c) White continues immediately from the blocking technique to execute a double palm strike to Black's solar plexus and groin.

Method Three

Method Three Knee Strike

The hand posture for the third method of Tiger form discussed next is the same as the second method discussed previously. The difference with the third method is a double-handed block and raised knee strike in the middle of the form which is executed after the practitioner drives forward off the rear foot with the first double palm strike. After the knee strike and block the practitioner drives forward again with a repeat of the double-handed palm strike to complete the movement.

Tiger Form Method Three

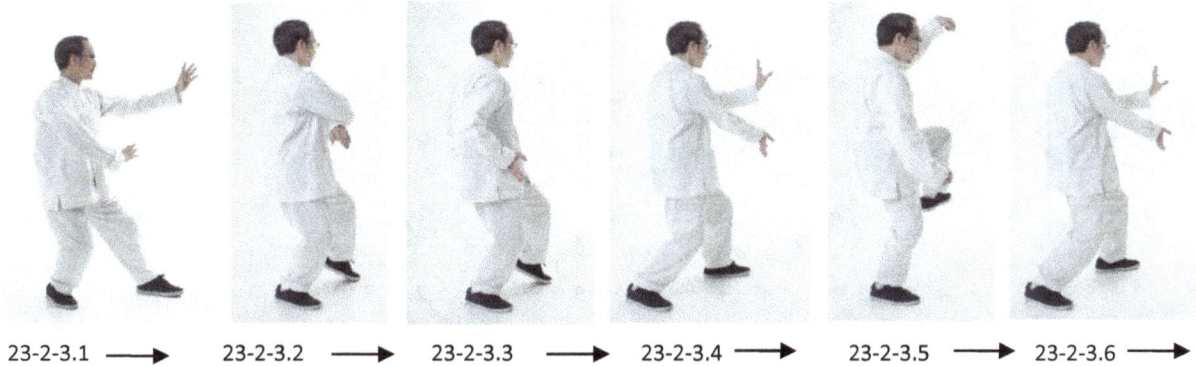

23-2-3.1 → 23-2-3.2 → 23-2-3.3 → 23-2-3.4 → 23-2-3.5 → 23-2-3.6 →

To open the form into (L) Pi Chuan (Figure 23-2-3.1) use the opening method shown in Chapter 19 previously.
(Figure 23-2-3.1) Starting from (L) Pi Chuan posture.
(Figure 23-2-3.2) Step forward with the (R) foot and turn the body to the left at a 45-degree angle and step out forwards with the (L) foot placing it on the ball of the foot into (L) cat stance. At the same time cross over both arms in front of the body at Tan Tien height with hands above the hips, held open and palms facing down.
(Figure 23-2-3.3) Whilst holding the (L) cat stance, the practitioner then pulls both hands equally apart across the body in a 'tearing' action and turns the hands to face palms outwards at their corresponding hips.
(Figure 23-2-3.4) Next the practitioner pushes forward from the back (R) foot and steps forward with the front (L) foot. The back foot follows up using the half-step method into a (L) Pi Chuan stance. At the same time both arms strike forwards with the (L) hand on top, at solar plexus height and the (R) hand directly underneath it at the height of the Tan Tien. This is (L) Tiger form.

(Figure 23-2-3.5) From (L) Tiger form, the practitioner then raises upwards onto the back (R) foot in a single leg stance and knee strikes with the (L) knee. At the same time both arms pull backwards with the (R) arm blocking low in front of the (R) hip and the (L) hand blocking high at the level of the head. The blocking hands both have the form of the cranes beak.

Note: When the practitioner draws back into single leg stance there should be minimal change in head height. The rear supporting leg should remain flexed throughout and maintain the forms height.

(Figure 23-2-3.6) Next the practitioner pushes forward from the back (R) foot and steps forward with the front (L) foot. The back foot follows up using the half-step method into a (L) Pi Chuan stance. At the same time both arms strike forwards with the (L) hand on top, at solar plexus height and the (R) hand directly underneath it at the height of the Tan Tien. The practitioner is now returned to (L) Tiger form.

23-2-3.7 → 23-2-3.8 → 23-2-3.9 → 23-2-3.10 → 23-2-3.11

(Figures 23-2-3.7 to 3.11) The practitioner then steps forward along the centreline of the form with their (L) foot and turns their body 45 degrees to the right and steps into a (R) cat stance. From this position, they then repeat the same sequence of movements discussed in (Figures 23-2-3.2 to 3.6) previously which finishes with the practitioner in (R) Tiger posture. (Figure 23-2-3.11)

At this point the same sequence of movements can be performed repeatedly forward in a straight line until the practitioner chooses to turn and change direction. The method of turning is the same as described in Method One at the start of this chapter. After turning the first time, the practitioner repeats the movements and turns again to finish the form facing the direction from which they started. From a (R) Tiger posture the practitioner steps through into (L) Pi Chuan and finishes the form in the manner discussed in chapter 19 of this book.

Method Three Fighting Application:

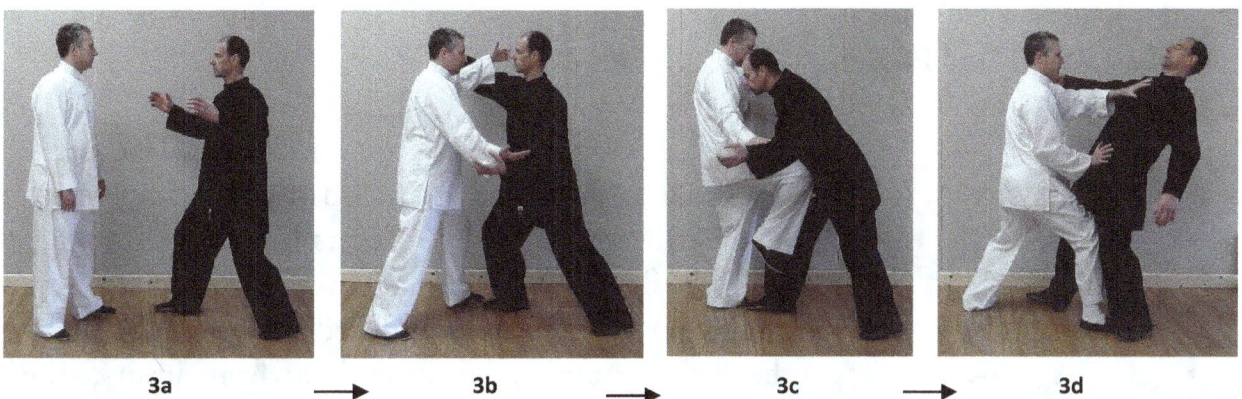

(Figure 3a) White faces off with Black in a neutral stance.
(Figure 3b) Black lunges forward to grab around White's. In anticipation, White steps into the attack and throws out a double-handed block to break the attempted grab of Black.
(Figure 3c) As soon as contact is made with Black's arms White simultaneously executes a (R) knee strike upwards along the centreline to Black's Tan Tien.
(Figure 3d) White continues immediately from the block and knee strike technique to execute a double palm strike to Black's solar plexus and stomach to drive him away.

Method Four

Method Four Hand Posture

The hand posture for the second method of Tiger form discussed below is a double-handed 'tigers claw' which is formed by the first two fingers (index and middle) partially flexed with the remaining two fingers (ring and little) held completely flexed against the palm by the flexed thumb to protect them from injury. The spirit of the hand is held in the first two fingers which allows for a target specific tearing action in application.

Tiger Form – Method Four

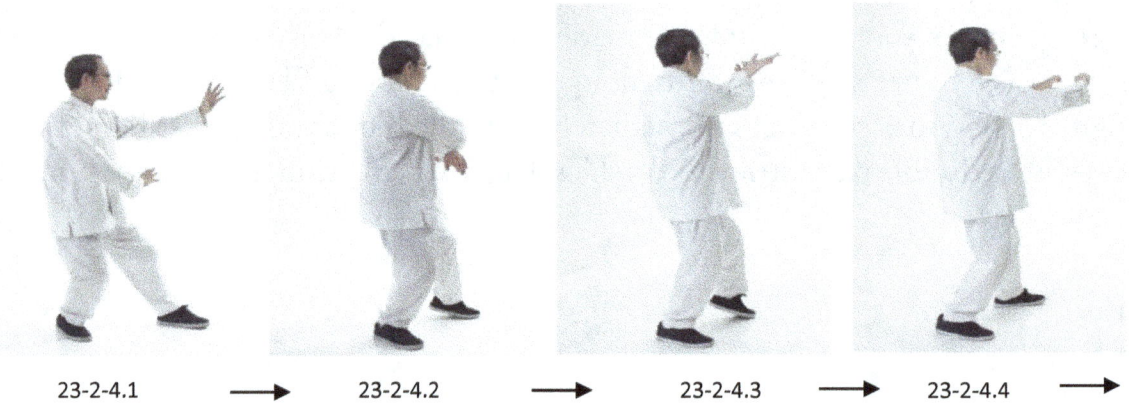

23-2-4.1 → 23-2-4.2 → 23-2-4.3 → 23-2-4.4 →

To open the form into (L) Pi Chuan (Figure 23-2-4.1) use the opening method shown in Chapter 19 previously.

(Figure 23-2-4.1) Starting from (L) Pi Chuan posture.

(Figure 23-2-4.2) Step forward with the (R) foot and turn the body to the left at a 45-degree angle and step out forwards with the (L) foot placing it on the ball of the foot into (L) cat stance. At the same time cross over both arms in front of the body at Tan Tien height with hands above the hips, held open and palms facing down.

(Figure 23-2-4.3) Whilst holding the (L) cat stance, the practitioner then pulls both hands equally apart across the body in a 'tearing' action and closes their hands at their corresponding hips to form fists. The two arms then cross over and drive upwards and outwards at an angle of 45 degrees to nose height. The index and middle fingers of both hands are held straight as they strike upwards and the remaining two fingers are held in place flexed against the palm by the flexed thumb.

(Figure 23-2-4.4) Next the practitioner pushes forward from the back (R) foot and steps forward with the front (L) foot. The back foot follows up using the half-step method into a (L) Pi Chuan stance. At the same time both hands open with palms facing outwards to form the two fingers 'tigers claw' posture and simultaneously tear downwards in perfect timing with the rear foot half-step striking the ground. This is (L) Tiger posture.

23-2-4.5 → 23-2-4.6 → 23-2-4.7

(Figures 23-2-4.5 to 4.7) The practitioner then steps forward along the centreline of the form with their (L) foot and turns their body 45 degrees to the right and steps into a (R) cat stance. From this position, they then repeat the same sequence of movements discussed in (Figures 23-2-4.2 to 4.4) previously which finishes with the practitioner in (R) Tiger posture. (Figure 23-2-4.7)

At this point the same sequence of movements can be performed repeatedly forward in a straight line until the practitioner chooses to turn and change direction. The method of turning is the same as described in Method One at the start of this chapter. After turning the first time, the practitioner repeats the movements and turns again to finish the form facing the direction from which they started. From a (R) Tiger posture the practitioner steps through into (L) Pi Chuan and finishes the form in the manner discussed in chapter 19 of this book.

Method Four Fighting Application:

4a → 4b → 4c

(Figure 4a) White's faces off with Black in a neutral stance.
(Figure 4b) Black throws a (R) straight punch to White's face. White counters

by stepping across to the outside with the (L) rear foot, at the same time White simultaneously blocks and strikes Black to the face with a (R) straight punch.

(Figure 4c) White continues immediately from the blocking technique to control Black's arm with his (R) hand and half-steps forward to strike Black's face with his (L) palm and then claw down across Black's eyes and face. Both hands tear apart in opposition to one another on execution of this technique

Method Five

Method Five Hand Posture

The hand posture for the fifth method of Tiger form discussed next is a double-handed palm strike which is formed by both the hands held out sideways, symmetrically in front of the body in line with the centreline. This method can be used to deliver tremendous internal power to destroy an opponent's organs if the practitioner has a high level of skill. It can also be used effectively to push or throw an opponent a great distance if the correct body mechanics and timing are applied to the technique.

Tiger Form - Method Five

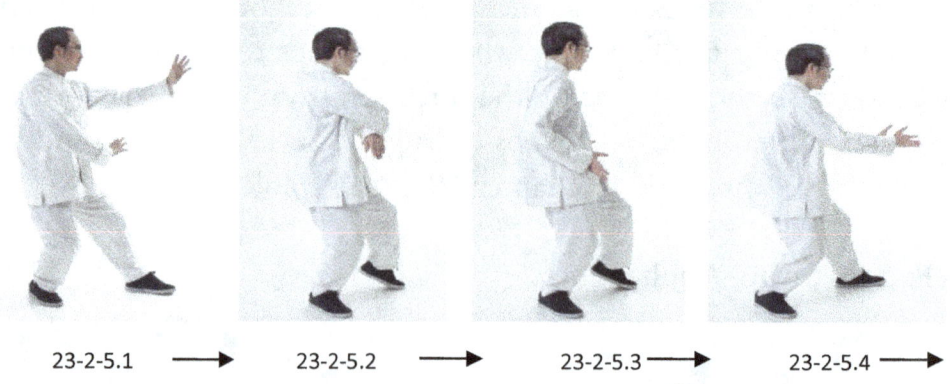

23-2-5.1 → 23-2-5.2 → 23-2-5.3 → 23-2-5.4 →

To open the form into (L) Pi Chuan (Figure 23-2-5.1) use the opening method shown in Chapter 19 previously.
(Figure 23-2-5.1) Starting from (L) Pi Chuan posture.
(Figure 23-2-5.2) Step forward with the (R) foot and turn the body to the left at a 45-degree angle and step out forwards with the (L) foot placing it on the ball of the foot into (L) cat stance. At the same time cross over both arms in front of the body at Tan Tien height with hands above the hips, held open and palms facing down.
(Figure 23-2-5.3) Whilst holding the (L) cat stance, the practitioner then pulls

both hands equally apart across the body in a 'tearing' action and turns the hands to face palms outwards at their corresponding hips.

(Figure 23-2-5.4) Next the practitioner pushes forward from the back (R) foot and steps forward with the front (L) foot. The back foot follows up using the half-step method into a (L) Pi Chuan stance. At the same time both arms strike forwards simultaneously at the height of the Tan Tien. This is (L) Tiger form.

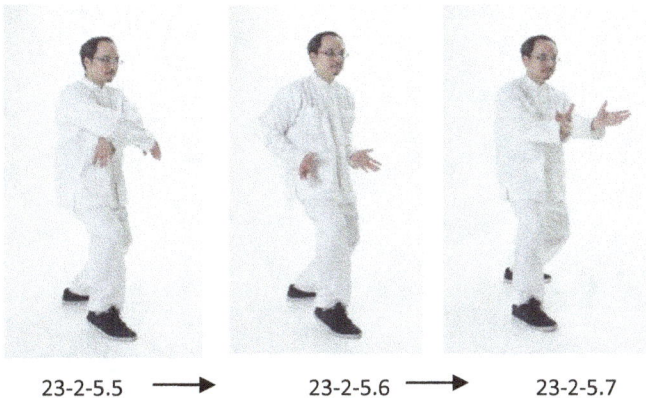

23-2-5.5 → 23-2-5.6 → 23-2-5.7

(Figures 23-2-5.5 to 5.7) The practitioner then steps forward along the centreline of the form with their (L) foot and turns their body 45 degrees to the right and steps into a (R) cat stance. From this position, they then repeat the same sequence of movements discussed in (Figures 23-2-5.2 to 5.4) previously which finishes with the practitioner in (R) Tiger posture. (Figure 23-2-5.7)

At this point the same sequence of movements can be performed repeatedly forward in a straight line until the practitioner chooses to turn and change direction. The method of turning is the same as described in Method One at the start of this chapter. After turning the first time, the practitioner repeats the movements and turns again to finish the form facing the direction from which they started. From a (R) Tiger posture the practitioner steps through into (L) Pi Chuan and finishes the form in the manner discussed in chapter 19 of this book

Tiger Form – Method Five Fighting Application:

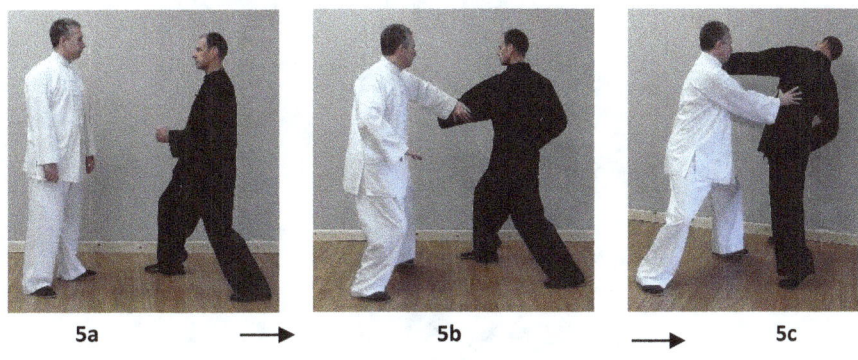

5a → 5b → 5c

(Figure 5a) White faces off with Black in a neutral stance.
(Figure 5b) Black throws a (L) reverse punch to White's Tan Tien. White counters by stepping right, outside Black's attack and blocking with an (L) open palm to the outside of Black's (L) arm and opening his ribs to a counter strike.
(Figure 5c) White continues immediately from the blocking technique to execute a double palm strike to Black's ribs and in time with his half-step uproots Black off his centre to push him away.

Monkey Form

3. Monkey Form – Hou Hsing

Introduction

Grand Master Chiao

Monkey form consists of a series of repeated postures in multiple directions that seek to imitate the features and attributes of this active and intelligent animal. By advancing and retreating with speed and agility the practitioner uses an open hand 'slapping' method combined with agile stepping techniques which serves to draw in and then overwhelm the opponent with speed and aggression in application. The nature of this form is quite complex and requires some flexibility in the waist to turn fully when changing direction, alongside the necessary leg strength to sit into stances and retain balance and stability. Further to this there are some large back stepping movements that can be progressed to jumping movements at the end of each straight-line sequence depending on the agility of the practitioner.

The pattern of Monkey form is set out in the shape of the letter 'T'. The practitioner moves along this 'T' pattern forwards, backwards and sideways repeating the same hand and foot movements and turning both 180 degrees and 90 degrees to replicate the set pattern of the form. Each line of movement, regardless of direction is however practiced in a straight line in accordance with Hsing-I theory. Traditionally the form moves five steps backwards and then five steps forwards in each direction before finishing facing the direction the practitioner started in. However, depending on the size of the practice area the form can be practiced in any odd number of steps appropriate to the space available (e.g. 3, 5, 7, 9 etc.).

Finally, when moving forward or backwards practicing Monkey posture each open hand strike should pass closely, one hand over the top of the other. The attacking/forward hand passes over the top of the defending/retreating had each time. Both palms face the ground throughout these repeated movements. When stepping forwards in Monkey posture it is always the same hand and foot which are forwards and when stepping backwards it is always the opposite hand and foot which are forwards in posture.

Monkey Form

To open the form into (L) Pi Chuan (Figure 23-3.1) use the opening method shown in Chapter 19 previously.

23-3.1 → 23-3.2 → 23-3.3 →

(Figure 23-3.1) Starting from (L) opening Metal posture.

(Figure 23-3.2) The practitioner draws in both the hands as fists towards the chin and at the same time sinks slightly, storing the weight heavily into the rear (R) leg. This posture is often referred to as 'Monkey eats banana' as the practitioner draws in both hands towards his face as if feeding himself.

(Figure 23-3.3) Next, the practitioner transfers his weight forwards into his (L) leg with the forward (L) foot twisting outwards to an angle of 90 degrees and the rear (R) foot lifts its heel with the weight now balanced in the front section of the foot. This is (L) cross stance. At the same time, the upper body turns 180 degrees to the left to look backwards over the left shoulder and at the same time both hands thrust outwards and backwards as fists with the (L) hand punching out to nose height and the rear (R) hand holding position near the (L) elbow. This hand posture is like Metal form.

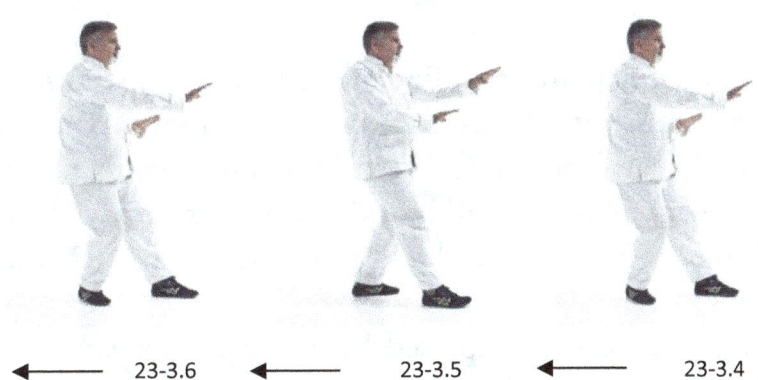

← 23-3.6 ← 23-3.5 ← 23-3.4

(Figure 23-3.4) Next, the (R) foot takes a step backwards behind the (L) foot, using the 'shock step method'. This completes the practitioners 180 degree turn to face the opposite direction from which they started the form. At the same time, the (R) hand strikes forwards directly over the top of the retreating (L) open hand. The (R) hand strikes as a palm strike at solar plexus height and the (L) hand moves backwards to protect the centreline. This is now (L) Monkey posture.

(Figure 23-3.5) Next, the practitioner repeats the same backward shock step on the opposite side. At the same time, the (L) hand strikes out with an open palm slapping method directly over the top of the retreating (R) hand which draws backwards to protect the centreline. This is now (R) Monkey posture.

(Figure 23-3.6) Next, the practitioner repeats the same backward shock step on the opposite side. At the same time, the (R) hand strikes out with an open palm slapping method directly over the top of the retreating (L) hand which draws backwards to protect the centreline. This is now (L) Monkey posture.

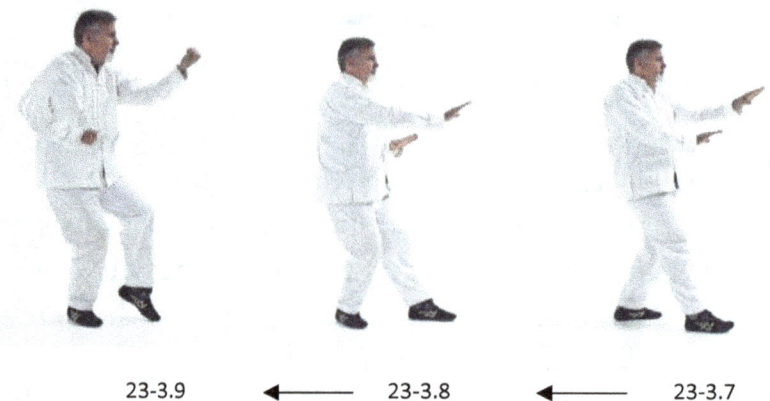

23-3.9 ← 23-3.8 ← 23-3.7

(Figure 23-3.7) Next, the practitioner repeats the same backward 'shock stepping' and open hand striking method described previously in (Figure 23-3.5) This is now (R) Monkey posture.

(Figure 23-3.8) Then the practitioner repeats the same backward 'shock stepping' and open hand striking method described previously in (Figure 23-3.6) This is now (L) Monkey posture.

Note: This completes the first line of five repeated Monkey posture stepping movements.

(Figure 23-3.9) To complete this first line of the form the practitioner next takes a large step/jump backwards with the (R) foot and the (L) foot draws in simultaneously into (L) cat stance. As the practitioner steps back, both hands pull in towards the body as fists with the (L) forward hand blocking across the body at the height of the face using an O/I block. The (R) rear hand pulls back to the (R) hip as a fist with the palm facing upwards.

Note: This large step can be replaced by a jump backwards as the skill level and balance of the practitioner develops however it should be noted that when jumping backwards the head of the practitioner should remain level throughout the movement.

Master James McNeil & Andrew Jackson

23-3.10 → 23-3.11 → 23-3.12 → 23-3.13 → 23-3.14 →

(Figure 23-3.10) Next, the practitioner repeats similar movements but this time in a forward direction. The practitioner steps forwards with the (L) foot and at the same time the (L) hand strikes forwards as a palm strike at solar plexus height and the (R) hand moves forwards from the hip also as an open hand palm strike to protect the centreline. This is now (L) Monkey posture.

Note: The speed of each step and hand movement when moving forwards allows no time for a half-step of the rear foot in this form. The hands and feet move rapidly forward in time with each other as though it were imitating a monkey walking along a tree branch.

(Figure 23-3.11) Next, the practitioner steps forwards with the (R) foot and at the same time the (R) hand strikes forwards as a palm strike at solar plexus height and the (L) hand moves backwards also as an open hand palm strike to protect the centreline. This is now (R) Monkey posture.

(Figures 23-3.12 to 3.14) The practitioner then repeats the forward stepping movements described previously in (Figures 23-3.10 and 3.11) a further three times. This sequence of steps ends with the practitioner in (L) Monkey posture.

Note: This completes the second line of five repeated Monkey posture stepping movements.

23-3.15 → 23-3.16 → 23-3.17

(Figure 23-3.15) From (L) Monkey posture, the practitioner draws in both the hands as fists towards the chin and at the same time sinks slightly storing the weight heavily into the rear (R) leg.

(Figure 23-3.16) Next, the practitioner transfers his weight forwards into his (L) leg with the forward (L) foot twisting outwards to an angle of 90 degrees and the rear (R) foot lifts its heel with the weight now balanced in the front section of the foot. This is (L) cross stance. The upper body turns to the left 180 degrees to look backwards over the left shoulder and at the same time both hands thrust outwards and backwards as fists with the (L) hand punching out to nose height and the rear (R) hand holding position near the (L) elbow. This hand posture is like Metal form. **(Figure 23-3.17)** Next, the (R) foot takes a shock step backwards behind the (L) foot and completes the practitioners 180 degree turn to face the opposite direction. At the same time the (R) hand strikes outwards as a palm strike at solar plexus height and the (L) hand moves backwards also as an open hand palm strike to protect the centreline. This is now (L) Monkey posture.

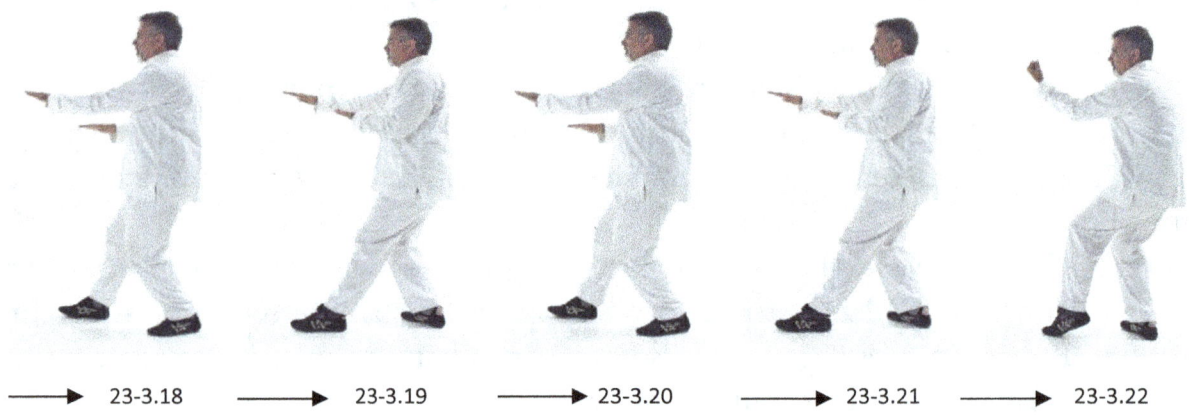

23-3.18   23-3.19   23-3.20   23-3.21   23-3.22

(Figure 23-3.18 to 3.21) Next the practitioner repeats the same backward 'shock stepping' and open hand striking method four times. As described previously in (Figures 23-3.5 and 3.6) This sequence of steps ends with the practitioner in (L) Monkey posture. (Figure 23-3.21).

Note: This completes the third line of five repeated Monkey posture stepping movements.

(Figure 23-3.22) To complete this line of the form the practitioner next takes a large step/jump backwards with the (R) foot and the (L) foot draws in simultaneously into (L) cat stance. As the practitioner steps back, both hands pull in towards the body as fists with the (L) forward hand blocking across the body at the height of the face using an O/I block. The (R) rear hand pulls back to the (R) hip as a fist with the palm facing upwards.

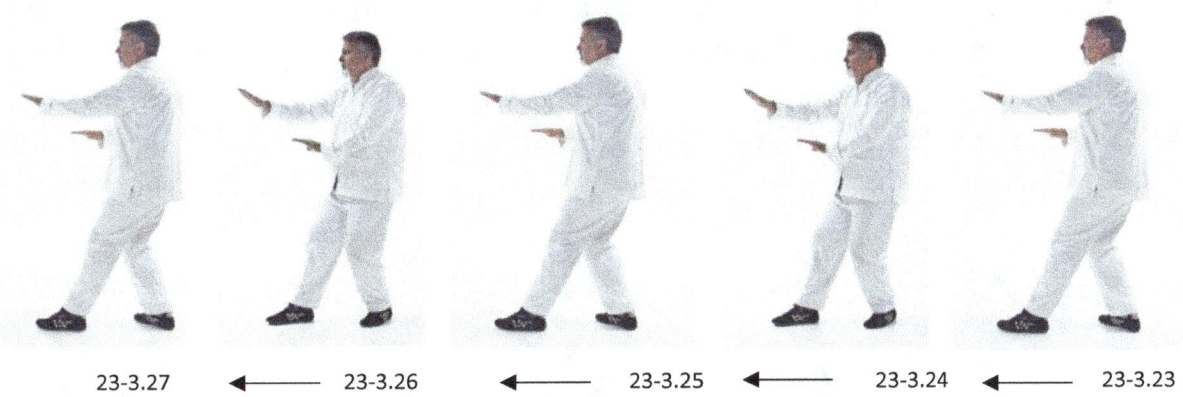

23-3.27 ← 23-3.26 ← 23-3.25 ← 23-3.24 ← 23-3.23

(Figure 23-3.23) Next, the practitioner repeats the same movements but this time in a forward direction. The practitioner steps forwards with the (L) foot and at the same time the (L) hand strikes forwards as a palm strike at solar plexus height and the (R) hand moves forwards also as an open hand palm strike to protect the centreline. This is now (L) Monkey posture.

(Figures 23-3.24 to 3.27) Next the practitioner repeats the same forward stepping and open hand striking method four times. As described previously in (Figures 23-3.10 and 3.11) This sequence of steps ends with the practitioner in (L) Monkey posture. (Figure 23-3.27).

Note: This completes the fourth line of five repeated Monkey posture stepping movements.

23-3.28 → 23-3.29 → 23-3.30 →

(Figure 23-3.28) From (L) Monkey posture, the practitioner draws in both the hands as fists towards the chin and at the same time sinks slightly storing the weight heavily into the rear (R) leg.

(Figure 23-3.29) Next the practitioner holds his weight in his (R) leg and cross over steps 90 degrees to the right with his (L) foot and the rear (R) foot lifts its heel with the weight now balanced in the front section of the foot. This is (L) cross stance. The upper body turns to the left 90 degrees to look backwards over the left shoulder and at the same time both hands thrust outwards and backwards as fists with the (L) hand punching out to nose height and the rear (R) hand holding position near the (L) elbow. This hand posture is like Metal form.

(Figure 23-3.30) Next, the (R) foot takes a step backwards behind the (L) foot and completes the practitioner's 90 degree turn to the side. At the same time, the (R) hand strikes forwards as a palm strike at solar plexus height and the (L) hand moves backwards also as an open hand palm strike to protect the centreline. This is now (L) Monkey posture.

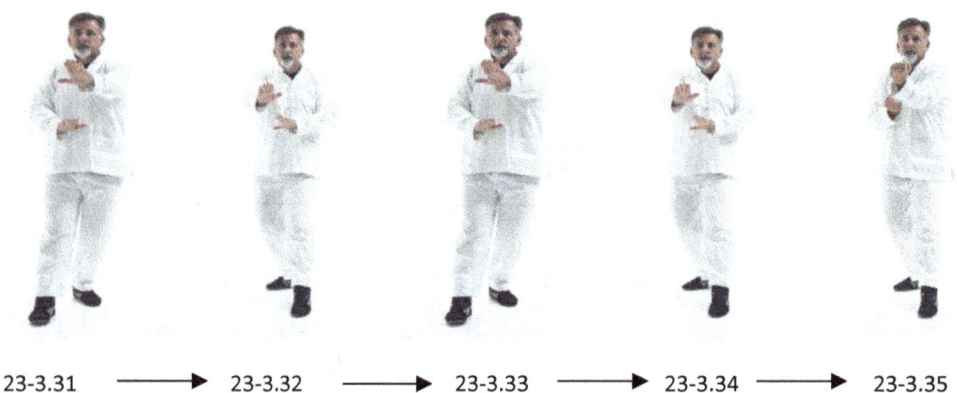

23-3.31 → 23-3.32 → 23-3.33 → 23-3.34 → 23-3.35

(Figures 23-3.31 to 3.34) Next the practitioner repeats the same backward 'shock stepping' and open hand striking method four times. As described previously in (Figures 23-3.5 and 3.6) This sequence of steps ends with the practitioner in (L) Monkey posture. (Figure 23-3.34)

Note: This completes the fifth line of five repeated Monkey posture stepping movements.

(Figure 23-3.35) To complete this line of the form the practitioner next takes a large step/jump backwards with the (R) foot and the (L) foot draws in simultaneously into (L) cat stance. As the practitioner steps back, both hands pull in towards the body as fists with the (L) forward hand blocking across the body at the height of the face using an O/I block. The (R) rear hand pulls back to the (R) hip as a fist with the palm facing upwards.

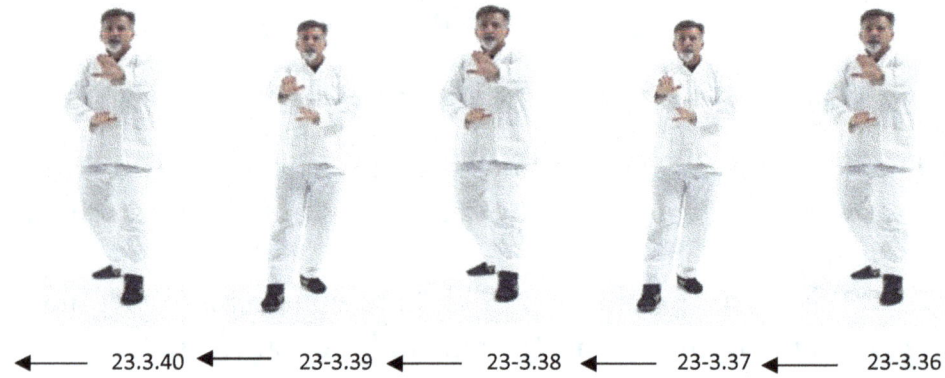

← 23.3.40 ← 23-3.39 ← 23-3.38 ← 23-3.37 ← 23-3.36

(Figure 23-3.36) Next the practitioner repeats the same movements but this time in a forward direction. The practitioner steps forwards with the (L) foot and at the same time the (L) hand strikes forwards as a palm strike at solar plexus height and the (R) hand moves forwards also as an open hand palm strike to protect the centreline. This is now (L) Monkey posture.

(Figures 23-3.37 to 3.40) Next the practitioner repeats the same forward stepping and open hand striking method four times. As described previously in (Figures 23-3.10 and 3.11) This sequence of steps ends with the practitioner in (L) Monkey posture. (Figure 23-3.40)

Note: This completes the sixth line of five repeated Monkey posture stepping movements.

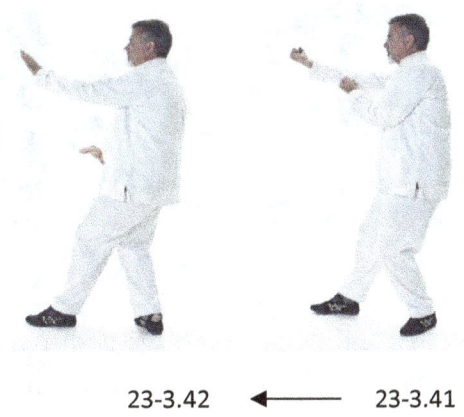

23-3.42 ⟵ 23-3.41

(Figure 23-3.41 and 3.42) To complete the form the practitioner turns 90 degrees to their right and steps forward with the (R) foot and then steps through with their (L) foot, using the half-step method into (L) Metal posture. The practitioner is now facing the same way as they originally started the form. From (L) Metal posture the form can now be finished correctly using the closing method described in Chapter 19 previously.

Monkey Form – Fighting Applications:

Application 1 – Movements 23-3.4 to 3.6

3a ⟶ 3b ⟶ 3c ⟶ 3d

(Figure 3a) White faces off with Black in a neutral stance.
(Figure 3b) Black throws a (R) Wood punch to White's midsection. White counters by blocking the punch using a (R) 'slapping' open palm strike.

(Figure 3c) Before Black can throw a counter strike, White continues immediately by striking again with an open palm along Black's extended (R) upper arm pulling him off balance.

(Figure 3d) White then finishes with a third (R) open palm strike to Black's face.

Application 2 – Movements 23-3.9 to 3.11

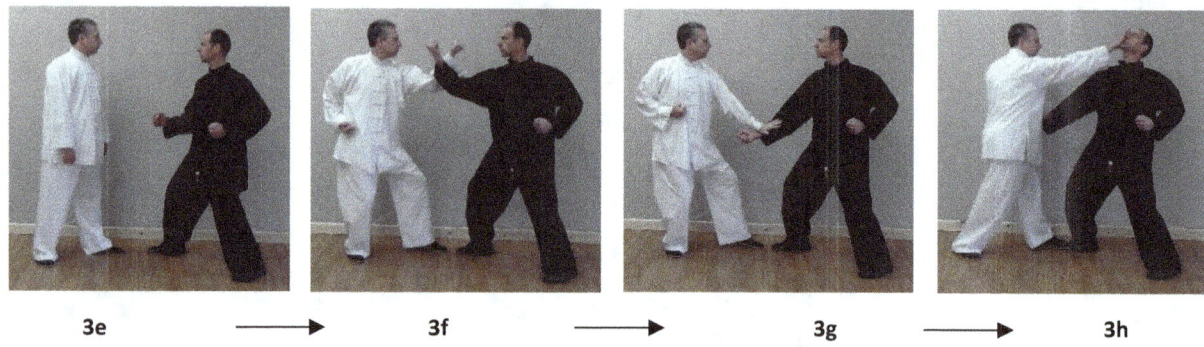

3e → 3f → 3g → 3h

(Figure 3e) White faces off with Black in a neutral stance.

(Figure 3f) Black throws a (R) straight punch to White's face. White counters by stepping back out of range of the attack and blocking the punch using a (L) O/I block.

(Figure 3g) Before Black can throw a counterstrike, White continues immediately by pressing down with an open palm along Black's extended (R) forearm to open up his centreline.

(Figure 3h) White then finishes with a (R) open palm strike to Black's face.

Application 3 – Movements 23-3.15 to 3.17

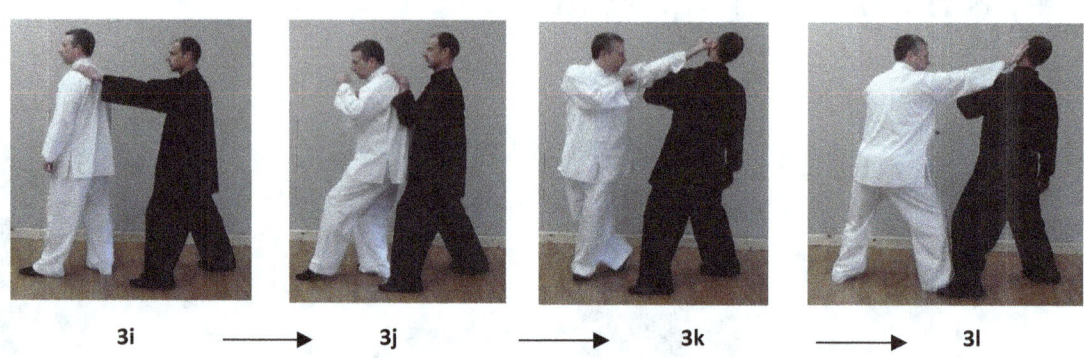

3i → 3j → 3k → 3l

(Figure 3i) Black attacks White from behind by reaching out to grab at White's (L) shoulder.

(Figure 3j) On feeling Black's grab, White quickly draws backwards, closing the distance between his attacker into a defensive posture to protect himself before turning to counter attack.

(Figure 3k) With limited space to counter, Black is forced off balance and White takes advantage by cross stepping to the side and turning his upper body 180 degrees and strikes using (L) Metal punch.

(Figure 3l) White then finishes by turning completely round and stepping forwards into (R) Pi Chuan stance and strikes Black's face with a (R) open palm strike.

Horse Form

4. Horse Form – Ma Hsing

Introduction

Grand Master Chiao

The horse is fast and renowned for its power. As previously stated in chapter 13 of this book this lineage has two different methods of Horse form. One form originates from Master Chiao and the other from Master Hsu. No one method is better than another. The differences between the different methods just allow for a wider variation of fighting applications to be derived from their postures.

The direction for each individual form is to move up and down in a straight line, repeating itself on both left and right sides as it advances. The form then turns 180 degrees and repeats its movements in the opposite direction before turning again to finish facing the direction the practitioner originally started in accordance with traditional Hsing-I practice.

Method One – Master Chiao

Method One Hand Posture

The hand posture for the first method of Horse form discussed below is a double, closed handed posture that resembles a 'horses hoof'. This posture is like a partially closed fist, however, the thumb supports the four flexed fingers underneath the second, third and fourth distal phalanges as shown in the picture opposite.

Horse Form – Method One

To open the form into (L) Pi Chuan (Figure 23-4-1.1) use the opening method shown in Chapter 19 previously.

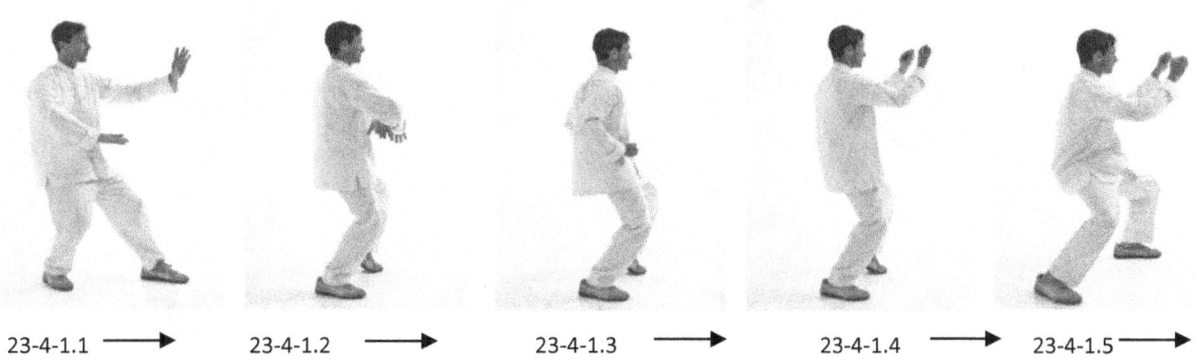

23-4-1.1 → 23-4-1.2 → 23-4-1.3 → 23-4-1.4 → 23-4-1.5 →

(Figure 23-4-1.1) Starting from (L) Pi Chuan posture.

(Figure 23-4-1.2) Step forward with the (R) foot and turn the body to the left at a 45-degree angle and step out forwards with the (L) foot placing it on the ball of the foot into (L) cat stance. At the same time, the practitioner crosses over both arms in front of the body at Tan Tien height with hands above the hips, held open and palms facing down.

(Figure 23-4-1.3) Whilst holding the (L) cat stance, the practitioner then pulls both hands equally apart across the body in a 'tearing' action and closes their hands at their corresponding hips to form the horse fists posture as shown previously. The two arms are then ready to drive upwards and outwards at an angle of 45 degrees to the body at nose height.

(Figure 23-4-1.4) Whilst holding the (L) cat stance, the practitioner then drives the fists upwards and outwards at an angle of 45 degrees to the body at nose height.

(Figure 23-4-1.5) Next the practitioner pushes forward from the back (R) foot and steps forward with the front (L) foot. The back foot follows up using the half-step method into a (L) Pi Chuan stance. At the same time both hands turn to face palms outwards and strike forwards and downwards in perfect timing with the rear foot half-step striking the ground. This is (L) Horse posture.

Note: The downward striking action of the hands in time with the stepping of the feet creates a whole body movement from which the technique derives its power. This striking action is not just executed with arm strength alone. Perfection of this timing is crucial to the effectiveness of the Horse form in any fighting application.

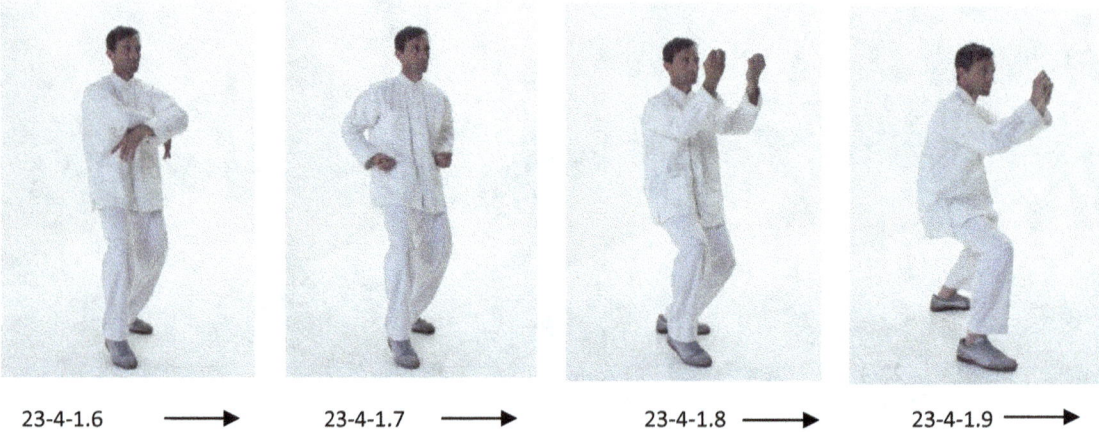

23-4-1.6   23-4-1.7   23-4-1.8   23-4-1.9

(Figures 23-4-1.6 to 1.9) The practitioner then steps forward along the centreline of the form with their (L) foot and turns their body 45 degrees to the right and steps into a (R) cat stance. From this position, they then repeat the same sequence of movements discussed in (Figures 23-4-1.2 to 1.5) previously which finishes with the practitioner in (R) Horse posture. (Figure 23-2-1.9)

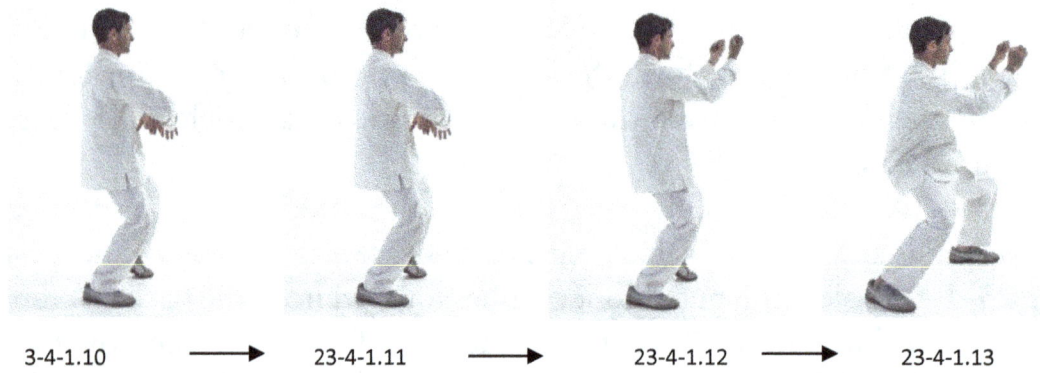

3-4-1.10   23-4-1.11   23-4-1.12   23-4-1.13

(Figures 23-4-1.10 to 1.13) At this point the same sequence of movements can be performed repeatedly forward in a straight line until the practitioner chooses to turn and change direction. Traditionally Hsing-I practitioners turn their forms on the (L) side; however, it is prudent to practise turns on both sides from a fighting application purpose.

23-4-1.16   23-4-1.15   23-4-1.14

(Figure 23-4-1.14) From (L) Horse posture (Figure 23-2-1.13) the (L) front foot is turned inwards in a clockwise direction approximately 45 degrees, the weight is transferred from the (R) foot to the (L) foot and at the same time both arms cross over the body at the height of the Tan Tien with the hands held above the hips.

(Figure 23-4-1.15) The practitioner continues to turn in a clockwise direction a further 180 degrees ending the pivot in (R) cat stance. At the same time both the hands pull equally apart across the body and then drive upwards and outwards at an angle of 45 degrees to nose height.

(Figure 23-4-1.16) Next the practitioner pushes forward from the back (L) foot and steps forward with the front (R) foot. The back foot follows up using the half-step method into a (R) Pi Chuan stance. At the same time both hands turn to face palms outwards and strike forwards and downwards in perfect timing with the rear foot half-step striking the ground. This is (R) Horse posture.

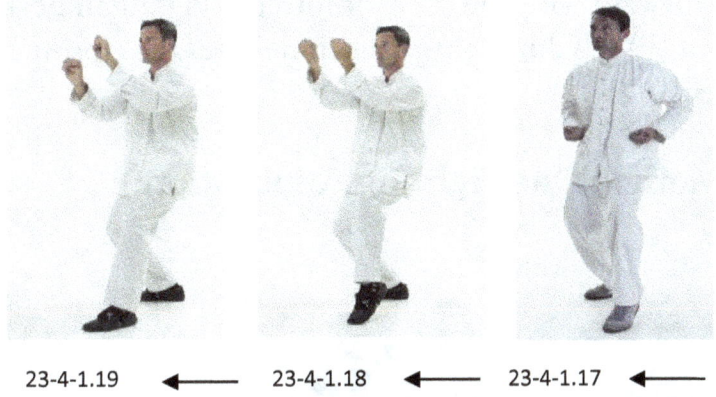

23-4-1.19 ← 23-4-1.18 ← 23-4-1.17 ←

(Figures 23-4-1.17 to 1.19) Continues the sequence stepping forwards into (L) Horse posture ready to turn.

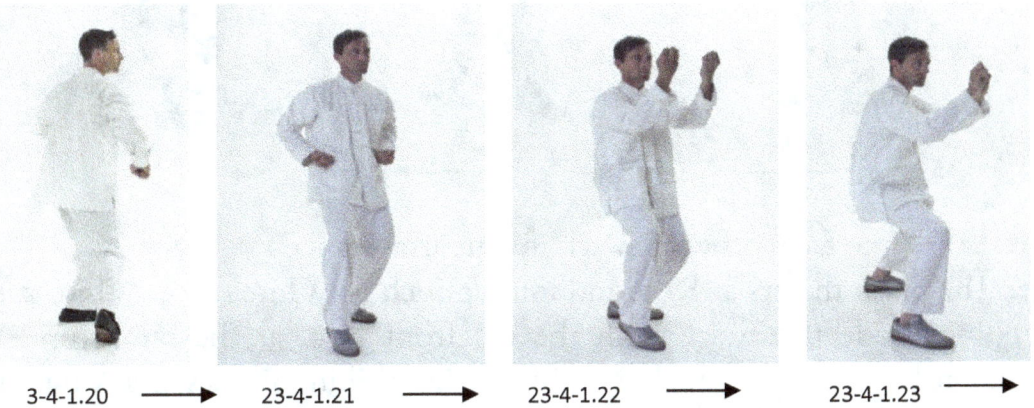

3-4-1.20 → 23-4-1.21 → 23-4-1.22 → 23-4-1.23 →

(Figures 23-4-1.20 to 1.23) Repeats the turn sequence and ends with the practitioner in (R) Horse posture.

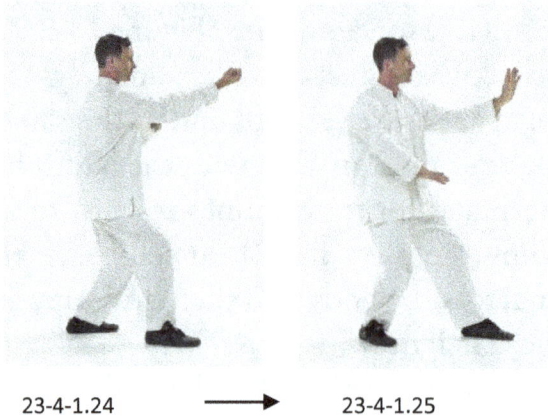

23-4-1.24   →   23-4-1.25

(Figures 23-4-1.24 and 1.25) Next, the practitioner turns to face the original centreline stepping forward with the (R) foot and punching forwards with the (R) fist simultaneously. The (L) fist is held at the (R) elbow as in Pi Chuan and the practitioner steps forward with the (L) foot into (L) Pi Chuan posture. To finish the form correctly from (L) Pi Chuan the practitioner uses the closing method described in Chapter 19 previously.

Horse Form – Method One Fighting Application:

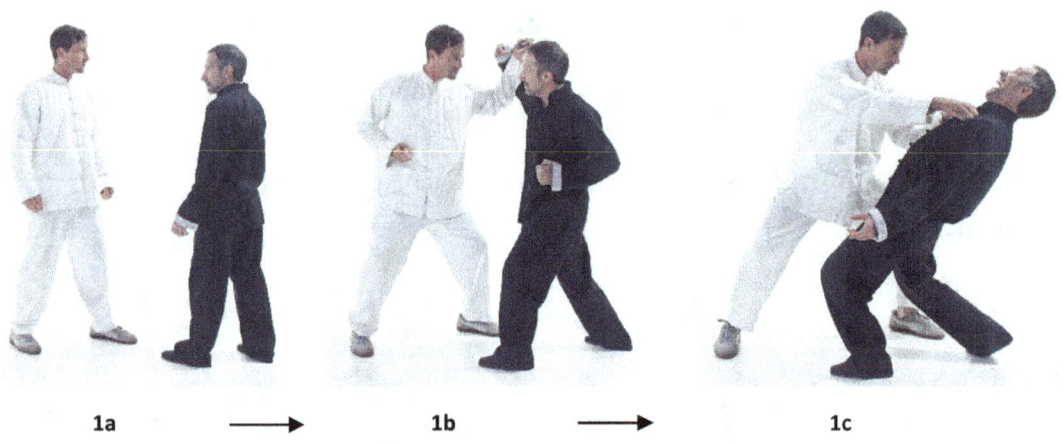

1a   →   1b   →   1c

(Figure 1a) White faces off with Black in a neutral stance.
(Figure 1b) Black throws a (R) roundhouse punch to White's face. White counters by stepping inside the attack with the (L) front foot, at the same time White simultaneously blocks the punch with his (L) fist striking Black's attacking arm.
(Figure 1c) Before Black can counterstrike, White quickly closes the distance by half-stepping forward and striking Black's centreline with a (R) punch forcing Black backwards and off balance.

Method Two – Master Hsu

Horse Form – Method Two

To open the form into (L) Pi Chuan (Figure 23-4-2.1) use the opening method shown in Chapter 19 previously.

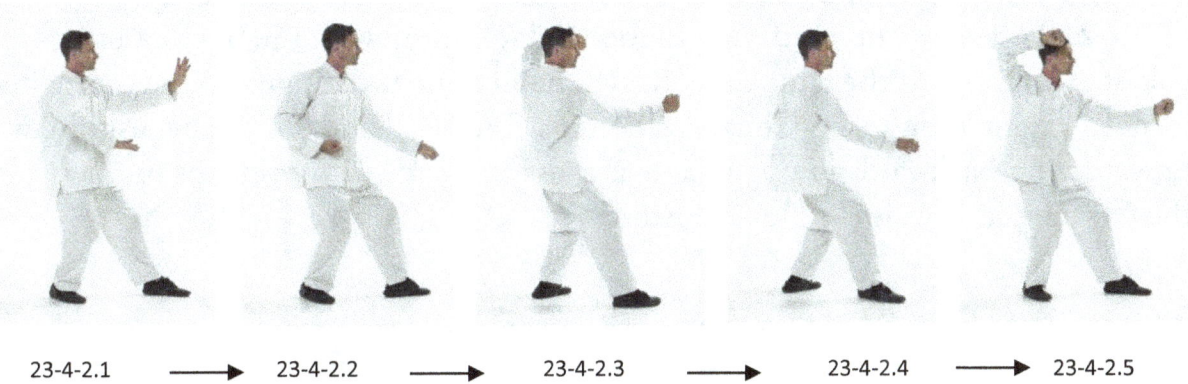

23-4-2.1 → 23-4-2.2 → 23-4-2.3 → 23-4-2.4 → 23-4-2.5

(23-4-2.1) Starting from (L) Pi Chuan posture.

(23-4-2.2) Step forward with the (L) foot at a 45 degree angle and block down to the centreline at Tan Tien level with the (L) hand as a crescent palm block. At the same time, the (R) hand draws back to the (R) hip as a fist facing 'eye' up.

(23-4-2.3) Step forwards with the (R) foot and follow up with the (L) foot using the half-step method. At the same time, the (R) hand punches straight up the centreline to nose height using Peng Chuan technique. The (L) hand simultaneously draws upwards and backwards in opposition as a fist and ends its movement in line with the (L) temple. This is (R) Horse posture.

(23-4-2.4 and 2.5) Movements (figures 23-4-2.4 and 2.5) repeat the sequence of movements (figures 23-4-2.2 and 2.3) on the opposite side. This ends in movement (figure 23-4-2.5) with the practitioner in (L) Horse posture.

Note: At this point the same sequence of movements can be performed repeatedly forward in a straight line until the practitioner chooses to turn and change direction. Traditionally Hsing-I practitioners turn their forms on the (L) side; however, it is prudent to practise turns on both sides from a fighting application purpose.

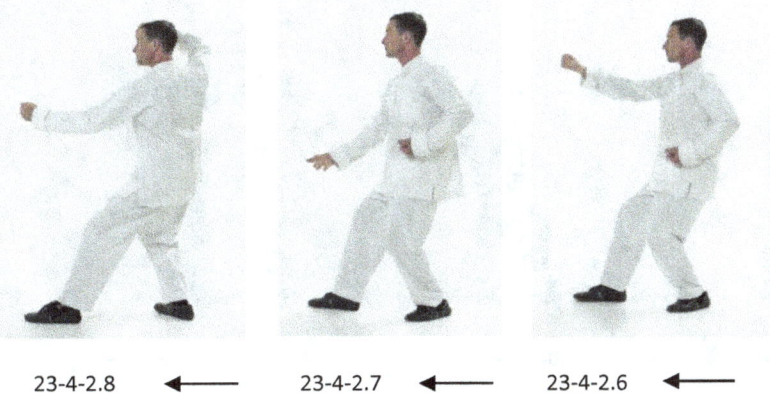

23-4-2.8 ← 23-4-2.7 ← 23-4-2.6 ←

(23-4-2.6) Next, turn 180 degrees into (R) Pi Chuan stance. At the same time, the (R) hand executes a back-fist strike at nose height, whilst the (L) hand pulls back to the (L) hip as a fist facing palm up.

(23-4-2.7) Step forward with the (R) foot at a 45 degree angle and block down to the centreline at Tan Tien level with the (R) hand as a crescent palm block. At the same time, the (L) hand draws back to the (L) hip as a fist facing 'eye' up.

(23-4-2.8) Step forwards with the (L) foot and follow up with the (R) foot using the half-step method. At the same time, the (L) hand punches straight up the centreline to nose height using Peng Chuan technique. The (R) hand simultaneously draws upwards and backwards in opposition as a fist and ends its movement in line with the (R) temple. This is (L) Horse posture.

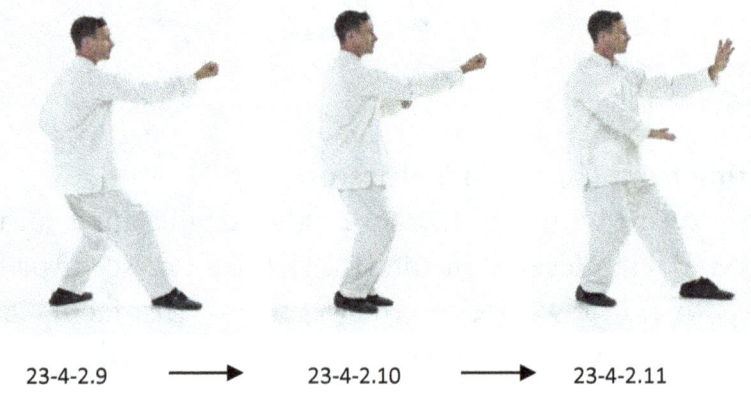

23-4-2.9   →   23-4-2.10   →   23-4-2.11

(23-4-2.9) Next, turn 180 degrees into (R) Pi Chuan stance. At the same time, the (R) hand executes a back-fist strike at nose height, whilst the (L) hand pulls back to the (L) hip as a fist facing palm up.

(Figures 23-4-2.10 and 2.11) Next, the practitioner steps forward with the (R) foot and punching forwards with the (R) fist simultaneously. The (L) fist is held at the (R) elbow as in Pi Chuan and the practitioner steps forward with the (L) foot into (L) Pi Chuan posture. To finish the form correctly from (L) Pi Chuan the practitioner uses the closing method described in Chapter 19 previous.

Horse Form – Method Two Fighting Application:

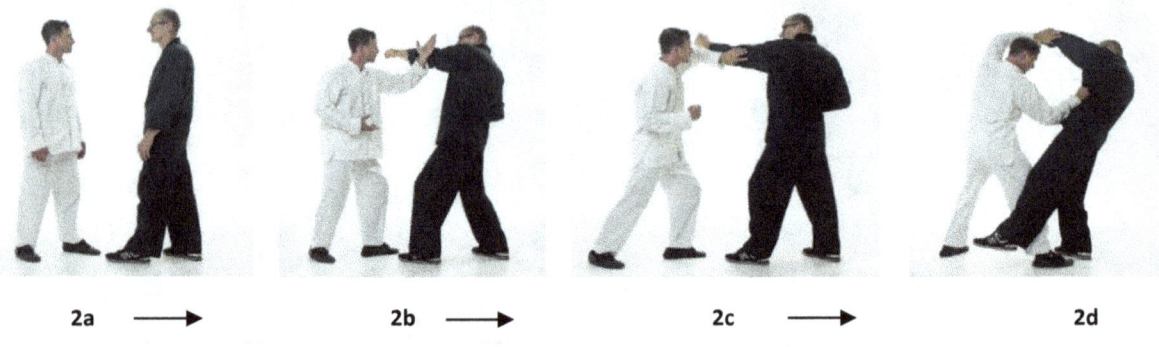

2a   →   2b   →   2c   →   2d

(Figure 2a) White faces off to Black in a neutral stance.
(Figure 2b) Black throws a high (L) straight punch to White's face. White steps to the outside of Black's attack and blocks the punch by cover blocking Black's elbow.
(Figure 2c) White then counters by stepping forwards and redirecting Black's (L) arm across his own centreline making it difficult for Black to counter strike.
(Figure 2d) White then presses Black's arm further away, opening Black's (L) side and delivers a (R) Peng Chuan punch directly into Black's ribs.

Tuo Form

5. Tuo Form – Tuo Hsing

Introduction

Grand Master Chiao

The Tuo (mythical animal) is a powerful animal, especially in the water. When training in this style it is particularly important to coordinate the movement of the upper and lower parts of the body. The whole body is lively and resilient, with the emphasis placed on the turning of the waist, which constitutes the centre of movement for the body.

In application, the sideways stepping pattern of Tuo form allows the practitioner to evade a direct attack and change the angle for counterstrike. Timing and coordination of both the hands and feet are crucial to making this technique effective in application.

The direction of practice for Tuo form is to move forwards in a straight line, repeating itself on both left and right sides as it advances. This form does not turn and repeat itself as with other animal forms. Instead when the practitioner is turned to the left they then step backwards and repeat the movements backwards in the opposite direction before again, stepping forwards to finish the form facing the direction they originally started in.

Note: This forms sequence of pictures has been shown from a head on view as it is the clearest way to show the forms sideways movements.

Tuo Form

To open the form into (L) Pi Chuan (Figure 23-5.1) use the opening method shown in Chapter 19 previously.

23-5.1 → 23-5.2 → 23-5.3 → 23-5.4 →

(Figure 23-5.1) Starting from (L) Pi Chuan posture.

(Figure 23-5.2) Using the hook step method, the practitioner steps forwards and turns the (L) foot outwards in a circular motion, away from their own centreline to an angle of 90 degrees from the starting position. At the same time, the (L) hand rotates to the left facing palm upwards. The (R) hand starts to move towards the (L) elbow from its starting position at the Tan Tien.

(Figure 23-5.3) The (R) foot immediately follows forwards, turning to the side in the same direction to support the (L) foot's advance. As the weight is transferred into the (L) foot the (R) foot comes to rest alongside the left but remains slightly off the ground with the legs pressed lightly together. The body is now turned 90 degrees to the left from the original line of the form. At the same time the (L) hand turns, palm up in time with the body holding its position at head height with the elbow flexed at 45 degrees. The (R) hand comes to rest under the (L) elbow with the palm facing down to the ground. The back is straight and the eyes look forwards in line with the centreline of the body throughout this movement.

(Figure 23-5.4) Next, the (R) foot takes a step forwards and to the right in a circular motion, using the hook step method and the body follows in a 180-degree forward turn. The right hand wipes off along the underside of the (L) forearm, rotating as it moves into an open-handed ridge hand block at face height. At the same time, the (L) hand drops down across the body to protect the centreline with its palm facing down to the ground.

23-5.5 ⟶ 23-5.6 ⟶ 23-5.7

(Figure 23-5.5) The (L) foot immediately follows forwards, turning to the side in the same direction to support the (R) foots advance. As the weight is transferred into the (R) foot the (L) foot comes to rest alongside the left but remains slightly off the ground with the legs pressed lightly together. The body has now turned 180 degrees to the right from the previous movement shown in figure 23-5.3. At the same time the (R) hand turns, palm up in time with the body holding its position at head height with the elbow flexed at 45 degrees. The (L) hand comes to rest under the (R) elbow with the palm facing down to the ground. The back is straight and the eyes look forwards in line with the centreline of the body throughout this movement. This is (R) Tuo posture.

(Figures 23-5.6 and 5.7) Shows the same sequence of movements as figures 23-5.1, 5.2 and 5.3 previous, which leaves the practitioner now turned to their left side. This is (L) Tuo posture.

At this point the same sequence of movements can be performed repeatedly stepping from side to side, whilst moving forward along a straight line until the practitioner chooses to change direction and begin moving backwards along the same straight line they originally came from. Traditionally Hsing-I practitioners turn their forms on the (L) side; however, both sides are repeatedly practiced throughout the form and therefore the practitioner can step backwards or forwards from either side which is useful in application of the form.

← 23-5.11   ← 23-5.10   ← 23-5.9   ← 23-5.8

(Figures 23-5.8 and 5.9) Next from a (L) Tuo posture the practitioner begins to move backwards by taking a step back with the (R) foot and simultaneously turning the body towards the right. The hands follow using the same wiping off method as discussed previously. The (R) hand turns, palm up in time with the body holding its position at head height with the elbow flexed at 45 degrees. The (L) hand comes to rest under the (R) elbow with the palm facing down to the ground. The back is straight and the eyes look forwards in line with the centreline of the body throughout this movement. This is (R) Tuo posture.

(Figures 23-5.10 and 5.11) The practitioner then repeats the same movements on the opposite side, stepping backwards with the (L) foot, turning the body to the left and this time and wiping the arms off to the side. This is now (L) Tuo posture.

23-5.13 ←   23-5.12 ←

(Figures 23-5.12 and 5.13) The practitioner then repeats the same movements on the opposite side, stepping backwards with the (R) foot this time turning the body to the right and wiping the arms off to the side. This is now (R) Tuo posture.

This same sequence of movements can be performed repeatedly stepping from side to side, whilst moving backward along a straight line until the practitioner chooses to change direction and begin moving forwards again.

23-5.14 →   23-5.15 →   23-5.16 →   23-5.17

(Figures 23-5.14 and 5.15) From the (R) Tuo posture shown in figure 23-5.13 previous the practitioner can now change direction and begin to move forwards using the same method discussed previously into (L) Tuo posture.

(Figures 23-5.16 and 5.17) From (L) Tuo posture the form can now be finished correctly by stepping forwards into (L) Pi Chuan posture and using the closing method described in Chapter 19 previous.

Tuo Form Fighting Application:

(Figure 5a) White faces off with Black in a neutral stance.

(Figure 5b) Black throws a (L) roundhouse punch to White's face. White counters by blocking the punch using a (L) O/I ridge hand block.

(Figure 5c) White continues immediately from the blocking technique by using his (R) hand to wipe off Black's attacking (L) arm to the outside.

(Figure 5d) Black attempts to counterstrike with a (R) roundhouse punch to White's head but White covers this with a (L) knife hand block.

(Figure 5e) White continues immediately counters Black by stepping into his centreline and striking his collar bone with a (R) knife hand strike and finishes attack by taking Black to the ground.

Cock Form

6. Cock Form – Gi Hsing

Introduction

Grand Master Chiao

Cock form consists of a combined series of movements that seek to imitate the features and attributes of this lively and aggressive bird. By advancing and retreating with speed and agility the practitioner uses a wide variety of both hand, foot and stepping techniques which serves to confuse the opponent in application.

This forms movements are more varied than some of the other animal forms and although it does follows the same straight-line movement pattern, however its different postures are not repeated in both directions. The direction for Cock form is to move up in a straight line. The form then turns 180 degrees and moves back in the opposite direction before turning 180 degrees again to finish facing the direction the practitioner originally started in accordance with traditional Hsing-I practice.

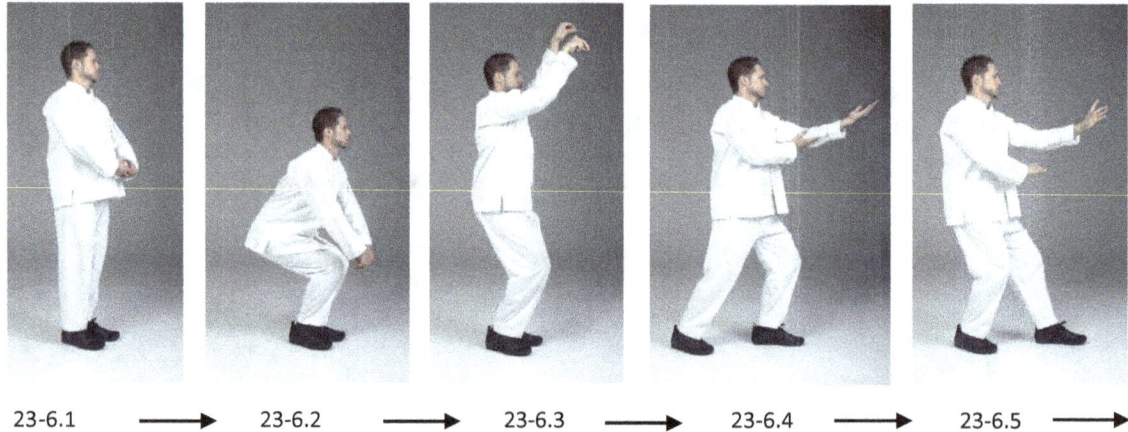

23-6.1 → 23-6.2 → 23-6.3 → 23-6.4 → 23-6.5 →

Note: Cock form starts from its own unique opening posture.

(Figure 23-6.1) Starting from (L) opening posture, the hands are held symmetrically as cranes beaks with palms facing up at the height of the Tan Tien. The front foot faces forwards and the back foot is places at 45 degrees with the heels touching.

(Figure 23-6.2) The practitioner bends at the knees and drops the body towards the ground until both hands are at the level of the knees. As the hands lower in a circular motion, they both turn over as cranes beaks with the palms now facing the ground. The feet remain static and the head and eyes look straight ahead.

(Figure 23-6.3) Next, stand back up with the feet remaining in the same static position. Both hands raise together above the head with hands remaining held in cranes beak postures.

(Figure 23-6.4) Both hands drop down the front centreline of the body to the height of the Tan Tien and then the hands open into spear hand postures with palms facing upwards.

Step forwards with the (L) foot into (L) bow stance and at the same time the (L) spear hand strikes straight out to throat height followed closely by the (R) spear hand which is kept close to the (L) elbow.

(Figure 23-6.5) To complete the opening sequence the practitioner then transfers their weight back into the rear (L) leg as in (L) Pi Chuan stance. Both spear hands turn over to face palms down with the rear (R) hand moving to the centreline to protect the Tan Tien. This is now (L) Pi Chuan posture.

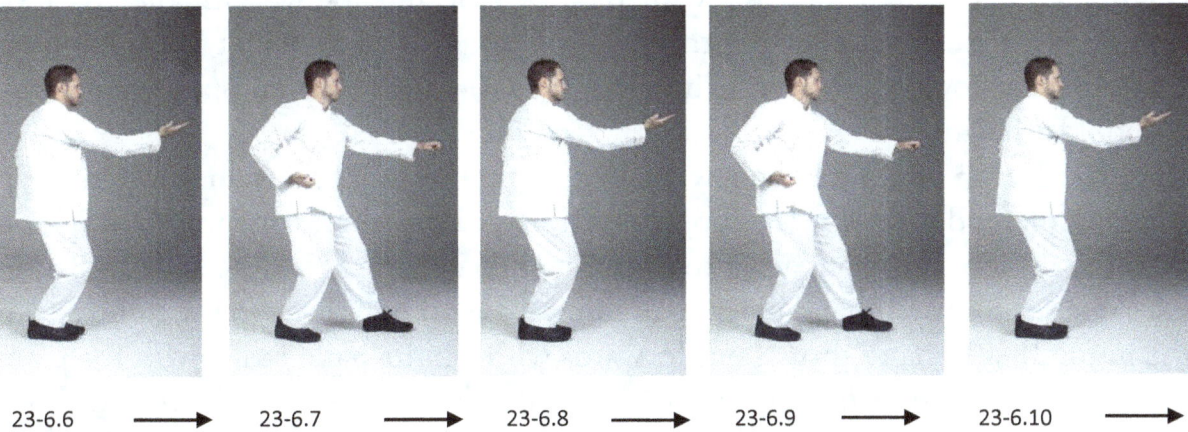

23-6.6 ➔ 23-6.7 ➔ 23-6.8 ➔ 23-6.9 ➔ 23-6.10 ➔

(Figure 23-6.6) From (L) Pi Chuan the (R) hand forms a spear hand posture and then strikes straight out approximately to the height of the Tan Tien/bladder. Simultaneously, the (L) hand forms a fist and pulls back to the (L) side of the waist, palm up. As the (R) hand strikes, the (L) foot takes a step forward followed closely by the (R) foot which steps forward, alongside the (L) foot, ending tight alongside the instep, about one inch behind the left toe. This foot position is the same as 'closed' Wood only the hands have a different posture.

(Figure 23-6.7) Next, the (L) hand forms a leopard fist posture and strikes out toward the centreline of the body at the solar plexus and passes by the (R) arm, which is simultaneously drawing back to the (R) side of the waist as a fist, palm up. At the same time, the (L) foot moves out and the (R) foot follows using the half-step method. This foot position is the same as 'open' Wood only the hands have different postures.

(Figures 23-6.8 to 6.11) Repeats twice, the sequence of (figures 23-6.6 and 6.7) above.

23-6.11 → 23-6.12 → 23-6.13 → 23-6.14 → 23-6.15

(Figure 23-6.12) Step forwards with the (L) foot and follow with the (R) foot using the half-step method. Punch straight forward at face height with (L) Peng Chuan whilst covering the centreline with the (R) hand using an open palm block at shoulder height.

(Figure 23-6.13 and 6.14) Follow on by stepping forward using the close the gap stepping method. The rear (R) foot moves forward up to the forward (L) foot and then the (L) foot, steps out again to open the stance back to (L) Pi Chuan again. At the same time, the (R) hand blocks palm upwards and pulls back to the right side of the head. The (L) hand thrusts out forwards with a knife hand strike with the palm facing down aimed at mid-rib height. Both hands and feet must start and finish their movements together.

(Figure 23-6.15) Next, the feet remain static while the (R) hand forms a fist and executes an O/I block across the centreline coming to rest with the (R) fist in line with the (L) shoulder opposite. The (L) hand also forms a fist and pulls back to the (L) hip with palm facing upwards.

← 23-6.19 ← 23-6.18 ← 23-6.17 ← 23-6.16

(Figure 23-6.16) The practitioner then turns 180 degrees on the spot with both feet turned to opposing 45-degree angles. As the body turns the (R) arm drops down towards the (L) opposite hip and the (L) hand executes a O/I block across the centreline at head height. This combined turning movement causes the arms to become tightly coiled across the body like a spring waiting to recoil.

(Figure 23-6.17) Next the weight transfers from the (L) foot into the forward (R) foot and the practitioner executes a (L) 45-degree kick (rising) at knee height. Both arms simultaneously explode diagonally outwards with the (R) hand striking upwards to head height in a cranes beak hand posture and the (L) hand striking out to the side at hip height also as a cranes beak hand posture.

(Figure 23-6.18) As the (L) kicking foot lands on the ground the weight is transferred into it and the practitioner drops straight down into a low cross sitting stance. The (L) hand covers across the centreline at face height as an open palm block and the (R) hand strikes straight down towards the ground in a finger thrust hand posture.

(Figure 23-6.19) From the previous low cross sitting position the practitioner explodes upwards changing feet in mid-air so as the (R) foot becomes the forward foot with the weight evenly balanced between both legs on landing as a (R) bow stance. Again, both hands strike outwards as cranes beak hand postures with the (R) hand reaching head height and the (L) hand striking out to hip height on their respective sides.

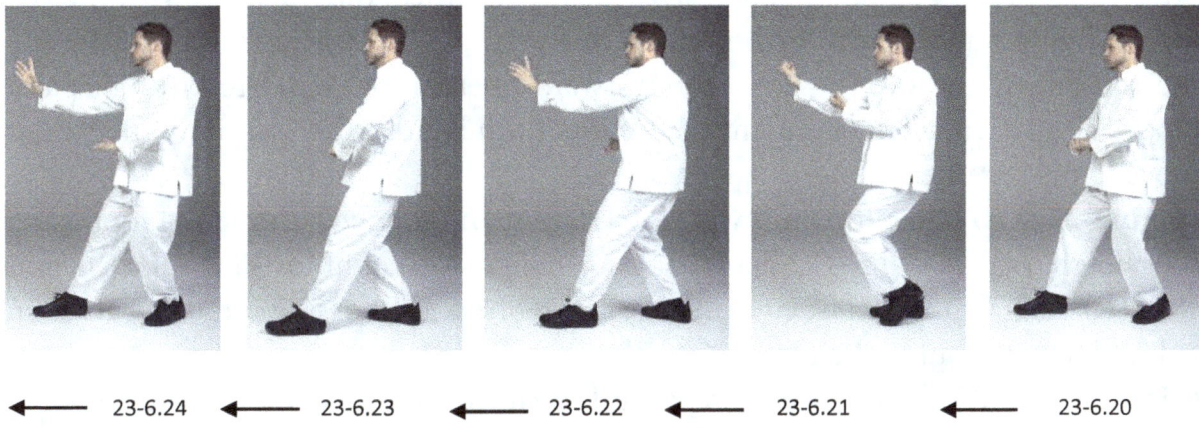

← 23-6.24   ← 23-6.23   ← 23-6.22   ← 23-6.21   ← 23-6.20

(Figure 23-6.20) Next, draw in the both hands to Tan Tien height as fists facing palm down.

(Figure 23-6.21) Step forwards with the (R) foot and at the same time the (R) fist punches straight out to nose height followed closely by the (L) fist which is kept close to the (R) elbow.

(Figure 23-6.22) Step through with the (L) foot and follow up with the (R) foot using the half-step method. At the same time as stepping execute a (L) punch straight up to nose height (not shown) following the line of the previous (R) punch and as soon as the (L) punch reaches its full extension open the hands dropping the (R) hand down to the midsection, protecting the Tan Tien and the (L) hand chops forward and down the centreline in a splitting action. At the end of this sequence the practitioner should now be in (L) Pi Chuan posture.

(Figures 23-6.23 and 6.24) Repeats the same sequence as (figures 23-6.20 to 6.22) on the opposite side returning the practitioner to (R) Pi Chuan posture.

23-6.29 ← 23-6.28 ← 23-6.27 ← 23-6.26 ← 23-6.25

(Figure 23-6.25) Next, the (R) foot is drawn back into (R) cat stance and at the same time the (R) fist circle blocks low from outside to inside to protect the centreline at Tan Tien level. The (L) fist remains at the (L) hip throughout.

(Figure 23-6.26) Both feet then rapidly exchange positions using the chicken step method. The head stays level throughout this change of stance. The practitioner is now in (L) cat stance. Simultaneously with the feet the hands change, with the (R) fist circling around as if to grab with an open hand and the drawing in to the (R) hip as a fist again. The (L) fist comes forward opening the hand to crescent palm block at Tan Tien height along the centreline. Both hands must start and finish their movements together.

(Figure 23-6.27) Step forwards with the (L) foot and follow with the (R) foot using the half-step method into (L) Pi Chuan stance. Punch straight forward at face height with (R) Peng Chuan whilst covering the centreline with the (L) hand using an open palm block at shoulder height.

(Figure 23-6.28) Follow on by stepping forward using the close the gap stepping method. The rear (R) foot moves forward up to the forward (L) foot and then the (L) foot, steps out again to open the stance back to (L) Pi Chuan again. At the same time, the (R) hand blocks palm upwards and pulls back to the right side of the head. The (L) hand thrusts out forwards with a knife hand strike with the palm facing down aimed at mid-rib height. Both hands and feet must start and finish their movements together.

(Figure 23-6.29) Next the feet remain static whilst the (R) hand forms a fist and executes an O/I block across the centreline coming to rest with the (R) fist in line with the (L) shoulder opposite. The (L) hand also forms a fist and pulls back to the (L) hip with palm facing upwards.

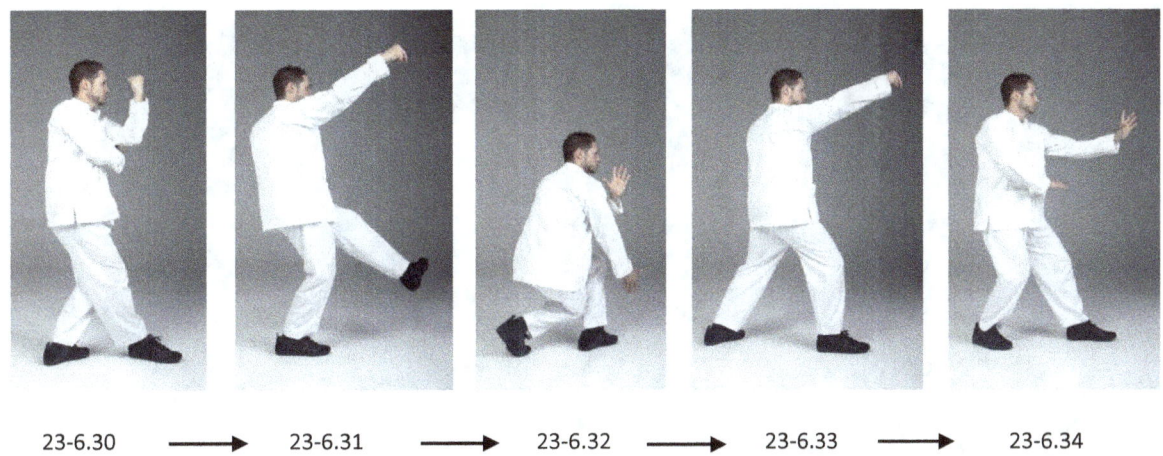

23-6.30 → 23-6.31 → 23-6.32 → 23-6.33 → 23-6.34

(Figure 23-6.30) The practitioner then turns 180 degrees on the spot with both feet turned to opposing 45-degree angles. As the body turns the (R) arm drops down towards the (L) opposite hip and the (L) hand executes a O/I block across the centreline at head height. This combined turning movement causes the arms to become tightly coiled across the body like a spring waiting to recoil.

(Figure 23-6.31) Next the weight transfers from the (L) foot into the forward (R) foot and the practitioner executes a (L) 45-degree kick (rising) at knee height. Both arms simultaneously explode diagonally outwards with the (R) hand striking upwards to head height in a cranes beak hand posture and the (L) hand striking out to the side at hip height also as a cranes beak hand posture.

(Figure 23-6.32) As the (L) kicking foot lands on the ground the weight is transferred into it and the practitioner drops straight down into a low cross sitting stance. The (L) hand covers across the centreline at face height as an open palm block and the (R) hand strikes straight down towards the ground in a finger thrust hand posture.

(Figure 23-6.33) From the previous low cross sitting position the practitioner explodes upwards changing feet in mid-air so as the (R) foot becomes the forward foot with the weight evenly balanced between both legs on landing as a (R) bow stance. Again, both hands strike outwards as cranes beak hand postures with the (R) hand reaching head height and the (L) hand striking out to hip height on their respective sides.

(Figure 23-6.34) Next, draw in the both hands to Tan Tien height as fists facing palm down. Step forwards with the (R) foot and at the same time the (R) fist punches straight out to nose height followed closely by the (L) fist which is kept close to the (R) elbow. [Not shown (see figures 23-6.20 and 6.21 previous).] Step through with the (L) foot and follow up with the (R) foot using the half-step method. At the same time as stepping execute a (L) punch straight up to nose height (not shown) following the line of the previous (R) punch and as soon as the (L) punch reaches its full extension open the hands dropping the (R) hand down to the midsection, protecting the Tan Tien and the (L) hand chops forward and down the centreline in a splitting action. At the end of this sequence the practitioner should now be in (L) Pi Chuan posture.

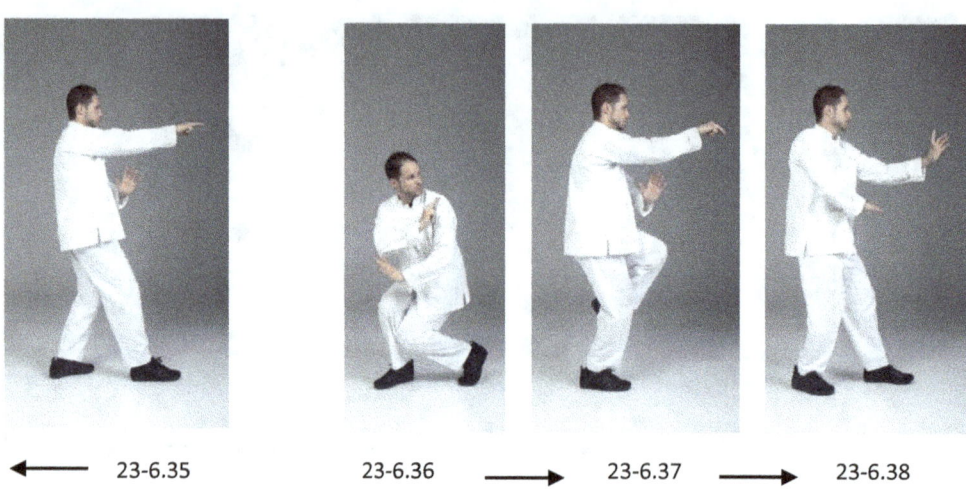

← 23-6.35   23-6.36 →   23-6.37 →   23-6.38

(Figure 23-6.35) From the previous (L) Pi Chuan posture slide the (L) foot backwards using the shock step method. At the same time, the (L) hand blocks down the centreline as an open palm facing downwards to Tan Tien height. Simultaneously the (R) hand strikes upwards and out along the centreline to the height of the eyes using the sword finger hand technique with the palm facing downwards. This is (R) Cock form.

(Figure 23-6.36) Next, hook sweep around with the forward (R) foot and turn 360 degrees to the left in a counter clockwise direction. As the body turns, both knees flex lowering the height of the practitioner like a 'cork screw' into the ground. At the same time as sweeping the (R) hand, ridge hand blocks at face height across the centreline, coming to rest firmly against the (L) shoulder. The (L) hand remains protecting the Tan Tien throughout.

(Figure 23-6.37) From the lowered position in movement (figure 23-6.36) the practitioner stands straight up on the (R) leg into (R) single leg stance. The (L) hand guards the Tan Tien and centreline, whilst the (R) hand thrusts straight out to the height of the throat using the sword finger hand technique with the palm facing downwards.

(Figure 23-6.38) Next, step forwards with the (L) foot and follow with the (R) foot using the half-step method. At the same time, the (R) hand pulls down to an open palm at Tan Tien level and the (L) hand chops forward and down the centreline in a splitting action. At the end of this sequence the practitioner should now be in (L) Pi Chuan posture.

Note: To finish the form correctly the practitioner uses the closing method described in Chapter 19 of this book.

Cock Form Fighting Applications:

Application 1 – Movements 23-6.1 to 6.3

6a → 6b → 6c

(Figure 6a) White faces off with Black in a neutral stance.
(Figure 6b) Black throws a (R) straight punch to White's ribs. White counters by blocking the punch using a (L) I/O cranes beak block.
(Figure 6c) White continues immediately from the blocking technique by using his (R) hand to cover block Black's attacking (R) arm and counter strikes along the centreline with a (L) cranes beak strike to the underside of Black's jaw.

Application 2 – Movement 23-6.6

6d → 6e → 6f

(Figure 6d) White faces off with Black in a neutral stance.
(Figure 6e) Black throws a (L) straight punch to White's ribs. White counters by blocking the punch using a (L) O/I covering palm block.
(Figure 6f) White continues immediately from the blocking technique, striking Black under the armpit using a (R) spear hand strike.

Application 3 – Movement 23-6.7

6g → 6h → 6i

(Figure 6g) White faces off with Black in a neutral stance.
(Figure 6h) Black throws a (R) straight punch to White's ribs. White counters by blocking the punch using a (L) O/I covering palm block.
(Figure 6i) White continues immediately from the blocking technique by using his (R) hand to strike Black's throat with a leopard fist technique.

Application 4 – Movements 23-6.35 to 6.38

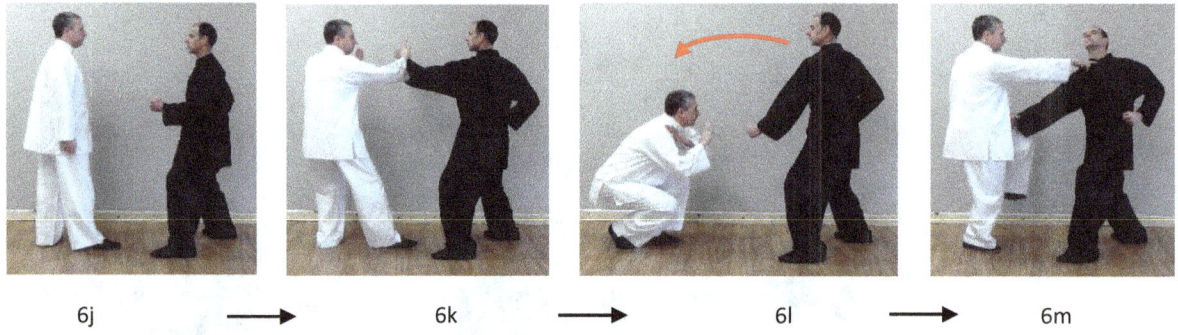

6j → 6k → 6l → 6m

(Figure 6j) White faces off with Black in a neutral stance.
(Figure 6k) Black throws a (L) straight punch to White's face. White counters by blocking the punch using a (R) O/I ridge hand block.
(Figure 6l) To avoid a (R) roundhouse punch, counter strike, White continues immediately from the blocking technique by dropping underneath the attack.
(Figure 6m) White then springs upwards, covering the spent roundhouse punch with his (L) open palm and strikes forwards with a (R) sword finger strike to Black's throat.

Phoenix Form

7. Phoenix Form- Tai Hsing

Introduction

Master McNeil

The phoenix is a bird of mythical legend, considered to be strong and powerful, rising upwards and capable of destroying all in its way with its mighty wings. When the phoenix flaps its wings, this emphasises its form and intention. The Phoenix form in this lineage of Hsing-I seeks to imitate the flapping technique with the arms and fists.

As previously stated in Chapter 13 this lineage has two different methods of Phoenix form. The first method to be discussed originates from Master Chiao's lineage and will be referred to as Method One in this chapter. The second method originates from Master Hsu and will be referred to as Method Two. No one method is better than another. The differences between the different methods just allow for a wider variation of fighting applications to be derived from their postures.

The direction for each individual form is to move up and down in a straight line, repeating itself on both left and right sides as it advances. The form then turns 180 degrees and repeats its movements in the opposite direction before turning again to finish facing the direction the practitioner originally started in accordance with traditional Hsing-I practice.

Phoenix Form – Method One (Master Chiao)

To open the form into (L) Pi Chuan (Figure 23-7-1.1) use the opening method shown in Chapter 19 previously.

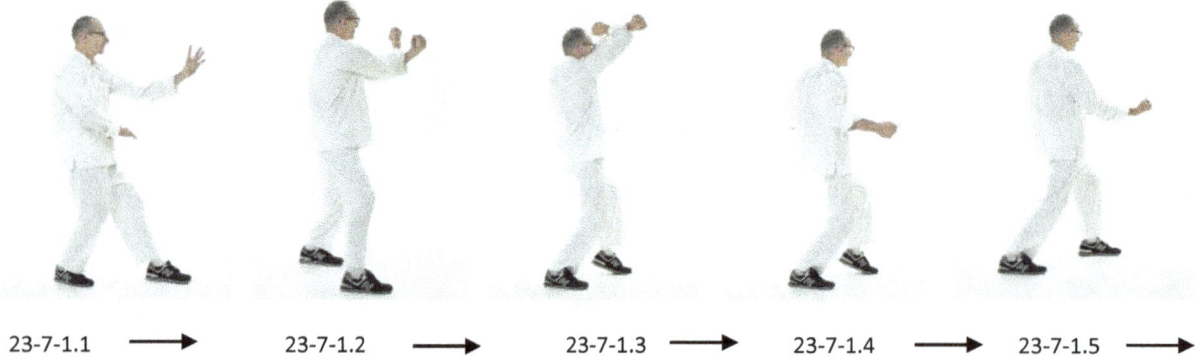

23-7-1.1 → 23-7-1.2 → 23-7-1.3 → 23-7-1.4 → 23-7-1.5 →

(Figure 23-7-1.1) Starting from (L) Pi Chuan posture.
(Figure 23-7-1.2) The practitioner steps forward with the (R) foot and crosses both arms in front of the body with hands held as fists at the height of the face.

Note: Make sure the crossed hands do not block the line of vision.

(Figure 23-7-1.3) Next, turn the body to the left at a 45-degree angle and step out forwards with the (L) foot placing it on the ball of the foot into (L) cat stance. At the same time both arms rise symmetrically upwards above head and in front of the body with both hands held as fists.

(Figure 23-7-1.4) Whilst holding the (L) cat stance, the practitioner then circles both hands downwards at the sides of the body.

(Figure 23-7-1.5) Next the practitioner pushes forward from the back (R) foot and steps forward with the front (L) foot. The back foot follows up using the half-step method into a (L) Pi Chuan stance. At the same time, both arms then drive upwards and outwards at an angle of 45 degrees to the body resembling to a double-handed uppercut strike to rib height. This is (L) Phoenix posture.

Note: The downward circling action of the hands in time with the stepping of the feet creates a whole body movement from which the technique derives its power. This circling action is not just executed with arm strength alone. Perfection of this timing is crucial to the effectiveness of all the Phoenix form method in any fighting application.

23-7-1.6 → 23-7-1.7 → 23-7-1.8 →

(Figure 23-7-1.6) The practitioner then steps forward along the straight line direction of the form with their (L) foot and turns the body to the right at a 45-degree angle and step out forwards with the (R) foot placing it on the ball of the foot into (R) cat stance. At the same time both arms rise symmetrically upwards above head and in front of the body with both hands held as fists.

(Figure 23-7-1.7) Next, whilst holding the (R) cat stance, the practitioner then circles both hands downwards as fists at the sides of the body.

(Figure 23-7-1.8) Next the practitioner pushes forward from the back (L) foot and steps forward with the front (R) foot. The back foot follows up using the half-step method into a (R) Pi Chuan stance. At the same time, both arms then drive upwards and outwards at an angle of 45 degrees to the body resembling to a double-handed uppercut strike to rib height. This is (R) Phoenix posture.

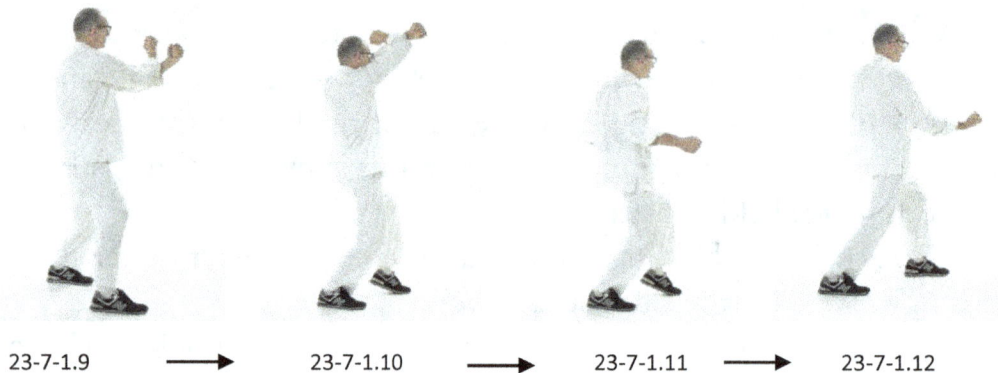

23-7-1.9 → 23-7-1.10 → 23-7-1.11 → 23-7-1.12

(Figures 23-7-1.9 to 1.12) The practitioner then steps forward along the straight line direction of the form with their (R) foot and turns their body 45 degrees to the left and steps into a (L) cat stance. From this position, they then repeat the same sequence of movements discussed in (Figures 23-7-1.2 to 1.5) previously which finishes with the practitioner in (L) Phoenix posture. (Figure 23-2-1.12)

Note: At this point the same sequence of movements can be performed repeatedly forward in a straight line until the practitioner chooses to turn and change direction. Traditionally Hsing-I practitioners turn their forms on the (L) side; however, it is prudent to practice turns on both sides from a fighting application purpose.

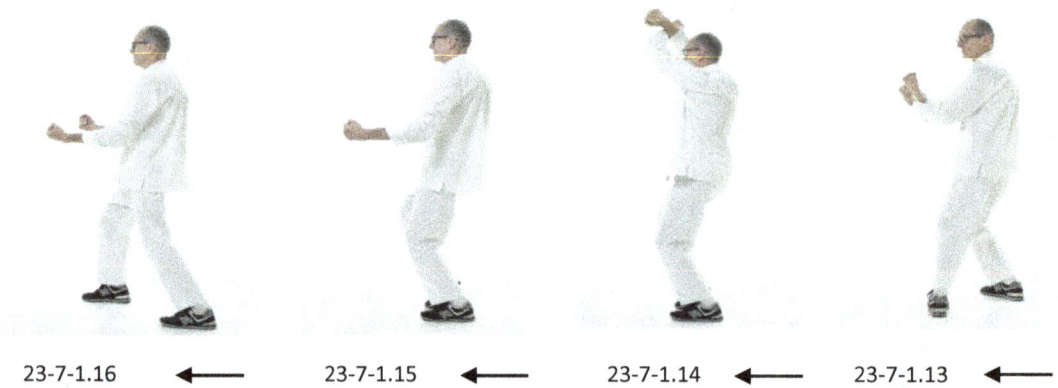

23-7-1.16 ← 23-7-1.15 ← 23-7-1.14 ← 23-7-1.13 ←

(Figure 23-7-1.13) From (L) Phoenix posture (figure 23-7-1.12) the (L) front foot is turned inwards in a clockwise direction approximately 45 degrees, the weight is transferred from the (R) foot to the (L) foot and at the same time both arms cross over in front of the body with hands held as fists at the height of the face.

(Figure 23-7-1.14) The practitioner continues to turn in a clockwise direction a further 180 degrees ending the pivot in (R) cat stance. At the same time both arms rise symmetrically upwards above head and in front of the body with both hands held as fists.

(Figure 23-7-1.15) Whilst remaining in a (R) cat stance, the practitioner then circles both hands downwards as fists at the sides of the body.

(Figure 23-7-1.16) Next the practitioner pushes forward from the back (L) foot and steps forward with the front (R) foot. The back foot follows up using the half-step method into a (R) Pi Chuan stance. At the same time, both arms then drive upwards and outwards at an angle of 45 degrees to the body resembling to a double-handed uppercut strike to rib height. This is (R) Phoenix posture.

23-7-1.20 ← 23-7-1.19 ← 23-7-1.18 ← 23-7-1.17 ←

(Figures 23-7-1.17 to 1.20) The practitioner then steps forward along the straight line of the form with their (R) foot and turns their body 45 degrees to the left and steps into a (L) cat stance. From this position, they then repeat the same sequence of movements discussed in (Figures 23-7-1.2 to 1.5) previously which finishes with the practitioner in (L) Phoenix posture. (Figure 23-7-1.20)

Note: At this point the same sequence of movements can be performed repeatedly forward in a straight line until the practitioner chooses to turn and change direction.

23-7-1.21 → 23-7-1.22 → 23-7-1.23 → 23-7-1.24 →

(Figure 23-7-1.21) From (L) Phoenix posture (figure 23-7-1.20) the (L) front foot is turned inwards in a clockwise direction approximately 45 degrees, the weight is transferred from the (R) foot to the (L) foot and at the same time both arms cross over in front of the body with hands held as fists at the height of the face.

(Figure 23-7-1.22) The practitioner continues to turn in a clockwise direction a further 180 degrees ending the pivot in (R) cat stance. At the same time both arms rise symmetrically upwards above head and in front of the body with both hands held as fists.

(Figure 23-7-1.23) Whilst remaining in a (R) cat stance, the practitioner then circles both hands downwards as fists at the sides of the body.

(Figure 23-7-1.24) Next the practitioner pushes forward from the back (L) foot and steps forward with the front (R) foot. The back foot follows up using the half-step method into a (R) Pi Chuan stance. At the same time, both arms then drive upwards and outwards at an angle of 45 degrees to the body resembling to a double-handed uppercut strike to rib height. This is (R) Phoenix posture.

23-7-1.25 ⟶ 23-7-1.26

(Figures 23-7-1.25 and 1.26) Next, the practitioner turns inwards to face the original straight line direction of the form, stepping forward with the (R) foot and punching forwards with the (R) fist simultaneously. The (L) fist is held at the (R) elbow as in Pi Chuan and the practitioner steps forward with the (L) foot into (L) Pi Chuan posture. To finish the form correctly from (L) Pi Chuan the practitioner uses the closing method described in Chapter 19 previously.

Phoenix Form – Method One Fighting Application – Movements 23-7-1.4 to 1.5

1a ⟶ 1b ⟶ 1c

(Figure 1a) White faces off with Black in a neutral stance.

(Figure 1b) Black steps in and throws a (L) straight punch to White's face. White counters by stepping to the outside of Black's attack with the (L) rear foot into cat stance and at the same time White simultaneously blocks with a (L) I/O block to Black's (L) punch.

(Figure 1c) White continues immediately from the blocking technique to press

Black's arm away, turning him and opening his (L) flank. Then White counter strikes by stepping in at a 45-degree angle with a short (R) uppercut to Black's open ribs.

Phoenix Form – Method Two (Master Hsu)

To open the form into (L) Pi Chuan (Figure 23-7-2.1) use the opening method shown in Chapter 19 previously.

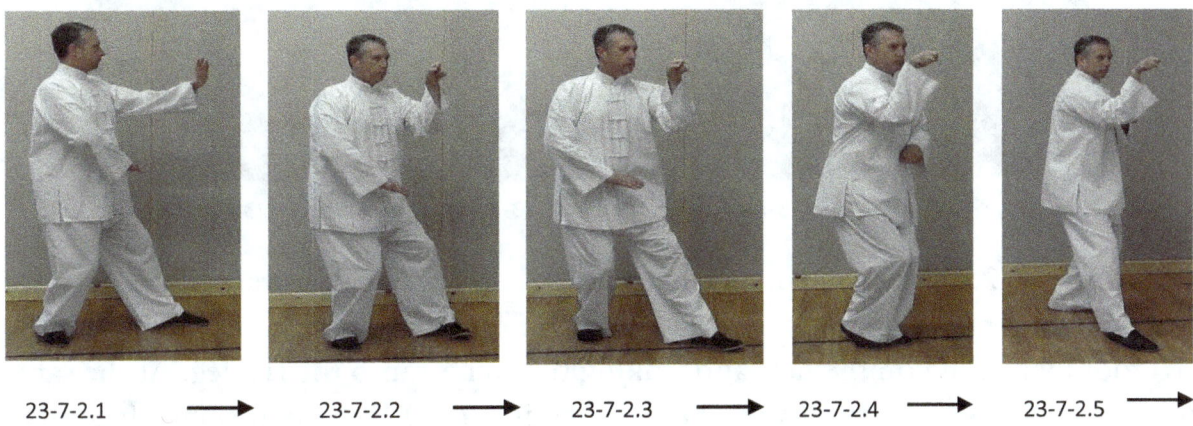

23-7-2.1 → 23-7-2.2 → 23-7-2.3 → 23-7-2.4 → 23-7-2.5 →

(Figure 23-7-2.1) Starting from (L) Pi Chuan posture.
(Figure 23-7-2.2) The practitioner turns inward on the heel of the (L) foot and this action also turns the body inwards to an angle of 45 degrees. The practitioners weight stays loaded in the rear (R) foot. At the same time, the (L) hand makes a Phoenix eye fist hand posture and strikes forwards in a 'pecking' type motion at the height of the face. The (R) hand remains facing palm down protecting the centreline of the body at the height of the Tan Tien.
(Figure 23-7-2.3) Next, the practitioner continues to step out at a 45-degree angle to the straight line direction of the form with the (L) foot. At the same time, the (L) arm circles forwards at the shoulder joint, with the elbow held flexed at a 45-degree angle and the (L) hand strikes forwards for a second time, in a 'pecking' type motion at the height of the face. The (R) hand remains facing palm down protecting the centreline of the body at the height of the Tan Tien.
(Figure 23-7-2.4) Next, the (R) rear foot, steps forwards continuing in a 45-degree angle to the straight line direction of the form and as it passes alongside the standing (L) front foot the (R) hand also circles at the shoulder joint and forms a Phoenix eye fist to strike using the same 'pecking' technique as described previously (Figure 23-7-2.3) to the height of the face. Simultaneously the (L) hand draws downwards across the centreline retaining the Phoenix eye hand posture throughout.
(Figure 23-7-2.5) Next, as the practitioner completes the forward step of the (R) foot the (L) foot follows up using the half-step method. In time with the step the (R) arm repeats the same shoulder circling, Phoenix eye hand strike a second time to

face height as described previously in figure 23-7-2.4. Simultaneously the (L) hand continues to draw downwards finishing at the height of the solar plexus retaining the Phoenix eye hand posture throughout.

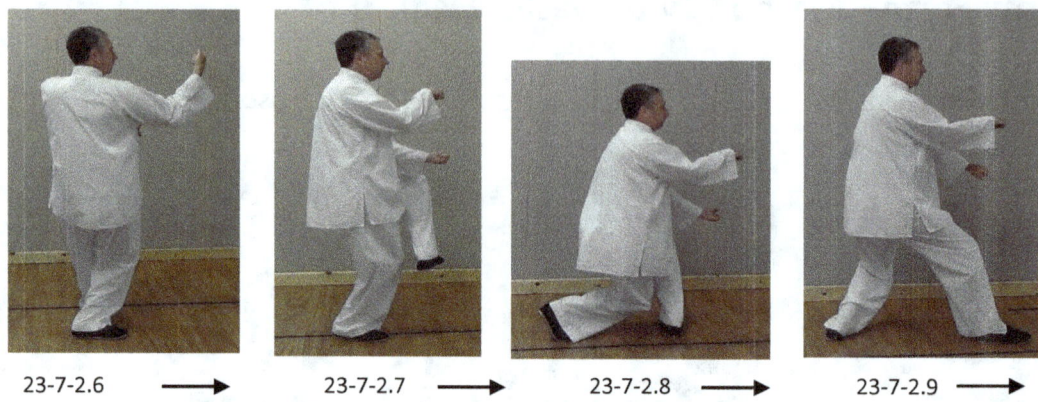

23-7-2.6 → 23-7-2.7 → 23-7-2.8 → 23-7-2.9 →

(Figure 23-7-2.6) Next, the practitioner turns the upper body inwards, back towards the original straight line direction of the form. The weight is then switched to the (R) foot by turning on the heel and sinking the weight into the (R) leg. At the same time, the (L) foot also pivots on its heel creating a (L) Pi Chuan stance facing 45 degrees to the left of the original straight line direction of the form. The practitioners weight stays loaded in the rear (R) foot and at the same time, the (R) hand retains its Phoenix eye fist hand posture and strikes forwards along the original straight line direction of the form in a 'pecking' type motion at the height of the temple. Simultaneously the (L) hand draws downwards across the centreline finishing at the height of the solar plexus retaining the Phoenix eye hand posture throughout.

(Figure 23-7-2.7) Next, the practitioner sweeps in a circular upwards motion with the instep of the (L) foot, raising it to the height of the opposite knee. The head must remain level throughout this sweeping action. At the same time both hands rotate symmetrically in an anti-clockwise direction finishing in line with the centreline of the body with (R) hand held at solar plexus height with its palm facing downwards, directly above the (L) hand which is held at Tan Tien height with its palm facing upwards.

(Figure 23-7-2.8) Next, the (L) raised foot, steps forwards along the original straight line direction of the form and is placed with a 'stomping' action into (L) cross stance which lowers the height of the practitioner. Both hands remain held as fists throughout in the same posture as described previously in Figure 23-7-2.7.

(Figure 23-7-2.9) Next, the practitioner steps forward with the (R) foot and the (L) foot follows up using the half-step method. In time with the step both hands strike straight out forwards as fists at their respective heights. The (R) upper fist strikes straight out and the (L) lower fist rotates as it strikes thus ending the double fist strike with both hands facing palm downwards.

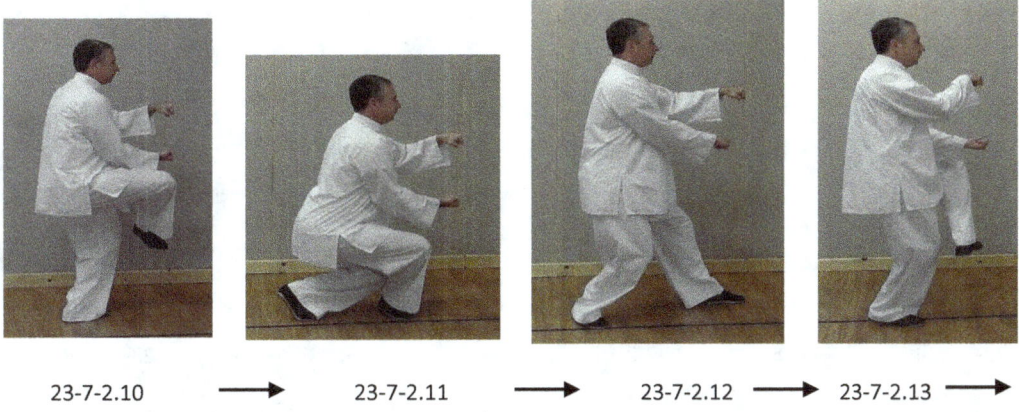

23-7-2.10 → 23-7-2.11 → 23-7-2.12 → 23-7-2.13 →

(Figure 23-7-2.10) Next, the practitioner sweeps in a circular upwards motion with the instep of the (R) foot, raising it to the height of the opposite knee. The head must remain level throughout this sweeping action. At the same time both hands rotate symmetrically in a clockwise direction finishing in line with the centreline of the body with (L) hand held at solar plexus height with its palm facing downwards, directly above the (R) hand which is held at Tan Tien height with its palm facing upwards.

(Figure 23-7-2.11) Next, the (R) raised foot, steps forwards along the original straight line direction of the form and is placed with a 'stomping' action into (R) cross stance which lowers the height of the practitioner. Both hands remain held as fists throughout in the same posture as described previously in Figure 23-7-2.10.

(Figure 23-7-2.12) Next, the practitioner steps forward with the (L) foot and the (R) foot follows up using the half-step method. In time with the step both hands strike straight out forwards as fists at their respective heights. The (L) upper fist strikes straight out and the (R) lower fist rotates as it strikes thus ending the double fist strike with both hands facing palm downwards.

Note: This sequence (Figures 23-7-2.10, 2.11 and 2.12 repeats the previous sequence (Figures 23-7-2.7, 2.8 and 2.9) but on the opposite side.

(Figure 23-7-2.13) Next, the practitioner sweeps in a circular upwards motion with the instep of the (L) foot, raising it to the height of the opposite knee. The head must remain level throughout this sweeping action. At the same time both hands rotate symmetrically in an anti-clockwise direction finishing in line with the centreline of the body with (R) hand held at solar plexus height with its palm facing downwards, directly above the (L) hand which is held at Tan Tien height with its palm facing upwards.

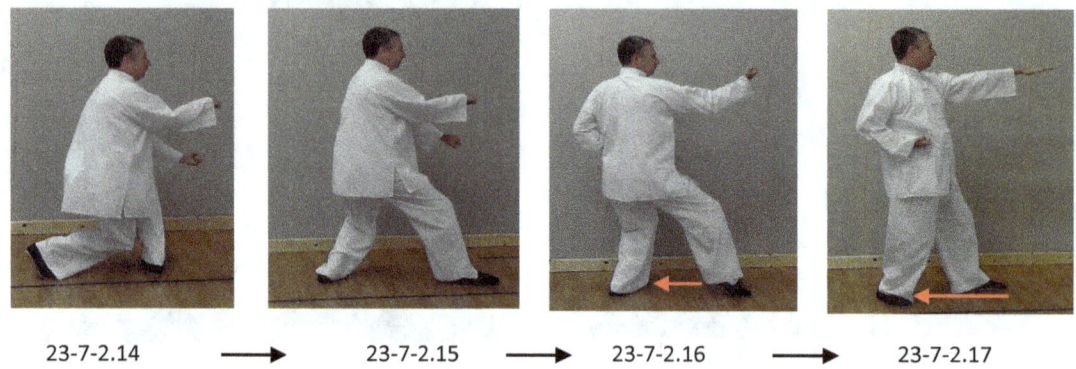

23-7-2.14 → 23-7-2.15 → 23-7-2.16 → 23-7-2.17

(Figure 23-7-2.14) Next, the (L) raised foot, steps forwards along the original straight line direction of the form and is placed with a 'stomping' action into (L) cross stance which lowers the height of the practitioner. Both hands remain held as fists throughout in the same posture as described previously in Figure 23-7-2.8.

(Figure 23-7-2.15) Next, the practitioner steps forward with the (R) foot and the (L) foot follows up using the half-step method. In time with the step both hands strike straight out forwards as fists at their respective heights. The (R) upper fist strikes straight out and the (L) lower fist rotates as it strikes thus ending the double fist strike with both hands facing palm downwards.

Note: This sequence (Figures 23-7-2.13, 2.14 and 2.15 repeats, exactly the previous sequence (Figures 23-7-2.7, 2.8 and 2.9).

(Figure 23-7-2.16) Next, the practitioner takes a step backwards with their rear (L) foot and simultaneously draws back their (R) foot onto its toe into a (R) cat stance. At the same time, the (R) forward hand turns over and executes a back-fist strike to nose height and the (L) hand is reciprocally drawn back to the (L) hip as a fist facing palm upwards.

(Figure 23-7-2.17) Next, the practitioner 'shock steps' backwards with the (R) foot placing themselves into a (L) Pi Chuan stance. In time with the back step the (L) hand executes a palm strike to head height and the (R) hand draws back to the (R) hip as a fist facing palm upwards.

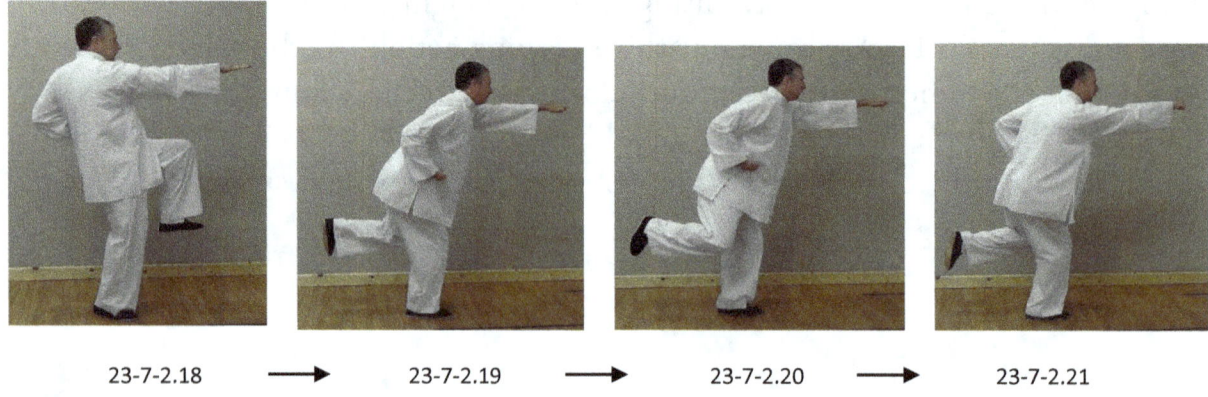

23-7-2.18 → 23-7-2.19 → 23-7-2.20 → 23-7-2.21

(Figure 23-7-2.18) Next, the practitioner leans backwards and raises their (L) foot placing themselves into a (R) single leg stance. In time with the back step the (R) hand executes a palm strike to head height and the (L) hand draws back to the (R) hip as a fist facing palm upwards.

(Figure 23-7-2.19) Next, the practitioner leans forwards whilst remaining balanced on the (R) foot and strikes straight forwards at the height of the face with a (L) Phoenix eye fist. The (R) hand draws back to the (R) hip as a fist facing palm upwards.

(Figure 23-7-2.20) Next, the practitioner takes a big leap forwards with the (L) foot and strikes straight forwards a second time at the height of the face with a (L) Phoenix eye fist. The (R) hand remains held at the (R) hip as a fist facing palm upwards.

(Figure 23-7-2.21) Next, the practitioner takes a second big leap forwards with the (R) foot and strikes straight forward at the height of the face with a (R) Phoenix eye fist. The (L) hand draws back to the (R) hip as a Phoenix eye fist.

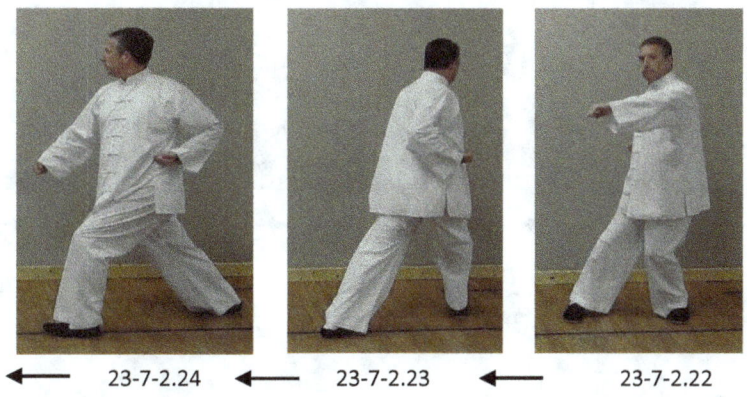

← 23-7-2.24   ← 23-7-2.23   ← 23-7-2.22

(Figure 23-7-2.22) Next, the practitioner takes a third big leap forwards with the (L) foot and striking out with the (L) Phoenix eye fist. Immediately on landing the (L) foot the practitioner pivots completely on the (L) foot in effect turning 180 degrees whilst using the outstretched (L) arm to hook and circle in time with the clockwise rotation of the upper body at the height of the neck.

Note: As the practitioner leaps forwards over three steps (Figures 23-7-2.19 to 2.22) the head should be held at the same height throughout the movements.

(Figure 23-7-2.23) As the practitioner rotates their upper body clockwise the weight of the body is transferred from the (L) foot into the (R) foot which allows the (L) leg to continue to rotate fully. The (L) arm continues to circle round in time with the body lowering itself to the height of the hips. The (R) rear hand pulls back to the (R) hip as a Phoenix eye fist facing palm up.

(Figure 23-7-2.24) Next, the practitioner rotates their upper body back anti-clockwise, with the weight of the body being transferred back from the (R) foot into the (L) foot. The (R) arm then strikes round in a circular motion over the height of the shoulder and then ending its strike downwards as a Phoenix eye fist at the height of the hips. The (L) rear hand pulls back to the (L) hip as a Phoenix eye fist facing palm up.

Hsing-I Chuan | The Practice of Heart and Mind Boxing

← 23-7-2.29 ← 23-7-2.28 ← 23-7-2.27 ← 23-7-2.26 ← 23-7-2.25

← 23-7-2.34 ← 23-7-2.33 ← 23-7-2.32 ← 23-7-2.31 ← 23-7-2.30

← 23-7-2.39 ← 23-7-2.38 ← 23-7-2.37 ← 23-7-2.36 ← 23-7-2.35

23-7-2.44 ← 23-7-2.43 ← 23-7-2.42 ← 23-7-2.41 ← 23-7-2.40

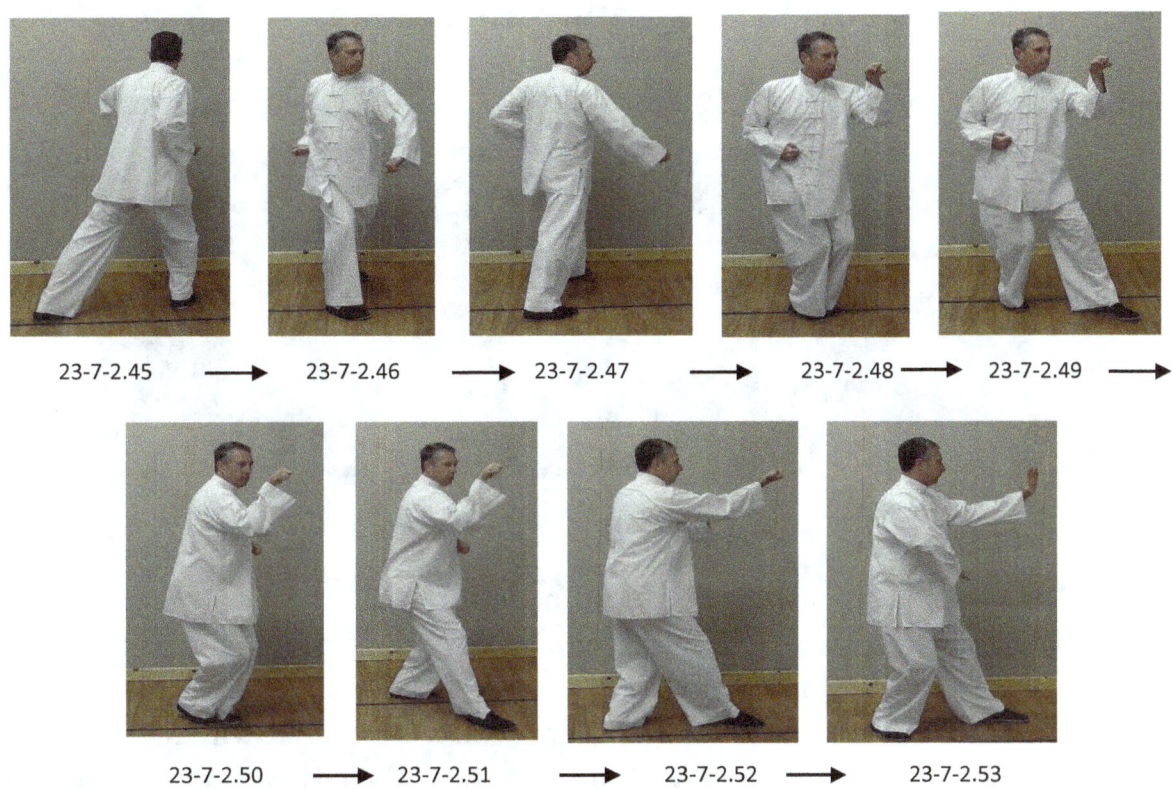

23-7-2.45 → 23-7-2.46 → 23-7-2.47 → 23-7-2.48 → 23-7-2.49 →

23-7-2.50 → 23-7-2.51 → 23-7-2.52 → 23-7-2.53

(Figures 23-7-2.25 to 2.51) The practitioner then repeats the same movements in the opposite direction before turning again 180 degrees to face the direction in which they originally started the form.

(Figures 23-7-2.52 and 2.53) Next, the practitioner turns to face the original straight line direction of the form by stepping forward with the (R) foot and punching forwards with the (R) fist simultaneously. The (L) fist is held at the (R) elbow as in Pi Chuan and the practitioner steps forward with the (L) foot into (L) Pi Chuan posture. To finish the form correctly from (L) Pi Chuan the practitioner uses the closing method described in Chapter 19 previously.

Phoenix Form – Method Two Fighting Applications:

Application 1 – Movements 23-7-2.4 to 2.5

1a → 1b → 1c

(**Figure 1a**) White faces off with Black in a neutral stance.
(**Figure 1b**) Black throws a (L) straight punch to White's ribs. White counters by stepping onto Black's (L) forward foot and at the same time simultaneously covering the attack with his (L) rear hand (unseen). As he redirects the strike with his rear hand, White also block/strikes the attack with his with his (R) elbow striking downwards directly into the inside, exposed aspect of Black's elbow joint.
(**Figure 1c**) White continues immediately from the (R) elbow block/strike technique to strike directly to Black's (L) temple pressure point with a (R) Phoenix eye fist.

Application 2 – Movements 23-7-2.6

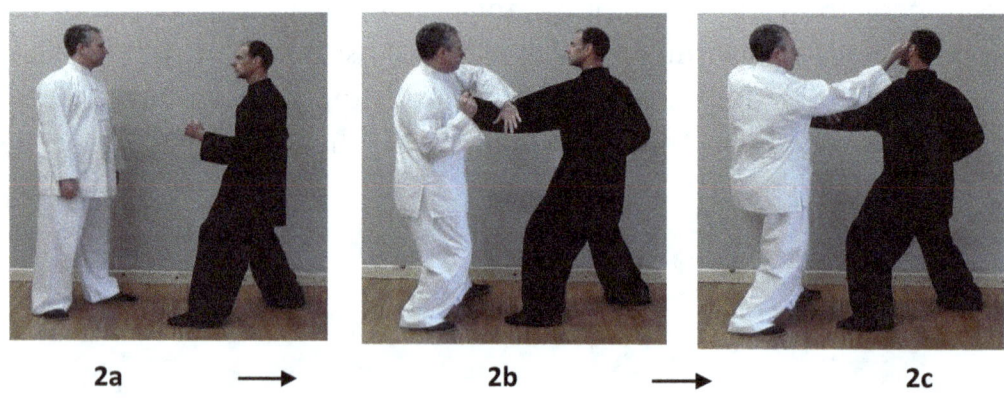

2a → 2b → 2c

(**Figure 2a**) White faces off with Black in a neutral stance.
(**Figure 2b**) Black throws a (L) straight punch to White's ribs. White counters by turning his body outside of the direction of the strike and covering it with his (L) arm to defend his centreline. By twisting outside of the attack this allows White to stay in perfect range to counter strike.
(**Figure 2c**) White completes the evasive manoeuvre by following up with a strike directly to Black's (L) temple pressure point with a (R) Phoenix eye fist.

Application 3 – Movements 23-7-2.10 to 2.12

3a → 3b → 3c

(Figure 3a) Black attempts to cross grab White's (R) wrist.
(Figure 3b) White counters by stepping to the outside of the direction of the grab, turning his body and breaking Black's grip by rotating his arm/wrist through the weakened thumb and index finger of Black's attack. This action also unbalances Black and makes any counter strike more difficult.
(Figure 3c) Before Black can react, White completes the move by lunging forward and executing a double fist strike to Black's exposed ribs, knocking him completely of balance.

Application 4 – Movements 23-7-2.10 to 2.11

4a → 4b → 4c

(Figure 3a) Black attempts to cross grab White's (R) wrist.
(Figure 3b) White counters by quickly rotating his (R) hand around Black's wrist and taking control of Black's elbow with his rear (L) hand. From this position White can then sweep Black's forward leg with the instep of his (R) foot to destabilise Black's stance.
(Figure 3c) Before Black can react, White completes the move by executing a (R) 45-degree stomping kick straight out into Black's rear (L) leg damaging the medial ligament and knocking Black to the ground.

Application 5- Movements 23-7-2.17 to 2.19

5a → 5b → 5c → 5d

(Figure 5a) White faces off with Black in a neutral stance.
(Figure 5b) Black throws a (L) straight punch to White's ribs. White immediately covers the strike with a (R) open palm block.
(Figure 5c) Black then issues a counterstrike by executing a (R) straight punch at White's solar plexus. White takes quick evasive action by leaning his body backwards into (L) single leg stance, out of range of the strike and simultaneously covering it with his (L) palm to defend his centreline.
(Figure 5d) White completes the evasive manoeuvre and counter strike by stepping forward and following up with a Phoenix eye fist strike directly to Black's throat.

Application 6- Movements 23-7-2.21 to 2.24

6a → 6b → 6c →

6d → 6e

(Figure 6a) White faces off with Black in a neutral stance.

(Figure 6b) Black throws a (R) straight punch to White's face. White immediately cuts off the strike by stepping in with a (R) Phoenix eye fist strike directly aimed at Black's eye.

(Figure 6c) Before Black can respond White steps around the outside of Black and simultaneously hooks his (L) arm around Black's neck and at the same time controlling his outstretched (R) arm.

(Figure 6d and 6e) White completes the attack by rotating his waist and arm pulling Black round and throwing him down to the ground by his neck.

Sparrow-Hawk Form

8. Sparrow-Hawk Form – Yao Hsing

Introduction

Master McNeil

Sparrow-Hawk form consists of a series of repeated postures that seek to imitate the physical and spiritual qualities of this bird. The form moves smoothly from mid to high postures and twists from side to side as it moves forwards. The unique footwork of the 45-degree hook step method allows for the practitioner to rapidly change angles and heights of attack whilst applying this form.

It should be noted that on opening this form using the Hsing-I method the practitioners first two movements are Horse form, before transitioning to the hook step method and Sparrow-Hawk posture thereafter.

The direction for each individual form is to move up and down in a straight line. The form opens and moves forwards, then turns 180 degrees and continues its movements in the opposite direction before turning again, 180 degrees to finish facing the same direction the practitioner originally started in accordance with traditional Hsing-I practice.

Sparrow-Hawk Form

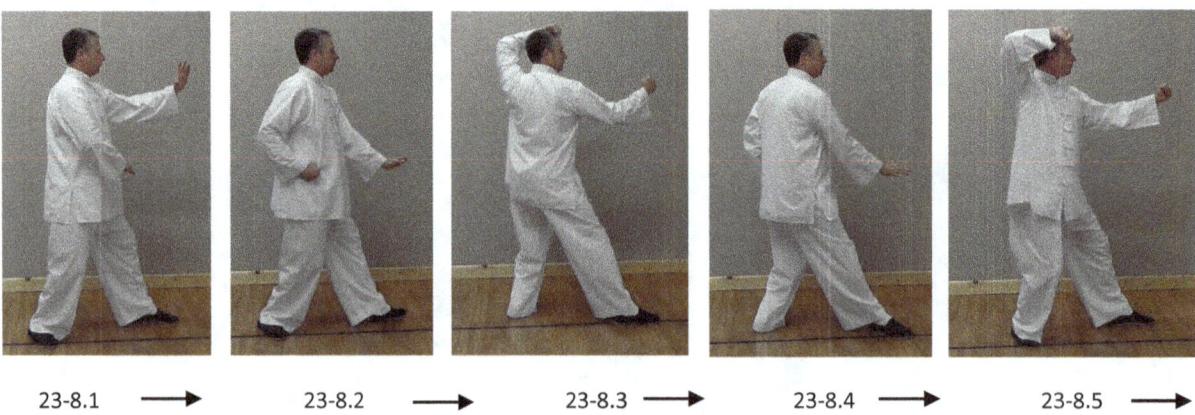

23-8.1 → 23-8.2 → 23-8.3 → 23-8.4 → 23-8.5 →

To open the form into (L) Pi Chuan (Figure 23-8.1) use the opening method shown in Chapter 19 previously.
(Figure 23-8.1) Starting from (L) Pi Chuan posture.
(Figure 23-8.2) Step forward with the (L) foot and block down to the centreline at Tan Tien level with the (L) hand as a crescent palm block. At the same time, the (R) hand draws back to the (R) hip as a fist facing 'eye' up.

(Figure 23-8.3) Step forwards with the (R) foot and follow up with the (L) foot using the half-step method. At the same time, the (R) hand punches straight up the centreline to nose height using Peng Chuan technique. The (L) hand simultaneously draws upwards and backwards in opposition as a fist and ends its movement in line with the (L) temple. This is (R) Horse posture.

(Figures 23-8.4 and 8.5) Movements (figures 23-8.4 and 8.5) repeat the sequence of movements (figures 23-8.2 and 8.3) on the opposite side. This ends in movement (figure 23-8.5) with the practitioner in (L) Horse posture.

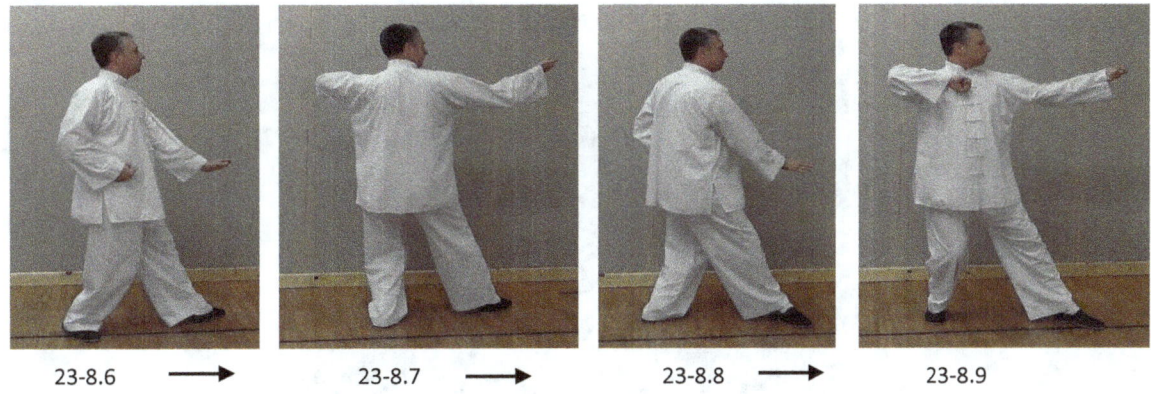

23-8.6 → 23-8.7 → 23-8.8 → 23-8.9

(Figure 23-8.6) Step forward with the (L) foot and block down to the centreline at Tan Tien level with the (L) hand as a crescent palm block. At the same time, the (R) hand draws back to the (R) hip as a fist facing 'eye' up.

(Figure 23-8.7) Step forwards with the (R) foot and follow up with the (L) foot using the 45-degree hook step method. At the same time, the (R) hand strikes straight up the centreline to throat height using eagles claw technique. The (L) hand simultaneously draws upwards and backwards in opposition as a fist and draws directly backwards across the chest, ending its movement with the fist turned palm outwards at the height of the solar plexus. (See figure 8.9 for hand position) This is (R) Sparrow-Hawk posture.

(Figures 23-8.8 and 8.9) Movements (figures 23-8.8 and 8.9) repeat the sequence of movements (figures 23-8.6 and 8.7) on the opposite side. This ends in movement (figure 23-8.9) with the practitioner in (L) Sparrow-Hawk posture.

Note: At this point the same sequence of movements can be performed repeatedly forward in a straight line until the practitioner chooses to turn and change direction. Traditionally Hsing-I practitioners turn their forms on the (L) side; however, it is prudent to practice turns on both sides from a fighting application purpose.

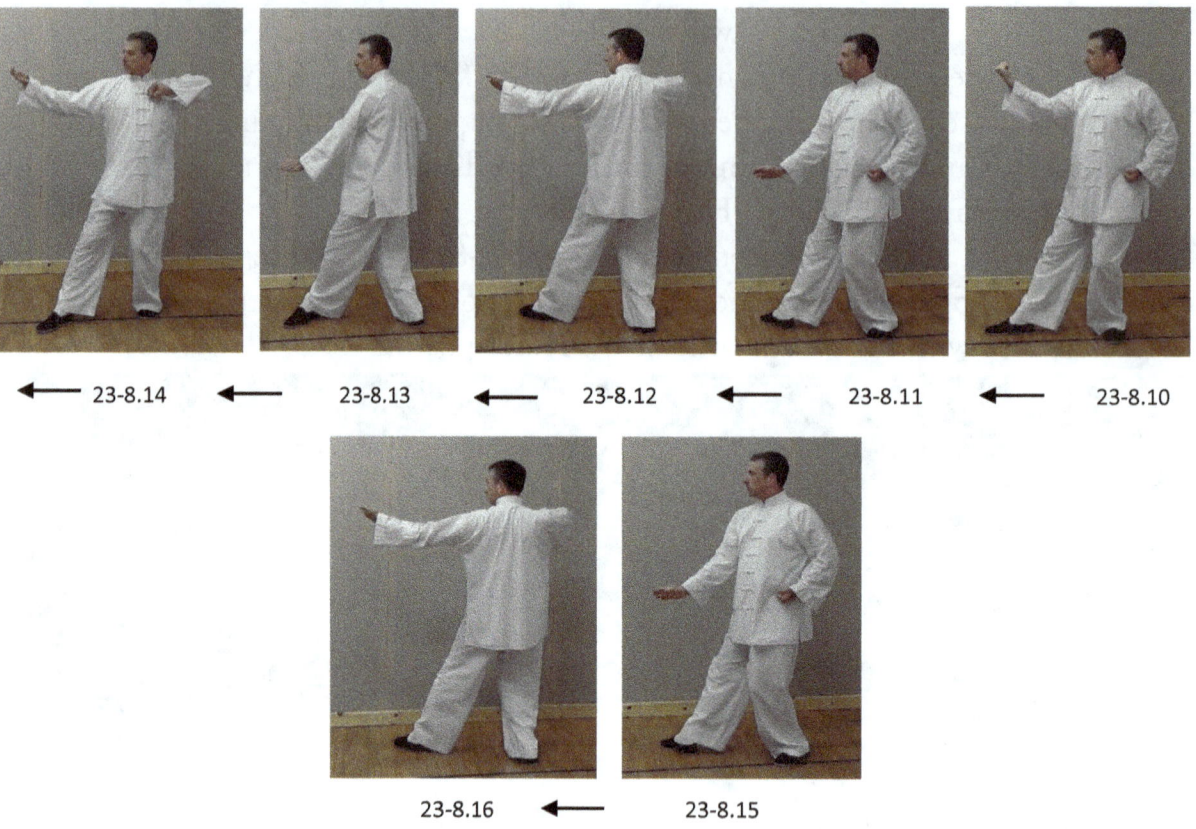

(Figure 23-8.10) Next, turn 180 degrees into (R) Pi Chuan stance. At the same time, the (R) hand executes a back-fist strike at nose height, whilst the (L) hand pulls back to the (L) hip as a fist facing palm up.

(Figure 23-8.11) Step forward with the (R) foot and block down to the centreline at Tan Tien level with the (R) hand as a crescent palm block. At the same time, the (L) hand draws back to the (L) hip as a fist facing 'eye' up.

(Figure 23-8.12) Step forwards with the (L) foot and follow up with the (R) foot using the 45-degree hook step method. At the same time, the (L) hand strikes straight up the centreline to throat height using eagles claw technique. The (R) hand simultaneously draws upwards and backwards in opposition as a fist and draws directly backwards across the chest, ending its movement with the fist turned palm outwards at the height of the solar plexus. This is (L) Sparrow-Hawk posture.

(Figures 23-8.13 to 8.16) Movements (figures 23-8.13 to 8.16) repeat the sequence of movements a further two times. This ends in movement (figure 23-8.16) with the practitioner in (L) Sparrow-Hawk posture.

Note: At this point the same sequence of movements can be performed repeatedly forward in a straight line until the practitioner chooses to turn and change direction. Traditionally Hsing-I practitioners turn their forms on the (L) side; however, it is prudent to practice turns on both sides from a fighting application purpose.

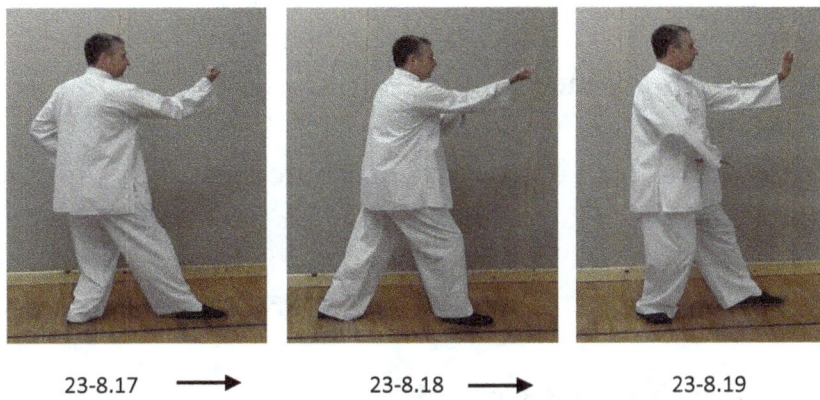

23-8.17 → 23-8.18 → 23-8.19

(Figure 23-8.17) Next, turn 180 degrees into (R) Pi Chuan stance. At the same time, the (R) hand executes a back-fist strike at nose height, whilst the (L) hand pulls back to the (L) hip as a fist facing palm up.

(Figures 23-8.18 and 8.19) Next, the practitioner turns to face the original centreline stepping forward with the (R) foot and punching forwards with the (R) fist simultaneously. The (L) fist is held at the (R) elbow as in Pi Chuan and the practitioner steps forward with the (L) foot into (L) Pi Chuan posture. To finish the form correctly from (L) Pi Chuan the practitioner uses the closing method described in Chapter 19 previously.

Sparrow-Hawk Form Fighting Applications:

Application 1 – Movements 23-8.8 and 8.9

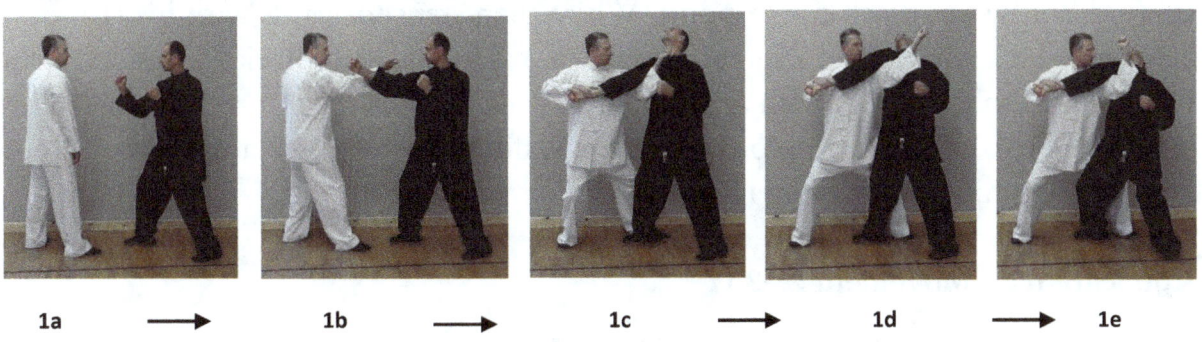

1a → 1b → 1c → 1d → 1e

(Figure 1a) White faces off with Black in a neutral stance.

(Figure 1b) Black throws a high (R) straight punch to White's face. White steps forwards into Black's centreline and at the same time blocks the attack with a (R) eagle claw strike to the back of Black's elbow.

(Figure 1c) Before Black can respond, White then steps forwards with his (L) foot, behind Black's forward foot and slips his (L) hand under Black's extended arm striking him in the throat with a (L) eagle claw technique.

(Figure 1d) From this position White controls Black's arm at the wrist and sharply pulls it down across his own chest whilst simultaneously extending his own arm forwards and delivering a (L) shoulder strike to the underside of Black's (R) shoulder. The lever effect of the combined pull and strike can easily dislocate the shoulder when timed correctly.

(Figure 1e) To complete the counter attack White then drops his weight straight into the ground by flexing his knees and keeping his back straight. At the same time, White sinks his elbow into Black's solar plexus and forces Black to bend backwards, off balancing him and making it easy to take him to the ground.

Application 2 – Movements 23-8.8 and 8.9

(Figure 2a) White faces off with Black in a neutral stance.
(Figure 2b) Black throws a high (R) straight punch to White's face. White steps forwards into Black's centerline and at the same time blocks the attack with a (R) eagle claw strike to the back of Black's elbow.
(Figure 2c) Before Black can respond, White then steps forwards with his (L) foot, behind Black's forward foot and slips his (L) hand under Black's extended arm striking him in the throat with a (L) eagle claw technique.
(Figure 2d) To complete the counter attack White then sweeps Black's forward foot off balancing him and making it easy to take him to the ground.

Application 3 – Movement 23-8.17

(Figure 3a) Black grabs at White's (R) shoulder from behind.
(Figure 3b) White immediately places his own (L) hand across his body and directly

on top of Black's grabbing hand. (not clearly shown), at the same time turning 180 degrees clockwise to face Black. At the same time, White circles up his (R) arm as a fist to protect his face and centreline.

(Figure 3c) Whilst maintaining a hold to Black's extended hand and arm, White then strikes down on the back of Black's arm with a back fist creating a hyperextension injury to the (R) elbow joint.

Swallow Form

9. Swallow Form – Yen Hsing

Introduction

Grand Master Chiao

The swallow is a small, agile bird with long and powerful wings. The movements of Swallow form aim to imitate the spirit and features of this lively bird. The nature of this form can be physically challenging as it requires the switching of heights from extreme low postures to high with speed and confidence of balance. It also requires flexibility and strength in the legs to achieve some of its postures. For this reason, Swallow form is usually studied towards the end of the twelve animals training when the practitioner has gained sufficient skill level to practice this form with precision.

The direction of Swallow form is to move up and down in a straight line. The form then turns 180 degrees and repeats its movements in the opposite direction before turning again to finish facing the same direction the practitioner originally started in accordance with traditional Hsing-I practice.

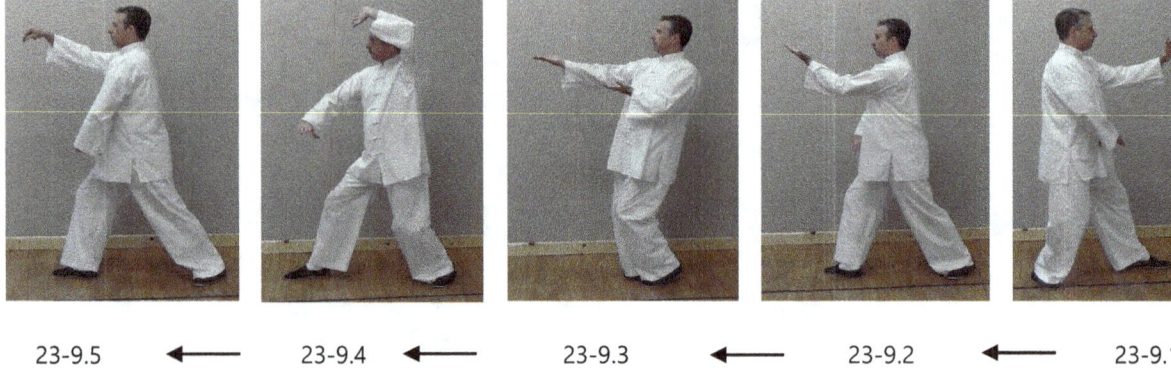

23-9.5 ← 23-9.4 ← 23-9.3 ← 23-9.2 ← 23-9.1

To open the form into (L) Pi Chuan (Figure 23-9.1) use the opening method shown in Chapter 19 previously.

(Figure 23-9.1) Starting from (L) Pi Chuan posture. (Pictured far right above)

(Figure 23-9.2) From the opening Pi Chuan posture turn immediately 180 degrees and take a small step forwards with the (R) foot and place it at 45 degrees to the centreline of the form. The (L) foot turns reciprocally on its heel to place the practitioner in (R) bow stance with a 45-degree foot. At the same time, the (L) hand chops from O/I as a knife hand strike palm to throat height. The (R) hand holds its position facing palm down at the height of the Tan Tien.

(Figures 23-9.3 and 9.4) Follow on by stepping forward using close the gap stepping method (Figure 23-9.3) to move one step forwards ending with the practitioner in

(R) Pi Chuan stance (23-9.4). At the same time, the (R) hand blocks palm upwards at the height of the head (Figure 23-9.3) and is closely followed by the (L) palm blocking up in a 'rolling' circular motion which changes the hands positions. The (L) hand terminates at the height of the forehead, along the left side of the centreline and the (R) hand thrusts out forwards with a knife hand strike with the palm facing down aimed at ribs height (Figure 23-9.4). Both hands and feet must start and finish their movements together.

(Figure 23-9.5) Next, take a small step forwards with the (R) foot into (R) bow stance. At the same time, the (R) hand forms a cranes beak and strikes directly up the centreline to jaw height. The (L) hand blocks down the centreline with an open palm to protect the Tan Tien.

23-9.6 → 23-9.7 → 23-9.8 → 23-9.9 →

(Figure 23-9.6) Next slide the rear (L) foot backwards and turn the body 180 degrees. At the same time flex the (R) knee and lower the body into (L) drop stance. At the same time, the (L) hand follows the line if the (L) leg and scoops round with the palm in a 'hooking' action as close to ground level as the flexibility of the practitioner allows. The (R) hand remains as a cranes beak and lowers only in time with the body.

(Figure 23-9.7) Staying as low as possible transfer the weight forwards into the (L) foot and cross step forwards with the (R) foot into (R) cross stance. At the same time, the (R) rear hand strikes downwards along the centreline of the form as a spear hand with palm facing away from the body. In opposition, the (L) hand blocks upwards as a spear hand to protect the head with its palm facing towards the body. Both hands and feet must start and finish their movements together.

(Figure 23-9.8) From the low cross step position stand straight up into (R) single leg stance. The body is turned completely to 90 degrees from the straight line direction of the form and the (L) raised knee should be flexed to an angle of 90 degrees. As the practitioner stands up the (R) hand also extends straight up as high as possible with the palm facing away from the body. In opposition, the (L) hand presses palm down, inside the raised (L) knee, to the height of the Tan Tien to protect the centreline.

(Figure 23-9.9) Next, the practitioner executes a (L) side kick at midsection height whilst simultaneously the (L) hand thrusts forwards, palm facing outwards in time and in line with the kick. The (R) hand reciprocally thrusts backward to counter balance the technique with its palm facing backwards. Both arms should appear symmetrical at the end of this kicking technique.

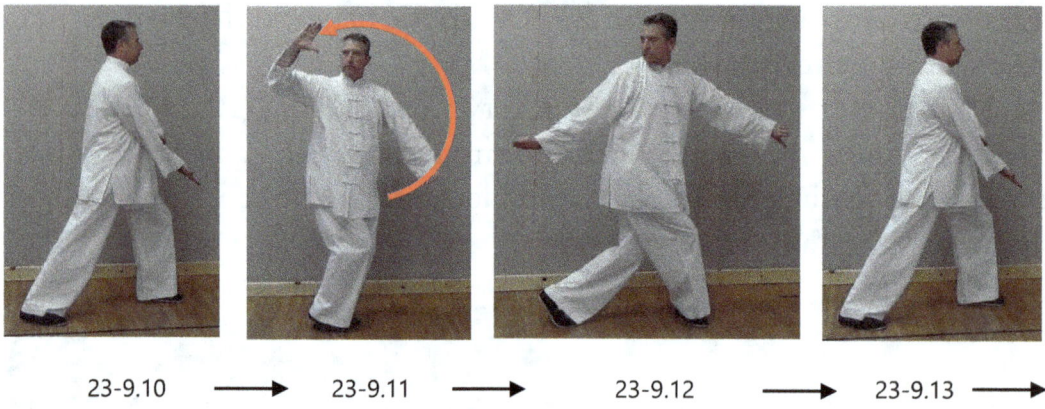

23-9.10 → 23-9.11 → 23-9.12 → 23-9.13 →

(Figure 23-9.10) Next, the (L) kicking foot is planted firmly on the ground and the (R) rear foot adjusts itself using the half-step method. This places the practitioner into a (L) bow stance. At the same time, the rear (R) hand circles downwards and strikes using a palm strike in time with the turn of the body, up the centreline to the height of the groin. The (L) hand moves downwards from its outstretched position and rotates inwards with its palm towards the body at the height of the Tan Tien. As both hands complete their movements, the inside of the (R) forearm should come to rest firmly against the palm of the (L) hand.

(Figures 23-9.11 and 9.12) Next, step forward with the (R) foot into (R) cross stance. At the same time, the (R) hand circles up and over the head coming to rest above the rear heel of the (L) foot as a crescent palm block behind the practitioner. The (L) hand simultaneously circles downwards to the height of the groin and then up 'warding off' to the height of the Tan Tien. As the (L) hand wards off the palm turns to face palm out, away from the body.

(Figures 23-9.13 to 9.18) Next, repeat the same sequence of movements (Figures 23-9.10, 9.11 and 9.12) a further two times moving forwards along the straight line direction of the form.

(Figure 23-9.19) With the (R) forward foot planted firmly on the ground, execute a (L) rear straight leg kick down the centreline. The (L) hand holds its forward guarding position and the rear (R) hand moves forward in time with the body's momentum, with the palm open.

(Figures 23-9.20 and 9.21) The (L) kicking foot should be brought to the ground under control and is planted firmly alongside the inside of the standing (R) foot. As soon as the (L) foot is planted the (R) foot executes a back-heel kick technique behind the practitioner to groin height. Next the (R) kicking foot should be brought to the ground under control and planted firmly alongside the inside of the standing (L) foot. At the same time, the (L) forward hand turns to face palm down and the rear (R) hand circles straight up the centreline facing palm up coming to rest by 'slapping' firmly against the palm of the opposite hand.

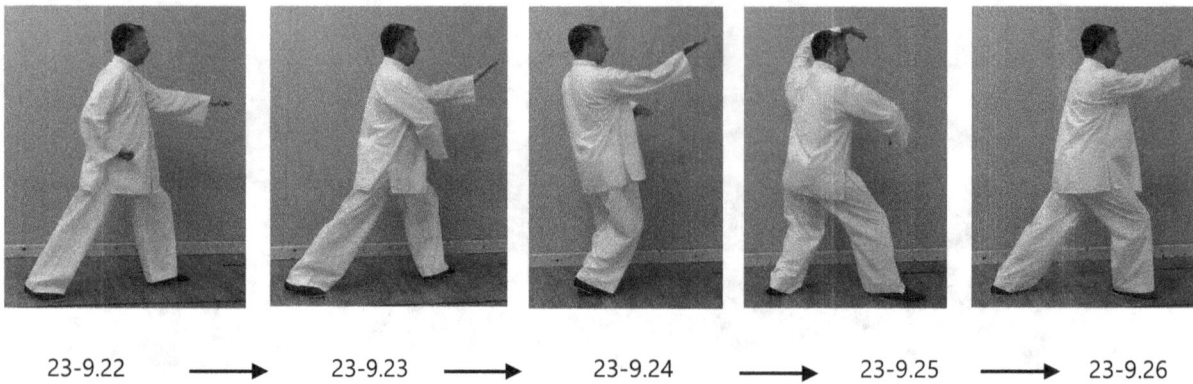

23-9.22 → 23-9.23 → 23-9.24 → 23-9.25 → 23-9.26

(Figure 23-9.22) Next, the (L) foot takes a step forwards into (L) bow stance. At the same time, the (L) forward hand strikes out along the centreline with a leopard fist to Tan Tien height and the rear (R) hand draws back in opposition to the (R) hip as a fist facing palm upwards.

(Figure 23-9.23) Next, take a small step forwards with the (L) foot and place it at 45 degrees to the centreline of the form. The (R) foot stays firmly planted to the ground. At the same time, the (L) hand drills palm upwards as a spear hand to throat height. The (R) hand blocks down the centreline with palm down protecting the Tan Tien. This is the first posture of Tsuan Chuan.

(Figures 23-9.24 and 9.25) Follow on by stepping forward using close the gap stepping method (Figure 23-9.24) to move one step forwards ending with the practitioner in (R) Pi Chuan stance (23-9.25). At the same time, the (R) hand blocks palm upwards at the height of the head (Figure 23-9.24) and is closely followed by the (L) palm blocking up in a 'rolling' circular motion which changes the hands positions. The (L) hand terminates at the height of the forehead, along the left side of the centreline and the (R) hand thrusts out forwards with a knife hand strike with the palm facing down aimed at ribs height (Figure 23-9.25). Both hands and feet must start and finish their movements together.

(Figure 23-9.26) Next, take a small step forwards with the (R) foot into (R) bow stance. At the same time, the (R) hand forms a cranes beak and strikes directly up the centreline to jaw height. The (L) hand blocks down the centreline with an open palm to protect the Tan Tien.

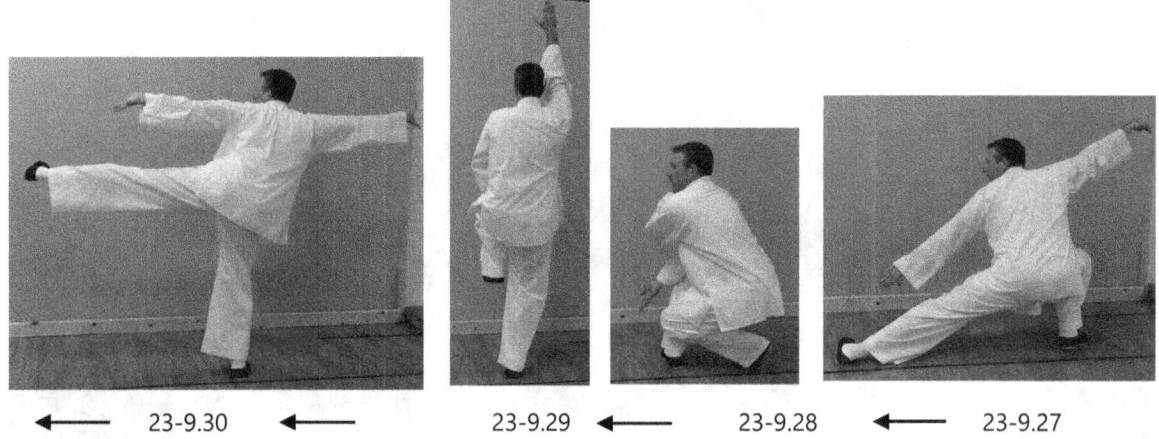

← 23-9.30 ← 23-9.29 ← 23-9.28 ← 23-9.27

(Figure 23-9.27) Next slide the rear (L) foot backwards and turn the body 180 degrees. At the same time flex the (R) knee and lower the body into (L) drop stance. At the same time, the (L) hand follows the line if the (L) leg and scoops round with the palm in a 'hooking' action as close to ground level as the flexibility of the practitioner allows. The (R) hand remains as a cranes beak and lowers only in time with the body.

(Figures 23-9.28 to 9.47) The practitioner then repeats the same sequence of movements described previously in figures 23-9.7 to 9.26 in the opposite direction.

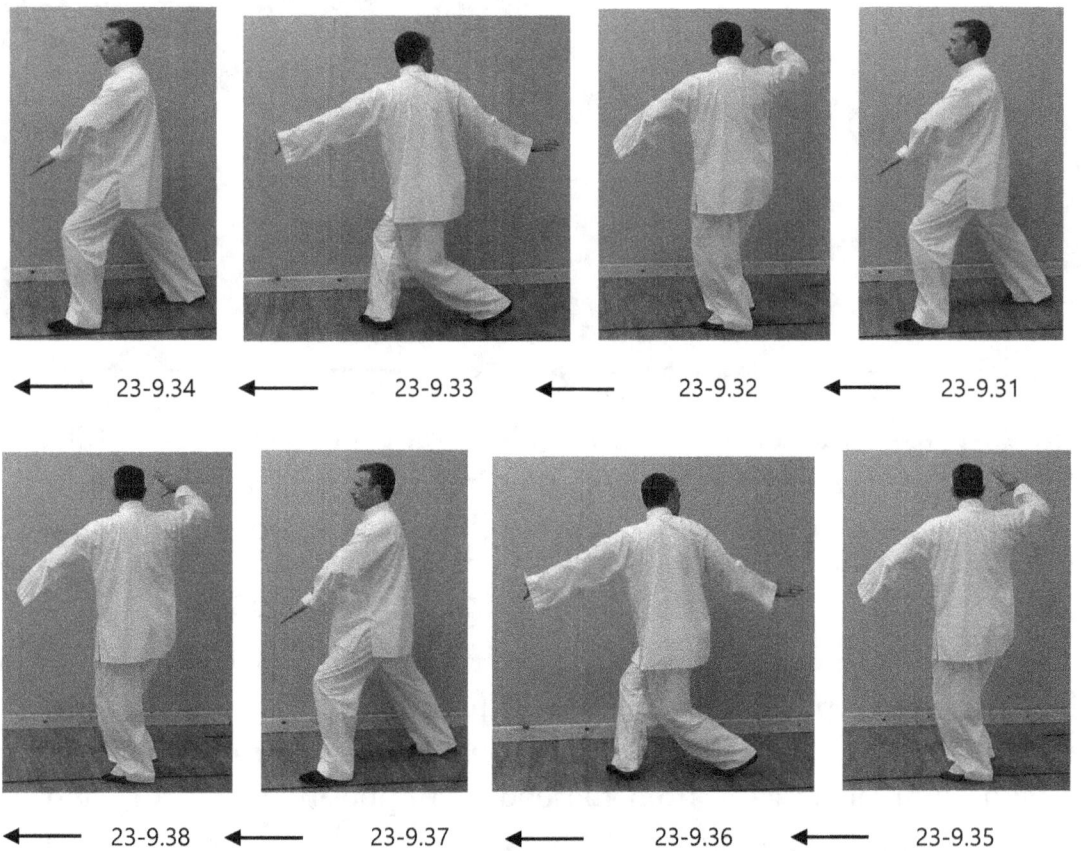

← 23-9.34 ← 23-9.33 ← 23-9.32 ← 23-9.31

← 23-9.38 ← 23-9.37 ← 23-9.36 ← 23-9.35

(Figure 23-9.48) Next slide the rear (L) foot backwards and turn the body 180 degrees. At the same time flex the (R) knee and lower the body into (L) drop stance. At the same time, the (L) hand follows the line if the (L) leg and scoops round with the palm in a 'hooking' action as close to ground level as the flexibility of the practitioner allows. The (R) hand remains as a cranes beak and lowers only in time with the body.

(Figure 23-9.49) Staying as low as possible transfer the weight forwards into the (L) foot and cross step forwards with the (R) foot into (R) cross stance. At the same time, the (R) rear hand strikes downwards along the centreline of the form as a spear hand with palm facing away from the body. In opposition, the (L) hand blocks upwards as a spear hand to protect the head with its palm facing towards the body. Both hands and feet must start and finish their movements together.

(Figure 23-9.50) From the low cross step position stand straight up into (R) single leg stance. The body is turned completely to 90 degrees from the centreline of the form and the (L) raised knee should be flexed to an angle of 90 degrees. As the practitioner stands up the (R) hand also extends straight up as high as possible with the palm facing away from the body. In opposition, the (L) hand presses palm down, inside the raised (L) knee, to the height of the Tan Tien to protect the centreline.

(Figure 23-9.51) Next, with the (R) foot firmly planted the practitioner rotates the upper body and raised (L) leg 90 degrees to the left to face the straight line direction of the form. At the same time, the (R) hand simultaneously punches forwards to nose height along the centreline. The (L) hand is drawn to the inside of the (R) elbow as in Pi Chuan technique.

(Figure 23-9.52) Step down and through with the (L) foot and follow up with the (R) foot using the half-step method. At the same time as stepping execute a (L) punch straight up to nose height following the line of the previous (R) punch and as soon as the (L) punch reaches its full extension open the hands dropping the (R) hand down to the midsection, protecting the Tan Tien and the (L) hand chops forward and down the centreline in a splitting action. At the end of this sequence the practitioner is now in (L) Pi Chuan posture.

Note: To finish the form correctly the practitioner uses the closing method described in Chapter 19 of this book.

Swallow Form Fighting Applications:

Application 1 – Movements 23-9.1 to 9.2

1a → 1b

(Figure 1a) Black walks up behind White and grabs his (R) arm by the wrist.
(Figure 1b) White counters by quickly turning 180 degrees and at the same time breaking Black's grip by rotating his hand around Black's wrist. This action also unbalances Black and makes any counter strike more difficult. Before Black can react, White completes the move by executing a (L) knife hand strike from O/I directly to Black's neck.

Application 2 – Movement 23-9.5

2a → 2b → 2c → 2d

(Figure 2a) White faces off with Black in a neutral stance.
(Figure 2b) Black throws a (R) straight punch to White's ribs. White immediately covers the strike with a (L) open palm block.
(Figure 2c) Black then issues a counter strike by executing a (L) roundhouse punch at White's head. White takes quick evasive action by blocking directly upwards using the (R) hand cranes beak strike as a defensive technique.
(Figure 2d) White completes the evasive manoeuvre and counterstrike by following up with a second repeated cranes beak strike with the (L) hand to Black's jaw.

Application 3 – Movement 23-9.6

3a → 3b → 3c → 3d

(Figure 3a) White faces off with Black in a neutral stance.
(Figure 3b) Black throws a (R) straight punch to White's face. White immediately covers the strike with a (R) open palm block, deflecting the strike and drawing Black into the counter attack.
(Figure 3c) Before Black can respond White drops quickly down to grab at Black's forward supporting leg.
(Figure 3d) White completes counterstrike by pulling up Black's rooted foot and completely throwing him to the ground.

Application 4 – Movement 23-9.8

4a → 4b → 4c

(Figure 4a) White faces off with Black in a neutral stance.
(Figure 4b) Black throws a (R) straight punch to White's ribs. White immediately steps in and covers the strike with a (L) open palm block.
(Figure 4c) White then counter strikes by following up with a (R) knee to Black's groin and simultaneously strikes Black's throat with a (R) palm strike.

Application 5 – Movements 23-9.11 to 9.13

5a → 5b → 5c → 5d

(Figure 5a) White faces off with Black in a neutral stance.
(Figure 5b) Black throws a (L) straight punch to White's ribs. White immediately steps in and covers the strike with a (R) open palm circle block.
(Figure 5c) White then counters by cross stepping to Black's outside and simultaneously circles up Black's attacking arm and presses it across his own body making any further attack from Black difficult.
(Figure 5d) White completes counter strike by stepping directly into Black's off balanced body and striking him to the liver with an (R) open palm and pushing him away with his (L) forearm.

Application 6 – Movements 23-9.21 and 9.22

6a → 6b → 6c → 6d

(Figure 6a) White faces off with Black in a neutral stance.

(Figure 6b) Black throws a (R) straight punch to White's ribs. White immediately steps in and covers the strike with a (L) open palm block.

(Figure 6c) White then counters by continuing his (L) hand as a finger thrust strike along Black's forearm striking into the inside vulnerable tendons of Black's (R) elbow joint.

(Figure 6d) Black tries to evade by stepping back with his (L) leg, but white quickly closes the distance by counter stepping forwards onto Black's (R) foot. White then completes counterstrike by striking him to the solar plexus with a (R) leopard fist technique.

Snake Form

10. Snake Form – Sher Hsing

Introduction

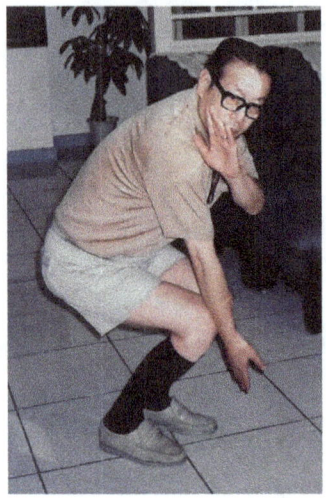

Grand Master Chiao

Snake form consists of a series of repeated postures that seek to imitate the physical and spiritual qualities of the snake. The form moves smoothly from high to low postures and strikes out with speed and accuracy to selected targets. The arms of the practitioner coil and twist like the snake allowing control and manipulation of the opponent in application.

As previously stated in Chapter 13 this lineage has two different methods of Snake form. One form originates from Master Chiao which is generally simpler to look at, yet as with all things simple the application of this method is ruthless and effective. In comparison Master Hsu's Snake form is more complex to learn and offers a wide range of techniques in its application. Regardless of their differences in appearance the spirit in which the movements are practiced remains the same and no one method is better than the other.

The direction for each individual form is to move up and down in a straight line. The form opens and moves forwards, then turns 180 degrees and continues its movements in the opposite direction before turning again, 180 degrees to finish facing the same direction the practitioner originally started in accordance with traditional Hsing-I practice.

Snake Form – Method One (Master Chiao)

To open the form into (L) Pi Chuan (figure 23-10-1.1) use the opening method shown in Chapter 19 previously.

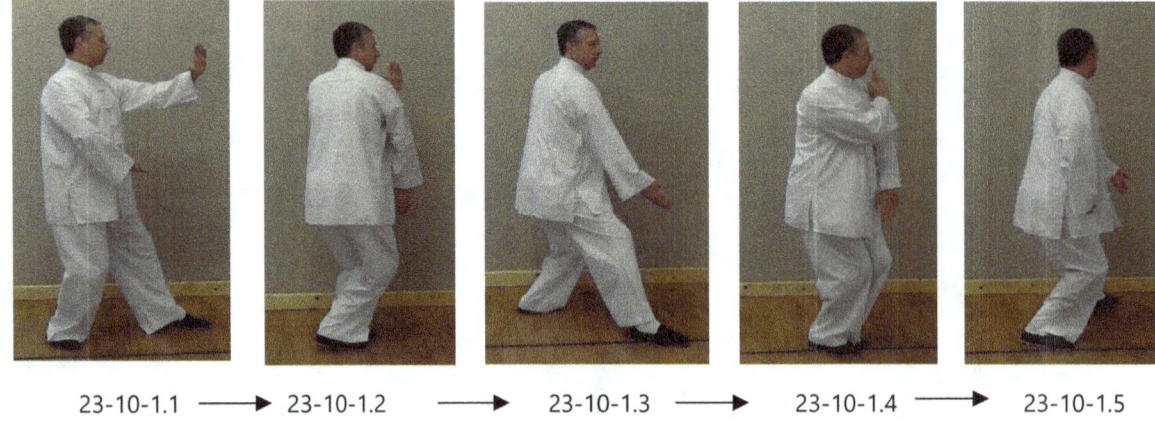

23-10-1.1 → 23-10-1.2 → 23-10-1.3 → 23-10-1.4 → 23-10-1.5

(Figure 23-10-1.1) Starting from (L) opening Metal posture.

(Figure 23-10-1.2) Next, the (L) foot takes a step forwards and the (R) foot follows coming to rest on the toes at the instep of the (L) foot. At the same time, the body turns to an angle of 45 degrees to the left of the straight line direction of the form. The (R) hand thrusts downwards across the centreline with its knife edge facing forwards at the height of the groin. Simultaneously the (L) hand blocks across the centreline with an open palm at the height of the face. The eyes stay looking straight ahead and the back remains straight throughout.

(Figure 23-10-1.3) Next, the (R) foot, steps out at angle of 45 degrees back across the straight line direction of the form and the (L) foot follows using the half-step method. At the same time, the (R) arm follows striking forward with the (R) hand striking with the ridge hand strike to groin height. Simultaneously the (L) hand pulls backwards in opposition down to the level of the (L) hip (shown clearly in figure 23-10-1.8).

(Figure 23-10-1.4) Next, the (R) foot takes a step forwards and the (L) foot follows coming to rest on the toes at the instep of the (R) foot. At the same time, the body turns to an angle of 45 degrees to the right of the straight line direction of the form. The (L) hand thrusts downwards across the centreline with its knife edge facing forwards at the height of the groin. Simultaneously the (R) hand rises and blocks across the centreline with an open palm at the height of the face. The eyes stay looking straight ahead and the back remains straight throughout.

(Figure 23-10-1.5) Next, the (L) foot steps out at angle of 45 degrees back across the straight line direction of the form and the (R) foot follows using the half-step method. At the same time, the (L) arm follows striking forward with the (L) hand striking with the ridge hand strike to groin height. Simultaneously the (R) hand pulls backwards in opposition down to the level of the (R) hip.

Note: At this point the same sequence of movements can be performed repeatedly forward in a straight line until the practitioner chooses to turn and change direction. Traditionally Hsing-I practitioners turn their forms on the (L) side; however, it is prudent to practice turns on both sides from a fighting application purpose.

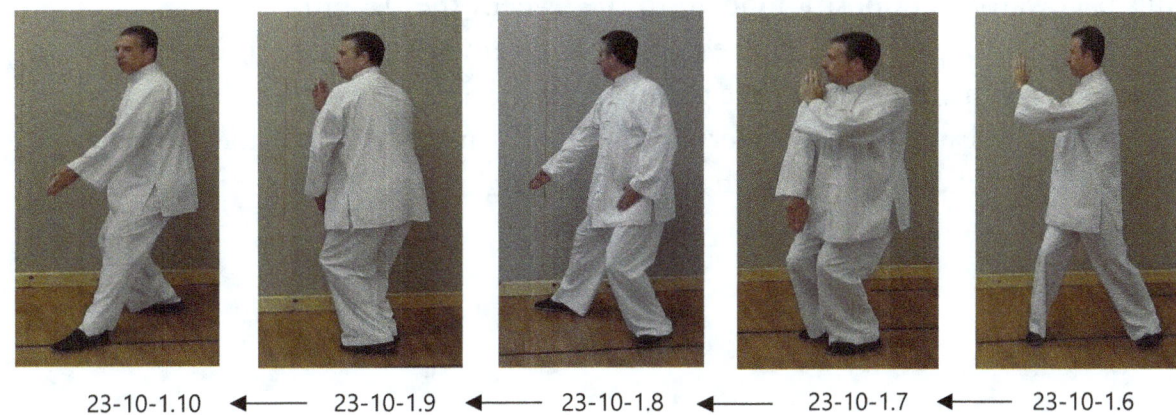

23-10-1.10 ← 23-10-1.9 ← 23-10-1.8 ← 23-10-1.7 ← 23-10-1.6

Figure 23-10-1.6) The practitioner then turns 180 degrees to face the direction from which they came. The (L) front foot steps across the body and turns inwards in a clockwise direction approximately 45 degrees, the weight is transferred from the (R) foot to the (L) foot. At the same time, the (L) arm circles round blocking with a (L) hand open palm across the height of the face. The (R) hand remains held at the (R) hip as an open hand.

(Figure 23-10-1.7) Next, the (R) foot follows coming to rest on the toes at the instep of the (L) foot. At the same time, the body turns to an angle of 45 degrees to the left of the straight line direction of the form. The (R) hand rises from (R)hip to the height of the (R) shoulder and then thrusts downwards across the centreline with its knife edge facing forwards at the height of the groin. The (L) hand completes its open palm block across the centreline at the height of the face.

Note: Throughout the turn sequence both hands must start and finish the movements together.

(Figure 23-10-1.8) Next, the (R) foot, steps out at angle of 45 degrees back across the straight line direction of the form and the (L) foot follows using the half-step method. At the same time, the (R) arm follows striking forward with the (R) hand striking with the ridge hand strike to groin height. Simultaneously the (L) hand pulls backwards in opposition down to the level of the (L) hip.

(Figure 23-10-1.9) Next, the (R) foot takes a step forwards and the (L) foot follows coming to rest on the toes at the instep of the (R) foot. At the same time, the body turns to an angle of 45 degrees to the right of the straight line direction of the form. The (L) hand thrusts downwards across the centreline with its knife edge facing forwards at the height of the groin. Simultaneously the (R) hand rises and blocks across the centreline with an open palm at the height of the face. The eyes stay looking straight ahead and the back remains straight throughout.

(Figure 23-10-1.10) Next, the (L) foot, steps out at angle of 45 degrees back across the straight line direction of the form and the (R) foot follows using the half-step method. At the same time, the (L) arm follows striking forward with the (L) hand striking with the ridge hand strike to groin height. Simultaneously the (R) hand pulls backwards in opposition down to the level of the (L) hip.

Note: At this point the same sequence of movements can be performed repeatedly forward in a straight line until the practitioner chooses to turn and change direction. Traditionally Hsing-I practitioners turn their forms on the (L) side; however, it is prudent to practice turns on both sides from a fighting application purpose.

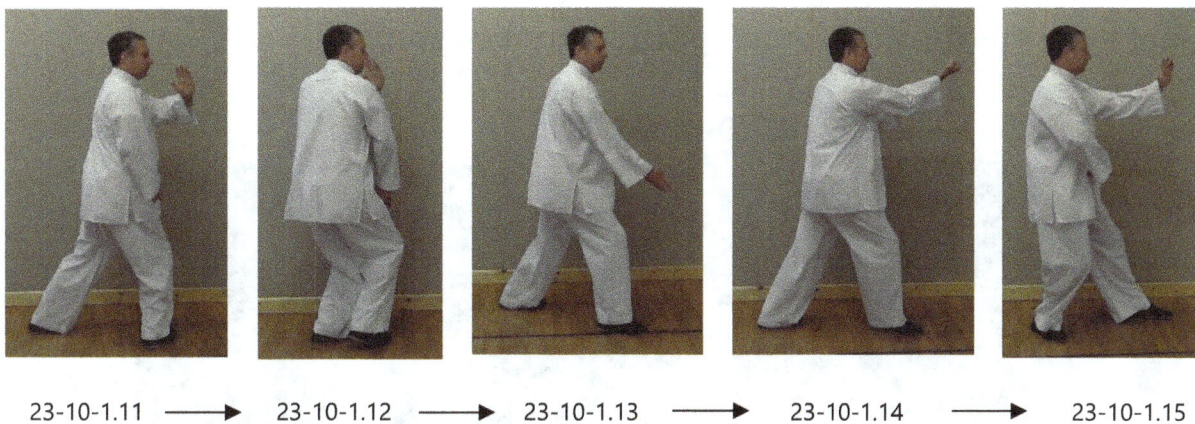

23-10-1.11 → 23-10-1.12 → 23-10-1.13 → 23-10-1.14 → 23-10-1.15

(Figure 23-10-1.11) The practitioner then turns 180 degrees to face the direction from which they came. The (L) foot steps across the body and turns inwards in a clockwise direction approximately 45 degrees, the weight is transferred from the (R) foot to the (L) foot. At the same time, the (L) arm circles round blocking with a (L) hand open palm across the height of the face. The (R) hand remains held at the (R) hip as an open hand.

(Figure 23-10-1.12) Next, the (R) foot follows coming to rest on the toes at the instep of the (L) foot. At the same time, the body turns to an angle of 45 degrees to the left of the straight line direction of the form. The (R) hand rises from (R)hip to the height of the (R) shoulder and then thrusts downwards across the centreline with its knife edge facing forwards at the height of the groin. The (L) hand completes its open palm block across the centreline at the height of the face.

Note: Throughout the turn sequence both hands must start and finish the movements together.

(Figure 23-10-1.13) Next, the (R) foot, steps out at angle of 45 degrees back across the straight line direction of the form and the (L) foot follows using the half-step method. At the same time, the (R) arm follows striking forward with the (R) hand striking with the ridge hand strike to groin height. Simultaneously the (L) hand pulls backwards in opposition down to the level of the (L) hip.

(Figures 23-10-1.14 and 1.15) Next, the practitioner turns to face the original centreline stepping forward with the (R) foot and punching forwards with the (R) fist simultaneously. The (L) fist is held at the (R) elbow as in Pi Chuan and the practitioner steps forward with the (L) foot into (L) Pi Chuan posture. To finish the form correctly from (L) Pi Chuan the practitioner uses the closing method described in Chapter 19 previously.

Snake Form – Method One Fighting Application:

Application 1 – Movements 23-10-1.2 to 1.3

1a → 1b → 1c

(Figure 1a) White faces off with Black in a neutral stance.
(Figure 1b) Black throws a low (L) straight punch to White's ribs. White steps in to the inside of Black's attack and block/strikes with a spear hand thrust, cutting off Black's attack and continuing to strike out at Black's groin.
(Figure 1c) Before Black can respond, White then lunges forwards with his (R) leg directly into Black's centreline and simultaneously strikes him with a shoulder strike to the solar plexus and a (R) ridge hand strike to the groin [unseen in picture].

Snake Form – Method Two (Maser Hsu)

To open the form into (L) Pi Chuan (figure 23-10-2.1) use the opening method shown in Chapter 19 previously.

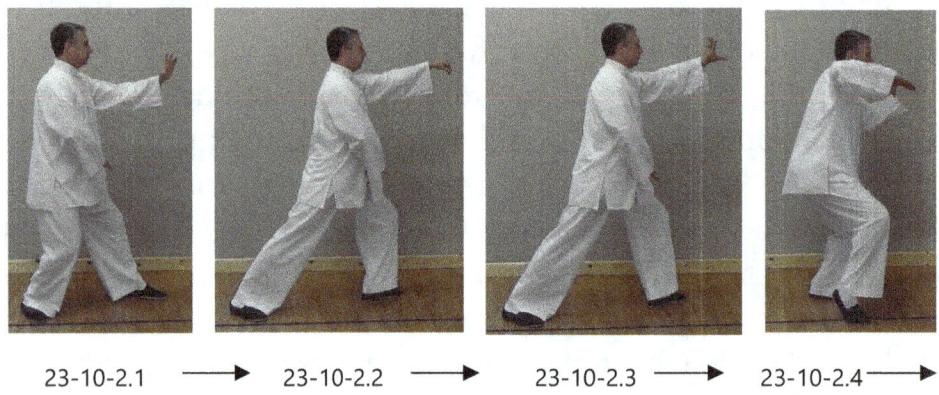

23-10-2.1 → 23-10-2.2 → 23-10-2.3 → 23-10-2.4 →

(Figure 23-10-2.1) Starting from (L) opening Metal posture.
(Figure 23-10-2.2) Next, take a small step forwards with the (L) foot placing it at a 45-degree angle into (L) bow stance. At the same time, the (L) hand forms a cranes beak and strikes directly up the centreline to jaw height. The (R) hand remains palm down along the centreline to protect the Tan Tien.

(Figure 23-10-2.3) Next, the practitioner remains in the (L) bow stance whilst the (L) arm holds its extended position and the (L) hand opens and circles tightly at the wrist in anti-clockwise direction, grabbing into a tight fist as it circles [not clearly shown in picture]. The (R) hand remains protecting the Tan Tien throughout.

(Figure 23-10-2.4) Next, the weight transfers fully into the forward (L) foot and the rear (R) foot circle sweeps round, drawing into the (L) foot on its toes as in cat stance. At the same time, the (R) hand rises upwards to the height of the (R) shoulder and the (L) arm blocks across the centreline at face height.

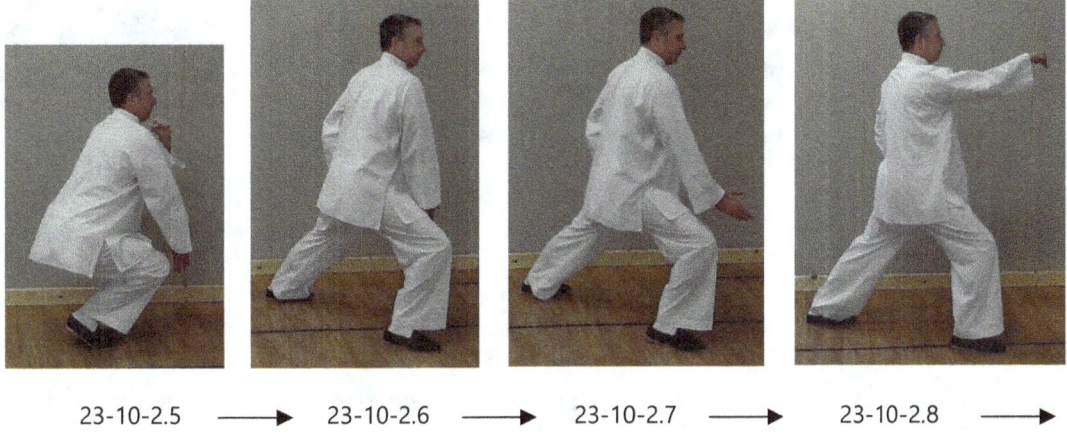

23-10-2.5 ⟶ 23-10-2.6 ⟶ 23-10-2.7 ⟶ 23-10-2.8 ⟶

(Figure 23-10-2.5) Next, the practitioner drops to the ground in a low crouched stance with the (R) foot remaining on its toes. The (R) hand simultaneously drops straight down the centreline rotating as it goes in a drilling motion towards the ground, coming to rest inside the flexed (R) knee, facing knife edge away from the body. The (L) hand remains as a fist protecting the centreline at head height.

(Figure 23-10-2.6 and 2.7) Next, the (R) foot, steps out at angle of 45 degrees to the right of the straight line direction of the form and the (L) foot follows using the half-step method. At the same time, the (R) arm follows, leading with the (R) shoulder, and rotating at the wrist forward with the (R) hand striking with the ridge hand strike to groin height. Simultaneously the (L) hand pulls backwards in opposition down to the level of the (L) hip as a closed fist, facing palm up.

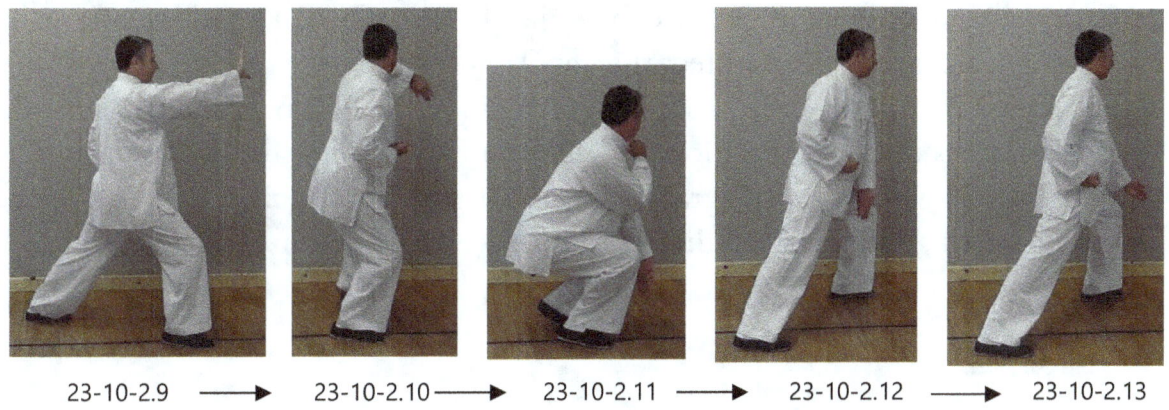

23-10-2.9 ⟶ 23-10-2.10 ⟶ 23-10-2.11 ⟶ 23-10-2.12 ⟶ 23-10-2.13

(Figure 23-10-2.8 to 2.13) The practitioner then repeats the same sequence of movements described previously in figures 23-10-2.2 to 10-2.7 on the opposite side.

Note: At this point the same sequence of movements can be performed repeatedly forward in a straight line until the practitioner chooses to turn and change direction. Traditionally Hsing-I practitioners turn their forms on the (L) side; however, it is prudent to practice turns on both sides from a fighting application purpose.

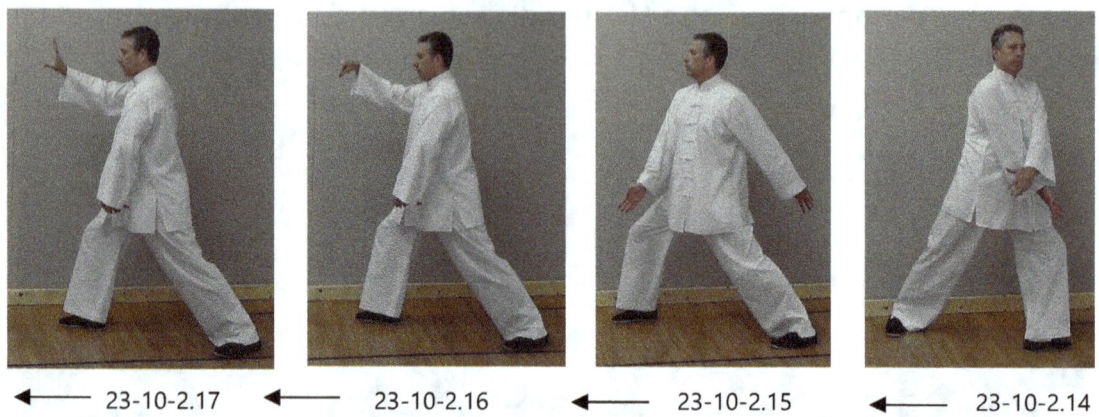

← 23-10-2.17   ← 23-10-2.16   ← 23-10-2.15   ← 23-10-2.14

(Figure 23-10-2.14) The practitioner then steps across the centreline of the form with the rear (L) foot and turns 180 degrees to face the direction from which they came. At the same time, both arms cross over at the wrists as open palms. The (L) arm blocks over the (R) arm as the body turns to protect the centreline of the practitioner at Tan Tien height.

(Figure 23-10-2.15) Next, the (R) foot completes the turn and the weight is loaded into the (R) forward foot as a (R) bow stance. Both hands strike out together, with the (R) forward hand striking straight along the centreline as a ridge hand strike. The (L) hand strike backwards behind the practitioner along the centreline as a knife hand strike.

Note: Throughout the turn sequence both hands must start and finish the movements together.

(Figure 23-10-2.16) Next, take a small step forwards with the (R) foot placing it at a 45-degree angle into (R) bow stance. At the same time, the (R) hand forms a cranes beak and strikes directly up the centreline to jaw height. The (L) hand remains palm down along the centreline to protect the Tan Tien.

(Figure 23-10-2.17) Next, the practitioner remains in the (R) bow stance whilst the (R) arm holds its extended position and the (R) hand opens and circles tightly at the wrist in clockwise direction, grabbing into a tight fist as it circles. The (L) hand remains protecting the Tan Tien throughout.

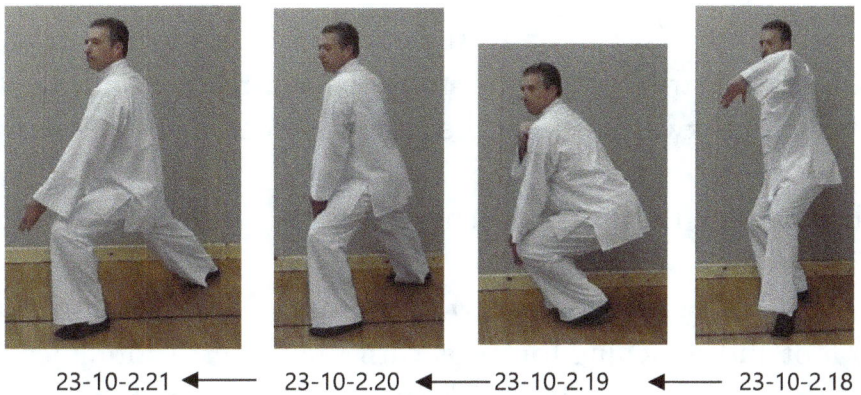

23-10-2.21 ← 23-10-2.20 ← 23-10-2.19 ← 23-10-2.18

(Figure 23-10-2.18) Next, the weight transfers fully into the forward (R) foot and the rear (L) foot circle sweeps round, drawing into the (R) foot on its toes as in cat stance. At the same time, the (L) hand rises upwards to the height of the (L) shoulder and the (R) arm blocks across the centreline at face height. (Not clearly shown)

(Figure 23-10-2.19) Next, the practitioner drops to the ground in a low crouched stance with the (L) foot remaining on its toes. The (L) hand simultaneously drops straight down the centreline rotating as it goes in a drilling motion towards the ground, coming to rest inside the flexed (L) knee, facing knife edge away from the body. The (R) hand remains as a fist protecting the centreline at head height.

(Figure 23-10-2.20 and 2.21) Next, the (L) foot, steps out at angle of 45 degrees to the left of the straight line direction of the form and the (R) foot follows using the half-step method. At the same time, the (L) arm follows, leading with the (L) shoulder, and rotating at the wrist forward with the (L) hand striking with the ridge hand strike to groin height. Simultaneously the (R) hand pulls backwards in opposition down to the level of the (R) hip as a closed fist.

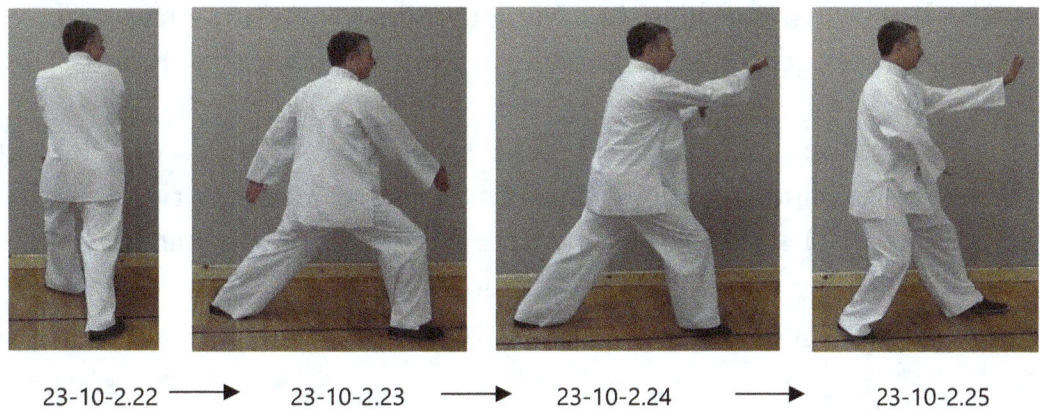

23-10-2.22 → 23-10-2.23 → 23-10-2.24 → 23-10-2.25

(Figure 23-10-2.22) The practitioner then steps across the centreline of the form with the rear (L) foot and turns 180 degrees to face the direction from which they came. At the same time, both arms cross over at the wrists as open palms. (not clearly shown) The (L) arm blocks over the (R) arm as the body turns to protect the centreline of the practitioner at Tan Tien height.

(Figure 23-10-2.23) Next, the (R) foot completes the turn and the weight is loaded into the (R) forward foot as a (R) bow stance. Both hands strike out together, with the (R) forward hand striking straight along the centreline as a ridge hand strike. The (L) hand strike backwards behind the practitioner along the centreline as a knife hand strike.

Note: Throughout the turn sequence both hands must start and finish the movements together.

(Figures 23-10-2.24 and 2.25) Next, the practitioner takes a small step forward with the (R) foot and punching forwards with the (R) fist simultaneously. The (L) fist is held at the (R) elbow as in Pi Chuan and then steps forward with the (L) foot into (L) Pi Chuan posture. To finish the form correctly from (L) Pi Chuan the practitioner uses the closing method described in Chapter 19 previously.

Snake Form – Method Two Fighting Applications:

Application 1 – Movements 23-10-2.8 to 2.13

2a → 2b → 2c → 2d → 2e

(Figure 2a) White faces off with Black in a neutral stance.

(Figure 2b) Black throws a high (R) straight punch to White's face. White steps forwards into Black's centreline and at the same time blocks the attack with a (R) cranes beak strike.

(Figure 2c) Before Black can respond, White then steps forwards with his (L) foot and opens his (R) hand, circling it around Black's extended wrist grabbing and controlling Black's (R) arm. At the same time, White circles his rear (L) hand across Black's extended elbow putting it into an elbow lock.

(Figure 2d) White then drops his weight straight into the ground by flexing his knees and keeping his back straight. This forces Black to bend forward to avoid the pressure applied in the elbow lock.

(Figure 2e) From this controlling position White simply moves his weight forward, knocking Black off balance with his (L) hip and simultaneously strikes Black's throat with a (L) ridge hand strike.

Application 2 – Movements 23-10-2.8 to 2.12

3a → 3b → 3c → 3d

(Figure 3a) Black throws a high (R) straight punch to White's face. White steps forwards into Black's centreline and at the same time blocks the attack with a (R) cranes beak strike.

(Figure 3b) Before Black can respond, White then steps forwards with his (L) foot directly behind Black's forward (R) foot. At the same time, White opens his (R) hand, circling it around Black's extended wrist grabbing Black's (R) arm and simultaneously covers Black's elbow to effectively control the arm.

(Figure 3c) White then hook sweeps Black's forward leg with his (L) foot taking Black completely off balance.

(Figure 3d) Next, White simply moves his weight forward delivering a (L) hip strike to Black's (R) side knocking Black backwards and simultaneously strikes Black's groin with a (L) ridge hand strike.

Eagle/Bear Form

11. Eagle/Bear Form – Ying/Xiong Hsing

Introduction

Master McNeil

Eagle/Bear form is unique in the twelve animals of Hsing-I practiced in this system as it contains the physical and spiritual qualities of two animals combined into one form. The movements are a constant interchange between the energies of the two animals. The form moves swiftly from light and agile footwork to bold, solid and centred footwork. The form's hands also switch from precision grasping and striking to heavy pounding of open palms. The body is held straight throughout the movements and power is generated through the rotation of the waist.

The direction for each individual form is to move up and down in a straight line. The form opens and moves forwards, then turns 180 degrees and continues its movements in the opposite direction before turning again, 180 degrees to finish facing the same direction the practitioner originally started in accordance with traditional Hsing-I practice.

Eagle/Bear Form

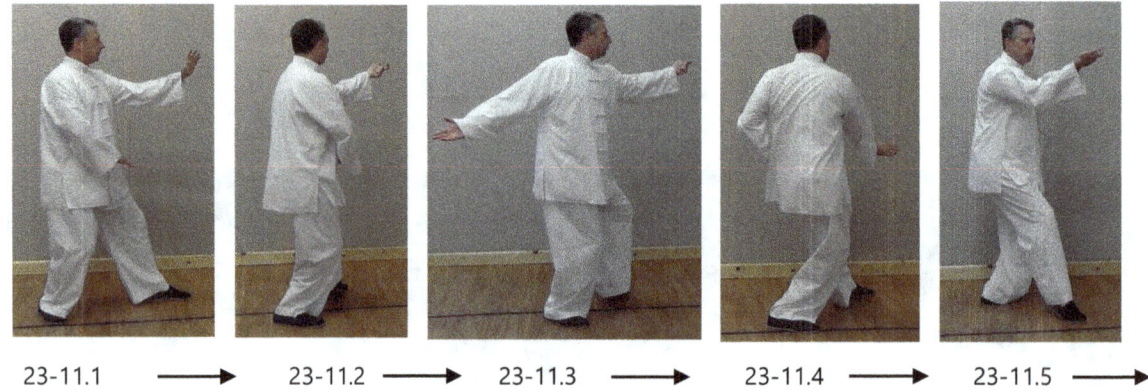

23-11.1 ⟶   23-11.2 ⟶   23-11.3 ⟶   23-11.4 ⟶   23-11.5 ⟶

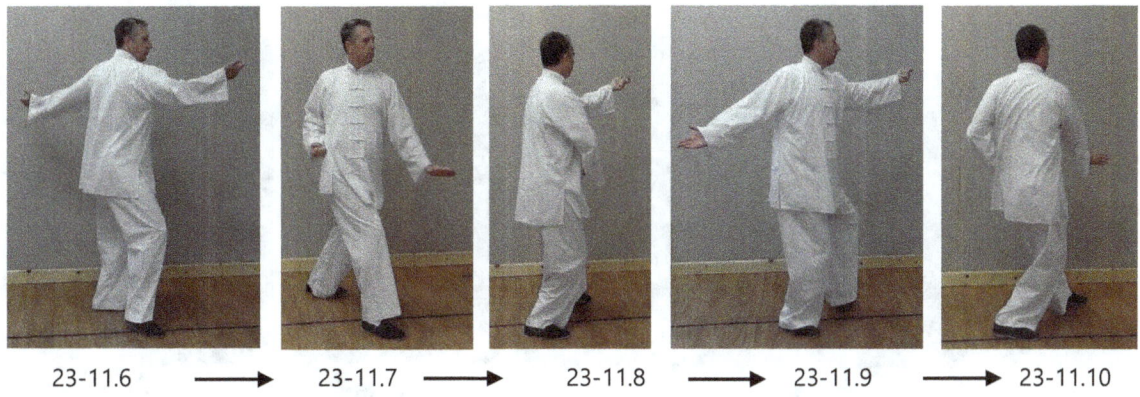

23-11.6 → 23-11.7 → 23-11.8 → 23-11.9 → 23-11.10

To open the form into (L) Pi Chuan (Figure 23-11.1) use the opening method shown in Chapter 19 previously.

(Figure 23-11.1) Starting from (L) Pi Chuan posture.

(Figure 23-11.2) Begin by stepping out with the (R) foot at a 45-degree angle. Next turn the body outward 45 degrees, counter clockwise to the left into a (L) cat stance. The right foot is flat, the left foot is on its ball and toes. The (L) hand simultaneously strikes out at throat height along the centreline using the eagle claw hand posture. At the same time, the (R) hand holds its position as an open palm protecting the Tan Tien. This is (L) Eagle posture.

(Figure 23-11.3) Next, the practitioner holds the (L) cat stance and opens the hips, by turning the waist backwards. At the same time, the (R) arm stretches backwards in a circular motion in time with the turning of the waist. The (L) forward hand retains its eagle claw posture and extends forwards slightly in time with the waist turn. The back remains straight throughout the rotation of the waist.

(Figure 23-11.4) Next, step forward at a 45-degree angle to the left of the straight directional line of the form, pushing off the rear (R) foot and leading with the forward (L) foot, using the half-step method. At the same time, the (R) arm and hand circles from behind, high over the height of the head and continues down across the centreline, in front of the practitioner as an open palm strike, ending at the height and level of the opposite (L) hip. The (L) hand reciprocally pulls back to the (L) hip with fist facing palm up. This is (L) Bear posture.

(Figures 23-11.5 to 11.10) Movements (figures 23-11.5 to 11.10) repeat the sequence of movements (figures 23-11.2 to 11.4) on the opposite side. This ends in movement (figure 23-11.10) with the practitioner in (L) Bear posture.

Note: At this point the same sequence of movements can be performed repeatedly forward in a straight line until the practitioner chooses to turn and change direction. Traditionally Hsing-I practitioners turn their forms on the (L) side; however, it is prudent to practise turns on both sides from a fighting application purpose.

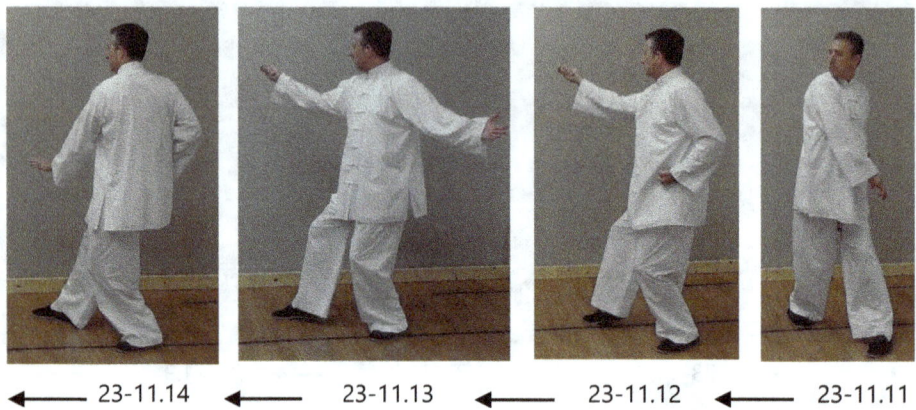

← 23-11.14   ← 23-11.13   ← 23-11.12   ← 23-11.11

(Figure 23-11.11) From (L) Bear posture (figure 23-11.10) the (L) foot steps across the body and turns inward, in a clockwise direction, approximately 45 degrees. The weight is transferred from the (R) foot to the (L) foot and at the same time the (R) hand protects the centreline as an open palm.

(Figure 23-11.12) The practitioner continues to turn in a clockwise direction a further 180 degrees ending the pivot in (R) cat stance facing an angle of 45-degrees to the straight directional line of the form. The (R) hand turns upwards along the centreline and forms an eagle claw hand posture, thrusting upwards and out at the height of the throat. The rear (L) hand is retained at the (L) hip as a fist facing palm up.

(Figure 23-11.13) Next, the practitioner holds the (R) cat stance and opens the hips, by turning the waist backwards. At the same time, the (L) arm stretches backwards in a circular motion in time with the turning of the waist. The (R) forward hand retains its eagle claw posture and extends forwards slightly in time with the waist turn. The back remains straight throughout the rotation of the waist.

(Figure 23-11.14) Next, step forwards at the 45-degree angle to the right of the straight directional line of the form, pushing off the rear (L) foot and leading with the forward (R) foot, using the half-step method. At the same time, the (L) arm and hand circles from behind, high over the height of the head and continues down across the centreline in front of the practitioner as an open palm strike, ending at the height and level of the opposite (R) hip. This is (R) Bear posture.

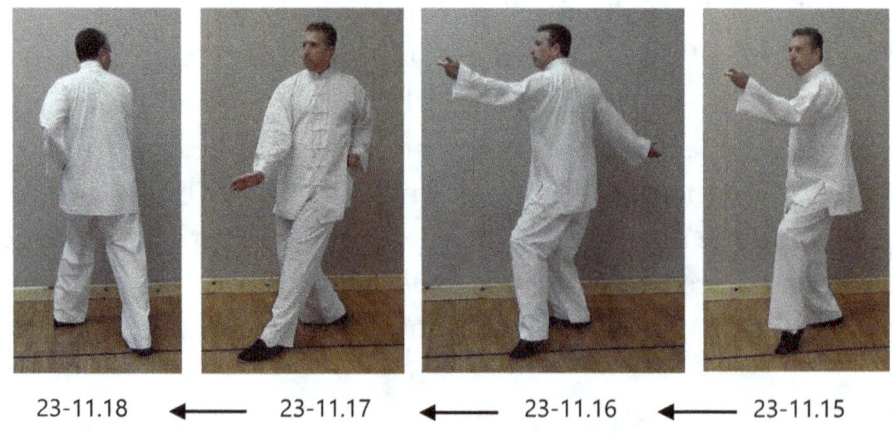

23-11.18   ← 23-11.17   ← 23-11.16   ← 23-11.15

(23-11.15 to 11.17) Movements (figures 23-11.15 to 11.17) repeat the sequence of movements (figures 23-11.12 to 11.14) on the opposite side. This ends in movement (figure 23-11.17) with the practitioner in (L) Bear posture.

Note: At this point the same sequence of movements can be performed repeatedly forward in a straight line until the practitioner chooses to turn and change direction. Traditionally Hsing-I practitioners turn their forms on the (L) side; however, it is prudent to practice turns on both sides from a fighting application purpose.

(Figure 23-11.18) From (L) Bear posture (figure 23-11.17) the (L) foot steps across the body and is turned inward, in a clockwise direction, approximately 45 degrees. The weight is transferred from the (R) foot to the (L) foot and at the same time the (R) hand protects the centreline as an open palm.

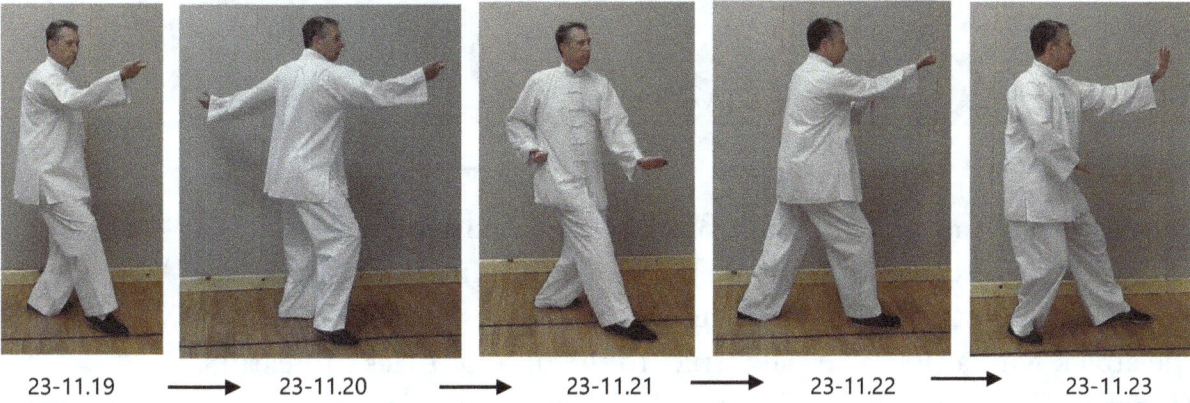

23-11.19 → 23-11.20 → 23-11.21 → 23-11.22 → 23-11.23

(Figure 23-11.19) The practitioner continues to turn in a clockwise direction a further 180 degrees ending the pivot in (R) cat stance facing an angle of 45-degrees to the straight directional line of the form. The (R) hand turns upwards along the centreline and forms an eagle claw hand posture, thrusting upwards and out at the height of the throat. The rear (L) hand is retained at the (L) hip as a fist facing palm up.

(Figure 23-11.20) Next, the practitioner holds the (R) cat stance and opens the hips, by turning the waist backwards. At the same time, the (L) arm stretches backwards in a circular motion in time with the turning of the waist. The (R) forward hand retains its eagle claw posture and extends forwards slightly in time with the waist turn. The back remains straight throughout the rotation of the waist.

(Figure 23-11.21) Next, step forwards at the 45-degree angle to the right of the straight directional line of the form, pushing off the rear (L) foot and leading with the forward (R) foot, using the half-step method. At the same time, the (L) arm and hand circles from behind, high over the height of the head and continues down across the centreline in front of the practitioner as an open palm strike, ending at the height and level of the opposite (R) hip. The (R) arm reciprocally pulls back to the (R) hip as a fist, facing palm up. This is (R) Bear posture.

(Figure 23-11.22 and 11.23) Next, the practitioner turns to face the original centreline stepping forward with the (R) foot and punching forwards with the (R) fist simultaneously.

The (L) fist is held at the (R) elbow as in Pi Chuan and the practitioner steps forward with the (L) foot into (L) Pi Chuan posture. To finish the form correctly from (L) Pi Chuan the practitioner uses the closing method described in Chapter 19 previous.

Eagle/Bear Form Fighting Applications:

Application 1 – Movements 23-11.5 and 11.8

1a → 1b → 1c

(Figure 1a) White faces off with Black in a neutral stance.
(Figure 1b) Black throws a high (R) straight punch to White's face. White steps outside Black's attack turning to angle of 45-degrees. At the same time, White blocks the attack with a (R) eagle claw strike to the back of Black's forearm.
(Figure 1c) Before Black can respond, White grasps Black's extended arm, clawing deeply into the tendons of the wrist, and then steps forwards with his (R) foot and at the same time strikes into Black's armpit with a (L) eagle claw technique to attack the tendons and vessels.

Application 2 – Movements 23-11.5 and 11.8

2a → 2b → 2c

(Figure 2a) White faces off with Black in a neutral stance.
(Figure 2b) Black throws a high (R) straight punch to White's face. White steps outside Black's attack turning to angle of 45-degrees. At the same time blocks the attack with a (R) eagle claw strike to the back of Black's elbow.

(Figure 2c) Before Black can respond, White grasps Black's extended arm, clawing deeply into the tendons of the inside elbow, and then steps forwards with his (R) foot and at the same time strikes into Black's throat with a (L) eagle claw technique.

Application 3 – Movements 23-11.3 and 11.4

3a → 3b → 3c → 3d

(Figure 3a) White faces off with Black in a neutral stance.
(Figure 3b) Black throws a low (R) straight punch to White's Tan Tien. White quickly steps into the attack cutting it off with a (L) crescent palm block.
(Figure 3c) Black counters with a (L) roundhouse punch to White's head which White swipes away with a (R) bear open palm strike.
(Figure 3d) Before Black can respond, White delivers a second bear open palm strike directly to Black's jaw.

Application 4 – Movements 23-11.2, 11.3, 11.4, 11.6 and 11.7

4a → 4b → 4c → 4d

(Figure 4a) White faces off with Black in a neutral stance.
(Figure 4b) Black throws a high (R) straight punch to White's face. White steps outside Black's attack turning to angle of 45-degrees. At the same time blocks the attack with a (R) eagle claw strike to the back of Black's elbow.
(Figure 4c) White steps in and grasps Black's extended arm to control him. At the same time, he strikes the back of Black's shoulder with a (R) open palm strike, forcing Black to bend forwards and over balance.
(Figure 4d) Before Black can recover, White delivers a second (R) open palm strike directly to Black's (R) ear.

Fighting Chicken Form

12. Fighting Chicken Form – Dou Gi Hsing

Introduction

Master McNeil

The fighting chicken has great physical power and courage. The movements of this form are quick and aggressive in their application. There are some switching from high to low postures which can be challenging of both balance and leg strength, however the applications gained from this form are many and although it may appear odd to look at when practiced in single form, with exploration of its techniques in application it soon becomes apparent as to its effectiveness in fighting.

The direction of Fighting Chicken form is to move up and down in a straight line. The form then turns 180 degrees and repeats its movements in the opposite direction before turning again to finish facing the same direction the practitioner originally started in accordance with traditional Hsing-I practice.

Fighting Chicken Form

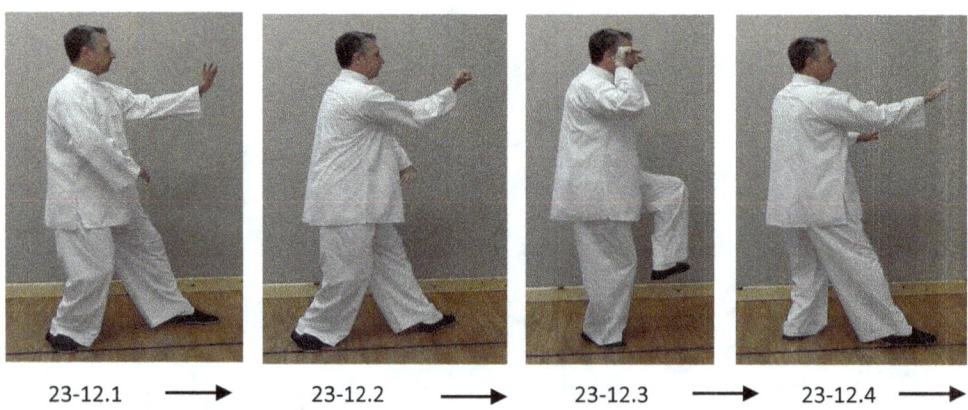

23-12.1 → 23-12.2 → 23-12.3 → 23-12.4 →

To open the form into (L) Pi Chuan (Figure 23-12.1) use the opening method shown in Chapter 19 previous.

(Figure 23-12.1) Starting from (L) Pi Chuan posture.

(Figure 23-12.2) Step forward with the (L) foot, placed at 45 degrees to the centreline of the form. At the same time, the (R) hand punches straight up the centreline in a drilling motion the same as Tsuan Chuan to the height of the nose. The (L) hand blocks down the centreline at the height of the Tan Tien as an open palm.

(Figure 23-12.3) Next, the (L) foot is raised and drawn back into (R) single leg stance and at the same time both the hands are drawn into the side of the head in cranes beak postures to the height of their corresponding temples. The elbows are held close to the body to protect the upper ribs.

(Figure 23-12.4) Both feet then rapidly exchange positions using the chicken step method. The head stays level throughout this change of stance. The practitioner is now in (R) Pi Chuan stance. Simultaneously with the feet the hands change, with both hands striking forwards as open palms. The (R) hand attacks slightly ahead of the (L) hand and on completion of the movement the (R) hand remains above the forward (R) foot and the (L) hand remains protecting the centreline at the height of the solar plexus. Both hands remain palms facing downwards and pointing in the direction of the centreline. Throughout the sequence, both hands must start and finish their movements together.

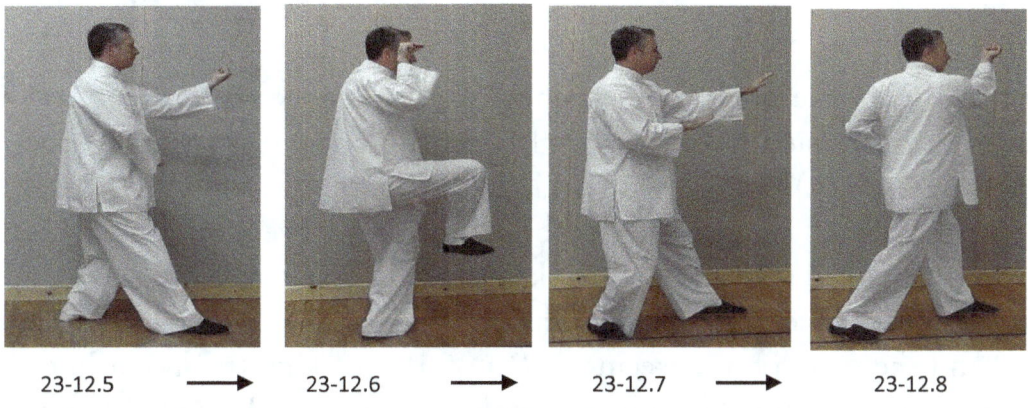

23-12.5 → 23-12.6 → 23-12.7 → 23-12.8

(Figure 23-12.5) Next, step forward with the (R) foot, placed at 45 degrees to the centreline of the form. At the same time, the (L) hand punches straight up the centreline in a drilling motion the same as Tsuan Chuan to the height of the nose. The (R) hand blocks down the centreline at the height of the Tan Tien as an open palm.

(Figure 23-12.6) Next, the (R) foot is raised and drawn back into (L) single leg stance and at the same time both the hands are drawn into the side of the head in cranes beak postures to the height of their corresponding temples. The elbows are held close to the body to protect the upper ribs.

(Figure 22-12.7) Both feet then rapidly exchange positions using the chicken step method. The head stays level throughout this change of stance. The practitioner is now in (L) Pi Chuan stance. Simultaneously with the feet the hands change, with both hands striking forwards as open palms. The (L) hand attacks slightly ahead of the (R) hand and on completion of the movement the (L) hand remains above the forward (L) foot and the (R) hand remains protecting the centreline at the height of the solar plexus. Both hands remain palms facing downwards and must start and finish their movements together.

(Figure 22-12.8) Next the feet remain static whilst the (R) hand forms a fist and executes an O/I block across the centreline coming to rest with the (R) fist in line with the (L) shoulder opposite. The (L) hand also forms a fist and pulls back to the (L) hip with palm facing upwards.

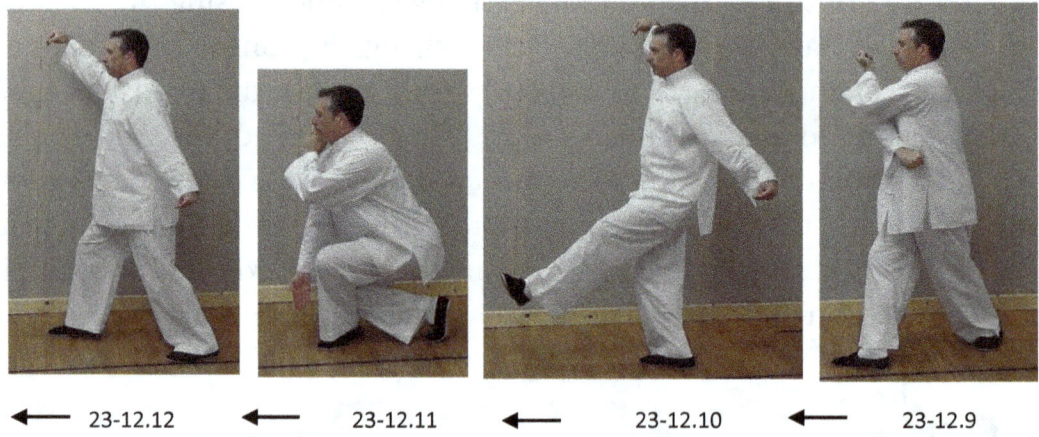

← 23-12.12   ← 23-12.11   ← 23-12.10   ← 23-12.9

(Figure 22-12.9) The practitioner then turns 180 degrees on the spot with both feet turned to opposing 45-degree angles. As the body turns the (R) arm drops down towards the (L) opposite hip and the (L) hand executes a O/I block across the centreline at head height. This combined turning movement causes the arms to become tightly coiled across the body like a spring waiting to recoil.

(Figure 22-12.10) Next the weight transfers from the (L) foot into the forward (R) foot and the practitioner executes a (L) 45-degree kick (rising) at knee height. Both arms simultaneously explode diagonally outwards with the (R) hand striking upwards to head height in a cranes beak hand posture and the (L) hand striking out to the side at hip height also as a cranes beak hand posture.

(Figure 22-12.11) As the (L) kicking foot lands on the ground the weight is transferred into it and the practitioner drops straight down into a low cross sitting stance. The (L) hand covers across the centreline at face height as an open palm block and the (R) hand strikes straight down towards the ground in a finger thrust hand posture.

(Figure 22-12.12) From the previous low cross sitting position the practitioner explodes upwards changing feet in mid-air so as the (R) foot becomes the forward foot with the weight evenly balanced between both legs on landing as a (R) bow stance. Again, both hands strike outwards as cranes beak hand postures with the (R) hand reaching head height and the (L) hand striking out to hip height on their respective sides.

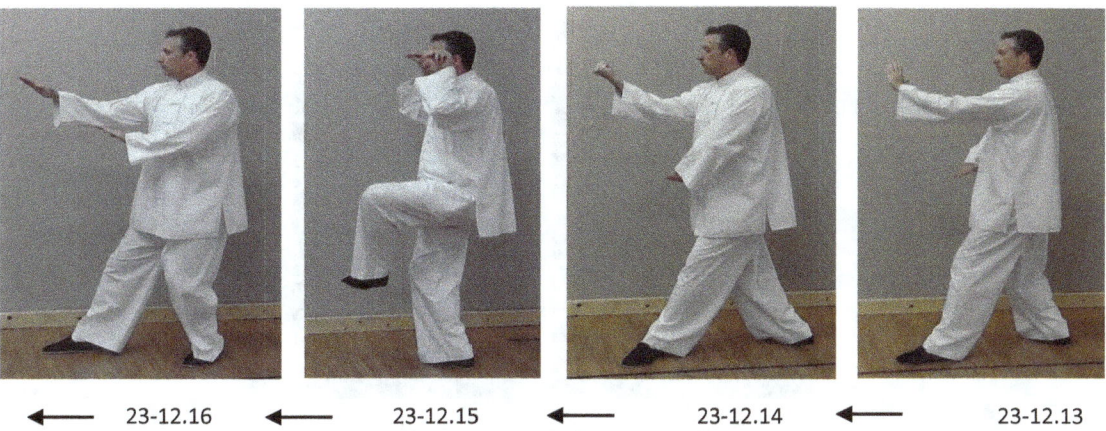

← 23-12.16   ← 23-12.15   ← 23-12.14   ← 23-12.13

(Figure 22-12.13) Next, draw in the both hands to Tan Tien height as fists facing palm down. Step forwards with the (R) foot and at the same time the (R) fist punches straight out to nose height followed closely by the (L) fist which is kept close to the (R) elbow. Step through with the (L) foot and follow up with the (R) foot using the half-step method, this puts the practitioner into (L) Pi Chuan posture.

(Figures 23-12.14 to 12.24) The practitioner the repeats the same movements as described in figures 23-12.2 to 12.12 previously, in the opposite direction before turning again 180 degrees to face the direction they originally started the form.

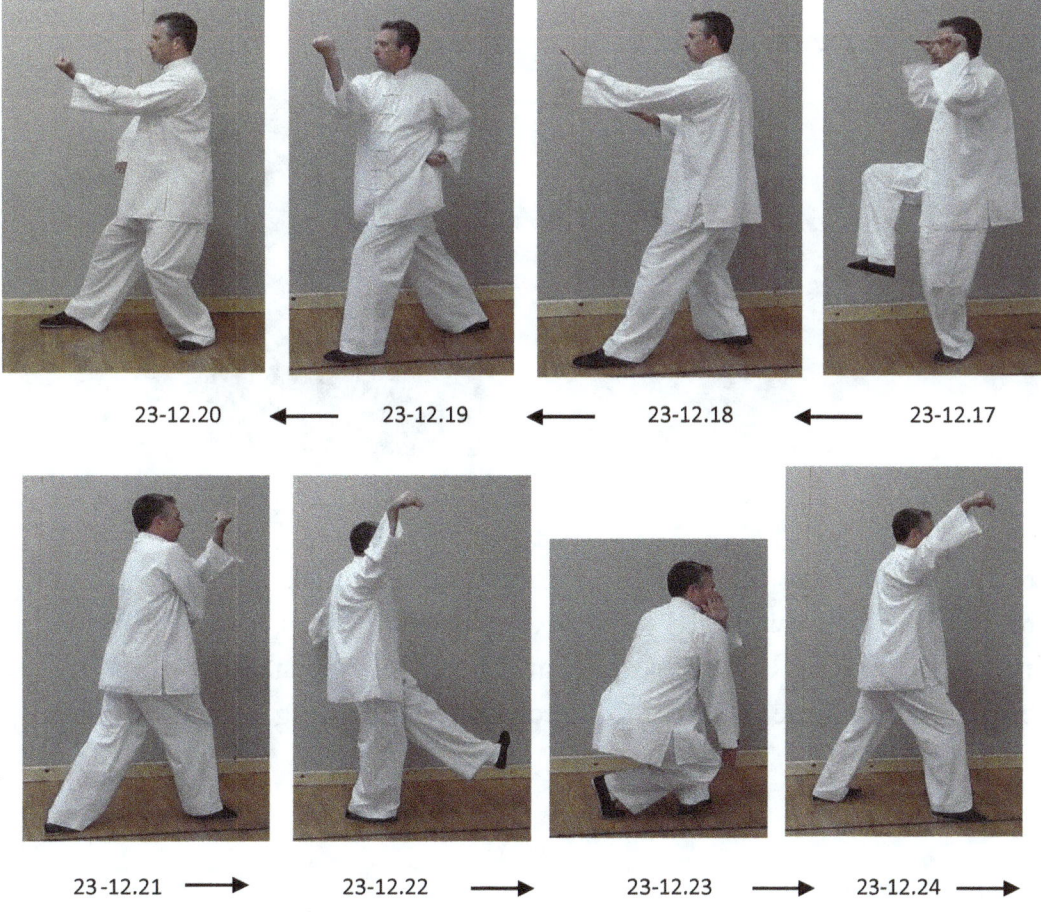

23-12.20 ← 23-12.19 ← 23-12.18 ← 23-12.17

23-12.21 → 23-12.22 → 23-12.23 → 23-12.24 →

23-12.25 → 23-12.26

(Figures 23-12.25 and 12.26) Next, the practitioner turns to face the original straight line direction of the form by stepping forward with the (R) foot and punching forwards with the (R) fist simultaneously. The (L) fist is held at the (R) elbow as in Pi Chuan and the practitioner steps forward with the (L) foot into (L) Pi Chuan posture. To finish the form correctly from (L) Pi Chuan the practitioner uses the closing method described in Chapter 19 previously.

Fighting Chicken – Fighting Applications:

Application 1 – Movement 23-12.2

1a → 1b

(Figure 1a) White faces off with Black in a neutral stance.
(Figure 1b) Black throws a (R) straight punch to White's ribs. White counters by stepping onto Black's (R) forward foot and blocking the strike with a (L) covering palm block. At the same time White executes a (R) drilling punch to Black's jaw.

Application 2 – Movements 23-12.3 and 12.4

2a → 2b → 2c → 2d

(Figure 2a) White faces off with Black in a neutral stance.
(Figure 2b) Black throws a (R) straight punch to White's ribs. White counters by blocking the strike with a (L) covering palm block.
(Figure 2c) Black then counter strikes with a (L) roundhouse punch to White's head. White draws back into a (L) single leg stance and blocks the attack with a (R) cranes beak block.
(Figure 2d) White then counter strikes by dropping the foot and stepping into Black's centre and delivering a (R) knife hand strike to Black's (L) clavicle.

Application 3 – Movements 23-12.8 and 12.9

3a → 3b → 3c → 3d

(Figure 3a) White faces off with Black in a neutral stance.
(Figure 3b) Black throws a (R) straight punch to White's face. White counters by blocking the strike with a (R) O/I hammer fist block.
(Figure 3c) Black then counterstrikes with a (L) roundhouse punch to White's head. White counters by blocking the strike with a (L) O/I hammer fist block.
(Figure 3d) White then counter strikes by delivering a third O/I hammer fist strike to Black's jaw.

Hsing-I Chuan | The Practice of Heart and Mind Boxing

Application 4 – Movement 23-12.10

4a → 4b → 4c → 4d

(Figure 4a) White faces off with Black in a neutral stance.
(Figure 4b) Black throws a (R) straight punch to White's face. White counters by covering the attack with a (R) open palm, redirecting Black's attack. As White draws Black in he steps behind Black's forward leg.
(Figure 4c and 4d) White then counters by controlling Black's outstretched (R) arm and hooking round Black's forward (R) foot to sweep him completely off balance and force him to the ground.

Application 5 – Movements 23-12.12 and 12.14

5a → 5b → 5c

(Figure 5a) White faces off with Black in a neutral stance.
(Figure 5b) Black throws a (R) straight punch to White's face. White counters by blocking the strike with a (L) cranes beak block.
(Figure 5c) Black then throws a (L) upper cut, which White blocks with a (L) covering palm block and then executes a (R) drilling punch to Black's jaw.

Master James McNeil & Andrew Jackson

Chapter 24

Lo-Shu Training

The Ancient History of the Lo-Shu Diagram

Emperor Fu Xi

The 'Lo-Shu' is a Taoist diagram of change and part of the legacy of the most ancient Chinese mathematical and divinatory I-Ching traditions. The Lo-Shu Square literally translates as 'Luo River Scroll', or the 'Nine Halls Diagram' and reveals the unique normal magic square of order three.

Ancient Chinese myth would have it that the authorship of both the I-Ching and the Eight Trigrams are attributed to the Chinese Emperor Fu Xi, said to be a Shaman King who lived approximately 5000 years ago and was thought to have been half-man and half-dragon. Fu Xi was accredited with the development of civilisation, the teaching of writing and the concept of organised agriculture to his subjects amongst many other things.

One day he was said to have seen a Dragon-Horse rise from the 'Huang Ho' (Yellow River) and on its side, were markings, which were recorded as the Ho-Tu, or Yellow River map. From this diagram, the emperor interpreted the eight directions of the Ho-Tu in terms of the so-called 'Earlier Heaven' arrangement of the Eight Trigrams. This pattern was said to describe the underlying nature of all things.

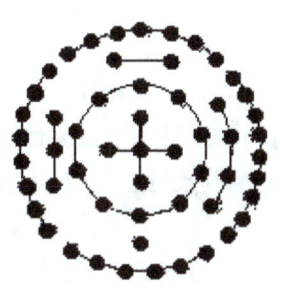

The Ho-Tu

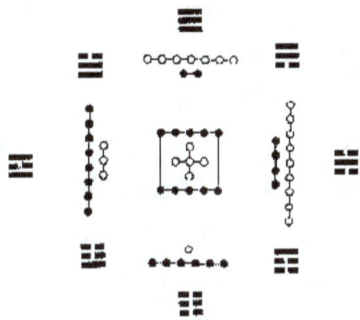

The 'Earlier Heaven' Sequence of Trigrams

Emperor Yu

Approximately 1000 years later ancient Chinese legend tells of another Shaman Emperor named 'Yu' who founded the Xia Dynasty although historical facts and dates are vague and conflicting. According to several ancient Chinese records, Emperor Yu was the eighth great-grandson of the Yellow Emperor Huang-Di and believed to have grown up on the slopes of Mount Song, just south of the Yellow River. During the reign of Yu's father, the Chinese heartland was frequently plagued by floods that prevented economic and social development. Yu's father spent more than nine years building a series of dykes and dams along the riverbanks which had limited success. When Yu came to power he continued his father's work and made a careful study of the river systems to learn why his father's great efforts had failed.

Over the next thirteen years Emperor Yu instigated the construction of a carefully planned system of irrigation canals which relieved floodwater into fields, as well as spending great effort dredging the riverbeds. This huge project was successful and allowed Chinese culture to prosper and flourish. The great achievement earned Emperor Yu renown throughout Chinese history and is referred to in Chinese history as 'Great Yu Controls the Waters' or 'Yu the Great'.

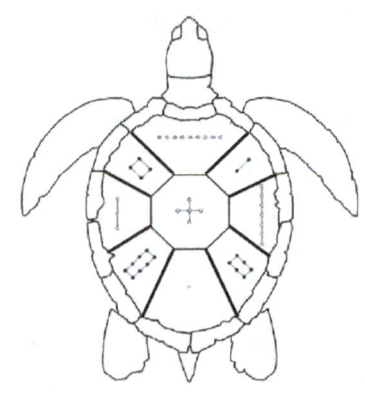

In a mythical version of this story Emperor Yu was assisted in his work by a divine turtle. It was said that one day whilst Yu was swimming in the River Lo (a major tributary of the Yellow River) the emperor sought solitude at the river's edge and as he gazed into the water he saw a turtle at his feet. Emperor Yu knew it was the same turtle he had seen formed by a pattern of stars in the night sky each night before he went to bed. On closer inspection, the Emperor noticed the special pattern on the turtle's shell and realized it was the 'Divine Turtle'.

From this realisation, it was deduced that the gods had provided Emperor Yu with a magic map containing information that allowed him to perform a ritual dance and save the country from the torrential flooding that was upon it at that time. This map was set out on the cracks of the turtle's shell and revealed a 3 x 3 magic square. The Lo-Shu sets out the eight trigrams about a central number and all numbers connect as a pattern of zig-zag lines. The map that Emperor Yu received was that of the 'Later Heaven' sequence of trigrams. It is believed that the 'Earlier Heaven' sequence refers to the archetypal order of things before creation (pre-creation) and the 'Later Heaven' sequence refers to the order of change in the manifest world (post-creation).

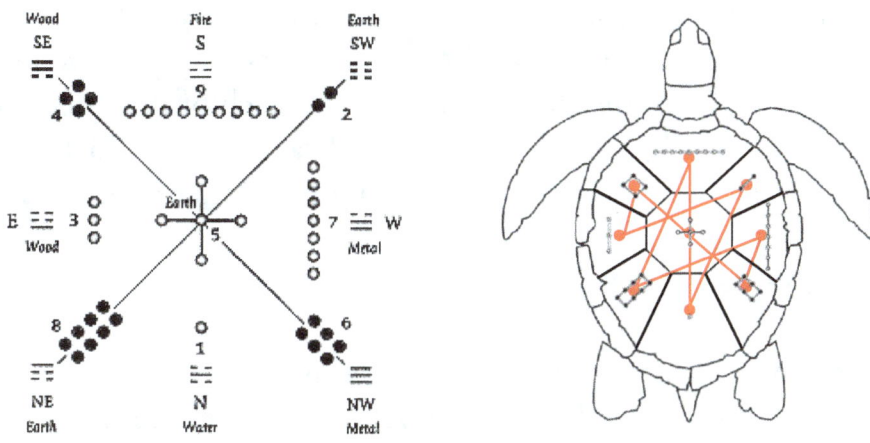

**The 'Later Heaven'
Sequence of Trigrams**

Since the discovery of the Lo-Shu it has been absorbed by later followers of the Tao and is often used in their rituals and magic practices. Taoist temples periodically perform the Chiao (Jiao) ritual, as a renewal of their cosmic mandate and efficacy. The secret part of the rituals take place inside the temple, where very few outsiders may attend. Inside the temple the core rituals themselves require a combination of reading ritual texts, making appropriate hand gestures, special meditation practices, offerings and dance movements, where the use of the Lo-Shu as a basic floor plan is drawn on the floor of the sacred ritual area. By dancing around the Lo-Shu, one is said to be able to summon the spirits. Through the course of the ritual, the Taoist sage concentrates their mind and energy to achieve union with the Tao where internally their body achieves harmony with the external universe. When this ritual is completed, the power and purity of the temple is renewed.

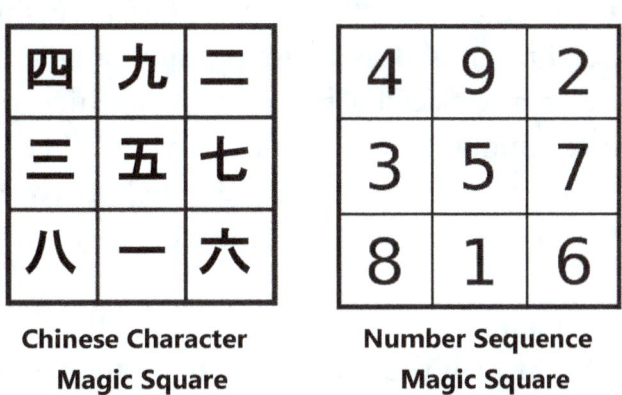

**Chinese Character
Magic Square**

**Number Sequence
Magic Square**

The 'Lo-Shu' is also known as a 'magic square' because the pattern of the magic square on the Divine turtle's shell was the first formula used to depict the energy of the universe. In the time of the ancient Chinese, the simple nine square grids of the magic square could be used to explain the balance and function of everything in the universe. The odd and even numbers alternate in the periphery of the Lo-Shu pattern; the four even numbers are at the four corners, and the five odd numbers form a cross in the centre of the square. The sums in each of the three rows, in each of the three columns, and in both diagonals, are always fifteen, which is the number of days in each of the twenty four cycles of the Chinese solar year.

Hsing-I Training using the Lo-Shu Diagram

As Hsing-I is an internal art that follows with Taoist principles its practice can also utilise the 'Dance of the Lo Shu' at a higher level where any of the systems movements can be practiced in either a single form or as a combination of movements which are repeatedly performed in the pattern and number sequence of the Lo-Shu.

Through regular training the practitioner aims to become skilled at a technique or random combination of techniques switching angles in an increasingly tight space mapped out by the placement of marker sticks in the Lo-Shu pattern. This skill when refined down to a small area is a useful development for fighting where switching from technique to technique in different directions without hardly moving and still being able to generate power is crucial to defeating an opponent.

Further to this when the skill level of the practitioner is at a high level the concentration and focus of the mind during this practice allows the practitioner to become in union with the 'Tao' achieving it is said unity in body, mind and spirit. This is the true goal of Hsing-I Chuan.

Practice method for Lo-Shu Training

The remainder of this chapter shows a series of nine diagrams which explains the order, direction and movements that a practitioner of Hsing-I performs when practicing this method of training. It is advised to start simple with the nine marker sticks of the Lo-Shu diagram placed a few feet apart which gives the practitioner space to execute their techniques correctly with power. When moving between the sticks, they must make sure they are blocking and punching correctly with every step. Each stick should be visualised as an opponent which the practitioner is evading, blocking or striking.

It is also advisable to start with the Metal Form, the first form usually learned in the system and progress through the Five Elements individually in sequence before practicing the more complex animal techniques of the system. As the practitioner becomes familiar with a technique they close in the Lo-Shu marker sticks until they are shoulder width apart and continue to train the technique until they can develop maximum power in the tightest possible space. When this is achieved they move on to the next technique and repeat the process.

At first the practitioner moves through the sticks in the number order of the 'magic square' (1-9) and later when this skill is mastered they can move through the pattern randomly. As the map of directions practiced when following the Lo-Shu were deemed to be provided by the gods, this training if practiced correctly will move the practitioner closer to the Tao spiritually.

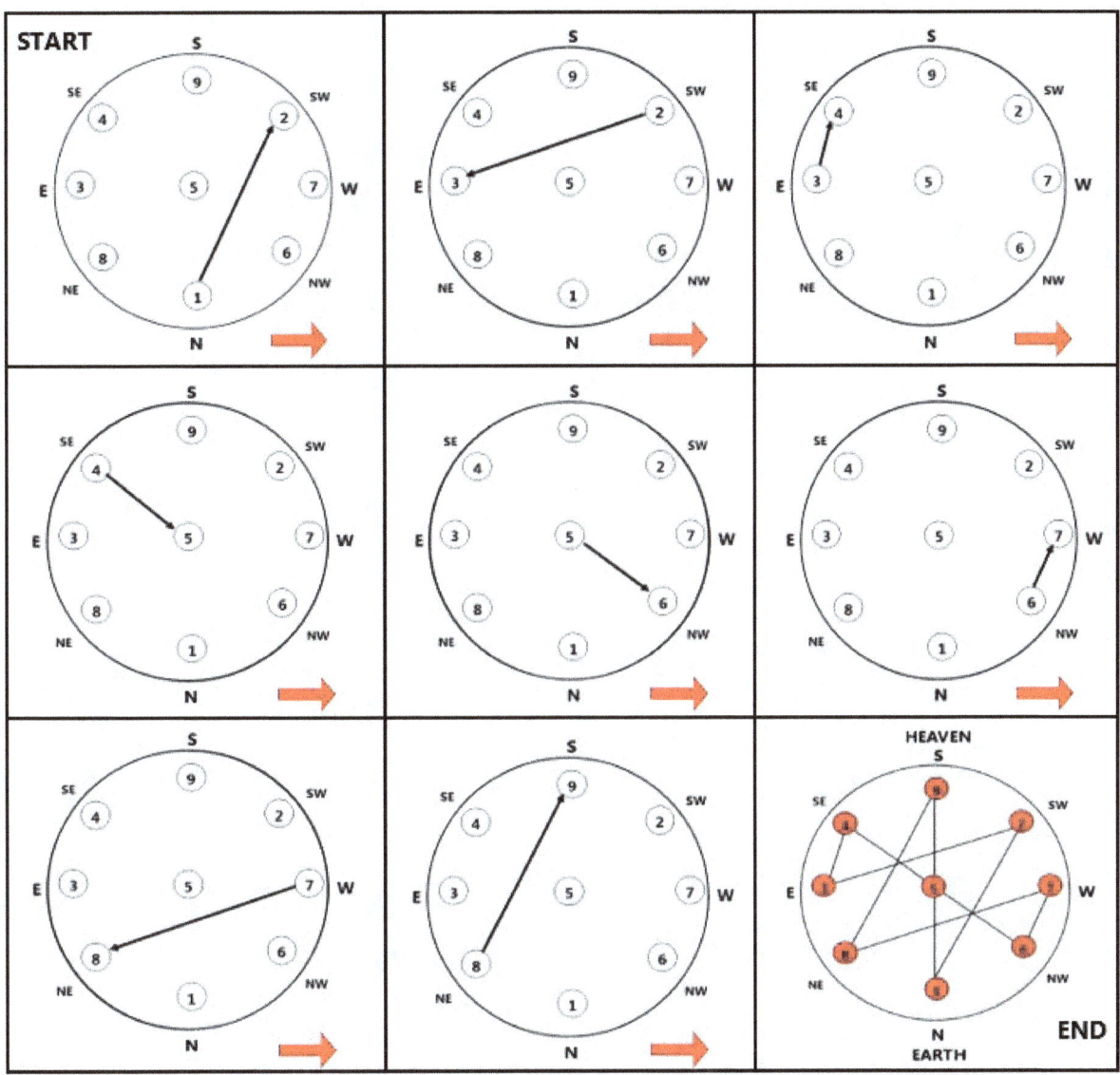

Chapter 25

Common Mistakes in Practice

Introduction

In order to understand how to develop the power attributed to Hsing-I, the novice practitioner must avoid making some common mistakes. However, it is inevitable that in learning something new a beginner will make mistakes. This is why all practitioners must all learn from knowledgeable teachers, so that these errors can be pointed out and corrected as they occur.

Regular correction over time is the key to successful learning. A novice who simply learns a form in a short time but never seeks future correction is much more likely to remain at a low level of skill and understanding. Many students learn forms and then leave their teacher, believing they can develop their training on their own and unfortunately wander completely off the path without realising it. Even worse, some go off and proclaim themselves a teacher, teaching others an art form they have not yet perfected themselves. Some students even when they have reached an ability to teach suddenly feel they can no longer learn from their teacher because now they are a teacher themselves. They believe they can only attend a class if they are teaching and no longer feel the need to continue their own learning. They forget why they started to learn in the first place, their own self-development and now focus only on standing at the head of the class wanting respect from others. Unfortunately these paths can lead to the practitioner developing a self-inflated ego, thinking they are better than they truly are.

Of course all practitioners must experiment and train by themselves, but they should also be reviewed by their teacher as regularly as possible in order to develop their skills and correct bad habits. When the time is right and usually with the permission and encouragement of the student's teacher the step up to teaching aspects of the system they have perfected will enhance the practitioner's abilities too. Respect as a teacher is earned by the hard work of being a student and this should never be forgotten no matter what level the practitioner is at. Most honest and reputable teachers would tell you that if their teacher was still in this world they would still be learning from them as a student. Therefore, the purpose of this chapter is to highlight some of the most common mistakes made by many Hsing-I students, regardless of the lineage from which they practise and the need to keep being reviewed by their teacher.

On this subject Andrew Jackson states:

"Once when training with my teacher Master McNeil I asked him about the difficulties I felt in trying to be a teacher in one sense whilst still learning at the same time and he said to me: 'When I was with my teacher, I was his student. When I am with my students I am their teacher.'

To this day I have never forgotten this simple yet truthful answer and as I have developed my training over the years I remain comfortable and happy with the role of being both a teacher and student. While my teacher is in this world, I will remain his student, seeking guidance and correction wherever possible. I know I can never be too experienced or too 'long in the tooth' to learn more from my teacher."

The following part of this chapter highlights six of the most common mistakes made when learning the basic principles of Hsing-I. A practitioner should constantly check every movement of their forms and try to eliminate these mistakes. These mistakes may seem obvious to most martial artists and yet when they practise their own techniques they seem to be completely oblivious when they make the same mistakes themselves. Ask yourself constantly, do I make these mistakes? Do I seek guidance and review from my teacher to make sure bad habits have not crept into my practise? Have I changed the way I practice without realising it and if so why have I done this? It is not only beginners who make mistakes. When more experienced practitioners self-develop their techniques, they can easily start to make mistakes without realising. Never think you are too skilled to be corrected, this is one of the biggest mistakes any practitioner can make!

On this subject Master McNeil states:

"Every movement and every posture of the body has a meaning when practising Hsing-I. The movements and postures of each of the forms have been preserved over time for special purposes. Whether or not the practitioner can comprehend this depends on the quality of their instruction and the length of time they have studied.

To modify an art, which has been in existence for over a thousand years, takes a special person of great skill, and in most cases they are making the assumption that by modifying a posture or movement they are improving it. In reality though, they are really only adapting it for themselves. Generally speaking, attempts to modify an ancient art such as Hsing-I should not be made, since the essential elements may be lost in the process. In my opinion, it should be kept as pure and as close to its origins as possible."

Mistake (1)

Figure 25-1a

Incorrect: Don't ever over extend your body when attacking an opponent.

Figure 25-1b

Correct: Keep your back straight and keep your feet and hands aligned throughout delivery of your technique.

Mistake (2)

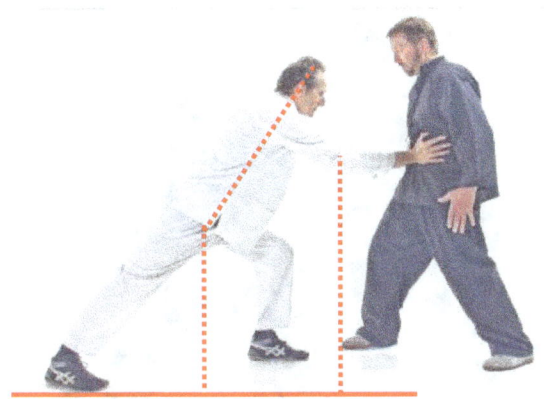

Figure 25-2a

Incorrect: Don't overextend the elbow past the knee when pushing an opponent.

Figure 25-2b

Correct: When pushing, you should always have your back straight, elbows down and feet aligned.

Mistake (3)

Figure 25-3a

Incorrect: You will have reduced power pulling an opponent when you bend forward at the waist.

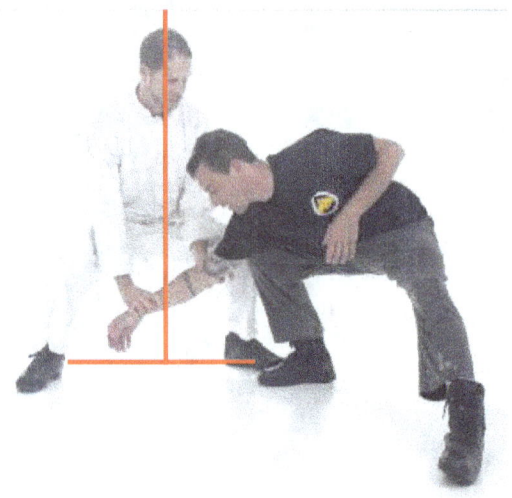

Figure 25-3b

Correct: Sink your weight and keep your back straight. This will allow you to pull any opponent down with tremendous force.

Mistake (4)

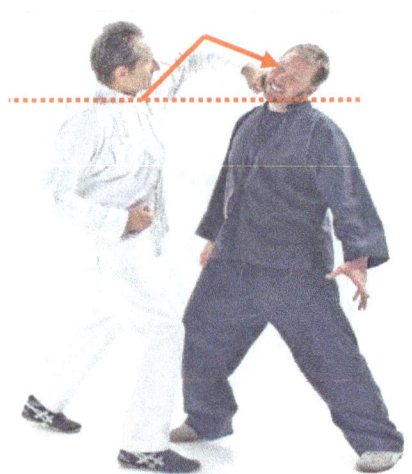

Figure 25-4a

Incorrect: With the elbow raised, there is a loss of power in the delivery of the punch and this arm position leaves the ribs exposed to a counter attack.

Figure 25-4b

Correct: Keep the elbow down for increased power in your punch. This method allows for the efficient use of internal power in your technique and protects the body from counterstrike.

Mistake (5)

Figure 25-5a

Incorrect: With the heel off the ground, the supporting leg straight and the knee held in extension, the foundation of your technique will be unstable and there will be less power generated in your kick.

Figure 25-5b

Correct: With the foot firmly planted to the ground, the supporting leg bent and the knee positioned in line with the foot below, you will have better balance and more driving power in your kick.

Mistake (6)

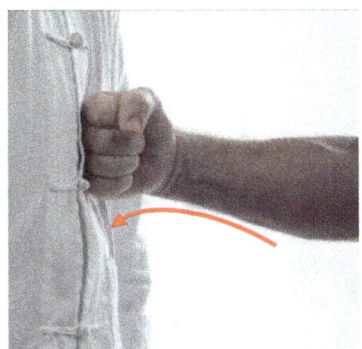

Figure 25-6a

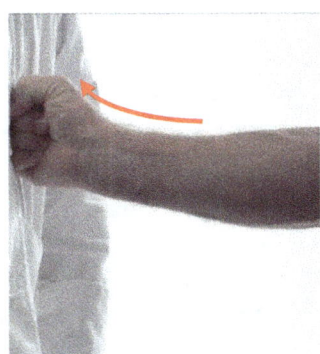

Figure 25-6b

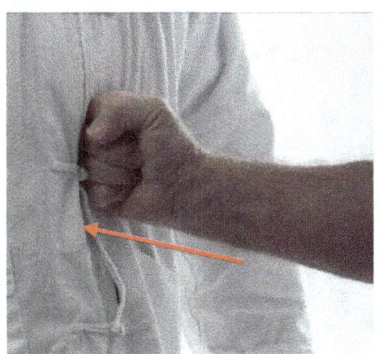

Figure 25-6c

Figure 25-6a, 6b
Incorrect: When punching, if the wrist is bent then the tendons will be loose on impact with the target. This results in you having less strength in the direction of your technique, which could easily lead to injury.

Figure 25-6c
Correct: If the wrist is straight in the direction of your punch you will have much more penetrating power in your punch's delivery and less likely to injure the wrist on impact with the target.

Chapter 26

Five Element Staff

Introduction

Historical background of weapons development
The documented use of weapons in martial arts dates back over thousands of years. In fact man utilised simple objects found around him in his environment, provided by nature such as sticks and stones to defend himself or hunt for food in order to survive and this proof can been seen in cave paintings and artifacts found in excavations around many parts of the world including china, dating back to prehistoric times.

As time progressed and man's ingenuity advanced, weapons with sharp edges and projectiles with deadly accuracy were developed allowing man to fight more effectively with reduced chance of injury to himself when hunting as he could remain at a further, safer distance from his prey and still bring it down.

Ancient Chinese civilisation was no different than any other part of the world in this development. As it advanced so did the need to defend itself from neighbouring civilisations. In the fight for supremacy and control, warlords headed groups who fought to conquer one another trying constantly to eradicate their enemies and assert their dominance over the lands they controlled.

As society within these civilisations developed into more complex structures each element required means and methods to defend its own position and keep it in control. Emperors, Kings, Warlords and politicians would develop more advanced weapons with Blacksmiths working bronze, iron and eventually developing steel to produce many types of lethal weapons and protective armour of great quality. They also trained great armies and even religious factions would train their monks to protect their temples and the treasures contained within them.

Rivalling civilisations constantly needed to expand their territory to provide for their ever-increasing population. As their population expanded, so did their yield of taxes and their wealth. Maintaining their growth and dominance led to many battles between great armies and it was these battle grounds that led to the rapid development of weapons and the skills required to utilise them.

Most traditional Chinese martial arts systems have many weapons attributed to them. Some very simple and practical, others very exotic and requiring great skill to use them effectively. Hsing-I was no different, originally attributed to General Yue Fei as the leader of a great army his warriors were trained to use weapons alongside their empty hand skills. In a battle, his soldiers would have been skilled with a weapon but further to this the need to understand a range of weapons would also be necessary including understanding the weapons and tactics of their enemies. Therefore, a soldier often trained in multiple weapons so that on the battle field they could pick up any type of weapon and use it effectively. If a soldier knew how to use a weapon he could attack with it but he could also understand its strategy and therefore understand how to defend against it too.

Hsing-I Weapons

Most lineages of Hsing-I have some form of weapons training as a part of their curriculum. The most commonly trained weapons are Staff (Guen), Spear (Chiang), Broad Sword (Dao Jian) and Straight Sword (Zhang Jian). A few lineages have some unique weapons of their own but the four mentioned here are the most common and reflect some of those most commonly utilised in Chinese armies of the past.

The most important thing for the practitioner of Hsing-I to understand when they start their weapons training is that they need to utilise the same theories and skills they have developed in their empty hand training and apply them correctly in the use of the weapon. It is for this reason that weapons training usually starts after or towards the end of empty hand training when learning Hsing-I.

First the theories of Hsing-I must be understood before they can be utilised with a weapon in the hands. Whole body power must be applied to the weapons technique just the same as in the empty hand techniques for them to be effective. This allows the practitioner to extend the range of their chi beyond their body and through the weapon energising it to apply devastating and lethal blows to defeat an enemy.

This method of training makes the Hsing-I method of using weapons quite distinct and recognisable from other systems of martial arts in that the structure and shape of the techniques trained in the empty hand forms can be clearly seen in the weapons form. If the practitioner doesn't understand the basic skills of Hsing-I then training any weapon at this stage will only serve to make the practitioner less effective in its use.

The weapons commonly favoured in the practice of Hsing-I are usually much heavier and larger than those seen in other systems and modern martial arts today. This probably stems back to ancient times where practical weapons needed to be strong enough to survive the rigours of battle. As weapons technology developed then it is logical to assume weapons became smaller, lighter and more flexible as they were made of stronger more durable materials. Training with heavier weapons also helps to develop the practitioner's chi, balance and strength.

The staff was usually the first weapon to be trained as the skills and strength learned from this training served to prepare the practitioner for the more dangerous training of weapons with bladed edges such as sword and spear. If a mistake is made training with the staff the practitioner ends up with bruises and embarrassment. When a mistake is made with a live bladed weapon and the practitioner may seriously injure themselves and their training could be finished forever.

The Hsing-I training staff was often over six feet in length and had a diameter of three inches or more. It appeared more like a slim log than the type of staff often seen in today's martial arts. Made from hard and dense wood, it was heavy and designed to defend against all types of weapons including those with bladed edges. The method of the Hsing-I staff was to incorporate both double and single ended techniques, making its application effective at long and medium range in either attack or defence. Later after the skills of staff were learned the practitioner could move onto the spear which is required a higher level of skill manoeuvre the bladed spear tip accurately and effectively.

When considering sword training it is usually the broad sword that was learned first as the skills are more basic. Again, it was usually the heavier of the swords and so gave good grounding in strength and agility required to utilise it. The techniques of the broad sword are more circular in general with 'hacking' and 'slashing' movements designed to cut down the enemy. Its thick heavy blade reduced its speed, but the blunt back side of the blade could be used to block and the fashioned edge used to cut. It was an effective weapon even with a less skilled soldier and for that reason was often provided to the lower ranking soldiers within the armies.

The more skilful method of sword was the straight sword which requires many hours of practice to master its technique. Hsing-I straight swords are often double handed and long in length making them a challenge to master. The skills learned from this practice can also be transferred to the shorter straight sword which is more commonly seen in most martial arts today.

In conclusion, the staff and broad sword were quicker to learn than the spear and straight sword respectively. Therefore, these were the weapons taught initially to basic low ranking troops. As a soldier progressed in their career and if they survived the many battles they encountered they would then rise in rank and so learn and master more skilful weapons.

In times of peace the natural method of learning the different weapons were progressed in the same order. The quality and time required to make a spear or straight sword was considerably longer and more expensive than a staff or broad sword therefore it was often the lower classes who trained in staff and broad sword opposed to the higher more wealthier classes who had time and money to develop the skills required for the spear and straight sword. It was for this reason the staff and broad sword were referred to as 'peasant' weapons and the spear and straight swords were referred to as 'scholar' weapons. However, in today's society where all weapons can be learned without such class prejudice it should be recognised that all the weapons are deadly when placed in a skilled practitioners' hands and using the Hsing-I method.

In this lineage of Hsing-I the only weapon that is taught is the staff. However, this weapon provides the basic skill set required to understand the theory of applying Hsing-I mechanics to the use of almost any weapon. It is the most practical weapon to learn in today's society as the staff is easily accessible as any long stick could be used, it is currently still legal to walk round with a stick and therefore more practical with today's laws.

The remainder of this chapter will discuss the staff from a Hsing-I, five elements prospective, looking at each individual element and applying its energy and form to an individual staff technique and fighting application. This is the starting point for understanding Hsing-I staff training just as it is in empty hand practice. Once these techniques and the mechanics associated with them are understood the practitioner can then move onto the more complex Hsing-I staff form.

Even though there is only one main staff form associated to this lineage when a practitioner is training the five element techniques they can execute them continuously in a straight line and turn in effect creating a five-element form. After the individual element techniques of Metal, Water, Wood, Fire and Earth have been trained and their energies understood they can be further combined to create another form similar to the empty hand version of the Five Element Linked Form which are shown earlier in this book. Practicing the individual elements in this way gives the practitioner more variation and structure to their staff training regime.

Within the lineage discussed in this book the sole staff form is called 'Jou Torng Bong', which originates through Master Hsu and serves to combine the energies of the Five Elements and Twelve Animals into the use of the staff. Unfortunately, the exact translation of this name is not clear and appears to have been lost over time. Due to the size and complexity of this form it makes it too difficult to show and describe in photo format, so it has not been illustrated in this book. Instead the individual Five Element techniques alongside their associated energies and applications will be discussed. These skills then can be transferred directly into the practice of the staff form which would need to be learned directly from a knowledgeable teacher of this lineage.

The benefits attributed to training in Hsing-I Staff are:
- Improves stability of footwork
- Improves hand/eye coordination
- Develops combined 'whole body' power
- Improves physical strength
- Improves understanding of Hsing-I techniques
- Improves strategy awareness in applying Hsing-I techniques at different ranges

Hsing-I Staff Training Method

1. San-Ti Posture Training

26-1a ← 26-1b   26-1c ← 26-1d

Left Side San-Ti Posture   **Right Side San-Ti Posture**

Training in the Hsing-I Staff follows the same protocol as learning the empty hand forms. Prior to learning the complex staff form of Jou Torng Bong the practitioner must first understand the basic principles of San-Ti posture and the individual Five Elements techniques, because these principles and their techniques are embedded within the staff form.

Training first begins with standing in San-Ti posture in both left and right sided variations until the practitioner becomes used to standing whilst holding the staff and familiarising their body and mind to this structure. If the practitioner has a sound grounding in Hsing-I empty hand forms and San-Ti standing practice this first practice method should be quite quick to assimilate. However, it should never be ignored or underestimated.

It should be noted that (L) San-Ti posture with the staff is a mirror of (L) Reverse Metal posture shown above in Figures 26-1a and 1b and not (L) Metal posture as practiced in empty hand training. This is because the staff method usually has the (R) hand holding the midsection and the (L) hand holding the rear section of the staff as its basic default hand position. Therefore, it differs slightly from empty hand practice of San-Ti training. When standing in (R) San-Ti, the mirror position is (R) Metal as shown in Figures 26-1c and 1d above.

Practice Method
Stand in both (L) and (R) San-Ti posture holding the staff with the hands placed just like Metal form for periods of five to twenty minutes until the body and mind feel comfortable in both the posture and holding the weight of the staff physically. Try practising with longer, heavier staffs when this standing practice appears to be getting easier, as this will increase the mental and physical strength, endurance, and chi flow of the practitioner.

2. Staff Form Opening Sequence

When stepping into San-Ti posture or any of the Five Elements postures the method of opening and closing the sequence is the same. The closing method is simply a reverse of the opening method. When practising any of the Five Element staff techniques or the staff form the practitioner should always open and close from a (L) San-Ti posture in line with traditional Hsing-I theory.

The opening movements are shown below from both side and front to enable the reader to get a clear view of the sequence.

← 26-2c   ← 26-2b   ← 26-2a

Side View

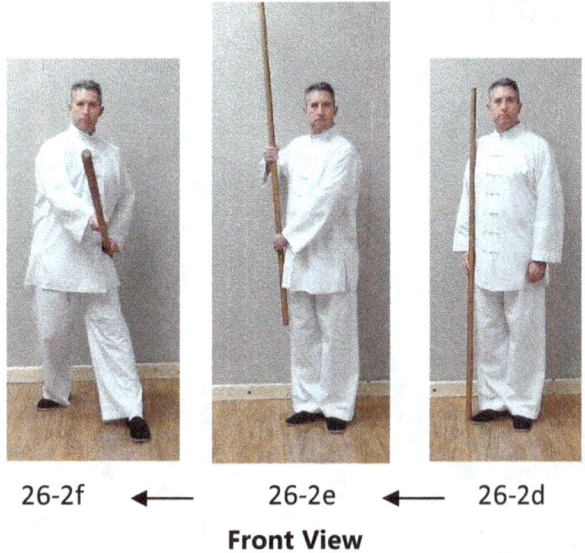

26-2f ← 26-2e ← 26-2d
Front View

Starting sequence from far right to left

(Figures 26-2a and 2d) Standing facing forward in a neutral Wuji posture with the front (L) foot facing straight and the back (R) foot angled to 45 degrees. The staff is held in the (R) hand at the height of the hip and parallel to the (R) side of the body with the lower end resting on the ground. The upper section of the staff rests lightly against the front of the (R) shoulder.

(Figures 26-2b and 2e) The practitioner raises the staff with their (R) hand to the height of their shoulder and at the same time grasps the lower section of the staff with their (L) hand, whilst turning their body 45 degrees to the right. This movement across the body with the (L) hand takes the staff away slightly from the (R) shoulder and keeps it raised and perpendicular to the ground.

(Figures 26-2c and 2f) Next the practitioner steps forward with the (L) foot into left side San-Ti posture and brings the staff forward and down in a straight line to an angle of 45 degrees to the ground, this movement is executed in a 'chopping' action as in Metal form. The (R) hand and (L) foot are forward as in a reverse metal posture in empty hand forms practice. This movement completes the opening sequence and places the practitioner in a guard stance from which all other staff techniques can be executed.

3. Staff Closing Technique

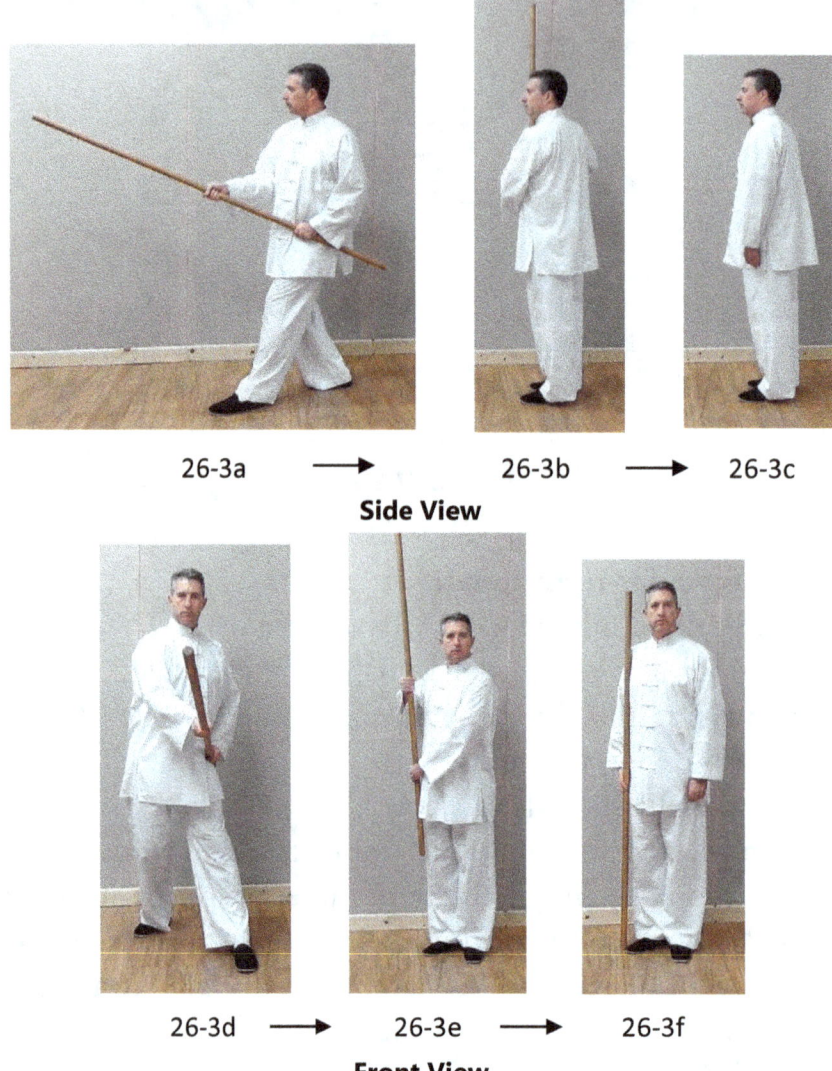

Starting sequence from far left to right
(Figures 26-3a and 3d) Starting from a (L) San-Ti posture
(Figures 26-3b and 3e) The practitioner takes a step backwards with the rear (R) foot and at the same time draws the forward (L) foot backwards until the heels of the two feet come together. The rear foot is placed at 45 degrees and the forward foot faces straight ahead. As the feet move backwards and draw together, the (R) hand draws the staff backwards to the (R) side of the body and the (L) hand simultaneously comes across the body retaining its grip on the lower section of the staff. The body is now facing 45 degrees to the right with the staff raised and held perpendicular to the ground.
(Figures 26-3c and 3f) Finally the staff is lowered by the (R) hand to the ground with the upper section of the staff coming to rest against the front of the (R) shoulder. The (L) hand is holding the rear section of the staff at the height of the (L) hip. The body turns back to face front and finishes in Wuji posture.

4. Five Element Staff Turn Method

When practising the Five Element staff techniques the practitioner moves up and down in a straight line repeating the chosen technique on both left and right sides. When the practitioner elects to turn they first step forward from which ever element technique they are training into (L) Metal posture. From this posture, they can then execute the turn sequence as shown in this chapter and then continue to train the element of choice. By using this method of returning always to (L) Metal at the end of each sequence the turn method will always be the same regardless of the element being practiced.

Note: Some lineages of Hsing-I have a different turn sequence for each of the Five Elements like the empty hand forms.

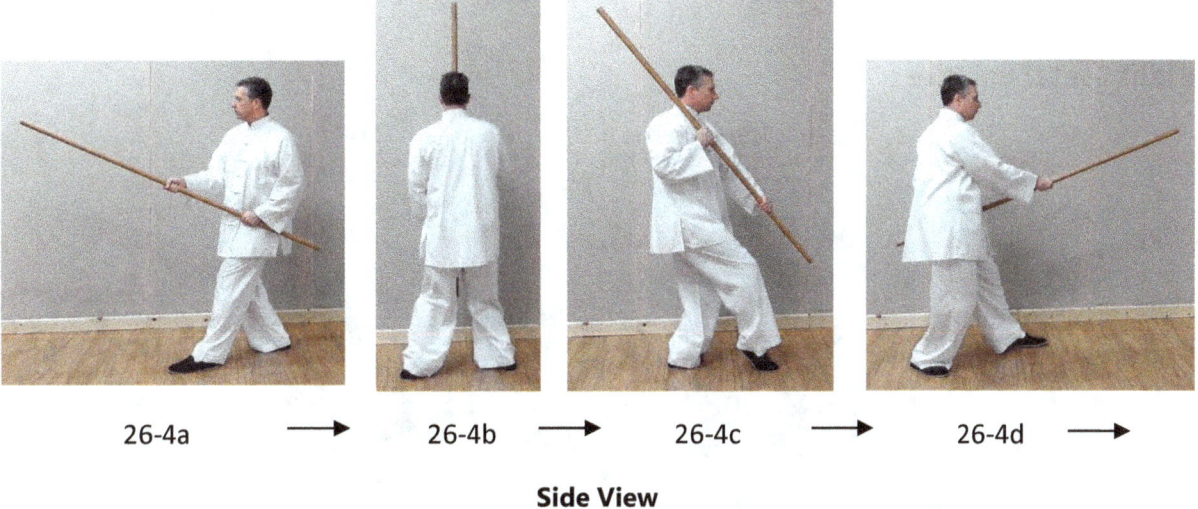

26-4a → 26-4b → 26-4c → 26-4d →

Side View

Starting sequence from far left to right
(Figure 26-4a) Starting from a (L) reverse Metal posture
(Figure 26-4b) Next the practitioner turns 90 degrees to their right stepping the forward (L) foot into a pigeon-toe stance as when practising Metal form in empty hand practice. At the same time, the (R) hand draws upwards towards the direction of the (R) shoulder and the (L) hand brings the lower section of the staff across the centreline of the body until the staff is held perpendicular to the ground.
(Figure 26-4c) Next the practitioner then continues to turn a further 90 degrees to their right placing the (R) foot into a (R) cat stance. At the same time, the (R) hand draws the upper section of the staff backwards over the direction of the (R) shoulder and the (L) hand reciprocally raises the lower section of the staff to an angle of 45 degrees.
(Figure 26-4d) Next the practitioner takes a small step forwards with the (R) foot and then steps through with the (L) foot using the half-step method. At the same time, the (L) hand pulls backwards and down on the lower section of the staff drawing into

back to the (L) hip and the (R) hand simultaneously presses forward on the upper section of the staff to produce a forward 'chopping' action as in Metal form.

Note: The practitioner ends the turn sequence in a (L) reverse Metal posture and is now ready to continue the form or end the form using the closing method discussed previously in this chapter.

The remainder of this chapter discusses each of the individual Five Element techniques. After each technique, has been explained there will be a few examples of possible fighting applications for some of the movements, however it should be noted that there are many possible fighting applications for each of the movements and the examples shown are simply to give the reader a basic understanding of how they may be applied.

5. Metal Form

Right Metal Posture

26-5a   26-5b

The first element to be trained in the Five Elements staff generating cycle is Metal. This is logical because the practitioner utilises this posture as the 'guard' position. They also open and close their practice of all the elements by passing both into and from (L) reverse Metal posture. In empty hand training the energy of Metal form is 'splitting' and this is the same when training the staff. Often in staff training the energy is described as 'chopping' but essentially this is the same as splitting. Pictures (figure 26-5a and 5b) above show the similarity in empty hand and staff posture of Metal form. Unlike San-Ti staff training discussed previously and the traditional method of turning from the left side, when practising Metal form the practitioner should familiarise themselves with training and turning from the right side too as when fighting it is essential to be skilled in moving, turning and applying the staff technique in any direction.

Left Metal Posture

26-5c   26-5d   26-5e

When training (L) Metal posture (figure 26-5c) using the staff, there are two main variations of posture to be considered. The first method is the same as San-Ti posture (figure 26-5d) and the second shown in (figure 26-5e) where the hands appear crossed. This is because the (L) hand retains hold of the rear section whilst the (R) hand holds the midsection. To keep the posture structurally aligned and bring the rear section of the staff across from the left side to the right side of the body, the arms must cross whilst executing the low block and 'chopping' strike associated with the element of Metal.

The first variation utilises a high blocking technique appropriate to defend against a strike to the head or upper part of the body. The second variation utilises a low block technique to defend against an attack to the legs. These two methods of blocking can be practiced individually or alternating and can also be executed high or low with either left or right foot forward. This gives complete versatility to the technique and creates maximum possibilities for applications.

Metal Form – High Block Method

← 26-5h   ← 26-5g   ← 26-5f

Starting sequence from far right to left

(Figure 26-5f) Open the form from Wuji into (L) Metal posture using the opening method discussed previously in this chapter.

(Figure 26-5g) Take a small step forward with the (L) foot and then begin to step through with the (R) foot using the half-step method. As the (R) foot passes through the inside of the (L) foot the (R) hand brings the mid and upper section of the staff upwards to the side of the (R) shoulder and the (L) hand reciprocally drives the rear end of the staff upwards in a striking motion until the angle of the staff is at 45 degrees to the ground to the rear of the practitioner.

(Figure 26-5h) As the (R) foot, steps thorough to complete the transition into (R) Pi Chuan stance it is followed up by a (L) foot half-step. In time with the (L) foot half-step the practitioner strikes forward and down with the (R) hand in a straight 'chopping' action to the level of 45 degrees to the ground in front of the practitioner. The (L) hand reciprocally draws the rear section of the staff back to the (L) hip.

Note: From this position, the sequence can be repeated always drawing the staff upwards to block to the (R) side of the body. The only difference between the left and right postures with this sequence of movements are the legs and feet. The hands and upper body movements are practised in the same way as described previously.

Metal Form – Low Block Method

← 26-5m ← 26-5l ← 26-5k ← 26-5j ← 26-5i

Starting sequence from far right to left.

(Figure 26-5i) Starting from (L) Metal posture.

(Figure 26-5j) Take a small step forward with the (L) foot and then begin to step through with the (R) foot using the half-step method. As the (R) foot passes through the inside of the (L) foot the (R) hand brings the mid and upper section of the staff downwards to the side of the (R) hip and the (L) hand reciprocally moves across the centreline of the body towards the (R) shoulder until the staff is held perpendicular to the ground.

(Figure 26-5k) As the (R) foot continues to step through and out in front the staff continues it circular blocking motion with the (R) hand pushing the staff upwards and over, whilst the (L) hand presses the rear section of the staff downwards in a chopping action simultaneously anchoring the rear section of the staff firmly against the (R) ribs of the practitioner. The staff should now be parallel to the ground. This is (R) Metal posture.

(Figure 26-5l) Take a small step forward with the (R) foot and then begin to step through with the (L) foot using the half-step method. As the (L) foot passes through the inside of the (R) foot the (R) hand brings the mid and upper section of the staff across the centreline and downwards to the side of the (L) hip and the (L) hand reciprocally moves across the centreline of the body towards the centreline until the staff is held perpendicular to the ground.

Note: The movement of crossing over the arms allows the waist to turn maximally to the left in readiness to generate the power of the forthcoming strike.

(Figure 26-5m) To complete the sequence the practitioner steps thorough to transition back into (L) Metal posture and is followed up by a (L) foot half-step. In time with the half-step the practitioner strikes forward and down with the (R) hand in a straight chopping action to the level of 45 degrees to the ground (to the front). The (L) hand reciprocally draws the rear section of the staff back to the (L) hip.

Note: From this position, the whole sequence can be repeated if required.

Metal Form – Staff Fighting Applications

Metal Form – High Block Application

26-5n → 26-5o → 26-5p

(Figure 26-5n) White faces off to Black in (R) Metal ready stance.
(Figure 26-5o) Black steps sideways to the left and strikes out with a cross cut to White's head. White counters the strike by withdrawing his staff into a high block technique.
(Figure 26-5p) White keeps control of Black's staff by maintaining contact and staying inside of its reach. This enables him to use it a guide to counter strike. White steps through with his (L) foot, sinking his body and uses the chopping action to strike Black on his (L) side clavicle using Metal technique.

Metal Form – Low Block Application

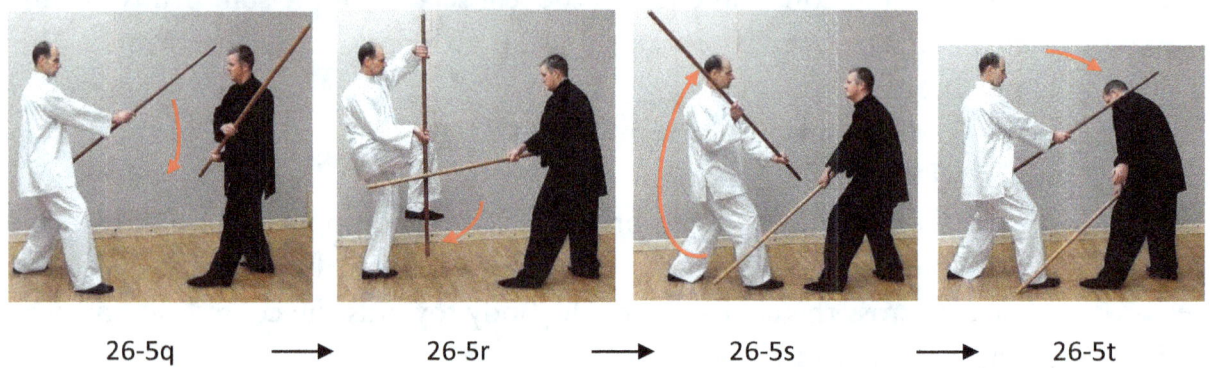

(Figure 26-5q) White faces off to Black in (R) Metal ready stance.

(Figure 26-5r) Black strikes out with a low cross cut to White's forward (R) knee. White counters the strike by raising and withdrawing his (R) foot into (L) single leg stance and at the same time he circles his staff downwards into a low block technique and blocks the incoming strike.

(Figure 26-5s) White stays inside of Black's attacking staff to make a further attack difficult. And continues to circle his staff around in the same direction bringing it up to the level of his head in preparation to strike.

(Figure 26-5t) As Black tries to withdraw, White then steps through with his (R) foot, sinking his body and uses the chopping action to strike Black on his (L) side clavicle using Metal technique.

6. Water Form

Water Posture

Following on in the order of the five elements generating cycle is Water. Water form has the energy of drilling and when training with the staff this transfers to the weapon as an upwards twisting action, often striking with the tip in a 'flicking' action. (Figures 26-6a and 6b) show the similarity in empty hand and staff posture of Water form.

When practicing Water form using the staff, there are two main variations to be considered. The first method utilises a low block technique to defend against an attack to the legs. The second method utilises technique appropriate to defend against a strike to the head or upper part of the body.

Water Form – Low Block Method

In this method, the practitioner utilises a low block technique to defend against an attack to the legs, sweeping backwards as the practitioner steps forwards to then drill upwards in attack. This technique is repeated always sweeping to the outside of the advancing (R) leg and then stepping through with the (L) leg to deliver the strike. As the rear (L) hand remains in control of the rear section of the staff it is not practical to practice this technique on alternate sides. To practise this method on the opposite side the practitioner would start from a (R) Metal form.

26-6e ← 26-6d ← 26-6c

Starting sequence from far right to left.

(Figure 26-6c) To open the form from Wuji into (L) Metal posture use the opening method discussed previously in this chapter.

(Figure 26-6d) Take a small step forward with the (L) foot and then step through with the (R) foot into (R) Bow stance with a 45-degree foot as in Water form. As the (R) foot, steps forward the (R) hand brings the mid/upper section of the staff downwards and backwards behind the advancing (R) leg. The (L) hand reciprocally moves across the centreline of the body towards the (R) shoulder until the staff is held at an approximate 45-degree angle to the ground.

(Figure 26-6e) Next the (R) foot, steps through using the half-step method and the staff circles upwards along the centreline and strikes up from below in a forward 'flicking' motion. This striking action is delivered by the (R) hand pushing the staff upwards, whilst the (L) hand presses downwards on the rear section simultaneously. When the strike is complete the staff should be at an angle of 45 degrees to the ground, with the tip at approximately face height.

Note: From this position, the sequence can be repeated until the practitioner elects to turn or finish in the appropriate manner discussed earlier in this chapter.

Water Form – High Block Method

In this method, the practitioner blocks against a high attack before counter striking with the opposite end of the staff. This method for practising Water technique allows for practice of the 'drilling' method to be trained on both sides alternatively. In this method, the practitioner simply steps forward whilst executing the drilling strike with the same side hand and foot in an 'uppercut' type movement. This method requires the use of both ends of the staff alternating with each step as the practitioner moves forward and therefore the hands must swap over from one end of the staff to the other when executing each strike. The method of switching ends of the staff alternatively to strike with also gives the option to shorten the range of the weapon and strike from mid-range to the opponent. This ability to change the range of attack by switching ends of the staff to strike is a characteristic of the Hsing-I staff method.

Water Method 2

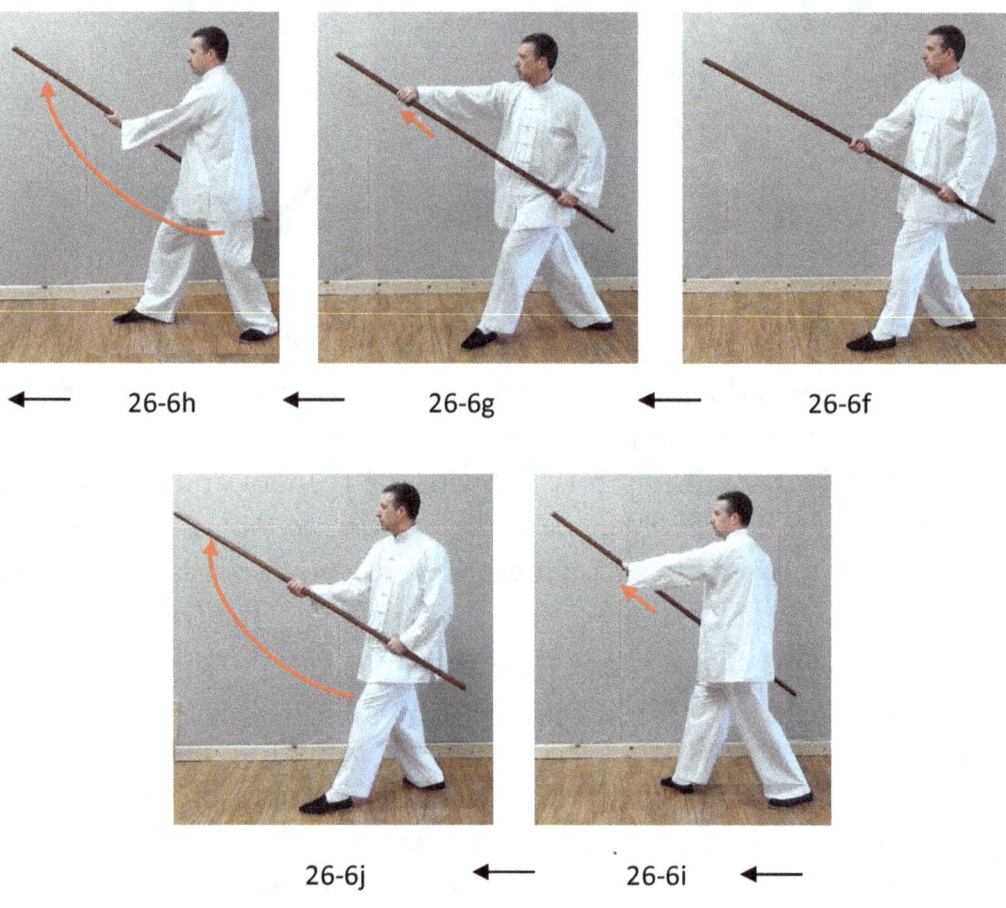

Starting sequence from far right to left
(Figure 26-6f) To open the form from Wuji into (L) Metal posture use the opening method discussed previously in this chapter.

(Figure 26-6g) Take a step forward with the (L) foot into (L) bow stance with a 45-degree foot as in Water form. At the same time, the (R) forward hand slides upwards to the forward section of the staff.

(Figure 26-6h) Next, the (L) foot, steps through using the half-step method and the (L) hand circles the staff upwards along the centreline and strikes up from below in a forward 'flicking' motion. This striking action is delivered by the (L) hand pushing the staff upwards, whilst the (R) hand presses downwards on the rear section simultaneously. When the strike is complete the staff should be at an angle of 45 degrees to the ground, with the tip at approximately face height.

(Figure 26-6i) Next, take a step forward with the (R) foot into (R) bow stance with a 45-degree foot as in Water form. At the same time, the (L) forward hand slides upwards to the forward section of the staff.

(Figure 26-6j) Next, the (R) foot, steps through using the half-step method and the (R) hand circles the staff upwards along the centreline and strikes up from below in a forward 'flicking' motion. This striking action is delivered by the (R) hand pushing the staff upwards, whilst the (L) hand presses downwards on the rear section simultaneously. When the strike is complete the staff should be at an angle of 45 degrees to the ground, with the tip at approximately face height.

Note: From this position, the sequence can be repeated until the practitioner elects to turn or finish in the appropriate manner discussed earlier in this chapter.

Water Form Fighting Applications

Water Form – Low Block Application

26-6k → 26-6l → 26-6m

(Figure 26-6k) White faces off to Black in (R) Metal ready stance.

(Figure 26-6l Black strikes out with a low cross cut to White's forward (R) knee. White counters the strike by stepping forwards and circling his staff downwards into a low block technique to block the incoming strike.

(Figure 26-6m) As Black tries to raise and withdraw his staff to counter, White sinks his weight into his rear (L) leg and delivers a drilling uppercut strike to Black's throat.

Water Form – High Block Application

26-6n → 26-6o → 26-6p

(Figure 26-6n) White and Black both face off in (R) Metal ready stance.
(Figure 26-6o) White takes the initiative and on contact with the forward section of his staff he steps forward into 45-degree (R) bow stance and presses Black's staff to the outside.
(Figure 26-6p) Before Black can react, White steps forward with his (L) foot to close the distance and delivers a quick, circular flicking uppercut strike to Black's ribs.

7. Wood Form

Wood Posture

26-7a 26-7b

Open Wood Posture

26-7c   26-7d

Closed Wood Posture

Following on in the order of the Five Elements Generating Cycle is Wood. Wood form has the energy of expanding, shooting out straight and when training with the staff this transfers to the weapon as a driving straightforward action. This straight out striking with one end of the staff is often referred to as 'poking' when describing staff techniques. Throughout the 'poking' movement the strike contains a subtle twisting, rotation of the staff allowing the strike to 'bite into' and penetrate the opponent on contact. Figures 26-7a and 7b and 26-7c and 7d show the similarity in empty hand and staff posture of both open and closed Wood postures.

When practicing Wood form using the staff the practitioner utilises a mid-level circular blocking technique to defend against an attack to the midsection. This method of blocking opens up the opponent by moving their weapon to the side and allows the practitioner to take advantage of the full length of the staff when driving forward and shooting straight out into the opponent. This straight attack of Wood is a classic example of Hsing-I efficiency in taking the shortest route to the target in a straight line and this method can penetrate even the smallest gap in an opponent's defence.

Wood form can be practiced and applied using both open and closed stances as seen above. When practising the form as a sequence the Wood strike technique can be practised on both the left and right sides.

Wood Form

Starting sequence from far right to left

(Figure 26-7e) To open the form from Wuji into (L) Metal posture use the opening method discussed previously in this chapter. Before taking a step, circle block the staff round from inside to outside in a counter clockwise direction.

(Figure 26-7f) Next the practitioner takes a small step forward with the (L) foot and step up to closed Wood posture with rear (R) foot. As the (R) foot steps up to the inside of the (L) foot the (L) rear hand simultaneously drives the staff out forwards, as the (R) hand stays fixed to the midsection of the staff and applies a twisting action as it projects forwards whilst keeping it straight and parallel to the ground. Both hands are now holding the rear section with the forward section held fully extended along the centreline.

(Figure 26-7g) Before stepping forwards into open Wood posture the practitioner first circle blocks the staff round from inside to outside in a counter clockwise direction. Next, the (R) foot, steps through using the half-step method. As the (R) foot steps forward into (R) open Wood stance, the (L) hand draws the staff backwards through the (R) hand until it rests at the (L) hip. Then on completion of the half-step the (L) hand simultaneously drives the staff out forwards, as the (R) hand stays fixed to the midsection of the staff and applies a twisting action as it projects forwards whilst keeping it straight and parallel to the ground. Both hands are now holding the rear section with the forward section held fully extended along the centreline.

(Figure 26-7h) Next the practitioner takes a small step forward with the (R) foot and step up to closed Wood posture with rear (L) foot. As the (L) foot steps up to the inside of the (R) foot the (L) rear hand simultaneously drives the staff out forwards, as the (R) hand stays fixed to the mid-section of the staff and applies a twisting action as it projects forwards whilst keeping it straight and parallel to the ground. Both hands are now holding the rear section with the forward section held fully extended along the centreline.

(Figure 26-7i and 7j) Before stepping forwards into open Wood posture the practitioner first circle blocks the staff round from inside to outside in a counter clockwise direction. Next, the (L) foot, steps through using the half-step method. As the (L) foot steps forward into (L) open Wood stance, the (L) hand draws the staff backwards through the (R) hand until it rests at the (L) hip. Then on completion of the half-step the (L) hand simultaneously drives the staff out forwards, as the (R) hand stays fixed to the midsection of the staff and applies a twisting action as it projects forwards whilst keeping it straight and parallel to the ground. Both hands are now holding the rear section with the forward section held fully extended along the centreline.

Note: When practising Wood form the sequence of movements can be practiced on alternate sides or can be just practised form the left side like the empty hand form of this lineage. Whichever side the practitioner chooses to step forward on the hands remain the same with the (L) hand at the rear and the (R) hand forward.

Wood Form – Fighting Application

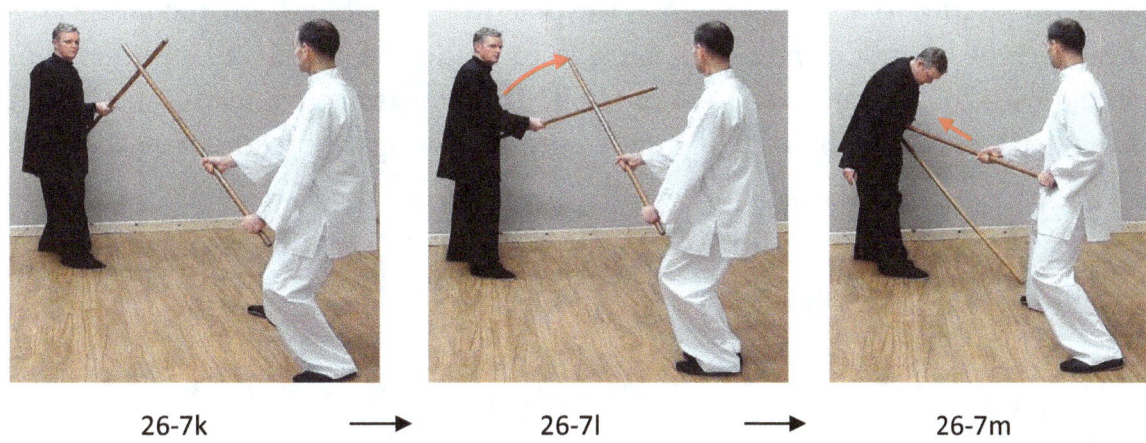

26-7k → 26-7l → 26-7m

(Figure 26-7k) White faces off to Black in (R) Metal ready stance.
(Figure 26-7l) Black strikes out with a straight thrust to White's face. White counters the strike by stepping forwards with his rear (L) foot into closed Wood posture and simultaneously circling his staff to the outside to deflect Black's attack.
(Figure 26-7m) As Black tries to withdraw his staff to counter, White steps straight forwards into (R) open Wood posture and delivers a straight thrusting strike to Black's solar plexus.

8. Fire Form

Fire Posture

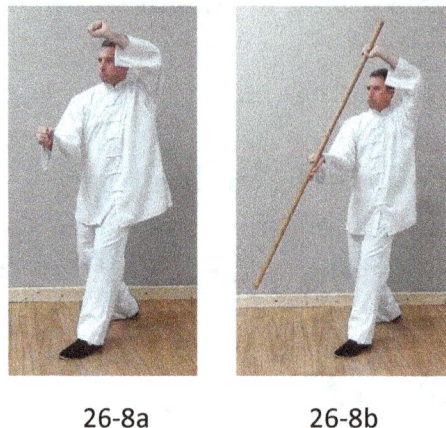

26-8a   26-8b

Following on in the order of the five-element generating cycle is Fire. The element Fire has the energy of rising like heat and flames from a fire. The Hsing-I definition of fire is that it 'pounds' as a ball being fired from a cannon against a wall. When training with the staff this transfers to the weapon as a rising, pounding action, often striking with either end of the staff in application. Figures 26-8a and 8b above show the similarity in empty hand and staff posture of Fire form.

When practising Fire form using the staff, the practitioner utilises both ends of the staff to block and strike. The footwork is the same as the empty hand form of Fire and the initial turn to 45 degrees allows the practitioner to block any incoming attack at head height by first stepping to the side to evade the strike and simultaneously blocking with the forward section of the staff. This blocking movement is then swiftly followed up from below, by a circular uppercut strike along the practitioner's centreline.

Fire Form

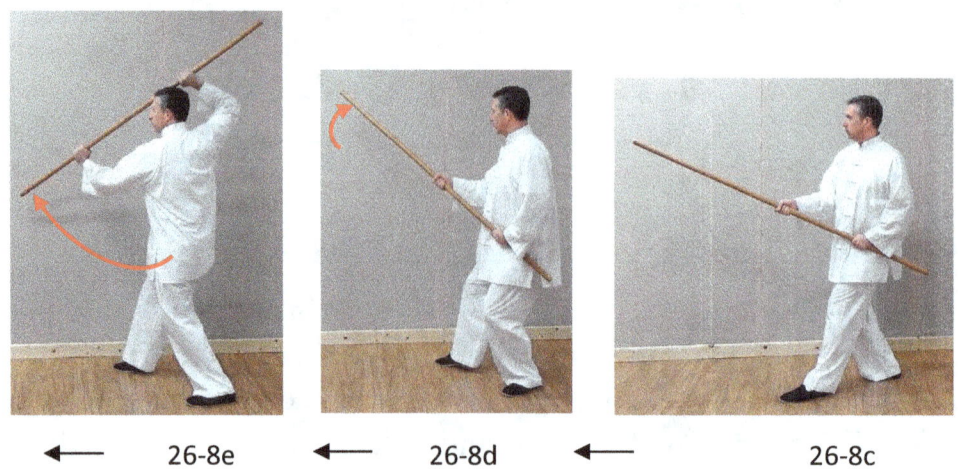

← 26-8e   ← 26-8d   ← 26-8c

26-8g ← 26-8f ←

Starting sequence from far right to left

(Figure 26-8c) Open the form from Wuji into (L) Metal posture using the opening method discussed previously in this chapter.

(Figure 26-8d) Take a small step forward with the (L) foot and then turn to 45 degrees to the right into (R) cat stance. Throughout the stepping sequence the staff is retained at a 45-degree angle to the ground.

(Figure 26-8e) The (R) foot then steps forward at the 45-degree angle using the half-step method. At the same time, the (L) hand drives the rear section of the staff forwards and upwards to the height of the ribs. The (R) hand assists this circular rising movement by drawing the midsection of the staff upwards and backwards to the right side of the head.

(Figure 26-8f) The (R) foot then takes a small step forwards down the line of the form before the practitioner turns 45 degrees to the left into a (L) cat stance. At the same time, the (L) hand circles upwards with forward section of the staff and the (R) hand assists by drawing down the rear end of the staff towards the (R) hip. The staff should be at a 45-degree angle to the ground at the end of this movement.

(Figure 26-8g) The (L) foot then steps forward at the 45-degree angle using the half-step method. At the same time, the (R) hand drives the rear section of the staff forwards and upwards to the height of the ribs. The (L) hand assists this circular rising movement by drawing the midsection of the staff upwards and backwards to the left side of the head.

Note: Fire form is practiced and applied alternatively on both the left and right sides. When turning or finishing the form the practitioner steps into a (L) Metal posture and turns or finishes using the method described earlier in this chapter.

Fire Form – Fighting Application

26-8h → 26-8i → 26-8j → 26-8k

(Figure 26-8h) White and Black both face off in (R) Metal ready stance.
(Figure 26-8i) Black draws back to strike White with a straight chop to White's head.
(Figure 26-8j) White anticipates the attack and steps 45 degrees to the left into (R) cat stance, positioning himself on the outside of Black's attack and simultaneously blocks the attack with his staff which is retained throughout the stepping movement at 45-degree angle to the ground.
(Figure 26-8k) White then steps forward with his (R) foot using the half-step method and attacks Black with the (L) hand using the rear section of the staff in a circular uppercut motion, to strike Black in the (R) midsection, rib area.

9. Earth Form

Earth Posture

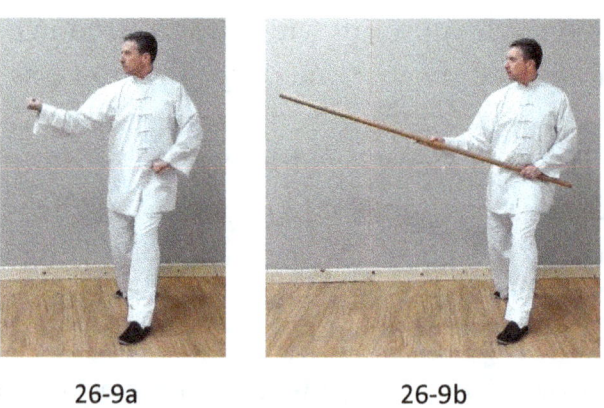

26-9a   26-9b

Following on in the order of the Five Element generating cycle is Earth. The element Earth has the energy rolling, crossing and moving in a sideways manner. The Hsing-I definition of Earth is that it rolls like a marble or rather like the planet earth rotating on its axis. When training with the staff this transfers to the weapon as a turning sideways, in a crossing, shearing like action. Striking with a round circular swinging motion of the staff in application. Figures 26-9a and 9b above show the similarity in empty hand and staff posture of Earth form.

When practising Earth form using the staff, the footwork is the same as the empty hand form of Earth and the initial turn to 45 degrees allows the practitioner to block any incoming attack at head height by first stepping to the side to evade the strike and simultaneously blocking with the forward section of the staff. This blocking movement is then swiftly followed up by a circular sideways or crosscut strike. The long ranging circular motion of the strike makes this technique very powerful when transferred from the ground through the rotation of the waist and all the way into the striking tip of the staff.

Earth Form

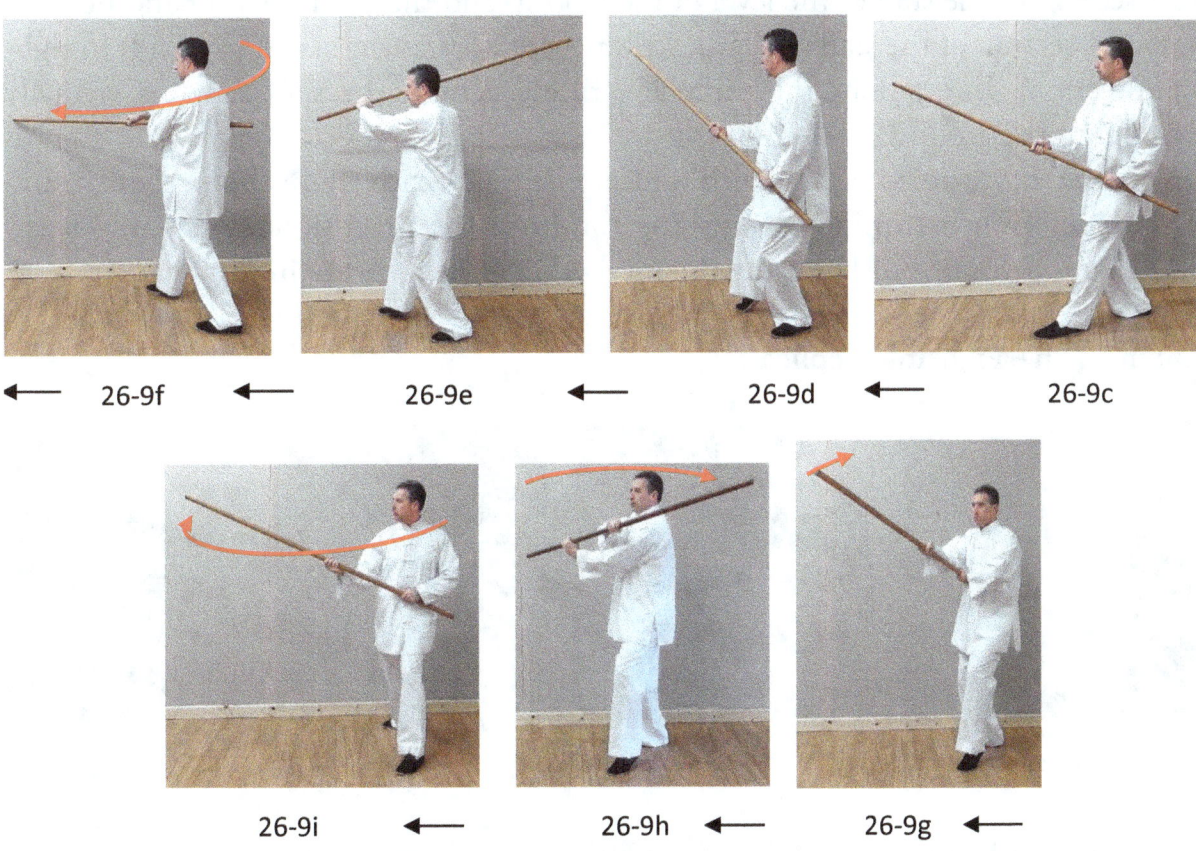

Starting sequence from far right to left

(Figure 26-9c) To open the form from Wuji into (L) Metal posture using the opening method discussed previously in this chapter.

(Figure 26-9d) Take a small step forward with the (L) foot and then turn to 45 degrees to the right into (R) cat stance. Throughout the stepping sequence the staff is retained as a blocking technique and held at a 45-degree angle to the ground.

(Figure 26-9e) As the (R) foot begins to step forward at the 45-degree angle using the half-step method. At the same time, the practitioner circles the staff around the head one complete circle.

(Figure 26-9f) This circular motion of the staff ends with both the arms crossed and the rear section of the staff held by the (L) hand coming to rest under the (R) arm pit and the (R) forward hand striking sideways as a crosscut. Throughout this circular striking action, the staff remains parallel to the ground.

(Figure 26-9g) Take a small step forward with the (R) foot and then turn to 45 degrees to the left into (L) cat stance. Throughout the stepping sequence the staff is retained as a blocking technique and held at a 45-degree angle to the ground.

(Figure 26-9h) As the (L) foot begins to step forward at the 45-degree angle using the half-step method. At the same time, the practitioner circles the staff around the head one complete circle.

(Figure 26-9i) This circular motion of the staff ends with the (L) hand holding the rear section of the staff at the level of the (L) hip and the (R) forward hand holding the mid-section of the staff forward, striking sideways as a crosscut from left to right in direction. Throughout this circular striking action, the staff remains virtually parallel to the ground.

Note: Earth form is practiced and applied alternatively on both the left and right sides. When turning or finishing the form the practitioner steps into a (L) Metal and turns or finishes using the method described earlier in this chapter.

Earth Form – Fighting Application

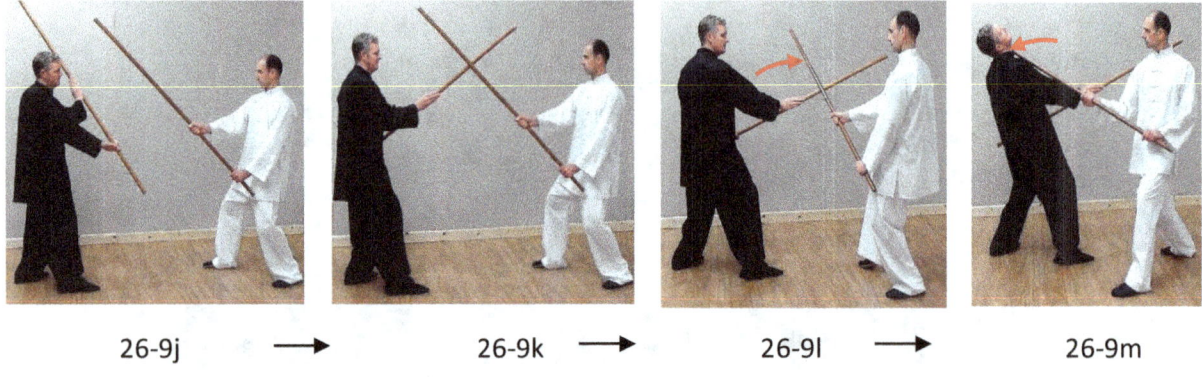

(Figure 26-9j) White faces off to Black in (R) Metal ready stance.
(Figure 26-9k) Black draws back to strike White with a straight chop to White's head.
(Figure 26-9l) White anticipates the attack and turns 45 degrees to the right into (R) cat stance, positioning himself on the outside of Black's attack and simultaneously blocks the attack with his staff which is retained throughout the stepping movement at 45-degree angle to the ground.
(Figure 26-9m) White then steps out sideways with his (L) foot using the half-step method and attacks Black with a short sideways cross cut attack to Black's throat.

Chapter 27

Tien Gunn Exercises

Introduction

"'Tien Gunn', meaning 'Celestial Stem' or 'Heavenly Stem', is a series of exercises beneficial for maintaining the body's health and the techniques contained within each exercise can also be applied to protect the body as a form of self-defence. Taken from the Taoist theoretical framework found within the classical Chinese internal styles known as Hsing-I and Pa-Kua, these exercises combine the health benefits of Chi-Kung methodology with the application of powerful fighting techniques found within the internal martial arts. When practised correctly, the practitioner becomes centred and solid in their technique and a powerful root connection to the earth is established. Within the body, the spine or 'celestial stem' becomes strong and flexible, increasing the circulation of chi and blood to the five internal organs, the brain and the extremities.
Master McNeil

Historical background of Tien Gunn theory:

The development of the Celestial Stems theory is vague and several different accounts are recorded. The most commonly accepted version is that in ca. 2698–2597 BCE Huang Di, the Yellow emperor was said to have instructed one of his ministers, Da Rao Shi, to create a calendar system which could be utilised in aiding the growing of crops. Da Rao Shi explored the rule of changes between sky and earth, as well as that of the four seasons. From these studies, he then created the Ten Celestial Stems and the Twelve Earthly Branches to make accurate calculations to form a calendar cycle.

Through this study of the universal cycles came a method of counting time which became the cornerstone of time calculation in ancient China and which still exists today. As Taoists view all cycles within the universe as being reflected within the body, the Ten Celestial Stems reflect the relationship and function of the ten organs in the human body.

When discussing the body from a TCM viewpoint there are normally twelve organs to be considered. To reduce this count to ten in fitting with the Stems and Branches theoretical model, the following considerations must be made. First the San-Jiao organ is not a physical organ per se and secondly, the Pericardium organ directly surrounds the heart to protect it and therefore, the two are seen to be combined as one. This now leaves ten organs contained within the torso which directly relate to the internal classification of the ten Celestial Stems.

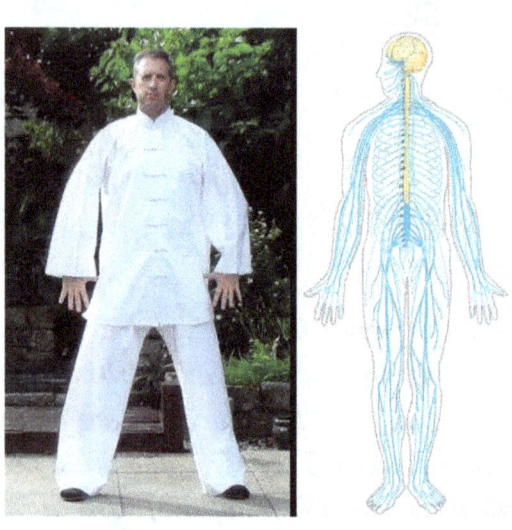

Relevant to the theory of Tien Gunn are the structures of the spinal column which contains the spinal cord and the brain which are classed separately and are referred to as extraordinary organs in TCM. These two extraordinary organs in fact represent the central nervous system (CNS) in western medical terms, whose function is to command and control the ten organs. Therefore, the celestial stem is seen to be the commander of the ten organs within the body. The ten organs are the origins of the Twelve Earthly Branches which take the form of the twelve main meridians and represent in western medical terms the peripheral nervous system (PNS) within the body.

The Ming dynasty book *San Ming Tong Hui* [*Confluence of the Three Fates*] describes the celestial stems and earthly branches: *"Stems are like the trunk of a tree, strong and sturdy, and considered as Yang; and branches are literally like the branches of a tree, weaker yet flexible, and therefore considered as Yin."* This would infer that the practice of Tien Gunn exercises seeks to strengthen the trunk and root of the body and at the same time make the peripheries more pliable and flexible.

On a physical level, the rotating movements of the exercises seek to free up tension within the spinal column and surrounding soft tissues and musculature. They also help massage the ten organs contained within the torso keeping them healthy and providing an abundance of blood, which can be distributed to the peripheral tissues, or branches of the body. The stances associated with each exercise give strength to the legs and make the practitioner rooted to the ground.

On an energetic level, the celestial stem comprises of essentially the longitudinal meridian that passes through the centre of the body (Thrusting meridian). It begins at the perineum (Huin point) and passes through the Tan Tien, up the centre of the spine and into the brain to the top of the head (Bai Hu point). When this central meridian is free of blockages, the 'Little Nine Heaven' circulation is opened which in turn stimulates the circulation of chi in all the meridians of the body.

Figure 27-01

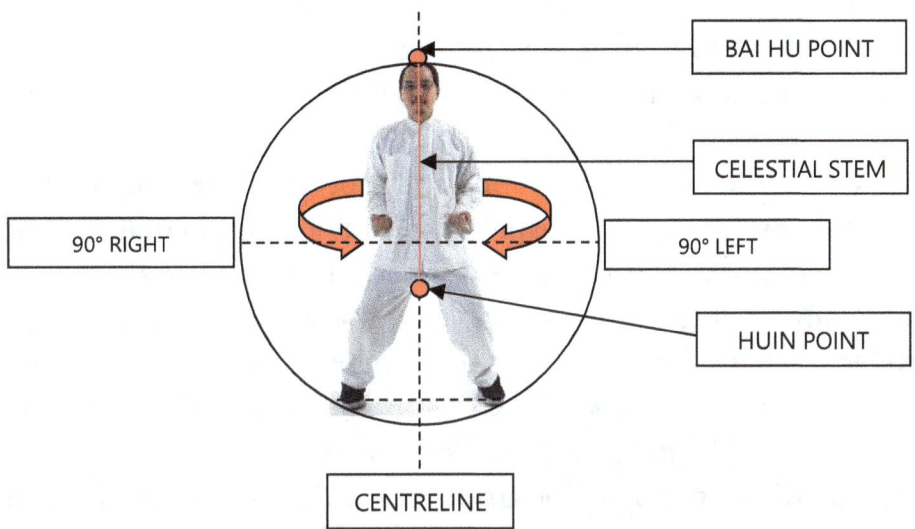

Therefore, Tien Gunn is a combined body and mind conditioning Chi-Kung practice. Whilst variations of these exercises can be found within the different lineages and styles of internal arts, this form of Tien Gunn taught through Master Hsu's 'Tang Shou Tao' lineage comprises a series of twenty-five exercises that develop both internal and external conditioning of the practitioner. These exercises can be performed in a relaxed or strenuous manner and when combined with correct breathing methods, they help to develop the coordination, timing, power and flexibility required for both improving the chi flow and health of the practitioner, while also helping to improve the effectiveness of fighting techniques learned within the Hsing-I Chuan system.

Externally, Hsing-I practitioners use these exercises for physical conditioning to help develop increased power and harmonious connectivity through its individual joints. These traditional exercises are used to link the rotational power of the torso via the direct connection of the spine, legs and feet to the earth. The understanding gained from this method of power generation is very similar to 'Chan Xi' or 'silk reeling energy' made famous by the internal style of Chen Tai Chi Chuan.

Internally, Hsing-I practitioners use these exercises from the beginning of their study to systematically help develop their sensitivity and an ability to lead chi to all parts of the body. This practice helps clear blockages and allows chi to flow efficiently to the organs, especially upwards to the brain which in turn allows clear thinking and efficient decision making to take place.

Once the basic movements of these exercises are learned they can be practised at many levels of skill and will improve the practitioner in the following ways:
- Natural alignment of physical bone structure
- Stretching and lengthening of soft tissues
- Opening of joints and increase of chi and blood flow through the joints
- Internal massaging of organs

- Improving connection of body segments throughout movement
- Improving biomechanical efficiency of the body
- Strengthening of muscles, tendons, ligaments for functional activity
- Quiets the mind and focuses the spirit (Shen), reducing emotional tension
- Increases aerobic capacity
- Harmonises the energetic and physical aspects of the body together

In the following section of this chapter there is a description of the twenty-five Tien Gunn exercises practised in this lineage of Hsing-I. These exercises should be practiced daily with a minimum of ten repetitions on each side to be beneficial to a practitioner's health. With each exercise, the first sequence of pictures starts with the practitioner turning to the left. Arrows accompany these where appropriate to aid understanding the exercise's movements. The second sequence of pictures shows the same exercises performed in the opposite direction without arrows. The arrows below the pictures highlight the direction of the sequence from left to right or vice versa. Finally, the third sequence of pictures shows a single fighting application for each exercise where appropriate.

Note: There are many possible fighting applications for each of the exercises and the examples shown are simply to give the reader an understanding of how they may be applied. A second point to understand is that when applying any of the Tien Gunn movements for self-defence the practitioner should learn to apply the understanding of rotational power gained from single standing practice and apply it to their Hsing-I fighting stance as to stand square on to an opponent when fighting presents an easy target area.

The breathing sequence for each exercise is to always inhale and exhale through the nose with the tongue touching the roof of the mouth as in line with Taoist internal practice. One complete cycle of breath is usually performed with each repetition of a technique. Where this is not the case the appropriate breathing method will be explained in the exercises description.

1. Sword Hand

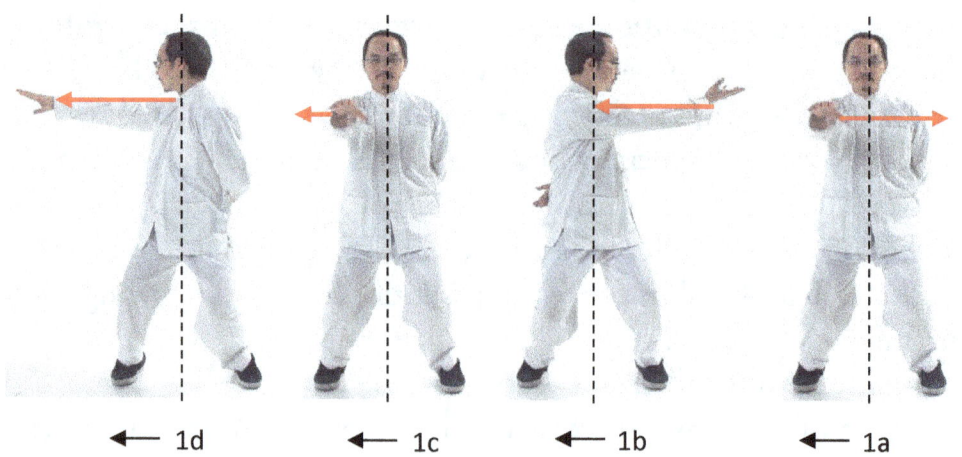

← 1d   ← 1c   ← 1b   ← 1a

(Figure 27-1a) The (L) hand is placed on the kidney with thumb pointing up. The (R) hand is held out front facing palm down. The feet are placed with toes facing forward and approximately shoulder width apart. The knees are slightly bent and the back held straight. The eyes look straight ahead and the tongue rests against the roof of the mouth.

(Figure 26-1b) The body rotates through 90 degrees to the left and at the same time the (R) hand rotates across the body, elbow slightly bent. Along the course of the 90-degree rotation to the left the (R) hand turns palm upwards. The feet remain static, firmly rooted to the ground throughout.

(Figure 26-1c to 1d) The body then rotates back to the right through the starting position, 180 degrees finishing with the (R) arm held out to the right side at 90 degrees to the centreline. The elbow is slightly bent and throughout the course of the 180-degree rotation the (R) hand is turned over to face palm down. The feet remain rooted and static throughout.

Note: Inhale as the arm moves across the body and exhale as the arm strikes out to the side away from the body.

1e → 1f → 1g → 1h →

(Figures 27-1e to 1h) Next repeat the same sequence on the opposite side.

Sword Hand Fighting Application

1i → 1j → 1k → 1l →

(Figure 27-1i) White faces off to Black in a neutral stance.

(Figure 27-1j) Black throws a (R) straight punch to White's face. White counters by stepping (L) into the attack and cover blocking the punch from I/O with the (R) knife hand block.

(Figure 27-1k) White continues immediately from the blocking technique to strike out along the line of Black's (R) extended arm attacking the neck of Black and at the same time covers Black's (L) counter attacking punch with a (R) knife hand block.

(Figure 27-1l) To finish, White draws back his (L) hand to cover any attempt at another counter strike and delivers a (R) knife hand strike to Black's neck.

2. Transverse Palm (High and Low)

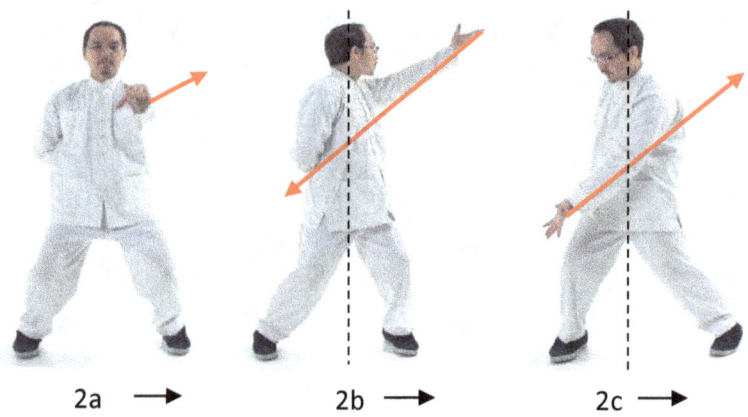

2a →   2b →   2c →

(Figure 27-2a) The (R) hand is placed on the kidney with thumb pointing up. The (L) hand is held out front facing palm down. The feet are placed with toes facing forward and approximately shoulder width apart. The knees are slightly bent and the back held straight. The eyes look straight ahead and the tongue rests against the roof of the mouth.

(Figure 27-2b) The body rotates through 90 degrees to the left and at the same time the (L) hand rotates outwards to the (L) side, away from the body with elbow slightly bent. Along the course of the 90-degree rotation to the left the hand raises upwards above head height and the (L) hand turns ridge (thumb side) upwards. The feet remain static, firmly rooted to the ground throughout.

(Figure 27-2c) The body then rotates back to the right through the starting position, 180 degrees finishing with the (L) arm across the body the right side at 90 degrees to the centreline. The elbow is slightly bent and throughout the course of the 180-degree rotation the (R) hand moves downward in a diagonal pathway is turned over to face knife edge (little finger) down. The feet remain rooted and static throughout.

Note: Inhale as the arm blocks low across the body and exhale as the arm block high away from the body.

2d → 2e → 2f →

(Figures 27-2d to 2f) Next repeat the same sequence on the opposite side.

Transverse Palm Fighting Application

2g → 2h → 2i

(Figure 27-2g) White faces off to Black in a neutral stance.
(Figure 27-2h) Black throws a (R) straight punch to White's face. White counters by stepping (L) and cover blocking the punch from I/O with a (L) ridge hand block.
(Figure 27-2i) To finish, White continues immediately from the blocking technique to strike out along the line of Black's (R) extended arm attacking the neck of Black with a (L) knife hand strike.

3. Direct Clamping

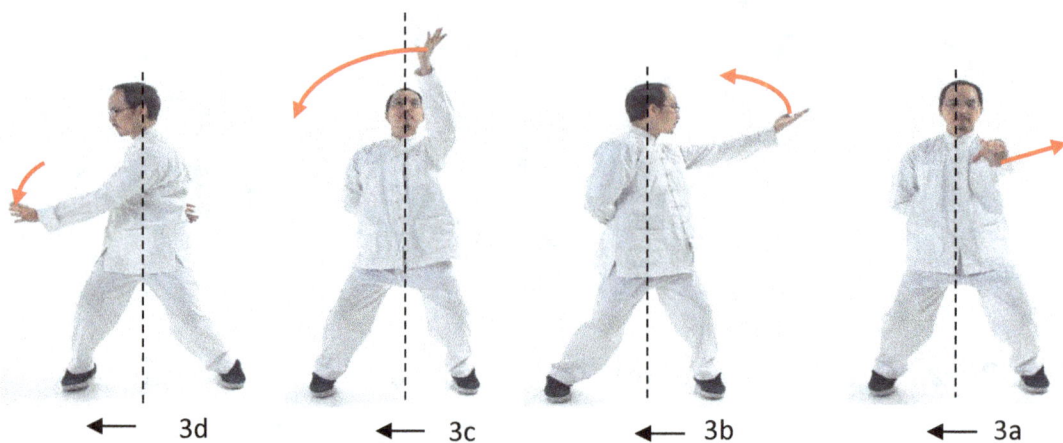

(Figure 27-3a) The (R) hand is placed on the kidney with thumb pointing up. The (L) hand is held out front facing palm down. The feet are placed with toes facing forward and approximately shoulder width apart. The knees are slightly bent and the back held straight. The eyes look straight ahead and the tongue rests against the roof of the mouth.

(Figure 27-3b) The body rotates through 90 degrees to the left and at the same time the (L) hand rotates outwards to the (L) side, away from the body with elbow slightly bent. Along the course of the 90-degree rotation to the left the hand raises upwards above head height and the (L) hand turns ridge (thumb side) upwards. The feet remain static, firmly rooted to the ground throughout.

(Figure 27-3c) The body then rotates back to the right through the starting position with the (L) arm arcing over and across the body at face height.

(Figure 27-3d) The body continues its rotation to the right to a total 180 degrees finishing with the (L) hand blocking at the level of the (L) hip using a crescent palm block. The feet remain rooted and static throughout.

Note: Inhale as the arm blocks high away from the body and exhale as the opposite arm circles over across the body to palm strike.

(Figures 27-3e to 3h) Next repeat the same sequence on the opposite side.

| 3e → | 3f → | 3g → | 3h → |

Direct Clamping Fighting Application

| 3i → | 3j → | 3k → | 3l |

(Figure 27-3i) White faces off to Black in a neutral stance.

(Figure 27-3j) Black throws a (R) straight punch to White's face. White counters by stepping (L) to the outside of the attack and cover blocking the punch from O/I with a (R) ridge hand block.

(Figure 27-3k) White continues immediately from the blocking technique to press down Black's attacking arm across his own centreline, making a counter attack more difficult.

(Figure 27-3l) To finish, White strikes back across the centreline and upwards with his (R) hand, delivering a (R) palm strike to Black's jaw.

4.　High Block and Grab

4a → 　 4b → 　 4c → 　 4d → 　 4e →

(Figure 27-4a) Both hands are held as fists at the height of their corresponding hips. The feet are placed with toes facing forward and approximately shoulder width apart. The knees are slightly bent and the back held straight. The eyes look straight ahead and the tongue rests against the roof of the mouth.

(Figure 27-4b) The body rotates through 90 degrees to the left and at the same time the (R) hand rises to head height at an angle of 45 degrees to the starting centreline. Along the course of the body's rotation to the left the (R) hand turns palm upwards as a spear hand. The feet remain static, firmly rooted to the ground throughout.

(Figure 27-4c) At the end of the (L) rotation the (R) spear hand forms a fist, facing palm down.

(Figure 27-4d) The body then starts to rotate back to the right with the grasping (R) fist pulling downwards across the body, back towards the (R) hip.

(Figure 27-4e) At the end of the sequence the body rotates 90 degrees back to the (R), finishing in its original starting position. Both hands are held as fists at the height of their corresponding hips. The feet remain rooted and static throughout.

← 4j 　 ← 4i 　 ← 4h 　 ← 4g 　 ← 4f

(Figures 27-4f to 4j) This exercise is practised on each side in alternate movements. Inhale as the hands reach out to the side and exhale as the hands are drawn in to the Tan Tien.

High Block and Grab Fighting Application

(**Figure 27-4k**) White faces off to Black in a neutral stance.

(**Figure 27-4l**) Black throws a (R) straight punch to White's face. White counters by stepping (L) to the outside of the attack and cover blocking the punch from O/I with a (R) ridge hand block.

(**Figure 27-4m**) To finish, White draws back his (R) hand to grab and cover any attempt at Black retreating and simultaneously delivers a (L) straight punch to Black's Jaw.

5. Turn, Block and Strike

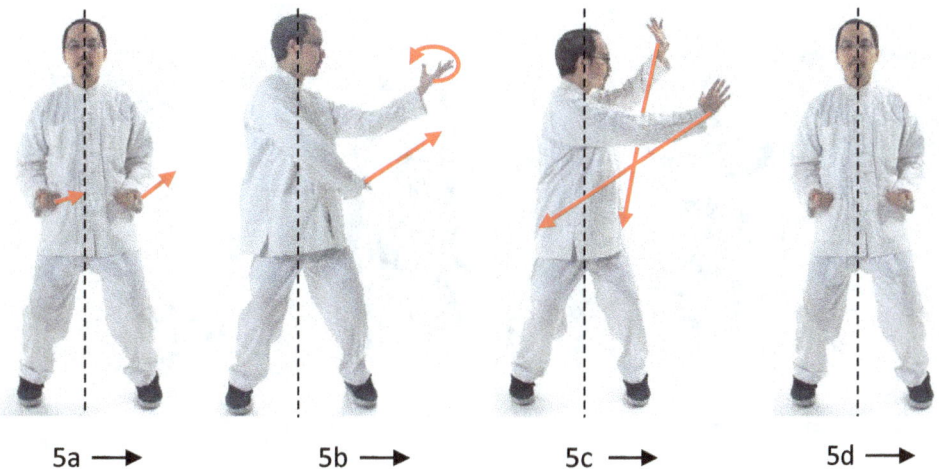

(**Figure 27-5a**) To start, both hands are held as fists at the height of their corresponding hips. The feet are placed with toes facing forward and approximately shoulder width apart. The knees are slightly bent and the back held straight. The eyes look straight ahead and the tongue rests against the roof of the mouth.

(**Figures 27-5b and 5c**) The body rotates through 90 degrees to the left and at the same time the (R) hand rises to head height with the elbow and forearm blocking at an angle of 45 degrees. At the same time, the (R) hand palm strikes to the left side at solar plexus height. The feet remain static, firmly rooted to the ground throughout.

Note: This upper body movement is the same as Pao Chuan in the five elements although the hands are open and not fists on striking/blocking.
(Figure 27-5d) Next, the body rotates back 90 degrees to its original starting position (figure 25-5a) and as both hands become fists they strike the abdomen at the height of the Tan Tien simultaneously.

← 5h   ← 5g   ← 5f   ← 5e

(Figures 27-5e to 5h) This exercise is practiced on each side in alternate movements. Inhale as the fists are drawn in to the Tan Tien and exhale as the hands block/strike to the side.

Turn, Block and Strike Fighting Application

5i →   5j →   5k

(Figure 27-5i) White faces off to Black in a neutral stance.
(Figure 27-5j) Black throws a (R) roundhouse punch to White's face. White counters by stepping (L) and cover blocking the punch from I/O with a (L) ridge hand block.
(Figure 27-5k) To finish, White continues to cover Black's attack whilst immediately executing a (R) palm strike to Black's solar plexus.

6. Reverse Clamping

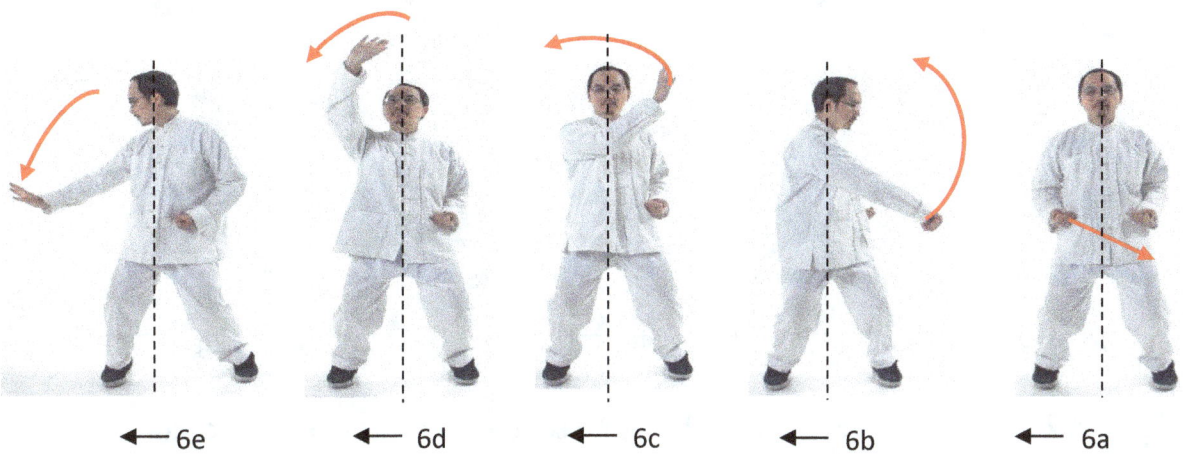

←— 6e   ←— 6d   ←— 6c   ←— 6b   ←— 6a

(Figure 27-6a) To start, both hands are held as fists at the height of their corresponding hips. The feet are placed with toes facing forward and approximately shoulder width apart. The knees are slightly bent and the back held straight. The eyes look straight ahead and the tongue rests against the roof of the mouth.

(Figure 27-6b) The body rotates through 90 degrees to the left and at the same time the (R) hand circle blocks low across the midsection to approximately 45 degrees to the left. At the same time, the (R) fist rotates in time with the arm rotation, creating a spiralling effect within the muscles and tendons of the forearm. The feet remain static, firmly rooted to the ground throughout.

(Figures 27-6c and 6d) Next, the (R) arm arcs overhead in time with the (R) rotation of the body back through the centreline. The feet remain static, firmly rooted to the ground throughout.

(Figure 27-6e) Continue to rotate the body to the right a total 180 degrees, allowing the (R) arm to continue its natural arc downwards across the body to the level of the hips, terminating in a crescent palm block to the right. The feet remain static, firmly rooted to the ground throughout.

Note: Inhale as the arm crosses the body and circle blocks low and exhale as the opposite arm circles over and palm strikes out to the side.

(Figures 27-6f to 6j) Next repeat the same sequence on the opposite side.

Reverse Clamping Fighting Application

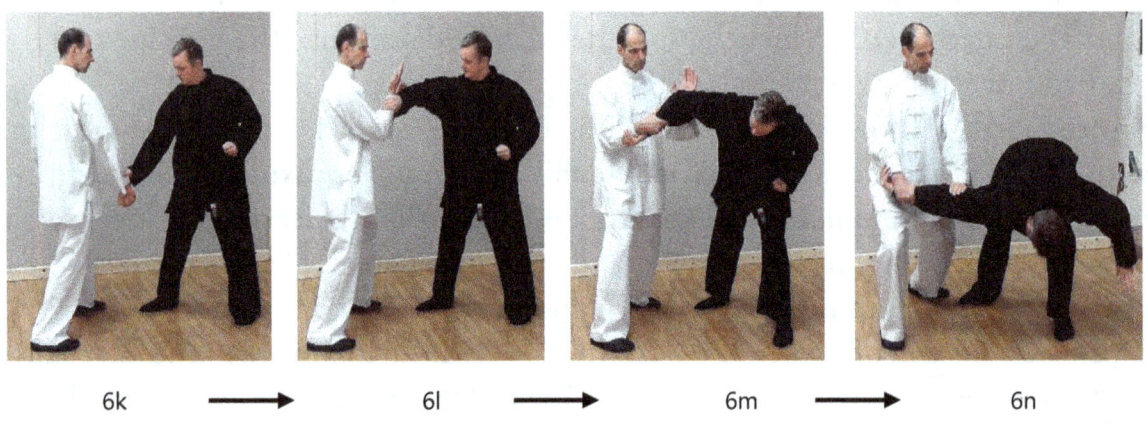

(Figure 27-6k) Black lunges forward and grabs White's (R) wrist.
(Figure 27-6l) To counter the grab, White rotates his (R) open hand around the outside of Black's grabbing hand and at the same time covers Black's rising elbow with his (L) hand.
(Figure 27-6m) White continues to grab and rotate Black's (R) wrist and turns Black's (R) elbow completely over with his (L) open hand.
(Figure 27-6n) To finish, White sinks his weight and presses Black downwards to the ground whilst maintaining a firm wrist grip and arm bar at Black's (R) elbow joint.

7. Circle Block and Back Fist

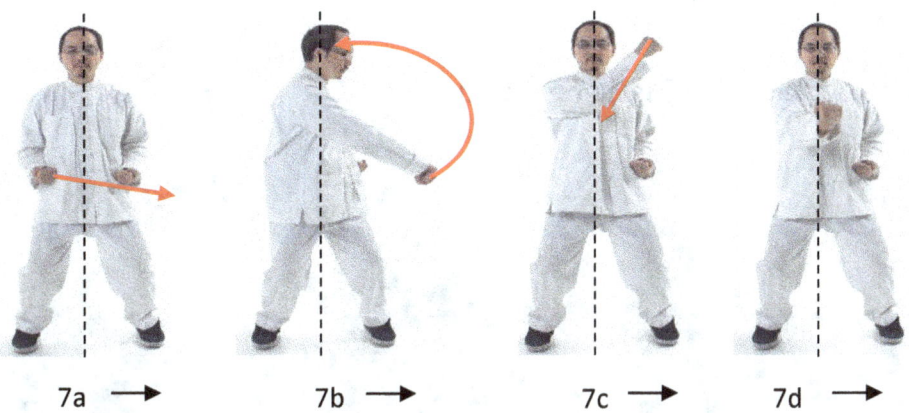

(Figure 27-7a) To start, both hands are held as fists at the height of their corresponding hips. The feet are placed with toes facing forward and approximately shoulder width apart. The knees are slightly bent and the back held straight. The eyes look straight ahead and the tongue rests against the roof of the mouth.

(Figure 27-7b) The body rotates through 90 degrees to the left and at the same time the (R) hand circle blocks low across the midsection to approximately 45 degrees to the left. At the same time, the (R) fist rotates in time with the arm rotation, creating a spiralling effect within the muscles and tendons of the forearm. The feet remain static, firmly rooted to the ground throughout.

(Figure 27-7c) Next the (R) arm turns over into a back-fist at nose height in time with the (R) rotation of the body back through the centreline. The feet remain static, firmly rooted to the ground throughout.

(Figure 27-57d) Continue to rotate the body back to the right allowing the (R) arm to continue its natural arc downwards along the centreline, terminating in a back fist at solar plexus height, directly down the centreline. The feet remain static, firmly rooted to the ground throughout.

(Figures 27-7e to 7h) This exercise is practised on each side in alternate movements. Inhale as the arm crosses the body and circle blocks low and exhale as the back fist strikes along the centreline.

Circle Block and Back Fist Fighting Application

(Figure 27-7i) White faces off to Black in a neutral stance.
(Figure 27-7j) Black throws a (R) straight punch to White's Tan Tien. White counters by turning his body to the outside of the attack and covers Black's attacking hand with a (R) crescent palm block. White simultaneously (L) circle blocks to the back of Black's (R) elbow joint, forcing it into hyperextension.
(Figure 27-7k) To finish, White continues immediately from the circle blocking technique to strike upwards along the line of Black's (R) extended arm with a (L) back fist strike to Black's face.

8. Double Block, Turn and Thrust

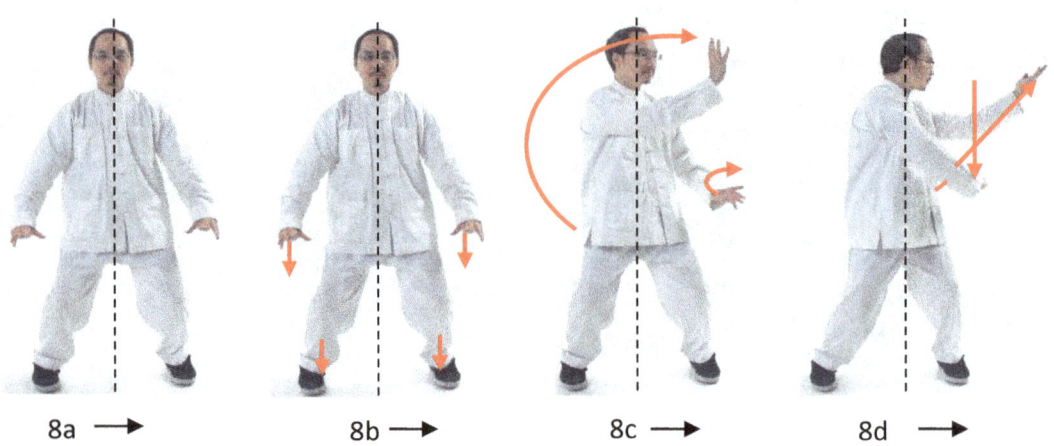

(Figure 27-8a) To start, both hands are held as open hands, facing palm down at the height of their corresponding hips. The feet are placed with toes facing forward and

approximately shoulder width apart. The knees are slightly bent and the back held straight. The eyes look straight ahead and the tongue rests against the roof of the mouth.
(Figure 27-8b) From the starting position sink the knees a little and block down with the palms of both hands simultaneously.

(Figure 27-8c) Next, rotate the body 90 degrees to the left. At the same time the (R) hand arcs upwards and across the body, passing the face whilst the (L) hand takes the form of spear hand and starts to rise in time with the opposing hand. The feet remain static, firmly rooted to the ground throughout.

(Figure 27-8d) Whilst the body is fully rotated to the left, both hands pass each other. The (L) spear hand drives up the centre inside the downward blocking (R) hand. The (L) spear hand terminates at the height of the throat and the (R) hand faces palm down at the height of the Tan Tien. Both hands protect the body's centreline. The feet remain static, firmly rooted to the ground throughout.

⟵ 8h ⟵ 8g ⟵ 8f ⟵ 8e

(Figures 27-8e to 8h) This exercise is practiced on each side in alternate movements. Exhale as the hands press down into double block. Inhale as the arm circle blocks high across the face and exhale as the spear hand strikes along the centreline.

Double Block, Turn and Thrust Fighting Application

8i ⟶ 8j ⟶ 8k

(Figure 27-8i) White faces off to Black in a neutral stance.
(Figure 27-8j) Black throws a (R) straight punch to White's Tan Tien. White counters by stepping (L) to the outside of the attack and cover blocking the punch with a (L) palm block to Black's extended forearm.
(Figure 27-8k) To finish, White continues immediately from the blocking technique to strike out along Black's centreline, attacking the throat of Black with a (R) spear hand strike.

9. Wave Hands

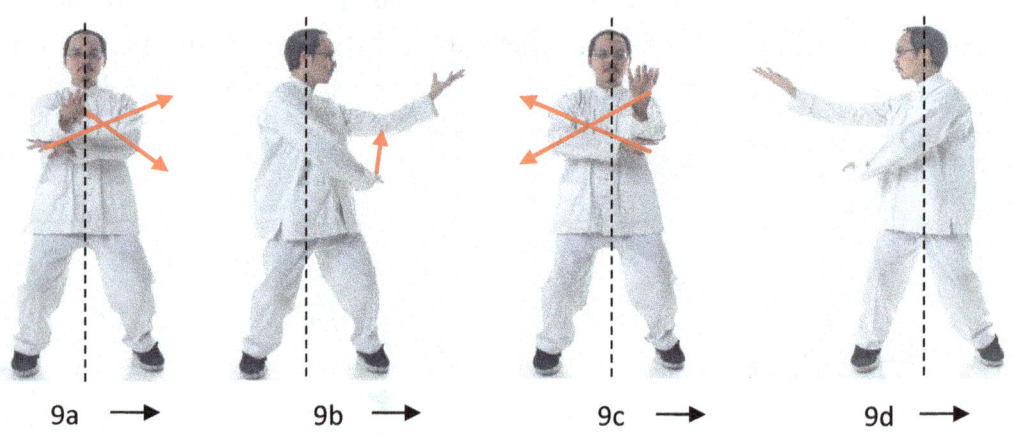

(Figure 27-9a) To start, the (R) hand is held straight out with palm facing down. The (L) hand is placed under the (R) elbow with the back of the hand touching the (R) elbow. The feet are placed with toes facing forward and approximately shoulder width apart. The knees are slightly bent and the back held straight. The eyes look straight ahead and the tongue rests against the roof of the mouth.
(Figure 27-9b) Next, rotate the body 90 degrees to the left. At the same time, the (L) hand wipes off along the underside of the (R) forearm, rotating as it moves into an open-handed ridge hand block at face height. At the same time, the (R) hand drops down across the body to protect the centreline terminating as an open palm down block directly under the (L) elbow. The feet remain static, firmly rooted to the ground throughout.
   Note: This upper body movement is the same as Tuo form.
(Figure 27-9c) Next, the body rotates back 90 degrees to its original starting position; however, the hands have swapped positions with the (R) hand now wiping off along the (L) forearm. The feet remain static, firmly rooted to the ground throughout.
(Figure 27-9d) Continuing its rotation a further 90 degrees to the right, both hands continue their pattern of movement, terminating with the (R) hand ridge hand blocking at face height and the (L) hand covering palm down under the (R) elbow.
   Note: This exercise is practised on each side in alternate movements. Inhale before you rotate and exhale as you rotate to the left. Then, inhale before you start to rotate and then exhale as you rotate back to the right. Repeat this process with each rotation sequence.

Wave Hands Fighting Application

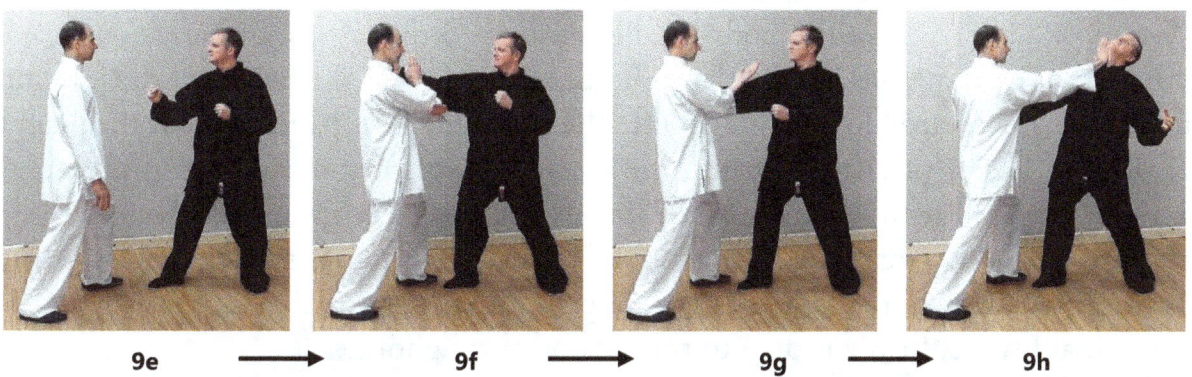

9e → 9f → 9g → 9h

(Figure 27-9e) White faces off to Black in a neutral stance.

(Figures 27-9f and 9g) Black throws a (R) straight punch to White's face. White counters by stepping into the attack and cover blocking the punch from I/O with a (R) palm block. At the same time White brings his (L) open hand across his centreline in case of a second counterstrike from Black.

(Figure 27-9h) Before Black can attack again, White continues immediately from the blocking technique to strike out with his (L) hand along the underside of his own (R) arm to replace the original block and simultaneously strikes out with a (R) knife hand strike to Black's neck.

10. Cranes Beak Striking

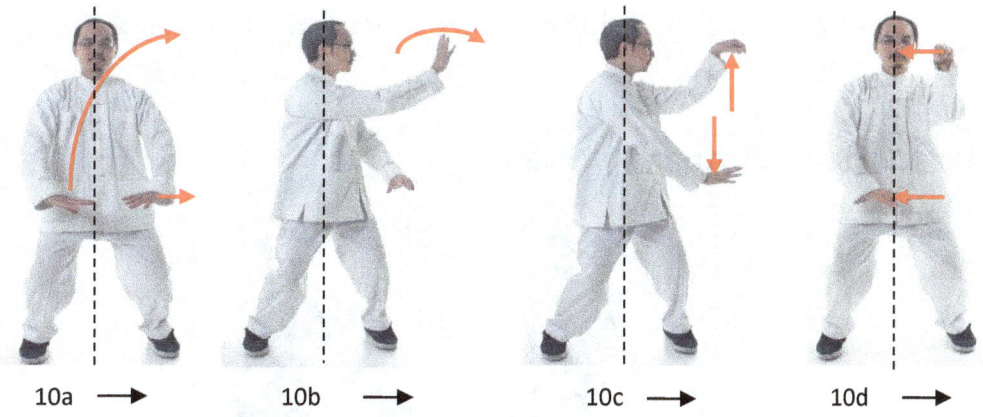

10a → 10b → 10c → 10d →

(Figure 27-10a) To start, both hands are held as open hands, facing palm down, in front of the body at the height of the Tan Tien. The feet are placed with toes facing forward and approximately shoulder width apart. The knees are slightly bent and the back held straight. The eyes look straight ahead and the tongue rests against the roof of the mouth.

(Figure 27-10b) Next, rotate the body 90 degrees to the left. At the same time the (R) hand arcs upwards and across the body, passing above the face whilst the (L) hand takes the form of the cranes beak and starts to rise in time with the opposing hand. The feet remain static, firmly rooted to the ground throughout.

(Figure 27-10c) Whilst the body is fully rotated to the left, both hands pass each other. The (L) cranes beak hand drives up the centreline to the height of the jaw and inside the downward blocking (R) hand. The (R) hand faces palm down at the height of the Tan Tien. Both hands protect the body's centreline and end their movements simultaneously. The feet remain static, firmly rooted to the ground throughout.

(Figure 27-10d) Next, the body rotates back to the right, through the starting position. The hands remain in the same position as (figure 27-10c) previous. The feet remain static, firmly rooted to the ground throughout.

(Figures 27-10e to 10h) This exercise is practised on each side in alternate movements. Inhale as the hand arcs up to the height of the face and exhale as the hand presses down into a low palm block and the opposing cranes beak arm concludes its striking movement.

Cranes Beak Striking Fighting Application

(Figure 27-10i) White faces off to Black in a neutral stance.
(Figure 27-10j) Black throws a (R) straight punch to White's Tan Tien. White counters by stepping into the attack and cover blocking the punch from above to

press down on Black's extended (R) forearm. White continues immediately from the blocking technique to strike directly upwards along the centreline of Black attacking with a cranes beak strike to the underside of Black's jaw.

11. Crane's Beak Blocking and Palm

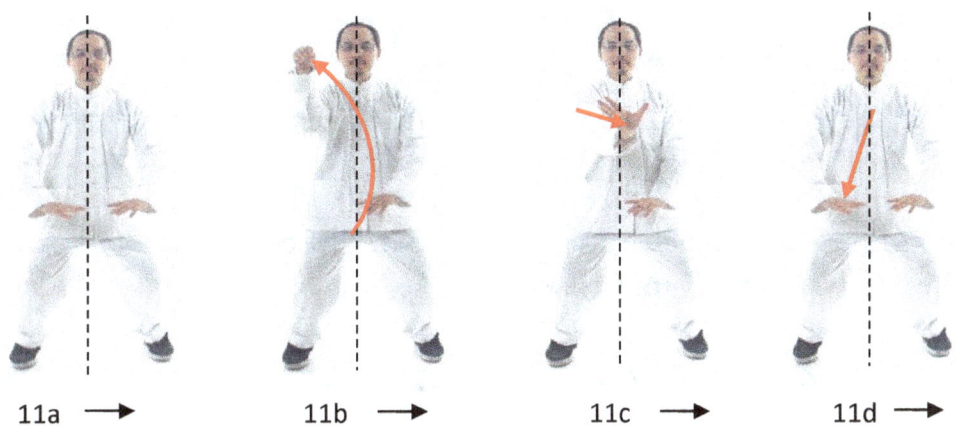

11a →   11b →   11c →   11d →

(Figure 27-11a) To start, both hands are held open with palms facing down and in front of the body at the height of the Tan Tien. The feet are placed with toes facing forward and approximately shoulder width apart. The knees are slightly bent and the back held straight. The eyes look straight ahead and the tongue rests against the roof of the mouth.

(Figure 27-11b) Next, the (R) hand forms a cranes beak and arcs upwards and across the body's centreline, circling from inside to outside in an anti-clockwise direction, to the height of the face whilst the (L) hand holds its position at the Tan Tien level. During this circle block movement, the waist leads by rotating subtly to the left a few degrees in time with the (R) arm. The feet remain static, firmly rooted to the ground throughout.

(Figure 27-11c) As the (R) hand reaches face height it then begins to drop to the height of the solar plexus and the hand opens into a palm strike along the centreline. The waist continues to subtly lead this movement, rotating a few degrees to the right and then back to the centre on finishing the palm strike. The feet remain static, firmly rooted to the ground throughout.

(Figure 27-11d) The (R) hand is then drawn back to the initial starting position at the Tan Tien level.

11e → 11f → 11g → 11h →

(Figures 27-11e to 11h) This exercise is practised on each side in alternate movements. Inhale as the hand arcs up to the height of the face and exhale as the hand strikes outward in a palm strike.

Crane's Beak Blocking and Palm Fighting Application

11i → 11j → 11k

(Figure 27-11i) White faces off to Black in a neutral stance.
(Figure 27-11j) Black throws a (R) straight punch to White's face. White counters by stepping into the attack and uses the cranes beak to block the punch from I/O with the (R) arm.
(Figure 27-1k) White continues immediately from the blocking technique to strike at Black's ribs with a (R) palm strike technique.

12. Phoenix Fist

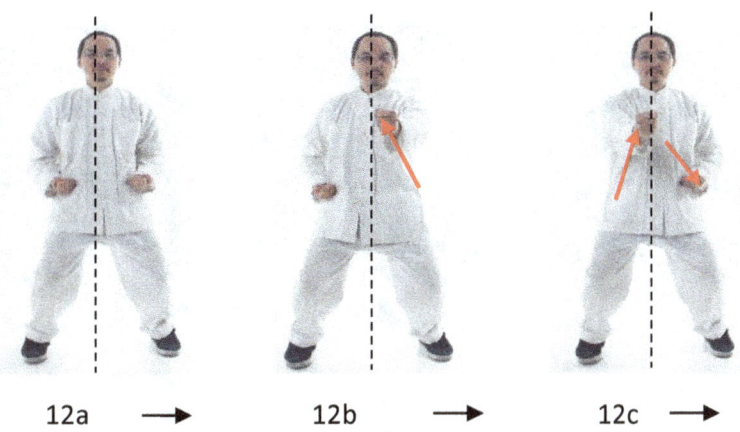

12a → 12b → 12c →

(Figure 27-12a) To start, both hands are held as fists at the height of their corresponding hips. The feet are placed with toes facing forward and approximately shoulder width apart. The knees are slightly bent and the back held straight. The eyes look straight ahead and the tongue rests against the roof of the mouth.

(Figure 27-12b) Next, the (L) hand forms a Phoenix eye fist and punches straight out down the centreline at the height of the solar plexus. At the same time, the (L) hip drives forward in time with the punch. As the (L) punch reaches its full extension, the (L) hip pulls back to its original starting position in a relaxed but intentional 'snapping' motion. This combined hip movement is referred to as 'reverse hips'. The back is straight and the feet remain firmly rooted throughout.

(Figure 27-12c) As the (L) fist is drawn back, the (R) fist forms a Phoenix eye and punches straight down the centreline at the height of the solar plexus. On swapping positions, the arms and hands pass close, almost touching each other. The reverse hip action is used, with the (R) hip driving forward and then snapping back as previous, but on the opposite side. The back is straight and the feet remain firmly rooted throughout.

Note: This exercise is practiced on each side in alternate movements. Inhale between each punch. Exhale as the hand punches outward in a Phoenix eye fist.

Phoenix Fist Fighting Application

(Figure 27-12d) White faces off to Black in a neutral stance.
(Figure 27-12e) Black throws a (R) straight punch to White's Tan Tien. White counters by stepping (L) directly into the line of attack and simultaneously blocking and striking the oncoming attack with a (L) Beng Chuan punch utilising the Phoenix eye fist to target the rib of Black.
(Figure 27-12f) White continues immediately from the first strike to deliver a second (R) Beng Chuan punch, this time utilising the Phoenix eye striking method to target the solar plexus of Black.

13. Rocking, Side to Side

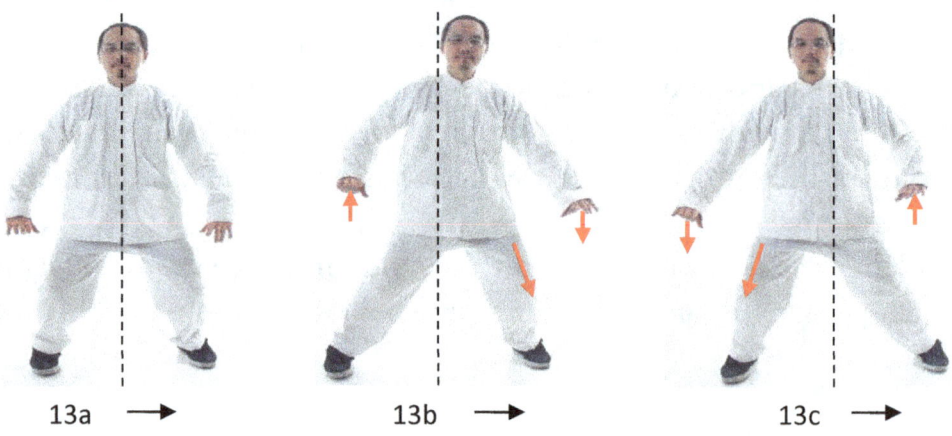

(Figure 27-13a) To start, both hands are held as open hands, facing palm down at the height of their corresponding hips. The feet are placed with toes facing forward and approximately shoulder width apart. The knees are slightly bent and the back held straight. The eyes look straight ahead and the tongue rests against the roof of the mouth.

Note: This shoulder width stance can be opened into a wider horse stance if the practitioner wants to make the exercise lower and more physically challenging. The same rules of alignment apply to the knees and feet.

(Figure 27-13b) Next, gently move the weight over to the (L) leg by allowing the (L) knee to move over the direction of the (L) foot below it. Don't let the knee go beyond the toe as this leads to poor alignment and potential injury to knee ligaments if overstressed. At the same time press gently down with the (L) palm in time with the body's natural sinking.

Note: This combined movement should be very subtle and almost undetectable in the movement of the head. Allow the legs to do the work and keep the upper body relaxed.

(Figure 27-13c) Repeat the same sequence on the opposite (R) side.

Note: This exercise is practised on each side in alternate movements. Inhale between each movement. Exhale as the palm presses down towards the ground.

Rocking, Side to Side Fighting Application

(Figure 27-13d) Black lunges forward and grabs White's (L) wrist.
(Figure 27-13e) To counter the grab, White rotates his (L) open hand around the outside of Black's grabbing hand.
(Figure 27-13f) White continues immediately to sink his weight and use the circling, pressing technique to break the grip of Black.
(Figure 27-13g) To show the exercise clearly and enable the reader to visualize this technique the final picture depicts the exercise posture with both hands pressing down, although in reality only one hand is used in application, with the free hand able to counter strike the opponent as required.

14. Spear Hand

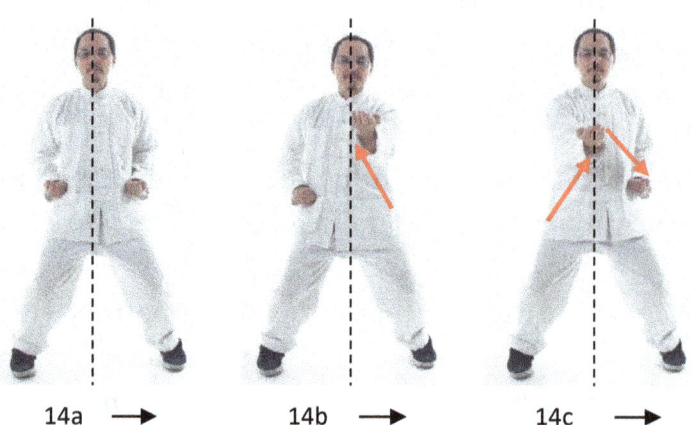

14a → 14b → 14c →

(Figure 27-14a) To start, both hands are held as fists at the height of their corresponding hips. The feet are placed with toes facing forward and approximately shoulder width apart. The knees are slightly bent and the back held straight. The eyes look straight ahead and the tongue rests against the roof of the mouth.

(Figure 27-14b) Next, the (L) hand forms a spear hand facing palm up and thrusts straight out down the centreline at the height of the solar plexus. At the same time, the (L) hip drives forward in time with the punch. As the (L) spear hand strike reaches its full extension, the (L) hip pulls back to its original starting position in a relaxed but intentional 'snapping' motion. This combined hip movement is referred to as 'reverse hips'. The back is straight and the feet remain firmly rooted throughout.

(Figure 27-14c) As the (L) spear hand is drawn back, it returns to a fist at the hip. At the same time, the (R) fist forms a spear hand and thrusts straight down the centreline at the height of the solar plexus. On swapping positions, the arms and hands pass close, almost touching each other. The reverse hip action is used, with the (R) hip driving forward and then snapping back as previous, but on the opposite side. The back is straight and the feet remain firmly rooted throughout.

Note: This exercise is practised on each side in alternate movements. Inhale between each spear hand thrust. Exhale as the hand thrusts outward in a spear hand strike.

Spear Hand Fighting Application

(Figure 27-14d) White faces off to Black in ready stance.
(Figure 27-14e) Black throws a (R) straight punch to White's Tan Tien. White covers the oncoming attack with a (L) covering palm block and counters by immediately dropping his stance into a low horse stance, simultaneously striking Black's groin with a spear hand technique.

15. Rolling the Shoulder

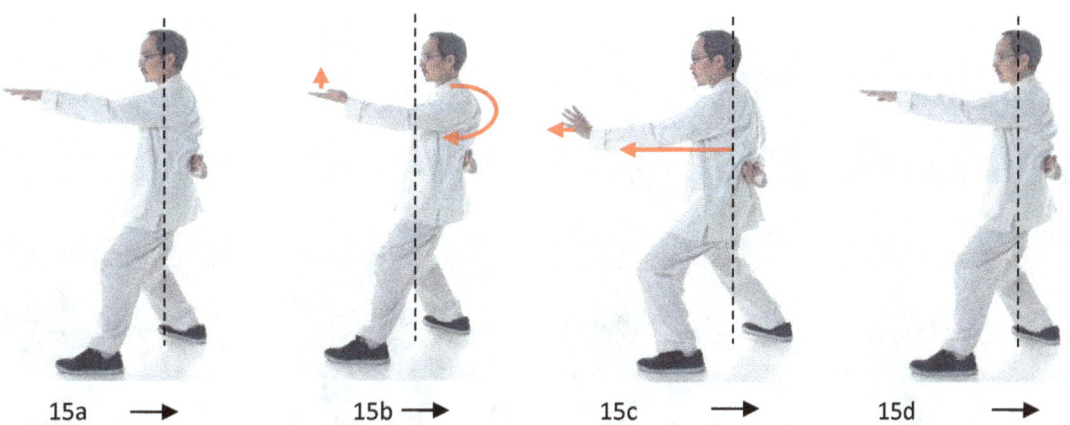

(Figure 27-15a) Start with the feet as in (L) Pi Chuan posture with the weight 70:30 on the back leg. The (L) arm is held out in front with the elbow straight and the palm facing down. The (R) hand is held behind the back with the back of the hand resting at kidney level. The upper body is at 45 degrees to the centreline. The knees are slightly bent and the back held straight. The eyes look straight ahead and the tongue rests against the roof of the mouth.

(Figure 27-15b) Next, push backwards through the front (L) foot and rotate the body 45 degrees to the left, until it is aligned with the shoulders square to the centreline. At the same time, the (L) shoulder complex rotates upwards and backwards, in effect pulling the arm backwards towards the body. The elbow remains straight throughout and the (L) hand turns palm up. The head remains level throughout this movement.

(Figure 27-15c) Next, push forwards from the back (R) foot and return the body 45 degrees to the right, until it is aligned with the shoulders back at 45 degrees to the centreline. At the same time, the (L) shoulder complex rotates downwards and forwards, in effect pushing the arm/hand forwards from the body. The elbow remains straight throughout and the (L) hand turns palm forwards. The head remains level throughout this movement.

(Figure 27-15d) From figure 27-15c the body repeats the sequence, passing through the staring position shown in figure 27-15a above.

Note: Inhale as the arm draws backwards and exhale as the arm pushes forwards.

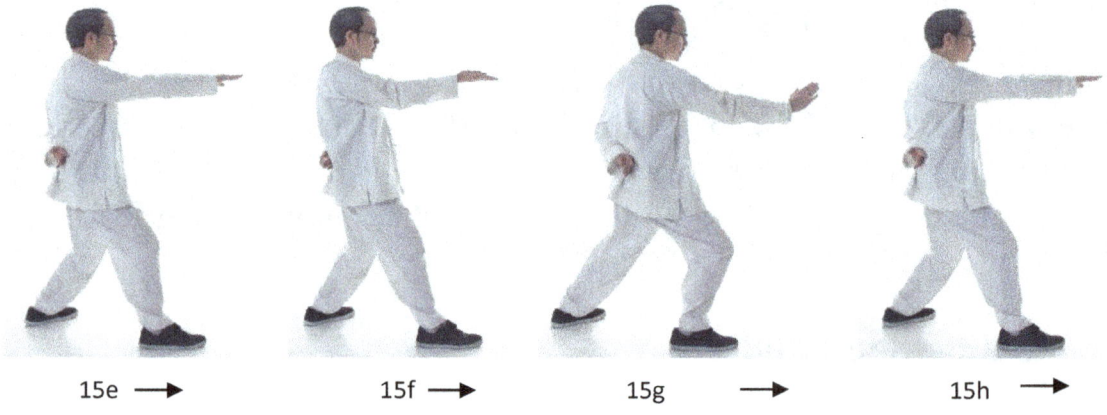

(Figures 27-15e to15h) Next repeat the same sequence on the opposite side.

Rolling the Shoulder Fighting Application

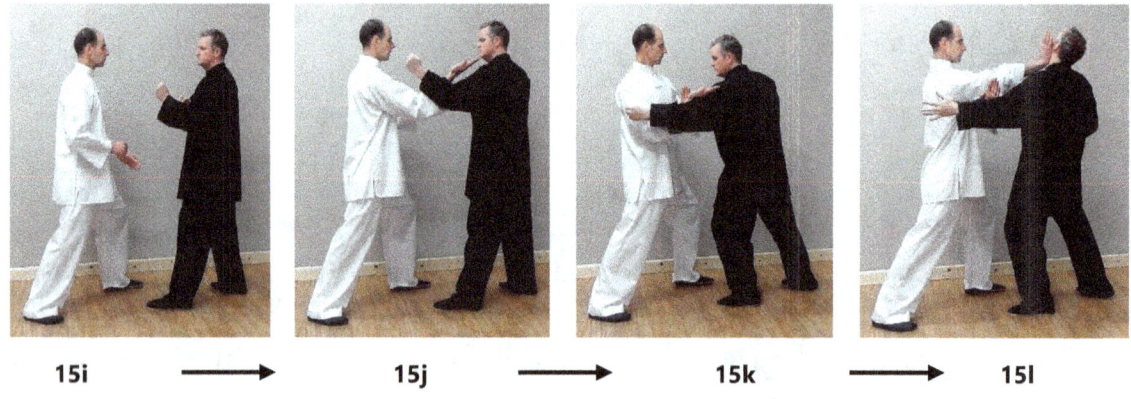

(Figure 27-15i) White faces off to Black in ready stance.

(Figure 27-15j) Black throws a (L) straight punch to White's face. White counters by turning the (R) shoulder and body allowing the incoming attack to be received without moving the feet. The attacking punch is blocked by White's (R) turning, retreating forearm.

(Figure 27-15k) White continues immediately from the blocking technique to strike out along the line of Black's (L) extended arm whilst at the same time White covers his own centreline to guard against any counter attack by Black.

(Figure 27-15l) To finish, White completes his attack with a straight (R) palm strike to break Black's jaw.

16. Tiger Push

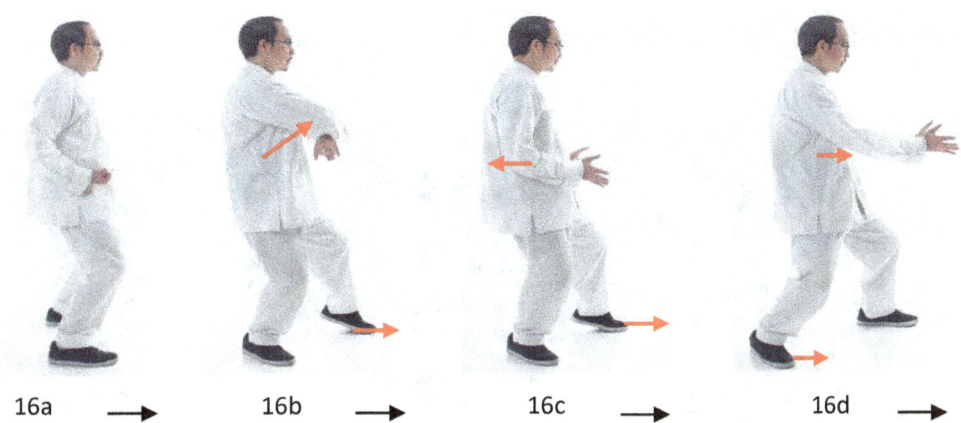

(Figure 27-16a) To start, both hands are held as fists at the height of their corresponding hips. The feet are placed with toes facing forward and approximately shoulder width apart. The knees are slightly bent and the back held straight. The eyes look straight ahead and the tongue rests against the roof of the mouth.

(Figure 27-16b) Step out forwards with the (L) foot placing it on the ball of the foot into (L) cat stance. At the same time cross over both arms in front of the body at Tan Tien height with hands open and palms facing down.

(Figure 27-16c) Pull both hands equally apart across the body in a 'tearing' action and turn the hands at their corresponding hips to face palms forward.

(Figure 27-16d) Push forward from the back (R) foot and step forward with the (L) foot. The back foot follows up using the half-step method of Hsing-I. At the same time both hands push forwards in perfect timing with the body.

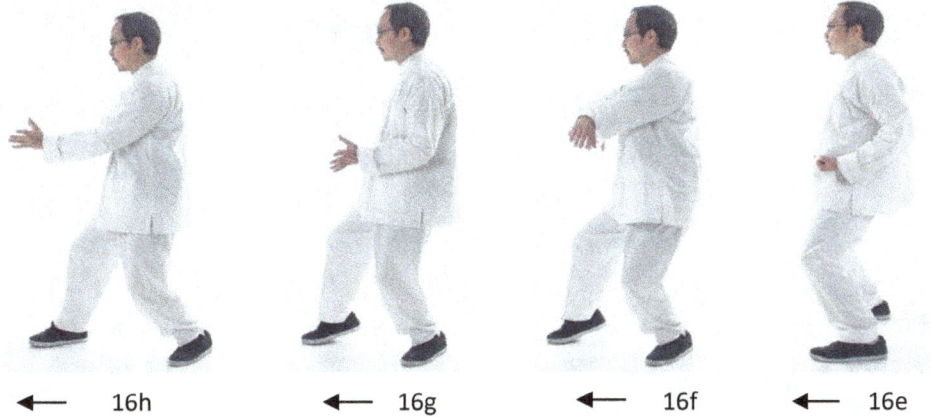

(Figures 27-16e to 16h) The practitioner then turns 180 degrees into (R) cat stance using the same footwork as Tiger form whilst simultaneously crossing both arms across the body and bringing both hands to their corresponding hips. They are now ready to repeat the movement on the opposite side.

Note: Inhale as the arms cross and pull to the sides and exhale as the hands push forwards.

Tiger Push Fighting Application

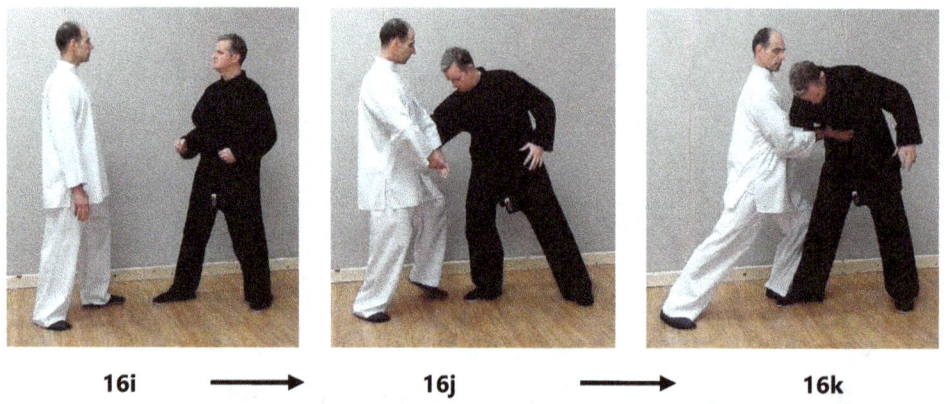

(**Figure 27-16i**) White faces off to Black in a neutral stance.
(**Figure 27-16j**) Black throws a (R) straight punch to White's Tan Tien. White counters by stepping across with the (R) rear foot, 45 degrees to the inside of the attack into (L) cat stance. At the same time, White counters with a (L) double handed tearing block to the attacking punch.
(**Figure 27-16k**) White continues immediately from the blocking technique to strike out with both tiger palms to break Black's ribs and drive him away.

17. High Block and Strike

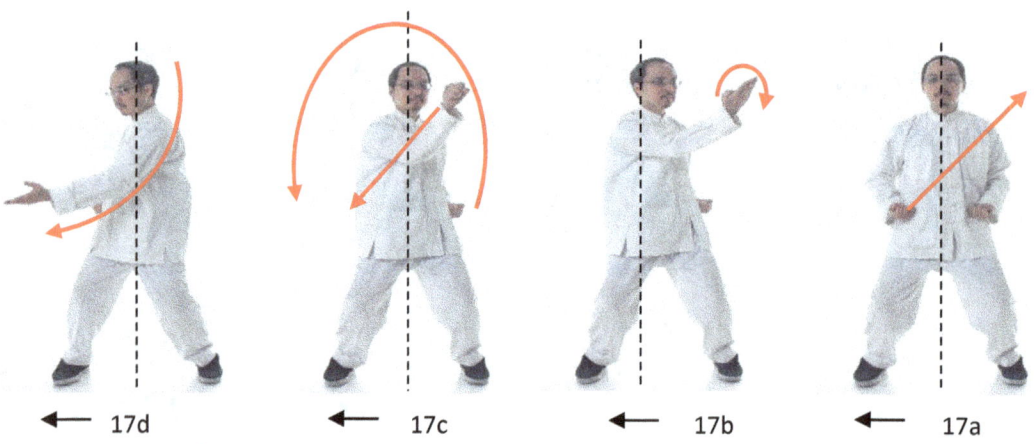

(**Figure 27-17a**) Both hands are held as fists at the height of their corresponding hips. The feet are placed with toes facing forward and approximately shoulder width apart. The knees are slightly bent and the back held straight. The eyes look straight ahead and the tongue rests against the roof of the mouth.

(Figure 27-17b) The body rotates through 45 degrees to the left and at the same time the (R) hand rises to head height at an angle of 45 degrees to the starting centreline. Along the course of the body's rotation to the left the (R) hand turns palm upwards as a spear hand. The feet remain static, firmly rooted to the ground throughout.

(Figure 27-17c) At the end of the (L) rotation the (R) spear hand forms a fist, facing palm down.

(Figure 27-17d) The body then starts to rotate back to the right with the grasping (R) fist pulling downwards across the body, back towards the (R) hip. At the same time, the (L) hand is brought from the (L) hip in a wide arc over the (L) shoulder with the hand open at head height. The (L) arm makes a wide circular arc in time with the body's rotation to finish 45 degrees to the starting centreline. The (L) hand cuts with the knife edge facing down towards the ground at its termination. From here the sequence begins again, starting at figure 27-17b.

Note: Inhale as the arm blocks upwards across the body and exhale as the opposite arm circles over and down, to strike.

17e →   17f →   17g →   17h →

(Figures 27-17e to 17h) Next repeat the same sequence on the opposite side.

High Block and Strike Fighting Application

17i →   17j →   17k

(Figure 27-17i) White faces off to Black in a neutral stance.
(Figure 27-17j) Black throws a (R) straight punch to White's face. White counters by stepping (L) into the attack and blocking the punch from I/O with a (L) ridge hand block.
(Figure 27-17k) To finish, White continues immediately from the blocking technique to strike out with a (R) knife hand strike to Black's neck.

18.   Circling the Eyes

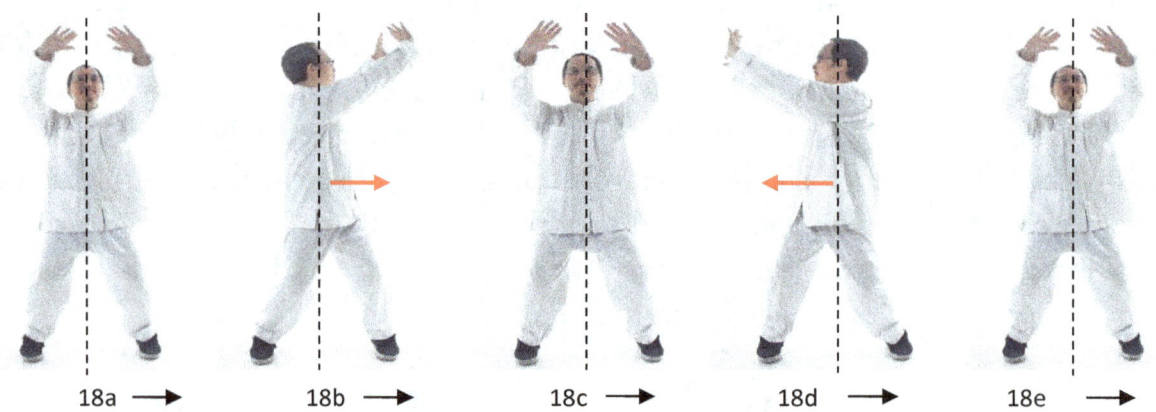

(Figure 27-18a) To start, both hands are held as open hands, with palms facing outwards above head height. The feet are placed with toes facing forward and approximately shoulder width apart. The knees are slightly bent and the back held straight. The eyes look straight ahead and the tongue rests against the roof of the mouth.
(Figure 27-18b) With the arms held in a static position the body rotates 90 degrees to the left. Using the hands as a guide allow the head to follow, keeping the chin in line with the centreline of the body throughout. Whilst the head and body are rotating, circle the eyes to the left making the eye muscles work to their maximum. Try to take in as much of the visual field as possible without moving the head.
(Figure 27-18c) When the body has reached the end of its 90-degree (L) rotation then start to rotate back through the starting position, this time circling the eyes to the right, taking in the maximum visual field possible.
(Figure 27-18d) Continue the (R) rotation with eye circling until the body is fully rotated 90 degrees to the right. Keep the hands held out in the same position as from the start.
(Figure 27-18e) Change back to the left until the original starting position is reached. Always circle the eyes in the direction the body is rotating.
   Note: This exercise is practiced continually from side to side. Breathe naturally through the nose, with the tongue placed on the roof of the mouth throughout.
   Health Note: According to TCM theory, many problems with the eyes are related to the energetic health of the liver organ system. It is said "the liver opens

into the eyes." Regular practice of this chi-kung exercise utilises the muscles and tissues of the eyes and helps to restore the livers chi flow to its optimal level and consequently improve the overall health of the eyes.

19. Rotating Hips

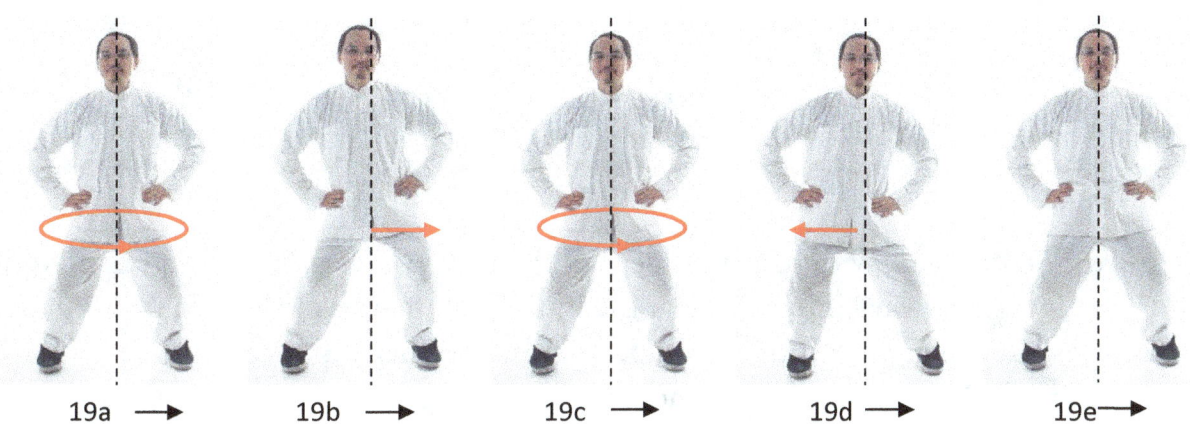

19a → 19b → 19c → 19d → 19e →

(Figure 27-19a) Both hands are held with palms resting on their corresponding hips. The feet are placed with toes facing forward and approximately shoulder width apart. The knees are slightly bent and the back held straight. The eyes look straight ahead and the tongue rests against the roof of the mouth.

(Figures 27-19b to 19e) Start by circling the hips in a clockwise direction to the left. Continue round a full circle until the hips have returned to their starting position. The upper body should remain almost still, whilst the lower back and pelvis rotate. Repeat rotations at least ten times and then change to the opposite direction.

Health Note: When rotating the hips, the rotations should be kept small. This is not a 'hula hoop' exercise. The idea is to loosen up the base of the spine, sacrum and especially the sacroiliac joints which become stiff and fused into older age. Breathe naturally through the nose, with the tongue placed on the roof of the mouth throughout. This lower lumbar area should be kept flexible as it houses an important energy gate called Ming Men along the pathway of the spine. Obstructed chi flow at this gate will lead to chi deficiency of the brain and hinder the flow of the Little Nine Heaven energy circulation.

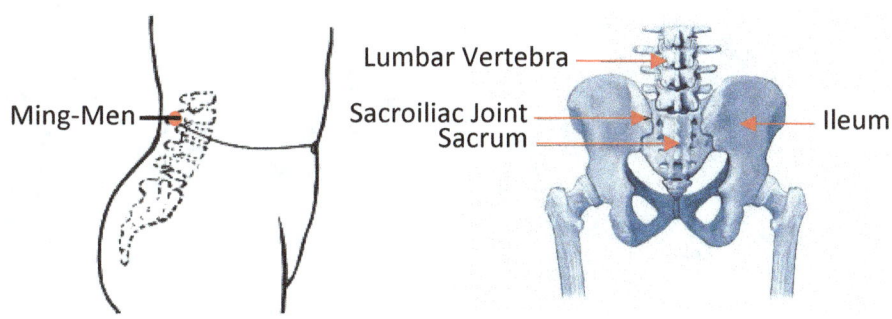

20. Bend to the Earth and Twist

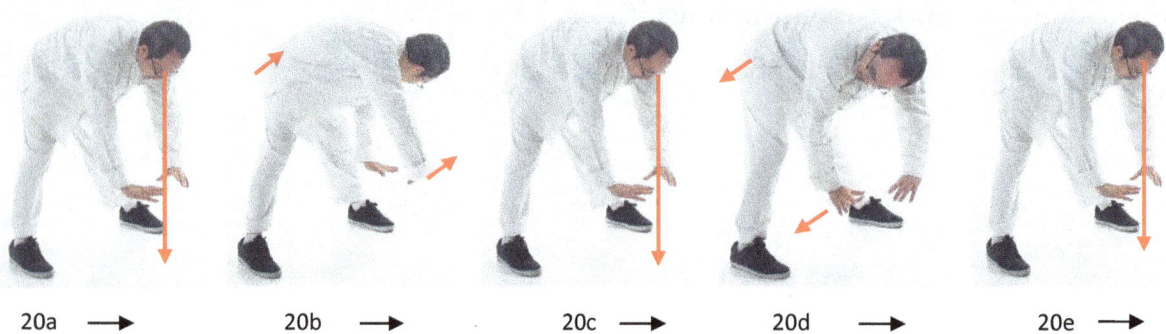

(Figure 27-20a) Start with feet shoulder width apart. The legs are held straight and the body is bent forward into flexion at the waist. Both hands are held in front of the body with the palms facing the ground. The practitioner looks through the hands at the ground. Breathe through the nose with the tongue on the roof of the mouth. **(Figure 27-20b)** Start by rotating your body to the left whilst maintaining a flexed position at the waist. As the body twists to the left the arms and hands should also turn to the left in line with the body. The hands should twist also as though turning a car steering wheel to the left at the same height as the starting position shown in figure 27-20a. The head must look round to the left also, as though trying to look at the left hip. At the same time as the body twists to the left, the left hip and buttocks must also push to the left. This creates the effect that the practitioner is attempting to look at their own rear end.

Health Note: This method of twisting will rotate and loosen up the whole spine and benefit the general flow of chi through the spinal column and cord within it leading to nourishment of the brain.

(Figures 27-20c to 20e) Return to the starting position and then repeat on the opposite side.

Note: This exercise is practiced continually from side to side. Breathe naturally through the nose, with the tongue placed on the roof of the mouth throughout.

21. Squat and Strike

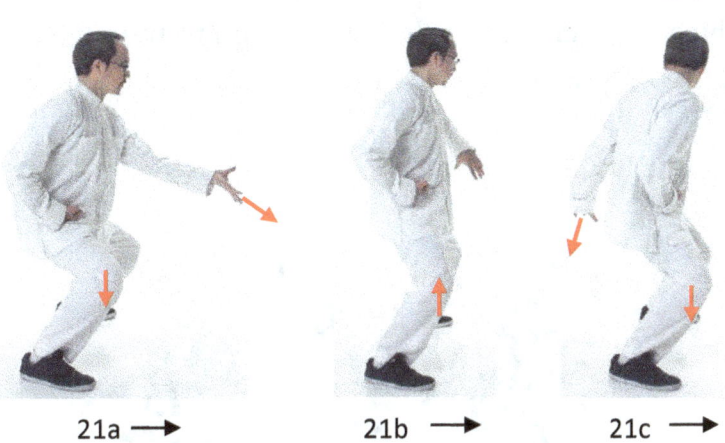

21a →   21b →   21c →

(Figure 27-21a) First, place the feet shoulder width apart. Keep the back straight. Both fists start from the hips. Next, squat down, keeping the back straight throughout and reach forward with a (L) spear hand as though to strike out directly down the centreline at groin height. Make sure the knees stay in line with the toes below.

(Figure 27-21b) From the termination of the (L) spear hand strike make as though to scoop up an imaginary object with the (L) open hand and at the same time twist round to the left, raising your height back to the starting level as you turn.

(Figure 27-21c) Continuing the turn to the left with your waist rotating to its maximum without moving the feet, bend the knees again and sink down as though to place the imaginary object on the ground behind. The back must stay straight and the feet rooted to the ground throughout this whole sequence.

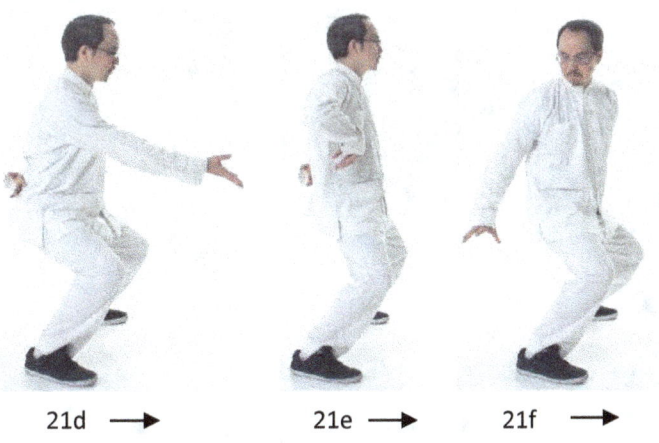

21d →   21e →   21f →

(Figures 27-21d to 21f) Then repeat the sequence on the same side again, for a minimum of ten times before changing to the opposite side. Breathe only through the nose with the tongue on the roof of the mouth throughout. Inhale as you pick up and exhale as you put down the imaginary object.

Health Note: The knees should remain bent to varying degrees and never totally straighten during this sequence of movements. This helps develop strong legs alongside a flexible waist which helps create a strong foundation to train from. It also encourages increased chi and blood flow throughout the whole body, especially the lower limbs.

Squat and Strike Fighting Application

21g → 21h

(Figure 27-21g) Black lunges forward to grab White from behind with both arms in a bear hug technique.
(Figure 27-21h) White steady's his balance by dropping his weight into a low Horse stance and at the same time rotates his waist to the left to break Black's grip. As Black is forced to release his grip, White strikes to Black's groin with a (L) palm strike.

22. Grasp and Kick

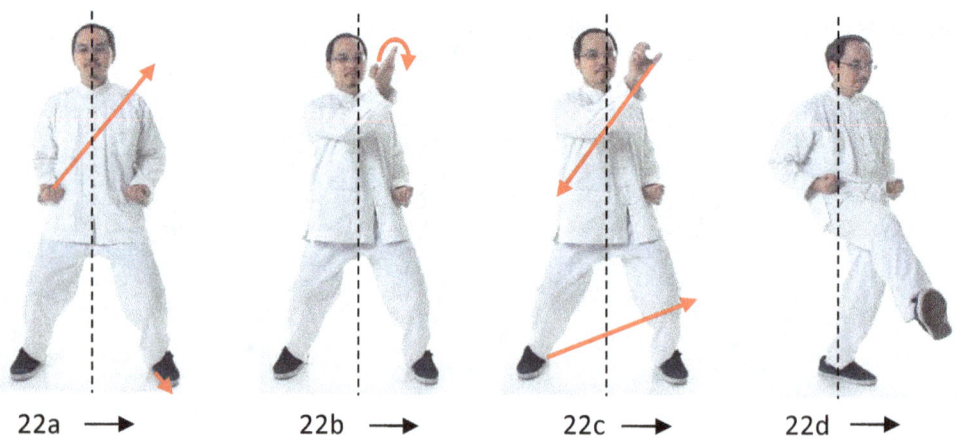

22a → 22b → 22c → 22d →

(Figure 27-22a) Both hands are held as fists at the height of their corresponding hips. The feet are placed with toes facing forward and approximately shoulder width apart. The knees are slightly bent and the back held straight. The eyes look straight ahead and the tongue rests.

(Figure 27-22b) First, step forward with the (L) foot and at the same time strike out with a (R) spear hand to face height across the centreline of the body, with the palm facing up. The opposite (L) hand remains held as a fist at the (L) hip.

(Figure 27-22c) Turn the palm of the (R) spear hand over and make a 'grabbing' action to form a fist facing palm down. At the same time move the weight forward into the front, (L) foot.

(Figure 27-22d) Grasp and pull back with the (R) fist to the (R) hip and at the same time step forward and through with the (R) foot to execute a (R) 45 degree rising kick to knee height. As you step down use the half-step method to place your feet in (R) Pi Chuan stance.

(Figures 27-22e to 22g) From (R) Pi Chuan stance you can now repeat the sequence on the opposite side, ending in (L) Pi Chuan stance.

Note: Inhale as you block out with the spear hand across the body and exhale as you pull the hand back and kick forward.

Grasp and Kick Fighting Application

(Figure 27-2h) White faces off to Black in ready stance.

(Figures 27-22i) Black throws a (R) straight punch to White's face. White counters by stepping (L) to the outside of the attack and blocking the punch with a (R) spear hand technique.

(Figure 27-22j) To finish, White continues immediately from the spear hand technique to take control of Black's extended (R) arm at the wrist and elbow to control him whilst delivering a (R) 45-degree rising kick to White's (R) knee.

23. Muscle, Tendon and Wipe Off

23a → 23b → 23c → 23d →

Exercise Part 1. Muscle/Tendon

(Figure 27-23a) Continuing to walk forward the practitioner uses the (R) foot to kick the back of the (L) lower leg at the height of the calf muscle (gastrocnemius). At the same time, the (L) lower arm strikes the (R) lower arm at the height of the forearm muscles (extensor and flexor carpi). This sequence conditions the muscles.
(Figure 27-23b) Stepping forward again the practitioner repeats the same muscle striking sequence on the opposite side.
(Figure 27-23c) Continuing to walk forward the practitioner uses the (R) foot to kick the back of the (L) lower leg at the height of the Achilles tendon. At the same time, the (L) lower arm strikes the (R) lower arm at the height of the wrist extensor and flexor tendons. This sequence conditions the tendons of the upper and lower limbs.
(Figure 27-23d) Stepping forward again the practitioner repeats the same tendon striking sequence on the opposite side.

Note: Repeat the sequence (figures 27-23a to 23d) again a minimum of 10 times before changing to the final 'wiping off' exercise of this sequence. Breathe only through the nose with the tongue on the roof of the mouth throughout. Inhale as you step forward and exhale as you strike the muscles or tendons.

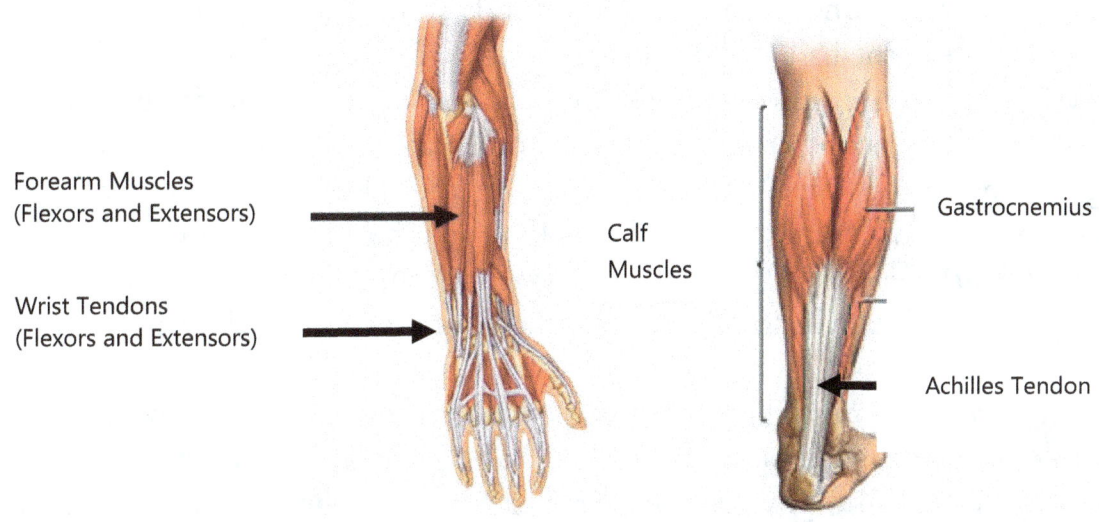

Exercise Part 2. Wipe Off

After striking the muscles and tendons has finished the practitioner 'wipes off' by simply continuing to walk whilst trying to kick their butt with their own heels and simultaneously wiping one forearm against the other in the areas that have been striking. This simple method encourages the chi and blood to flow back into the tissues that have received trauma from previous striking.

24. Heel and Toe

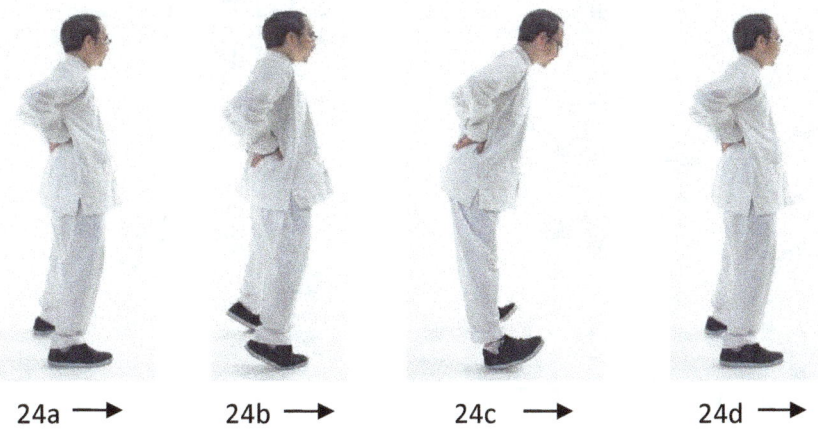

(Figures 27-24a and 24b) Start with feet placed shoulder width apart. Stand up straight and place both hands on the lower back at the height of the kidneys.

Vigorously rub the kidney area with both hands simultaneously and at the same time stand up onto the balls of both feet by raising the heels off the ground.

(Figure 27-24c) Continue to rub the kidney area with both hands as you drop back down onto the soles of your feet and then immediately rock back onto the heels, raising the toes of both feet off the ground together. The upper body will move forwards to compensate and balance the rocking action of the exercise.

(Figure 27-24d) Next, lower both toes back to the ground and return to the original starting position. Continue to rub the kidney area of the lower back throughout this exercise.

Repeat this exercise a minimum ten times. Inhale as you raise the body on its toes and exhale as you drop the body and rock back onto the heels.

Health Note: On a physical level, this exercise stretches and strengthens the muscles and tendons of the lower limbs and improves standing balance. On an energetic level Taoist texts state that rubbing the kidney area puts heat and chi into the kidney organs which is beneficial for all the organs and as it is the kidneys that store the ancestral energy of the body and is the root of both Yin and Yang chi. Further to this, by raising and lowering the heels on the toes helps stretch the Bladder meridian which is paired to the kidneys via the Five Element Theory and this 'dropping' of the heels to the ground creates a beneficial vibration through the bladder meridian which also stimulates the kidneys energy.

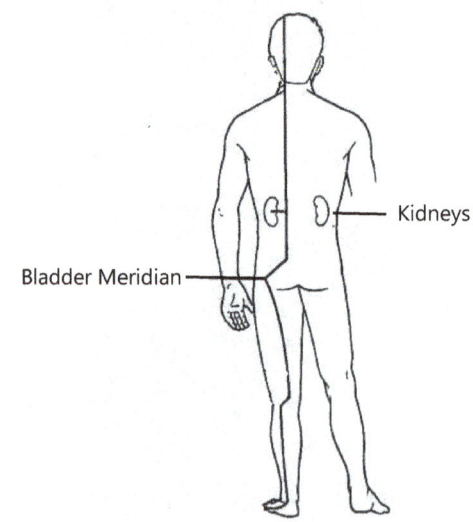

25. Pat the Head

25a →   25b →   25c →

(Figures 27-25a to 25c) Start with feet placed shoulder width apart. Stand up straight and place both hands on the sides of the head. Rotate the waist from side to side whilst firmly patting the head with both hands simultaneously, covering all areas of the head, sides, back, top and forehead.

Health Note: This exercise is practiced continually from side to side and all over the head. Breathe naturally through the nose, with the tongue placed on the roof of the mouth throughout. Stimulation of the brain is achieved by firmly patting the head. This action in effect 'wakes up' the brain and is an excellent exercise to practice if you are feeling tired and lethargic or in the morning on waking. As the brain is the command centre for all the organs, its stimulation is therefore beneficial to the whole body.

www.ingramcontent.com/pod-product-compliance
Lightning Source LLC
Chambersburg PA
CBHW080826010526
44111CB00016B/2618